Chrome Colossus

ED CRAY

Chrome Colossus

General Motors

AND ITS TIMES

McGRAW-HILL BOOK COMPANY

New York   St. Louis   San Francisco
Düsseldorf   Mexico   Toronto

Book design by Anita Walker Scott.

Printed in the United States of America.

Library of Congress Cataloging in Publication Data

Cray, Ed.
Chrome colossus.
Bibliography: p.
Includes index.
1.   General Motors Corporation—History.   I.   Title.
HD9710.U54G375   338.7′6292′0973   80-14256
ISBN 0-07-013493-6

The author gratefully acknowledges the assistance of the following publishers who granted permission to quote from copyrighted material:
    Wright Enterprises, for quotations from *On a Clear Day You Can See General Motors,* copyright © 1979 by J. Patrick Wright;
    Dow, Jones & Company, Inc., for quotations from Vermont Royster's column in the *Wall Street Journal;*
    Ludlow Music, Inc., for lines from "Talking Dust Bowl," words and music by Woody Guthrie, TRO—copyright © 1961 by Ludlow Music, Inc., New York, N.Y. Used by permission.

Published in association with
SAN FRANCISCO BOOK COMPANY

FOR ALL THE CHILDREN:

Rachel and Olivia Adams,
Joshua and Naomi Kovacs,
Duncan and Blake Martell,
Nick and Matt Myerhoff,
and, of course,
for Jennifer,
who grew from a little girl to a co-worker
while her father was writing this book.

Contents

Part III The Ozymandias Syndrome 383

Photographic sections follow pages 182 and 382

Introduction

Such men strode confidently.

Around him a flurry of reporters and photographers elbowed for position, slowing him momentarily to snap a question before his escort brushed them aside.

The white-haired man in the conservative blue suit ignored the newsmen as he crossed the sidewalk and started up the granite steps. The questions fell harmlessly behind as the reporters skipped to keep up.

"Are you going to sell your holdings, Mr. Secretary?"

"What did the president tell you to do?"

Charles Erwin Wilson, "Engine Charlie," president of the world's largest corporation, followed the company-provided escort into the building. A closely barbered public-relations man turned at the top of the stairs and yelled, "Later. Later. We'll have a statement after the hearing."

His eyes fixed straight ahead, Charles Erwin Wilson, President-elect Eisenhower's nominee for secretary of defense, marched past the public-relations man. The trailing swarm crowded through the double doors held open by two younger men from the company's Washington office. Wilson ignored them too.

The president of General Motors expected doors to be opened for him; he would have to get used to opening them himself when he came down to Washington. Other things would change too, the white-haired man realized. He was taking one hell of a salary cut—from $626,000, the highest executive pay in the world, to a mere $22,500. The youngster holding the door was making that much. Twenty-two five just might have been enough to keep the six kids in school a few years ago.

But the president-elect had insisted. It was Charles Erwin Wilson, sixty-two, whom he wanted as his secretary of defense, "to cut military expenditures without cutting military strength," as Eisenhower had promised during the campaign. And Charlie Wilson, a small-town boy from Minerva, Ohio, was not a man to spurn either his friend or his president.

He had agreed to come for a lot of reasons, but most of all for the challenge, he admitted. After thirty-three years with the company, twelve of them as its president, he had done it all. More than once. Bringing out the small car might have made it interesting, but Mr. Sloan and the board of directors had scotched that.

Still, there were accomplishments. Under him Chevrolet had become the first in twenty-two years to sell more than one million cars a year. Two years earlier, the company had racked up a record profit of $834 million. Last year's sales were $7.5 billion; no other firm had come even close. He had converted the corporation from peacetime to wartime production and back again, with fair profits all the while. No one better appreciated the ability of good men working in the free-enterprise system to get things done.

Now it was over. The Saturday before, he had gotten up from his desk for the last time, stuffed the carton of cigarettes in his briefcase, shook hands with his secretary, and put it all behind him. He would miss the executives on the fourteenth floor—all "regular men," he told his wife, Jessie—but the Wilsons would make other friends in Washington.

Money they didn't need. Not with their savings and $400,000 in cash bonuses still owed him by the company. Not with 39,470 shares of General Motors stock selling on the market at around $65. Not with the farm and the prize cow herd. He'd sell some of the little holdings and just hang onto the Motors. And the pipeline. And the 15,000 shares in the National Bank of Detroit.

President Eisenhower had agreed. Wilson could hold the stock and avoid the $200,000 capital-gains tax he would have to pay if he sold it. It was one thing to give up a big salary, but it was another to sacrifice everything he had worked for all these years in order to serve his country. If matters came up involving the company—they would, he knew, for General Motors was now Defense's biggest contractor—he would stand aside and let deputies decide. It was the only honorable way to handle it.

The warmly paneled hearing room was unnaturally quiet after the roiling parade through the Senate Office Building. Still, there were far too many people standing in small knots, gossiping quietly, occasionally glancing over to appraise Wilson, as if to determine what it was about this slightly jowly man in the expensive suit that qualified him to head the largest industrial enterprise in the world.

Wilson had requested that the confirmation hearing be closed; he did not relish the frankly appraising stares, or the public disclosure of his assets. Yet it had to come out, Senator Leverett Saltonstall had warned him. Senator Lyndon Johnson of Texas was concerned, and Lester Hunt of Wyoming was muttering about the Millionaires' Cabinet. They could not bar the press.

"Engine Charlie" Wilson *was* well-fixed, a millionaire, but he had earned every penny of it. Fresh out of Carnegie Institute of Technology, he had gone to work at Westinghouse as an apprentice electrical engineer for eighteen cents an hour. He spent ten years there, working his way up, before Charles Kettering hired him away to be chief engineer and sales manager for Remy Electric Company.

Nine years more and he had proved himself a comer in Remy's parent corporation, General Motors, his salary going up, his stock bonuses accruing. Then ten years of rotating assignments, learning the ropes here and there throughout the corporation: household appliances, aviation, real estate, auto accessories, and finally assistant to General Motors President William S. Knudsen for five years.

When Knudsen resigned in 1940 to head the war mobilization effort, Charles E. Wilson was ready to step into the presidency. He was well-seasoned, conservative, a Republican of course, and a staunch supporter of free enterprise—even if, by General Motors' standards, he was much too friendly with labor.

One by one the members of the committee straggled in, shook his hand, chatted a moment, then took their places at the raised table. Wilson was irritated. He was on time; they could be too. Courtly Leverett Saltonstall, the senior Republican on the committee, finally tapped the gavel. Aides and staff members broke off in mid-sentence to scatter to their appointed seats. The reporters jammed into the first rows of chairs took out notebooks, flipping through for blank pages to record the confrontation of Charles Erwin Wilson and the fifteen United States senators on the Armed Services Committee.

Wilson was prepared for them. He had copies of his letters of resignation—from GM, from the oil company and the bank, and from the Automobile Manufacturers Association. Two board memberships he thought he could keep: Carnegie Institute and Kettering's foundation. There were no conflicts of interest there. He had a statement on the details of his pension plan from GM, and the board of directors' explicit assurance—more for the record than for Wilson—that "any action or conduct by you while serving as Secretary of Defense will not be regarded as inimical or in any way contrary to the best interests of General Motors Corp."

Wilson's request for the letter was unprecedented, but so, too, was his decision to take early retirement to go into government work. Bill Knudsen's case had been different; the country was about to go to war, and most of them in business and finance knew it. "As a matter of fact," Wilson would tell the committee when he got a chance, "it has been a little difficult to intrigue any of us to come down. We have been very backward about it." But they hadn't been personally offered cabinet posts by the president either. "Maybe they were not asked by the right man."

Another letter outlined the bonuses due him over the next four years: the cash and 1,737 shares of GM stock. There was an uneasy stir in the hearing room when Wilson said he intended to hold onto these shares.

Senator Johnson interrupted. "What is the value of that stock, the par value?"

"The par value is $5. The market value is about $65 or $66, something like that." Wilson spoke slowly, carefully. What did the value of the stock matter? He had earned it all under the terms of the company's bonus plan years before. "Some of you probably have some. I doubt if I am the only man in this room that has any."

Johnson, himself busily amassing a fortune in Texas land, drawled, "Well, I do not have any or I would know what it was worth."

Charles Wilson slowly stroked the edge of his chin, keeping a tight check on his anger. Antagonizing a senator was not the way to start as secretary of defense.

"I would like to point out in the case of General Motors," Wilson continued, "my holdings may sound like a lot, and they are a nice asset for anyone, but as a percentage of General Motors they are less than half of a tenth of one percent. In other words, there are eighty-eight-million-and-some-odd shares of General Motors stock, so my ownership is very small, from that angle."

Senator Saltonstall, who would formally become the committee's new chairman when Congress convened the following week, began the questioning. As senior Republican on the committee, he was responsible for getting the nomination through; he intended to allay any doubts immediately.

"Do you have any relationship with General Motors," asked Saltonstall, "in connection with your stock ownership, the bonus that is coming to you over the next five years, which makes you feel you cannot be perfectly impartial and do your very best possible in the interest of the Government of the United States in the very important job which you will hold?"

"Certainly not," Wilson replied. The reporters writing their idiosyncratic shorthand notes called that kind of a question a "home-run ball," soft and easy to hit. "Now, no one has any finger on me in any way, except our government, and the single purpose that I have in mind is the security and welfare of our country, and I have so much bigger stake in our country than I have in any one of these little bits of business."

"If you have a renegotiation of contracts with General Motors, will that be embarrassing to you?"

"I would have nothing to do with that." Wilson paused, lighting a fresh cigarette off the old, groping for just the right words. "Somebody else will have to settle that. I think I reasonably know what is right or wrong in business, otherwise I would not have gotten along in General Motors, because in General Motors if I wanted to do something crooked, there are too many honest men that would not go along."

Senator Johnson took up the questioning. "Mr. Wilson, have you disclosed to the committee all of your financial holdings?"

"Yes. Some of them I have had for a long time. If I sold them I would have to pay a good bit of tax, which I do not care to do."

"I am not interested in what you sell, provided you answer the question."

"If there was a nice clean way without too much penalty for me personally to sell everything I had and put it in government bonds, I would do it; but the penalty is too great, gentlemen, and I do not know why you should ask me to do it."

"I am not suggesting that you do it."

Now the Texan was being more reasonable, if dubious.

"Your relationship with General Motors is such that, in your opinion, you would have no hesitancy in passing on any matter that would involve you in the future?"

"I would not, no, any more than I would with the Chrysler Company, the Ford Company, Curtiss–Wright, John Doe's company. They are all going to be on their merits."

Senator Robert Hendrickson of New Jersey, a Republican stalwart, followed. "Mr. Wilson, you have told the committee, I think more than once this morning, that you see no area of conflict between your interest in the General Motors Corporation or the other companies, as a stockholder, and the position you are about to assume."

"Yes, sir." It was almost a sigh. They were in still waters.

"Well now, I am interested to know whether—if a situation did arise where you had to make a decision which was adverse to the interests of your stock and General Motors but in the interests of the United States Government—could you make that decision?"

"Engine Charlie" Wilson leaned forward. His voice was firm, assured. "Yes, sir. I could. I cannot conceive of one because for years I thought what was good for our country was good for General Motors—and vice versa. The difference did not exist.

"Our company is too big. It goes with the welfare of the country. Our contribution to the nation is quite considerable."

As it was, so it would be, time out of mind.

One oligopoly dominates the nation and its economic prosperity. As long ago as 1939, *Fortune* magazine saw the city of Detroit, Michigan, and the automobile industry as "probably the birthplace of both good times and bad." In the years since, General Motors has become the bellwether of Detroit. A bad model year in 1957 produced a recession in 1958, with Wall Street ruefully joking, "General Motors sneezed, and the country caught a cold." With an Arab-imposed oil embargo in late 1973, General Motors' sales plummeted 34 percent, and the nation slipped into its longest recession in history. The economic brownout lifted only when "car and truck sales helped spark the national economy to a dramatic comeback in 1976, reaffirming the axiom that the motor vehicle industry has a major impact on national economics," the manufacturers' trade association proclaimed with undue modesty. "The giant GM swings so much weight among supplier businesses that, economists say, a strike against it could significantly reduce gross national product and deepen unemployment—just as in 1970, the last time GM and the UAW [United Auto Workers] collided head-on," the *Wall Street Journal* noted.

Eighty-five percent of American families own one or more of the 140 million motor vehicles registered in the United States. Each year, 26,000 dealers will sell as many as fourteen million new cars, as well as another twenty million used automobiles.

One of every six Americans employed, some fourteen million, serves the internal combustion engine, working for more than 800,000 businesses which are either dependent entirely on the automobile, or are automobile-related.

One out of every six wage earners, joining with the other five to spend over $140 billion, one of every four retail dollars, on their family cars. The automobiles they drive consume 13 percent of their salaries. Over the ten-year life span of the vehicle—and fewer than one of every five autos built actually survives the rigors that long—its owner will have spent as much as forty-five cents for every mile driven.

Ten, twelve, fourteen million new motor vehicles each year. One hundred thirty-eight million people licensed to drive them, more than one-half of the nation's population, annually traveling 1.4 trillion miles in sedans, coupes, station wagons, vans, pickups, compacts, sports cars, roadsters, dune buggies, and half a hundred other configurations of body and internal combustion engine.

Every billion dollars in automobile sales means jobs for some 57,000 workers; every billion dollars in sales lost produces a two-billion-dollar decline in the gross national product.

What is good for General Motors *is* good for America. What is good for America is good for General Motors as well.

From its earliest faltering miles on unpaved streets, the automobile conferred mobility on those who otherwise would have none. It offered privacy—often the only available—for millions of teenagers and changed a nation's courtship customs. Its chromium accouterments and accessories offered status, or the badge of status, which in the anonymous, mobile society the automobile created were at once the same thing. The automobile slowly but surely eviscerated public-transportation systems, transformed the delivery of goods and services, molded the size and shape of the nation's cities, and altered the very nature of life in twentieth-century America.

It had given life, and it had killed—49,700 in 1977, 55,000 and more in the years before the 55-mile-per-hour speed limit on the nation's highways. How many thousands more have died, and will die in the future, because the automobile contributed 47 percent of all air pollution until 1970, is incalculable. The noxious brown haze that wreathes the world's cities shortens lives, public-health officials aver.

The automobile had birthed vast satellite industries, powerful principalities in their own right: oil, rubber, and glass companies, service stations and garages, highway-construction combines and motor-hotel chains, even parking lots, whose owners make up the largest landholders in most urban centers. The automobile also beguiled the nation into enormous programs of mixed benefits: a massive interstate highway system, 45,000 miles of concrete and asphalt that cost $72 billion, quartered the nation, sliced cities apart, and garroted neighborhoods in a noose of motor vehicles.

And astride it all loomed the colossus of roads, the fourteenth richest "nation" in the world, the greatest industrial empire ever assembled, the employer of more people worldwide than live in Washington, D.C.

General Motors.

Producer of one out of every four automobiles manufactured in the world, six of every ten in the United States. Larger than Ford and Toyota—the second- and third-ranked auto manufacturers—combined.

Consumer of one out of every ten tons of steel manufactured in the United States, one of every four tons of iron, more than one-third of the natural rubber imported. The world's largest industrial hydra is itself a $30-billion-per-year customer, buying from 40,000 suppliers on five continents.

Owner of a private air force of thirteen planes, the cost of which is "under $10 million per year to operate," the company once reported disingenuously. Owner of thirty-five subsidiaries in twenty-six foreign countries, of 121 factories in seventy-seven American cities. Owner of General Motors Acceptance Corporation, whose $45 billion in outstanding loans make it the largest seller of short-term commercial notes in the United States.

Producer of diesel locomotives, digital computers, rifles, steel tubing, fork-lift trucks, inertial navigation systems, earthmovers, jet engines, armor plating, airplane propellers, garden tools, buses, helicopter engines, fiber optics, electric motors, ball bearings, and, of course, automobiles and trucks—9.4 million in 1978 alone.

Of a size barely comprehensible, General Motors grows each year. Between 1970 and 1977, while the gross national product of the United States doubled, General Motors' sales tripled. The world's largest meganumerical eats longest at the groaning board.

General Motors' sales are more than five times those of the

nation's largest grocery chain, Safeway; almost four times greater than those of the largest mercantile dealer, Sears. Were the Chevrolet Motors Division split from the parent company, each of the severed parts would rank among the five largest industrial corporations in the United States.

Such size generates vast power, well beyond the palpable financial influence. "There is probably no company in the United States that affects the lives of the citizens of the country as much as General Motors," the staff of a Senate subcommittee concluded in 1956. Seventeen years later, critical economist John Kenneth Galbraith noted, "The public decisions of General Motors in the course of any year are far more consequential than those of any state legislature." Decisions made and ratified on the fourteenth floor of the brooding building on West Grand Boulevard in Detroit directly and indirectly affect every man, woman, and child in the United States, as well as uncounted millions around the world. This is power undreamed of seventy years ago by the company's founder, a one-time cigar drummer who couldn't resist taking a flier.

Part I

BEGINNINGS

The car stood in the middle of the yard, quite unattended, the stable-helps and other hangers-on being all at their dinner. Toad walked slowly round it, inspecting, criticizing, musing deeply.

"I wonder," he said to himself presently, "I wonder if this sort of car *starts* easily?"

Next moment, hardly knowing how it came about, he found he had hold of the handle and was turning it. As the familiar sound broke forth, the old passion seized on Toad and completely mastered him, body and soul. As if in a dream, he pulled the lever and swung the car round the yard and out through the archway; and, as if in a dream, all sense of right and wrong, all fear of obvious consequences, seemed temporarily suspended. He increased his pace, and as the car devoured the street and leapt forth on the high road through the open country, he was only conscious that he was Toad once more, Toad at his best and highest, Toad the terror, the traffic-queller, the Lord of the lone trail, before whom all must give way or be smitten into nothingness and everlasting night. He chanted as he flew, and the car responded with sonorous drone; the miles were eaten up under him as he sped he knew not whither, fulfilling his instincts, living his hour, reckless of what might come to him.

—Kenneth Grahame, *The Wind in the Willows*

1

A Matter of Timing

Billy Durant flogged the coughing black machine through the mud and dust of the Michigan countryside, damning mechanical gods and all inventors in one breath, exalting them in the next. His excitement rose and fell as the borrowed Buick lumbered up hills, teetered on the crests, and hurtled down again, belching a pungent wake of smoke and gasoline fumes.

The farmers around Flint, Michigan, had grown accustomed to goggled Billy Durant, shrouded in an overly large linen duster, racing along the rutted tracks that bounded their sections. More than a few in this autumn of 1904 had hitched a team to the suddenly spavined machine after a chagrined Durant had come walking up to a farmhouse to ask for a tow.

By early October the chagrin and rueful second thoughts had vanished. Durant was elated. The Buick was miles ahead of the steam-powered Mobile, the first motorcar in which Durant had ever ridden. That ride two years earlier, with the ponderous vehicle lurching and rumbling under his unsteady seat, had been more alarming than he had cared to admit.

13

William Crapo Durant knew little about automobiles, and even less about their mechanical innards. Which was why James H. Whiting, president of the Flint Wagon Works, had asked Durant to try out this first of David Dunbar Buick's Model-B's. Comfortable? Reliable? See for yourself, the older man urged.

Stern J. H. Whiting—his portrait suggests a man with a tumultuous ulcer and a plague of vexations—wanted Billy Durant to take charge of the Buick. He needed a younger man to run the new company, to sell the automobile handcrafted in Whiting's carriage works. So he had arranged for Durant to borrow Buick number one, owned by Flint's town doctor.

Durant was intrigued with the idea of a new product in a new industry, though "industry" might be too grand a word just yet. But Durant could see the possibilities; what the Buick, and the automobile in general, needed was a salesman like Billy Durant.

If he could find the time. The stock market had been going down all year, sometimes precipitously, in what Hearst and Pulitzer doomcriers were calling the "Rich Man's Depression." Warily following the market-dominating moves of men the likes of Morgan, Hill, and Brady, Durant had devoted most of the year in the New York offices of the Durant–Dort Carriage Company simply trying to get out of the Street alive.

The slide proved temporary, a wringing-out of the market, with Hill and Harriman scrambling for another railroad and the Mellons cornering copper or aluminum or whatever else caught their eye. Certainly the panic was nothing to dampen the far-seeing optimism of a man like Billy Durant, who could recognize signs of progress all around him: great industries, growing cities, even a few improved roads—too few, Durant might admit, perched on the high seat of the motorized carriage.

A hundred railroads cobwebbed the nation. Thomas Edison's incandescent bulb lighted buildings and Detroit's city streets. Just a year before, two bicycle mechanics from Ohio had flown an aeroplane 852 feet over the sand dunes at Kitty Hawk, North Carolina. George Eastman's roll film had transformed photography from an arcane science to an everyday hobby—and a million-dollar business. The glorious St. Louis Exposition had opened in the spring of 1904 to celebrate the manifest progress in the hundred years since the Louisiana Purchase, and the entire country was singing a musical invitation to "Meet Me in St. Louis, Louis." The Exposition's contribution to this orgy or social advancement was the hot dog and the ice-cream cone.

Growth and progress were everywhere. New York's first subway, a marvel in itself, would open later that October, but would be overshadowed quickly by the new Williamsburg Bridge and by the world's tallest building—the twenty-two-story, 280-foot-tall "Flatiron" building. There was excitement in the air, a zest for expansion; twenty-two stories was just a start. This was to be the American Century, and "they were optimistic, optimists to the point of belligerence," as Booth Tarkington wrote of the citizens of Midland City, in *The Magnificent Ambersons*.

As if to affirm that optimism, the United States occupied the Canal Zone; surveyors already were sighting their way across the isthmus in what was to be the largest, most costly engineering endeavor in history. That took confidence, and a man like Teddy Roosevelt in the White House to bully the project through.

Durant admired the brash go-getter in Roosevelt, the president's ability to get things done. Wall Street was wary of him, but Durant had scant respect for the opinions of pusillanimous bankers and old-maid brokers. As long as Roosevelt went after only the biggest of the trusts—James Duke's United States Tobacco Company or Rockefeller's Standard Oil—Billy Durant would find a way to create his financial empire.

Billy Durant meant to be a part of this Age of Gold and Steel. Already the major figure in the nation's largest carriage manufactory, Durant had kept an eye on these new automobiles, possible competition for his Blue Ribbon carriage line. Nearly every newspaper in the country had an automotive column; the weekly magazines outdid each other putting forward this or that new motorcar, this or that new accessory to enhance the pleasures of fun-loving motorists.

The public was eager for the novelty. What Durant wanted was a reliable machine he could believe in, one he could sell. If he had it in David Dunbar Buick's valve-in-head engine, forget the noise, forget the complaints of oily fumes and nauseous stench; what horse could go thirty miles per hour, hour after hour? So for six weeks during September and October of 1904, William Crapo Durant, grandson of a Michigan governor and self-made millionaire, sat regally at the tiller of the two-cylinder Buick loaned to him by Dr. Herbert H. Hills. Or waited impatiently for the hot-tempered Walter Marr, Buick's chief mechanic, to repair a mysterious gear or obscure valve.

Investment in the Buick Motor Company tickled the gambler in Durant. The industry was new, but was growing rapidly. In 1903, some sixty producing automobile companies had sold more than 11,000 vehicles. Automobile men who thronged the bar of Detroit's Pontchartrain Hotel assured the ever-smiling, abstinent Durant that sales surely would double that year. While twice as many firms had failed, and the industry was rife with promoters who had nothing more than vast stock offerings to sell, the expensive experimental phase of the automobile's development was about over.

There were enough horseless carriages on the muddy roads of America to prove the worth of the gasoline engine. Ransom E. Olds alone had sold more than 4,000 of his one-cylinder, curved-dash runabouts at $650 each in 1903, proving the automobile was something more than a rich man's amusement. Six hundred fifty dollars—more than a year's wage for a laborer—was dear enough, but the swell of middle-class America, owners of comfortable homes built and furnished for as little as $3,000, would be able to afford this newest creation of capitalist enterprise. All the market needed was a sound automobile at a fair price—the Buick would do—and a Billy Durant to sell it.

If there was one thing Billy Durant could do, it was sell. It was for just that reason J.H. Whiting had arranged for Dr. Hills' loan of the first Model-B. The year before, Whiting had bought control of the Buick Motor Company, and now he needed someone to run it; his own carriage business was too demanding to allow him time enough. Buick, Marr, and head engineer Eugene C. Richard were mechanics more interested in tinkering with their machines and tools than businessmen concerned with putting the enterprise on a firm basis. The Buick Motor Company urgently needed a promoter, someone to line up distributors and convince them of the worth of the Buick.

At the Chicago convention of carriage manufacturers early in 1904, Whiting had sounded out an old friend, F. A. Aldrich, secretary of Flint's largest carriage maker, Durant–Dort. Aldrich agreed that his boss, Billy Durant, would be the man for the job at the Buick Motor Company. With the right kind of inducement, Durant—well, you never could be sure with Rushabout Billy.

At forty-three, Durant was a success, a millionaire several times over, and Flint's leading citizen, though he spent little time in that self-proclaimed "Vehicle Capital of the World." Born in 1861 in Boston, the son of William Clark and Rebecca Durant, "Willie," as the family called him, and a younger sister were brought to live in his mother's home town of Flint when the boy was eleven. They were good New England stock, his mother would point out frequently. Rebecca Crapo Durant was a direct descendant of Resolved White, one of the 102 voyagers who first saw Massachusetts' stern and rockbound shore from the deck of the leaking *Mayflower,* and in later years would serve as a vice-regent of the Daughters of the American Revolution, buoyed into office by her son's prominence. Billy's father was nominally an investment banker of good prospects, though career and sobriety both had vanished in soft companions and hard liquor. Given an opportunity to recoup, William Durant had failed in 1863 to secure Boston investment money for his father-in-law's Flint and Holly Railroad. An erratic provider, the alcoholic Durant drifted from one stock promotion to another, then disappeared entirely from Boston, Flint, and the lives of his aristocratic wife and two children.

While Billy Durant was a favored grandchild—grandfather Henry Howland Crapo, governor of Michigan from 1865 to 1869, enrolled him when he was seven as an honorary colonel in the state militia—Rebecca Durant and her two children had little money. For the first three years they lived in Flint, Billy an impressionable eleven- to fourteen-year-old, the Durants lived on relatives' generosity. Only with the death first of her father, then of her mother in 1875, did inheritance free Rebecca Durant of financial concern.

Billy Durant adored his doting mother and never spoke of his absent father. Man and boy apparently had had little contact, though the son's lifelong abstinence may well have been a lesson learned indirectly from the alcoholic father. Yet something of the father lingered in the son: a penchant for the big flier, the business gamble others disdained. Billy was just more successful.

Seven years in the Flint public schools were enough for the restless youth. Willie-grown-to-Billy left high school in his senior year in order to supplement the family income. *Plutarch's Lives* was as nothing compared to the world of commerce.

Billy Durant took a job in the lumberyard founded by his grandfather. He turned over his millhand's salary to his mother, saving only enough of that $3.00 per week to buy himself snappy clothes purveyed in Flint's leading haberdashery. Though he listed himself in the city directory as a laborer, Durant was an impeccable dresser even then. The derby, the boutonniere, the nipped-waist jacket later to be called Edwardian proclaimed him a young man on the go.

Durant did not stay long in the lumberyard. In short order, he went to work at the company store, then on to a night clerk's job in a drug store. There he spotted a patent medicine he thought had potential and took it on the road, selling to farmers in the Flint vicinity. The patent-medicine business palling—the restive Durant was always on the lookout for new enterprises—he became a drummer for a cigar company. So successful was Durant that the cigar manufacturer laid off three other salesmen and turned their territories over to the not-yet-twenty-one-year-old. In Horace Walpole's phrase, he had "just enough parts to lead him astray from common sense."

But Durant quickly tired of the cigar business too; besides, he had responsibilities at home. His mother objected to his constant travel, and the Flint City bandmaster wanted him back at his post as drum major and sometime cornet player. Dutiful "Willie" complied, and with former schoolmate I.W. Whitehead to handle administrative details, opened an insurance office in Flint. He was at last peddling something that matched his capabilities as a salesman.

With each move, Durant's fortunes had improved; now that he was in insurance—real estate and construction would follow—he was marked as just the sort of up-and-comer needed to restore the near-bankrupt Flint Waterworks Company to solvency. A delegation of the town's leading businessmen called on the ambitious young man, asking him to assume management of the privately owned utility. As secretary, he would make twenty-five dollars a month—not a great deal of money when a millhand could earn seventy-five cents for a ten-hour day—but he would not have to relinquish his partnership in the prospering insurance business. Durant accepted.

Within eight months Billy Durant had the company back on its feet, had expanded patronage, and had improved service by personally soliciting complaints from each of the waterworks' subscribers. He had restored the business by personal salesmanship, this time door-to-door, often working into the early-morning hours.

Capable of eighteen- to twenty-hour days, often for long periods, Durant was a man of driven energy. Of medium height, never weighing more than 135 pounds, he functioned on enthusiasm and blue-plate specials served up in all-night cafes. People who met him invariably were impressed: by the brown eyes crinkled at the corners in a perpetual smile; by the punctilious manners; by the soft voice, never raised, never harsh.

Durant's capacity for work set him apart. He had few friends or confidants, no chums, only associates, men who played checkers with cigar-smoking Billy, exchanging pleasantries and little more. Everyone knew him, he knew everyone; yet no one was truly close. If he took on a job, he insisted on being the boss, a condition he imposed when he accepted the waterworks post; he could delegate authority only sparingly. It was his reputation that was at stake, and only he, Billy Durant, could make certain the job would be done as he wanted it.

The waterworks firmly in hand, Durant conceivably might have become an entrepreneur in the burgeoning utilities industry but for a chance discovery in 1886. An acquaintance offered Durant a ride in a novel two-wheeled cart much like a racing sulky. Assured the lightweight vehicle would not tip over, and impressed by the unique suspension system which imparted such stability on the worst of roads, Durant sought out the manufacturer in Coldwater, Michigan. Durant had intended only to se-

cure a sales territory, but the virtually bankrupt Coldwater Road
Cart Company would go him one better. For $1,500 he could buy
the entire assets, including the patent for the little cart.

Durant plunged. No matter that he lacked the $2,000 it would
require to buy and move the company to Flint. Durant turned to
J. Dallas Dort, a friend then rusticating as part owner of a Flint
hardware store. Clerking was not a fit career for the heir to
Detroit's largest brickyard, a graduate of Michigan State Normal
College at Ypsilanti; the restive Dort agreed to put up half of the
money, selling his interest in the hardware store and borrowing
the rest. Durant convinced a local bank to lend him the other
$1,000.

At the age of twenty-five, Durant was a manufacturer. The
simply designed cart was easily fabricated in the factory of W. A.
Paterson, then Flint's largest carriage builder. Paterson charged
the newly organized Flint Road Cart Company, which itself had
no factory, $12.50 for each finished cart. The two partners sold
the carts to dealers for $17.00.

On the strength of orders for 600 of the carts, sold by Durant
before one had even been manufactured, the partners placed an
order with Paterson for 1,200 vehicles. The cart was an immediate success, the Flint Road Cart Company selling 4,000 in its first
year and realizing a profit of $18,000. William Crapo Durant was
on his way.

By 1904, the renamed Durant–Dort Carriage Company was
the nation's largest carriage manufacturer, with fourteen factories in the United States and Canada, and the owner of stands
of hickory in Mississippi and Arkansas. A half-dozen subsidiaries supplied parts and paints and varnishes for the full line
of 50,000 "Blue Ribbon" carriages, wagons, and carts the company assembled annually in its factories. Capitalized at $2 mil-
lion, Durant–Dort had a $3-million payroll each year.

Dort was president, but no one doubted that it was Billy Durant who provided the driving force behind Flint's largest employer. In the years since he had created the company, Durant
had made just one mistake: he had organized subsidiaries to
build bicycles and replacement parts with money invested by
friends in Flint. The bicycle craze of the 1880s subsequently

withered, and Durant's companies with it, yet Durant himself had come out of his first business failure with his personal reputation greater than ever. On the grounds that he and Dort had encouraged their friends to invest in the bicycle companies, he insisted that Durant–Dort repay each of the investors. If it was Durant's company in good times, it was also his responsibility in bad times. Dozens of Flint residents learned one could get rich by investing with Durant; you never went broke on his fliers. Billy made sure of that.

While building the Durant–Dort Carriage Company, Durant had learned more about the mass marketing of road vehicles than anyone else in the country. He also had evolved a theory to explain his success as a salesman: "Assume that the man you are talking to knows as much or more than you do. Do not talk too much. Give the customer time to think. In other words, let the customer sell himself."

The best product was a "self-seller. If you cannot find one, make one." First with a novel suspension system, then with a low-cost line of buggies, then with a lavishly appointed carriage, Durant found the "self-sellers."

Sometime after 1902 and his unsettling ride in the steam-powered Mobile, Durant first looked into the motorcar industry. Long-established carriage makers such as the Studebaker Brothers were investing. The well-known Peerless Wringer Company had brought out an automobile with a gasoline engine, and the White Sewing Machine Company had marketed a steam-powered vehicle. Bird-cage manufacturer George A. Pierce was offering an automobile he called the Arrow. The Pope Manufacturing Company, the nation's largest bicycle manufacturer, was reorganizing to sell automobiles. Nordyke and Marmon—their heavy machinery rumbled in Durant's own factories—was going to build a Marmon automobile.

Until such established manufacturers entered the business, the American automotive industry was a precarious web of garage experimenters. No one man actually could prove he invented the automobile, though a Rochester, New York, patent attorney by the name of George Selden had applied for a United States patent in 1879 for a four-wheeled wagon powered by a three-cylinder, internal-combustion engine. Selden was seemingly one of the few Americans to keep abreast of experiments and technical developments in Europe, where shopfuls of Englishmen, Germans, and Frenchmen were painfully handcrafting automobiles.

In Cologne, Germany, Herr Doktor Nicholas Otto compressed first illuminating gas and then gasoline—that petroleum distillates had explosive qualities had been known at least since 1799—to fuel a series of stationary engines that operated on a four-cycle principle. (The theoretical sequence' was accorded a French patent in 1862; Otto was merely the first to apply it practically.) The piston of Otto's patent *Gasmotor* made four strokes in a single cycle: the first to take in the fuel and air mixture, the second to compress it, the third to ignite it by a timed spark, and the fourth to exhaust the resultant gases before the four-stroke cycle began again. Only one of the four strokes actually powered the crankshaft; a flywheel provided momentum for the three unpowered strokes.

Though Otto produced a significant number of stationary and semi-portable engines to compete with the well-established steam engine, a fifty-year-old engineer, Gottlieb Daimler, was dissatisfied. Leaving his post as manager of the Otto *Gasmotorwerke* in 1882, Daimler started a business of his own, hoping to reduce the size of Otto's cumbersome engine and install it on a road vehicle. It took Daimler seven years to build a four-wheeled, four-seat *Gaswagen*. Fourteen years later, Crédit Lyonnais banker and diplomat Emil Jellinek would commission a specially built Daimler racing car and name it after his daughter Mercedes.

Meanwhile, Karl Benz, a twenty-eight-year-old graduate of Karlsruhe's technical high school, had opened his own firm, first building stationary engines on the Otto principle, then a gasoline-powered automobile with water-jacketed cylinders and electric ignition of the fuel mixture. Patented in 1886, the machine was in quantity production almost immediately.

By 1891, the French automotive firm of Panhard–Levassor had secured rights to the Daimler and Benz engines, installing them with a combination of clutch, reduction gears, and chain drive to deliver power to the rear wheels. The Panhard–Levassor was the first to place elliptical springs between the chassis and the body, with the upright engine in front of *l'automobiliste* to take advantage of whatever cooling air currents the fifteen-mile-per-hour vehicle generated.

Most American mechanics were unaware of all these developments, or even that the word "automobile" had been coined by the French Academy—in recognition not so much of the gasoline-powered vehicle as of the ponderous steam omnibuses which were threatening life and property in both England and France by 1875. In half a hundred machine shops and garages across the United States, mechanical-minded men were attempting first to perfect a stationary gasoline engine and then reduce it in size so that it could be fit to a carriage. Fifty more were struggling with cumbersome steam- or electric-powered vehicles. As one pioneer mechanic-engineer, Hiram P. Maxim, put it: "I was blissfully ignorant that Benz and Daimler in Germany; DeDion, Panhard and a host of others in France; Napier and a few others in England; Duryea Brothers, Haynes, Apperson Brothers, Winton, and others in the United States were working might and main on gasoline-propelled road vehicles [in 1892]. I was also blissfully ignorant of the existence of one George B. Selden of Rochester, New York, who had applied for a patent on my idea when I was a little boy at school. As I look back, I am amazed that so many of us began work so nearly at the same time, and without the slightest notion that others were working on the problem."

The year after Maxim, then superintendent of the American Projectile Company of Lynn, Massachusetts, began work on his gasoline-powered automobile, Charles E. and J. Frank Duryea finished their first car in nearby Springfield. By September 1895, the Duryea brothers had abandoned their bicycle-repair business altogether and incorporated the Duryea Motor Wagon Company, offering a "two-seater" for $1,000 and a "four-seater" for $2,000. In 1896, Charles having migrated to Illinois after an argument over further development of the wagon, J. Frank alone built thirteen Duryeas. In the accepted trade custom of the day,

America's first new-car buyer, George H. Morill, Jr., of Norwood, Massachusetts, paid cash for his Duryea.

By November 1895, the workshops of ignorance had been breached. That month, the first magazine solely devoted to the automobile, *The Horseless Age,* bravely proclaimed: "Those who have taken the pains to search below the surface of the great tendencies of the age, know what a giant industry is struggling into being there. All signs point to the motor vehicle as the necessary sequence of methods of locomotion already established and approved. The growing needs of our civilization demand it; the public believes in it, and await[s] with lively interest its practical application to the daily business of the world."

Before the end of the month, sixty people, mostly would-be manufacturers, met in Chicago to form the American Motor League. No man among them outstanding, none was elected president. Instead, the assembled members picked four vice-presidents, including Hiram P. Maxim and Charles E. Duryea.

It was the group's newly elected treasurer, railroad mechanic Charles Brady King, who was to provide the next significant accomplishment of the "industry struggling into being." On the night of March 6, 1896, King drove his four-cylinder, four-cycle automobile around downtown Detroit, all the while followed by an interested bicyclist furiously pedaling through the snow flurries. The Detroit *Journal* reported the next day: "The first horseless carriage seen in this city was out on the streets last night. . . . The apparatus seemed to work all right, and it went at the rate of five or six miles an hour at an even rate of speed." The bicyclist who trailed behind King was a lanky, thirty-two-year-old mechanical engineer employed by the Edison Illuminating Company. Henry Ford's parallel efforts on the "Quadricycle" in the garage behind his Bagby Avenue home had lagged behind those of his friend King.

Two new automobile manufacturers entered the lists in 1897: Alexander Winton in Cleveland, and the Olds Motor Company, Michigan's first. Both Winton and Olds previously had manufactured stationary engines for marine and industrial use and intended to adapt those engines to the horseless carriage. At the same time, the Electric Vehicle Company, the creation of Columbia Bicycle's Colonel Albert A. Pope and some of Wall Street's most venturesome entrepreneurs, launched a fleet of two-and-one-half-ton electric taxicabs on the streets of Manhattan. (It was one of these cumbersome taxicabs that was responsible for the first recorded automobile accident.) The enterprise, promptly dubbed the "Lead Cab Trust," died within two years. By 1905, a trade journal would dismiss its few surviving two-passenger hacks as "a relic of an earlier period of automobile development."

Though few automobiles actually were constructed in these first years, there was widespread public interest in the industry's fitful progress. Newspapers created a new sport, publicizing automobile races as speeds increased from 1895's fifteen miles per hour to fifty miles per hour in 1900. More than a few promoters stood ready to tap the interest enthusiastic press accounts stirred, the bemused Ray Stannard Baker pointed out in a summary of the fledgling industry: "Between the 1st of January and the 1st of May, 1899, companies with the enormous aggregate capitalization of more than $388,000,000 have been organized in New York, Boston, Chicago, and Philadelphia for the sole purpose of manufacturing and operating these new vehicles. At least eight establishments are now actually engaged in building carriages, coaches, tricycles, delivery-wagons and trucks, representing no fewer than 200 different types of vehicles, with nearly half as many methods of propulsion."

Ransom E. Olds became the ninth manufacturer when, with $500,000 invested by Detroit copper and lumber magnate Samuel L. Smith, he incorporated a new Olds Motor Works on May 9, 1899. The firm lost $80,000 in its first year. Ironically, the Olds Motor Works would have gone under but for a fire on Saturday, March 9, 1901, which totally destroyed not only the building but the huge electric sign on the roof that had proclaimed this "the largest automobile factory in the world." James J. Brady, a young timekeeper, skittered into Mr. Smith's fast-disappearing factory and pushed to safety a lightweight, experimental car that Olds earlier had decided not to build.

Olds took one last gamble with Mr. Smith's money. He moved the surviving model with its distinctive curved dashboard to his former factory in Lansing, drew plans directly from the model itself, and farmed out the fabrication to subcontractors. The successful bidders were an odd group. Patriarchal Henry M. Leland of Leland–Faulconer, Detroit's premier machine shop, undertook to build the engines. The fun-loving John and Horace Dodge, having abandoned their Windsor, Ontario, factory when the bicycle boom collapsed in 1896, made the transmissions. The Briscoe brothers, though busy stamping out garbage cans in their sheet-metal shop, contracted for the radiators. Barney Everitt, a Detroit carriage builder, went to Norwalk, Ohio, to lure close-mouthed Fred Fisher from his family firm, then put him in charge of building the curved-dash's distinctive body. All would become major figures in the automobile industry.

That lightweight phoenix raised by a spunky timekeeper was to become one of the most famous automobiles in American history. "No accidents with the Oldsmobile," the company advertised in 1901. "Mechanical skill and mathematical exactness eliminate the danger of the horse's uncertain temper, sudden fright and unruly disposition."

Olds Motor Works sold 425 of its curved-dash runabouts in 1901, and 2,500 the following year. The Oldsmobile was the nation's first mass-produced automobile, and it eventually inspired the still-familiar song of 1906, "[Come Away with Me, Lucille,] In My Merry Oldsmobile." Priced to sell to a middle-class market of professional men and merchants, the Olds became a favorite of the upper class as well—a snooty cachet that added even more to the automobile's appeal.

Involved in the stock market himself, Billy Durant watched as others tentatively entered the automobile business. One of his competitors, Studebaker Brothers, carriage makers since 1852, began distributing an electric-powered vehicle in 1902. Though its electric motor was both quieter and cleaner than the rival gasoline engine, the automobile had two serious drawbacks: the great weight of the batteries slowed the vehicle's top speed, and the short range of the "fuel" supply required incessant, expensive recharging. Eventually these two faults doomed the electric auto.

Public interest—curiosity, anyway—grew apace. Forty-eight thousand people, paying fifty cents admission, attended the first national automobile show in New York's Madison Square Garden from November 3 through 10, 1900. There were fifty-one exhibitors amid the rented potted palms and patriotic bunting. Thirty-one had salesmen at the ready to take orders for autos then in production or promised for some future, albeit indefinite, delivery. Like social-climbing parents everywhere, the would-be industrialists were spending meager resources in a bravura launching of their child in polite society.

The bicycle was surely dead, after a brief boom that had put four million cyclists on inadequate roads. No less a figure than Colonel Albert A. Pope, creator of the short-lived bicycle trust and president of the new American Bicycle Company, proclaimed in the business press: "The automobile will in time be the universal means of transportation, and the future of the American Bicycle Company [for which Pope was attempting to float a $4.2-million stock issue to build two new automobiles] rests on the adoption and development of the automobile. . . . I predict that inside of ten years there will be more automobiles in use in the large cities of the United States than there are now horses in these cities." This self-confident captain of capitalism was wrong by only half a decade, but by then he was long bankrupt.

Public enthusiasm for the automobile in the first years of the century—humorists called it "auto-mania"—was matched only by Wall Street's restraint. Bankers and stock brokers alike were wary of the industry, disturbed by the ephemeral character of so many of the erstwhile manufacturers. The collapse of the "Lead Cab Trust" did nothing to enhance the reputation of the industry, for if such financial rakehells as Thomas Fortune Ryan and William C. Whitney came a cropper, the time was premature for prudent men to consider serious investments.

Billy Durant, already a Wall Street veteran, was well aware of the financial community's disdain. Unlike the Morgans, the Mellons, or Kuhn, Loeb, though, he recognized the opportunity. No matter that it was impossible to predict public preferences: one-, two-, or four-cylinder engines; planetary, cone, or pneumatic transmissions; tiller or wheel steering; buggy or "French" body;

front or rear drive; chain or leather drive; the tubular frame or the Peerless' new pressed-steel frame. The automobile was commercially viable, providing one had a reliable motor and gear drive. Design changes could be made to accommodate public demand; indeed, a manufacturer could offer more than one model, each incorporating various alternatives. The important thing was, as *Scientific American* editorialized in January 1904, that "the period of experiment is over, and the growing confidence of the public in the automobile is resulting in a remarkable growth in the industry. . . ."

There were, in reality, two automobiles—the high-wheeled wagon and the low-wheeled "French" body—as well as a variety of hybrids: wagon carriages with small-diameter wheels, motor-bicycles, and motorized tricycles. Each had its advocate. The tall wagon wheels allowed clearance over poor roads; the lower French bodies were more stable. In the earliest years, the motorized buggy was the favored design—in large part because the body craftsmen were carriage makers who left off only the harness and singletree. (Even that omission, one man proposed in a letter to *Scientific American,* might be overcome. A full-sized horse's head, with horn mounted in the mouth and the eyes converted into headlamps, would "humor the skittish horse" which might encounter this annoying imposter. It would "prevent the fear often experienced by the novice of being pitched over the dashboard of his car.")

Though even such an authority as Charles Duryea would reject the European body as "unsuited to American needs" and "demanded [only] by a few snobs who wish to show off the fact that they have been abroad and acquired a motor vehicle taste," the low-slung body prevailed. It would not be the last time European styling would be forced upon reluctant American manufacturers.

The French design prevailed over the American buggy simply because the bathtub bodies could be adorned with ever more lavish appointments. Passengers sat in high comfort, lording it over pedestrians, while running boards and small doors in the body made mounting the car easier than clambering onto a high-wheeled carriage. Given the hobble skirt demanded by contemporary fashion, it was no small advantage. Further, the

French body moved the engine to the front of the vehicle, out from under the passengers' well-padded buttocks; it soothed nerves unsettled by staccato, timed explosions beneath the *gluteus maximus*.

Although the automobile's great weight offered a semblance of solidity and reliability, neither condition actually prevailed. Buggy or French body, the automobile was a sickly conveyance, prone to mechanical difficulties bewildering to most drivers. Magnetos, differential gears, connecting rods, fuel pumps, and spark retarders were so many puzzles for most motorists, who either learned to cope or permanently garaged their ailing vehicles. As late as 1906, *Motor Age* was urging "a policy of extreme simplicity" to aid the grease-spattered motorist. "The simple car will not only be the car for the masses but will be easier to make, more satisfactory to sell and more sensible for the ordinary man to use . . ."

Whatever the mechanical or financial problems of James H. Whiting and the Buick motorcar in 1904, Billy Durant was certain he could overcome them. The investment required was small—once the engineers had finished their experimentation. In June 1903, Detroit coal merchant Alexander Y. Malcolmson had invested only $28,000 in the Ford Motor Company—the lanky engineer's third effort at manufacture after two false starts—and had sold 658 two-cylinder vehicles at $1,200 each. Henry Leland of Leland–Faulconer had resurrected the corpse Ford abandoned in 1903; the next year he sold 1,895 one-cylinder automobiles called the Cadillac. Henry B. Joy and a handful of his devil-may-care friends from Detroit's fashionable Woodward Avenue had invested in a company and sold 250 Packards in 1904.

The minimal investment required was made possible by the very structure of the industry. The automobile manufacturer did not so much build a horseless carriage as assemble parts made by a host of subcontractors. There were machine shops, carriage builders, and die makers aplenty to fashion engines, bodies, and transmissions; these companies normally expected thirty-to-ninety-day payment. At the same time, assembly of the completed components did not take long, nor require a large payroll.

The manufacturer then could ship his automobiles to dealers, who, in exchange for territorial franchises, were required to pay in advance at least 20 percent, and frequently much more, of the wholesale cost. Payment of the balance was in cash, immediately upon receipt of the motorized carriages from the factory. Cautious or impecunious manufacturers often shipped C.O.D.

Given this structure, the dealers' early deposits provided the manufacturer with working capital to build more cars to meet the hoped-for orders. In effect, the shrewd manufacturer could use a combination of credit from his suppliers and cash advances from his dealers to stay in business until he amassed sufficient working capital to expand his assembly plant.

Beyond the appearance of financial stability, which Durant could provide, a manufacturer most needed a proven design. Six weeks of driving Dr. Hills' Buick had convinced the skeptical Durant he had such a motorcar. It would be an automobile for a nation confident in its destiny, sure of a God-given prosperity, a nation of shopkeepers turned merchant princes, to whom the world looked for industrial leadership. Moreover, Durant intended the Buick to be built by a company that would rival the greatest industrial combines fashioned on Wall Street.

Durant meant to show the way.

2

The Founder

Billy Durant took six weeks to make up his mind about the automobile industry and the Buick motorcar. He had been slow getting into the bicycle business and had been caught just as the bubble burst. More cautious this time, Durant was convinced the automobile industry would continue to grow. Poor roads, which had limited the bicycle's range, hampered the automobile too, but gasoline engines powered vehicles where bicyclists dared not pedal.

As for the Buick itself, Durant was apparently swayed by a cautious endorsement of the vehicle in the technically inclined *Cycle and Automotive Trade Journal*. After an afternoon ride with David Buick's young son, Tom, at the tiller, writer Hugh Dolnar concluded: "The car was simply more than enough at every point, that day and that run." Dolnar also reported that his driver was fined twelve dollars for speeding during the test ride.

Durant's decisions made, it took two evenings of calculating and two conferences with Whiting and the directors of the Flint Wagon Works to settle the bargain on November 1, 1904. As

31

a director—he declined the presidency in favor of Whiting—Durant would reorganize the Buick Motor Company. The firm would be recapitalized immediately from $75,000 to $300,000 and again "in a few months" to $500,000. Durant's first responsibility was to sell this stock to raise working capital. In exchange, he was to have a free hand in setting company policy and directing Buick's fortunes, such as they were. Durant would take no weekly salary; instead, the company would give to him personally $325,000 in Buick shares after the entire stock issue was subscribed. To make his water-logged holdings valuable, Durant would have to sell Buicks. It was the sort of challenge he could savor, but then it was Durant who had structured the deal.

David Dunbar Buick himself paid little notice to the fifth reorganization his motor-building company was undergoing since it had been founded three years earlier as the Buick Auto-Vim and Power Company. Buick had never in his fifty years devoted much attention to business matters anyway. Raised in Detroit after his parents emigrated from Scotland, Buick had apprenticed in a local machine shop. By the mid-1880s, he was in business with a friend, the Buick and Sherwood Manufacturing Company successfully marketing plumbing supplies.

Buick's tinkering produced first a patented lawn sprinkler, then seriatim innovations in indoor plumbing, and finally a process of enameling porcelain to cast-iron bathtubs that broke a German monopoly. In a very direct way, Buick made possible the contemporary bathroom; architects were quick to incorporate his innovations in the Eastlake, Romanesque, and Shingle style homes then in fashion.

By the turn of the century, David Buick had lost interest in lawn sprinklers and water closets. The gasoline engine fascinated him. Buick sold his interest in his company and the patented enameling process, and with the $100,000 proceeds organized the Auto-Vim enterprise. First undertaking development of a stationary engine for marine and factory use, Buick later decided to follow the example of Ransom Olds and build a gasoline-powered automobile.

Buick and the two engineers working successively with him, Walter Marr and Eugene C. Richard, had an innovative idea.

They would place the air-intake and exhaust-outlet valves in the head, above the piston, rather than in the foot of the cylinder. Which of the three was responsible for this more efficient concept and which for its refinement would be a matter of argument for years to come—both Buick and Marr were quick-tempered, and Richard was excitable.

Engrossed in developing the engine, and building at least one auto in their Detroit workshop, none of the three engineers paid close attention to finances. By 1902, Buick's savings were gone, Auto-Vim was broke, and its founder was forced to seek additional financing. New capital led to the founding of the Buick Manufacturing Company, which absorbed Auto-Vim, if not David Buick's financial attention. By the fall of 1902, the firm was again short of cash, though Buick was closer to building a car with his new "valve-in-head" engine in it.

To complete the pilot model, Buick turned to Benjamin and Frank Briscoe, owners of a thriving Detroit sheet-metal plant. Already fabricating Oldsmobile radiators, the Briscoes had envisaged deeper involvement in the new industry. Benjamin Briscoe in particular fancied the family name gracing the radiator of a motorcar; the automobile had a status denied the backyard garbage can.

Benjamin Briscoe recognized opportunity when Buick knocked. His interest in David Dunbar Buick was directly correlated to his interest in the valve-in-head engine: he saw a Buick engine powering a grand Briscoe automobile. The brothers periodically advanced small sums to Buick, never as much as he needed and increasingly more than they cared to put out. The small amounts totaled $2,000 in May 1903, when the Briscoes proposed to advance a final $1,500 in exchange for a reorganization of the company.

Buick had no place else to turn. On May 19, the Buick Motor Company was incorporated, the Briscoes owning $99,700 and Buick $300 of the company's stock. The inventor could regain all the shares merely by repaying the $3,500 he owed to the Briscoes by September.

Early in the summer of 1903, the Briscoes realized Buick would be unable to repay the debt. The new engine still eluded completion—Buick would never consider it perfected—and the prospective Briscoe autocar was no closer to the showroom. The disenchanted brothers began looking for a buyer, and, while visiting relatives in Flint, Benjamin Briscoe accidentally found one.

His handlebar mustache finely twirled, strands of hair oiled by Macassar to his balding skull, James H. Whiting of the Flint Wagon Works was a formidable figure. Twenty years earlier he had converted a flagging sawmill into a prosperous carriage manufactory. Suspecting now that he would have to convert once again—this time from carriages to automobiles—Whiting snapped up the Briscoe offer: an automobile design in exchange for $3,500 to buy out the two brothers and some $11,000 of the wagon works' money to clear up debts Buick had incurred with various Detroit suppliers.

On September 10, 1903, Whiting took control of a new Buick Motor Company, David Buick accepting a 20-percent interest in the $50,000 worth of stock as compensation for his work to date. Whiting apparently intended the new Buick motor to power a perfected Whiting Wagon Works machine sometime in the future; in the interim, the company would make and sell conventional stationary and marine engines. When David Buick's valve-in-head engine was ready, there would be ample opportunity to build a chassis and body in the waiting wagon works.

For a man of Whiting's sobriety, caution was not unreasonable. Advertisements in trade magazines offering for sale "four-passenger, side-entrance car bodies, in good condition, at considerably reduced prices" were not unusual epitaphs for the speculative dreams of automobile entrepreneurs. The same issue of the Flint *Journal* announcing the arrival of the Buick in Flint also reported that Michigan's blacksmiths, in convention assembled, had voted $5,000 to create a state college of horseshoeing. (Buick or no, horses outnumbered automobiles 3,000 to 1 in the United States; indeed, horse droppings were condemned as a public-health hazard in large cities.)

Even more telling, because a capable friend was involved, Alexander Brownell Cullen Hardy, the one-time works manager of the Durant–Dort Carriage Company, had decided to leave the automotive business. Hardy had managed to build fifty-two vibrant red and burnished-brass Flint Roadsters and sell his low-priced cars at a profit. Suddenly confronted with a demand that he pay royalties to the holders of the Selden patent, the disgusted Hardy was quitting the automobile industry for a manager's job in a Waterloo, Iowa, wagon factory. It was a keen loss for Flint's close-knit carriage industry.

Whiting waited through the winter of 1903–04. The Buick Motor Company produced conventional stationary engines, selling them through the wagon works' carriage dealers. Sales were promising, but not enough to satisfy either David Buick's capacity to spend money perfecting the recalcitrant valve-in-head engine or for Whiting to consider proper expansion.

David Buick finally completed a pilot model of a two-cylinder, valve-in-head engine on May 27, 1904; the wagon works then owned the most powerful engine, pound-for-pound, in the world. Nothing would do, Buick and Marr argued, but to fit the engine to an automobile chassis, to fulfill its destiny.

The stationary engines were selling well at this point. Wary of an unprofitable diversion too soon in the company's career, Whiting gave nervous assent only for the construction of a single prototype. Mass production, he insisted, was dependent upon successful completion of test runs over a course that he would choose. If the Buick Motor Company were to produce an automobile, it would be a proven one. The Whiting Wagon Works' and Whiting's own reputations were at stake.

Perched atop the prototype, Tom Buick and derby-topped Marr set off on a 230-mile, circuitous run from Flint to Detroit and back—the actual distance between the two cities was sixty-five miles—on Saturday, July 9, 1904. Stopping at small towns along the way for the publicity value, the two men arrived in Detroit the following Monday. They made the return trip, with Marr driving the entire 115 miles, in 217 minutes the next day. Whiting was satisfied.

With orders prompted by the well-publicized test run, Whiting finally agreed to put the Model-B into production. (Six cars produced by Buick in Detroit in 1903 were now belatedly labeled "Model-A.") The first of the sixteen Model-B's produced in 1904 was delivered on July 27 to Dr. Herbert H. Hills; this was the vehicle Billy Durant was to pilot along the roads surrounding Flint.

To some extent it was affection for his home town that prompted Billy Durant to take on the struggling Buick Motor Company. If Buick failed, three of Flint's banks would follow, bringing on a local depression and inevitably leading to the collapse of a covey of smaller manufacturing firms and local merchants.

On November 1, 1904, Durant took over as general manager and director of the Buick Motor Company. Within a week he set off on a series of moves which transformed the poverty-hounded Buick of 1904 into the nation's largest-selling car by 1908. He transferred operations from the crowded Buick factory in Flint to an empty building in Jackson, Michigan, that had housed the Imperial Wheel Company, a Durant–Dort subsidiary. Motor and transmission construction continued in Flint, where the W.F. Stewart Carriage Company also built the Model-B body, but final assembly and sales were conducted in Jackson.

On a trip to the Jackson plant about this time, Durant was serenely confident. "E.W.," he proclaimed to a friend on a tour of the new facility, "they claim this motor car business is a mystery—has an electric plant, a water plant and a whole lot of other gadgets. But after all, it is nothing but organization. Organization. Organization," he reiterated. "Bricks and mortar," Durant snapped, rapping his visitor on the knee. "Men and machinery and organization. And E. W., I am going to be one of the big motor car manufacturers of this country."

The organization-minded Durant's next move was to purchase the license granted by the Association of Licensed Automobile Manufacturers (A.L.A.M.) to the Pope–Robinson Company of Hyde Park, Massachusetts, so as to avoid patent-infringement problems that had throttled the earlier Flint Roadster. The A.L.A.M. held the rights to the patent granted to Rochester, New York, attorney-inventor George Selden, a patent that seemingly covered the automobile.

An outraged Henry Ford had elected to challenge the Selden patent in court; Durant preferred to pay the 1¼ percent on the retail selling price the A.L.A.M. demanded as a license fee. With the Buick Model-C then taking shape in the Jackson assembly plant priced at $1,200, Durant would be tithing $15 for each car he sold in order to avoid the threat of a lawsuit, the outcome of which was uncertain.

The Model-C was introduced to the public at the New York Automobile Show in January 1905. Catalogs distributed at the show described the twenty-two-horsepower Model-C as finished in royal blue with gold-and-black striping, brass moldings, and thirty-inch wheels on an eighty-seven-inch wheelbase. It was virtually identical to 1904's Model-B, except for one major attribute: Billy Durant was selling it.

The least expensive car in its price range, the Model-C was also the most powerful, a reporter for *Horseless Age* noted. George Otis Draper enthused: "The general finish and design of the Buick are excellent, and it should attract a large class of purchasers who want all the power possible with a necessarily limited price." (The magazine's enthusiasm for the Buick would wane quickly when Durant declined to advertise.)

Durant was at the show to take orders for his new vehicle. According to another writer for *Horseless Age,* the smiling Durant "had found the people at the show more critical than ever before, and believed that they really understood the mechanism and construction of cars and appreciated the honest efforts made to give them a reliable and desirable machine at a fair price." Durant "was well pleased with the show, business and prospects," the magazine continued. He had good reason to be. He had taken orders, and deposits, for 1,108 Model-C's, more cars than he would be able to produce that year. Equally important, he had enlisted a handful of dealers with enough capital to buy Buicks as they were produced. For the moment, the master salesman had to restrain himself to avoid overselling.

The automobile was a seasonal beast. Without a heater, and with a top, windshield, and storm screens sold as optional accessories, it hibernated during the winter. After "preparing a car for the winter's rest," as *Horseless Age* put it, "the automobilist is almost the first of all created things to show signs of coming spring." Sales reflected the machine's seasonal habits: brisk during spring and summer, slacking off in the fall, and ending before cold weather set in.

Production was carried on in the winter and spring, ending in midsummer, when development of the next year's model began. Unlike the settled carriage business, annual model changes were necessary to incorporate refinements and innovations. For many companies, the problem was one of funding design and then producing prototypes in the summer, six months before the New York Automobile Show generated that model's first sales. Cash-short companies—that is, most of the industry—failing to make annual changes often discovered at the New York show that a competitor had stolen a march on them.

To conserve scarce cash, auto makers laid off workers by the hundreds in the summer and rehired later in the year, when production on the following year's models began. While engineers planned the new motorcars, the out-of-work craftsmen fared as best they could; a working man with a family saved little on wages of $2.50 per day. (The practice of annual model changes and cyclical employment born of economic necessity would persist well into the fourth quarter of the century.)

Durant's immediate problem was underproduction. The Jackson plant could produce five to eight Model-C's per week, fewer than one-fifth of his sales. He needed to expand as quickly as he could, trusting his ability to sell the increased factory output in future years, when he had no large backlog of orders. Durant pondered the gamble in New York between visits with his brokers and evenings at the opera, where the new Italian tenor, Enrico Caruso, had swept all before him. The Metropolitan and the Philharmonic had become passions for the one-time cornet player in the Flint City Band; the men he met on the Street, the "very best" people, were all patrons; so, too, would be the Michigan industrialist William Crapo Durant.

Durant returned to Michigan committed to expansion. His first move was to purchase land on the undeveloped north side of Flint. Although it was farmland, Durant could see it as the heart of a burgeoning industrial city. But that was for the future; to meet his immediate problem, he expanded the Jackson assembly plant.

Fulfilling the agreement reached earlier with Whiting and the directors of the wagon works, the capitalization of the Buick

Motor Company was increased to $500,000. The additional stock—there was no money behind it at all—was to be used for what Durant euphemistically called "promotional purposes": his own salary. Of the company's total stock, Durant received shares worth $325,000.

Shortly thereafter, Durant transferred $101,000 of his personal holdings to Whiting as payment for managing the Flint factory, and $22,000 to Charles M. Begole, president of the Buick board of directors, for his aid in Jackson. The balance Durant turned over to the Durant–Dort Carriage Company's treasury with the explanation that since his own $25-per-week salary was being paid by that company and its stockholders, they therefore deserved to share in whatever success Buick enjoyed. It also made Durant–Dort the largest stockholder in Buick after Whiting, a significant part of Durant's plans. The carriage company had a national reputation and considerable resources.

His vision growing with each Model-C sold, Durant nurtured a scheme for even further expansion. On June 4, 1905, he wrote to Charles Stewart Mott, president of the firm supplying Buick with its axles, asking, "Would you entertain a proposition of removing or establishing a branch factory at Flint, Michigan, *provided the business of three or four large concerns* [emphasis added] was assured for a term of years? Flint is the center of the automobile industry, a progressive city, good people, with conditions for manufacturing ideal."

That Flint was a progressive community could not have endeared the city to Mott, an ever-watchful guardian against Eugene Debs' socialists. The Progressives in the Republican Party—Johnson, Norris, LaFollette—were troublesome enough to a man of Charles Mott's conservative nature.

Weston–Mott was well established in Utica, New York, and its thirty-year-old owner was reluctant to move from the settled comforts of upper New York State to a provincial town of 14,000 in Michigan. A branch factory, Mott believed, would prove difficult to manage from Utica. Yet Michigan, not solely Flint as Durant's letter had it, *was* increasingly the center of the new industry; a large portion of Weston–Mott's business was supplying axles for two of the largest-selling automobiles, Cadillac and Oldsmobile, one built in Detroit and the other in Lansing.

Mott and his partner were interested. The clinching argument for the ever-practical Mott, who had no patience for Durant's evanescent fantasies of future industrial empires, was Durant's promise to secure additional local financing for Weston–Mott were it to move.

By investing in Weston–Mott, Durant was taking the first step to vertical integration of his new auto company. Already producing most of the major components of the new Model-C in his own factories, Durant was assuring himself of a reliable source of supply for the one major part Buick did not fabricate itself. The Weston–Mott move was Durant's first step, too, in creating congeries of companies as he had earlier heaped together to supply parts and raw materials for the carriage works.

But Billy Durant conjured bigger things for Buick and himself. Too late into the carriage business, with other firms solidly established by the time Durant–Dort became a significant factor, Durant had missed his first opportunity to be a titan among giants. A second had gone aglimmering when the bicycle boom withered. The automobile business was new, however, and but haphazardly structured; no one firm dominated. As long as the large banks were outspoken in their disdain of the new industry, the financial mandarins of New York and Boston would not move to form a predominant organization. The way was open for an entrepreneur with the brass to gamble.

In the previous quarter of a century, Durant had watched powerful men fashion trusts in virtually every American industry from copper and candles to candy and coal, from matches and buttons to meat and boats. In 1904, economist H.R. Seager estimated, 318 industrial trusts held control of 5,300 different concerns, manipulating 40 percent of the nation's manufacturing capital. Durant himself had been forced to organize subsidiaries of Durant–Dort to provide parts when successive attempts were made to impose trusts over carriage-supply businesses and linseed-oil production. A defensive move, vertical integration from raw material to finished carriage had made Durant–Dort the more powerful.

That power was heady, but comparatively slight. Men such as John D. Rockefeller, the son of a patent-medicine salesman;

Peter A.B. Widener, a one-time butcher; and Andrew Carnegie, a Scots immigrant, had amassed enormous influence and the ability to control markets and prices, to manipulate great wealth and huge corporations. For Durant there was fascination in the power of these men, and that of McCormick, Armour, Swift, Marshall Field, and Elbert Gary; of the railroad barons, Hill and Harriman, Vanderbilt, and the House of Morgan. That all were men of wealth was incidental; it was their influence, their capacity literally to move mountains for mines or for railroads, to build industrial cities, and to shape great events that Durant envied.

Had Billy Durant organized Durant–Dort ten years before he did, he might have been able to convert it from the *largest* carriage manufacturer to the *predominant* carriage manufacturer. But he was too late; by the time Durant–Dort had become pre-eminent, the Supreme Court of Ohio had struck down Standard Oil's trust and ordered it dissolved. By 1901, Durant's efforts merely to consolidate a loose confederation of carriage manufacturers on a national scale had foundered on the individuality of owners who would yield no prerogatives even if it meant greater profits. That effort failing, the restive Durant had lost interest in the routine of the carriage business, had left Durant–Dort in his partner's hands, and had decamped for Wall Street. There, by his own wits, he hoped to accrue the influence that so tantalized him.

The trusts of old had metamorphosed during the first years of the twentieth century. Because an amendment to New Jersey state law permitted a company chartered in that state to own the stock of corporations chartered elsewhere, the New Jersey holding company was the favored form of business organization in those industries where trusts had once flourished.

Committed now to automobile manufacturing, Durant intended to create the dominant automobile holding company, and to raise himself to a position of power in financial circles. He would have to move quickly, before scoffing bankers awoke to the automobile's potential. Only by size could he keep them at bay.

First, however, he had to harden the nucleus: Buick. With Whiting and Begole overseeing production—Billy Durant had never cared for that aspect of manufacturing—Durant concentrated on sales. He recruited dealers and sought out customers. "We do with two cylinders what others try with four," Buick advertisements trumpeted during 1905. Durant added his personal assurance to the advertising copy: "We build nothing but high grade automobiles and when better automobiles are made, Buick will build them."

Though Durant was moving all the vehicles the factory could produce, the financing problem still pressed him. Production in two cities, then shipping parts by train from Flint for assembly in Jackson, was both uneconomical and slow. The two facilities had to be combined into a single factory on the fallow farmland outside of Flint. Consequently, in the spring of 1905, a coy Durant moved to entice Flint's investors to underwrite the expansion. He publicly asked the banks of rival Jackson for $100,000 to build the consolidated factory in that city. Spurned there, Durant turned to the residents of the Michigan port community of Bay City. That town too might have the Buick works for a mere $100,000.

Durant's appeal had its intended effect. Faced with the prospect of losing a fast-growing industry, Flint investors responded with money earned first in lumbering and then in the carriage industry. On April 24, two local banks and a group of the town's influential citizens agreed to buy $80,000 worth of Buick stock. Durant sweetened the deal by offering a 20-percent stock bonus to his Flint neighbors. (That bonus had not been offered to investors in Jackson or Bay City, but then neither of those communities had the farmland Buick already owned.) As a condition of the arrangement, Durant happily agreed to "the understanding that the Buick Motor Company will discontinue its Jackson plant and locate its entire business at Flint, commencing construction work upon its new buildings as soon as plans can be prepared and the weather will permit." Br'er Rabbit had been thrown into Flint's choicest briar patch.

At the same time, Durant moved to reorganize the Buick Motor Company once again, increasing its capitalization to $1.5 million. The firm's inventive attorney, former Speaker of the State Assembly John J. Carton, had some difficulty justifying the radical increase, since good will and patents constituted 60 percent of Buick's assets. "In the application presented to the secretary of state," Carton later admitted, "I listed all the assets quite generously up to the legal requirements, but nevertheless we were still $60,000 short, and this was taken up by the following item: 'Ownership of invention of combustion engine not patented for business reasons—$60,000.' " The schedule survived nominal state scrutiny, Carton explained, for political rather than financial reasons: "The fact that I was very well acquainted at Lansing, the state capital, may have been beneficial in getting such a hazy item passed." Carton himself had reservations; his client "just soared high, wide and handsome."

Durant now had additional stock to sell with a face value of a million dollars. Necessarily relying upon his local reputation, he raised $500,000 in forty-eight hours. The balance of the million-dollar issue would be sold too, but long afterward Durant proudly would recall that first two-day period when the citizens of Flint put a price upon his character. They had little else to go on in buying the stock; the company was badly watered, and "few of the subscribers had ever ridden in an automobile," Durant later recalled.

Once again the board was reconstituted. Six of the nine directors were carriage makers, there to protect their companies' investments; two others had been in the carriage business before taking posts at Buick. Only Genesee County Bank President Arthur G. Bishop, who would outlast all his colleagues on the board, had no direct connection with Flint's major industry.

By the end of 1905, Buick had built and sold 725 cars, held a backlog of orders, and had a set of books that listed "good will" as one-third of its watery assets. The company also had discovered in road racing a potent form of free advertising. Buick's catalog for the year boasted that a regular stock Buick had won its class in the hazardous Eagle Rock, New Jersey, hill-climbing contest. Durant himself drove a Model-C in an endurance run from Chicago to St. Paul, the field of four ending its grand tour in the mud of Waterloo, Iowa, when heavy rains turned rural roads into impassable wallows. Undaunted, Durant entered the prestigious Glidden Tour the following year, along with such other automobile executives as Percy Pierce (Pierce–Arrow), J.D. Maxwell (Maxwell), and Ransom E. Olds (Reo). Typically, Durant was disqualified because he stopped to aid a woman motorist.

A chivalrous Durant was also an expanding Durant. By March 1906, the Jackson plant was turning out as many as seventeen cars per day; in one unusual week, Buick shipped 250 of its new Model-F's. While that automobile accounted for 1,200 of the 1,400 vehicles the firm would sell that year, Durant had broadened his offerings to the public by also adding a runabout for $1,150 and a four-cylinder luxury car priced at $2,500.

The company braved 1907 with no less than six models and Buick's first truck, dubbed, for obvious reasons, "the plumber's body." The automobiles ranged from a two-cylinder Model-G, priced at $1,150, to the top-of-the-line $2,500 runabout. The six motorcars—three of which were holdovers from 1906—strategically bracketed all but the lowest-priced market. The automobile industry informally placed its products into four price classes: from $500 to $850; from $900 to $1,450; from $1,500 to $2,400; and from $2,500 up. Durant's six models covered the top three price ranges, or 80 percent of the market.

Henry Ford's first Model-T, priced at $950, was a year off and four years of production away from proving that a market existed at all for an inexpensive, workingman's automobile. The industry was skeptical that such an auto could succeed; one by one, lower-priced, motor-driven carriages had crashed in the marketplace.

The motor vehicle was by no means a universal mode of transportation. Its tufted cushions, burnished brass, and japanned woodwork priced the automobile far beyond the reach of most, however much they might envy the growing number of drivers careening about city streets. Unskilled workers in Durant's clangorous factories earned as little as twenty cents an hour. New England's cotton mills paid weavers an average of $1.02 for the standard ten-hour day. Women workers suffered even more, New York society matron Bessie McGinnis Van Vorst learned during a winter-long masquerade as a factory girl. Unskilled, she earned seven cents an hour canning pickles for the H.J. Heinz

Company of Pittsburgh. At the end of a week, she paid $3.00 of her $4.20 in wages for her room and board.

"Here and there I see a new girl whose back is flat, whose chest is well developed," Mrs. Van Vorst reported. "Among the older hands who have begun work early there is not a straight pair of shoulders. Much of the bottle washing and filling is done by children from twelve to fourteen years of age. On their slight, frail bodies toil weighs heavily; the delicate child form gives way to the iron hand of labor pressed too soon upon it. Backs bend earthward, chests recede, never to be sound again."

For pennies per hour, children worked in the pickle factory, picked coal, or tended looms because the "sturdy mechanic" of political oratory could not by his "honest labor" alone earn enough to support a family. Farmers were little better off, imprisoned still in a barter economy, averaging but $200 in cash income annually. The Sears and Roebuck catalog might feature page after page of nipped-waist, ankle-length dresses—rural and urban bluenoses sniffed at the prominent bosoms that resulted from overlaced stays—but Mrs. Van Vorst's coworkers and farm wives alike still bought yard goods to make their own clothes.

Little wonder, then, that rural America—60 percent of the nation's population—was hostile to the horseless carriage it could not afford. Resentful farmers in some states were able to impose severely restrictive laws. In 1900, the state of Vermont adapted a fifty-year-old English statute and decreed that all automobiles must be preceded by "a person of mature age" walking at least one-eighth of a mile ahead of the onrushing vehicle; that worthy's task was to wave a red flag and thereby warn approaching horsemen of impending motordom.

Automobiles frightened horses and raised dust, which settled on fruit trees and ruined produce, while speeding cars made rural roads dangerous for hapless carriage drivers. According to one farm-journal editor with a passionate rhetoric rooted in a century of bucolic conservatism, the smoking motorcar hazarded all life, "driven by a reckless, blood-thirsty, villainous lot of purse-proud, crazy trespassers upon the legitimate avenues of trade."

Worst of all, those "crazy trespassers" wanted better roads throughout the country, roads for which farmers would be either taxed or forced to tithe labor in lieu of cash. Not until 1908 would State Senator G.W.F. Gaunt, master of the New Jersey Grange, signal rural cooperation, and then not without demanding a *quid pro quo:* "We farmers are not opposed to the motorcar . . . It will be an important feature in making farm life more attractive. When the motorcar becomes cheaper in price through more general use, the farmer will be the first to adopt it for business and pleasure." As chairman of the New Jersey State Senate's Agricultural Committee—to which all road bills were referred— Gaunt would consent "to better not only the condition of the roads but the lot of the motorist" when a cheaper automobile was available. But any bill that passed would still need the Democratic governor's signature, and Woodrow Wilson was skeptical. As president of Princeton University a few short years before, he had concluded, "Nothing has spread socialistic feeling more than the use of the automobile . . . a picture of the arrogance of wealth."

Maintenance was also costly, prohibitively so. At the American Medical Association's convention in 1906—as a profession, physicians were the first to use the automobile widely—one Dr. Stinson of San Francisco noted he spent $566 in four months for repairs on his $983 one-cylinder car. Similarly, the newly introduced pneumatic tire could be expected to last 1,000 miles, with replacements costing from $60 up for a set. Bessie Van Vorst's haggard coworkers might buy a set of tires with the $1.20 they had left after paying their weekly room and board—if they saved for a year.

The handcrafted automobile could be produced and sold at a profit only to a middle- and upper-class market. William E. Metzger, who opened the nation's first automobile showroom in 1898, recorded that eighteen of the first twenty steam-powered Mobiles he sold went to those he described as Detroit's "capitalists, manufacturers, physicians and general business men." The following year *Horseless Age* gratefully acknowledged "the gracious patronage [of] our American aristocracy" for having motored that summer to Newport.

The market had changed little when the E.M.F. (Everitt-Metzger-Flanders) was introduced in 1907: "Sales were to man-

ufacturers, capitalists, merchants, and physicians; not to salesmen, small shopkeepers, clerks, mechanics or artisans. The only
exception was an occasional plumber or steam fitter, and such
men were in a sense proprietors; they were masters, not jour-
neymen."

Durant, too, was offering motorcars to satisfy the fancy of
these higher-income, better-educated buyers; there were enough
such new motorists to double his company's 1907 sales over the
previous year's figure. Still, Durant was impatient with the pace.
He dispatched John L. Poole to open a Paris-based foreign department, assuring the trade press as he waved good-bye to
Poole that "there is a growing demand for American medium-
priced cars in foreign countries." Poole's one-man office would
become, in time, a division of General Motors employing 300,000
people.

At the same time, Durant signed a fifteen-year contract with
R.S. McLaughlin to provide engines and power trains to the
McLaughlin Carriage Company of Oshawa, Ontario. Until the
Second World War, McLaughlin's Canadian Buicks were considerably more elaborate and well-finished than the American versions. Ultimately, McLaughlin's factories would metamorphose
into General Motors of Canada, and its products would lose their
individuality.

Though Buick's sales had been exceptional during the summer
of 1907, there were portents of the company's first major crisis.
Stock prices throughout most of the year had been wavering on
the New York Stock Exchange, up one day and down the next.
Investors' confidence waned, waxed, and waned again. New
stock issues of established firms went undersubscribed, and the
languor seeped into the municipal-bond market as investment
capital dried up. Prices began sliding on the New York and
European stock exchanges in September, and, as the market
worsened, bank credit tightened. The major New York banks,
which controlled the flow of cash in the country by adjusting
their interest rates, had become too heavily involved in the declining market. They no longer had funds to lend.

The 738 employees of the Buick Motor Company were at work
on an expanded line for 1908 when the panic struck. On October

22, 1907, the Knickerbocker Trust Company in New York City—with only 5 percent reserves to back its deposits—closed its doors. A rumor on Wall Street had provoked mass withdrawals by brokers who believed the bank had been entangled in a dubious and ultimately disastrous stock escapade. Though not a gold-plated firm like Guaranty, with its ties to the House of Morgan, Knickerbocker was still a major bank on the Street. Anyone might be the next to fall. First in New York, and then across the country, banks became defensive, calling in loans and hoarding cash just when only a more open-handed credit policy could shore up investors' confidence.

Buick, for the first time in its five-year history, was in an outwardly sound financial condition. Durant apparently had been forewarned of the impending panic by one of the few who had predicted it, New York traction magnate Anthony N. Brady. At first from afar, then more closely as he gained confidence, Durant had followed the portly Brady's moves. His sagacity equaled only by his rapaciousness, Brady was a figure to behold, when he was seen on the Street at all.

Brady preferred to work his mysterious ways through intermediaries. J. Pierpont Morgan and Jacob H. Schiff—ever-confident advocates of American growth—made their fortunes in bull, or rising, markets. Brady, with a hunter's sense of the kill, made his in the worst of times. Selling stock at peak prices, he waited for the plunge he had predicted; when it came, he was in a position (that is to say, he was heavy with cash) to buy those same shares back when the market was at its lowest.

Either by deliberate warning or by close observation of Brady's covert actions on the Exchange, Durant sensed the coming panic and prepared. In June, Durant secured the board of directors' approval of an increase in Buick's common stock from $900,000 to $2 million. This was the firm's first common stock to be sold instead of awarded as a bonus to those who purchased the preferred shares; it was intended to provide Buick with a cash reserve when the expected break in the market set in. At the same time, the board declared Buick's first dividend of $250,000, an announcement calculated to enhance interest in the new common stock. Meanwhile, auditors appraised the company's value at $2.8 million. They also wrote off the books all such intangibles as good will and lawyer Carton's unpatented gasoline engine.

Still, Buick remained hard-pressed for cash. No matter how great Durant's reputation was in Flint, there was only so much money to be squeezed from that turnip. Beyond Michigan, would-be investors in the remaining common shares were wary.

Durant staked Buick's future; he had little respect for banks and their too-conservative judgments anyway. While other automobile manufacturers curtailed production of the 1908 models, laying off workers to await the easing of the financial spasm, Durant plunged. Fending off creditors on one telephone while ordering from suppliers on the other, he built Buicks. Because his hundred cash-short dealers around the country were unable to buy cars from him, Durant stored the completed autos throughout Flint and Jackson in empty warehouses, barns, even in open fields before the winter snows. Through September, inventories grew and cash reserves vanished. Each completed car represented an investment of approximately $900, half of that the two-dollar-per-day wages for his factory hands. Even with production curtailed and the work force cut back, each one hundred cars represented a minimum of $45,000 spent for labor with no immediate prospect of sales.

By October, the rows of Buicks in begrimed ranks around Flint had doubled; but once committed to production, Durant had to continue, lest creditors become alarmed and force Buick into bankruptcy. Continued production was a nostrum for anxious suppliers, a sham assurance that Buick had adequate capital, even if the creditors weren't being paid promptly. Through October the panic prevailed, Durant ever more glib and Buick ever more precarious.

As cold November came, made colder by the strain of anxiety on the quiet Exchange, the hymn-singing J. P. Morgan put aside the affairs of the Episcopal church to take up the affairs of a nation. Little men had precipitated a panic, and little men had deepened it. Now the House of Morgan—imperious J.P., he of the bulbous red nose and riveting eyes—would set things to rights.

From his marble library at Thirty-sixth Street and Madison Avenue—younger members of the firm at 23 Wall Street had taken to calling the library "the uptown branch"—Morgan summoned the barons of his realm. On these lesser lords of finance he levied assessments, $25 million to be loaned by the soundest of New York banks to buttress the tottering institutions. When the bankers balked, Morgan literally locked the library doors and stared down his swollen nose at the cards of a solitaire game, waiting until the imprisoned bankers capitulated one by one.

Buick's inventory and its creditors' anxiety swelled while Morgan parceled out the money, at 20-percent interest rates, to the poor relations. The hard-hit banks in turn began to loan money to brokers again, and a weak confidence returned to Wall Street. As Morgan had foretold, the stock market turned around.

Credit requirements eased across the country as stock prices inched upward throughout the winter. The panic waning, Buick dealers once again were able to borrow money from local banks and order from the factory's inflated inventory. Fretful merchants who had hoarded small cash reserves found new resolve and started visiting automobile showrooms.

Durant's showrooms anyway. Buick was virtually the only manufacturer to have automobiles available as the selling season began. There were six different models, including the new, four-cylinder Model 5 touring car priced at $2,500, introduced "in order to complete the Buick line." The second new entry was a low-priced Model 10, at $900, built "for men with red blood who don't like to eat dust." Accommodating three passengers—the third person rode over the rear axle in a single bucket seat the catalog called, for obvious reasons, "the rumble seat"—the Model 10 "White Streak" was an instant success.

Despite the industrial depression that inevitably followed Wall Street's alarums and excursions, Buick sales ballooned to 8,487 automobiles during 1908, more than twice the previous year's figure. At a time when as many as five million workers were unemployed nationally, Flint's city fathers boasted that the depression existed everywhere but there. Buick leapt from eighth to first place in industry sales; Henry Ford ranked second with

6,181 automobiles sold, including the first of his new Model-T's; and Cadillac came in a distant third with 2,380.

If Durant had had any doubts that Morgan's strong-arm financial tactics would work, he never expressed them. Instead, he kept up his cyclonic work schedule, a cigar in his mouth all the while, a covey of aides trailing after him as he strode through his factory. Sixty years later, the last survivor of Buick's precarious balancing act of 1907–08, C. S. Mott, would recall, "He was one hell of a gambler. To this day, I don't know how he was able to handle it financially, but he did it."

Ground was broken in August 1907 for the long-delayed three-story factory on the farmland north of Flint, and by the spring of 1908, Durant was employing as many men in construction work as he had building Buicks. A tent city and shantytown sprouted around the Buick factory site, first to house construction crews, then auto workers and their families in housing-short Flint.

Meanwhile, Durant was promoting the Buick, any Buick, as a racing vehicle. Bob Burman, a one-time wheel painter in the Durant–Dort carriage factory, had become first a new-car test driver and then a race driver for Buick. An aw-shucks, toe-in-the-sand American archetype, Burman made his debut as a racer in 1905, when he motored one of the first Buick Model-C's from Jackson to Grosse Pointe's racetrack, an unprepossessing entry permitted to compete only to fill out the field of nationally known racers. "That small car really was rolling after it got started," another of the entrants later recalled. "Burman took awful chances on the turns. But he won the contest and beat [Henry] Ford and me," Barney Oldfield added ruefully.

Because racing victories and hill-climbing triumphs generated publicity—even the staid *Wall Street Journal* reported the results of major events—Durant detailed Walter Marr, Vandyke beard and temper bristling, to build a high-powered racing machine. Marr's racer was to challenge the Peerless Green Dragon, which was then setting records in race after race as Barney Oldfield transformed himself into a household name.

To drive his racing cars, Durant invited two members of the Fiat racing team to come to Flint for a trial spin on Buick's test track behind the newly opened factory. When mustachioed Louis Chevrolet won the match race, Durant prudently nominated the loser to do double duty as his personal chauffeur. Arthur Chevrolet took fewer chances while driving than did his brother Louis.

Marr's racing car, the Buick 60 Special, swept the field for three years. With Burman at the wheel, the "Bug" would set a 105-mile-per-hour speed record the day the Indianapolis Motor Speedway opened in 1910. By 1911, the Buick racing team of Burman, the Chevrolet brothers, and Louis Strang would have accrued more than five hundred trophies, uncounted inches of free newspaper publicity, and a reputation as the fastest team in the world. Such success prompted Durant's generosity; at the end of the 1909 racing season, he personally gave the team $10,000 to be divided among its members.

Durant made two other significant additions to his staff during this period. William H. Little, called "Wild Bill' behind his back, left a declining Massachusetts carriage company to become production manager at the new Flint factory. Under Little's punishing direction, Buick managed a production peak in June 1908 of one finished automobile every twelve minutes; working eighteen- to twenty-hour days, Buick shipped 1,654 cars to meet the demand in that post-Panic month.

Shortly thereafter, Durant enticed Alexander B.C. Hardy, the one-time Durant–Dort production manager, back to Flint. Carriage building in Iowa was as nothing now for the creator of the defunct Flint Roadster. A master of production, Hardy was to hold a succession of jobs with Buick, one of the few men willing or able to nay-say the strong-minded Durant and still remain his friend. The adroit diplomat would outlast Durant at Buick and become wealthy in the process.

There were two losses: David Dunbar Buick and his son Thomas. Though the motorcar bore his name, the elder Buick had been shunted off to a quiet workshop. There he could continue his tinkering without demanding that production be halted so that each tiny improvement could be immediately installed on his auto. Further, the pace Durant set was not to the elder Buick's liking: "There wasn't an executive in the place who ever knew what time it was. We worked until we had the day's job done and were ready for tomorrow and then we went home—and not until then." Buick traded in most of his stock in 1906 and left his workshop; he also left behind his name on the successful automobile he had dreamed about in 1900.*

With production near capacity and the company's reputation sound, Billy Durant began thinking once again about the consolidation that would give him the power to influence events. He had caused a tent city to be built; now he intended to move mountains.

---

* Buick remained a director through 1907, then joined with the Briscoes to make Scoe carburetors. He became involved in a number of unsuccessful business ventures and eventually, at age seventy-two, took a job as an instructor-clerk at the Detroit School of Trades. In 1928, he was interviewed by a young Detroit newspaperman, Bruce Catton, who talked to the old man in his office at the trade school. Over the door, Catton reported, was a sign reading, "No Trials, No Triumphs." The impoverished Buick—he could not afford a telephone—asked neither pity nor charity, only a job. "It's kind of hard," he told Catton, "for a man of my age to be uncertain about the future." General Motors, which might have afforded him a small annuity from its $200 million in annual earnings, ignored Buick. He died penniless in Detroit on March 5, 1929, at the age of seventy-four. Young Tom founded Genesee-brand tires in Flint, then dropped out of sight after 1908.

3

Morgan's Minions

His self-confidence buoyed by his successful gamble during the Panic of 1907, Durant turned again to his long-nurtured plan for a larger enterprise. He was no longer alone, though; others now harbored similar schemes for an amalgamation of automotive companies under the ultimate control of a single group of owners.

As early as 1904, the formidable Anthony N. Brady, member of the board of directors of the Association of Licensed Automobile Manufacturers, had considered such a move. Requiring its members to be in good financial condition, lest the failure of one tarnish the reputation of all, the A.L.A.M. had detailed Hermann F. Cuntz, a mechanical engineer, to tour the constituent companies as its financial policeman. Brady then secretly engaged Cuntz to relay confidential company records to him.

Cuntz, in turn, suggested that Brady combine the healthiest of the companies into a single moving force in the nascent industry. If Brady had any qualms about the propriety of his private investigation, it would have been unusual. Whatever scruples he pos-

54

sessed had not hindered him from becoming one of the most powerful of Wall Street's overlords. Brady was also one of the most secretive of the buccaneers on the Street, a still-mysterious figure seventy years later, yet a man powerful enough to send a host of mercenaries to do battle with J.P. Morgan's duchy.

Born in Lille, France, in 1841, of Irish parents, Brady had been raised in Troy, New York. At the age of twenty-one he entered the tea business in Albany, then pyramided a small investment into a local monopoly on tea and coffee. By the time he also had secured control of a local granite quarry and Albany's construction industry, he decided to remove his talents to larger horizons—New York City's financial center.

In the next forty years, the florid Brady amassed a personal fortune to equal J.P. Morgan's. Only Brady was able to hold out against Rockefeller's Standard Oil trust, only Brady powerful enough to then propitiously merge those oil holdings on his own terms with Standard.

As president of New York Edison and the major figure in building the Brooklyn Rapid Transit, Brady had backed George Westinghouse's efforts to keep his electric company from being engulfed by J.P. Morgan's General Electric. By the turn of the century, Anthony N. Brady was the single most powerful figure in the nation's fragmented street traction, subway, and public-utilities industries. To him was attributed one of Wall Street's more enduring phrases: "The straphangers pay the dividends."

Already a hidden power in half a hundred companies, Brady was covetous of the new automobile industry. With Cuntz as his stalking horse, he opened negotiations with a handful of manufacturers, Durant among them. The Michigan millionaire was impressed with the scheme put forward by the Wall Street multimillionaire. (Durant's letter to C. S. Mott promising the business of four or five large automotive concerns apparently was a step in fashioning the combine Brady envisioned.) But Brady had sniffed the winds of panic early in 1907, and took himself out of the stock market entirely. His auto amalgamation plan was tabled until a more opportune moment. He told engineer-agent Cuntz that the A.L.A.M. companies had an inflated notion of their value and could be purchased for much less after the expected panic had shaken their confidence.

Brady, the straphanger's friend, was wrong. The Panic of 1907 left the automobile industry comparatively unscathed. The tightening of credit had come on before the production lines started up; automotive companies simply cut their work forces to wait out the winter's credit freeze, contributing to the industrial depression that followed, but not to their own demise. Though few companies had automobiles in the spring of 1908 to greet awakening buyers, only a handful of the weakest succumbed. And the weakest did not interest Anthony N. Brady.

Nor were Brady and Durant alone in their visions of combine. Benjamin Briscoe, by 1907 the largest producer of automobile parts in the country, was not a man to be satisfied with merely stamping metal fenders and coiling radiators for others. After selling the Buick to Whiting, Briscoe had invested in John Maxwell's automotive works. The Maxwell–Briscoe firm was among the industry's most successful, but one of the more overextended in the Panic of 1907. Briscoe would weather the panic, like so many other industrialists, by summarily closing his factory. Yet who knew what trials for the fledgling industry lay ahead? Briscoe, too, conceived of an industrial combine to offer mutual support in the next crisis.

To such a union Briscoe offered the Maxwell and an entrée to the counting rooms of J. P. Morgan. In 1903, the Briscoe brothers had borrowed $100,000 from Morgan for their sheet-metal works; five years later, Morgan partner George Walbridge Perkins had invested his own money in the automobile company. Briscoe had credit and a Morgan partner in tow. Given a sound plan, perhaps he could influence Morgan to finance the combine Brady had delayed.

Brady, because he was Brady, had intended an offensive combine, an amalgam powerful enough to set prices in the marketplace or drive out those who attempted to compete by underselling. Briscoe, on the other hand, wanted a defensive combination large enough to spread the risk of a bad model. "If we should ever experience a 'silly season,'" he explained, "should we ever drop so far behind competition as to make it difficult for us to sell our product 'off the fire,' we . . . would find ourselves in a very unfortunate financial position.''

Moreover, if the combine were large enough, Briscoe believed, it could police the entire industry, intimidating the under-capitalized from entering production and curbing stock promotions for phantom automobiles: ''Many of us thought that the industry was beset with difficulties and so came the desire of some of us to form a combination of the principal concerns in the industry, not with the desire to sell all of the automobiles that were to be sold, but rather for the purpose of having one big concern of such dominating influence in the automobile industry, as for instance, the United States Steel Corporation exercises in the steel industry, so that its very influence would prevent many of the abuses that we believed existed . . .''

Briscoe was thirty-nine at the time, eight years Durant's junior, and if not as wealthy as his friend Billy, every bit as ambitious. Ill-printed news photographs, his family complained, made him look like a beefy pugilist or an overage professional ballplayer—resolute enough, but lacking any trace of good breeding.

Sometime late in 1907—the exact date is lost in the faulty memories of the two participants—Briscoe called Durant, suggesting they meet to discuss ''the biggest thing in the country. There's millions in it.'' Over breakfast the next morning, Briscoe explained that George W. Perkins, one of the major partners in the House of Morgan, was interested in creating a combine of automobile firms. There was no definite plan, other than amalgamation. The details were left to Briscoe; the final decision would be Perkins'.

Durant was tantalized by a possible collaboration with the House of Morgan, at the height of its prestige as a result of its timely actions during the October Panic. Briscoe had no well-defined plan; he suggested only that he and Durant convene a meeting of twenty of the largest automobile makers and see who might be interested.

Durant was dubious: ''I told him frankly that I did not believe the plan was workable. The proposition in my opinion was too big, too many concerns involved, too many conflicting interests to be reconciled." Rather, Durant proposed that they confine their talks to a handful of the largest companies in the medium-priced field. Briscoe ticked off four nominees: Ford, Reo, Buick, and Maxwell–Briscoe, at that point the four leading automobile manufacturers in the nation. Durant suggested Briscoe "first see Henry Ford, who was in the limelight, liked publicity and unless he could lead the procession would not play."

On January 17, 1908, the four company heads met for a private lunch in Detroit. Fearing publicity, Olds, Ford, and Briscoe "gumshoed separately" to Durant's rented room at the ten-story Pontchartrain Hotel on Cadillac Square.

In terms of automobile experience, Olds was senior. He had been building steam-powered vehicles since 1887 and gasoline engines since 1893. A well-grounded, practical engineer, he was even more accomplished in human terms. Probably no pioneer in the automotive wilds was more adept at spotting capable men, recruiting them to the motorcar's cause, and giving them responsibilities to match their ability. In large measure, the growth of Detroit as the automotive center of the United States, not to say the world, was the result of Olds' training the cadre of young men who would build companies of their own in later years.

If any of the four were to resist a merger, it certainly would be the fiercely independent Henry Ford. As driven as was Durant, headstrong unto stubborn, Henry Ford meant to build automobiles, his way, without let or hindrance. In 1902 when investors had questioned his judgment, he had abandoned the firm bearing his name. When investors later sought dividends from the Ford Motor Company that Ford wanted to put into capital investment, willful Henry bought them out—for $75 million. Moreover, Ford never could bring himself to trust these sophisticated men sitting in Durant's hotel room. Born on a Michigan farm in 1863, he was still a farm boy, hair parted in the middle, imbued with the suspicion that glib sharpers from the city preyed upon good rural folk. James C. Couzens, his business manager, was perhaps the only man Ford could or would trust in all of Detroit. None among the four men eating lunch in Durant's room at the Pontchartrain was less interested in partners, mergers, combines, or trusts than Ford.

The table cleared of all but coffee and cigars, Briscoe opened the meeting by suggesting a consolidation of their companies. There was an uncomfortable silence. Durant then sought a way to open the discussion, which seemed stillborn in the defensive reserve of the participants. If Ford were valued at $10 million, he asked the group, did Ford himself object to settling Reo's value at $6 million? Or Maxwell's at $5 million?

Foolishness. Dour Henry Ford snapped that he did not have any idea of the value of his competitors. Already planning his Model-T for introduction late in the year, Ford would be a reluctant member of the wedding—if there were a wedding at all. Still, Ford had been rattled by the Panic of 1907; his production was running 30 percent behind last year's. He could perceive some advantages in the right kind of merger, one that left him free to run his business the way he saw fit.

The discussion turned elsewhere, to questions of organization, of who would manage the combine. Briscoe suggested that the purchasing, engineering, advertising, and sales departments of the four manufacturers be merged, and that policy for the four companies be set by a single operations committee. It was precisely such a scheme that Henry Ford most feared.

Durant sensed Ford's reserve and objected. Why interfere with four successful companies? It was unnecessary. A holding company, governed by a super-board of directors setting only the broadest policy, would be better. Each then would be free to operate as he saw best.

Briscoe's proposal was of a piece with his background as a manufacturer. It was in the four departments he suggested merging that the success of a manufacturing firm was made. Durant, for his part, was more interested in the financial aspects of the proposed merger, in blocs of stock to be manipulated and suppliers to be brought into the combine by the judicious exchange of shares. "Durant is for states' rights," Briscoe summarized. "I am for a union."

Through the early afternoon they hammered out a proposal. The four men tentatively settled upon the organization of a holding company that would purchase the assets of the four manufacturers by paying out the new firm's preferred stock in amounts

equal to the appraised value of their companies. Briscoe said he
would relay their proposal to the Morgan partners; the three
other men elected to go along. They might otherwise never see
the innermost sanctum of finance: 23 Wall Street.

A week later, Durant, Briscoe, Olds, Ford, and James
Couzens, Ford's business manager, met in the New York law
offices of Ward, Hayden, and Satterlee. The wary Ford and
Couzens had a second reservation, objecting to Herbert L. Satterlee as the instrument of their merger. Satterlee was, after
all, J.P. Morgan's son-in-law; Ford and Couzens preferred
Job Hedges, their representative in New York. According to
Durant, this first meeting in New York was exploratory, rather
more for the benefit of Satterlee than to consummate the marriage.

Why consolidate? Having multiple "makes" would reduce
catastrophic risks to virtually nothing should a manufacturer
bring out a poor seller.

How big was the market, and what share did each firm claim?
Statistics were imperfectly compiled, and no one at the meeting
knew just how large the industry was. Fifty thousand automobiles with an average selling price of $1,200 seemed reasonable.
Ford alone had 30 percent of the market; Buick, Reo, and Maxwell together accounted for another 25 percent of all automobiles
sold in 1907.

Admittedly, the industry had no great reputation as a financial
investment. Hundreds of firms had announced bewildering
squadrons of automobiles amid fanfares of promotional literature, but had collapsed before production began. However, of
the sixty-odd firms commercially marketing vehicles, only one
had failed in 1907. The bulk of the business failures that plagued
the industry came during the early, promotional stages of a company's existence, rarely after the firm put an automobile on the
road. The public was buying motorcars, as many as the manufacturers could produce. And, in the four companies represented in
the room, Satterlee had four of the least likely to fail.

Satterlee also had a well-tested product, if he could but see it.
A *Harper's Weekly* writer in February 1908 would shortly conclude: "It is very rare, indeed, that an automobile has such a

serious breakdown as to require towing to a repair shop, or to necessitate its abandonment by the passengers. Such stoppages as have to be made on the road are usually only for simple adjustments, the cleaning or changing of a spark plug, connecting up a fresh ignition battery cell or the substitution of a new inner tube for a punctured tube in a tire." The autoist of the day—the male, in any event—was expected to be able to make these simple repairs. The daring female driver, as good breeding demanded, was expected to wait for masculine assistance in such arcane pursuits as cleaning a spark plug.

The American automobile was lighter than its European counterpart and vastly overpowered by comparison. If the grand European touring car favored by men of Satterlee's position was opulently appointed and finished, the American car was built for a larger, mass market willing to sacrifice some luxury for price. American or foreign, automotive design was essentially fixed: a two- or four-cylinder engine mounted in front of the four passengers, producing from twenty to thirty horsepower; a sliding-gear transmission with three speeds forward and one in reverse; magneto ignition with a battery auxiliary; a pressed-steel frame of 100 to 115 inches in length, with elliptical springs to cushion the passenger from the vicissitudes of the roads.

Of the manufacturers in the room, only the visionary Ford had any reservations. The tendency of consolidations, mergers, trusts, holding companies—whatever form the proposed amalgamation took—was to increase prices, he pointed out. Ford, according to Durant's autobiographical notes, "was in favor of keeping prices down to the lowest possible point, giving to the multitude the benefit of cheap transportation."

Herbert L. Satterlee was more than J.P. Morgan's son-in-law; along with J. Pierpont, Jr., he was ever at the old man's side. The brothers-in-law each had an ear. Exceptionally adroit in finance and corporation law, Satterlee, against the advice of his father-in-law, was then working to reorganize the shuttered Knickerbocker Trust Company. If he could keep it from receivership, he would save $47 million of depositors' funds. Satterlee was skeptical of the automobile industry and the men in it. The senior Morgan was sternly opposed to investment in automobiles, and his son-in-law did not wish to flout J.P.'s counsel twice in a short span of time.

The doubts husbanded at 23 Wall were confirmed soon enough. At a later meeting, Couzens suddenly announced that whatever the appraised valuation of his company, Ford wanted an additional $3 million in cash. "Mr. Satterlee was quite put out," Durant wrote later, "and after giving the matter a few moments' thought, went back into the other room and very diplomatically stated that there had been a misunderstanding, but that the matter of finance was entirely up to the bankers, and when they had perfected their plans, another meeting would be called." The House of Morgan did not pay "good will" or "key-money."

The bankers had no intention of paying out cash to form the combine at all. They had expected to exchange the stock of a purposefully formed holding company to buy the firms to be amalgamated in the new combine. Now one of the key figures was demanding a cash bonus, and a second, Ransom E. Olds, not to be outdone, was insisting that if Ford got $3 million, then he also wanted $3 million. Fair's fair.

At this point, Ford declared that he was no longer interested and decamped. The chair stood on three legs. Olds attended meetings through May, then fell away. The chair toppled.

The bankers formally shelved the plan, and Satterlee, its good shepherd, went off to Washington for a brief stint as assistant secretary of the navy in Theodore Roosevelt's second administration. (Satterlee, a thirty-five-year-old naval lieutenant during the Spanish-American War, was awarded the post in repayment for his successful reorganization of Knickerbocker Trust and his pivotal role in helping J.P. Morgan, Sr., crush the panic the year before. As a further mark of his gratitude, trust-busting T.R. invited the senior Morgan to dine at the White House and then ended antitrust proceedings against various Morgan enterprises.)

The House of Morgan no longer was participating in merger negotiations, though one partner in the firm still harbored an interest. George Walbridge Perkins was the most powerful of the partners Morgan had taken into the banking house. With Morgan, Sr., spending more time in recent years attending to Episcopalian church affairs and collecting art, Perkins operated with virtual autonomy.

The son of an Ohio reformatory warden, Perkins had prospered mightily, despite his father's conclusion early on that young George was "slow in the head." Starting as a seventeen-year-old clerk at New York Life Insurance Company, Perkins had raced through the corporate hierarchy to become a vice-president. Under his shrewd direction, New York Life had become the largest insurance company in the world.

In 1900, J.P. Morgan, Sr., had invited the thirty-eight-year-old Perkins to become a partner. Perkins accepted only on the condition that he retain his vice-presidency of New York Life, the better to assure that the company's $500 million in premiums found their way into Morgan-sponsored stock flotations. There was no conflict of interest, Perkins maintained firmly, because the interest of both the insurance company and the bank were identical: to make money.

It was Perkins who welded the McCormick and Deere families into International Harvester, a combination that Morgan himself had not been able to bring about and a coup that made Perkins first among the princelings in the House of Morgan.

Now, although Morgan and Company as a bank no longer was interested in a holding company of automobile firms, investment banker George Perkins was. Durant and Briscoe took up negotiations with Perkins and Francis Lynde Stetson, the very proper Morgan and Company legal advisor. Perkins and Stetson had worked together in fashioning the Harvester trust and were now inseparable counselors. What gods of finance had joined, no speculative venture could sunder.

By the end of June 1908, the four men had reached a general agreement to merge Buick and Maxwell–Briscoe into a new, aptly named United Motors Company. On July 1, the firm of Ward, Hayden, and Satterlee advised Buick attorney John J. Carton that the certificate of incorporation had been filed and stock for the new United Motors could be issued in a few days. Carton was to prepare Buick's stock for the exchange.

The agreement was broadly written, the details not at all set-

tled. Durant believed—"assumed" might be more accurate—he
was to be the new company's general manager. Perkins and
Stetson reserved a definite commitment. Perkins agreed to put
up only $500,000 of the $1.5 million Durant and Briscoe needed
to launch the firm and to buy other companies. A frustrated
Durant wrote to Carton on July 2: "Had a long, hot session with
our friends in New York yesterday and was pretty nearly used up
at the finish. If you think it is an easy matter to get money from
New York capitalists to finance a motor car proposition in
Michigan, you have another guess coming. Notwithstanding the
fact that quoted [interest] rates are very low, money is hard to
get owing to a somewhat unaccountable feeling of uneasiness
and a general distrust of the automobile proposition."

Of less importance, though it required reprinting the stock
certificates, Perkins now wanted the firm's name changed to the
International Motor Car Company. Stetson fancied the name
"International" as well; the two had used it first on the successful Harvester trust and later with International Mercantile
Marine, Morgan's effort to control world shipping. It was a lucky
name, and the two were fond of it.

While Perkins nagged at details, Durant cast about for other
companies that might be brought into International Motors. He
lighted upon the Olds Motor Works of nearby Lansing, Michigan.

Ransom E. Olds had left his namesake in 1904, stalking out to
organize Reo after a bitter argument with Frederic L. and Angus
Smith. Though the company had produced some 5,000 curved-
dash Oldsmobiles that year—the nation's largest-selling
automobile—the Smith brothers wanted to build more prestigious, expensive machines. Since their father, S.L. Smith, controlled two-thirds of the Olds Motor Works' stock, the two
young men prevailed.

At the moment of his departure, Olds left behind a prosperous
company that he had begun in the obscurity of his father's Lansing machine shop twenty-three years earlier. Olds and Son had
begun building stationary engines, both gasoline and steam, and
then experimented with a steam-powered automobile. Through a
succession of metamorphoses, Pliny F. Olds and Son became the

Olds Motor Works in 1899, with Smith, the first capitalist of note to value automobile production, as its major backer. The business then moved from Lansing to Detroit, the better for Smith to watch his company and his two sons. There Olds set to work designing an electric-powered car as the company's first production model. They sold but four in the entire year of 1900.

The fire of March 9, 1901, forced Olds to change his plans. Some years later, a wry Frederic Smith wrote: "The fire was beyond question the best move ever made by the management, in that it put an end to the experimenting and chasing after strange electric gods . . ." As timekeeper Brady pushed the pilot model of a gasoline-powered runabout to safety, "the last of our electric 'Stanhope' two-seaters came crashing down from an upper floor and landed a-sprawl on top of the steel safe in my office. The safe was empty and the Stanhope a charred skeleton. Somehow the combination seemed chock-full of significance— emblematic, prophetic."

In-for-a-penny, in-for-a-pound, S.L. Smith underwrote the removal of the surviving one-cylinder runabout to Olds' former plant in Lansing. Though starting from scratch, by the end of the 1901 sales season Olds had sold 425 of the one-cylinder runabouts, the first automobile to be mass-produced in the world. Three years later, production topped 5,500 vehicles annually, and the company was financially secure.

When he huffed off in 1904, Olds left behind designs for a new runabout, a straight-dash model incorporating many of the advances made in the early years of the industry. Olds Motor Works sold 6,500 of these vehicles in 1905, the one year it was produced, making Oldsmobile the largest-selling automobile in the nation for the third straight year. Since then, the company had fallen upon evil days. Abandoning the straight-dash runabout at $650, the Smith brothers increased the size of the engine to six cylinders and the cost of the car to $4,500. As the size of the car and the price grew, sales shrank to 1,055 in 1908, when Durant began looking for additional companies to bring under the protective wing of International Motors. The Smiths were eager to be wooed.

In a single midnight visit to Oldsmobile's Lansing works, Du-

rant and the Smith family came to terms. Durant raced through
the dimly lighted plant in a fifteen-minute, early-morning tour,
with his secretary, W. W. Murphy, and the three Smiths trailing
behind, made his appraisal, and adjourned to a corner of the
factory to bargain. "We came to a provisional understanding
before daylight," Frederic Smith recalled, then qualified the
comment. "Durant did the understanding; the rest of us just
thought we understood."

The elder Smith was the company's only creditor. Though the
motor works already had paid cash dividends under Olds' management amounting to more than 100 percent of investment,
Smith had been forced to reinvest $1 million under his sons'
stewardship. Even so, he valued the company at $2 million.

Durant was not a man to haggle; he offered $2 million of pre-
ferred stock in International Motors. Smith declined. International's stock in itself was worthless, and both his firm and
Maxwell–Briscoe were in poor shape.

Durant countered confidently, sensing that Smith, too, was
tantalized by the prospect of Morgan interest. If Smith would
take $2 million in International shares for three-quarters of the
Olds firm, Durant would take those shares off his hands within
one year. He would buy them personally for $1.8 million,
thereby guaranteeing Smith a $300,000 profit on his Olds Motor
Works investment to date. In effect, Durant was promising that
International Motors would earn at least $1.8 million with which
to pay off Smith, or Durant himself would personally come up
with the money. The proposal was irresistible; by dawn, the
Smiths had agreed to sell.

But if the Smiths were willing, George Perkins was cooling.
Drilled in the restrained circles of insurance, he had difficulty
appreciating the flamboyant style of his fellow midwesterner. He
distrusted Durant's headstrong enthusiasms—such as the Olds
deal, consummated without Durant even looking at the company's books, but merely taking Smith's word for the worth of
the firm. It was all very well for Durant to offer $1.8 million in
cash—Perkins himself was putting up $500,000—but not for a
failing property. Men like Perkins sold companies whose greatest
asset was good will; they did not buy them.

Durant's incessant optimism might be tolerated, or curbed, but his ridiculous suggestion that the automobile industry soon would be producing 500,000 vehicles a year smacked of madness. Yet this was the man who was politely, but persistently, insisting that he be placed in charge of the new company's finances.

By the end of July, the proposed merger of Buick, Olds, and Maxwell–Briscoe was in the hands of lawyer Francis Stetson. Stetson raised two questions about the Buick stock then amassed in a trust awaiting the expected stock exchange. First, did Buick's stockholders understand the terms of the deal? Durant's answer was typical, if exasperating. The stockholders did not know the terms but had deposited their stock in trust on the basis of their confidence in Durant. The decision was entirely within his hands, Durant assured Stetson.

The Wall Street lawyer was dissatisfied. He doubted if a title of that kind would be sufficient and said he thought it might be necessary to have the Buick stockholders execute a new set of papers. "I questioned the wisdom of changing or even suggesting a change in the agreement. Mr. Stetson insisted that he must have a better title," Durant wrote in his autobiographical notes.

There was a second stumbling block, which Durant did not mention. Apparently, Stetson had learned that some Buick stock had changed hands during the course of the negotiations. He coldly insisted that the sellers be permitted to buy back their shares since they had sold in ignorance of a pending merger that would make their stock far more valuable. Placed on the defensive, Durant could plead only that he was acting on the advice of his lawyer, John Carton, and would continue to do so. It was a tacit admission that he, Durant, had been buying stock in Buick so as to shore up his own holdings. As Buick's leading investor, he would be in a better position to insist that he be named general manager of International Motor Car Company.

Durant's demand that he manage the combination's finances—Briscoe apparently would be responsible for manufacturing—was more than the Morgan people would permit. "There is no place in the world where jealousies prevail to the extent that they do in the Wall Street district," a bitterly frustrated Briscoe wrote later. "The dominating forces and personalities there brook no interference. They permit no outsider to have his way if they can help it, and they aim at the very start, when any project comes to them, to control all the ways and means of finance and management. They do so without apparently taking any of the responsibilities of management upon themselves, yet, by their adroitness, making sure to dictate the policies at any and all times."

On July 31, the New York *Times* got wind of the merger and published a story detailing "the first big combination in the automobile world." International Motors, scheduled to begin operations on September 1, the *Times* reported, would be formed by merging Maxwell–Briscoe and Buick, and would have a capitalization of $25 million. "About half a dozen other plants will be brought into the organization with these two companies, and options have been obtained on other properties."

At that moment, Durant had Olds, and Briscoe had an option on Cadillac, a bit of information that only those two men shared. The remarkably accurate newspaper story only further alienated the Morgan people, Briscoe wrote to Durant in Flint: "Why they should feel it as deeply as they do I can't quite fathom myself . . . [and] the position taken by Mr. Stetson, that a full disclosure to each stockholder must be made whose stock is exchanged will, I imagine, somewhat interfere with your plans."

Perkins and Stetson had procrastinated for months, Briscoe conceded, their delays "very disappointing and disconcerting . . . ." Briscoe then made a suggestion that was to change the history of industrial America: "It would be possible for you and myself, and perhaps one or two others that we could attach to us, to take hold of this matter and work it out without waiting on anybody. We have both concluded that a million dollars in cash would be enough to finance the proposition and I will eat my shoes if we can't raise a million dollars between us."

The would-be partners temporarily shelved their plans for a Morgan-sponsored merger, to remain friendly competitors for the moment. While building up his own newly incorporated United States Motors Company, Briscoe intended to keep open their line to the House of Morgan. Meanwhile, Durant-inspired events would clear up Stetson's lofty objections to those inside stock purchases. With or without the Morgans, a merger was still possible. Briscoe had a shell organized for a holding company, as well as an option to purchase Cadillac. Durant too held an option on an extant firm—Olds—but he lacked the holding company that would be his dower in an eventual merger with Briscoe.

At the end of August, Durant met with Curtis R. Hatheway, a younger member of Ward, Hayden, and Satterlee to whom Durant had taken a liking. Durant told Hatheway that he intended to pursue a merger—in fact, had the Olds company in mind. Were he to relinquish the Buick stock he then held in trust, it would be difficult to gather it again. The ambitious Hatheway agreed to become the attorney for the new company. For capital, Durant would use a number of patents taken out by Walter Marr. The engineering success of the Buick was largely due to Marr, Durant assured Hatheway; additionally, Marr was fond of Durant and had named his only son after him. Durant was certain Marr would set aside sufficient patents against which stock could be issued. Hatheway the opportunist was more inclined to accept Durant's glib assurances than was Stetson the moralist.

Finances settled, the next question was a name for the firm. Perkins had kept "International" for his own use. Durant pulled a list from his pocket and casually scanned the entries; the name didn't matter very much. He selected one, suggested in an earlier discussion by Oldsmobile's Frederic L. Smith: General Motors Company.

4

L'Audace, Toujours L'Audace

On September 15, 1908, in a wash of deliberate anonymity, Curtis R. Hatheway filed articles of incorporation with the county clerk of Hudson County, New Jersey. The three required incorporators were unknown to clerks who routinely tipped off reporters to good stories in exchange for tickets to the ballpark; capital stock was listed as an unprepossessing $2,000. When the papers were forwarded to the New Jersey secretary of state's office the following day, the General Motors Company was formally incorporated.

Six days later, the three unknown directors selected one of their number, George F. Daniels, as the company's first president. Increasing the capitalization to $12.5 million—half the amount Durant and Briscoe had believed necessary to organize a holding company in the industry—the figurehead board then entertained its first business proposition.

70

"Mr. W. C. Durant present," in the circumspect wording of the board's minutes, and being "advised" that the new firm had among its various purposes the intention of building automobiles, Mr. Durant offered to sell the Buick Motor Company to General Motors.

On October 1, the formal purchase was completed, General Motors exchanging its stock for the 20,000 shares of Buick that Durant controlled. The price was $150 for each Buick share, two-thirds paid out in General Motors preferred and one-third in common stock. In addition, Durant personally invested $500,000 in the new holding company, receiving $500,000 in preferred stock and a bonus of $250,000 in common shares. (The bonus was a customary inducement in the corporation's early years.) Finally, for Durant's promise to underwrite the sale of $2 million of General Motors' preferred stock—the underwriter, in effect, agreeing to buy those shares he could not sell to the general public—the company issued to him personally $1 million in common stock. That last million dollars worth of stock Durant promptly gave back to the company, to be reissued as a 50-percent bonus with the preferred stock Durant later sold to other investors. He was far more excited by the reality of manipulating securities than he was by potential riches.

One-half of the $2 million in stock Durant pledged to sell was purchased by the Durant–Dort Carriage Company. That firm no longer needed its large cash reserves and was just four years away from discontinuing active operations. Typical of Durant's unending stock promotions, the sale would be completed on February 20, 1909, just three days before General Motors announced its first semiannual dividend of $3.50 for each preferred share. Durant–Dort's stockholders, Durant included, thus obtained 10,000 shares in General Motors preferred, a bonus of 5,000 shares of common, and an immediate $35,000 cash rebate in the form of a dividend.

By June 5, 1909, all of the common stock and all but fifteen of Buick's 5,000 outstanding shares of preferred would be exchanged, a testament to the faith placed in Durant by Buick's investors. The total Buick purchase price was $3.75 million worth of stock.

Its formative work done, on October 20, 1908, the triumvirate of figureheads amended General Motors' bylaws to provide for a seven-member board of directors. At that point, they promptly voted themselves out of office by electing Durant's slate of officers. The new president was William M. Eaton, a prominent businessman in Jackson, Michigan, upon whom Durant could rely to superintend the administrative details he so disliked. Durant, as was his wont, chose to be vice-president. Young Wall Street attorney Curtis R. Hatheway, who was to play a significant role in the corporation's early years, was elected secretary and treasurer.

With the remaining $8.75 million in General Motors shares, as well as Buick's cash receipts, which now flowed to the parent corporation, Billy Durant went on a buying spree unequaled in American business for another fifty years. For the next eighteen months, Durant swept up companies large and small—at turns capricious, then deliberate; at one moment the businessman, the next seemingly a boy in a candy shop with a nickel weighing heavily in his hand. There were repeated trips on the "Yellow Kid," the Pennsylvania Railroad's limited; or the less sumptuous "Michigander"; the pressing problem always seemed to be in Flint if Durant was in New York, and in New York if he was at the Buick factory. There were pell-mell journeys to inspect factories Durant considered buying and hasty visits to Chicago banks for quickly arranged loans.

Durant roundly enjoyed it all—the midnight conferences, the unending stretch of eighteen-hour days, the frenetic bidding and bargaining. Only two things interrupted: visits to his doting mother and evenings at the theater and concerts with his second wife, Catherine, twenty-five years his junior.

Durant's first move was to purchase, for $240,000 in General Motors stock, the W.F. Stewart Body Company, which had been building Buick bodies. To weld closer the second critical supplier, Durant exchanged shares for a 49-percent interest in Weston–Mott, with C.S. Mott holding control of the balance.

His next step was something more of a gamble. While on a trip to Boston earlier in 1908 to open a Buick sales branch there, Durant had been approached by a young Frenchman seeking to

sell him electrical parts for automobiles. Durant was not interested in the parts themselves, but he was impressed with the
young man, Albert Champion, a sometime motorcycle racer.
Would Champion consider selling Durant his manufacturing
company—actually a small workshop in Toledo, Ohio—for
$2,000?

Champion was interested, but his backers were not. Promised
25 percent of the stock in a new firm, the young Frenchman was
induced to abandon his Albert Champion Company for a new
and larger Champion Ignition Company in Flint. Durant promised a guaranteed market for the special spark plugs Champion
would produce for Buick's valve-in-head engine.

Forced to leave his name firmly attached to the company he
was leaving, Champion adopted his initials, as Olds had done
earlier, for his new product. His first production of forty A-C
spark plugs per day in a corner of the Buick plant cut the price
Durant had been paying from thirty-five to twenty-five cents.
Within a year, the Champion Ignition Company was producing a
thousand plugs daily in its own factory, with Durant crowing that
he was thus saving himself $100 a day.

On November 12, 1908, General Motors acquired its second
line of automobiles, exchanging General Motors' stock for a 75-
percent interest in the Olds Motor Works. The price was approximately $3 million (a million more than Durant had offered when
trying to bring Olds into International Motors earlier in the year),
again in shares, plus $17,000 in cash to buy out a handful of
reluctant shareholders. According to terms reached with S.L.
Smith earlier, two Oldsmobile representatives were added to
General Motors' board of directors: Frederic L. Smith and
Henry Russel.

By now there were major problems with Oldsmobile. The
company had steadily lost money on its luxurious automobiles
since 1906. Looking at the books after the purchase, Olds president Henry Russel asked Durant if he had found anything of
value. Durant shook his head. "Neither have I," Russel admitted.

Oldsmobile had one major asset: considerable production experience. There also was name recognition with the buying pub-

lic, the result of the popular song and a string of company-owned billboards around the country. Durant shrugged off both with the comment: "That's a hell of a price to pay for a bunch of road signs."

Oldsmobile desperately needed a new model for 1909, a car that would put the company back into the burgeoning middle-class market. Olds had nothing planned, though, a problem Durant solved with some dispatch. He ordered a Buick Model 10 body culled from the production line and trucked to Olds-mobile's Lansing factory. At Durant's direction, workmen placed the unfinished wooden body on two sawhorses and promptly sawed it into quarters. Durant commanded that the four sections be spread some inches apart, lengthening and widening the body, and rather immediately changing its appearance. Oldsmobile now had a new automobile, with a finish and trim somewhat more lavish than that of the Model 10, priced at $1,200.

Durant's design-by-quartering proved successful; a writer at the New York Automobile Show in January 1909 decided that Olds "presented an especially striking array of body designs . . . ." Compatible in price rather than competitive with the $1,000 Model 10, sales of the new Oldsmobile Model 20 would reach 6,575 that year, putting the company in the black for the first time since 1906.

Durant was moving as quickly as possible, and as quietly, so as not to drive higher the prices of companies in which he was interested. Still, the purchase of a firm with Oldsmobile's prestige, whatever its current financial condition, provoked rumors of even more mergers. Successively, Maxwell's Benjamin Briscoe, Angus Smith of Olds, and Buick's William Mead denied a tripartite merger to a reporter for the *Automobile Trade Journal* late in November 1908. The gentlemen were not telling the truth.

Durant and Briscoe both nurtured their plan for a single, grand holding company in automobiles. Backed now by Anthony N. Brady, Briscoe was accumulating properties for United States Motors, properties rather less valuable than their ledger sheets puffed. One such had $6 million in debts to its suppliers, a little matter never entered on the company's books and discovered

only after Briscoe had taken possession. It was of no conse-
quence; neither Briscoe nor Brady intended their company to
survive long.

From his offices at Forty-first Street and Park Avenue in New
York, crowded with hat-in-hand automobile manufacturers and
parts suppliers, Durant, too, scouted for available properties.
The first addition to the Buick–Oldsmobile fold was Oakland, the
General Motors board of directors authorizing Durant to purchase a 50-percent interest late in 1908. The company had been
organized in 1907 by Edward M. Murphy, a Pontiac, Michigan,
carriage manufacturer. Oakland's first automobile did poorly
and was replaced by the powerful four-cylinder Model-K, which
quickly became a hill-climbing champion. Sales in the panic-
wary year of 1908 totaled just 278 vehicles, however, and Oakland was in a precarious position when Durant approached Murphy.

The two were friends of about the same age, familiars from the
carriage days. Durant considered the reluctant Murphy an
energetic, "high-type" leader with an exceptional capacity for
business organization. "I cultivated Murphy," Durant later
wrote, "and paid attention to what he was doing, saw him frequently, offered suggestions as to where important materials at
very much lower prices could be obtained, and helped him in
many ways."

Durant's was an onslaught of charm. Courteous, deferential
even, Durant acknowledged that he wanted Murphy's organizational skills. Assured he would not lose his autonomy, Murphy
succumbed, turning over his stock to Durant. A few days after
the stock was transferred, Durant received a telegram informing
him that Murphy had died.*

---

* It is not clear from General Motors' corporate records, but it would appear that Durant
was exceptionally generous to Murphy's heirs. The Federal Trade Commission's *Report
on Motor Vehicle Industry*, 76th Congress, House Document No. 468 (Washington, D.C.,
1939) notes ". . . that part or all of the 11,217 outstanding Oakland shares finally acquired were purchased from W. C. Durant, who exchanged personally owned General
Motors stock for some of the shares, the company not being in a position to hand over
any of its own stock; and that, although Mr. Durant had acquired some of the shares at a
cost, in par value of General Motors stock exchanged, exceeding $10 per share, he had
sold such shares to General Motors at a price of $10 per share." The $10-per-share price
had been fixed by board vote and Durant knew he would be out of pocket. It was an act of
quiet magnanimity to Murphy's heirs.

The acquisitive Billy Durant had two goals in mind as he set off on his buying rampage: to broaden General Motors' base with multiple lines of automobiles and to assure a continuous flow of component parts. Dealing largely in stock exchanges, husbanding his cash when he could, in the next year he gathered up five suppliers and a brace of automobile companies.

On February 23, 1909, at Durant's urging, the board of directors authorized the purchase of the Reliance Motor Truck Company. Reliance, Durant told the board, "had a high reputation in the trade" and would give the corporation a commercial vehicle division it lacked. Organized in 1903, Reliance had abandoned its early passenger-car lines to concentrate on producing trucks and delivery vans. Shortly after, General Motors added a second truck manufacturer, the Rapid Motor Vehicle Company.

Learning that the four-year-old Rainier Motor Car Company was bankrupt, Durant personally incorporated the Marquette Motor Company, then used his new corporation to buy out Rainier. Founded in 1904 to build a heavy touring car styled the "Pullman of Motor Cars," Rainier never had been able to gain a large enough portion of the highest-priced market. Proper promotion and a national sales network, Durant believed, would make Rainier the top-of-the-line vehicle he lacked, a competitor to Pierce–Arrow, Franklin, Peerless, and Packard.

In June 1908, General Motors purchased the newly organized Welch Motor Car Companies of Pontiac and Detroit. The firms had announced four models for the year, ranging in price from $4,675 to $7,000, but had suffered scant production. Amalgamation with General Motors offered the Welch brothers, well-known automobile engineers, the money they needed to increase production. Again, Durant's plan suffered a setback: Fred Welch, the company's moving force, drowned shortly after the sale. Within five months, Welch–Pontiac would be up for sale.

None of his acquisitions compared with the coup Durant counted when he snared the Cadillac Motor Car Company. Cadillac was one of Detroit's premier manufacturers, ruled with autocratic majesty by sixty-three-year-old Henry Martyn Leland. A religious fundamentalist, Leland had earned a reputation for equally rigorous adherence to precision machine-making.

After a succession of early jobs—including a Civil War stint in the Springfield, Massachusetts, armory—Leland had gone to work in 1872 for the nation's leading machine-tool maker, Brown and Sharpe of Providence, Rhode Island. Within six years, he was the head of that company's sewing-machine division— making the firm's major product—and had acquired the fanaticism for precision of cofounder Joseph R. Brown. (Brown already had invented the vernier caliper and later would patent the micrometer.)

After eighteen years with Brown and Sharpe, during which time he perfected hair clippers for both horse and man, Leland had saved enough money to organize his own company. His choice of location narrowed to either Chicago or Detroit, there being less competition in the West. Leland picked Detroit because it was firmly an open-shop city. A rate-buster himself, he had quit the nascent machinists' union decades earlier, after just three meetings; he preferred to work at his own speed rather than one dictated by his coworkers.

Established in Detroit, the white-bearded Leland became involved in the automobile industry in progressive stages. In 1901, Ransom Olds had contracted with Leland & Faulconer for 2,000 engines for the curved-dash Oldsmobile. Working to tolerances within one-thousandth of an inch, Leland produced engines delivering more horsepower than the ostensibly identical motors built for the Olds by the Dodge brothers. The Dodges were content with commonly accepted tolerances no greater than one-sixty-fourth of an inch.

Leland, however, was not satisfied with the design of the three-horsepower motor; inferior design offended his craftsmanship. Ransom Olds had been building gasoline engines since 1885, true enough, but the determined Leland had almost as much experience with stationary engines. On his own initiative, Leland redesigned the motor to produce ten horsepower, only to have it rejected by the Smiths, who were unable to afford the retooling costs.

Leland then had an engine, but no automobile in which to mount it, a deficiency remedied when Henry Ford parted heated company with the backers of the Henry Ford Company. The investors, with an automobile design but no one to build its cars, and Leland, with an engine but no automobile, found common cause.

In August 1902, Leland and the Ford investors jointly organized the Cadillac Motor Car Company, named after the French explorer who had founded the city of Detroit, his coat of arms borrowed for the new auto's insignia. Three pilot models of Cadillac's Model-A were built in the last months of 1902, then delivered to New York and the January 1903 auto show. Sales manager William E. Metzger took hand-over-fist orders, and deposits, for 1,000 automobiles. Nine months later, Cadillac had forty-eight sales offices across the country selling the $750 Model-A and the $900 Model-B.

Cadillac's automobile production rose steadily to 4,300 vehicles in 1906, but fell off severely in the wake of the Panic of 1907. That year Cadillac sold 2,696 cars as demand for the one-cylinder engine slackened, and the company's larger, four-cylinder models failed to attract buyers.

Fearing that the firm was near bankruptcy, Leland elected to be the only entrant in the Royal Automobile Club of England's exacting Standardization Test. The judges selected three cars from the stock of Cadillac's London sales representative, drove them to Brooklands racetrack twenty miles from the city center, and entirely stripped them down. The disassembled parts from the automobiles were painted yellow, blue, and red. Choosing parts from each of the three piles, and an occasional substitution selected by the judges from a fourth pile of spares, the three automobiles were entirely rebuilt.

To complete the test, the three variegated automobiles were then driven five hundred miles, proving not only the exacting mechanical standards in Leland's Cadillac which allowed such interchangeability, but the durability of the auto itself. Cadillac's reputation was secured, the resultant publicity creating a demand for the vehicle that the factory, starting late in the wake of the panic, could not meet.

Durant first eyed the Cadillac in the winter of 1908, dispatching a representative to arrange a meeting with the bearded autocrat Henry Leland and his son Wilfred, a self-effacing man who was responsible for Cadillac's finances. The Lelands, alarmed by their near-bankruptcy, already had given an option to buy to Benjamin Briscoe. That option lapsed on November 12, 1908, and by the time Briscoe was able to return to the Lelands with a firm offer, Durant had stepped in.

As was his custom, Durant's negotiations were briskly conducted, decisions rapidly made. Durant had one question: "Can you produce at a fair profit the new four-cylinder Cadillac car which you are offering to the public at $1,475 and give a proper discount to your retail dealers and distributors?"

"It can be and is being done," Wilfred Leland calmly assured Durant.

That settled, Durant asked Leland to write out on a piece of hotel stationery Cadillac's costs to produce the new Model 30. Satisfied with the figures, Durant asked Cadillac's price.

The Lelands wanted $3.5 million in cash. Durant asked for a few days to discuss the purchase with his board. General Motors did not have that much money in its treasury; to obtain it, the company would be forced to issue bonds, and that required board approval.

Durant presented the proposed deal to four of the seven members then on the board at a New York meeting. To Durant's surprise, Frederic Smith objected. The company already owed $1.8 million to Smith's father. If cash was to be paid out, Smith had first claim. Regretfully, Durant telegraphed to cancel the offer.

Sometime after the first of the year, Durant dispatched Arnold H. Goss, secretary of the Buick Motor Car Company, to do what Durant would not, bargain down the $3.5 million asking price. The Lelands, however, were less anxious to sell. The Panic was well behind them, and the Cadillac Model 30, introduced shortly before Durant's first meeting with the Lelands, an encouraging success.

Goss proposed a $3 million sale price, and sought to tempt Wilfred Leland with a personal bonus in return for Leland's urging Cadillac investors to accept the lower figure. Leland declined. He also rejected any stock exchange, insisting upon cash.

Goss left empty-handed—to return some weeks later, again

asking the sale price. Leland was even more secure; anticipated profits for the year were higher than expected, and the Model 30 was on its way to selling 7,868 vehicles. The price now, Leland told Goss, was $4,125,000, in cash, with a ten-day option. Since General Motors still had not paid Smith, Goss declined the option.

In June 1909, Durant himself returned to the negotiations. More than a little perturbed by his persistence, the Lelands raised the selling price to $4.75 million cash, with $500,000 to be deposited, and forfeited, if Durant did not complete the purchase. The bargaining had grown tiresome.

Durant agreed, providing the Lelands, father and son, took some stock in General Motors. After thinking it over—Durant *was* constructing a sizable automobile company with enormous potential—they agreed to take $75,000 in General Motors stock. Durant asked for a management contract with the two, offering a percentage of the net profits as well as a salary if the two would remain. The Lelands accepted, but only with the stipulation that they were to have a free hand in managing Cadillac's affairs; Durant's reputation for insisting that things be run his way had preceded him. The white-bearded Leland had a clear plan in mind for his automobile, intending to upgrade it year by year, emphasizing its advertised "dignity, proportion and richness." He wanted no interference.

Within ten days Durant had raised the money, using Buick as collateral against the bank notes. The announcement of the sale at $4.75 million on July 29 was a sensation. It was the largest bank transaction in Detroit to that time, but more important, it melded two of the five largest auto makers, Buick and Cadillac, into one company. Cadillac employed 3,400 men in its Detroit factory, and turned out an average of thirty-six cars per day. In its peak production period, the company had produced seventy-five automobiles in one day, one every twelve minutes for fifteen hours.

Sensitive to their reputation and that of Durant—the advocate of precision as opposed to the onrushing emperor—Wilfred Leland released a statement to the press stipulating the terms of the management agreement:

We have the written assurance of the purchaser that the Cadillac Company will continue to carry on its business as though it were an entirely independent organization. It is not tied to any company, or to any policies. On the contrary, Cadillac standards, Cadillac policies, Cadillac methods and the entire Cadillac organization will be carried on without alteration, and exactly as though the transaction recently consummated had never taken place. Mr. H.M. Leland will continue to have full charge of the management of the company.

We are entering into these new relations in good faith, and with the full expectation and belief that the statements above made will be actually carried out.

For his part, Durant ignored the implicit skepticism of the Lelands, the deliberately distant reference to himself and General Motors as "the purchaser." If it was a slight, he could afford to ignore it; within the month, Cadillac would announce its 1908–09 profit of $2 million, all of it paid into the General Motors treasury. The practical effect was to reduce Cadillac's purchase price of $4.75 million to some $2.75 million, something less than the first asking price of $3.5 million.

By the end of September 1909, Durant had acquired, largely by paying out General Motors stock, eleven automobile companies, eight automotive-parts makers, and two commercial-vehicle producers. Within three months, Durant had added yet another motor manufacturer, a wheel-rim fabricator, and two more automobile lines: the two-cycle Elmore, which would survive but three years while paying for itself; and the Ewing, introduced earlier in the year as the "debutante of the season." Like Osiris, Ewing soon would be dismembered, its corporate parts scattered to the four corners of General Motors' kingdom.

Hardly pausing to digest these, Durant weighed the purchase of the Goodyear Tire Company; John Willys' rousing success, Willys–Overland; and the Thomas Flyer. The Goodyear price was $3 million; master salesman Willys wanted $2.5 million; E.R. Thomas, flush with the international success of his New York-to-Paris-via-Siberia race winner, demanded as much or more. None was interested in a stock exchange. Durant was unable to find banks willing to lend him the money to exercise his options and broke off negotiations.

Years later, Alexander B.C. Hardy explained Durant's apparent whimsies:

Durant bought a lot of different companies, most of which were not much good; but he paid for them largely in stock. He didn't want the actual assets of these companies; most of them were head over heels in debt, anyway. He wanted to have a lot of "makes," so that he would always be sure to have some popular cars. I heard him explain this one day in this way:
"They say I shouldn't have bought Cartercar," he said. "Well, how was anyone to know that Carter wasn't to be the thing? It had the friction drive and no other car had it. How could I tell what these engineers would say next? And then there's the Elmore, with its two-cycle engine. That's the kind they were using on motor-boats; maybe two-cycles was going to be the thing for automobiles. I was for getting every kind of car in sight, playing it safe all along the line."

Never soundly grounded in the mechanics of the automobile, Durant not only wanted "every kind of car in sight," but every kind of component as well. "Nobody at the time knew what would work best—what types of motors, gears, axles, magnetos, wheels, springs, radiators would become permanent or practical and useful. Everybody in the business was experimenting. We scrapped what wasn't considered practical. But the essential and tried product of the several companies was kept and developed," Durant told a Flint enthusiast many years later.

Though he was strapped for working capital, Durant's was a bedazzling feat of corporate legerdemain. By the end of its first fiscal year in September 1909, General Motors had sold $29 million worth of automobiles and parts. Profits amounted to more than $9 million, enough to justify a $3.50 cash dividend on the preferred stock and a stock dividend of 150 percent on the common.

The stock dividend was significant; General Motors' cash position was poor, too weak for the company to pay dividends on both preferred and common stock and still retain needed working capital. Investments had been heavy for plants and machinery in the twenty-two companies then flying Durant's pennant. Further, General Motors had 14,250 people on its payroll at the height of the production season, with a cash drain of $192,000 in salaries every two weeks.

To remedy the situation, the board of directors increased General Motors' capitalization to $60 million; Durant could continue to buy companies only if he could still sell stock—to pay for the firms he was shepherding into the fold. In October 1909, the cash shortage cost Durant the biggest acquisition of all.

Durant had coveted the Ford Motor Company since the abortive amalgamation of the year before. He had since toured the Ford factory with the hard-nosed James C. Couzens, then had asked Couzens to see if Ford still wished to sell. If so, Durant suggested that the three meet in New York at their earliest convenience.

Henry Ford was uncertain of his future. His long-nurtured Model-T had been introduced that year, only to encounter considerable sales competition from the new six-cylinder automobiles only slightly higher priced. Ford was publicly disdainful— "I've got no use for a motor that has more spark plugs than a cow has teats"—but privately dispirited. Even sales of 10,000 Model-T's could not assuage his disappointment. He wanted to refine existing automobiles, increasing production as he did so; that would bring down the Model-T's $950 price tag and thereby increase sales. Instead, he was confronted with an ever-enlarging list of competitors, each with its own transient innovation to attract customers.

Worse still, Ford's five-year suit against the holders of the Selden patent had been decided against him on September 15, the judge holding that Selden's combination of motor and drive-train was entitled to primacy. It had been a long battle, and though it had won for Ford a popular reputation as an opponent of monopolistic trusts, he would file an appeal less from righteous resolve than from stubbornness. The zest was gone.

In late October, Couzens came alone to Durant's Park Avenue office. Ford, he explained, was in bed at the Hotel Belmont across the street, suffering from nervous dyspepsia. Something he had eaten on the train from Detroit had disagreed with him.

Whatever illness of spirit sapped Ford's resolve, no such

malaise troubled Couzens. In six years he had transformed himself from Alexander Malcolmson's clerk into keeper of Henry
Ford's exchequer, as well as business manager, publicist, and
salesman. Brusque to the point of bad manners, he was a punishing taskmaster respected by the men who worked for him, but
never revered as was the equally authoritarian Ford. Ford was
responsible for design and production—his name was on the roof
of their burgeoning factory—but as Couzens' successor later recalled, "All matters of importance at the Ford Motor Company
were decided in Mr. Couzens' office."

Couzens, the one-time bookkeeper, and Durant, the former
drummer, understood each other. Couzens had come to do business.

Ford was willing to sell out for $8 million—in cash. Durant had
to put down $2 million immediately and pay the balance with
5-percent interest within three years. Ford himself, Couzens told
Durant, was going to concentrate on building farm machinery;
his contemplated tractor would do as much or more as any automobile for the farmer, the man to whom Ford felt closest.

The following day Durant met with officers of the National
City Bank of New York, the largest in the country, long identified with Rockefeller and Standard Oil, and more recently with
J.P. Morgan and Company. The bank officers were interested in
making the loan, especially in view of Ford's $3-million profit
that year, but a loan of that size would have to be approved by
the bank's board of directors, a body firmly controlled by Morgan.

On October 26, the General Motors board approved the purchase of Ford for $8 million in cash, figuratively keeping its
fingers crossed that National City would provide the first $2
million. National City would not. Morgan the father, Morgan the
son, somebody in authority at 23 Wall Street had vetoed any
involvement in the unsettled automobile industry. Durant reluctantly dropped his option, Ford recovered from his dyspepsia,
and Couzens soon went into politics.

Within days of National City's refusal to loan the money, Durant took a small step to assuage what he now believed was the
natural hostility of bankers to the automobile industry. There

were 200,000 vehicles on the nation's roads, valued at $419 million. Investors had put down as much as $200 million in motorcar ventures—a diversion of funds from the bond market, which sorely vexed bankers. More than 180,000 workers were building automobiles, earning $80 million annually, but still the bankers refused to accept Durant's reality. His was one of the largest, with Ford, in a growing industry; yet Durant had to go hat in hand to banks for loans.

Perhaps the banks were ill-informed. Durant summoned a reporter for the *Wall Street Journal* to give a rare public statement, purportedly because "the nature of the General Motors Company . . . has never been clearly understood in the automobile trade," the paper dutifully reported. (Had Durant wished to inform the auto industry, rather than Wall Street, there were at least four trade journals that offered a larger audience of automotive executives.)

Durant detailed General Motors' growing list of holdings, including the newly gained controlling interest in Bedford Motors, Limited, its first European acquisition. As good as 1909 sales had been—Durant claimed $34 million, exaggerating by $5 million— the following year would be even better. He had estimated that General Motors would produce 40,000 vehicles, but was revising this figure in light of the orders in hand for 68,000 automobiles and trucks valued at $60 million.

The *Wall Street Journal* reporter was obviously impressed. "The strides taken in the industry," he wrote, enthusiasm overtaking grammar, "is evident in the fact that the number was the total output of the country in 1908."

Outwardly, Durant was confronting the new year with a thriving organization. He had settled his own feud with the holders of the Selden patent, reportedly paying $1 million in back royalties shortly after the patent was upheld by the trial court. While payment of the royalties mooted the legal actions filed and threatened against his companies, it also reduced his available cash. Durant needed money to fund the incessant demands of expansion, including a new, million-dollar factory in Flint for Buick and a new headquarters and group of plants in Detroit "of hitherto unequalled size and capacity."

Production in 1910 would strain General Motors' capacity to the "utmost," Durant happily assured the *Wall Street Journal* reporter. General Motors was offering twenty-one different models for 1910, in a variety of body styles, produced by ten different manufacturers. The cars ranged in price from Buick's $1,150 Model-F, "the foundation on which the great structure of the Buick Motor Company was built," to the overweight Rainier's $4,500.

If General Motors was "strained to the utmost," Durant was not. He was everywhere in his domain. He served as host amid the elaborate trappings of a special twelve-car train of executives who journeyed from Detroit to Flint for an inspection of the new seventeen-acre Buick plant. He flitted to Chicago, stopping only long enough to repay one loan, before returning to Detroit to seek another. Since Oldsmobile had its unofficial theme song, nothing would do but that the top-selling Buick should have its ode too.* Oldsmobile needed room to expand its plant; Durant was off to Lansing. Oakland needed major expansion; Durant personally laid out the site. Durant involved himself in everything, even minor details if they interested him.

Lee Dunlap, general manager at Oakland in the hectic days of 1910, later recalled the sight of Billy Durant in full career: "When Mr. Durant visited one of his plants it was like the visitation of a cyclone. He would lead his staff in, take off his coat, begin issuing orders, dictating letters, and calling the ends of the continent on the telephone, talking in his rapid easy way to New York, Chicago, San Francisco. That sort of thing was less common than it is now; it put most of us in awe of him. Only the most phenomenal memory could keep his deals straight; he worked so fast that the records were always behind."

General Motors had two fast-selling automobiles, Buick and Cadillac; a revived Oldsmobile, which by the beginning of 1910 had earned back its purchase price; and the promising Oakland,

---

* A fair sample of Victor H. Smalley's 1909 doggerel:
  I love my horse and wagon, but oh! you Buick car.
  You leave the folks a-laggin' and wonder where they are.
  I'll chop the wagon into kindling wood; tie Old Dobbins to the pasture bar.
  I love my horse and wagon, but oh! you Buick car.

expected to sell 4,000 vehicles that year. The two truck companies, Reliance and Rapid, were profitable. Other members of the wedding were not: Ewing, the "debutante" of the year before; the overweight Rainier; the death-stricken Welch; and the obsolete Cartercar.

Still Durant bought: the Randolph Motor Car Company, which had yet to build its first vehicle; a power company in Flint; 42.5 percent of the McLaughlin Motor Car Company of Canada; and a 100,000-share interest in Benjamin Briscoe's newly consolidated United States Motors.

The $1 million paid for the United States Motors stock was more than a gesture to a friend. It was part of the still-cherished plan Durant and Briscoe shared to combine their holdings into the dominant force within the young industry. Through 1909, while each went his separate way, they continued to dream of the amalgam that had been scotched by Perkins' withdrawal; Durant even had taken options to buy for General Motors in July 1909 the three major Briscoe companies: the original sheet-metal works, the Maxwell–Briscoe Automobile Company, and the Brush Runabout Company, builders of a $500, all-wooden-body car designed by Allison Brush, who was by 1910 Buick's chief designer. But, once again, J.P. Morgan and Company had blocked a merger, demanding that Durant pay $2 million *cash* for the bank's share of the Briscoe holdings. J.P. Morgan and Company wanted nothing to do with a man who repeatedly predicted the automobile industry soon would sell 500,000 vehicles a year, who insisted the saturation point would be reached "only when they stop making babies." Twelve years after, Briscoe wrote bitterly: "The $5 million of General Motors stock the [Morgan-backed] Maxwell-Briscoe Company would have obtained at that time would have mounted by the stock dividend declarations . . . to more than $100 million."

Frustrated, Briscoe had then turned to Anthony N. Brady. The first of Wall Street's mighty to realize the potential of the industry, Brady intended to rectify his earlier mistake of not paying the comparatively low prices the automobile companies had demanded prior to the Panic of 1907.

Briscoe publicly announced the formation of United States

Motors in February 1910, "at a time when it is freely admitted," one trade journal wrote, "that the automobile business is passing through a second formative period." The company's ultimate aim—its self-extinction—was so carefully masked that *Automobile* reported, with an obliquely critical reference to Durant: "To what extent this nucleus will gather force is a matter which will have to be confined to speculation . . . It is anticipated by the knowing ones in the inner circle that the United States Motor Company is destined to rival the Napoleonic movements of the most ambitious effort in recent times."

It was Brady who organized the complicated plan designed to bring about first parity, then merger, of fledgling United States Motors and "Napoleonic" General Motors. Brady induced former associates to join him in investing an additional $1 million in their jointly owned, moderately successful Columbia Motor Car Company. Briscoe as promptly exchanged United States Motors shares for Columbia; the investors got the stock they actually wanted, and Briscoe had obtained another automobile line, as well as the $1 million in working capital he needed.

The second and simultaneous step was to deliberately water or reduce the value of General Motors stock, a tactic frowned upon in financial quarters but frequently practiced anyway. On January 4, 1910, Billy Durant had secured the approval of his board of directors to purchase the assets of the Heany Company, authorizing a $7.1-million payment in General Motors stock and cash for what charitably may be described as a clutch of clouded patents on the tungsten-filament electric light.

John Albert Heany had filed for a patent in 1904 on an improved electric light bulb. When the patent was granted in 1907, J. P. Morgan and Company's General Electric, a rival claimant for the tungsten-filament invention, brought suit. As an outgrowth of the civil suit, Heany, his attorney, and a clerk in the United States patent office were indicted in federal court on a charge of falsifying Heany's original patent application. Though Heany himself was exonerated, both attorney and clerk were dispatched to federal prison in 1907. Their convictions all but destroyed any opportunity the inventor had of maintaining the primacy of his patent and its value.

Even so, Nathan Hofheimer, Durant's stockbroker, organized the Heany Company on September 28, 1908, just twelve days after General Motors' incorporation. Curtis R. Hatheway, the one-time Ward, Hayden, and Satterlee attorney, served as secretary-treasurer. Durant was a major stockowner, though the company's sole assets consisted of the dubious patents; its major creditor was Anthony Brady, who had earlier backed the Heany patents as a ploy in his ongoing struggle against Morgan and Morgan-supported General Electric. With Durant's purchase of Heany's assets, Brady would be exchanging virtually worthless Heany for valuable, if diluted, General Motors. No matter—for their intent, as Briscoe wrote later, was "to sweeten the deal."

The deal was very sweet indeed. In exchange for two-thirds of Heany's outstanding stock, Durant agreed to pay $1.1 million in General Motors preferred, $5.9 million in common, and $112,000 in cash. The stock, previously unissued, was taken from General Motors' treasury and thus diminished the equity in the company any other shareholder previously had enjoyed. The stock issuance would have been of no great consequence had the Heany Company been worth anything approaching $7.1 million; it wasn't. (Eventually, General Motors would sell various ex-Heany facilities for $1.2 million to rival General Electric.)

With the value of its outstanding stock diluted by the additional shares issued—"watered" in Wall Street's term—General Motors shares were closer to parity with United States Motors stock. Briscoe, Brady, and the others holding stock in United States Motors could get more General Motors shares in exchange than they would have had the Heany deal not been consummated. Additionally, Brady, Durant, Hofheimer, and Hatheway benefited by unloading their virtually worthless Heany stock.*

* In June 1915, inventor John Albert Heany filed suit in federal district court in New York asking $1 million in damages from Hofheimer, Durant, and Hatheway. (Brady had died two years earlier.) Heany's petition, reported in the New York *Times* of June 30, 1915, alleged that he had been cheated in his exchange of Heany for General Motors stock. The three respondents had received proportionately more General Motors stock for their interest in Heany than had the inventor, he claimed. In his suit, Heany asserted that at the time of the merger, his company had a net worth of $3 million. General Motors had paid $7 million. Heany's suit was settled out of court, the settlement apparently unreported in the press.

By the spring of 1910, Durant had run out of cash. The rapid expansion, both in additions to holdings and in plant construction, had been predicated on a continued high volume of sales. But inexplicably, public taste shifted, and the Buick, which had been the guarantor, or security, for repeated midwestern bank loans, fell behind its projected sales totals.

Buick sales totaled 8,820 vehicles in 1908, the year General Motors was formed. In 1909, the company produced 14,606 cars, half of these the $900 Model 10. This sporty roadster would account for one-third of the 30,000 vehicles manufactured in 1910, but not enough to meet the demands for profits Durant placed upon it.

Bankers who had granted loans to General Motors, on the assurance that the Buick was doing well, became skittish, and began to call in their notes. In May 1910, Durant suspended construction on the new Buick factory in Flint so as to conserve cash. He cut the work force, then cut it again. Euphoric Flint, said to be the fastest-growing city in America, suddenly came to its senses. Employment in Durant's works had tripled in just two years, but now 15,000 carriage and automobile workers faced layoffs. Increasing numbers sat helplessly in the tent cities and shacks surrounding the Buick complex on Flint's north side. Lured to the city by the promise of what the Detroit *News* six months before had called "the great new life that has come to the state," the workers found themselves without jobs, without savings, and without hope of public relief.

The shock reverberated for years; in 1910, Flint, Michigan, home of motordom's greatest capitalistic venture, elected a Socialist mayor. The resentments would last a lifetime, the bitterness handed from father to son. Laborers made $2.20 per day at Buick's Flint works in the booming year of 1909. Few workers could afford the chariots of privilege they produced; at the beginning of 1910, only 100 automobiles were licensed in the city.

In June 1910, Durant turned to his own Durant–Dort Carriage Company and the Flint Wagon Works to borrow money to meet payrolls and pressing bills. Cadillac secured a $500,000 loan after an emergency meeting with two Detroit banks only hours before a payroll was due. Harry K. Noyes, Buick's Boston distributor, became the company's sometime paymaster. On one occasion he literally shipped from Boston to Flint suitcases of money to pay bills; had Noyes banked the funds, they would have been confiscated by banks to meet Buick's overdrafts. Another time, Noyes deposited Buick money in his own name, then wrote a cashier's check payable to the company.

By midsummer, the once-flourishing Buick, which had served as security for General Motors' loans, owed $2.7 million in short-term borrowings to banks and $5 million to suppliers. The foundation of Durant's empire was cracking under the strain of rapid expansion.

His sources of funds in Michigan and New York exhausted, Durant and Cadillac's Wilfred Leland canvassed the Midwest for further loans. It was a two-man road show for rural bankers, who were no more ready to shower down coin than big city banks had been, Leland recalled:

He would explain with evident satisfaction, that General Motors had acquired Cadillac, and that he wanted the bank official to become acquainted with me and wanted me to tell him a little about the financial condition of Cadillac . . . We made trips to many different banks and in every instance the substance of the statement made by the bank official was, "Well, Mr. Leland, if the Cadillac stood alone, we would be glad to loan up to the limit. But the Cadillac is now a part of General Motors and is involved in all the complications and entanglements of that organization and we cannot loan a dollar."

Durant secured a momentary reprieve in early September. Colonel Ralph Van Vechten, vice-president of Chicago's Continental and Commercial Savings and Trust Company, agreed to consider a $7.5 million loan to General Motors. Elated, Durant returned to Michigan to assemble a current corporate financial statement from the casually kept ledgers of his scattered detachments. The returns were worse than anticipated; General Motors actually needed $9.5 million to stay afloat.

Still optimistic, Durant, cunning Arnold H. Goss, and Alexander B. C. Hardy returned to Chicago. If Van Vechten were willing to loan $7.5 million, surely he would loan $9.5 million to the largest automobile manufacturer in the world.

Van Vechten was cool, however. Staring out the window at the distant elevated transit line, he explained that the bank's directors had had second thoughts. There would be no loan—not $9.5 million, not $7.5 million. Continental had decided that General Motors was far too precarious. The three stunned mendicants found their own way out.

Even in the wake of the last rejection, with the corporation he called "my baby" slipping away, Durant managed to retain something of his sense of humor. Hardy recalled the trip home after Continental's refusal: "The train stopped in Elkhart, Indiana, in a pouring rainstorm. Far down the dark and dismal street shone one electric sign—'Bank.' Durant shook Goss, who was dozing dejectedly in a corner. 'Wake up, Goss,' said the leader. 'There's one bank we missed.' "

Sales for the 1910 fiscal year, which ended in September, had doubled those of 1909, but profits had not kept pace. The 1910 profit of $10.2 million was only $1.1 million greater than the year before. The retrenchment continued. A portion of Welch was offered for sale; Michigan Auto Parts and then Marquette–Rainier went on the block. There were no buyers. Durant took to walking Flint's streets alone at night.

His chauffeur at the time, Laverne Marshall, recalled a lonely Durant waiting for a train on a cold autumn morning: "Mr. Durant wore a long, straight overcoat with a fur collar which gave him a military appearance. He paced up and down the platform, his arms folded snugly in front of him. His head, covered by his fur collar, was drawn down closely to his shoulders. To me he was the image of Napoleon heading his staff."

He was a Napoleon whose army no longer had reserves and no hope of reinforcements until John H. McClement, a stockholder in the company, approached Durant with a proposition. In exchange for a finder's fee—he would take it in stock—McClement would explore the possibility of a loan with various New York banking interests.

A one-time auditor and controller for various railroad companies, McClement had gravitated into orbit around the Morgan bank as comptroller of the Edison Electric Company. From there he had moved on to the Northern Pacific Railroad, another Morgan investment. He had been one of the appraisers of the Deere and McCormick family holdings that George W. Perkins had fused to create the Harvester trust, a particularly delicate task since the appraisals determined which family would control. As a director of Colorado Fuel and Iron, he was John D. Rockefeller's watchdog, a shrewd accountant who served successive masters. At the age of forty-six, McClement became what a later age would call a "consultant." He retired "from active business" to give himself over, as his approved biography put it, to accepting retainers from "leading banks and railroads for his advice on important financial matters."

By the third week of September 1910, McClement had put together a consortium of East Coast banking firms with the express intention of cannibalizing General Motors or taking control for themselves. Twenty-two representatives of the nation's largest financial institutions, summoned by the influential Boston and New York investment banking houses of Lee, Higginson and Company and J. & W. Seligman, gathered in the directors' room of the Chase National Bank in New York. Among other things, the minutes of the meeting stated, they were there "to effect a reorganization of the management and a restriction of enthusiasm" among those in control of General Motors.

Through a long day, Durant and the general managers of the automobile companies, Mead, Dunlap, and Smith, discussed the corporation's position and the prospects for Buick, Oakland, Oldsmobile, and the smaller automobile companies.

Chase National: Was not the corporation growing rather rapidly?

J. & W. Seligman: You do have a consolidated purchasing department, do you not?

Continental Bank: No audit of the books? Of accounts receivable?

Lee, Higginson's James J. Storrow, his patrician sensibilities ruffled: What did Welch, Rainier, Randolph, Seager Motor, and Packard Electric contribute? Or Ewing, Marquette, and Cartercar?

The day wore longer for Durant, his midmorning enthusiasm pummeled under skeptical questioning. Enthusiasm, then hope, faded.

The bankers assembled were openly critical of Durant's ferocious empire-building, the lack of firm management in his loose confederation, and the uncoordinated buying of parts and raw materials. The corporation's books were in fearful need of repair; Dunlap did not know how much Oakland owed at the moment.

General Motors' and Durant's prospects had reached a low point by four o'clock in the afternoon, when wearied Wilfred Leland began presenting Cadillac's financial report in the paneled board room. Durant had honored his agreement, leaving the Lelands autonomous; they had pursued their conservative ways, husbanding resources and paying for expansion out of income. Producing forty vehicles per day, with a profit that year of $3 million, Cadillac had no outstanding bank debts. The Lelands' was a form of business management the bankers could appreciate.

The meeting adjourned shortly before six that evening, according to Wilfred Leland's account, the only one to survive. The nominal chairman, J.C. Van Cleaf, called young Leland aside. Would he wait in an adjoining room while the bankers discussed the situation privately? Leland stayed behind as a dejected General Motors delegation gathered its papers and left the directors' room.

A half-hour later, Van Cleaf summoned Leland before the tribunal of bankers, telling him: "Up to the time of your testimony, we were convinced that nothing was possible except the complete dissolution of the General Motors Company. The operations you have explained to us have deeply interested us." A committee of five bankers had agreed to stay in New York, to meet that evening in the Belmont Hotel, and Van Cleaf wanted Leland, pledged to secrecy, to attend while they discussed the situation.

That night, in Parlor B of the Belmont Hotel, across the street from General Motors' New York office, where Durant waited in dark silence, Wilfred Leland argued with the committee of bankers. As wild-eyed as Durant's predictions seemed, the automobile industry was one of unlimited possibility, Leland urged. Quiet, conservative, deeply principled Wilfred Leland was as infected with auto-mania as had been the most dedicated of garage tinkerers a decade before.

The five-member committee remained skeptical. Over coffee, a warm Spanish port, and Cuban cigars, Leland pressed his argument. True, many of those in the industry were poor businessmen, but they were selling as many automobiles as they could produce—even in this post-Panic depression. The problem was to find the capital to expand, as rapidly as possible, to meet the demand.

If General Motors were broken up, Leland insisted, the investors would lose their money, the banks their $3 million in outstanding loans, and suppliers some $5 million. If General Motors fell, it could trigger a nationwide panic; it certainly would damage investors' confidence just as the economy was rebounding from the depression. All the company needed, Leland pleaded, was time—and cash to meet its past-due bills.

"If you will only reorient your thinking in the direction of how General Motors might be saved," urged Leland, "rather than why it should be dissolved, you will find many good portents of success. General Motors made ten millions last year. Surely fifteen millions was not such a great sum to loan to a business earning at that rate."

Throughout the night, Durant waited in his company's New York office while Leland talked to the bankers in Parlor B. Durant never revealed his feelings during that death watch, though surely he must have wondered if Leland were fashioning a new motors holding company with himself as its president. He and the rest of the General Motors delegation ordered a catered supper and then left it uneaten, no longer interested in food. The longer the talks across the street wore on, the less the exiles could believe their own reassurances. Durant slumped lower in his chair; his baby was dying while he sat helpless.

At 2:30 in the morning, the meeting at the Belmont Hotel broke up. Leland had prevailed, the committee of five finally convinced that General Motors was worth salvaging. Apparently, too, Leland had declined the bankers' bid that he become the corporation's chief operating officer. Durant had been especially solicitous of the Lelands, father and son, and had honored his agreement fully. Though theirs was not a friendship so much as a business arrangement, Wilfred Leland had no desire to repay Durant's respect by taking his corporation from him.

The group of twenty-two bankers reconvened the following morning at ten, a downcast Durant waiting to hear word of his corporation's premature death. Durant later said that the unexpected decision was "the surprise of his life."

Colonel Ralph Van Vechten, vice-president of Chicago's Continental and Commercial, which earlier had declined to lend $9.5 million, announced the committee's recommendation of a $15 million loan to General Motors. Urging a supportive policy, Van Vechten then polled the bankers in the room, asking each to subscribe some portion of the necessary loan. The twenty-two bankers, who had assembled the day before to dismember the corporation, overpledged $17.5 million, five million more than actually was needed to pay outstanding debts and provide working capital.

The terms of the loan, however, were to be exceptionally severe. In exchange for $15 million underwritten by a syndicate of banking houses, General Motors would mortgage all of its physical properties. Though the loan was for $15 million at 6-percent interest, the bankers immediately discounted it, as was their custom, and gave the corporation just $12.75 million. Additionally, the bankers were to receive a bonus of $6.17 million in preferred stock, a total profit on a no-risk, mortgage-backed loan of over 62 percent—plus whatever dividends their shares earned. Durant had fallen among the barracudas of Wall Street.

There were additional terms to the loan. The incumbent board of directors was to resign, to be replaced by a group hand-picked by the bankers. Moreover, and most galling to Durant, a five-member committee was to manage the company during the five-year term of the loan. Its avowed purpose was to restrict Durant's enthusiasm.

The five members of the voting trust that would run the company's affairs were Durant; Albert Strauss, prime figure in the

New York investment house of J. & W. Seligman; James J. Storrow, senior partner in Boston's Lee, Higginson, who would
serve as General Motors' interim president; James N. Wallace,
president of Central Trust Bank in New York, the third of the
three institutions that underwrote the loan; and Anthony N.
Brady, who by virtue of the Heany–United States Motors deal
was now a major stockholder in General Motors.

Durant's was a helpless rage: "The $15 million loan finally
offered had outrageous terms which I was forced to accept to
save my 'baby,' born and raised by me, the result of hectic years
of night and day work . . ."

Billy Durant had lost control of General Motors.

5

The Interregnum

The banker's collar chafed. For months Durant fretted under the restraints the voting trust imposed while James Storrow, its chairman, moved to reorganize the company. Still caught up in his "Napoleonic" frenzy, Durant urged that General Motors press on. The new, decidedly more conservative leadership chose instead to regroup the scattered subsidiaries, consolidating and reappraising.

There was little chance that Durant and Storrow would or even could agree. However proper the two men were, they were palpably dissimilar: Durant the trader, with a hussar's dash; sober Storrow the Brahmin, a Beacon Street familiar, moving partner in one of the nation's largest bond-marketing houses. Durant could muster little patience for either the protocol of mandarins imposed by Storrow or with Storrow's confreres, who represented an elite of commerce from which Durant, and his father before him, had been excluded.

Born in 1864, the great-grandson of naval hero Oliver Hazard Perry, James Jackson Storrow represented the banking fraternity in all its somber conservatism. He moved with ease among those who in a less reverent time would be dubbed the "Establishment." An oarsman on the Harvard eight for three years, and captain in 1885, he had matriculated in Harvard Law School. Oliver Wendell Holmes, then chief justice of the Massachusetts Supreme Court, was a frequent guest at the home young Storrow rented while still in law school.

After twelve years of legal practice, Storrow became a partner in the investment house of Lee, Higginson and Company. He also had taken the interest in civic affairs expected of his ilk, successfully shepherding a plan to clean up the Charles River basin. More importantly for his business career, he had redirected Lee, Higginson's business from marketing railroad bonds to municipals. If municipals were less lucrative, they were also less risk-laden.

Risk was anathema to men like Storrow; they took few gambles, and those but cautiously. There certainly was little risk in the $12.5 million loan to General Motors; yet ostensibly because of financial peril, the bankers had exacted usurious terms. To raise the money, the banks bought $100 shares in a voting trust, taking as a bonus a grant of $6.17 million in General Motors stock. With personal funds, Durant bought a block of voting-trust shares—in effect, loaning the corporation his own money while retaining a voice in its management. (Under the terms of the voting trust, for the next five years holders of the company's common stock would have no veto power over management decisions.)

The $12.5 million, for which General Motors was obligated to repay $15 million, was totally secured by mortgages on property and machinery the company owned. While Durant's haphazard books overestimated the fixed investment at $37 million, McClement, reevaluating their inflated worth for the new investors, knocked off $16 million. Even the lower figure was sufficient to repay the loan if General Motors failed, and would provide a handsome profit besides.

The Eastern bankers ultimately wrung $9.35 million in cash and securities, Durant complained, for a loan of $12.5 million. The fees were more costly to the corporation than had been the

Heany purchase, which was commonly believed to have been the capstone on Durant's tomb.

In the two years of its existence, General Motors had posted a $15.3 million profit on total sales of $88.4 million. The demand for its automobiles appeared to be increasing. Indeed, the entire auto industry in the coming year of 1911 was expected to produce 185,000 vehicles, an 819-percent increase since 1904, Buick's first year. Such palpable guarantees coupled with the industry's favorable prospects transformed the loan notes from dicey fliers to virtual sureties as Wilfred Leland had argued in Parlor B. The twenty-two lenders themselves first bought up a large percentage; insiders, friends of friends, scavenged the remains left by the lions.

On October 18, 1910, the authoritative Boston News Bureau reported: "Private subscriptions have been coming in so rapidly to the $15 million First Lien Five-Year General Motors notes that it seems doubtful whether there will be any public issue or any chance for the general public to subscribe." Less than one month later, the notes had been totally subscribed, without a public offering.

Durant might have gained rueful satisfaction from the fact that Eastern investors now shared his enthusiasm for the automobile generally, and General Motors particularly, but there could be only bitterness in the knowledge that he had been so deliberately slapped down compared to the treatment accorded Daniel Guggenheim, president of American Smelters, a month later. The two most prestigious New York investment banks—Kuhn, Loeb and J. P. Morgan and Son—together underwrote a $15 million bond issue for the hard-pressed copper magnate to pay $11 million in debts and to provide new working capital. Guggenheim had fallen behind in a speculative industry that had made more on Wall Street than it had in production, yet the underwriters had imposed no voting trust. Guggenheim was one of their own.

Durant would know no such solicitude; Storrow now commanded General Motors. Even before the voting trust took control on November 15, 1910, Durant sought to mollify his new colleagues. Because Storrow insisted that Durant concentrate on the corporation's management, Durant had nominated Charles W. Nash to replace himself as president of Buick.

A veritable protégé of Durant and his carriage-works partner, J. Dallas Dort, Nash had risen from a laborer's job sorting scrap iron at the carriage works to become its general manager. Though expert at carriage production, Nash knew nothing about automobiles. Storrow, however, was taken with other qualities in the new Buick president.

Born in DeKalb, Illinois, in 1864, Nash was bound out to a farmer at the age of seven by his impoverished mother and spent six hated years in virtual servitude before running away. For eight years more he had shuttled from one job to another—carpentry in the winter, farm labor in the summer. At the age of twenty-one, responsible for a wife, Nash was managing a farm near Flint; his wages consisted of twenty dollars per month, a house to live in, and free milk. He managed to save $150 of his $240 wages that year, he told a friend proudly.

Five years of farm life wore hard on his young wife, so Nash packed it in for a clerk's job in a Flint grocery store. Though he couldn't save as much money, he could make his wife happy, the only consideration in Charlie Nash's mind equal to thrift. Because clerking paid little and offered no opportunity for advancement, Nash next took a job as a blacksmith's helper in the Flint Road Cart Company's modest works for $1.25 a day. He was twenty-eight.

The specter of his boyhood poverty hovered over Charlie Nash. Penury in his youth had bred parsimony in the man. Hard work, he believed, meant advancement, and pennies more in wages. Those pennies, carefully husbanded, became dollars.

Within six months after Nash went to work sorting scrap iron, Dort had singled him out for promotion to foreman in the expanding carriage factory. In time he would become works superintendent, then vice-president and director of the largest carriage manufactory in the world. "I craved responsibility," he explained in a later interview.

Nash was forty-six when Durant tapped him as president of Buick—a humorless, driven man, self-conscious about his meager grade-school education. Sure of his skills as a production manager, Nash was confident he knew how to get work out of factory hands. His credo was simple, Calvinist, and inflexible: with devotion and hard work a man could rise in the world. Piece rates assured production. It was an appealing argument to the "hunkies" and "bohunks" living in the tar-paper-and-packing-box shantytown around the Buick works, immigrants desperately anxious to succeed in the New World. Nash knew well how to take advantage of his workers' sensibilities.

Storrow was impressed with Nash. The poor boy from Michigan and the Boston Brahmin became close, if improbable, friends. Nash, who had never known his own father, found a substitute in the friendship of Storrow, just as he had earlier found it in the friendly sponsorship of J. Dallas Dort. Storrow "was an extraordinary man," Nash later wrote. "I doubt if a man ever lived who had a warmer, bigger heart than Mr. Storrow, and who, on the other hand, was so unable to show it in his daily contact with men. A great many men felt that Mr. Storrow was of the 'banker' type—rather cold-blooded—which was entirely contrary to his real make-up. . . ."

Durant, effectively an outsider, never would so penetrate Storrow's reserve. Durant might be chairman of the pivotal finance committee, but it was Storrow, as interim president of General Motors, who made the executive decisions. Nash was responsible for Buick and confident enough of his carriage-works experience to call upon Durant but little. After all, most of the techniques of auto production had been borrowed directly from the familiar carriage business long before Nash arrived.

The second bulwark of the corporation, Cadillac, was firmly and efficiently managed by the Lelands. The balance of the company's lines were contracting and regrouping. Because the majority of the voting trust was hostile to further acquisitions or financial derring-do, Durant was left only with the tedium of ledger sheets and accounts receivable. It was not enough for so restless an emperor.

"I had been given a title and a position, but the support, the cooperation, the spirit, the unselfishness that is needed in every successful undertaking was not there," Durant fretted. "In a way, it was the same old story, 'too many cooks'; a board of directors comprised of bankers, action by committees, and the lack of knowledge that comes only with experience." Durant lamented that "Opportunities that should have been taken care of with quickness and decision were not considered." The company lacked "the very thing that counts for progress and success—quick decisions and leadership."

Others agreed. Much later, a General Motors vice-president noted: "The bankers were too skeptical about the future of the automobile industry. They were chiefly interested in trying to realize savings, so they closed down some plants, concentrating in others. They didn't take advantage of the opportunities. Under Durant, the company might have had a little financial difficulty now and then, but it would have grown much faster and its earnings would have been much greater."

Storrow and his colleagues were purblind. By training, cultivated temperament, and position, they were men with a vested interest in the status quo. They dealt as equals with similar men in matters of commerce; their wives were the arbiters of Society. (It is significant that their class had, with a capital letter, usurped the word "society" itself.) Theirs was a settled order ossified to caste in the half-century since the Civil War, so insulated that it failed to appreciate this last moment of careening, unchecked opulence before the chaos of world war.

With the industrial-born prosperity of the first decade of the century had come a gradual dispersion of wealth. The poor remained grimly poor; indeed, there were industrialists who considered it morally repugnant to pay anything more than a subsistence wage. Nonetheless, the onrushing middle class had so burgeoned that sociologists now sought to subdivide it into more distinct income groups: lower-middle, middle, and upper-middle. This group, or groups— artisans, clerks, shopkeepers, small businessmen—found new leisure time and the money to enjoy it.

The pursuits of the middle class fashioned new industries and new fortunes. Broadway songwriter-producer George M. Cohan, *Variety* estimated, was worth $1.5 million; producer David Belasco, $1 million. In half a thousand converted stores, shop girls and bank tellers watched the one reel of flickering spasms evolve into the first six-reel feature, *Tillie's Punctured Romance,* which incidentally introduced a young British comic, Charles Chaplin to America. Nickel admissions created empires in a dusty suburb of Los Angeles.

What some praised as sophistication and others damned as license animated all of the arts. In 1907, stunned Metropolitan Opera directors prohibited a second performance of Richard Strauss' *Salome* on the grounds that it was licentious. Six years later, some maturity having been gained, New York *Times* music critic Henry E. Krehbeil, reviewing Strauss' masterwork *Der Rosenkavalier,* perceived an underlying moral tone that justified the opera's "frank salaciousness." Paul Emile Chabas' coy nude, *September Morn,* drew titters when it was displayed, while the revolutionary Armory Show of 1913 provoked outraged Chicago art students to try Matisse for "artistic murder, total degeneracy of color, and criminal misuse of line" and to burn three of his paintings as punishment.

Social critics and art students notwithstanding, a striving for the new, the American, challenged the formal arts dominated by European academies. The fashionable New York architectural firm of McKim, Mead, and White still looked to Swiss chalets, English inns, and French chateaux for its inspiration. Meanwhile, in restless Chicago, pushy Detroit, and aspiring St. Louis, Daniel Burnham, Frank Lloyd Wright, Louis Sullivan, and Albert Kahn were creating an American architecture.

The "American tradition" developed most surely within the popular arts and in industry—over the protests of the tradition-minded. A horrified New York *Sun* editor condemned the wave of new dances—the grizzly bear, the turkey trot, the bunny hug—as perpetrated "by the habitués of low resorts, by strumpets and their patrons." It was in these low resorts, among the strumpets and their patrons, in tenements and railway yards, that John Sloan, George Luks, George Bellows, and their colleagues of the "Ash Can School" found their inspiration. And in the least reputable of these dance halls what would come to be known as the Jazz Age had begun. Paul Whiteman, a young musician of indifferent talent, organized a band to play uptown

the new "syncopation" popular in Chicago's black neighborhoods. In Baltimore, H.L. Mencken already was referring to
the more daring young women, their ankle-length skirts slit to
the calf, as "flappers." The slit skirts themselves, blamed on
the necessity of mounting the automobile, were damned as im-
moral by the *Ladies' Home Journal* in 1913.

As the financial gap between the upper and middle classes
narrowed, shopkeepers emulated their social betters by building
summer homes where only the most wealthy had dared in other
times. Newport and Long Island flourished. The leisures of the
rich were to be democratized, and nothing so typified the new
wealth abroad in the land, the new leisure, as the American
automobile.

The automobile became the badge of the *arriviste*. Meanwhile,
at a nickel a ride, factory workers still paid the dividends of the
nation's 1,260 street railways. Women working in Chicago's
largest mercantile houses drew paychecks each Saturday totaling as little as five dollars. In New York City, between hunting
trips, former President Theodore Roosevelt found girls in the
garment industry's sullen lofts earning just three dollars for a
seventy-two-hour work week.

The jobholder was virtually powerless: confronted with
wholesale firings if he sought to organize; court injunctions,
lockouts, and federal troops if he went out on strike. Among the
nation's major industries, only the railway brotherhoods, essentially mutual-benefit societies, were able to assert some measure
of industrial control.

By 1911, Henry M. Leland's Employers Association of Detroit
had used mass firings during successive slumps to purge the city
of organized union activity. Out of a labor force of 175,000, just
15,000 held union cards. Leland the rate-buster, insisting he
wished only to protect the employer from the abuses of labor,
had become a union buster. The Employers Association lobbied
in Lansing, killing child-labor restrictions and various Progressive efforts at workmen's-compensation and factory-safety laws;
at its beck and call, magistrates issued anti-union injunctions,
and police became strike-breakers.

Leland was a paragon of restraint compared to John D. Rockefeller, a law unto himself within the sovereign state of Colorado. When desperate miners employed at Rockefeller's Colorado Fuel and Iron went on strike in 1913, the attorney general of the state organized two National Guard companies of the state's hard cases to put down "the civil war in Southern Colorado." The lawless militia did just that in April 1914, assaulting the miners' tent city near Ludlow and massacring twelve children and two women.

Though the right to organize, to bargain collectively for wages and working conditions, was to be denied for another thirty years, reform was afoot elsewhere. In 1906, Upton Sinclair's *The Jungle* loosed a flood of letters upon a laggard Congress demanding an end to the jackalry of the "beef trust"; then-President Theodore Roosevelt petulantly retorted: "Tell Sinclair to go home and let me run the country for a while." Congress passed the Pure Food and Drug Act the same year nevertheless.

With muckrakers to the right of them and Socialists to the left—the one alarming the public, the other, business—politicians fumbled toward reforms. Massachusetts passed the first minimum-wage law—for women and children only—despite employers' arguments that it infringed upon the liberty of ten-year-olds to bargain with mill owners for their wages. A half-dozen states adopted workmen's-compensation laws. In California, Governor Hiram Johnson brought down the Southern Pacific Railroad's statewide hegemony.

Nothing was more symbolic of Progressive reform than Louisiana Representative Arsene Pujo's 1912 hearings on the "money trust." Committee counsel Samuel Untermyer badgered J. Pierpont Morgan, who was bewildered by public resentment of his personal handling of the nation's financial affairs. Once crowds had saluted "Pierpontifex's" appearances on Wall Street, running after his black-and-gold carriage for a look at the great man within. Now there was an outcry, a demand for reform that even a compromised United States Senate could not ignore: Morgan was to be laid low. The Pujo investigation disclosed that just three banks controlled 112 corporations worth more than $22 billion. By the sheer size of their enterprises, Morgan and Rockefeller alone could determine the supply of money in the nation. Pujo's report was to presage even more changes.

Ponderous William Howard Taft, elected president in 1908, had sincerely tried to curb the worst excesses. The literal-minded Taft assumed it his responsibility to carry out the reforms of which his predecessor, Theodore Roosevelt, had only spoken. Taft authorized an antitrust suit against United States Steel in 1911, and Roosevelt, having personally assured J.P. Morgan three years before that no such action would be filed, took Taft's move as a personal affront. At the head of the Bull Moose Party, Roosevelt entered the 1912 presidential campaign against the incumbent. By splitting the Republican–Progressive vote—the only question remaining, said railroad mogul and United States Senator Chauncey Depew, "is which corpse gets the most flowers"—Taft and Roosevelt fell to the former Presbyterian college professor from New Jersey, Woodrow Wilson.

Propelled by the Pujo investigation, the first of Wilson's reforms was the Federal Reserve Act, adopted in 1913 despite opposition from such former legislative arbiters as the American Bankers Association and the United States Chamber of Commerce. (The *Texas Banker's Record* inveighed against "the communistic law" to rationalize the supply of money by imposing federal governors on privately owned regional banks.) Swept along by the countervailing political force of the middle class, Congress in 1914 passed Alabama Representative Henry A. Clayton's antitrust bill to buttress the older Sherman Act, and created the Federal Trade Commission. Big business would remain big, but the watch of government commissions had been mounted. The Sixteenth Amendment ratified by forty-two states, 357,598 people with incomes over $3,000 paid a total of $28 million in 1914's new federal income tax.

These were but reforms. It would be for Henry Ford to make a socioeconomic revolution by creating the blue-collar consumer of luxury goods. On January 5, 1914, the Ford Motor Company announced that it would begin hiring 5,000 men and raising wages to five dollars for an eight-hour day. The next morning, job seekers literally stormed the gates of Ford's newly automated Highland Park, Michigan, plant.

Skilled workers could earn as much as fifty-four cents an hour at Ford, yet few qualified in a factory that had no less than sixty-five different pay scales. The five-dollar-day, which ironically shrouded Henry Ford with an image of social enlightenment, was inaugurated for the most practical of reasons. Ford's turnover was staggering; for every 100 production jobs, 963 men were hired annually. Even as Ford was installing Philadelphia engineer Frederick Winslow Taylor's ultimate efficiency machine, the integrated, moving assembly line, production totaled just 11.7 automobiles per worker per year, only twice that of 1905, despite massive automation and investment in some ten thousand machine tools, more than one for each worker.

Ford is widely credited with having invented the moving assembly line, thereby creating mass production in America. In fact, Ford himself acknowledged borrowing the notion of moving the product to the worker, rather than the worker to the product, from the meat-packing industry. Ford was not even the first to do so in the auto industry; as early as 1904, Ransom Olds had rolled his curved-dash Oldsmobiles along the floor while workers added individual parts.

At Ford's new sixty-five-acre Highland Park plant, however, the entire process—the very building itself—was created for sequential assembly of first parts, then automobiles, from standardized, machine-made components. Engineers analyzed even the smallest phase of production, beginning with subassemblies and working up to entire motors and transmissions. Only after the components were flowing smoothly did Ford, in 1914, place chassis construction on a moving assembly line. Within the year, the time required to assemble a Model-T had been cut from twelve man-hours to one-eighth that.

Though not conceived as such, the five-dollar-per-day wage was a necessary palliative for the remorseless assembly line and the mindless repetition required to produce 1,000 cars every day. A wage that offered some promise of escape from squalor was more important to workers than working conditions. Ford, because he was Ford, coupled the five-dollar-per-day offer to a clutch of idiosyncratic conditions, the first being that only men qualified. Ford felt there was no need to pay women—who would only get married anyway—more than two dollars per day; besides, they didn't work on the assembly line and their turnover was low. To qualify for the five dollars, a man had to be over twenty-two and of such moral fiber that he, among other things, neither "spit on the floor at home," bought on credit, nor was separated or divorced. Only the pure of heart were to enjoy the bounty of what Ford called "neither charity nor wages, but profit sharing."

That rationalization of social value came later; for Henry Ford, it was simply a matter of economics. By slowing turnover to just 15 percent of the total work force, he could increase production. By instituting the eight-hour day, he could run his plant around the clock. Thus, with one self-serving reorganization, Henry Ford granted labor a condition of employment it had sought futilely for fifty years.

Few understood; the *Wall Street Journal* editorially complained Ford was "putting Biblical teachings in places where they don't apply." Other auto makers grumbled, cursing him as a "mad socialist," a traitor to his presumed class, but they would be forced to follow suit, doubling the prevailing wage of Michigan's auto workers. Not to do so risked the best workers hieing off to join the throngs in front of the Highland Park plant, where fire hoses and baton-flaying policemen scattered the mob of job-seekers who crushed against the locked factory gates.

On November 15, 1910, an expanded board of directors took charge of General Motors' fortunes. Four directors of Detroit's First National Bank joined Durant, Storrow, Strauss, Wallace, and Brady, along with the now ubiquitous John H. McClement. Durant was a single vote on the board; Storrow was president and in firm control. Yet among General Motors' leaders only Durant had the vision to grasp the implications of the economic turmoil of the time. In 1914 he saw that Ford was creating wider markets by ever-increasing production and by continually lowering prices. The five-dollar-per-day wage would come back to him in sales. Storrow, the bankers, and Charlie Nash sensed none of it.

While Nash had busied himself with learning about the automobile business, the industrial recession had eased and Buick's tenuous situation improved. Plant expansion that had been halted when cash ran short in 1910 was resumed in October of that year with the promise of bankers' money in the offing. Employment at Buick, which had fallen to a low of 2,300 in September 1910, was by February 1911 back up to 4,800.

Buick's rising fortunes pointed the way, and nothing in President Wilson's campaign promise of a New Freedom impinged on Durant's vision of ever-expanding sales for the automobile, indeed for all American industry. Near the end of 1912, the automobile manufacturers who convened in the bar of the Pontchartrain Hotel in Detroit established a pool to predict the following year's production. The industry had shipped 378,000 automobiles and trucks in 1912, and Durant estimated half a million in 1913, the pool's highest guess. He won; the industry produced 485,000 cars and trucks, and Durant said to his colleagues, "Gentlemen, you don't realize the purchasing power of the American people."

Though Storrow did not intend to serve long as president, he immediately inaugurated a series of money-saving salary cuts and corporate reforms. As captain of the Harvard eight, he had installed an entirely new rowing technique; he would do the same for General Motors. There were immediate personnel changes. The hapless Lee Dunlap, who had not been able to tell the bankers the size of Oakland's debt at the September 1910 meeting, was replaced. At Durant's request, William Little moved from his post as works manager at Buick to Durant's vice-presidential office, ostensibly to give Nash a freer hand in making changes, but actually to work on a plan Durant was to formulate. Another Durant loyalist, Louis Chevrolet, left as the racing program was curtailed.

The next six months were painful for Durant. At every turn he saw the main chance slipping away. A clutch of firms assembled by him in the halcyon days were cut loose. Those companies that couldn't be sold off, such as Ewing, were marked for an ignominious write-down. Most embarrassing to Durant, on May 15, 1911, he was forced to confess to the board of directors that the company's large holdings in Heany were virtually worthless. On Durant's motion, the board voted to attempt to sell what it could of the Heany holdings to General Electric, the only possible buyer, and to end the company's abortive foray into the electric-lamp business.

Storrow also was reorganizing and consolidating the company's scattered holdings. The Rainier purchase was completed with the expectation that it would become the firm's prestige automobile. The two complementary truck firms—Rapid built one-half- to three-ton trucks, Reliance from four- to seven-and-one-half-ton vehicles—were combined to form General Motors Truck Company. The firm also completed the purchase of England's Bedford Motors, where made-in-America Buick parts were being assembled into complete automobiles for sale in Europe. Bedford was, for the moment, the single manufacturing component of the newly organized General Motors Export Company. Meanwhile, an autonomous General Motors of Canada was incorporated as a sales office.

Slowly, the ungainly corporation lumbered into shape, but not without serious mistakes. Late in 1910, shortly after he took command of Buick, Charles Nash approved a decision to kill the company's most successful automobile, the Model 10. Nicknamed the Buick "White Streak," the automobile had been the bulwark of Buick's recent success. In the three years since its introduction, the $1,000 Model 10 had accounted for one-half of Buick's sales. It was, however, a light, four-cylinder car, and comparatively low-priced; Nash needed a more profitable vehicle. The loss of the Model 10 was felt immediately. Buick sales skidded from 30,000 to 14,000 in 1911.

As Storrow and Nash rang the changes, Durant grew ever more restless. His friend R.S. McLaughlin concluded that Storrow feared Billy as "too much of a plunger. Mr. Durant was in durance vile; he had nothing to do." One of the New York bankers who had underwritten the General Motors loan sought to explain Durant's discomfort in a letter to Storrow: "Durant is a genius, and therefore not to be dealt with on the same basis as ordinary businessmen. In many respects he is a child in emotions, in temperament, and in mental balance, yet possessed of a wonderful energy and ability along certain other well-defined lines. He is sensitive and proud; and successful leadership, I think, really counts more with him than financial success."

Still, there was some progress of which Durant approved. Reflecting the corporation's new-found financial footing and the status of its sponsors, on July 31, 1911, General Motors became the first automotive stock to be listed on the New York exchange. The first sale was recorded on August 4, when 200 shares of common were sold for $50.50 per share. By the end of the first week's activity, the common stock had dipped to $48 and the $100 par value preferred to $84. There they would essentially remain through the doldrums of the reorganization, becalmed by a lack of dividends. (The lack of public confidence was shared by some of the banker-officers themselves. Several declined to buy General Motors stock when it was offered to them in 1911.)

While Durant idled and the stock wallowed, Storrow kept at his reorganization. He staffed the export company, sending Johnson Martin to Buenos Aires as the company's South American manager in December 1911. Martin's qualifications as an automobile salesman were dubious, but he was "a Princeton man of excellent background." Martin's major accomplishment seems to have been driving a Buick roadster across the South American continent from Buenos Aires, over the Andes, to Santiago, Chile, in 1914. It was a triumphant feat in an era of automotive adventures.

True to caste and university, Storrow also sought to recruit at the Harvard Engineering Society. "Most of the time I am suffering from a grievous dearth," he wrote in a letter in February 1911:

You might tell the men at the dinner, if it is sufficiently informal, that in the reorganization of the General Motors Company I am looking for anywhere from two to six sound, level-headed mechanical engineers. The output of the company last year was $58,000,000 and this was almost entirely accomplished without the advice and assistance of technically trained mechanical engineers. We also need a few managers and superintendents of factories. If some of the Harvard engineers have developed along administrative lines, you can say privately to some of the chaps at this dinner, if it won't do to say it outright, that if they know of the right men for any of these positions we are sore in need of them, and will give tender consideration to any man who applies for a job.

Whatever Harvard chaps Storrow recruited—and it was the last time General Motors looked East for its executive talent—Storrow's most important selection sported no Ivy League ties. Walter Percy Chrysler was a Kansas farm boy whose earliest memories were of Indian raids on the family homestead. As a young man he had gravitated to the railways, first as a janitor and then as a workman in the shops of the Chicago and Great Western Railway in Oelwein, Iowa. Mechanical-minded, Chrysler rose through the shops to become the railroad's superintendent of motive power in just nine years.

It was in Oelwein that Chrysler first became interested in automobiles. That interest became a passion after he spent his life's savings in Chicago in 1905 to buy a steam-powered Locomobile. Even before he drove the $5,000 machine, Chrysler had completely stripped it, laying out the unfamiliar parts on the floor of the barn behind his home, where he studied them individually. His profanity oiling its reassembly, Chrysler pondered the re-erected steam-powered car. "As I visualized its future," he recalled later, "it far outran railway development, which in a sense had reached its zenith, because the automobile provided flexible, economical, individual transportation."

Frustration, too, kindled Chrysler's disaffection with the railway industry. At thirty-three, he had reached the pinnacle of advancement; the railroads hewed to the absolute dictum that no grease-spotted mechanic was to become an executive. Around him he saw ample opportunity to save money for the railroad, to apply his own skills. Yet he was categorized as a mechanic; any business or financial skills he possessed were unwanted.

Chrysler applied for the position of works manager of American Locomotive's Allegheny erection shop. The firm built steam engines—it did not run them—and there was room for advancement. The pay was $275 per month, with room to advance, enough of a lure for an ambitious Kansas farm boy with a "rich railroadman's vocabulary, a short temper, and a showman's pride." Within eighteen months he was named works manager of the firm's Pittsburgh shops, American Locomotive's most important.

Storrow knew that Charles Nash needed help at Buick. Though Nash was competent, his experience producing wooden carriages was inadequate to the task of manufacturing iron and steel machines. Under Nash, production was up to forty-five vehicles per day, but it was not enough to meet the demand expected for the 1912 models. The experience would teach Charlie Nash a lesson he converted into a much quoted homily: "Selling is 90 percent a production problem."

As a director of American Locomotive, Storrow knew Chrysler. It was Storrow who personally wooed Chrysler from the erection shop, assuring him that Nash, his new boss, was "a Flint man of sterling character." Chrysler hardly needed the assurance. The new position offered an opportunity to satisfy two passions: an interest in the automobile and his wish to expand his administrative responsibility. Chrysler would have to take a pay cut, for tight-fisted Nash would give the railroad man a salary of only $6,000 a year. Chrysler paused only momentarily. He was making $8,000 at American Locomotive and had been promised a $4,000 raise if he stayed on.

Chrysler had more vision and was less miserly than Nash. Buicks were not steam cars, to be sure, but they were automobiles, and Chrysler was fascinated. At the age of thirty-six, Walter Chyrsler began a new career.

Chrysler came prepared to make changes. "I saved the Buick Motor Company my first year's salary the first week I was in Flint," he later said. As the cars were finished, Chrysler noticed, they were taken from the factory for a test drive in and around Flint. Neither cars nor drivers were logged as they left and returned; Chrysler kept a private tally and discovered that from one to four cars left the plant each day never to return. At his suggestion, Nash installed a check-out system.

The manufacturing process itself stunned Chrysler. "Every minute of my time we were figuring out further ways to adapt carriage-craft operations to automobile building," he noted. It was wasteful. The Buick factory was a weed-choked garden to Chrysler: "I was a machinist, and I was looking at workmen trained to handle wood. . . . With wood they were admirably skillful, for most of them had been carriage builders, but wherever they were handling metal it seemed to me there was opportunity for a big improvement." Within months of his arrival,

Chrysler had initiated production reforms that would anticipate the assembly line Henry Ford was planning to install the next year. He pushed factory production to seventy-five autos per day and cut construction time from four to two days.

As Chrysler settled in at Buick, Durant withdrew from General Motors. Though he retained his post as a director of the corporation, Durant resigned as finance committee chairman and corporate vice-president. Bill Little went with him. Some privately nurtured plans required their full attention.

The year 1912 marked an upturn for the corporation Durant left behind. Buick sales climbed to 20,000 from the previous year's dismal 13,000. Though still below Durant's record of 30,000, it established Nash and Chrysler as automotive manufacturers. Elsewhere in General Motors, Northway and Elmore had become profitable, and there was still some hope for Cartercar and that vehicle's unique friction drive.

For the third year, Oldsmobile was producing its massive Limited—a sixty-horsepower, six-cylinder behemoth. The Limited was overwhelming in size (it required two steps to mount to the seats) and in price: $4,600. In 1912, the Limited had a more modest four-cylinder companion, priced at $3,000. The vainglorious dreams of the Smith brothers finally had come true.

Oakland was still struggling, and Storrow had yet to find a solution for Rainier and Welch–Detroit. Cadillac, steady in its sales growth under Henry Leland, provided the major impetus for General Motors in 1912—and the automobile industry as a whole in 1913. A fatal accident was responsible.

Byron T. Carter was one of the early-in, early-out experimenters in the automobile industry. He had designed and marketed the Cartercar, with its friction drive, but had sold the company to Durant so that he could return to his career in vocational training in Michigan prisons. On a bitterly cold December day in 1910, Carter had stopped to aid a woman motorist who had stalled on an approach to one of the bridges in Detroit's Belle Isle Park. As Carter spun the crank on her auto to turn over the flywheel, the motor backfired. The crank, suddenly thrown into reverse, snapped Carter's forearm and smashed his jaw. Two Cadillac engineers, on a Sunday outing with their wives, took Carter to the hospital. Though neither a broken arm nor jaw were critical injuries, Carter developed pneumonia and died shortly after the accident.

Ernest Sweet, nominally Cadillac's premier engineer, told Henry Leland of the mishap and Carter's subsequent death. Mourning the well-known Carter, the patriarch lamented, "I'm sorry I ever built an automobile." Remorse became resolve: "Those vicious cranks! I won't have Cadillacs hurting people that way!"

The cranking start was the bane of the motorist—and the industry. The strength required was often beyond customers' capacities; by and large, it barred women from driving. Injuries were not uncommon—six workers in Cadillac's own factories had received broken forearms while cranking recalcitrant engines—and automobile guides were full of not always helpful hints on how to avoid what doctors had taken to calling "starter's arm": "Always pull up on the crank, never push down. It is even better to always use the left hand. In this way should a backfire result you will be unhurt, the crank simply unbending your fingers as it flies back. If you are so nervous as to still be afraid, buy a self-starter or a safety starting crank."

The safety cranks themselves were none too safe, and self-starters abjectly unreliable. For two years, the Winton had incorporated a testy compressed-air system to turn over the engine, but Winton owners cranked as often as did those with mechanical starters. Before the turn of the century, Thomas Alva Edison had taken out patents on a self-starter, but the device was both cumbersome and undependable. Others were no more successful, for if the Wizard of Menlo Park was unable to reduce the size of the battery and motor required to turn the heavy flywheel, what chance did lesser magicians have?

For some weeks after Carter's death Leland prodded Sweet and a group of Cadillac engineers, first for a design and then for a practical working model of a starter. It was a group effort, with no one individual responsible for the final innovation. There was a snag, though; the experimental starter motor the engineers had rigged was far too large to fit into the auto.

Cadillac's assistant sales manager, Earl Howard, suggested a solution. Some years before, when Howard was secretary to the sales manager of the National Cash Register Company in Dayton, Ohio, a young engineer there had invented a compact electric motor to replace the hand crank on the company's products. The innovative electric cash register had become the backbone of the National line.

Wilfred Leland called Charles F. Kettering at the small Dayton Engineering Laboratories Company. The company had been organized in 1909 by Kettering and National's sales manager, Edward A. Deeds. The two had prudently gone into business only after Deeds had sold the Lelands a Kettering-patented, improved automobile-ignition system. With a contract from Cadillac for 5,000 of the devices in hand, Deeds had returned to Dayton to set up the company to manufacture it.

Dayton Engineering Laboratories Company (Delco) opened for business in the hayloft of the disused barn behind Deeds' home, where Kettering and William A. Chryst earlier had puttered at night. It was staffed largely by moonlighting National Cash Register employees, who mockingly called themselves the "Barn Gang." Within two years, Delco was out of the loft at 319 Central Avenue and into rented offices in Dayton. Subcontractors actually manufactured the widely used ignition system, while Kettering and Chryst continued to work in the laboratory.

Charles Franklin Kettering was an inventive tinkerer with an inquisitive mind that ranged far beyond his university training as a chemical engineer. Born in 1876 on a farm near Loudenville, Ohio, Kettering had raced through public schools and had become a teacher in order to earn money to put himself through Ohio State University. The threat of blindness interrupted his studies, delaying his graduation until he was twenty-eight; poor eyesight would trouble him the rest of his life.

A gangling owl, his eyes widened in perpetual surprise behind rimless spectacles, Kettering joined National Cash Register in the summer of 1904 and worked for fifty dollars a week at a workbench in the building known as "Inventions 3" at the plant. His country-boy appearance and his backcountry drawl belied a formidable capacity for solving technological problems. Though he ultimately would achieve an international reputation as a scientist, he was not; rather, he was an inventor with a practical bent, intent upon immediate applications. He endorsed the concept of basic research, but did none himself.

Within four years, Kettering's work in Inventions 3 resulted in four devices that transformed National Cash Register: an electrically operated cash register, a charge-approval system for retail stores, an accounting machine, and a low-cost printing register. These four products, coupled with National president John H. Patterson's overweening ambition, had secured the company's virtual business-machine trust.

Wheels, gears, and springs were hardly enough to keep the curious Kettering occupied. Other projects interested him, including the need for a precise automobile-ignition device brought to his attention by Cadillac assistant sales manager Earl Howard in the summer of 1908. The hayloft workshop was the result. A year later, Kettering had worked out a practical system, Chryst had built a prototype, and Deeds had sold it.

The self-starter Leland now wanted was easier for Kettering; it was simply a matter of adapting the small electric motor invented earlier for the cash register. Opening a cash register's drawer and turning over a heavy flywheel essentially required the same thing: a very short burst of intense power, after which the motor could "rest."

A demonstration on February 27, 1911, just two months after Kettering and Chryst had begun work on the project, convinced Henry Leland that the self-starter was satisfactory. The engineers went one step further, removing from the running board the acetylene tank that provided fuel for the Cadillac's headlights. The headlights, too, would be linked to the ignition-electrical system, to be run off a battery that would be continually recharged by the motor.

Leland offered a production contract for 5,000 of the integrated starting and electrical systems to be installed on Cadillac's 1912 models. Dayton Engineering Laboratories agreed to give Cadillac one year's exclusive use of the system before offering it to other manufacturers. After all, the basic concept belonged to Cadillac's engineers; Kettering's major contribution had been his adaptation of the older cash-register motor.

The self-starter helped to boost Cadillac sales from 10,000 in 1911 to 14,000 the following year. The device had implications far beyond Cadillac's or Delco's balance sheets, however. It made it possible for older people and women who did not have a sturdy left arm to drive with comparative ease. An almost immediate effect was to further the new sense of independence that animated the once-sheltered "weaker sex"; Mrs. Carrie Chapman Catt and her sister suffragists now campaigned for women's rights from the back seats of beribboned automobiles.

Cadillac's advertising for 1912 did not make great mention of the self-starter—a reflection perhaps of the fact that neither the company nor Delco thought it a great invention, but rather a technological application. The Lelands did change their advertising emphasis from workmanship and quality, which had been Cadillac's byword, to laud "the handsome lines, the deep, soft upholstery, the yielding springs, the riding qualities of almost velvety smoothness." It was no way to sell a machine, the patriarch grumbled, but it was the way to sell a new method of transportation.

Purchasers no longer bought automobiles as mechanical curiosities; they presumed their reliability. With the sheer marvel of a horseless carriage no longer an inducement, automobile manufacturers began catering to a taste for status among the middle class of parvenus. Even the workaday Model-T became "a car of extraordinary smartness and distinction," though still "the most reliable, the most serviceable, practical and economical. . . ." The switch in emphasis from performance to comfort and status would be reversed in time, then reversed again and again; the three major themes in automotive advertising had been fixed.

A year after Cadillac's introduction of the self-starter, there were no less than forty-four manufacturers of electrical starting and lighting equipment for automobiles, all taking advantage of the industry's patent pool to use the basic Cadillac–Delco system. Dayton Engineering starters were standard equipment, for a premium, on all General Motors automobiles; in addition, Delco furnished starters for Hudson, Packard, Cole, and Jackson, establishing itself as a major automotive-parts supplier.

By the end of 1912, Storrow had fundamentally regrouped Durant's sprawling conglomerate, Nash and Chrysler had turned Buick's fortunes around, and the central office of the corporation had been considerably strenghthened. In the fiscal year ending July 12, 1912, General Motors sold 49,538 vehicles, its income amounting to $64.7 million. Net profits reached $8.1 million, of which $6.4 million was reinvested in plant expansions and new machinery. Even more important, from Storrow's point of view, the installment payment on the loan owed to the banks had been met promptly.

The corporation running smoothly, the bankers relinquished day-to-day management. On November 11, 1912, Charles Nash became president of General Motors and a month later, Walter P. Chrysler succeeded him as president of Buick.

Nash continued Storrow's reforms. Despite a general business downturn, which would intensify as Europe tensed for the upheaval of war, the corporation prospered. Desultory Oakland sales reached a new high of 8,600. Buick ranked third in industry sales, its production up to 26,666, though far behind the 182,000 of Henry Ford's first year of assembly-line production.

Following Storrow's dictates, Nash continued the rationalization of General Motors' automobile lines. Welch–Detroit, Rainier, and Elmore were dropped; Marquette was marked for early extinction, along with the obsolete Cartercar; the moribund Randolph properties were sold. By the end of 1913, General Motors had but four viable automobiles: Buick, Cadillac, Oakland, and Oldsmobile. Among themselves they were still competitive; Storrow's notion of each car appealing to a different income group had not been well enforced. Nevertheless, they had narrowed both the gaps between the prices of the cars and the range of models. The luxurious Oldsmobile Limited was dropped, the highest-priced Olds selling for a mere $3,200. At the other extreme, Buick offered its Model 30 at General Motors' low price of $1,075.

Sales and profits for 1913 increased, though there was grumbling from some holders of General Motors common stock when they once again were denied a stock dividend; the profitless common stock dropped to a low of $25 a share. Total production for the year fell slightly below 1912's mark, but income, because of higher prices, topped $85 million, a lesson not lost on later managers. Repayment of the bank loan continued on schedule.

Nash still had problems, notably with Henry Leland, who insisted on running Cadillac without interference. Continually demanding mechanical precision, Leland increased production costs in comparison to other General Motors autos. Once the second-lowest-priced car in the General Motors array, Cadillac now vied with the more expensive Oakland. Leland stared down suggestions that he adapt to faster assembly-line production so as to make the Cadillac again non-competitive with Oakland; if there were to be changes, he replied, Oakland could make them—up or down, Leland cared not which. He, for one, was going to make his automobile his way—as a craftsman.

Nash retaliated in what to him was the most satisfying way. Despite Cadillac's continued success, and despite the Lelands' constant technical assistance to the other companies in the corporation, Nash declined to terminate the salary cuts the Lelands had taken voluntarily in 1910, when Storrow first began his economies.

In 1914, Henry Leland provided another technological innovation, this one conceived by his son Wilfred, ostensibly the man responsible for Cadillac's business affairs. Despite harassment from Nash and Storrow's accountants, Leland had supervised the development of an eight-cylinder engine with the pistons angled into the engine block.

When word of Leland's V-8 leaked out of Cadillac's Detroit factory, there was substantial criticism. Six-cylinder engines were troublesome enough, afflicted with periodic vibration in the drive shaft and plagued with timing problems. Eight cylinders merely compounded the difficulties.

Leland persevered, installing the new engine in his 1914 models. The critics carped the louder, rankling Leland; in response, he placed a classic advertisement still considered a copywriter's touchstone. In the January 2, 1915, issue of the *Saturday Evening Post,* Cadillac described "The Penalty of Leadership":

In every field of human endeavor, he that is first must perpetually live in the white light of publicity. Whether the leadership be vested in a man or a manufactured product, emulation and envy are ever at work. In art, in literature, in music, in industry, the reward and the punishment are always the same. The reward is widespread recognition; the punishment, fierce denial and detraction. When a man's work becomes a target for the whole world, it also becomes a target for the shafts of the envious few. If his work be merely mediocre, he will be left severely alone—if he achieve a masterpiece, it will set a million tongues a-wagging. Jealousy does not protrude its forked tongue at the artist who produces a commonplace painting. . . .

There is nothing new in this. It is as old as the world and as old as the human passions—envy, fear, greed, ambition, and the desire to surpass. And it all avails nothing. If the leader truly leads, he remains—the leader. Master-poet, master-painter, master-workman, each in his turn is assailed, and each holds his laurels through the ages. That which is good or great makes itself known, no matter how loud the clamor of denial. That which deserves to live—lives.

Wilfred Leland's V-8 engine was installed in every Cadillac built between 1914 and 1927.

The depression year of 1914 was enigmatic. Henry Ford's Highland Park assembly lines produced 45 percent of the 569,000 motor vehicles manufactured that year in the United States. Some 180 other companies scrambled for the balance even as they tried to install their own assembly lines. When sales slackened in the business downturn, the single-minded Ford cut his prices—from $550 at the beginning of the model year to $490. Ford sales skyrocketed.

While Ford prospered, others failed. In the five-year period between 1910 and 1914, 151 new companies announced their intention to produce automobiles. Two out of three faltered in the same period. Despite this high mortality rate, the ample profit figures intrigued bankers heretofore cool to automotive investments. Chase National Bank's President A. Barton Hepburn told the New York *Times*: "Everybody has predicted that whenever hard times came the automobile industry would crumble. Not so; revolutions never go backward, and the motor car is to continue in use. The public is beginning to know the solid condition of the automobile trade."

With the industry well established, bankers were happy to claim credit. ". . . [I]n fostering this growing industry bankers of this country have played a most important part with practically no loss," William Livingstone, president of Detroit's Dime Savings Bank, told the American Bankers Association. Perhaps with an eye on General Motors' erratic career, Livingstone continued: "Discerning bankers in the past few years especially have appreciated the stability of the industry and the standing of the men in charge, and have cooperated to a marked degree in establishing the business on its present high plane."

Annual sales reached three-quarters of a million vehicles; automobile registrations in the nation totaled 1.8 million in 1914. There was one car for every forty-five people, one for each mile of surfaced highway in the nation, one for each 1.3 square miles of land in the continental United States. Though not universally owned, the automobile had become ubiquitous.

The benefits of the automobile were manifest, but it also could be blamed for any number of problems. Discussing the loss of the World Series by John McGraw's New York Giants to Connie Mack's Athletics, *Spalding's Official Baseball Guide* blamed the McGraws' weakness at bat on "too much driving in motor cars. Some of the most expert oculists insist that athletes, who are dependent upon clearness of vision for success in physical competition, should under no circumstances become addicted to the motor car habit."

General Motors had recovered, buoyed along by national optimism, President Wilson's promise of continued neutrality in the European war, and generally increased prosperity in the country. General Motors sales in 1914 totaled $85.3 million, fractionally less than the year before; the corporation had sold 59,000 vehicles, 13,000 more than in 1913. Still there was no dividend on the common stock, though there was enough market activity to boost the price to $37 per share at its lowest point during the year. The bankers' trust had but one year to run; the $15 million would be fully repaid.

His eyes crinkling in their perpetual smile, Billy Durant was watching. They had taken his baby from him, but he had plans to redress that grievance. And he had a stalking horse: Louis Chevrolet's new car.

6

Second Empire

The inevitable cigarette dangling from his lip, nicotine staining his bushy mustache, Louis Chevrolet admired the hammered sheetwork on his new automobile. Painted and trimmed, with its rolled-leather seats installed, the touring car would justify the long hours he had devoted in the grimy workshop on Detroit's Grand Boulevard—and every penny of Billy Durant's money he had spent. Louis Chevrolet had created this grand automobile, splendid and solid, a machine of distinction to match his reputation as the finest motorcar racer in America.

Chevrolet had worked slowly, cursing his way through each engineering problem. Durant had been patient at first, stopping by rarely to see how his former race driver was coming on the new car, complaining only about the ever-present cigarette hanging from Chevrolet's lip. Now, late in 1911, Durant was hurrying him, forcing compromises, even suggesting that Chevrolet substitute a puny engine that Arthur C. Mason was building in Flint for the powerful motor Chevrolet envisioned. Durant needed a car to launch another of his automobile companies.

124

Just how early Durant fastened on the exact plan to recapture control of General Motors from the bankers he never disclosed, but from the moment he was ousted he vowed to return. Early in 1911 he told Chevrolet only that he was planning "a comeback. We're going to need a car." Within months Durant had such a vehicle: the coughing, clattering runabout that Bill Little, another of Durant's cronies from Buick, was designing in Flint. The trouble was that the Little car was just that—little, hastily engineered to be built in the former factory of the Flint Wagon Works. Besides, who could be inspired to buy an automobile named the "Little"?

By the end of October 1911, Chevrolet had completed the prototype of his touring car, with a projected selling price of $2,150. Production would be another hurdle, for the new enterprise was precariously financed. With only $275,000 in the treasury—much of it already committed—Alexander B.C. Hardy, yet another General Motors refugee, was compelled to liquidate the remaining parts inventory of the Flint Wagon Works even while selling the new Little Four runabout. The 3,500 automobiles, 3,600 buggies, and 8,000 sets of wagon wheels Hardy dealt off in 1912 managed to finance Chevrolet's fancy.

Meanwhile, Durant rented an empty garage in Detroit, where Chevrolet began production of his Classic Six. Production of the Chevrolet reportedly reached 2,999 in its first year, 1912, but the figure seems generous. As in so many of Durant's promotions, the bookkeeping was haphazard. Durant himself was not happy with his new enterprise. "I had found a name for my company— the Chevrolet," he wrote in sketchy notes for an autobiography that he never completed. "My next job was to find a car worthy of the name, a car for power, speed, stability, appearance and price that would outclass any other car in the country. Some job."

While Bill Little and Art Mason searched for a new design, Durant was busy elsewhere. He bought a large plot of land directly across the street from Ford's Highland Park factories and erected a billboard impudently announcing that the world's largest automobile plant would be built on the spot. Durant launched the Republic Motor Company in 1912, with an announced capitalization of $65,000,000, though he undoubtedly had as little as one-thousandth of that sum in hand at the time. He opened a small factory in New York City to build the under-powered Little—not so much for the production, but to impress Wall Street investors, who could come and marvel at the man-ufacturing miracle taking place before their very eyes. "Grown-up people are very much like children in many respects, they like to see the wheels go 'round," Durant noted wryly. He inveigled his old carriage-business partner, J. Dallas Dort, into a reorganized Chevrolet Motor Company. Dort brought with him other investors from the Durant–Dort Carriage Works, and that company bought one-half of Chevrolet's $2.5 million in stock. Either at Dort's insistence, or perhaps from instinct—Billy Du-rant always swam back to Flint to spawn new enterprises, even late in life, when age had sapped his strength if not his vision—Durant announced in March 1913 that he would move the Chev-rolet factory to his home town.

With yet another burst of energy Durant organized a fourth automobile company, Sterling Motors, still looking for the right combination of price, power, and appurtenances. He abruptly scuttled Republic and moved managers from plant to plant—the most important, Hardy, taking over as general manager of Chev-rolet. Little and Sterling Motors disappeared into Chevrolet; Mason Motors would follow later. Durant was groping.

His marketing strategy fell to him by default. Durant spotted an ever-widening gap in the market between such medium-priced cars as Hupp, Maxwell, and Reo at $1,000 and Henry Ford's Model-T, selling as low as $600. It was with the medium-priced White Streak that Durant had first impressed motordom; it was with a medium-priced car that John Willys had turned the bank-rupt Overland into the third-largest auto company in the country in just three years. Durant meant to have such a car, but Chev-rolet's Classic Six at $2,500 would not do. The Frenchman could conceive of a handcrafted luxury car but lacked the engineering skills to transform it into a mass-produced, medium-priced vehi-cle. Hardy and Little would have to do it, replacing milled parts with castings, steel alloys with more readily shaped and cheaper metals, and aluminum with pressed steel.

A troubled Louis Chevrolet returned from a European trip late in 1913 to discover his touring car cast aside in favor of a new Light Six, priced $1,000 cheaper. More important, two other models—the $750 Royal Mail roadster and the $625 Baby Grand touring car—entered the line, aimed at the mass market between Ford's Model-T and the Willys–Overland. The Light Six, the Royal Mail, and the Baby Grand were the first to sport the "bow-tie" insignia, a design Durant spotted in a Sunday newspaper in Hot Springs, Virginia.

Like David Buick before him, Louis Chevrolet was less a businessman than an inventor, less concerned with ledger sheets and markets than engineer's drawings and the new demands of mass production. He was overwhelmed by Durant; Louis Chevrolet had discovered you didn't work *with* Billy, but *for* him. Chevrolet's disappointment exploded in a petty spat after Durant again chided him about smoking cigarettes: "I sold you my car, and I sold you my name, but I'm not going to sell myself to you. I'm going to smoke my cigarettes as much as I want. And I'm getting out."

Chevrolet's departure hardly interrupted Durant's accelerating enterprise, which found itself morally borne along by President Woodrow Wilson's New Freedom. Speaking for "the man on the make, the risk-taking entrepreneur who asked only a fair chance to make his fortune"—there were no better words to describe Billy Durant—the new president asked Congress: "Are you not eager for the time when the genius and initiative of all the people shall be called into the service of business? When newcomers with new ideas, new entries with new enthusiasms, independent men, shall be welcomed? when your sons shall be able to look forward to becoming not employees, but heads of some small, it may be, but hopeful business?" Durant's new enterprise was small but hopeful, for no man better understood that the automobile was now established, both as transportation and as an industry.

As the second decade of the century opened, motoring was still perceived as primarily a high-income, high-status avocation. Writing in *Suburban Life* in July 1911, an unblushing Mrs. A. Sherman Hitchcock noted that, amongst her peers, "there is no more important factor in the social life of the suburban town than the motor-car. It has been adopted universally, and is used for calling, shopping, the opera and theater, and all social functions, while for near-by spins and tours the motor-car is the ideal method of locomotion. . . . Motor parties are a delightful social pastime for the woman who has a country home, and enjoys entertaining her city friends or those nearer by. . . . Taken purely as a means of amusement, relaxation and pleasure,'' the good matron concluded, "the motor car is the finest product of modern civilization. . . .''

A scant two years later, Mrs. Hitchcock's insular world was shattered. Modern civilization, *Country Life* decided in 1913, "is adapting itself to the motor car, not the motor car to civilization.'' Nothing seemed quite to symbolize American progress—not the telephone, the nickelodeon-turned-cinema, nor the Marconi wireless telegraph—as did the lurching, top-heavy automobile. To own one was to gain not only mobility, but status; to be able to live farther from the crowded central cities in more wholesome suburbs while working still in those decaying sumps. Where once suburban development had clustered along interurban railroad lines, the automobile opened up the entire countryside; a developer no longer needed to engage a rail company as an unwanted partner, but only to clear a road to the railroad station and lay out plots in what once had been a pasture or plowed field.

The year 1913 was pivotal. For the first time, automobile manufacturers outproduced buggy and wagon factories, with the nation's press heralding "the motor conquest.'' Early the following year, Reginald McIntosh Cleveland concluded in *World's Work* that with 485,000 vehicles produced in 1913, "the market is pretty well saturated.'' Cleveland was the first of a dozen false prophets unable to comprehend any better than investment bankers the revolution overtaking the country. But then there never had been anything like the sprawling Highland Park factories designed by Albert Kahn for Henry Ford—factories which themselves transformed industrial architecture ever after—buildings in which Ford was installing the final elements of the moving assembly line. Ford himself could not grasp the social upheaval inherent in a bare-boned $490 roadster, priced below cost with the expectation that the sale of such accessories as windshields, tops, electric starters, and spare tires would produce the firm's profits. Ford would go to his grave yearning for the pastoral village life he had known as a boy in the town of Dearborn—a village he literally recreated as a testament to the lifestyle his automobile had destroyed.

If there was one problem for the automobile industry, it was the difficulty in motoring itself. Cars had been much improved and were far more reliable than the mechanics' puzzles of just five years earlier. No longer did the motorist stock an inventory of spare parts in the tool kit, though the wise driver still carried two spare tires. An automobilist might drive as much as two hundred miles before a flat tire forced him to stop, and the new demountable rims trimmed the former two-hour repair time to just minutes. The carefree driver might reasonably expect to motor at speeds as high as forty miles per hour for as long as he might, roads and weather permitting.

Most automobiles could be fitted with folding tops that could be raised or lowered by just one person—a distinct improvement over the cumbersome buggy tops of prior years. Electric lights had replaced acetylene torches; windshields and speedometers were standard equipment on all but the Ford. Meanwhile, the first truly all-weather cars had appeared, following Henry Leland's order for 150 closed bodies from Fred J. Fisher in 1910. (Fisher immediately had organized the Fisher Closed Body Corporation with his six brothers, the forerunner of the mammoth Fisher Body Corporation.) By 1914, the most expensive autos sported closed bodies with roll-up windows and primitive heaters, making them somewhat more practical in the hostile winters of New England and the Midwest.

One problem still remained: the lack of good roads. While the nation claimed 2.4 million miles of rural roads, just 10 percent of them were surfaced. (The toppings varied in quality, too, ranging from concrete, brick, and asphalt to gravel and crushed seashells.) To meet that need, a group of auto manufacturers, led by Cadillac's Henry Leland, Packard's Henry Joy, and Roy Chapin of Hudson Motors, organized the Lincoln Highway Association.

Pledging to raise $10 million from within their industry, they proposed building a highway from New York to San Francisco. Their offer to the counties through which the highway would pass was straightforward: the auto companies would provide both plans and material; the counties were to furnish the labor and equipment. Construction actually began in October 1914, after the highway association allotted just enough money to complete a dashed line of one-mile-long paved strips in each county. As expected, local politicians and other motorists suffered the lengthy unpaved stretches only one year before mounting a lobbying effort in Washington, seeking federal assistance. The result was the Federal Road Aid Act of 1916, quickly nicknamed the "Ford Act," which was to provide $75 million over a period of five years to aid the states in building highways "on any public road over which the United States mails now are, or may hereafter be, transported."

The highway act itself was a turning point in federal–state relations. It incorporated a matching-fund provision, forcing states to follow Oregon's lead and impose gasoline taxes with which to build roads. Moreover, it mandated the creation of state agencies to oversee local construction, an invasion of the prerogatives of the forty-eight states until then avoided by a Jacksonian democracy.

Automobile sales boomed. At the beginning of 1914, Durant asked Alexander Hardy to produce 25,000 of the new Chevrolet models; he had use for the money their sales would generate. One of the few men who could nay-say Durant, Hardy promised capacity production—5,000 vehicles. Denied by Hardy, Durant turned to an old ally, Nathan Hofheimer, one of the titular officers in the water-logged Heany Lamp, which General Motors was then trying to unload. Hofheimer ferreted out Louis J. Kaufman, president of the Chatham & Phoenix Bank in New York City. For the next six years, Kaufman sometimes stood at Durant's right hand, sometimes at his throat, but always where Kaufman would most benefit.

Unlike his Wall Street confreres, Kaufman recognized the potential of the automobile industry, especially as tense Europe rushed to arms. (In that, Kaufman was more far-sighted and more calculating than Durant, for whom a European war was a remote squabble of no concern to the United States.) President Wilson's proclaimed neutrality assured American business of increased sales to both sides. Within months the automobile industry would be selling cars, trucks, and parts directly to the armies grappling in the muddy trenches of the Marne; as the war ground mindlessly on, American exports of 12.3 billion—especially food and munitions—doubled, then tripled. The wealth of Europe drained steadily into Detroit through the fingers of newly affluent American farmers, merchants, and mechanics proudly driving well-polished Buicks, Chalmers, Packards, and Pierce–Arrows.

Turning out twenty Chevrolets a day, Durant rushed to double production. Kaufman underwrote a stock issue of 50,000 shares with a par value of $100, paying Durant but $55 a share and pocketing the balance. With the $2.75 million, Durant went on one of his customary shopping sprees. He picked up the empty Tarrytown, New York, plant of Maxwell–Briscoe, by then bankrupt; formed yet another motor company, Monroe; and opened six regional Chevrolet sales offices. Durant's son Clifford, a celebrated auto racer, scouted up California investors and launched an assembly plant in Oakland to meet western orders for Chevrolets. In the meantime, Durant contacted former associates from Durant–Dort days: Russel E. Gardner in St. Louis and the McLaughlins in Oshawa, Ontario. Both opened privately owned assembly plants for a new model with which Chevrolet meant to challenge Ford's growing dominance of the industry.

Durant was finally ready for his *coup de main*. He moved his headquarters from Detroit to New York, the better to be near the stock exchange for what he planned. From his office above a saloon and restaurant on Fifty-seventh Street at Eleventh Avenue, he began placing judicious buy orders for General Motors shares on Chevrolet's account.

Billy Durant was doing what Billy Durant did best. He privately urged his midwestern friends to hold onto their General Motors stock despite the bankers' refusal to pay dividends until the $15 million loan had been fully repaid. As the bankers continued to withhold dividends, disgruntled stockholders began unloading, and the price dropped steadily to a low of $24 per share.

Durant bought just as steadily, mostly shares once held by Eastern bankers who had decided to cash in their bonus stock of 1910. He even snared a portion of Lee, Higginson's holdings; James Storrow was concerned only with the repayment of the loan, not with investing in General Motors' future.

More far-sighted men would have clutched tightly to their "worthless" shares. Charles Nash had stitched together Durant's crazy quilt; he, after all, understood Durant's method of vertical and horizontal integration from their days together in the carriage business. At the same time, Walter Chrysler had pushed Buick sales to 32,889 in 1914. Under the no-nonsense Lelands, Cadillac was the largest seller in its price class, while Oldsmobile and Oakland held their own. Had Nash more of the gambler and less of the once-threadbare farm boy in his penurious soul, he might have seized the opportunity. Instead, General Motors lagged. Durant had left the company holding 21 percent of industry sales in 1910; by 1915, largely because of Ford's increases, General Motors sold but 8.5 percent of the automobiles manufactured. Despite that, Kaufman found men willing to gamble on Durant's baby—notably John Jacob Raskob, treasurer of the Du Pont company and a man who would figure heavily in Durant's life for the next fifteen years.

Johnny Raskob was an ambitious thirty-five when Kaufman introduced him to Billy Durant in 1914. Though Raskob himself was not yet wealthy—his adventures in the stock market were noted more for cunning than size—he represented access to the vast du Pont family fortunes. Fourteen years earlier, Raskob had gone to work for Pierre S. du Pont as a $1,000-per-year bookkeeper in Lorain, Ohio, where du Pont was striving to establish his independence of the powder works upon which the family fortune was based. The two had become close friends despite their dissimilar backgrounds. Raskob, a devout Catholic and the son of an Alsatian cigar maker, had worked his way through business school with the idea of becoming a stenographer; du Pont, an heir to the family fiefdom on the Brandywine River in Delaware, had enjoyed wealth and position all his life. They were even a contrast physically: Raskob short, with small hands and feet, graceful in his movements; du Pont stiff, awkward in anything remotely physical.

Despite the power both family name and fortune conferred, the reserved du Pont struggled against what he later judged to be faulty genes: "Somewhere in the remote generations of the du Pont family the spirit of what has recently been called inferiority complex crept in. Formerly it was known as shyness, a word that does not altogether express the exact nature of the fault, for fault it is." He was not only shy, but sensitive about his large nose—his "Hebraic" nose ran the whispers, for his great-grandmother was Jewish. Du Pont himself was a stout Episcopalian—all the du Ponts were—but having a Jewish great-grandmother apparently made Pierre more tolerant than his social peers; he had no hesitancy about doing business with the sons of Abraham, scorned by others of his class.

Never athletically inclined, Pierre had been something of a disappointment to his father. Lammot du Pont also had intimidated the youth, making him afraid to excel scholastically—the one area in which the boy was gifted—reminding Pierre often that those who excelled in academe "rarely amount to much in their after life." Lammot du Pont warned his son about such weaklings as men who smoked cigarettes, wore pince-nez, and liked music. Years after his father's death, Pierre would stage a mild rebellion, switching between spectacles and pince-nez and secretly teaching himself to play piano at the family-sponsored Tankopanicum Musical Club.

The death of his father left fourteen-year-old Pierre Samuel, the oldest son, as head of the house; Lammot, Sr., blown apart in one of the periodic explosions at the powder works, had left a wife, ten children, and $750,000. Throughout their lives, his brothers and partners called Pierre "Dad," sometimes humorously. The family responsibility, especially the management of its investments after he graduated in 1890 as a chemist from the Massachusetts Institute of Technology, made him the most cautious of businessmen, a conservative in all things but his splendid estate near Wilmington. Shyness and a conservative mien brought to Pierre du Pont a reputation for magisterial reticence and sobriety, a reputation that would play a major part in du Pont's automotive career.

In the fourteen years Raskob had worked for the du Ponts, he had risen steadily both in rank and Pierre's esteem. The two men became reverse sides of the same coin: Raskob proposed; du Pont disposed. The canny Raskob was the only outsider to sit in on the meeting of the three cousins—T. Coleman, Alfred I., and Pierre S. du Pont—when they fixed on an offer to buy the entire E.I. du Pont de Nemours & Company for $15.3 million in 1902. Typically, in a deal arranged by either Raskob or Pierre, the cousins put up no money, but arranged instead for a long-term loan to be paid from the corporation's future profits. The total cash outlay to buy the 100-year-old firm, with its $24 million in assets, was $2,100 for new incorporation papers.

With Pierre, the youngest, assuming leadership, E.I. du Pont expanded until 1907, when it produced three-quarters of all the explosives made in the United States. That year the federal government filed an antitrust suit, finally winning, in 1912, an order to split off both the Atlas and Hercules powder companies. Characteristically, Pierre took the antitrust suit as a personal affront; he was more sensitive to criticism than he ever could admit.

The qualities that had attracted the shy Pierre to Johnny Raskob intrigued Durant as well. Raskob was outgoing, as confident as Durant himself, and, like Durant, ever an optimist. In addition, Raskob possessed a keen mind, with an unusual capacity for corporate financial manipulations. Right now du Pont needed both Raskob's confidence and his fiscal talents, for he was buying out cousin Coleman's share of E.I. du Pont. With Raskob negotiating with the House of Morgan for an $8 million loan to purchase the controlling interest, du Pont and his younger brothers, Lammot and Irénée, would assume command of a corporation capitalized at $60 million.

Like Durant, Raskob had an eye for the main chance, the unknown company in a rising stock market. General Motors appealed. Its stock reflected the barren returns since 1910, he told Pierre, and was "easily worth double what it is selling for. . . ."

In April 1914, Pierre du Pont bought his first shares of General Motors stock, some 2,000 for his own portfolio and a few hundred for the family trust he still managed. The $135,000 he paid was the beginning of a $50 million investment in an industry rushing to importance. There were then 1.8 million automobiles in America, and Ford alone would add a quarter-million more that year. Even the New York *Times,* as conservative in its views as was du Pont in his, had moved automotive news from the Sunday society pages to the financial section.

Equally important, there was a sense of prosperity in the air, a national confidence bred by industrial success. All seemed right with the nation. The Panama Canal, opened in 1914, proved America's capacity to accomplish big things. Jack Johnson reigned as heavyweight champion of the world, but the Great White Hope, Jess Willard, would set things to right soon enough. President Wilson alternately cajoled and blustered, but had kept the United States out of war despite the provocations of Kaiser Wilhelm's submarines. America intended to let Europe settle its own quarrels while savoring the good times. War-bred prosperity spread across the country.

The auto itself reflected the new-found affluence. According to one automotive magazine, the year marked "a turning point in American automobile design. The automobile, considered as an object viewed by itself, has ceased to present . . . a conglomeration of inharmonious and badly assorted shapes and has begun to move toward a distinctive and appropriate form." One- and two-cylinder engines had been supplanted by four-, six-, and eight-cylinder motors. Even the smallest cars boasted at least twenty-four horsepower and exhilarating forty-mile-per-hour speeds. Automobile designers invoked a new word, "streamlining," to describe the longer, lower bodies with sloping hoods and sweeping curves on their new models. The New York *Times* automobile supplement for 1915 proclaimed: "Newest Motor Cars Have Lines of Much Grace." Only Ford's Model-T remained "angular and functional in appearance, like maiden aunts in a throng of soignée and beautifully costumed women."

Automobile advertising blossomed with the machine itself. Cadillac ads boasted of that vehicle's "luxurious environment" and "appointments in quiet good taste." The Auburn promised "dignity, convenience and pride of ownership" and the Cole Eight "perfect performance and striking beauty" (this before the Federal Trade Commission began insisting that automobile companies document their advertised claims). The Marmon was "in every sense a luxury car." Hudson, Marion, Velie, Chandler, Locomobile, and Studebaker similarly claimed the pleasures of Xanadu for their owners.

A Chicago auto-show exhibitor sported an enamel button proclaiming, "It's Hell to be poor." The poor could not yet buy automobiles, though Henry Ford was striving to make even that possible. Ford fulfilled a pledge to buyers that if sales reached 300,000 in 1915, he would share the profits of mass production by rebating fifty dollars to each purchaser. He sold 308,213 autos and disbursed $15 million; when his minority partners protested that lost profit—and the prospect of another $25 million loss because of "unnecessarily" low prices—Ford offered to buy them out for $70 million. It was his company, and he brooked no interference.

Yet in such a seller's market as prevailed in secure America in that second year of the Great War, only the madman of Highland Park cut prices. The rest of the industry sold dearly, the market ever-growing, seemingly endless. Even such a sober figure as Henry Leland of Cadillac was swept up. Automobiles would grow "in number and utility until they cover the face of the earth," he promised the Society of Automotive Engineers.

To keep pace with the demand, automobile companies rushed to expand. Employment in the industry reached 150,000 in 1915, ranking it fourteenth largest in the country. Yet the high degree of automation embodied in Ford's new moving assembly line increased the value of the manufactured goods even faster than the number of employees. The effect was twofold: smaller manufacturers who were unable to raise the ever-larger sums of necessary investment capital withered; new firms unable to pay the mounting costs of entering the market never produced an automobile. According to *Motor Age,* the 270 companies that had produced 400 models in 1911 had shrunk in just four years to 119 firms putting out 200 models.

Seeking ever more workers, the automobile companies increased wages even faster than employment. Journeyman laborers earned as much as fifteen dollars per week. Even $2.50 a day for the janitorial jobs reserved for blacks seemed munificent to Southern Negroes living on the parched red-clay farms of Mis-

sissippi and Alabama. One by one the young men slipped away
to the cities of promise "up north," especially to booming Detroit. Michigan's black population jumped tenfold between 1910
and 1930, while the white population was growing 167 percent.
This immigration would engender three generations of bitter racial conflict in Detroit's Pleasant Valley hovels.

On the crest of the financial boom, with General Motors stock
pegged at $82, Durant pressed his buying campaign. The price
began creeping up on the stock market; still Durant bought, for
prices as high as $220, siphoning profits from Chevrolet to pay
for the shares.

In June 1915, Chevrolet launched its Model 490, equipped
with electric lights and self-starter. The model number was to be
the same as the auto's price—sometime in the future, Durant
advertised, when mass production justified lowering the intro-
ductory price of $550. Durant deliberately positioned his new car
at the low-priced, volume end of the market dominated by
Ford's Model-T, then priced by no coincidence at $490. Theoret-
ically, Chevrolet would garner the less affluent customers willing
to pay a bit more for some conveniences. Ford typically met the
competition, not by upgrading his Model-T to include Chevrolet's self-starter and electric lights, but by slashing his price
once again—to $440. (Model-T purchasers still cranked their
cars to a start, but Ford's strategy succeeded, there being more
people at the low end of the economic scale than in the middle;
Ford sales climbed 73 percent in 1915, a lesson seemingly lost
upon today's auto makers.)

Six weeks later, Durant wrote to Arthur Bishop, his long-time
Flint banker: "At the close of business June 19, the Chevrolet
Motor Company had accepted orders from dealers and
distributors—every contract secured by a cash deposit—for
46,611, valued at $23,329,390—a fairly good record for 17 work-
ing days. Since June 19, we have orders for more than 1,000 cars
per day."

"A Little Child Can Sell It," Durant's slogan insisted, though
sales came more easily than production. Hardy managed to deliver only 13,292 vehicles in 1915. The following year, with the
McLaughlins' first Canadian production of 7,000 cars boosting

the total, Chevrolet turned out 70,701 vehicles—including the company's first forty-one trucks.

With the fifth annual meeting of the bankers' trust scheduled for September 16, and the last $2.5 million of the loan to be repaid on October 1, 1915, Durant raced toward a confrontation. He sought proxies from old friends, bought shares as he could on the rising market, and begged allies to hold what they had or buy more, all to gain a majority of the voting stock and forestall a new threat.

Storrow finally had awakened to the potential of the motorcar. Once he had considered himself a mere custodian, the honest watchman; now he prickled with genteel avarice. Storrow intended to put up a slate of directors who, if elected by holders of the common stock, effectively would retain the debt-free company in the hands of the banks. The bankers began soliciting proxy votes too.

Durant laid siege, playing on the knowledge that the proud easterners would not risk the public rebuke of their slate being voted down. Early in September he asked Charles Nash to stay on as president of the corporation, *when,* not if, Durant regained control, expecting his one-time foreman to report the cheeky, premature offer to Storrow. To Albert Strauss, representing the private banking house of J. & W. Seligman on the board, Durant said he intended to propose a major stock dividend at the annual meeting: "General Motors has been lugging it for five years," he needled. In the interests of harmony, Strauss agreed to allow dissidents to offer minority statements for inclusion in the annual report. (The issue now in doubt, Strauss apparently feared the bankers would be in the minority. Durant did nothing to disabuse Strauss of his anxiety.)

In the last days before the directors' meeting, Durant scrambled for an absolute majority of the common stock, paying as much as $350 for shares that had gone begging at $25 two years earlier. Three days before the meeting, he confidently showed Wilfred Leland a vault full of proxy statements, certain the news would get back to Storrow. The night before the New York meeting, his long-time secretary, W.W. Murphy, counted and recounted the proxies. The count was close, very close, but they had fallen short of the necessary majority.

About noon on the day of the meeting, Durant met Storrow privately, triggering what contemporaries later called the greatest bluff in Wall Street history. Approached by an anxious Storrow, Durant reportedly agreed with the Brahmin princeling that there would be no quarrel at the meeting, adding, "I'm in control of General Motors today." The directors of the corporation were to meet at 2:00 P.M. on September 16 in a second-floor room of the Belmont Hotel in New York City. Instead they waited while Durant, Nash, Storrow, and "certain other parties" sought a compromise. For the next four hours, the factions bickered about the slate of directors to be put before the stockholders at the annual meeting in November. They squabbled over the dividend to be voted on by the new board, Durant insisting on a 25- to 30-percent cash return on the value of the stock. The bankers, still cautious, and treasuring cash reserves over the company's stock, proposed merely a stock dividend. (Even though each share was then worth $260 on the market, a stock dividend would cost the corporation nothing; the newly released shares of a dividend would merely dilute the value of those presently held by investors.)

Through the afternoon they argued about challenged proxy statements, neither side sure which would prevail at the corporation's annual meeting to come in November. Not all of the proxies had been returned; other stockholders called down a plague on both houses and remained neutral. Playing his busted flush, Durant calmly smiled and continually raised the bet. Rather than 25 to 30 percent, he then proposed a 50-percent dividend, fifty dollars for each share of common outstanding. Realizing that a mere stock dividend would have little appeal compared to an $8,250,000 cash payout, the bankers folded their hand. They helplessly agreed that Nash would make the motion, with Durant seconding it, for a $50-per-share dividend to be ratified at the annual meeting.

Still they quarreled: Durant steadily pressed the banking faction to authorize expansion of the company to meet demand. The conservators had wrung $12 million in watered assets from the company in their five-year reign and had spent as little as possible modifying the production lines to emulate Ford's moving assembly lines. They had not kept pace with the industry's growth, and were the company not to be overwhelmed, it had to be expanded. Durant prevailed a second time.

That settled, Durant proposed that General Motors purchase Chevrolet. The bankers rejected the offer; for even though Chevrolet's estimated worth of $1.2 million would not seriously deplete their cash surplus of $19.5 million, the sale would give Durant even more money with which to buy up available shares of the larger company. To exchange stock instead, which Durant frankly favored, would be unthinkable; he was close to majority control now. Any more shares would simply settle the matter. Durant accepted the rebuff quietly; he had a hole card to be played later.

Invited by Louis Kaufman, Pierre du Pont attended the private meeting as one of the slate of directors Durant intended to nominate. Now he watched in some confusion. He had come with Kaufman's airy assurance that Durant and Kaufman were in firm control of the corporation, that any disagreements would be settled quickly. Instead, du Pont found himself a member of a slate on the opposite side of the table from the sort of men with whom he was most comfortable. Whatever his pique, du Pont could not help but be impressed with Durant, a man who seemed willing to challenge heaven and earth to reclaim what he believed was rightfully his. It would not be the last time that du Pont would be simultaneously upset with, and impressed by, Billy Durant.

The meeting ground on. In midafternoon Kaufman and du Pont stood in the hallway wearily reviewing the "absolute deadlock between the old and the new factions." After four hours, the two groups had struggled to agreement on twelve of the fifteen-man slate, six from each side. Three remained to be chosen, and they had reached an impasse.

Accounts vary as to who was responsible for the compromise—Kaufman, a board nominee from the Durant camp, who saw himself as an adroit puppet-master, or Storrow, the suddenly beleaguered leader of the Boston bankers. In any event, the two sides came to terms. The three vacant seats were to be filled by neutral directors nominated by du Pont. That Storrow was willing to trust du Pont, a nominal member of the opposition, was a tribute to the Delaware powder maker's reputation in banking circles; the great du Pont works had not been built by precipitous, headstrong rushes.*

By eight o'clock that evening, dinner long delayed, the two sides had worked out the details, with Durant seemingly giving up more than he was getting. Contrary to his original plan, he agreed to be one of the directors rather than remain merely the principal stockholder, guiding things from afar while he devoted his time to Chevrolet. Of the six members on his side, he could count on the votes of just two: Flint banker A.G. Bishop and John H. McClement, who had swum among the sharks since 1910 and the bankers' bail-out. Samuel S. Pryor, the president of Remington Arms, another Kaufman discovery, would vote with the bankers if it came to a showdown, Durant realized; Remington Arms was in grave financial difficulty, and Pryor himself soon would go to the bankers hat in hand. Nor could Durant count on Charles S. Mott, a member of the board since 1913, who had progressively surrendered his axle company to the corporation in exchange for General Motors stock. Kaufman was an ally, but his first loyalty lay with Kaufman, then with the du Ponts, whom he had long represented in New York.

If there was any leadership on the new board, it would come from the nominee for chairman, Pierre du Pont. However he came down on an issue, du Pont would strongly influence Kaufman, Pryor, and certainly the votes of the three neutrals du Pont had put forward: John J. Raskob; J. Amory Haskell, a retired Du Pont board member; and Lammot Belin, Pierre's cousin and brother-in-law. (Marital consanguinity was honored as much in the breach as in the observance along the Brandywine; du Pont himself would marry a first cousin by the end of the year.)

---

* It is possible that du Pont and Raskob, controlling some 3,000 shares, actually held the balance of power and thus could dictate terms. See Earl Sparling, *Mystery Men of Wall Street* (New York, 1930), pp. 209–10, citing Raskob as authority.

The unexpected turn of events stunned the financial press. From Boston, a correspondent telegraphed the *Wall Street Journal:*

General Motors' extra dividend on the $16,501,000 common stock has taken a decidedly different turn than Wall Street and State Street had been tacitly led to expect. It has taken a different turn than a majority of the directors themselves intended.

The action respecting this huge cash dividend of 50 percent . . . is simply a notice . . . that control of the company has changed hands.

Had there been no change in stock control, it is safe to say that General Motors would not have decided to pay out so large a sum as $8,250,000 cash. This 50 percent is probably the largest initial cash distribution on common stock ever made by a stock listed on the New York exchange.

News of the cash dividend—almost half of which Durant and his immediate allies would use to purchase more General Motors shares—sent the stock market into a frenzy. Overnight the stock jumped from $291 to $340. Much to Durant's pleasure, for he disliked "short selling," stock-market operators who had sold General Motors expecting it to fall in price had to scramble to fill the orders before the price went even higher.*

Durant offered to sell his Chevrolet company to General Motors and had been turned down. Since he could not remain idle and he could not sell, he would buy.

On September 23, Durant's lawyers incorporated the Chevrolet Motor Company of Delaware, with an authorized capital of $20 million. Significantly, H.M. Barksdale, one of the du Ponts' "Wilmington people," as Durant called them, joined the new corporation's board. The Delaware corporation became the owner of the separate New York and Michigan Chevrolet companies by exchanging $13.2 million in the new firm's stock for $1

---

* "Short selling" is a scheme sanctioned by federal regulations and stock-exchange rules. An operator who "goes short" sells borrowed shares of a stock at a high price, even though he does not at that moment actually own the shares. He is, in effect, gambling that the price will fall before he must return the borrowed shares. If the price falls, he then can buy more cheaply than he sold for, replace the borrowed shares, and pocket the difference. If anyone other than a member of the stock exchange sells an object he does not in fact own, he risks felonious fraud charges.

million of the old. The balance of the issue was to be sold to the public.

Durant's name was the lure. Announcing the new offering, Durant said that the Chevrolet was earning $2 million a month and the public offering was to triple production to 300 cars per day. Well before the public announcement, motor dealers and Durant's Flint neighbors oversubscribed the stock issue tenfold.

As the General Motors voting trust expired, the compromise slate of directors assumed control at the November 16 annual meeting. With Pierre du Pont installed as chairman, a post he would hold for the next thirteen years, the lulled bankers settled contentedly into the business of making money.

Durant hardly broke stride. With the $6.8 million from the sale of the new Chevrolet offering, he returned to the market, buying General Motors whenever he could. The price for shares that had hovered around $80 at the beginning of the year reached $395 on the day of the annual meeting and the formal announcement of the unprecedented dividend. (Significantly, Charles Nash reported at the meeting that "all companies in the group are on a paying basis," including the precarious Oakland, Cartercar, and Elmore enterprises.) General Motors' success and Durant's buy orders whipped the price to a peak of $558 on December 9.

Three days later, Durant personally held 71,218 shares, 44 percent of General Motors' common stock. On December 22, the New York *Times* reported that the "wizard of automobiles and friends had regained control by purchasing more than 100,000 shares, valued at present market prices at more than $50,000,000." The unnamed "friends" apparently held among themselves enough stock to give Durant a majority, were they to throw in with him. It was still too tenuous for Durant, especially when Pierre du Pont insisted on remaining neutral. Durant wanted autonomy.

The plan he devised to gain unrestrained authority was shrewd. With family members, and Flint neighbors loyalists like Alexander B.C. Hardy, he wielded overwhelming control of Chevrolet. On the day before Christmas, 1915, these allies held a meeting of Chevrolet stockholders—there were fewer than thirty present—to authorize an increase in the capitalization of the company from $20 million to $80 million. The new stock, Durant publicly announced, was to be exchanged until January 25, 1916, on the basis of one General Motors share for five Chevrolet shares. Because of a slight price differential, the month-long bargain sale favored holders of General Motors stock. In Boston, James Storrow was dismayed, "saying that it would be unfortunate if stockholders permitted control to pass to the Chevrolet."

But Durant was not done yet. To enhance the value of Chevrolet's shares, he put together a group of investors, a "syndicate" in Wall Street jargon, intent upon bulling Chevrolet's stock prices to new highs. At the same time, the syndicate would ignore whatever General Motors common or preferred shares came on the market. Since Durant's purchases had, until then, buoyed General Motors, withdrawing his support would tend to depress that stock.

Durant's backers included, for the first time, some of the most prominent of American industrialists: T. Coleman du Pont, Pierre's cousin "Coley," kicked in $500,000; Judge Elbert H. Gary of United States Steel contributed a like sum. Louis Kaufman headed a list of investment houses and brokerages that pledged at least $100,000 each. Buying and selling among themselves at premium prices, the syndicate members started Chevrolet on an upward spiral, enhancing the five-for-one trade offer. As the Chevrolet price rose and General Motors fell, Durant trimmed the offer to four-for-one; there was no sense being too generous. Even so, holders of General Motors common rushed to climb on the bandwagon, for unless both Chevrolet *and* General Motors went belly up, they could not lose.

Storrow and his banking allies were fighting a rear-guard action now. On the third day of the new year, they mailed a circular letter to General Motors' stockholders proposing a three-year voting trust to begin the following November, when the term of the incumbent board expired. The letter had no impact; Durant was about to furnish Wall Street "one of the most sensational and surprising incidents in its history."

Durant turned the screws. The new Chevrolet of Delaware corporation, he gleefully announced, had $28 million worth of vehicles on order, was producing more than 200 cars daily, and expected a net profit for the year of $6 million. Returns of 21-percent profit on sales would whet the appetite of any investor.

On March 1, a dozen General Motors stockholders "not connected with the management" urged their fellows to extend the voting trust. One market analyst snorted, "That the cause of the banking house interests has a decided flavor of weakness—not to say desperation—about it, is made clearly manifest upon an analysis of the signers of their circular. . . . The aggregate holdings of the entire list of signers is 8,047 shares, or less than 2½ percent of the entire outstanding stock—hardly a sufficient amount to impress the great body of shareholders that [a] voting trust is an urgent necessity."

The meager response to this bankers' second letter convinced Pierre du Pont and John Raskob that Durant had won high-low-jack-and-the-game. On April 16, 1916, Raskob wrote to Durant, asking if the du Ponts might still buy in at the five-for-one exchange rate, which had ostensibly expired in January. Three times before, du Pont had refused the exchange, insisting he and his three nominees had been elected as neutrals; for the same reason he had declined to endorse the two bankers' appeals.

In fact, du Pont and Raskob were playing a skilled waiting game. With H.M. Barksdale on the Chevrolet board and Coley a member of the syndicate, du Pont knew precisely what Durant was planning. He could appear to be taking a principled position while keeping his options open, well aware that his ultimate endorsement would bestow legitimacy upon Durant's apparent frenzies. The longer they held out, these sober men of capital, the more valuable their endorsement—and investment.

A delighted Durant readily arranged the deal. Du Pont not only was throwing in with the winner, but picking up a huge paper profit in the bargain. According to the New York *Times* of April 7: "Those who accepted the original offer have reason to congratulate themselves on the basis of present prices. General Motors closed last night at 460, off 25 points; Chevrolet at 196½, up 9. Five shares of Chevrolet are accordingly worth $522 more than one share of General Motors." Durant's syndicate had done its work well. In the middle of May, almost as an anticlimax,

Durant quietly announced that the minnow had swallowed the whale, that Chevrolet owned 54.5 percent of the General Motors shares outstanding.

Durant's overthrow of the regency left Charles Nash in an untenable position. Nash had cast his lot with the bankers—he and Storrow had become fast friends—but against Durant, the man who had first given him an opportunity to be something more than a laborer all his life. Still Nash understood, whatever *his* title or salary, that Billy Durant would run General Motors—Nash's abilities to be overshadowed by Durant's bravura, Nash's judgments to be countermanded by Durant's whims. Durant could forgive C.S. Mott for signing the bankers' letter, but not Charlie Nash, a Flint man. Their meeting some time before April's was brief. "Well, Charlie, you're through," Durant announced. Nash would be the first of the bankers' men to leave, Durant commenting, "I am not at all surprised, and, in view of the circumstances, think it is the honorable thing to do."

Events moved quickly in the presidential election year of 1916. Durant, the uncontested majority stockholder, was elected president in Nash's stead. One by one, the bankers followed Nash from the board room and were replaced by the heads of the motorcar companies, including Henry Leland and Walter Chrysler.

Chrysler's decision to stay on came as a last Durant-inspired slap to Nash and Storrow, who had expected the one-time Kansas farm boy to join them in a new automobile venture. But knowing he needed a strong, production-minded man at Buick, the backbone of General Motors, Billy Durant boldly pre-empted Chrysler's skills.

Shortly after Nash's resignation, Durant walked into the Buick general manager's office and summarily announced, "Mr. Chrysler, I'd like to hire you as president of the Buick Motor Company." Chrysler could be just as direct: "I want to be perfectly frank with you, Mr. Durant. If a plan on which I am negotiating goes through, I'm quitting here."

Fair enough, Durant conceded. Chrysler needed thirty days; Durant would be back in thirty days.

When Chrysler's bid for the Packard Motor Company with

Storrow's backing was rejected, and very reluctant to uproot his family for a dubious future with the failing Jeffery Motors where Nash had relocated, Chrysler called Durant. At seven o'clock the next morning—both men believed in an early start on the day—Durant confronted the works manager. Without preliminaries, Durant said, "I'll pay you $500,000 a year to stay on here as president of Buick."

Stunned, Chrysler could not respond. Just three years earlier he had been earning $6,000, that grudgingly raised first to $25,000 and then to $50,000. He numbly asked Durant to repeat the offer. Chrysler had intended to ask for a raise, something in keeping with his new title. "Mr. Durant, the salary you offer is, of course, far and away beyond anything I expected, but—"

Chrysler knew Durant as "the most winning personality of anyone I've ever known. He could coax a bird right down out of a tree, I think." Durant was not coaxing, but selling once again, this time a job and a corporation, asking Chrysler to delay going into business for himself. "I don't blame you for the ambition, but I ask you to give me just three years of yourself."

Chrysler succumbed, on the promise that he would have full authority over Buick, with just one boss: Billy Durant. Durant agreed, sweetening the agreement as he did so. Chrysler would draw a salary of $10,000 per month, taking the balance of the $500,000 in cash or in General Motors stock at the price on the day they signed the contract. Chrysler took the stock and went back to building automobiles.

He was needed. The demand for motor vehicles, especially trucks, had never been greater, the industry's already mercurial growth accelerated by the demands of war. General John Pershing was using Dodge Brothers trucks to support his cavalry units in the fruitless pursuit of Francisco Villa through the deserts of northern Mexico, and the French had resupplied Verdun with a hastily requisitioned fleet of horseless carriages. The two campaigns had proved the automobile's military value; by 1917 French Premier Clemenceau would beseech the United States to send 100,000 tons of oil—"as necessary as blood itself in the coming battles."

The nation entered the last half of 1916 nervously, Woodrow Wilson campaigning for "Peace with Honor! Preparedness!

Prosperity!'' and precinct workers reminding voters, "He kept us out of war.'' But German submarines might reopen their cat-and-mouse undersea warfare at any moment and drive the president to defend national honor by seeking a declaration of war. Meanwhile, the administration prepared for the possibility of such a conflict, creating a self-fulfilling prophecy. The National Defense Act reorganized the armed forces and created a Reserve Officers Training Corps (R.O.T.C.). Wilson's pacifistic secretary of state, the venerable William Jennings Bryan, resigned in protest. In July the farm-loan act established regional banks to provide farmers with long-term credit for machinery—including motor vehicles—that would expand acreage to meet the European demand for more foodstuffs. A month later, the Council of National Defense began overall military and civilian planning for America's entry into the war, and the juggernaut gathered force. On September 7, the federal Emergency Fleet Corporation came into being, with $50 million to build or lease merchant ships. The engines of commerce were no less determined than the dogs of war; if the Allies were buying, with payment on delivery, America meant to deliver the goods—whatever the risks.

Firmly in control at General Motors, and with that company apparently geared for the most successful year in its history, Durant turned to other projects. On May 12, 1916, even before the Boston bankers had accepted their humbling, the New York *Times* reported the formation of the United Motors Corporation, a $60 million combine of five parts-and-accessories manufacturers. Though United Motors was a separate company, Durant conceived of it as a functioning arm of General Motors; he was following his pattern of vertical integration from the carriage business of three decades earlier. As important as were the five parts manufacturers—the Durant-owned Perlman Rim Corporation, Dayton Engineering Laboratories, Remy Electric, New Departure Manufacturing Company, and Hyatt Roller Bearing Company—more important still were two men who came along with their firms: Charles Kettering of Dayton Engineering and Alfred P. Sloan, Jr., of Hyatt.

Alfred Pritchard Sloan, Jr., was forty-one in the spring of 1916, when he first met Billy Durant. With his father, a coffee and tea importer, Sloan owned 60 percent of the firm that produced bearings for Ford, Buick, Chevrolet, Willys, Packard, and half a dozen other, since-forgotten marques.

The grimy Hyatt works, located in a loft near the Trenton, New Jersey, railyards, was an odd place for the twenty-year-old fresh from the Massachusetts Institute of Technology with a degree in electrical engineering. Born in Waterbury, Connecticut, Sloan was, in the phrase of the times, "a sissy." Raised in Brooklyn—traces of that borough's accent lingered still, especially when he raised his voice—Sloan was a bookish sort, "naturally of a serious turn of mind," as he put it in his autobiography. Sloan's father once said of his son: "Alfred was everlastingly digging at some school problem. He had no inclination for shop-work or any mechanics. He wouldn't even bait his own fish-hook because he despised to get his hands dirty. But he would toil over his schoolwork until he talked about it in his sleep."

Considered precocious, Sloan was to justify that appraisal by rushing through M.I.T. in just three years, the youngest member of his class. He made few friends and grew to manhood the most private of persons—aloof and unable to unbend except with the handful of men whom he had known the longest. The energy he never learned to dispel in physical activities he discharged through fidgeting—drumming his fingers, tapping his foot, picking at his clothes. The effect was to make him seem impatient with wary subordinates; or worse, bored; or worse still, contemptuous. The prissy boy became a prissy adult, a fastidious dresser picked as one of the nation's ten best-dressed men in the 1930s, when he could well afford such finery as spats and camel-hair coats.

Six feet tall, thin to angularity, with an air about him that was frequently saturnine if not pessimistic, Sloan had taken a draftsman's job at Hyatt for twelve dollars a week. The firm was the precarious brainchild of John Wesley Hyatt, "an unsung American hero" according to one historian, but a man not overly blessed with penetrating business acumen. As the company edged toward insolvency in 1899, Sloan's father and a family friend invested $5,000 and gave the newly married Alfred, Jr., six months to see if he could revive the business. Thus Sloan became general manager of Hyatt at a salary of $175 a month, in charge of a ramshackle collection of antiquated machinery and twenty-five employees, a youth whose strongest expletive was "horseapples" amid men of earthy vocabulary. By dint of hard selling to various machinery manufacturers, Sloan showed a slight profit by the end of the six-months' trial. A photograph taken at the time showed the rising young businessman in celluloid collar and newly fashionable bow tie, his red hair parted in the middle and slicked to his head, facing the new century with unsmiling resolution.

In subsequent years, Sloan had built a new company employing 3,800 production workers on a piece-rate basis, its $4 million in annual sales based on the automobile industry's fortunes. Forced into precision production when he first tried, in 1903, to sell the demanding Henry Leland roller bearings for the Cadillac, Sloan himself had become an ever more stringent taskmaster, newly won over to the cult of scientific and technical management propounded by Frederick Winslow Taylor. By 1916, however, Sloan was privately worried: "More than half of our business came from Ford, and our other big customer, General Motors, dwarfed the remainder. If either Ford or General Motors should start making their own bearings or use some other type of bearings, our company would be in a desperate situation."

Durant's offer to buy was well timed. Sloan asked for $15 million, but settled finally for $13.5 million. Years later, Sloan admitted, "I have always thought I could have got the $15 million, if my nerve had held out—but it was a big transaction for me." Sloan received half of the money in cash and half in United Motors stock, then bought out his father and family friends. He ended up with some $5 million in United Motors stock and little cash. Durant's tender of the presidency of United Motors was welcome; at forty-one, Sloan was a little too old to go jobhunting, and as president of the new combine, he could at least have a hand in assuring the value of his holdings.*

* According to the June 8, 1916, issue of *The Automobile,* United Motors was to be the link between General Motors and a third automotive combine to be put together by Durant and Kaufman, an amalgam that would have fused Willys–Overland, then the third largest automobile company, with Hudson, Chalmers, and Electric Auto-Lite. The second merger apparently died aborning.

A mere $15 million acquisition was hardly enough to keep Durant occupied, especially with such men as Louis Kaufman around to arrange financing. Durant plunged on, still seeking the combination of companies that would blanket the automotive market.

Ever optimistic, Durant launched a $20 million expansion program to double the capacity of General Motors. He financed the effort by yet another stock arrangement, creating a new General Motors *Corporation* with 825,000 shares of common stock. The new $100 million company would acquire the old by exchanging five shares of the new stock for one of the old. While the change in names was a legal device—Durant meant to let the individual car companies retain their autonomy—the refinancing would provide him with as much as $70 million in new investment money with which to go shopping.

Nursing no more affection for the "Wilmington crowd" than he had for the moneylenders of New York and Boston, Durant had intended another innovation when he conceived the refinancing: a five-man board of directors with but a three-man executive committee. The du Ponts objected, and Durant, apparently fearing loss of their support, recanted his heresy. The board of the new company remained large; both finance and executive committees were retained.

It fell to Johnny Raskob to attempt to bring some administrative and financial order to the sprawling Durant enterprises. The two were like-minded. Raskob no less than Durant was enthusiastic about the future of motorcars, Raskob predicting $108 million in profits for General Motors over the next five years. Moreover, the two men well appreciated their common wizardry in corporate finance. Yet Durant played the skittish bride, resisting Raskob's proposed consolidation of General Motors and Chevrolet, despite the logic of the arguments and the proposed tax savings. (Holders of Chevrolet stock paid taxes first on the profits General Motors earned, then again on the dividends General Motors generated for Chevrolet.)

After months of fruitless negotiation, the United States' entry into World War I undercut Durant's unilateral control. The fear that military needs would curtail the use of steel in "pleasure cars" triggered a break in stock-market prices. (The industry would speak only of "passenger cars" ever after, thus removing the sybaritic taint to its product.) General Motors, the most volatile of the automotive stocks, suffered the heaviest. The price, which at the beginning of 1917 had stood around $200, fell to $115 six months later. Any merger was out of the question now, until the value could be restored.

For his own reasons, never explained, Durant formed a stock-buying syndicate with Kaufman and his long-time broker, Nathan Hofheimer. (The best guess—and it remains that—is that Durant was attempting to protect friends who had invested in either General Motors or Chevrolet at his suggestion, people who had put down the nominal 10-percent margin then required and subsequently found themselves unable to pay off the balance when brokers made demands for payment. They were caught in a bear market.) Despite the syndicate's timely purchases, the stock continued to fall. By the end of October, General Motors had slumped to $75, the syndicate had reached its limits, and Raskob had stepped in to help.

At Raskob's urging, the General Motors board voted the then-handsome salary of $500,000 per year to its president, risking whatever criticism might befall them because, as Raskob put it, Durant was fulfilling "his duty to protect the market of General Motors and its availability as collateral for the benefit of stockholders." Further, Durant's effort to stem the rush of the bears was "absorbing his time and attention to the detriment of the company's interests." The belated salary was to end the distraction.

Durant was sailing close to the wind by the end of the year when Raskob came up with a second plan to bail him out. In a multipage memorandum to the E.I. du Pont de Nemours board of directors, Raskob proposed that the explosives firm purchase $25 million in General Motors stock on the open market. The enthusiastic memorandum, dated December 19, 1917, was to torment the two companies forty years later.*

---

* General Motors Corporation's decision not to cooperate with the author was predicated on the legal department's warning, "Remember the Raskob memo," according to a source within the comapny.

Within 40 percent of the artillery shells fired on the western front propelled by Du Pont products, the powder works' profits from the sale of smokeless gunpowder were huge. Whatever the stalemate then existing along the Marne River, the war would end once the United States committed its full industrial might. Du Pont subsequently would be faced with finding new sources of income, and while the fledgling dyestuff and paint enterprises were promising, they could not in themselves support continued profits of $60 million a year. Automobiles were the solution, Raskob argued:

The growth of the motor business, particularly the General Motors Company, has been phenomenal as indicated by its net earnings and by the fact that the gross receipts of the General Motors-Chevrolet Motor Companes [*sic*] for the coming year will amount to between $350 million and $400 million. The General Motors Company today occupies a unique position in the automobile industry and in the opinion of the writer with proper management will show results in the future second to none in any industry. Mr. Durant perhaps realizes this more fully than anyone else and is very desirous of having an organization as perfect as possible to handle this wonderful business. . . . The evolution of the discussion of this problem is that an attractive investment is afforded in what I consider the most promising industry in the United States; a country which in my opinion holds greater possibilities for development in the immediate future than any country in the world. . . .

Raskob's summary of the arguments in favor of the stock purchase assured the Du Pont board that "with Mr. Durant we will have joint control of the companies. We are immediately to assume charge and be responsible for the financial operation of the Company . . . Our interest in the General Motors Company will undoubtedly secure for us the entire Fabrikoid, Pyralin, paint and varnish business of those companies."

Raskob closed with a locker-room pep talk: "During the past two years our Company has been doing big things. After the war it seems to me it will be absolutely impossible for us to drop back to being a little company again and to prevent that we must look for opportunities, know them when we see them, and act with courage. If our fundamentals are sound, as they certainly seem to be in this case, the control of the General Motors Company will be a task worthy of the best there is in us and will, I feel, afford many opportunities to keep our important men occupied with big things after the war."

The Du Pont directors were wary, both of the size of the investment Raskob proposed and of the automobile industry itself. Countering objections to Durant—since the bankers' ouster Durant had all but ignored the Du Pont people on his board of directors—Raskob stressed, "The Finance Committee will be ours." It was Pierre du Pont's support of the plan which carried the reluctant board members. They approved the investment on the second day, twenty-three to three.

Billy Durant now had new partners, men whose stock holdings would compel him to heed their counsel. As a condition of the investment, Durant agreed to establish functioning executive and financial committees on the board of directors rather than sycophants. While Durant would dominate the company's operations through the executive committee, five of the seven members of the finance committee were to be Du Pont people, with Raskob its chairman. The finance group held the purse strings; any expenditure larger than $150,000 was to be approved by the committee. The Wilmington people meant to watch Durant closely, Pierre du Pont conceded later, though nominally interested "only in the amount of appropriations that must be made, and the arrangement of finances. But principally they were interested in the character of the investments to be made." In agreeing to the investment, du Pont made one miscalculation—failing to appreciate the intoxicating effect automobiles would have on his good friend and Durant watchdog, John Raskob.

For his part, beyond ceding his autonomy, Durant had to agree to sell both United Motors and Chevrolet factories to General Motors in exchange for stock. The Chevrolet corporation was to become merely a vault for the General Motors shares Durant had acquired in its name.* It was to be a temporary arrangement

---

* These included some $9 million in General Motors stock Durant received for his portion of the United Motors sale. He voluntarily turned the shares over to the Chevrolet treasury, thus allowing other Chevrolet stockholders to split the booty. Durant explained the gift on the grounds that he had put together the United combine while working for Chevrolet.

only. Raskob would spend another two years manipulating the final purchase of Chevrolet's holdings, forcing the minnow to cough up the whale.

The fused corporations bounded into the new year expecting record sales. The war in France had hardly affected domestic production in 1917; sales boomed to nearly 1.9 million vehicles, snapped up at inflated prices by a suddenly affluent nation. Wages had never been higher, nor jobs so plentiful. The public, with money to spend, spent it on the new luxury—the automobile.

Amid such success, two casualties went unnoticed at General Motors. Henry and Wilfred Leland, perhaps remembering that first DeWars trophy that had established the Cadillac's reputation, were devoted Anglophiles. Intensely patriotic, and convinced that stopping the Hun would save the democracies of Europe, Wilfred Leland appeared in Durant's New York office the day after Congress declared war. As the Lelands later retold the story, they wanted permission to convert a new Cadillac factory for closed automobile bodies to the production of sorely needed airplane engines.

Durant refused. Flatly. "This war should stop tomorrow," he seethed. Leland was stunned. For ten years Durant had honored their verbal agreement, denying the Lelands nothing, giving them free rein. Now, at the most important moment, with democracy itself hanging in the balance, Durant was refusing them. "This is not our war and I will not permit any General Motors unit to do work for the government," Durant insisted.

Crestfallen, Wilfred returned to Detroit to confer with his father. The two men agonized for weeks, torn between the company they had built and a cause they felt for deeply. On June 18, they announced their resignation, and though Durant, recanting, spent an entire day asking them to reconsider, the Lelands left on July 3, 1917.*

Durant moved through the year, still buying, still building. He added the Scripps–Booth runabout to the line in July, outfitted it with a Chevrolet 490 engine and drive train, and sent it off to

---

* Six weeks later the Lelands incorporated the Lincoln Motor Company to build 6,000 Liberty airplane engines. In September 1920, they produced the first Lincoln automobile, a rival to their earlier Cadillac for prestige.

compete with the Buick and the Oakland Sensible Six, which was "Built to Serve and Save." Outmoded and underpowered, the Scripps–Booth would last but five more years.

Early in 1918, Durant discovered an undercapitalized, none-too-successful company in Detroit that was attempting to manufacture electric refrigerators. Guardian Frigerator's experiments were promising, and Durant, already worried about cutbacks in steel allocations for "pleasure" cars, suspected that a home refrigeration unit might offer a timely product to fill the gap. He invested personally, followed the inventors' progress closely, and gave a name to the new electric icebox—Frigidaire. Nine months later he sold the company to General Motors at the price he paid, promising the board of directors that this new unit alone eventually would pay the entire dividend on General Motors' preferred stock. Commenting later on Durant's sale, the fidgety Alfred Sloan, then a corporate vice-president, noted, "You might think he had reckoned on making a big profit for himself. Not Durant. I'd bet my life he did not make a dollar for himself in that or any similar deal. He was not that kind."

Early in June, Durant encountered an old nemesis, Bernard M. Baruch, chairman of the War Industries Board and as close to an economic dictator as the country had known. Baruch, who once frankly listed his occupation for a Senate committee as "speculator," had played a key role in the bear market that had sent Durant scampering the year before. Now, with the power to allocate raw materials to sixty industries, the man President Wilson called "Dr. Facts" confronted Durant again.

Two out of three automobiles and trucks built in America in this second year of the war were sold domestically, for pleasure use, Baruch scoffed. While truck production to meet military demands had soared, up more than tenfold since the war began, Baruch meant to curtail the use of steel alloys for frivolities. The Detroit manufacturers, including Durant, protested the cutbacks; Baruch, secure in the backing of President Wilson, applied pressure. While the manufacturers sat in Baruch's office listening, Baruch "telephoned the railroad administrator and suspended train service to their plants. Next he called the Secretary of War and asked that the Army seize the car companies' stockpiles of steel. After his third call, the General Motors man [Durant] stopped him and said, 'I quit.' The others followed suit.''

Baruch's stoppage order was delayed when the governor of Michigan pointed out that such a move would bankrupt the state. The War Industries Board finally decided that the automobile industry could have half the steel tonnage used during the last half of 1917 for the last six months of 1918. By year's end, automobile production had fallen 45 percent, to 943,000 vehicles. Truck production, almost doubled, could not take up the slack.

Noting the industry's cutbacks, Pierre du Pont fairly enthused: ''John [Raskob] and I agree that the opportunity of acquisition of shops manufacturing parts and accessories will be made broader through this slackening off in business and we will be able to liquidate quite a line of high price materials in preparation of after-war conditions.'' No less than Durant or Raskob, du Pont had become expansion-minded.

General Motors fared better than the industry as a whole. Buoyed by increased prices—cars equivalent to 1916 models sold for 50-percent higher prices by 1918, as manufacturers took advantage of what economists call ''excess consumer demand''—General Motors recorded sales of $269 million and profits of $35 million. The company had delivered $30 million of the $50 million in military supplies for which it had contracted—trucks, ambulances, automobiles, mortar shells, and airplane engines—but despite the abrupt cancellation of remaining contracts the armistice was welcome. There was an enormous, pent-up demand for automobiles, a demand so palpable that the automobile industry would rush to fill it without bringing out new models for 1919. Further, a nation only lukewarm to the war had, like Durant, rallied to the colors once war was declared; encouraged to save, the citizens had invested some $23 billion in Liberty Bonds, money that now would be available for the luxury purchases delayed since 1917.

To meet the estimated backlog of one-half million auto sales, General Motors planned a $52.8 million expansion effort for 1919. To fund it, Raskob arranged a massive corporate refinancing, increasing the capitalization to $370 million at the end of

1918 and then again to $1 billion the following year. General Motors thus became the second billion-dollar firm, after United States Steel, a move that Wall Street interpreted as proof of the automobile industry's arrival as a pillar of the economy. In General Motors' case, the image was illusory; less than a third of the billion dollars of common stock was issued.

Durant continued buying: Sheridan, yet another motorcar; Pontiac Body Company, melded into the Oakland; three Dayton companies Charles Kettering owned, including the promising Dayton–Wright Airplane; and a 60-percent interest in Fisher Body Corporation. The corporation made its first investment in the farm-implement business, Durant following the lead of Henry Ford and the Fordson tractor; bought total control of the McLaughlins' Canadian factories; set aside $9.5 million for new assembly plants; created a $1 million experimental laboratory for Kettering to which all proposed models from the car companies were to be submitted for review; began a building program in the housing-short company towns of Flint, Pontiac, and Lansing; started construction of a corporate headquarters in Detroit that ultimately would cost $20 million; and set up a company to finance consumer purchases of General Motors' automobiles. Durant's baby employed 86,000, a fourfold increase in six years.

Each of the investments was vital, some critical. The housing program was essential if newly paternal General Motors was to retain its workers; in a period of high wages and full employment, factory hands could move from job to job easily. Relative prosperity made them restive; war-aggravated disparities of affluence unleashed labor protests across the country. Led by Communist sympathizer William Z. Foster, steelworkers struck at the very core of American capitalism, United States Steel, demanding an end to the twelve-hour-day and seven-day-week, eighty-four hours of work for $28. Militant coal miners walked off the job in the anthracite fields. Seattle endured a general strike, the first time that European form of dissent had appeared in the New World, and Mayor Ole Hanson threatened to call out federal troops to stem the tide of Bolshevism in America. Even the thriving automobile industry was not immune. Machinists struck in Flint for two months. A Detroit axle plant shut down temporarily rather than boost its six-dollar-per-day wage. Only a labor injunction broke a strike by 14,000 assembly-line workers at the Willys plant in Toledo.

New York, Chicago—there were picket lines and bloody clashes between police and strikers everywhere. Bewildered industrialists, seeing socialism and anarchy all about, demanded action. Out of the turmoil would come the lawless era of the "Red Scare," when United States Attorney General A. Mitchell Palmer and his young special assistant, J. Edgar Hoover, staged a long series of roundups of aliens and suspected subversives. (To Palmer and Hoover, the words were synonymous.)

The restlessness in the auto industry extended into the ranks of management as well. The automobile was making some rich beyond belief, and the men who were making it possible sought a share for themselves. Given the task of working out a stock bonus plan for the corporation's executives, newly made millionaire Alfred Sloan noted: "Frankly there is nothing we need more at the present time than something of this kind. It is getting more and more difficult to keep our organization lined up. There seems to be an astounding amount of unrest everywhere, even among those that you would hardly think it possible."

Arguably, the most critical move in the boom years of 1918 and 1919 was the creation of the General Motors Acceptance Corporation (GMAC), a wholly owned subsidiary set up to finance the sale of the company's cars and trucks. John Willys, the master salesman, had created the industry's first captive lending agency in 1916, borrowing the hundred-year-old idea from the furniture industry. Disdainful banks disapproved of financing "pleasure" cars, and specialized lending agencies, such as Morris Plan, began to fill the gap in 1910. The business was profitable, and automobile manufacturers moved to set up their own finance plans. "Easy" credit in the flush years of the postwar boom heated automobile sales; in its first year of business, GMAC wrote $2 million in loans—one-quarter down, the balance in twelve monthly payments. By 1925, three of every four cars would be sold on the installment plan.

Predictions of a two-million-vehicle sales year no longer seemed figments of fevered imaginations. The industry rushed to expand production, Durant announcing another $37 million expansion program "as an answer to the uncertainty of postwar conditions."

Automobile prices rose steadily, and still the demand continued. Late in 1919, one trade journal calculated a 25-percent labor shortage in passenger-car plants. Another estimated that 33,000 auto workers had come to Detroit in the first months of 1919, along with their families, making a total new population of 75,000 to be housed, fed, and amused. No figure seemed too big or too preposterous in the heady prosperity of those years.

"The industry was possessed with a sense of destiny that the motor car was going to transform all of American life," a later historian wrote. Automobiles would remake the world, predicted Ralph Kaye, advertising manager of Kissel Motors:

. . . [B]y 1924, we will have highways built exclusively for automobile passenger traffic—that every hotel, office building and public institution will have "parking floors" for the cars of guests and visitors—that to live in certain parts of a city or suburban district it will be necessary to own an automobile. . . .

I predict that a house builder or contractor who builds a house without a garage as part of it would be as much out of fashion as one building it without roof or cellar . . . that the railroads will eliminate the short passenger route in favor of specially constructed passenger-carrying automobiles. . . .

I look for overhead tramways in the large cities—for educational laws making it necessary for every student to have a general knowledge of the construction and driving of automobiles, along with chemistry and geometry, and that to be unable to drive an automobile will be as bad as an inability to write a legible hand.

I look to see the time when the automobile will be as much a part of the household equipment as the kitchen range—that all marketing of fresh meat, vegetables, etc., will be done in the country, and that the housewife will think no more of driving 25 or 30 miles for her daily supplies of fresh food than she does now to walk around the corner to see the latest movie.

Amid the euphoria, there were cautionary voices. In early November 1919, the Federal Reserve Board moved to curb speculation on the varicose stock market; banks raised their interest rates, and brokers their margin requirements. During a week-long trip by private railway car introducing Du Pont officers to General Motors, Durant was apprehensive, one of the Du Pont party remembered. "On numerous occasions during that trip," Donaldson Brown wrote later, Durant "pointed out the economic storm warnings which were gathering on the horizon. Repeatedly he uttered gloomy prophecies, warning of a decline in the stock market. [Durant's] conspicuous pessimism was not shared by others on the journey. . . ."

Walter Chrysler was also upset. Chrysler, with the added title of vice-president in charge of operations, distrusted the company's headlong expansion. If sales slackened, General Motors would have enormous unused, and unpaid for, production capacity. "All my feeling, all my complaints, had to do with the physical expansion. . . . They kept buying things and budgeting this and budgeting that until it seemed, to me, we might come to a dismal ending. Buick was making about half the money, but the corporation was spending much faster than we could earn," Chrysler complained.

Durant himself had some misgivings about the expansion. Costs of the new office building were out of hand, and the workers' housing was overpriced, forcing the company to sell the new homes at a loss. Yet Durant felt bound by his agreement with the Du Pont interests. Each of the presidents of the constituent auto companies had operated as before, independent of each other, buying as he might at inflated prices, looking to the corporation only for capital to finance expansion. But Durant could not graciously object when Raskob now championed the growth, secured an additional $25 million Du Pont investment to fund it, and approved the wildest fancies of those seeking money.

The year 1920 appeared to be even better than 1919. A.H. Erskine, president of Studebaker, predicted sales of two million vehicles in the year. Manufacturers exhibited three hundred models at the bellwether New York Automobile Show in January, took orders, but would promise delivery of medium-priced cars only in June. All but chortling, Edward S. Jordan, the manufacturer of the Jordan Playboy, estimated that consumer demand would outrun production by one million automobiles.

Whatever the unfilled demand, the New York *Times* sourly noted that saturation of the market already had been reached on Fifth Avenue and Boston's Post Road, "and not a few highways in New Jersey and Long Island." In April, 1920, the Los Angeles City Council banned street parking in the downtown business district to alleviate traffic congestion; the ordinance was summarily rescinded two weeks later, after businessmen complained that sales had declined between 20 to 50 percent. "The vast majority of people in a queer way felt the business pulse of Southern California throbbed in unison with the purring motion of its automobiles," the Los Angeles *Times* commented.

Then the boom collapsed.

7

The Only Sports
in the Country

It came suddenly, a surprise, as financial busts always are. Throughout 1919, business and industry had battened on the pent-up demand and enforced wartime savings unleashed with the armistice. The boom could not continue—not with millions of mustered-out veterans seeking jobs and the oversupply of labor driving down wages—yet no manufacturer wanted to retrench prematurely and risk the loss of wondrous profits in postwar America.

Durant was concerned, the more so since the enthusiastic John Raskob as chairman of the finance committee happily assured everyone there would be funds enough for ever greater expansion. On October 31, an uncharacteristically worried Durant cautioned Raskob about "the enormous expenditures and capital commitments which are being authorized by the finance committee against prospective earnings—a method of financing which I

163

do not think is either safe or sound and which, in the event of industrial disturbance or paralysis, might seriously impair our position."

Through the balance of the year, Durant's resistance grew, especially to the fifteen-story, $20 million corporate headquarters, which Raskob had honorifically named the Durant Building. Still, both the finance and executive committees pressed on, authorizing both plant expansions and inventory accumulations for greater expected sales in 1920. Out of a sense of obligation, or perhaps deference to Raskob's judgment, Durant ratified or acceded to the pell-mell expansion. Besides, he wanted funds for his own favored project: farm tractors.

Following Henry Ford, whose Fordson tractor was as successful on farms as the Model-T was on roads, Durant had detailed Arthur Mason to design a tractor for the new Samson division. No sooner was that accomplished than Durant embraced the idea of a gasoline-powered tractor driven by reins held by the farmer, who rode behind his "Iron Horse." It was cumbersome, mechanically unruly, and finally a disaster.

Samson was to be more than a tractor company. Durant envisioned it supplying farmers with all their tool needs—including farm implements, "Sunnyhome" electric lighting and appliances (these developed earlier by Charles F. Kettering at Delco and still a project close to that farm boy's heart), and, finally, two trucks and a nine-passenger family car. Farmers had large families and hired hands, all of whom wanted to go to church on Sunday, Durant piously explained. Samson's light truck was a success, and the home appliances showed real promise; but the division required a disproportionate share of Durant's time and corporation funding.

Instead of reducing expenditures, the committees compromised by awarding everyone what he wanted: Raskob, $20 million for the headquarters; Sloan, $7.2 million to build a new ball-bearing factory; Cadillac, $7 million for plant expansion; and Durant, what ultimately would total $33 million for the farm-implement enterprise.

Raskob conceived two plans: one to raise money by selling $85 million in bonds on the market; the other to prop up the price of the common stock by splitting the $400 shares on a ten-for-one basis. (Such a split would allow smaller investors to buy blocks of company stock. Traditionally, such splits have had the inexplicable effect, too, of boosting prices, though a stock split is nothing more than an exchange of paper; it does not change a company's net worth.)

The bonds did not do well on the drifting market. By late February 1920, the corporation had sold only $7 million of the $85 million in bonds; by May, the total had reached just $12 million. With some retrenchments, chiefly slowing down construction on the headquarters building, they might get by with just $64 million in new funds. Raskob set out to find the money.

Durant's days stretched longer, far into the night, though he could still find time for checker games with the elevator operator, visitors from Flint, or employees. For a half hour, sometimes longer, executives needing decisions from him waited while Durant escaped into a game at which he was the acknowledged master.

Even Walter Chrysler, his sulphurous tongue momentarily in check, had begrudgingly accepted the long waits in Durant's outer office after a peremptory command to appear. (On one occasion, after a summons to New York from Flint, Chrysler had cooled his heels for four days before decamping once again for Flint—without ever seeing Durant and hearing nothing more about it.)

Chrysler may have been willing to accept such casual treatment from "the man who could charm birds from the trees," but he could not, he would not tolerate what he considered Durant's meddling in day-to-day operations. Chrysler thought those his prerogatives, and he resented Durant's inability to hew to a single strategy. "Walt, I believe in changing the policies just as often as my door opens and closes," Durant had chuckled. But Chrysler wanted consistency. The two quarreled, apologized, then quarreled anew. Worried also about his stock, his life's savings, Chrysler feared the devaluation of wartime inventories that he knew must come.

Having given Durant the three promised years and more, Chrysler abruptly quit in March 1920. All of Durant's arguments and Sloan's entreaties could not keep him on. His first move was to cash in his large block of General Motors shares, then to weigh a number of offers to take over faltering automobile companies. The loss of Chrysler would be laid to Durant, a criticism of his management of the corporation.

Meanwhile, in one of his periodic forays into the stock market, Durant began a carefully engineered scheme to punish those he considered his enemies—and turn a handsome profit while doing so. For weeks General Motors shares had drifted like a falling leaf—up, then down, inexorably down. Someone, or some group, was trying to depress the market.

The bear's usual device was to sell short during a period of financial malaise, trusting that investor disinterest would turn to anxiety as a stock failed to advance. Once that happened, the price would begin to fall, and the bear could pick up shares at low prices to fulfill previous sales. Short of a turnabout in the nation's business climate—still beyond Durant's capability— there was just one way a speculator might arrest a bear market and profit in the gamble.

But cornering a stock—that is, buying all the shares of a company offered and thereby depriving the bears of stock needed to repay their borrowings—was both risky and expensive. Durant began by recruiting a syndicate of old friends to join him in his venture, then dispatched telegrams to General Motors stockholders. Some he asked to buy stock, others to hold what shares they owned, and the third group to give him an option.* He timed the operation to coincide with the ten-for-one exchange, since the new shares could not be substituted for the old by stock-exchange rules. Durant's syndicate would be dealing in old shares only; once exchanged, an old share became a worthless token in the struggle for a corner.

Durant entered the market quietly, buying in ever-increasing lots. Unlike the average investor, who might be spooked into

* As with so much else surrounding Durant, his motives seem mixed. In attempting to manipulate the stock's price, Durant's actions would be illegal now. In asking for options, Durant may have been seeking to buttress his holdings at the expense of the "Wilmington crowd."

quickly reselling when the price faltered, Durant and his syndicate held onto their purchases. On paper, they were losing money so long as the market declined and would continue to do so until they had dried up the available stock. It took nerve, Durant's "upside" speculators against the bears' "downside" plungers. The bears were short-selling stock they didn't own, and Durant was buying it on 10-percent margin, gambling that his credit with brokerage houses was better than the opposition's.

By March 1920, the stock was over $350. Durant's purchases kept the price high—artificially high in the mind of unwary speculators, who themselves decided to go short. Still Durant bought. The price escalated, jumping $37 in one day as the bulls rushed to cover their shorts and found that General Motors shares were harder to come by.

The stock climbed to $410 by March 20, "only little removed from the 1919 record price," the New York *Times* marveled. "The spectacle of General Motors rising more than 45 points on a Saturday morning was so unusual as to stir up comment about a severely man-handled short interest." The "Topics on Wall Street" columnist concluded: "Apparently the shorts in this issue have had a bad beating."

Durant had won, and he might have driven the price even higher than its peak of $420 had not the New York Stock Exchange stepped in. A vigorous Durant partisan, magazine writer W.A.P. John, explained that Durant could have crushed the short-sellers "mercilessly": "But in so doing he would have ruined thousands of men, dozens of banks, and scores of brokers; and so after conferring with the officers of the New York Stock Exchange he placed a nominal value on the stock—the average price which he had paid in purchasing it—and the guilty were allowed to escape because the innocent were being ruined."

Durant was not wholeheartedly magnanimous. The stock exchange, in fact, had decided that the new shares, exchanged ten-for-one with the old, could be used to cover the shorts. Durant's corner depended upon dealing in a constricted market created when the bulk of the old General Motors shares was exchanged. Faced with the inevitable flooding of his corner with crisp new stockholders' certificates, Durant had gracefully accepted the compromise.

Durant's adventure would prove costly. The corner broken, he was left with sizable debts, just how much probably even Durant himself did not know at the time. He and his allies had bought on margin; in time, they would have to pay the balance due, as much as 90 percent of the purchase price. They might sell some of their stock immediately and take quick profits, but were they to dump too much, too fast, those sales alone would immediately depress the market.

Durant's triumph was short-lived. The bears came back—men like Bernard Baruch would always have reserves of cash and nerve to recover from temporary setbacks. Without Durant to prop it up, the stock began to sink again. A month after the corner fell in, ten shares of the new General Motors stock sold for $358, $62 less than the high of March 1920. Durant then had to be careful to sell stock just fast enough to avoid losing money. A number of his colleagues already were up against the wall—forced to pay their debts or sell. Durant began "to take over their accounts," in the parlance of Wall Street, taking responsibility for his own advice and buying them out.

Meanwhile, the sale of General Motors debenture bonds had fizzled to a halt. Increasingly anxious, Raskob, as chairman of the finance committee, scrambled to raise the money needed to pay for the company's ongoing expansion. He proposed that General Motors offer on a pro-rata basis 360,000 shares to its stockholders at $200 per share, less than half of the pre-split price. Durant, because he was strapped for cash as he completed his corner, and du Pont, because his board was opposed to further investment in the automobile company, both waived their rights to the new issues in favor of a new investor Raskob had located.

Raskob waxed enthusiastic about the new partner, Explosives Trades Ltd., England's counterpart to E.I. du Pont de Nemours. The English agreed to take $30 million of the issue, paying for it on the installment plan, 10 percent down and the balance in weekly installments until the end of the year. Another

$6 million was purchased by Canadian Explosives Ltd., controlled by the English firm. Still this left them $28 million short of the rock-bottom figure Raskob insisted the company needed to complete its expansion program. Raskob sought other investors, but in a generally declining market found no takers. He grew nervous.

In mid-April, over Durant's strident objections, which faded in the face of pressing financial needs, Pierre du Pont and a reluctant Raskob turned to J.P. Morgan and Company. However much Durant might dislike bankers in general, however much he might have remembered the arrogance of the Morgan investment house when he and Briscoe had gone hat in hand to 23 Wall Street twelve years earlier, Durant had to give way to his finance committee. "The company was headed towards the rocks," Durant later explained; J.P. Morgan was a last hope.

The Morgan partners were not any more enthusiastic about having Durant as a partner. The recent corner on General Motors had only enhanced Durant's reputation as a speculator rather than an industrialist—not the sort of person that august institution would prefer as a partner. "I need not tell you," Morgan partner Edward R. Stettinius, Sr., wrote Pierre du Pont, "that however attractive General Motors may have been to us, it would not have received the support we have given it had it not been for your active connection with, and interest in the company."

J.P. Morgan and Company agreed to underwrite the private sale of 1.4 million shares of stock at $20 per share, some $7 less than the still-falling market price. For its services, Stettinius demanded the right to purchase 100,000 shares at the insider's price of $10; well aware that Raskob's financial resources were at their limit, the Morgan partners struck a hard bargain.

Beyond this, Stettinius agreed to manage a $10 million syndicate to support the price of General Motors stock over the next six months. Stettinius would have "entire charge . . . to buy in the open market in such amounts and at such prices and at such time as the Managers may deem advisable." Durant subscribed $1 million, the Du Pont industries a like amount, and three of the newly made millionaires—Sloan, Deeds, and Kettering—

$500,000 each. John Raskob begged off, claiming he was worth but $2 million, and half of that, perhaps foolishly, was tied up in his Maryland estate.

Moreover, the bankers demanded six seats on an expanded board of directors: one for Stettinius himself, the other five for representatives of the major investors Morgan and Company had rounded up. As Raskob must have known—this accounting for his early reluctance—his finance committee was to be expanded to include two newly seated bankers and Stettinius. No more would John Raskob have a complaisant committee to rubber-stamp his proposals; as much as Durant he would find himself restrained.

More problems loomed. First domestic farm prices began fall-ing in the spring of 1920 as European agriculture recovered and American exports fell; the promising Samson tractor's sales suf-fered immediately, and the division became a severe drain on cash reserves. Then the demand for new automobiles slackened, first in rural areas and then in larger towns and cities. Inventories of raw materials and finished cars mounted in the yards of the automobile divisions. Each division operated autonomously—despite Durant's later reputation as a "dictator" who could not delegate authority. (In fact, Durant was more the dilettante, flit-ting in and out of divisions as his mood dictated.) Despite warn-ings from corporate headquarters and later orders to restrain purchases, the division managers continued to stockpile raw ma-terials at wartime prices, still bent on achieving record produc-tion in the next model year. Spring weather would stimulate sales, they believed; people still looked to the skies before buy-ing a car, even with closed bodies comprising more than half of the market. Beyond the warnings, however, Durant did nothing to curb the independent automobile divisions. It was, Alfred P. Sloan would write later, "decentralization with a vengeance," and the growing crisis would profoundly affect Sloan personally.

Then, in early June, the English investors found themselves in embarrassing circumstances. Sir Harry McGowan wrote to du Pont, saying, "Frankly, the difficulty of finding our proportion—around about $30,000,000—between now and the end of the year is going to be extraordinarily great." The postwar recession, long expected and long disdained, had begun to set in overseas.

Though he had withdrawn from the market, or so Pierre du Pont believed, Durant and his close allies inexplicably returned to the stock exchange. Durant's later rationale rang faintly hollow: "I was endeavoring to sustain General Motors stock so that the English interest to whom we had sold the stock at 20 when it was 38 would not get cold feet and repudiate their contract." Whatever the reason, Durant began buying heavily; ultimately, his private syndicate would accumulate one million shares. Durant bought despite an agreement with Stettinius not to do so, to allow the bank's own syndicate to operate freely in the marketplace.

The tide was running. Automobile sales across the country slowed in June. By July 10, General Motors stock had fallen to $27 per share. The rank of telephones on Durant's desk next to the Frederic Remington sculpted horseman rang constantly through the heat of the summer, Durant buying and buying. Still the price fell, to $25 on July 20.

Durant was spending a long weekend at Raymere, his great white Beaux Arts estate in Deal, New Jersey, when he received an urgent telephone call on July 27. Someone had dumped 75,000 shares of General Motors on the market that day, knocking the price down to $20.50. Alarmed, Durant returned to New York and put out feelers to learn the source of the stock. His distrust of bankers was reconfirmed. Edward Stettinius, the embodiment of financial rectitude, had sold more than 100,000 shares in the preceding few days—shares ostensibly accumulated by the syndicate in a parallel effort to *prop up* the price.

Challenged by Durant in front of Pierre du Pont and John Raskob, Stettinius could offer only the lame excuse that he believed the stock would continue to fall and the syndicate would be able to buy it back later at an even lower price. Indeed, the banker proposed that they take advantage of market conditions to sell 200,000 shares short. Durant refused, ever the uplifter, arguing "that our business was [on] the constructive and up-building side." Humiliated, Stettinius agreed that the syndicate would honor the decision to support the price of the stock so that it did not fall below $20 a share. Three days later, however, Durant again braced Stettinius, showing the Morgan partner purchase slips for General Motors at $19. The $10 million syndicate had *not* entered the market to shore up the price. None too discreetly, Durant was proving Stettinius a liar; later he would charge the banker with "almost a betrayal of trust."

Durant was now spending most of his time in the stock market. Automobile sales had slackened, leaving General Motors with unsold cars too expensive for the market, and inventories that tied up $210 million. First Chevrolet, then Buick (still the mainstay of the corporation), and then the other automobile divisions laid off workers or shut down factories entirely. The drain on cash eased while tens of thousands sat numbly in the heat of a Michigan summer, worrying how they would feed their families. Production of the new Scripps–Booth—which eventually was to become a low-cost challenger to Ford's Model-T—was shelved for the time being, to Charles Kettering's pleasure. The car had not been turned over to Kettering and his testing laboratory because Durant wanted it out quickly, without Kettering insisting upon immediate improvements.

The hasty improvisation of the Scripps–Booth was just another example of the disorganization within the sprawling enterprise that troubled the tidy mind of Alfred P. Sloan. Product development, he complained, "was something like a man wanting to get a new change of clothes, and he goes and buys a coat in one place and a pair of trousers in another and a vest in another and all different fits, and you don't get a complete ensemble, especially at less cost."

With seventy-five factories in forty cities and as many as fifty executives reporting directly to a harassed Durant, General Motors was just too large to operate as a one-man fiefdom. Encouraged by Pierre du Pont, Sloan took upon himself the job of writing a proposal for the company's reorganization. As time went on, the memoranda envisioned a complete restructuring of the corporation. Sloan worked alone, Durant too often distracted by the stock market or interrupted by the constantly ringing telephones lining his desk. Privately, Sloan might have resented the imperial Durant holding audience while a barber worked away at his chin, for Sloan preserved a strict sense of social courtesies. Still, it was impossible to dislike Durant, however cavalier he seemed about the gravity of business affairs.

Sloan submitted his memoranda to a distracted Durant. Durant glanced at them, placed them on a corner of his desk, and turned back to the ringing telephones. The documents sat there, while General Motors' inventories grew, sales declined, and Sloan grew more fretful. Like his friend Walter Chrysler, Sloan's personal fortune was tied up in company stock, and that was shrinking in value with each passing day. Sloan feared not only the declining market—which, after all, would reverse itself some day—but Durant's haphazard style of management, which could bring the company down. Durant was a "salesman-promoter, not a scientific operator or business administrator," Sloan worried. With Durant as president of General Motors, Sloan risked everything. The corporation's cash reserves of $100 million long since flown, its factories closed, and the yards piled high with rusting, overpriced inventories, General Motors could collapse. What then? Moreover, Sloan had a tempting offer from James J. Storrow of Lee, Higginson to join the Boston firm as a partner. Industrial analysis might not be as exciting as automobile manufacturing, but it was more stable.

Sloan hesitated, explaining later that he did not want to undercut Durant's desperate effort to prop up the price of the stock by dumping his own personal holdings—though why he would have to sell he did not explain. Instead, Sloan asked for a month's vacation to travel in Europe with his wife and to mull over Storrow's offer. In early September, his tour abandoned, his telltale order for a Rolls-Royce abruptly cancelled, Sloan returned to the United States to find that "the situation was coming to a head." Surprisingly, Durant himself was on vacation, his first in memory, certainly his first at General Motors. He was haggard, his smile worn thin, no longer the jaunty optimist.

By late September, Durant was backed to the wall. The British and Canadian investors had, as Durant feared, reneged on their agreement. They could put in no more than half of the $36 million they had pledged to invest. Raskob managed to paper over the shortage temporarily, hoping the crisis would soon ease.

It didn't. General Motors sold fewer than one-third the vehicles that September than it had a year earlier. Ford again responded to sluggish demand by cutting his prices as much as 30 percent, daring the rest of the industry to follow him down the rabbit hole. Other manufacturers, including Durant, declined to sell cars at a loss, and sales fell even more sharply. The stock market continued down; the recession deepened.

Dismay turned to anxiety, then to fear. A nation so confident that it could enforce peace that it rejected the Versailles treaty and the League of Nations less than a year earlier suddenly was clamoring to restrict immigration for fear of job competition. The antiforeign sentiment hardened with the arrest of two radical immigrants for the April 15, 1920, murder of two men in a payroll robbery in South Braintree, Massachusetts; Nicola Sacco and Bartolomeo Vanzetti would be executed seven years later, still protesting their innocence. On September 16, a bomb exploded in the very center of capitalism, the intersection of Broad and Wall streets in New York City. Thirty persons died seconds before noon that day, and a hundred more lay bleeding on the sidewalk in front of J.P. Morgan and Company. The explosion killed the Morgans' chief clerk and sent seventeen other employees to the hospital, but the partners in conference on the far side of the buff limestone temple escaped unharmed. J.P. Morgan, Jr., was out of the country. If the bombers had intended a lesson for the lords of capital, they were unsuccessful. The heart of the stolid Morgan bank barely fluttered.

Raskob wrote to Stettinius late in September at Durant's request, asking if any of the partners were selling stock again and urging the bankers' syndicate to begin buying. They had spent but $2 million of the $10 million entrusted to them. The bankers declined, Raskob wrote to Durant, on the grounds that General Motors' stock "was acting well in the market as compared to what other stocks were doing and under the circumstances thought our full buying power ought to be held in reserve to be used in the event of a more serious general situation developing." Durant was left as he had been in 1917, trying to support the stock price single-handedly.

Just why Durant continued to buy never has been adequately answered. To some extent, he was protecting friends who had joined him the previous spring in the successful corner of General Motors shares but now found themselves still holding too much stock worth too little. At least three times in the presence of his assistant, John L. Pratt, Durant relieved hard-pressed friends of the stock they held.

It was not altogether altruism that sent Durant to Stettinius. Quite as likely, in view of what was to happen within the next six weeks, Durant found himself overextended, having bought too much stock on margin over the year and subsequently finding himself caught between Scylla and Charybdis. Buying on margin, he had, in effect, asked brokers to loan him 90 percent of the stock's price at low interest rates. The brokers, in turn, went to banks to borrow that money, offering the stock itself as collateral. As the market price of the stock dwindled, its value as collateral also fell; the bank then asked the broker either for more security or for repayment of at least part of the loan. The broker passed the obligation on to Durant, who then had to come up with even more scarce cash or pledge more of his General Motors shares as security. To let the stock go at distress prices would be to undercut his own position; Durant had to keep buying, while meeting the new margin calls.

Stettinius waited while Durant faltered. On October 11, Durant announced the formation of a corporation to sell General Motors shares on the installment plan to small investors. Within five years, Durant told reporters, he would increase the number of stockholders "to such a point that the stock will be taken out of the stock market influences in Wall Street." Whatever the rationalization, the new effort was a token of his desperation; Durant had never before sold his personal shares in the company he called "my baby."

Still the price fell, to $17 by the twenty-seventh of the month. Pressed by banks and brokers alike, Durant was running short of cash. At the end of October, he borrowed 1.3 million shares of General Motors common from Pierre du Pont to meet new mar-

gin calls. The loan worried John Raskob all the more; Durant's
financial collapse would surely contaminate the corporation.
Anxiously, Raskob turned to Fred and Lawrence Fisher, suggesting that Fisher Body, half owned by General Motors, turn
that arrangement inside out. Because Fisher Body had good
credit with suppliers, it was "the only way open" to keep General Motors in good standing if Durant went down, Lawrence
Fisher explained later. While the dubious Fisher brothers pondered the strange bid, Raskob went elsewhere for aid.

Durant's advertisements in daily papers and financial journals
offering to sell General Motors stock on the installment plan
alarmed both the Morgan partners and du Pont. If Durant was
that desperate, he might have to surrender some of his stock put
up as collateral. A forced sale would destroy the price of the
stock, and the corporation with it.

Raskob arranged a meeting between the three uneasy allies on
Wednesday, November 10, at 23 Wall Street, urging that
"the partners in ownership of General Motors stock should
know each other's position." Dwight W. Morrow, a senior partner
in the banking firm, assured the others that J.P. Morgan and its
syndicate members were holding onto their shares. Du Pont said
the same. Durant gave no hint of his personal difficulties, even
after Morrow asked him directly, "Do you know of any weak
accounts in the market?"

"No," Durant assured his partners, leaving du Pont, for one,
"with the impression that his [Durant's] holdings were as clear
as our own." Morrow was suspicious, for no less than Durant
the bank had its collective ear to the ground. If Durant could not
meet the margin calls, as many as twenty brokers and at least
three banks could go under. Given the general state of business
and finance, Durant's failure could trigger a crisis as grave as the
1907 debacle; for good reason the cyclic troughs were referred to
as panics. At the same time, Durant's personal failure would be
tied to General Motors. Banks that had loaned the company
money could demand immediate repayment of the $80 million
outstanding. General Motors did not have the money. It was vital
the partners maintain appearances.

On November 11, Durant asked Pierre du Pont and John Raskob to lunch. While millions of people paused for two minutes at noon in memory of the men killed in World War I, the three sat down for the first in a series of embarrassing talks. Durant was distraught, his usual sang-froid worn away by anxiety. "The bankers," he told the surprised du Pont, "have demanded my resignation as president of General Motors." He was ready to accede, Durant continued, determined "to play the game," since both General Motors and he were "in the hands of the bankers." The men of J.P. Morgan had made their decision: Durant was to go. And, for the first time, Durant confessed that he was worried about his personal accounts, privately acknowledging that his own debts might be jeopardizing the company he had founded and built.

The following day, du Pont and Raskob discussed Durant's position, their own concern growing. Raskob met again with Durant to discuss Durant's financial condition in more detail—specifically, how much he owed. It could be $6 million or $26 million dollars, Durant conceded. In the face of the falling market—General Motors had slipped to $14 overnight—with brokers calling for ever more margin, and his books never very well kept anyway, Durant simply did not know.

Raskob and du Pont went off for long weekends on their estates on Friday, November 12, concerned but not alarmed. That night Durant and his wife went to the Metropolitan Opera with John T. Smith, General Motors' staff counsel, and Mrs. Smith. Throughout the opera—the traditional pairing of *I Pagliacci* and *Cavalleria Rusticana*—and a rubber of bridge in the Durants' apartment afterward, Durant "was as casual and amiable as ever," Smith recalled. "After a while he apologetically asked Mrs. Smith if she would be willing to go home alone so that he could talk business a little while with me. After she had gone he quietly told me how desperate the situation was. 'Something's got to be done. I've done all I can. And it means that there will have to be a new president for General Motors.' "

Durant's empire was unraveling.

Du Pont and Raskob returned to New York after their long weekend on Tuesday. Durant's office on Fifty-seventh Street was in a turmoil when they arrived. "Mr. Durant was very busy that day, seeing people, rushing to the telephone, and in and out of his room so that although we waited patiently for several hours, interrupted only by lunch time, it was not until four o'clock that afternoon that Mr. Durant began to give us figures indicating his situation," du Pont wrote.

Durant's plight was worse than Raskob and du Pont had imagined. He owed some $34 million, against which he had pledged four million shares of company stock—his own, du Pont's shares, and others loaned for that purpose. It was only a rough estimate; Durant had his brokers preparing statements even as he tried to meet new margin calls. Du Pont immediately called his brother Irénée, president of E.I. du Pont de Nemours, asking him to come to New York the following day. Raskob canceled his trip to New Haven for Saturday's Harvard–Yale football game. The panic was creeping through the paneled suites on Fifty-seventh Street.

The two du Ponts, Raskob, and Sir Harry McGowan of Explosives Trades Ltd. (still a heavy stockholder despite the default) drafted a plan to bail out Durant, General Motors, and themselves as well. Durant's revised total of his debts reached $38 million, more than enough to bring down himself, the corporation, as many as forty-four stockbrokers, and an unknown number of banks. The four men had to work fast, before Durant was forced to liquidate; brokers had been calling all day, demanding more collateral. Even as they talked, General Motors dipped again, to $13.50; the bottom might fall out at any moment.

Raskob stated their first offer, testing Durant's nerve. The Du Pont people would purchase the three million shares Durant held for $11 million in cash and $25 million in deferred payments, a total of $36 million—or $12 a share. Durant rejected the offer on the grounds that "he would be practically ruined."

Raskob then suggested the formation of a new company to hold Durant's stock. The holding company would issue its own shares to replace the stock presently in the hands of the brokers, plus as much as $10 million more in shares that the Du Pont interests would buy for cash. The cash then could be used by the company to retire the most pressing of Durant's debts. Durant would share ownership in the new company with the Wilmington crowd, Raskob explained. Durant asked for time to weigh the second offer.

Durant spent the following morning, Thursday, November 18, seeking an alternative escape route while he staved off his brokers. Meanwhile, du Pont and Raskob worked to revise the itemization of Durant's accounts; no matter how detailed it seemed, both men believed it to be incomplete. At two in the afternoon, Durant walked into his office and closed the door. The telephones between the Remington bronze and the "Please Do Not Smoke" sign were silent. Durant was at the end of both emotional and financial resources. There was nothing more he could give to his "baby." The corporation was slipping through his hands—had slipped, he finally admitted to himself. He reached toward the bank of telephones to place one last call.

George Whitney, the Morgan partner then responsible for the syndicate, was cool. Durant had been less than forthright before. Now, with rumors circulating throughout Wall Street, with the stock off at $13, would Durant be any more candid?

The continuing decline in prices—which already had cost Durant more than $60 million in paper value—"was proving very embarrassing to some of his friends," Durant told Whitney. They needed relief from the margin calls, relief that could come only if the Morgan-managed syndicate stepped in to buy 1.1 million shares from Durant at $13, the day's closing price. Whitney said he would call Durant back.

Durant waited. There was nothing more he could do.

Whitney talked with patrician Dwight Morrow, senior partner in J.P. Morgan and Company, a confidant of presidents, and later ambassador to Mexico. (His daughter Anne later married American aviation hero Charles A. Lindbergh.) Morrow would sentence Durant.

They needed some clarification, Morrow told Durant, turning the screws. "Are you in trouble?"

Durant couldn't admit his defeat. "Well, no. Only my friends."

Did Durant hold any interest in the profits or losses of these margined accounts of his friends?

"Well, under certain conditions, yes."

Then perhaps Durant should come down to 23 Wall Street to discuss the situation, Morrow suggested.

Once before, Durant had made a pilgrimage to J.P. Morgan and Company; he would not go, hat in hand, a second time. Instead, he suggested that Morrow stop by Durant's office uptown. It was on Morrow's way home, and by the end of the day Durant would have completed his financial statement; a typist was working on it even as they talked. Morrow agreed.

It was a long shot, even a risky one, but Durant thought he still might be able to retain a stake in General Motors—if Pierre du Pont and John Raskob would support him against the banks. He asked the two men, as they pored over the freshly typed list of Durant's debts, if they would join him in a meeting with the Morgan partners.

Du Pont refused: "We told him that his position differed so entirely from that represented to us and to Morgan and Co. that it was impossible for us to sit in a meeting with him and the Morgan partners, unless he agreed to make a complete statement to them." His pride still intact, Durant refused. He had played his last card.

At six-thirty that evening, Pierre du Pont, his brother Irénée, and John Raskob left their offices for dinner. In the lobby they met the three Morgan representatives: Dwight Morrow, Thomas Cochran, and George Whitney. Morrow took Pierre du Pont aside while the others exchanged uneasy pleasantries. Morrow explained that the three bankers had met with Durant and were to return at nine o'clock for further discussions. Before then, Morrow thought it best that he and du Pont discuss the situation.

Back in Raskob's office, du Pont asked if Durant had given the bankers a full accounting. Morrow handed over the typed list of accounts du Pont had seen earlier, adding the news that Durant needed $940,000 in cash to meet margin calls before the nine-thirty opening of the stock exchange the next morning. Otherwise, brokers would dump 300,000 shares onto the market—enough to drive the stock into the gutter. In Morrow's opinion, the situation was extremely serious. They risked "a panic that might result, in the event of Mr. Durant's failure." Irénée du

Pont was even more alarmed, fearing a complete financial crash. Their discussion lasted only half an hour. Morrow and Pierre du Pont canceled engagements they had for that evening, and the du Ponts, Raskob, and the Morgan representatives went for a hasty dinner.

At nine o'clock they returned to join Durant, his former son-in-law, and John T. Smith. In the next two hours the nine men arranged to bail out the hapless Durant, impelled by a sense of urgency to conclude negotiations that ordinarily would have stretched out for months. Even as the men talked, another broker waited in the outer office to ask for further margin from Durant.

Morrow was skeptical of Raskob's plan of the day before. The way to clean up Durant's debts, he insisted, was for the holding company Raskob proposed to pay cash for everything. Morrow estimated that Durant needed $27 million to meet his most pressing obligations. The du Ponts would contribute $7 million, with the balance to come from a consortium of banks the Morgans would put together. The Morgan partners would supply the money needed to meet the next morning's margin calls. For the $27 million, they would take over 2.5 million shares of General Motors stock owned by Durant, paying $9.50 per share.

Giving Durant cash to pay his debts also had the effect of buying him out. He would still own a minority interest in the holding company, but he would not directly own any General Motors stock. Without that stock, he was through as president. Durant helplessly agreed.

The Morgan partners were relieved by the arrangement. Cochran was elated. "There are only two firms in this country who are real sports," he blurted, "Du Pont and Morgan."

There remained only the matter of Durant's share in the new holding company. Morrow proposed a fourth. Durant argued those terms were too harsh and countered with a 40–60 division. They settled with Durant getting a third of the equity in the new company.*

---

* Ultimately, the agreement would be amended to give the banks that had furnished the $20 million one-fifth of the equity. The du Ponts voted to split the remaining 80 percent equally with Durant.

By five-thirty on the morning of November 19, the details had been settled. Durant wrote out his letter of resignation and left it for a secretary to type. Then he shook hands with du Pont—who was to personally loan Durant $530,000 to help him over the crisis—and thanked the Morgan partners for their assistance. As the Morgan contingent left for breakfast and the task of paying off Durant's creditors, Morrow shrugged. "Durant thanks us humbly now for saving his life, but within a week he will be cursing us for something else."

Durant had lost a personal fortune of more than $100 million, and the company he created just twelve years earlier along with it. In those twelve years, he had melded a gaggle of struggling automotive companies into the second-largest manufacturer in the country—a corporation worth $350 million, employing 100,000 workers in thirty-five cities, and selling $600 million worth of motor vehicles annually. In so doing, paradoxically, Durant became his own nemesis. While his flamboyant activities gained him public attention—and he was adroit in handling the newspapermen who looked upon him as a ready source of Wall Street news—the masters of finance had little regard for the unorthodox methods that had helped him build the corporation.

Wall Street demonstrated its delight in the new management immediately. On Saturday morning, November 20, while word of Durant's ouster and the consummation of the Du Pont–Morgan control worked its way through the financial district, brokers began buying General Motors stock. The price rose to $15.75 per share. By the following Monday, the New York *Times* reported in a story announcing the new order of things—significantly, it was the first time the corporation had made that august newspaper's front page—General Motors stood at $16.50.

What Durant had not been able to do with all his millions—turn the stock's plunge about—he accomplished with his resignation.

Henry M. Leland, about 1915, the patriarch who founded both the Cadillac and Packard automobiles and introduced precision manufacturing to the industry.

Henry M. Leland's first Cadillac, built in 1903.

Steered by a tiller, the 1903 Oldsmobile with its distinctive curved dashboard became the automobile industry's first mass-produced car.

Henry Ford, about 1900,
the industrialist-to-be.

David Dunbar Buick, about 1895, then in the plumbing supply business and soon to begin work on the "valve-in-head" engine.

FORD MOTOR CARS

Touring Car with Top

Henry Ford's first Model-T, 1909, from a contemporary advertisement for the four-cylinder, twenty-horsepower touring car.

The first Buick of 1904, at the Flint Wagon Works. Seated rear are Charles M. Begole (left) and James H. Whiting; the passenger in the front is Thomas Buick, the driver is either Walter L. Marr or David Buick.

Louis Chevrolet (left) and Bob Burman in their Buick "Bug" racers of 1908 and 1909.

The 1910 Buick White Streak in its racing configuration, that is, without the rumble seat astride the rear axle.

William C. Durant, about 1909, flush with General Motors' first success.

The 1910 Oldsmobile Limited, a seven-passenger touring car with a six-cylinder, sixty-horsepower engine which represented the zenith of General Motors' elegance at the time.

Louis Chevrolet at the wheel of a 1914 Buick.

C.F. Kettering in a characteristic posture, tinkering with the new self-starter on the 1912 Cadillac at the Delco shops in Dayton.

The "Royal Mail" Roadster is pleasing to the eye, coming or going.

The 1914 Royal Mail Roadster, which, with its companion Baby Grand touring car, established Chevrolet as a marque to be reckoned with.

William C. Durant, about 1915, characteristically confident.

Richard H. Grant, the cyclonic Chevrolet sales manager, beside the
Chevrolet 490, April 1915.

Pierre S. du Pont, about 1915,
near the time of his first purchase of General Motors stock.

Walter P. Chrysler, about 1920.

Part II

DOMINANCE

To George F. Babbitt, as to most prosperous citizens of Zenith, his motor car was poetry and tragedy, love and heroism. The office was his pirate ship but the car his perilous excursion ashore.

Among the tremendous crises of each day none was more dramatic than starting the engine. It was slow on cold mornings; there was the long, anxious whirr of the starter, and sometimes he had to drip ether into the cocks of the cylinders, which was so very interesting that at lunch he would chronicle it drop by drop, and orally calculate how much each drop had cost him.

This morning he was darkly prepared to find something wrong, and he felt belittled when the mixture exploded sweet and strong, and the car didn't even brush the door-jamb, gouged and splintery with many bruisings by fenders, as he backed out of the garage. He was confused. He shouted "Morning!" to Sam Doppelbrau with more cordiality than he had intended.

—Sinclair Lewis, *Babbitt*

8

The Wilmington Crowd

Pierre S. du Pont was reluctant. He was fifty, early and deliberately retired from the Du Pont corporation presidency. His real interest lay in the great new greenhouse at Longwood and the gardens he enjoyed cultivating; he wanted to spend more time as a reform-minded member of Delaware's state board of education. Furthermore, he knew almost nothing about the automobile industry, and it was not likely he would be able to make up for lost time in the years left to him. So, despite the urgings of the Morgan partners and his close friend, Seward Prosser of Bankers Trust, Pierre du Pont shied away from the presidency of General Motors.

The corporation itself was in wild disarray, its management sharply divided between Durant's men and the people du Pont and John Raskob had brought up from Wilmington. Each group was suspicious of the other. The Fisher brothers, supplying most

185

of General Motors' auto bodies, were avowedly in favor of Durant; their antagonism alone could destroy the harmony necessary to success.

Who else besides du Pont, argued Raskob, Prosser, and Morrow, had the reputation for financial probity the corporation most needed at this moment? Who else by his very presence as president could instantly assure Wall Street that the corporation was in the control of sound men? Raskob could not. He was a financial man with little interest in administration. Moreover, Raskob was too much like Durant, too much the risk-taker. Sloan, who worried a great deal about the bank loans, who might have been a serious candidate himself but for his lack of experience in finance, insisted that only Pierre du Pont "had the prestige and respect that would give confidence to the organization, to the public, and to the banks, and whose presence could arrest the demoralization that was taking place."

Moreover, Pierre du Pont was still "Dad," still the head of the family. *He* had ratified Raskob's enthusiasm for the motors venture, and he had accepted responsibility for the $50 million that E. I. du Pont de Nemours and Pierre's relatives subsequently had sunk into General Motors. The Durant bail-out had cost another $20 million and more deeply caught them in what appeared to be a quagmire; Pierre could not simply walk away with Du Pont industries so heavily involved, owning 43 percent of General Motors. Perhaps in time he might turn over the presidency to Sloan, when he had the assurance that Sloan could handle the job—*if* Sloan could handle the job. The reorganization plan that Sloan had sent to du Pont suggested that though Sloan might have been Durant's assistant, he had not been Durant's man, at least not like the headstrong managers of the automobile divisions.

For two days du Pont weighed his decision until Raskob's incessant urgings finally "set his mind at rest." Raskob prevailed by arguing that the automobile industry was still growing and that General Motors was already a major company in it, second only to Ford. The nucleus of a superb organization lay all about them: factories and equipment, at least two automobiles—Buick and Cadillac—making money, Kettering's research laboratory, the hugely successful acceptance corporation, and international distribution. "All is ready for a reorganization and advance toward better days," Raskob insisted. And better days were sure to come, once Warren Harding was inaugurated as president of the United States. Du Pont agreed. Longwood and the school children of Delaware would have to wait a bit longer.

It was not an auspicious time for du Pont to launch his automotive career. Detroit had luxuriated in the postwar boom, while manufacturers expanded their production capacity without regard to the total market or what competitors were doing. Each was intent on getting the greatest share of the pie in motor vehicles, at least the part Ford didn't swallow. The company that produced the most cars would sell the most.

With the September 1920 collapse, production had slowed. Throughout the rest of the year manufacturers had worked off swollen inventories, forcing overpriced automobiles onto captive dealers and shutting down production as they did so. Largely because of sales early in the year, the industry recorded a profit of $22 million, or $100 per car, in 1920. But by the end of the year, the mammoth Ford plants at Highland Park and River Rouge were closed entirely and automobile employment was just one-seventh what it had been twelve months earlier.

As du Pont took charge of General Motors, the country wallowed in the midst of the worst recession in its history. Nationally, five million men walked the streets looking for work. For the first time, dealers found themselves unable to deal off the used cars taken as down payments on new-car sales. Used-car prices fell 25 percent, and still the vehicles sat there. A "used-car problem," as it would become known, had surfaced.

Unemployment in auto towns such as Detroit and Flint ran twice as high as the national average. Seeking work, despondent laborers began returning to the mines of northern Michigan and the played-out farms of the South they had left in the boom years. By the end of 1920, as many as 200,000 people had left Detroit, the Michigan Manufacturers Association reported. That organization was not optimistic. "We do not expect them to return, for some time at least." Akron, Ohio, the center of the tire industry, lost 50,000 citizens in the last months of 1920.

No one was immune. The men of Hamtramck, a small Polish enclave that had welcomed the big new auto factory, now sat in grimy bars, drinking slivovitz and wondering when "Dodge Main" would reopen. At General Motors, Pierre du Pont muttered, "We are in a receivership of our own." Henry Ford raged against the unnatural stillness in the cavernous Rouge and decided that an international Jewish conspiracy was responsible. The anxiety was palpable. At first, businessmen and bankers had been outwardly confident, proclaiming that the slump—it was resolutely deemed a temporary decline—would pass quickly. All the experience of recent years—the Panic of 1907, the momentary pause in 1913—suggested that the economy would quickly right itself.

By year's end, the ringing resolve had been replaced by faintly desperate exhortations. "Cut out the hard times talk," *Automotive Trade Journal* commanded, "and instigate a policy of optimism which is bound to reflect itself in trade dealings. Conditions are not as gloomy as they appear." In a signed front-page editorial, B. C. Forbes, the business editor of papal majesty, assured the nation's businessmen, "Banks will extend credit to the man who has faith in himself and in his business. Sentiment is contagious. Talk panic and you foster panic. Talk optimism and you inspire optimism. Keep your head and you stand a good chance of keeping your business." The new year had good portents, Forbes assured his disciples, 100,000 of whom would go into bankruptcy in the next twelve months.

The first good sign, all agreed, was the election of Warren Gamaliel Harding, a small-town newspaper publisher who had risen to the United States Senate by dint of faithful, uneventful service to the Republican Party in Ohio. During the presidential campaign, the unpretentious Harding had decided, "America's first need is not heroics, but healing; not nostrums, but normalcy; not revolution, but restoration; not surgery, but serenity." It sounded reassuring, the president-elect judging the economy sound. The nation waited for his inauguration in March and the promised "return to normalcy."

Normalcy meant increased domination of business and industry by fewer and fewer combines, and a return to nineteenth-century capitalism with smug assurance that twentieth-century enlightenment would curb the worst excesses of laissez-faire—despite the Supreme Court's ruling that United States Steel was not to be blamed if it was so large that it could dictate steel prices. Normalcy meant a return to prewar wages and the end of union agitation; unions that called strikes were charged with violating the restraint-of-trade clause of the Sherman Antitrust Act and were held liable for triple damages.

There was special reason for optimism, the financial press pointed out. Beneficent forces had moved into the automotive industry: "The purchase of a big block of the stock of the General Motors Corporation, involving change of control of the property, is also important, and in a double sense. In the first place, it guards against the development of weakness in that quarter, and in the second place it cannot fail to be a stabilizing influence in the automobile industry, which has risen to such great dimensions within a relatively few years."

Du Pont could hardly take comfort in the blessing bestowed upon him. The task ahead was huge, with too few men to assume the burdens. First there was the need to root out Durant's abiding influence in the company. The former president had gone quietly, playing the game to the end, but there were men all around who knew only Durant's way of doing business, men who pulled long faces whenever Sloan talked about rational managerial controls.

Moreover, Durant's ouster had soured a large number of these people, who, whether they considered themselves "Durant men" or not, believed the former president had been badly used. They had gathered one last time at Durant's New York apartment, a sad evening of bittersweet reminiscences for men who had been together so long, through the good times and bad. The dinner was muted, funereal, with Durant the most ebullient of them all. He had given way to tears only briefly, once, tightly hugging his daughter the afternoon he resigned the presidency. Now he was smiling Billy Durant again, optimistic and generous.

"Boys," Durant explained to these friends from the carriage days who had worked their way into the automobile era, "I want you to know the Du Pont company treated me as fine as anybody could treat me. I was trying to support General Motors stock in the market," Durant continued, "and I became overextended." Without Pierre du Pont's help—Durant still could not bring himself to credit the Morgan bank—"the stock would have gone to practically nothing. I would have been broke and you boys who have got your money in General Motors would have been broke."

Unlike Durant, most of the men there were not speculators; they had put their savings into company stock, buying blocks at bargain prices because they believed in themselves, Durant, and the company they were creating. Investing was an act of faith, not a calculated risk, and for most of them their General Motors stock represented a lifetime's reward. Now Durant was asking them to support the Wilmington crowd, to stay with General Motors, even though he was leaving. "I'm sixty," Durant said with a shrug, adding that he would retire with the $6 million he had managed to extricate from the collapse. They should stay on, to rebuild the company and the value of its stock, the value of their own shares.

Still, "there was resentment down the line" toward the new managers, recalled John L. Pratt, the only Du Pont man to be accepted by the men from Flint. For their part, the Du Pont people were wary of Durant's "boys," a suspicion that hardened into distrust six weeks later, when Durant came out of foreshortened retirement to announce the formation of a new automobile company, Durant Motors. Despite Durant's reassurances that he only wanted "to make a real good car, limited to 50,000 per year," Raskob immediately suspected another Chevrolet gambit; the Street was alive with rumors and the prediction that Durant would be back in control within three years. Raskob could believe it. After all, Durant was nothing if not proud. He had thrown out the bankers before, and he might try again, especially with General Motors stock selling so cheaply. Raskob brushed aside Durant's reassurance to Pierre du Pont that he intended no third republic. After all, were Raskob planning such a palace coup, he would try to lull the opposition too.*

---

* Raskob's paranoia was unfounded. Durant launched the auto bearing his name, then followed his proven strategy of adding marques: the Star, the Flint, the Eagle, the

Of all the problems confronting Pierre du Pont on December 1, 1920, when he moved into Durant's Fifty-seventh Street office, the most pressing was a management reorganization of the loose confederation of often competitive firms operating under the General Motors banner. On a trip to Kettering's Dayton, Ohio, facilities at the end of his first week as president, du Pont reviewed Sloan's earlier proposals to realign the management.

With some minor modifications in the grouping of divisions, du Pont approved Sloan's plan. Despite inevitable changes brought on by expansion, that plan remained in effect more than fifty years. Reams have been written about it; business-administration students routinely study it as gospel; and Sloan's model has been adopted by virtually every major corporation in the United States and adapted by foreign companies to fit local circumstances.

Princeton, the Mason truck—all new—and the venerable Locomobile, plucked from bankruptcy. Ever the opportunist, he launched the low-priced Star—the name was no accident—after Henry Ford began to campaign against "the international Jew" in his wholly owned Dearborn *Independent*. The Star was meant to appeal to Jewish buyers who would not want to patronize a notorious anti-Semite, and thus has the distinction of being the only automobile ever sold on presumed ethnic identity. In less than a year, Durant Motors had booked $31 million in orders and Lazarus had risen again. But General Motors stock recovered just as quickly, pricing it beyond Durant's grasp, though as late as 1923 Raskob still was taking elaborate defensive measures. Durant eventually seemed to lose interest in automobiles. In the late 1920s, he gained a national reputation as "the bull of bulls," leading a clutch of investors with billion-dollar assets in the Great Bull Market of the period. Indeed, Durant was the very embodiment of the public's image of the financier of the time, saving fortunes for widows and orphans with transatlantic telephone calls, buying and selling great industries with as much regard as ordering dinner. By 1927, he was rumored to be worth $50 million. The Crash of 1929 apparently brought Durant low, though he reportedly had left the market early in the year. Durant Motors failed in 1933, and Durant publicly pledged to reimburse any investor who had lost money in a Durant venture. It was a last, futile gesture, a promise never honored; Durant himself filed for bankruptcy in 1936, claiming just $250 in assets and debts over $900,000. The next year he was photographed washing dishes, the pictures running in newspapers with the caption "Ex-financier turns dishwasher." Durant was merely showing employees of his newest business venture how he wanted the work done. Durant died in 1947 at the age of eighty-six. For the last three years of his life he had lived in shabby dignity with his wife, Catherine, in a Gramercy Park apartment, supported in part by C.S. Mott, R.S. McLaughlin, John Thomas Smith, and A.P. Sloan, who wrote, ". . . I owe him a great deal. He certainly was the pioneer who started the business as a result of which we have profited handsomely." (See Bernard Weisberger, *The Dream Maker, William C. Durant, Founder of General Motors* [Boston: Little, Brown, 1979], p. 361; Associated Press obituary number 2685, issued November 1, 1938, "for use as needed"; and James Flink, *The Car Culture* [Cambridge, Mass.: MIT Press, 1975], pp. 113–139.)

For all the thick manuals explaining the plan and its operations, Sloan's reorganization was neither original nor very complicated. It depended essentially on the staff-line division of effort developed by the German army in the last quarter of the nineteenth century. Sloan reached that point as a matter of necessity—the need to compromise between what he deemed the Du Pont Company's far too rigid centralization of command and Durant's live-and-let-live doctrines.

Business policy—what might correlate to military strategy—was to be the province of the central office, with staff positions carefully labeled "advisory." Tactics, providing they meshed with overall strategy (policy), would be left to the division managers. To coordinate the efforts of the divisions—sharing new technological developments, cooperative buying of parts and raw materials, advertising—du Pont and Sloan set up semipermanent committees drawn from representatives of the manufacturing divisions and staffed these committees with specialists drawn from the central office. Committee recommendations went to du Pont, then increasingly to Sloan for ratification, before becoming corporate policy.

The staffs controlled the decision-making process, and the staff members themselves were carefully chosen by Sloan. Only they had all the relevant information, which they could parcel out as they wished to influence ultimate decisions. While Sloan was fond of stressing that "General Motors has never been operated as an autocracy; it has been operated as a democracy," in actual practice, decision-making influence and veto power lay with the New York offices.

Keenly aware of the independence that the division managers had cherished under Durant, Sloan retained a measure of that in his reorganization plan. Managers still controlled manufacture, distribution, and sales; did their own hiring; and made their own purchasing decisions.

To implement the reorganization, du Pont and Sloan, newly named as vice-president for operations, first isolated the Durant men from policy-making functions. "Mr. du Pont didn't know, and I didn't know, as to the loyalty of those men," Sloan later explained. His plan transferred the auto-division managers from

the executive committee to a new advisory operations committee. Corporate policy would stem from a group of four: du Pont,
Sloan, Raskob, and a long-time Du Pont executive, J. H. Haskell.

Not all the division managers were happy with the realignment
of authority and what they considered an infringement of their
prerogatives. Fred Hohensee of Chevrolet—"a great driving
force who could get work done, but he didn't care too much how
well it was done"—was the first to leave. "Carload" Collins
abruptly quit Cadillac in March to take over the management of
competitor Peerless. Collins' loss was keenly felt; General
Motors needed salesmen, and Collins was that. The general
managers of the truck division, Oakland, and Oldsmobile were
gone before the end of September. Only Buick's successful
Harry Bassett—a great, friendly man with a face like his canine
namesake—stayed on.

"They tightened up the bolts and got the thing to really stick
together," John L. Pratt recalled, describing the internal upheaval as Sloan and du Pont realigned personnel. By and large,
Sloan selected men with engineering backgrounds, men whom he
believed had the intellectual discipline he favored.

Karl W. Zimmerschied, a Hungarian engineer who had headed
Chevrolet production, was promoted to division manager. In
sixteen months he would work himself to physical and mental
collapse trying to save the underpowered, poorly designed, and
now antiquated Chevrolet. Alexander B.C. Hardy moved from
Chevrolet to the advisory staff's purchasing section and, having
proved himself loyal, finally to Oldsmobile as general manager.
Needing a new head of the export division, Sloan tapped J.D.
Mooney, the president of Remy Electric, and a former mining
engineer who had worked for him earlier at Hyatt Roller Bearings. Mooney's promotion opened the way for Pratt to name
Remy's thirty-one-year-old chief engineer, Charles E. Wilson, as
head of that company. Du Pont's canniest move was to select
R.H. Grant, the president of Delco Light, as Chevrolet's general
sales manager. A veteran of John Patterson's National Cash Register school of high-pressure salesmanship, Grant was to transform automotive huckstering.

The more du Pont and Sloan shuffled and the more they realigned, the worse the morale became. Their biweekly trips to Detroit stretched out long enough for Sloan to order a spartan, hotel-like suite installed in the still-incomplete General Motors office building. Working there at night and visiting the plants by day, du Pont strove to reassure the remaining executives and to explain the reorganization. In time, he beat back the grumbles concerning absentee Eastern ownership—no less than Durant, the men he left behind had more than a little suspicion of bankers, a term that for many in the company quite comfortably stretched to cover chemist-industrialist Pierre S. du Pont.

The Delaware squire also had to contend with rumors that he would move factories eastward, to be closer to the gardens of Longwood. Real-estate prices in Detroit and Flint, already weakened by the recession, tumbled on the whisper. Back to Flint went austere traveling companions Sloan and du Pont to assure local businessmen that no such moves were contemplated. To prove it, General Motors subscribed to $300,000 worth of capital stock in the new Durant Hotel to be built in Flint; the name galled them—they had been virtually blackmailed—but what greater proof could they offer that they intended to stay?

With all their work—Sloan took to carrying his lunch to the office in a neatly folded paper bag—at half a dozen places the hastily thrown-up levee might give way. Pratt was detailed to continue the work begun under Durant to reduce inventories. His first move was to order the division managers to buy nothing and to stop shipments of materials already ordered. Pratt also persuaded suppliers to delay billing the corporation and to withhold lawsuits for noncompliance. One or the other might cripple the corporation before it could be turned around, leaving the suppliers without a good customer. It was a delicate task, for Pratt was, in effect, asking the suppliers to finance the company once again, as suppliers had in the earliest days of the industry. All but one steel mill agreed.

By the end of 1920, the car-building divisions had worked off $32.2 million in inventories; they used up another $6 million during the first quarter of 1921. Pratt might have expected more

progress, but he realized their cars were overpriced and therefore not selling up to expectations. By June, he reported that
Buick, Cadillac, and Oldsmobile were in good shape. Because of
poor sales, Chevrolet was overstocked; Oakland and Samson
Tractor were near collapse under the weight of too-optimistic
buying.

Du Pont, Sloan, and Pratt permitted themselves cautious
smiles. As the spring selling season progressed, they began paying off the $80 million in short-term bank loans that might have
sent the company into receivership. They still had not confronted the price and sales problems, but the sense of desperate
crisis seemed to have waned with the end of winter. They could
turn to long-range planning.

On April 6, 1921, du Pont set up a committee under Sloan's
chairmanship to study the product line-up and to recommend
revision of the lines. Du Pont also retained a group of consulting
engineers to provide the committee with an independent evalua-
tion of General Motors' automobiles—a move that would put
Sloan's committee on its mettle. Du Pont handed his vice-
president for operations one mandate: General Motors was to
enter the low-priced mass market, to compete directly with
Ford.

Sloan resisted. Pierre du Pont had become infatuated with a
new power plant that Charles Kettering had been working on
since 1918 and had decided that Kettering's air-cooled engine
was precisely the bold stroke needed to lure customers away
from Henry Ford. The engine was not revolutionary—the expensive Franklin automobile had used an air-cooled motor for
twenty years—but Kettering was having serious problems with
the shaped copper fins that surrounded each cylinder and passed
off the heat generated by the engine. Even if Kettering proved
that his copper-cooling concept was sound, there were still manufacturing obstacles to be overcome; there always were, Sloan
argued privately.

Making matters more difficult for Sloan, Kettering and du Pont
had hit it off well, perhaps because of their common interest in
chemistry and basic research—Kettering was forever talking

about investigating photosynthesis, why grass was green. Whatever the reason, the voluble Kettering had the president's ear, and a seat on Sloan's committee, where he could lobby for his new motor. In the interests of harmony—at that point the corporation needed it badly—Sloan would have to gag the other committee members. None of them seemed overly impressed with the air-cooled engine.

The report of the outside consultants came as a blow—or, rather, four blows. Chevrolet was in such poor shape that it could not hope "to compete with the market" and should be abandoned, the consultants recommended. Further, General Motors might consider changing the names of the Oldsmobile, Oakland, and Chevrolet because of their poor reputations.

While du Pont weighed the independent consultants' report, Sloan quietly argued against its recommendations. Sloan conceded that Chevrolet was "a mess," Oakland and Oldsmobile were in little better condition. But changing the names would mean, in effect, starting over, and a name change would do nothing to improve the models then being sold. Chevrolet should be continued; if it couldn't compete directly with Ford in price, it might skim off buyers willing to pay a bit more for a better-equipped car. Scuttling any of the divisions, and thus orphaning General Motors automobiles on the road, would alienate those who already owned Chevrolets, Oaklands, and Oldsmobiles. Two-year-old Sheridan, Sloan agreed, could be cut adrift, angering only a handful of owners. The not-yet-released Scripps–Booth could be disposed of easily, the company suffering some embarrassment and getting on with it. The greatest handicap to sales, Sloan insisted, was the sheer obsolescence of their designs, and the new models would obviate that. It would be easier to restore the reputation of the divisions than to build anew.

Before du Pont reached a decision based on the consultants' report, he might wait for a second, even more basic, report, Sloan pointed out. If the automobile lines floundered for another year—that is, if they merely worked off the bloated inventories—they could still count the year a success. Meanwhile, Sloan insisted, rather than changing product names and lopping off any divisions, they would be wiser to settle the broader and more basic policy question of the irrationality of their product lines.

For 1921, General Motors offered seven marques ranging in price from the Chevrolet 490 open roadster at $795 to Cadillac's closed, eight-cylinder behemoth tagged at $5,690. Three of the lines—Chevrolet's FB, Oakland, and Oldsmobile—overlapped in price, competing against each other, since each of the divisions independently set its own prices. Two cars in the line, Scripps–Booth and Sheridan, filled a gap in the pricing structure but had no real identity, no built-in demand, and no dealer organization; establishing those vehicles would divert time and money from the lagging divisions. Chevrolet, Oldsmobile, and Oakland were all sorely outmoded, prewar automobiles lacking the refinements of the previous five years. Only Buick and Cadillac were of good quality and reliability, and so had maintained their market position through the slump.

Du Pont agreed to hold off his decision on restructuring the lines, but Sloan was to incorporate in his final report an automobile *with an air-cooled engine* to challenge Ford. Sloan settled for the half-loaf.

Sloan's committee was made up largely of those he called "automobile men": C.S. Mott, newly named vice-president in charge of car, truck, and parts operations; Harry Bassett of Buick; Chevrolet's new manager, Karl Zimmerschied; Charles Kettering; and the most successful salesman the industry had known till then, Norval A. Hawkins. The one-time Ford sales manager, having fallen from Henry Ford's favor, had turned down a transfer to head the European sales office and abruptly quit. Hawkins was not out of work long; Sloan hired him in June 1920 to join the New York advisory staff as its sales expert.

Through two months of meetings, scheduled between peacemaking trips to the corporation's far-flung factories, the committee refined the corporation's product line. The first decision was the hardest, given their reservations; and the easiest, given du Pont's mandate: General Motors would compete head-to-head with Ford, even though most of the committee members believed it futile. Second, they decided to limit the number of lines, to achieve the maximum in economy of scale. Third, the divisions were not to overlap in prices, not to compete among themselves.

Sloan argued for language that was to have far-reaching effects, language that would be turned against him and his best-laid plans. The proposed policies, he said, would only work if the corporation's automobiles were the equal of the best the competition fielded. If they were competitive, Sloan reasoned, it would not be "*necessary* to lead in design," to gamble on untested innovations. While Sloan considered this an argument only against the air-cooled Chevrolet, that condition, hardened into general policy in later years, would come to dominate corporate thinking: don't innovate.

The committee outlined six price categories, the lowest of which had been mandated by du Pont, and thus effectively reduced the number of lines from seven to five. (Sloan privately intended to assign to Chevrolet two price categories, for if the new air-cooled program faltered, Chevrolet still would be left with a viable model.) To implement the strategy, "we proposed in general that General Motors should place its cars at the top of each price range [the air-cooled car excepted] and make them of such a quality that they would attract sales from below that price, selling to those customers who might be willing to pay a little more for the additional quality, and attract sales also from above that price, selling to those customers who would see the price advantage in a car of close to the quality of higher-priced competition. This amounted to quality competition against cars below a given price tag, and price competition against cars above that price tag."

Demurring from the du Pont mandate, the committee recommended that General Motors not confront Ford head-to-head, but manufacture a vehicle slightly better in quality and priced nearer to $600 rather than the Ford's $400. Chevrolet was to meet that mark; Oakland the $600 to $900 range; a new Buick four-cylinder the $900 to $1,200, effectively cutting out Scripps–Booth, Sheridan, and the four- and six-cylinder Oldsmobiles; the Buick Six from $1,200 to $1,700; the Oldsmobile

Eight from $1,700 to $2,500; and the top-of-the-line Cadillac the $2,500 to $3,500 price range.

For a number of reasons, the price categories never would be quite as discrete as Sloan's committee imagined, and the separation of automobile lines never as clear as envisioned. With shifting market conditions, the relative ranking of Oakland, Buick, and Oldsmobile would be scrambled; only Chevrolet and Cadillac would hold the sales positions assigned to them in 1921.

Meanwhile, Sloan and Hawkins struggled with the biggest of their sales problems: trying to determine if the industry had reached the saturation point. Their uncertainty mocked all the numbers Sloan compiled. The Fordists—Hawkins understood them well—pointed to ever-rising production and sales figures, arguing that steadily decreasing prices would steadily widen the potential market. Let the others complain; Henry Ford's market was not saturated and wouldn't be until every man, woman, and child of driving age owned an automobile.

Sloan fretted. Ford's success, his ability to sell 60 percent or more of all automobiles manufactured that year, meant there was less to be shared by other companies. The number of active automobile firms had declined steadily since the war and would fall even further, from 154 in 1920 to eighty-six three years later.* But in 1921 thirty of the eighty-six companies assembled less than 1,000 cars each, catering to limited, mostly carriage-trade customers. Many of these firms were in desperate condition, unable to keep pace by expanding sales and advertising to reach a national market. Even larger firms were not immune. Chandler and Briscoe, once formidable competitors, had folded. Maxwell, the last survivor of Benjamin Briscoe's ill-fated United States Motors combine, was in the hands of bankers; Walter Chrysler was taking it over, reorganizing it for the new owners. J. Dallas Dort, Durant's former partner from the carriage days,

---

* Estimates of the number of automobile manufacturers during this period vary due to definitions of "active" and "inactive" companies, usually based on attendance at the annual New York Automobile Show. The United States Census of Manufactures is no great help; it lumps automobile manufacturers with parts and accessories producers. The figures cited here are drawn from the May 1, 1925, issue of *Motor* magazine and the *Literary Digest* for May 16, 1925. By 1925, there were just forty-nine manufacturers, of which only sixteen seemed assured of survival, *Motor* concluded.

would announce he was liquidating, even after selling 85,000 vehicles in 1922. These were parlous times, and Durant's seemingly scattershot marketing of many lines to appeal to the widest possible corporate market seemed more justified than ever—especially with Oakland, Oldsmobile, and Chevrolet scarcely turning profits.

The crucial question was the market itself, for if the saturation point had been reached, or if it were close, new sales techniques, heavier advertising budgets, and greater persuasion would be required. General Motors' dealers would take on new importance, and *their* survival, too, would be important. Had they passed the saturation point? Were they still selling to people buying their first car, or to people replacing automobiles?

The answers were never clear. Sloan commissioned a private firm to gather nationwide automobile registration figures on a monthly basis and demanded more reports from the corporation's traveling field representatives. He created a general sales committee to ponder the saturation problem, for as late as March 1924, Sloan did not yet understand what had happened in dealers' showrooms.

The engineer in Sloan was affronted by the lack of precise information; engineers needed statistical tables, not vague shrugs or tentative guesses. Increasingly, Sloan turned from the division heads, who invariably were too optimistic in their forecasts, to rely instead on two unflinching financial experts.

Donaldson Brown and Albert Bradley were among the first of a new generation of financial specialists, men who cared little about machines and manufacture and even less about such intangibles as excitement or the romance of the industry. Trained as economists and accountants, they were hard-eyed, coldly dispassionate champions of financial analysis and, through analysis, control. They cared not whether the companies for which they worked produced steel thimbles or steel tanks; the principles of sound investment were the same—if they could but be discovered.

Oddly, the first and perhaps still the most influential of these analysts was a graduate electrical engineer who had gone to work reluctantly for E.I. du Pont de Nemours only because he could not find a job anywhere else. Donaldson Brown's tobacco-growing family had hated the "upstart" du Ponts almost as much as they favored the Confederacy, and Brown's father made the young man promise to quit as soon as Brown found another job.

Young Brown never did. Though the du Ponts considered the Browns "poor white trash," the chemical engineer from Maryland's Eastern Shore—across the bay from the du Ponts of Delaware—had flourished in the enemy camp. Truly gifted, Brown had worked his way up in the Du Pont organization, coming to executive attention with a report on the efficiency of the various factories comprising the powder works. Characteristically, the report emphasized capital turnover and profit margins as measured against corporate investment. Brown was detailed as "junior assistant treasurer—very junior" to Du Pont's finance department, headed then by treasurer Pierre S. du Pont, and seconded by John Raskob.

When Pierre du Pont became corporate president and Raskob treasurer, Brown moved up a notch. He replaced Raskob as treasurer, the good, gray corporate loyalist dutiful of service. Five years later, General Motors in desperate need of Brown's organizational talents, he transferred to the automobile company.

Because du Pont and Raskob believed General Motors needed the sort of financial controls that Brown had implanted at Du Pont industries—and the economists and statisticians he favored as coworkers—Donaldson Brown was named vice-president in charge of finance. Within weeks, the large-scale charts and graphs he brought to executive meetings and his pedantic lectures delivered with barely disguised impatience had established him as the company's most influential financial figure. "He is the brains of General Motors, but doesn't speak any known language," a senior executive later complained. Sloan served as Brown's translator.

Raskob would continue to deal with external financing, more closely scrutinized by Pierre du Pont, but he no longer would be the pre-eminent financial figure. Du Pont realized just how responsible his good friend John Raskob was for what they called "the Durant debacle," even if he never mentioned it. Though Raskob remained on the board for eight more years, his interest in General Motors waned in favor of Wall Street and national politics.

Quickly enough, the stiff-necked Brown recruited an ally, one of the few besides Sloan to grasp immediately the economically sophisticated controls Brown intended to implant. Young Albert Bradley had graduated Phi Beta Kappa from Dartmouth, held a doctorate in economics, and was teaching at the University of Michigan when Brown hired him to be the corporation's first statistician. If the friendly, cheerful Bradley found Brown's reserve hard to penetrate, it did not stop the two from working together effectively. They tended to divide the labor, with Brown working on theory and planning while Bradley adapted that theory to the reality of an automobile manufacturer faced with outstanding loans of $70 million in 1922, three sickly automobile lines, and a coterie of hostile executives.

Within five years, Brown and Bradley gave to the corporation two abiding strategies that would survive, with little modification, for the next fifty years. Brown created the concept of "standard volume," a method by which the company could avoid price adjustments upon its products, ignore seasonal variations (winter was still a slack period, despite closed cars carving out ever-larger shares of the market), and surmount the precipitous annual spikes and plunges in sales with steady profits. Brown was keenly troubled by the industry's rush to expand production capacity and the reality of idle factories draining away profits.

The great advantage of Brown's scheme to generate "the highest return consistent with attainable volume" was that the company could ignore temporary demand factors and still produce a handsome profit. General Motors intended to repeal one of the presumably inviolate laws of classical economics: prices rise and fall in relation to demand.

Brown's cautious "standard volume" plan asserted that in its best years General Motors was to operate at less than full production capacity. In an average year, it would produce and sell even fewer cars. The price of General Motors cars and trucks, the "standard price"—including a generous 20-percent return on investment—was to be figured on the average year's production.

Beyond that, in those years when the company sold more than the average, its profits would soar, since prices had been figured on lower production runs and thus higher overhead burdens on each car. By adopting conservative estimates of production—he hypothesized that in an average year General Motors would sell only enough vehicles to keep its factories running 64 percent of the time—Brown assured General Motors profits in even the worst of times. Some years would be better than others, but over a five-year span investors would annually reap an average 20-percent return on investment.

While Brown worked out the concept of standard volume that was to determine General Motors' pricing policies, Albert Bradley sought to forecast future demand and the actual production capacity the company would need. Begun first as an effort to find the elusive saturation point, the final study correlated automobile demand with income distribution in the nation; later this would be refined to be a correlation of automobile sales with overall economic activity.

Bradley attempted to feed into a "pyramid of demand" as many variables as he could obtain, building what would be called an "economic model" in the computer age a half-century later. In doing so, Bradley discovered one of the abiding truths of national prosperity, the factor that would make the automobile industry the bellwether of the economy: ". . . when business, and hence national income, was on an ascending trend, car sales increased at an even faster rate than income; and when business was on a declining trend, sales decreased at a faster rate than income." Bradley would continue to tinker with his formula, especially after he badly missed forecasting a downturn in 1924. One factor he would never quite master: the effect of changes in public taste, and especially the role of women in shaping those changes.

It baffled General Motors, the subtle, changing influence of women on automobile sales. Neither Bradley, Sloan, nor any of the executives had any experience to rely upon, for until this time the purchase of an automobile involved choosing among mechanical marvels, a task the industry assumed to be men's work, beyond the capacity of the frail sex. By the end of World War I, however, attitudes had changed. The automobile was no longer a wonderment; mechanical failure was not something to be tolerated as a concomitant to adventuring along rural lanes. Stressing the need for a research-and-testing laboratory, Kettering argued, "At first, when cars were novelties, people were interested in what made them go. Now they want to be unconscious of the mechanism."

Attitudes toward women also were changing. Women had filled production-line jobs during the war, and while "Tillie the Toiler" was largely replaced once the veterans were discharged, the "helpless" woman was an anachronistic conceit. Universal suffrage, gained in 1920, was in part belated recognition of women's contributions to the war effort—and a token of further change. Occupations closed to women opened grudgingly. Once confined to the role of homemaker, women in increasing numbers were working—some by choice, some by chance (the divorce rate would triple between 1890 and 1930). Widespread dissemination of birth-control information and the introduction of such labor-saving devices as the washing machine and the gas stove freed women from household drudgery.

A potential new market opened for automobile sales. "Is your wife marooned during the day?" a Chevrolet ad asked its male readers in 1921. Because men used the family car to go to work, the advertisement continued, "Architects and builders now find that all suburban and many city homes must be provided with twin garages." Families needed an "extra car. The wife finds it of everyday utility for shopping, calling, taking the children to school in bad weather, etc."

But women demanded more of the automobile than men did. A self-starter was mandatory, a closed body preferable; easier access—that is, automobile bodies with lower axles and running boards—appealed. Women also favored automobiles with lower roof lines (yet adequate headroom for hats), adjustable seats (their legs were shorter than their husbands'), and less-cumbersome gear shifts and steering.

Most of all, women sought grace. "Man made the automobile;

woman tamed it. Man utilized it; woman has socialized it,"
wrote Madelaine Ritza in an industrial journal. An unaccustomed attention to interior appointments confronted manufacturers, and spartan accommodations gave way to detailing that
virtually transformed the automobile into "an upholstered, silk-
curtained hallway between the boudoir and the theater," Ritza
enthused. "No manufacturer ever perfected the appointments of
his car to the extent of silver-plated handles and holders with
their vases of delicate cut glass, silk curtains and inlaid woodwork in the hope of pleasing the masculine heart."

As early as 1917, Edward S. Jordan, who marketed his Sports
Marine model as "essentially a women's car," made the telling
observation: "While men buy the cars, women choose them."
Those choices might be fickle and seemingly unpredictable, but
manufacturers could not ignore them. If blue cars sold this year,
manufacturers had to make blue cars; if yellow were the favored
color the next year, auto makers could continue to produce blue
automobiles only at the risk of financial disaster.

Over the years, women's influence would grow steadily. The
internal detailing of the automobile would become so important
that by 1968 General Motors would employ 3,500 stylists, including four women whose sole task was to choose fabrics and colors
for seats and padding that presumably would appeal to their sex.
(At the same time, the company would employ only 1,500 people
to work on all technological improvements.)

While Sloan's newly created central staff grappled with long-
range policies, the automobile divisions struggled with the immediate problem of dealing off their high inventories. As bad as
1920 had been for General Motors, 1921 was worse. In January,
the entire corporation sold just 6,150 cars. The managers' self-
reassurances had a hollow ring; what if sales didn't pick up in the
spring? Ford was going back to work on a limited basis, rehiring
5,000 of the 60,000 men laid off in the fall. Ford's price cut of
September was moving Model-T's, while General Motors stood
pat, waiting for warm weather.

Ford's production increased steadily. By March, both the
Rouge and Highland Park plants were back on a six-day week,

turning out 72,000 of the 105,000 motorcars and trucks produced that month by the entire industry. General Motors hung in the doldrums while Ford launched a savage speed-up that would characterize the automobile industry for generations to come. "Increased labor efficiency," a polite euphemism for the inexorably moving assembly lines, "has made it possible to operate the plant at approximately 80 percent of capacity with 60 percent of the normal labor quota," *Automotive Industries* benignly reported. Bone-weary men, frightened by the long winter layoff and knowing that work was still scarce, made Ford's September price cut possible. The speed-up would grind on, growing faster and growing worse for three more years, with production reaching 8,000 and then 9,000 automobiles per day.

Rueful auto workers joked of six pallbearers carrying Henry Ford's coffin, all drawing six-dollar-per-day wages, when the corpse sat up and barked, "What the hell is this? You call this efficiency? Put this thing on wheels! Lay five of these birds off and cut the other one's wages, 'cause the work is easy and the hours ain't long, and the pace is slow."

Ford plant executives competed for the old man's favor by the production figures they could wring from driven men. The image of Ford as the Enlightened Industrialist faded. In the smoky jukes and blind pigs of Black Chicago, bluesmen sang:

Say, I'm goin' to Detroit, I'm gonna get myself a job,
I'm tired of layin' around here workin' on this starvation farm.

Say, I'm goin' to get me a job now, workin' in Mr. Ford's place.
Say, that woman told me last night, "Say, you cannot even stand Mr.
  Ford's ways."

Warm weather came; buyers did not. One by one, the holdouts realized that their prices were too high and reluctantly began cutting them. Edward Jordan chopped $400 from his sporty Playboy. Dort and Maxwell followed. Marmon trimmed its lavish touring-car price by 20 percent, to $4,000.

Still Pierre du Pont held out. Price-cutting was foreign to his business experience; the chemical industry, joined informally in a vast international cartel, avoided unseemly battles in the marketplace based on anything so crass as the dollar. Frustrated division managers, ordered to freeze their prices, pleaded with Sloan, Pratt, Mott, anyone who would listen. Through April sales lagged as customers sought bargains elsewhere, but du Pont and Raskob remained adamant.

Finally du Pont relented, deciding to take his inventory losses in one great gulp, to clear the way for future profits. General Motors lowered prices from 11 to 21 percent through the month of May. The distressed Chevrolet fell to $645 for its cheapest model. Ford responded promptly, clipping another $25 from his touring car, opening up a $230 gap between his cherished Model-T and the upstart Chevrolet.

Despite the company's losses and the promise of more to come, du Pont felt more confident. General Motors was through "a most disquieting period," and despite his own acutely felt lack of knowledge about the burgeoning automobile business, du Pont felt more the master of the enterprise. He was getting reliable statistics—not always encouraging ones, but comforting in their reliability—and in such things the methodical du Pont took solace. Furthermore, he wrote the house of Morgan, "I am convinced that errors in expenditures are not as great as we had feared; in fact, I would not be surprised to find all the permanent investment [in plants and machinery] usable in a profitable way."

Du Pont's spirits rose. For all the travel, all the financial discussions with Raskob in their shared weekday suite at the Carlton Hotel in New York City, and all the tension of meetings in which each new decision was more critical than the last, du Pont was enjoying himself.

Once he was committed to what amounted to the industry's first price war, du Pont tried again. Chevrolet dropped to $625, General Motors losing $50 on each vehicle sold. While the Model-T went as low as $415, the gap was not as bad as it seemed, Sloan argued. The Chevrolet came equipped with demountable rims and a self-starter, both extra on the Ford; so the car was probably only $90 to $100 more expensive than the Model-T, just where Sloan's new pricing policy positioned them.

Aware of the narrowing gap and running at full capacity, Ford reduced his touring car another $60 in September, to a price of $355, or five dollars less than the same car had sold for in 1916. Chevrolet sales collapsed. By the end of 1921, Ford had garnered 62 percent of the 1.6 million autos sold, while all of General Motors had a total of but 14 percent. Chevrolet alone lost $8.7 million, selling a minuscule 4 percent of the industry's output. Stricken with fatal engineering flaws—a weak rear axle and drive shaft, its styling undistinctive—the Chevrolet hardly appeared to be a serious sales challenger to prosperous Buick, let alone mammoth Ford.

General Motors' annual report offered investors little encouragement. The corporation recorded a loss of $38.6 million, the first and last deficit in its history. But ledger sheets did not tell the entire story, du Pont and Sloan privately assured the bankers. In their first year, the new corporation heads had shored up or removed weak managers, curbed the runaway divisions, and ordered the chaos left in Durant's wake. They had settled on their permanent line, though anemic Samsom Tractor remained a problem. (Du Pont still nursed a belief that a market could be found for the tractor once farm prices turned upward. He would not agree to abandon the feeble machine for another six months, thus delaying another $27 million inventory write-off until 1922, when it would be more than made up by the profitable divisions.) Frigidaire showed promise, once a few mechanical problems were corrected, insisted its corporate defender, the reliable John Pratt. The divisions were working on new designs; by 1923, all but Chevrolet would have new models, the first in seven years. The air-cooled engine would soon make Chevrolet profitable.

Even the cautious Donaldson Brown conceded that there might be reason for optimism.

9

Waiting for the Circus

"Horse apples!" Alfred P. Sloan bellowed behind the locked door of his austere office. Secretaries he treated so deferentially at other times knew better than to interrupt the vice-president's periodic tantrums. This one was worse than most; they could hear Sloan's gravelly voice far down the halls of the fourteenth floor of the General Motors Building in Detroit.

Sloan raged at the delays and the wasted energy. The air-cooled engine had seduced Pierre du Pont and diverted the entire corporation. Sloan's plans to bring out new models awaited Kettering's long-promised engine. First George Hannum wanted it—he wanted anything to help his flagging Oakland—then he did not. Electric welding of the copper fins to the iron cylinders appeared too chancy for an assembly line. Alex Hardy considered it for Oldsmobile, in either a four- or six-cylinder version; then he, too, shied away. Chevrolet's Zimmerschied had rebelled until he suffered a physical breakdown and was hospitalized.

Only Zimmerschied's replacement, the new vice-president in

charge of Chevrolet's production lines, William Knudsen, seemed to think the air-cooled engine was within grasp. But that was encouragement enough for Pierre du Pont. After all, Bill Knudsen knew automobiles. He had built more motor vehicles than all of General Motors' division managers put together and had done it faster, so fast that even Henry Ford later would grudgingly concede that the former Danish bicycle mechanic was a "wizard of mass production." The men in the shop had another name to explain his wizardry: the "Speed-up King."

Signius Wilhelm Poul Knudsen was a bewildered twenty-year-old when he debarked at Hoboken, New Jersey, in 1899, confused by the immigration officer's shouted "Hurry up!" only learning later what the words meant, and, relishing their meaning, using them the rest of his life as an incantation that insured success. The son of a Danish customs inspector, the fifth of nine children, the beefy Knudsen—he stood six feet, three inches tall and weighed 235 pounds—had apprenticed as a bicycle mechanic in his native Copenhagen. Dissatisfied with the opportunities for a young man with only a degree from a technical school, and convinced by a few amateur fights that his pugilistic skills would not earn him a comfortable living, Knudsen had bought steerage passage to the United States.

With thirty dollars in his pocket to insure that he would not become a public charge, and obviously in good health, Knudsen cleared immigration. He found work in a Bronx shipyard—a laborer's job that paid $1.75 a day—his size his only recommendation. He needed no English for the task of reaming out rivet holes in steel plates, but Signius Wilhelm Poul did not intend to stay long in the shipyards.

Knudsen's first task was to relearn the pedagogic English he had studied in high school. In the evenings, the hulking laborer with the huge hands hunkered down on his brownstone stoop to learn from the children who played on the Bronx streets. In time, his English became excellent, though his accent remained. The accent bothered him, and to mask it, to avoid the smirks, he spoke little. Coworkers mistook his reticence for shyness; he was not shy, just more comfortable with machines than with people, paperwork, or politics. Knudsen became a man of few words, mostly profane; in later years he would refuse to have female secretaries for fear he would have to watch his language.

Within a year of his arrival, his English serviceable, Knudsen took a job repairing locomotives in the Erie Railroad shops at Salamanca, New York. After riveting boilers there for a year, he applied for a job as a bench hand at the John R. Keim Mills in Buffalo. Knudsen had experience in both of Keim's products: bicycles, two hundred a day, and a small, none-too-effective steam engine to be mounted on a wagon built in England. Refusing to struggle with "Signius Wilhelm Poul," the timekeeper entered him on the payroll as "Bill Knudsen," and William S. Knudsen he remained.

Keim Mills was expanding to meet the orders coming in for automobile parts from small firms in Michigan. The Olds Motor Works of Lansing wanted 4,000 brake drums, and the newly dubbed Bill Knudsen eventually was put to work on that. In 1906 Knudsen developed a method for forming and drawing steel, then went off to Detroit to underbid on a Ford contract for $75,000 in crankcases and rear-axle housings.

Partially due to Knudsen's production skills, Keim Mills had become one of the auto industry's major suppliers of pressed-steel parts when Henry Ford bought the company in 1911 and raised the salary of its twenty-nine-year-old assistant superintendent to $600 per month. Knudsen promptly married Clara Euler, who was to be the moderating force in his otherwise hard-driving life. It was she who cautioned Knudsen about his language and lectured him about his temper. Years later, an awed *Fortune* magazine unknowingly praised her polishing job: "Knudsen's physical presence is thrilling; it is like being in the room with a well-dressed and highly intelligent polar bear who speaks with a low, liquid accent." The docile bear of later years weekly vented six days of accumulated anger by hammering Sousa marches on the family xylophone during Sunday musicales.

In 1913, Ford ordered the Keim Mills moved to Detroit, and with them the assistant superintendent. The move completed quickly, Ford assigned Knudsen to the task of organizing and laying out new Model-T assembly plants as they opened. Knudsen outfitted fourteen identical factories in a two-year period, while his salary rose to $50,000 a year.

Knudsen was largely credited for the speed-up of Ford's production during World War I, when Model-T output more than doubled. "I learned to shout 'Hurry up' in fifteen languages," he later boasted. Once the United States entered the war, Knudsen took over production of the 204-foot-long Eagle submarine chasers under a $46 million government contract, building sixty of them in the first shops erected at the new River Rouge plant.

At the war's end, Ford turned his attention to Europe, detailing Knudsen to reorganize operations on that continent. In the process, Knudsen set up three more factories to assemble the Model-T from imported parts, one of them in his native Copenhagen. He was not a man to deny his roots.

The more Knudsen seemed to accomplish, the more dissatisfied Henry Ford became. Ford wanted no other giants about him; as big as the company was, there was room for only one titan. Even Ford's son Edsel would be brought to heel, reduced to serving King Henry, though Edsel realized the company was choking under his father's smothering hand.

Inevitably—for virtually all of Ford's ablest executives eventually left the company—the two men parted. There was dissatisfaction on both sides. Knudsen's colorful vocabulary offended Ford, who wanted men about him who neither smoked nor drank and certainly did not profane the Lord. Knudsen did all three. At the same time, Knudsen was continually irritated to find his orders as production manager summarily countermanded by Ford himself. Knudsen could hardly object to Ford wanting to run the company he now owned totally, but he refused to accept what amounted to repeated public rebukes. A clash was inevitable, he told his wife: "I can't avoid it if I stay, and I can't stay and keep my self-respect."

There were other irritants. Knudsen believed the Model-T was fast running its course, that the company needed a new automobile. Ford himself would have none of it; his car could sell indefinitely, he believed, so long as they could maintain production and keep cutting prices. The company could even afford to lose money on the basic automobile, for it turned an average profit of

$40 on accessories for each new Model-T, including self-starters, demountable rims, balloon tires, windshields, tops, gas gauges, and half a hundred other devices. Finally, there was a virgin market yet to be tapped, since half of America's families lacked automobiles. More production, along with price cuts, would make it possible for even those living on the national median income of $1,500 to buy a new automobile.

On February 28, 1921, Knudsen finally quit the Ford Motor Company. It was not a good time to be job-hunting, even for an executive of Knudsen's caliber. Knudsen spent ten months working as general manager of a stove factory that was converting to full-time production of automobile parts. Frustrated, he found the horizons too limiting; for, after all, he had whipped factories to produce more than 800,000 vehicles in a single year.

Knudsen approached C.S. Mott, vice-president of the accessories division of General Motors and Alfred Sloan's lieutenant. Mott hired Knudsen instantly to serve on the newly organized advisory staff, to make production suggestions to the division general managers.

Sloan knew Knudsen from earlier days, when Sloan had peddled Hyatt roller bearings to Ford, and he knew Knudsen's reputation as a punishing production man. Knudsen himself conceded that he had hounded Sloan "pretty hard for shipments."

"How much shall we pay you, Mr. Knudsen?" the saturnine Sloan asked.

Knudsen shrugged. "Anything you like. I am not here to set a figure. I seek an opportunity."

"How much did Mr. Ford pay you?"

"Fifty thousand dollars."

Sloan offered $6,000. One month later, he moved Knudsen to the lagging Chevrolet division as production vice-president to replace the worn-out Karl Zimmerschied. Knudsen's salary was to be $30,000 a year.

Knudsen effectively took charge of Chevrolet. Du Pont was far too preoccupied with the larger corporation; he held the title of president of Chevrolet only to push the copper-cooled engine into speedy production.

Knudsen's first year coincided with a general upturn in business. Even Chevrolet, without a new model, did well, helping General Motors convert the losses of 1921 into a $60 million profit in 1922. The corporation sold just over 450,000 vehicles—well behind Ford, but still 18 percent of the industry's production that year.

Knudsen promised that 1923 would be an even better year, though Chevrolet's improvements for the season consisted primarily of a new name—the "Superior." Priced at $510 for the two-passenger roadster, this "people's car . . . for the world's workers" was the first Chevrolet to implement the Sloan–Hawkins strategy of attacking the Model-T from above. "Pay a little less and you get much less," the company trumpeted, elliptically referring to the Ford.

Unimpressed with advertising executive Bruce Barton's claim for the Superior, Knudsen agreed it was "almost the perfect low-priced car—and it will really become perfect next year when we make one small change."

"What change?" Barton asked.

"We're just going to hang a small hammock under the chassis. Catch all the goddamn parts that fall out," a straight-faced Knudsen replied.

The Chevrolet was then seven years old, a relic long overdue for replacement, Knudsen told Sloan. If they would only decide what to do with Kettering's air-cooled engine, he would be able to get on with the production of a new model. Nevertheless, the more Sloan and du Pont discussed it, the more Sloan resisted. They were risking too much—$28 million on new plants—for an unproved, balky engine requiring a demanding new production technology, he argued. Of all the division managers and engineers, only Knudsen remained loyal, promising production of 500 copper-cooled automobiles a month by the end of 1922, in time for the 1923 season.

Knudsen's assurance was enough. Pierre du Pont, who rarely evinced anything approaching a smile, was openly delighted. "I am beginning to feel like a small boy when the long-expected circus posters begin to appear on the fences, and to wonder how each part of the circus is to appear and what act I will like best," he wrote the equally excited Kettering.

Yet even the capable Knudsen was having production difficulties. He managed to turn out 250 of the new air-cooled automobiles in time for the January 1923 New York Automobile Show, where the car predictably caused a gratifying stir. It was lighter and easier to maintain without a water-cooling system, and the engine got better mileage than conventional engines during Kettering's test rides around Dayton. The car cost $200 more than the Superior, but that cost inevitably would come down as Knudsen switched from the old to the new model.

The truth, slow to come to euphoric Pierre du Pont, shook him profoundly when it did. He and his brothers, Lammot and Irénée, and a handful of close friends—among them Seward Prosser and Philip Cook, the Episcopal bishop of Delaware—had received gifts of the air-cooled cars. They drove them through the first two months of the year, reporting successive problems to the suddenly sobered du Pont. The engine overheated, even in cold weather, misfired, and quickly lost compression and power.

The cooling system, so fine in theory, was not efficient enough. Kettering had made a classic mistake. The cool air entered the engine housing from the bottom and was expelled through the top, warming as it moved upward to the hottest part of the motor, the cylinders. Had Kettering designed the automobile to take in the cool air from the top, and expel it from the bottom, he might well have wrought the revolution he envisioned.

The polite criticisms of the Delaware squires were drowned out by the angry complaints from 350 field representatives and dealers driving air-cooled cars to stimulate sales, and, more important, from 100 customers who had snapped up the new Chevrolet by March. Knudsen moved quickly, recalling all the air-cooled automobiles. Only a handful survived the mass dumping into Lake Erie, including the car given to Henry Ford for his automobile collection. Bill Knudsen knew better than to ask Ford for anything; besides, there was even a perverse pleasure in dealing off such a balky machine to his former boss.

Pierre du Pont now realized that he had made a grave error in the air-cooled controversy, a mistake of which he felt ashamed in retrospect. He had become too personally involved in the copper-cooled engine's development, for whatever reasons. A last triumph to gild his reputation as an industrialist? The need to prove his judgment one last time? It didn't matter. Sloan was right; he had been right all along.

Du Pont's reappraisal was unsparing of himself. Despite the failure of the air-cooled engine, the corporation was in far better shape than it had been prior to the recession. The losses of 1920–21 had been concentrated in just ten of the corporation's thirty-four divisions; those ten had been reorganized, or in the case of the worst, such as Samson Tractor, discontinued. Du Pont and Sloan had installed firm financial and inventory controls, though the managers still tended to run off on their own, as Sloan complained. To remedy that, Sloan had suggested creating an executive vice-president with direct authority over the divisions. Only his own pettiness, du Pont acknowledged to himself, had kept him previously from appointing Sloan to the position the man so obviously wanted—and deserved. That was no way to manage a corporation worth almost a billion dollars.

Once recovered, General Motors had sent its stock prices climbing; investor confidence in motors appeared again. Du Pont's reassuring day-to-day presence was no longer vital for the investors, if it was needed at all. Sloan had been the steadier, more rational of the two of them, du Pont now understood, and had proven himself more than competent to assume active direction of the corporation. Du Pont could retain his chairmanship of the board of directors to maintain a watch on the 43-percent ownership E.I. du Pont de Nemours held, but it would be a more distant, less time-consuming overview. While du Pont's relationship with Sloan was more formal than cordial—they managed to call each other Pierre and Alfred—the two men generally agreed on business matters. Moreover, Sloan had built a solid staff, with a reassuring number of former E.I. du Pont executives who bespoke continued administrative sobriety. Du Pont had never intended his joint tenure as president and chairman to be permanent anyway. What better time to retire from the more demanding of the two posts, return to the gardens at Longwood, now blooming with spring, and take up the school reforms again?

On May 8, 1923, du Pont broached his retirement with an eager Sloan. Two days later, du Pont resigned, recommending to the board of directors that Alfred P. Sloan, Jr., vice-president in charge of operations, be named president of General Motors. The board ratified du Pont's decision. On May 21, Sloan was elected a director of E.I. du Pont de Nemours, binding the two corporations more closely.

Once installed, Sloan moved quickly. Before the end of May, he scuttled Oldsmobile's six-cylinder, air-cooled engine and directed that the division prepare a new model with a conventional engine. Before the end of June, Knudsen had ended Chevrolet's experimentation on the new engine.

Kettering was sorely wounded. He had vested energy and pride in the air-cooled concept, and now these hardheaded men had rejected it, and him. Dejected, "completely discouraged," according to one friend, Kettering wrote a letter of resignation:

My only regret, in severing my connection with the Corporation, would be the wonderful association I have had with yourself [*sic*], Mr. du Pont, Mr. Mott and others. There are many possibilities for work of the kind which I can do in industries where the problems which exist in getting new things over are not quite as difficult as in the motor industry.

Sloan suddenly faced his first crisis as president. He knew that Pierre du Pont was distressed by the abrupt termination of the air-cooled-engine project and now by the threat of losing Kettering. General Motors needed a research component as much as did Du Pont industries. If only the antiknock "doping compound" that he was working on panned out, Kettering would easily recoup the losses on the copper-cooled engine. Furthermore, if Kettering resigned, he would be free to patent automobile improvements General Motors would pay dearly to use; for all his bookish ways, Kettering was a shrewd businessman.

Sloan sought a diplomatic solution. In the face of an expanding market, he could not hold up competitive models to await uncertain developments while Studebaker, Dodge, Durant, or Chrysler ate into General Motors' sales. Beyond that, Sloan told

Kettering, it was not his policy to bring pressure on the divisions to adopt unwanted mechanical innovations. (That stance would be modified repeatedly in the years to come when Sloan himself wanted one of the automotive divisions to toe the mark.)

Conscious of the gap that yawned between Kettering, the laboratories, and Pierre du Pont on one hand, and the divisions and himself on the other, Sloan proposed a compromise. He suggested transferring development of the air-cooled engine to a new General Motors Research Corporation to be set up in Dayton. The new company would be staffed and managed by Kettering, with a raise in pay to $120,000, which was $20,000 more than Sloan himself made. It would be a small price to pay for keeping du Pont's hopes alive, however faintly, while retaining Kettering.

Kettering accepted the compromise, complaining that "accounting always kills research" and only grudgingly cooperating with the automobile divisions. To Sloan's pleasure, the copper-cooled car faded as an issue. Within a year, they were "Alfred" and "Ket" once again.

The unburdened Sloan turned to selling automobiles in what was to become a watershed year. For most of 1923, General Motors ran at capacity while the industry's production surpassed four million cars and trucks for the first time. Here were boom times again. Memories of the grim postwar recession were obliterated by ever-rising sales figures. The automobile industry luxuriated in optimistic predictions of the future. Finance, production, and, above all, selling—selling the nation on prosperity itself, on its divinely granted bounty—consumed businessmen. America believed in uplift, in progress. Prosperity was within everyone's grasp, the received wisdom of an age of untrammeled free enterprise.

The decade would be known popularly as the "Roaring Twenties," a time of increasing affluence and supreme confidence in the nation's grand get-rich-quick economy. As late as 1928, the campaigning Herbert Hoover assured his fellow pilgrims, "We shall soon with the help of God be within sight of the day when poverty will be banished from the nation." The attempted looting of oil reserves in the Teapot Dome scandal and rampant corruption in the Harding administration barely dampened the American carnival. Most voters preferred to believe that the philosophy of the Republican Party, the party of good times, stood above the corrupt politicians who had taken advantage of their good friend, the president of the United States. Even the death of the scandal-stricken Harding in August 1923 did not slow what had become a biblically sanctioned crusade for riches. The new president—"what you call a close chewer and a tight spitter," drawled Will Rogers—was no less committed than his predecessor to a complacent acceptance of an economy run amok; Calvin Coolidge assured his constitutents, "The chief business of the American people is business." The nation, or the affluent half, rejoiced; Warren Gamaliel Harding lived on in spirit. The stock market soared, sure proof that all was well in the world.*

By the end of 1923, the automobile industry had demolished previous sales records. The wholesale value of its products, $3.16 billion, ranked it for the first time as the largest industry in the country, surpassing steel by $9 million. The economy would never be the same. Motor vehicles loomed as the driving force behind the nation's prosperity. According to the Census of Manufactures, 351 automobile factories directly employed 318,000 workers in assembling cars and trucks; another 3.1 million people indirectly owed their weekly salaries and wages to the internal-combustion engine. The automobile devoured 10 percent of all tin, iron, and steel produced; half of the plate glass; 80 percent of all rubber; and 14 percent of the hardwood logged. The average car owner spent $500 annually to operate his Nash, Oldsmobile, or Packard. All this was new wealth, created by an industry that just twenty years earlier hardly deserved the label "industry."

* The messianic fervor reached a nadir of bad taste with the publication of advertising executive Bruce Barton's *The Man Nobody Knows,* the best-selling nonfiction book for both 1925 and 1926. Barton pictured Christ as "the most popular dinner guest in Jerusalem" and a superior administrator who "picked up twelve men from the bottom ranks of business and forged them into an organization that conquered the world." Jesus was thus "the founder of modern business," and were there a Second Coming, "He would be a national advertiser today." For the "Gospel According to Bruce Barton" and other religio-economic glosses, see Frederick Lewis Allen, *Only Yesterday,* reprint edition (New York, 1964), p. 149.

The giddy prosperity bemused even the dispassionate Donaldson Brown and Albert Bradley. Both discounted the disquieting figures buried under the roseate sales reports and the ever more optimistic estimates for the future. Nine out of ten families still lived on incomes of less than $2,500 per year; half of them could not afford new cars at all. "Time payment," a part of the language now, figured in seven of every ten car sales, "and in the case of cheaper cars, the average is much higher." The upper classes paid cash; the clerks and mechanics mortgaged themselves to join America's automobile age.

Customers had purchased 3.6 million new passenger cars by the end of 1923 but had traded in 2.8 million battered and bent vehicles to make their down payments. Those, too, had to be sold; the used car, quickly dealt off, was to become America's cheap car, the natural rival of the Model-T for sheer utility.

Only 800,000 customers had come into dealers' showrooms "clean"—that is, without a trade-in—while the year before there had been 950,000. The decline was ominous. Until now, auto manufacturers had not been so much competitors as colleagues rushing to meet the demand. There were sales enough for everybody. Now, with the saturation point at hand, they would be more directly competing for the relatively fewer first-time customers who entered the market each year. The weaker manufacturers and dealers would necessarily fail. They lacked distribution and the capital to use the new "science" of national advertising, a tool not only stimulating sales but creating demand based on needs the public had yet to recognize—until advertising made them aware.

There had been advertisements in American newspapers for 200 years, the acknowledgments of local merchants expressing gratitude to patrons who had "extended their custom," or announcements of the finest of French and English goods lately received at the docks. Throughout most of the nineteenth century, these advertisements had been local in nature, for particular merchants rather than particular products. But with increased transportation facilities and ease of distribution, manufactured goods no longer were necessarily confined to a sales territory close to the factory. Here and there, advertisements for nationally promoted goods—including cigars, cocaine-tinged Coca-Cola, Lydia Pinkham's and Carter's patent medicines—crept in between announcements of dry-goods sales at local emporiums.

By the 1920s, national advertising of brand-name products had come into its own. Newspapers and increasingly numerous magazines waxed fat on ads for toothpaste (Pepsodent proclaiming, "No excuse now for dingy film on teeth"), beverages (Coca-Cola without the cocaine, Postum, and Welch's grape juice), adding machines (Burroughs, Monroe, and Victor), radios (RCA's Radiola and Magnavox, "the reproducer supreme"), lubricating oils (Texaco and Mobiloil's Gargoyle brand), mouthwash (Listerine "for halitosis"), foods (twenty-one kinds of Campbell's soup at twelve cents a can and Heinz's 57 Varieties, still packed by the "neat, prim, white-capped Heinz girls"), and, of course, automobiles.

As competition intensified among auto manufacturers, as the industry shifted its emphasis from production to sales, as the market approached saturation, advertising budgets soared. General Motors' allocation for advertising went from one dollar to ten dollars per car in the decade between 1914 and 1924. For magazine advertising alone, the industry spent $3.5 million in 1921, a total that ballooned to $6.2 million two years later.

The major themes were utility—even Chevrolet sought a bit of that image so cherished by Ford—and freedom to travel. General Motors was "making the nation a neighborhood." Everyone could "be independent with a Chevrolet," the company urged in Fourth of July ads in 1923:

The Government of the United States, each of the states, counties and municipalities maintains at public expense splendid paved highways and graded roads, public parks and scenic natural reservations for the free use and enjoyment of all. But those who lack automobiles derive little or no benefit from such health-giving, useful and educational public improvements.

The Chevrolet brings to its owner a fuller freedom than is possible for those who lack this modern, economical utility. He is independent of steel rails, time-tables and even of the weather. He goes where he pleases, when he pleases, and stays until ready to go on or go home.

With a Chevrolet, a family might even move for the summer to
"a pretty little cottage in the country or at the seashore . . . .
where it is cool and quiet, miles from the railroad station." The
$680 utility coupe, a closed two-seater, "is ideal for the small
family on vacation or for use as an extra car." Back in the city at
the end of summer, the utility coupe—"built particularly for
business uses"—provided "most economical transportation for
sales on the road or for business men in daily trips to and from
office or factory."

At the same time, General Motors hesitantly sought to exploit
a potential women's market. For goodwives left at home when
their husbands drove off to work each day, advertisements in
women's magazines pointed out: "Artistic appearance, riding
comfort and refined interior appointments are characteristics of
the Fisher Bodies used on all closed models. You have reason to
be proud of your Chevrolet. It is an achievement."

If it provoked pride, the Chevrolet was also a sensible investment that allowed mother to "see the children safely to school.
Why worry about the safety of your little ones on the highways
or crossing city streets on the way to school? The low price and
small upkeep of a Chevrolet is cheap insurance against such
risks." Guilt might sell cars too.

Increasingly, the cachet of status figured in automobile promotion: "Ownership of a Buick sport model carries with it more
than the possession of a good automobile. Indicating an appreciation of car character and individuality, it reflects the dis-
criminating taste and judgment of its owner."

Just as families went into debt to secure the pleasures of the
new automobile age—status, independence, family togetherness,
and economy all guaranteed—so, too, did the national and local
governments. By the watershed year of 1923, highway expenditures had reached $1.5 billion annually, a staggering sum paid out
of the public purse to improve as many as 40,000 miles of highways each year. Motor-vehicle owners, paying gasoline taxes,
license and registration fees, and excise levies on cars, raised
less than one-third that amount. The balance was to be paid from
general revenues—revenues that increased progressively over
the decade to pay for America's new automobility. Politicians

who voted the increases did so with little fear they would be turned out of office. Half of American families owned automobiles, and the other half seemingly wanted to. If the "have-nots" could not enjoy the benefits immediately, when they did buy cars—they were intending to do so, certainly—the roads would be there to travel.

Increasing use of automobiles—first for work, then for leisure—inevitably hurt the nation's railroads. Rarely well managed, the railroads reached a peak in passenger miles in 1923, then began inexorably to lose business. Long-range travel suffered first, beginning a decline in 1924; commuter travel grew slightly as the suburbs expanded, but did not keep pace with either the population or the work force.

By unremitting exploitation, minimal service, and sheer lawlessness, the nation's railroads had alienated the public decades earlier. There was little sympathy for them by the 1920s, especially when the alternative was a locally owned trucking line or one's own automobile. New highways not only offered greater mobility but simultaneously satisfied a primal urge for revenge, especially in the West. "The way the motor truck has succeeded in getting itself subsidized as compared with the railroads is not only an economic mistake but a moral crime. . . . We have taxed the railroads and used the money to subsidize competition against them. We have made the railroads carry the cross on which they are crucified," a rare defender claimed.

Once the nation committed to the massive investment in, and upkeep of, automobiles and highways—well over $6 billion in 1923—more money inevitably would go to improve automobility rather than railroads. And as traffic increased on city streets, it drastically slowed public transit, especially streetcars and interurbans at street level. The 1922 timetable for the Pacific Electric Railway, the world's most extensive mass-transit system, allowed fifty-seven minutes to travel the seventeen miles from its Los Angeles terminal to the beaches at Ocean Park, and thirty-eight minutes to travel the eleven miles from that same terminal to Pasadena. By 1930, with the system losing money, those times had increased 50 percent because of blocked intersections and traffic tie-ups. The slower the trains ran, the more passengers turned to automobiles as an alternative; the more automobiles on the road, the slower the trains.

Critics of this new order were scorned as short sighted, meanly unable to envision the new society that machines had fashioned or the benefits the automobile bestowed. If there was congestion—which more highways would alleviate—the automobile had made possible such reforms as the nationwide consolidation of one-room schoolhouses. Children motored to a centrally located academy were benefiting from more modern facilities, better-trained teachers, improved curricula (including drivers' training classes after 1934), and even longer school days since they rode buses rather than walked to school.

The benefits were not unmixed, however. Criminals no less than the law-abiding were using automobiles. "Joy-riders," a term once contemptuously used to describe the wealthy cavorting in their horseless carriages, came to describe youthful car thieves. Despite passage of the Dyer Act in 1920, which made it a crime to transport a stolen car over state lines, auto thefts soared; haphazard registration laws made it easy to resell the stolen cars. "Highwaymen" lurked along the Lincoln Highway between New York City and Philadelphia, waiting to hijack likely-looking trucks. Owners responded by dispatching their motor fleets in armed convoys. Police were equally ineffectual in curbing the motorized bootlegger, as much for lack of zeal as lack of equipment.

But nothing was more pressing, more urgent, than the increasing traffic jams and the lack of parking in the nation's business districts. The swarm of automobiles alighting in the central cities from the prospering suburbs on weekdays had reached something approaching crisis proportions. Chicago's Automobile Trade Association warned it was "imperative that something be done to make room for the hundreds of automobiles being put on the streets by the dealers each week." Never mind the open road; the problem was just to make room.

Proposed solutions were but half thought through. Manufacturers and dealers joined with commercial truckers to oppose maximum-speed regulations on the grounds that "the faster the speed, the greater the number of machines." Minimum-speed limits were acceptable—eighteen miles an hour was suggested—since they would have the effect of barring not only pedestrians but cyclists and horse-drawn wagons from city streets, thus decreasing congestion. Streets no longer were for people, but were to be given over to the internal-combustion engine.

That increased speeds inevitably would cause more deaths was ignored by the automobile's advocates. The overwhelming cause of "gasoline rabies," the deaths of 15,000 people a year, and the injuries of another 1.7 million, was carelessness, the National Safety Council insisted. The automobile accident stood "pre-eminent among the preventable causes of death," that automobile-manufacturer-dominated body argued.

Beyond New York state, there were few if any restrictions on who might drive, a state legislative committee complained: "The child, the aged person, the lame, the blind, and the deaf [are] dealing out death to those who use the roads." Easy licensing regulations made for greater automobile sales, the New York *Times* noted editorially. The "silent, but effective" opposition of the sellers and makers of motorcars prevented passage of stricter licensing regulations and laws requiring permanent loss of license for actions as serious as drunk driving. The industry was already strong enough to overcome public approbation of Prohibition, just four years after the passage of the Eighteenth Amendment.

Yet even with increased legislation—state and local legislators were busily producing ever more detailed vehicle codes—the death toll continued to climb. Extensive education campaigns promised much and contributed little, leading one skeptic to note in 1923:

It is true, also, that there are occasional "safety" movements; but in observing some of them one is troubled by a most disturbing wonder whether they are not inspired and promoted to some degree by those whose primary interest is not in restraining the automobile, but in further exploiting it. The slogan used by some of these safety movements sufficiently suggests the point of view of those who inspire it. They say to the pedestrian, "Don't get hurt." They do not say to the automobile, "Don't hurt."

General Motors rushed into 1924 happily anticipating yet another record year as forecast by Albert Bradley. Reveling in profits real and potential, John Raskob finally had worked out a complicated bonus plan to fill a need Sloan had sensed for at least five years: a method "to keep our organization lined up."

The 2.5 million General Motors shares once owned by Billy Durant were to be turned over to yet another holding company, Managers Securities, which then would issue its own shares. The du Ponts would hold two-thirds of these and would skim off two-thirds of the dividends General Motors paid. The remaining third would be sold to eighty General Motors executives selected by Sloan. Over the next seven years, the chosen were permitted to pay $5 million on time payments for stock ultimately valued at $33 million. (The new $850-per-month president of Remy Electric, Charles E. Wilson, groused that he had expected a raise in salary upon his promotion, but found himself paying out money instead.)

Sloan apportioned the stock to each of the executives, weighing each man's value to the corporation as well as his seniority and rank. The plan to "make its executives partners" was calculated to hold the best managers. Those who left the company were required to sell their shares in Managers Securities back to the company; it was theirs only so long as they worked for General Motors.

The eighty men who bought in were imprisoned by "golden handcuffs," as such plans came to be known. The longer they stayed, the more valuable their stock, and the harder they worked to increase its worth. To leave meant to forfeit enormous dividends. By the end of the decade, their investment had sextupled in value, and the eighty were known enviously as "Raskob's millionaires." Though the concept was not original, the success of Raskob's plan would prompt other corporations to emulate General Motors' scheme.

The euphoria vanished in March. Inexplicably, demand failed to pick up after the winter, leaving dealers with large inventories of automobiles weathering in the spring rain. Goaded by a telegram from Pierre du Pont and the banker-controlled finance committee, Sloan summarily ordered the divisions to cut their production and to stop forcing cars upon beleagured dealers. "By cutting production schedules drastically we were able to reduce dealer stocks to manageable proportions in a few months' time, but not without considerable economic hardship to the employees of the corporation who were laid off," Sloan explained matter-of-factly. In slack times, dealers or employees would always bear the brunt of the hardship.

The slump of 1924 proved the value, however, of Donaldson Brown's conservative measure of standard volume. Despite a sales decline of $130 million from the previous year, General Motors still recorded a 20-percent return on investment. The stockholders prospered even if the workers and dealers did not.

Prompted by the unforeseen sales decline, Sloan instituted one further reform. To monitor sales more closely, he mandated that every ten days dealers report to the corporation actual sales of new and used cars, as well as stock on hand. The central office never again would be dependent upon the optimistic forecasts of the division managers. The corporate structure and controls that were to be the paradigm of rational business management were complete.

Despite the overall decline in the industry that year, some companies prospered. Dodge, Hudson, and Essex, marketing closed sedans for the price of open touring cars, cut deeply into competitor Buick's sales. Even Buick's new designs for that year could not stave off the onslaught—perhaps because the new radiator smacked too much of the Packard and set that company's miffed executives to whispering, "When nicer cars are designed, Packard will design them."

It was fast-failing Oakland that received the most attention in 1924. Late in the year, Sloan directed that Chevrolet's chief engineer, O.E. Hunt, begin design work for the Oakland division on a new six-cylinder, closed automobile. Hunt was to design the car to fill the gap that would open up below Oldsmobile the next year, after Bill Knudsen's new Model-K Chevrolet reached full production. The new car, which C.S. Mott dubbed "Pontiac" after an Ottawa chief who had besieged Fort Detroit in 1763, would deliberately incorporate as many Chevrolet parts as possible. Thus, even if it stole sales from Chevrolet below and Oldsmobile above, an inevitability, General Motors still would benefit from the economies of scale that resulted when two competing automobiles used the same parts. It was a deft way of helping Chevrolet increase its production without selling more Chevrolets, and thereby narrowing the 1.5 million vehicle sales differential between it and Ford.

At the same time, Sloan instructed Cadillac engineers to study the possibility of introducing a family car priced around $2,000 to fill the yawning gap between the $1,295 Buick Six and the $2,985 Cadillac. For the first time in the corporation's history, executives were planning for the future, anticipating needs rather than responding to market turns. Sloan's reorganization was firmly established.

Significantly, both new cars were to have the closed coupe and sedan bodies, which comprised half of all new cars sold. Both were to have six-cylinder engines, smoother and more powerful than the fours that dominated the market. Compared to the closed car, earlier open models seemed dated, and less functional and fashionable. Even Ford had fixed a heavier closed body to the four-cylinder Model-T chassis to meet the competition—one of every three Fords sold was a closed model—but in so doing had reduced the agility and endurance of his increasingly obsolescent auto.

Customers rushed to trade in open cars for closed. The first manifestation of what would become an annual stimulus to new-car sales—psychological obsolescence—came about inadvertently, even belatedly. "For twenty years we protected ourselves with a variety of rubber coats, hats, lap robes, and other makeshift things. For some reason or other, it took us a long time to realize that the way to keep dry in a motorcar was to keep the weather out of the car," Sloan noted wryly. Subsequently, the company would be quicker to recognize the sales potential in even slight model changes advertised properly.

In the meantime, the 1924 Oakland was given a new coat of paint and sent forth to do battle. But the Duco lacquer was more than an ordinary paint job, and with new cosmetics only, the "True Blue" Oakland managed to hold its own in a declining market. The basic concept for that new lacquer had been discovered accidentally in 1920, when a Du Pont chemist found a method of putting more pigment into a nitrocellulose suspension. It took three more years of experimentation, some of it by the still-irritated Kettering, to devise a way of spraying the quick-drying lacquer on metal bodies. The new paint speeded up the time required to finish an automobile body, drying in nine-and-a-half hours rather than the days or weeks older color varnishes required. This quickened the assembly time required for automobile bodies while saving space; drying bodies no longer filled vast factory lofts. (Ford would add the process of drying the paint by heat lamps in 1935, reducing drying time to just five minutes.)

General Motors sought an exclusive license for the new lacquer, only to be turned down by Du Pont. (It would not be the last time the sister companies stood at loggerheads.) With the individualistic Ford the notable holdout, the industry widely adopted the new paint the following year. It offered richer, deeper colors in wider variety. Equally important, it did not fade in sunlight or weather, nor would engine heat mottle the color on the hood. Dents could be pounded out and the metal repainted without telltale patches of mismatched color.

The new lacquer had drawbacks, the most immediate its dull finish. Owners who wanted a lustrous shine had to devote semiannual weekends to waxing the family car, giving birth to an American ritual that lasted until the introduction of acrylic paints in the 1960s. Waxing ostensibly helped the automobile retain its factory-fresh appearance—that is, if the lacquer continued to adhere to the untreated metal. Until Du Pont chemists developed a satisfactory undercoat for their lacquer, Oakland owners were likely to wake up one morning to discover that whole panels lay naked, stripped overnight of their "True Blue" paint by subversive chemical reactions.

The drawbacks worried the Fisher brothers, who preferred the shiny, hand-finished varnishes of old. Their reservations troubled Sloan, for they betokened "a very great inclination not to accept a change rather than the feeling that we should progress and improve things. I recognize the desirability of being conservative and all that sort of thing, but that can be overdone. . . ."

Only Chevrolet seemed free of what Sloan condemned as inertia. Knudsen had increased his production capacity, revamped
the assembly lines, reorganized the sales force, and created the
division's first new model since the war. Now the Model-K was
ready—longer, lower than Ford's Model-T, with more room and
more stylish lines. Most important, it was a closed car. Chevrolet was finally ready to take on Ford.

10

Vun for Vun

They could watch him coming down the production line, his derby bobbing over the tops of the car bodies or stacks of parts. "Knudsen!" one would yell over the explosion of the drop forge to the man at the next station, jabbing his head in the direction of the derby.

Knudsen would stop to talk briefly with a foreman, shouting to be heard over the shriek of the milling machines, or to watch the assemblers mechanically fitting the disc clutch and improved transmission to the moving chassis. Assistant plant managers scattered with instructions to the paint shop, the electrical department, and the foundry across the street. The message was always the same: "Hurry up!"

Knudsen wanted increased production. This was the best sales year the industry had ever known, so good that some even talked again of an automobile shortage. Chevrolet's Model-K was a resounding success. The four-cylinder automobile, built largely around the chassis developed for the air-cooled car, incorporated the latest in automotive technology and covered it all with a Duco finish. Only the newly introduced Chrysler, priced to compete with Buick, offered as many up-to-date improvements.

Hurry up! The seventeen-year-old Model-T could not match the 1925 Chevrolet. Knudsen had been right all along: Ford's universal auto was tired, a weaker competitor with each passing month. The addition this year of a second color, Brewster green, and modestly restyled bodies could only slow the Model-T's decline.

With Chevrolet's assembly lines in full cry, Sloan had fewer reasons to lock the doors of his spartan office and sail off into the tantrums that made secretaries wary. Only the company's disorganized truck production needed close attention, and John Pratt had found the solution: buying a majority interest in the faltering Yellow Cab Manufacturing Company of Chicago. Founder John Hertz had overextended himself and was willing to take on a partner. Nothing in Hertz's background as a sportswriter, fight manager, and automobile salesman had quite equipped him to cope with the problems of his patchwork enterprise founded on an auto-livery business.

Stuck with nine unsaleable Thomas Flyers in 1910, Hertz decided to rent them by the day. When that business slackened, he boldly painted them yellow to attract attention and dispatched them to cruise the Chicago streets, soliciting business. His Yellow Taxicabs doing well and his fleet growing, Hertz decided to build his own cabs capable of withstanding the rigors of constant use. Hertz Drivurself companies, Sterrett truck rentals, and bus tours followed—Hertz never lacked imagination—and he added a motor-coach manufacturing line to his factory.

General Motors paid $16 million for slightly more than half ownership of Yellow Cab Manufacturing and all its subsidiaries. Sloan and Raskob then created a new company—Yellow Truck and Coach Manufacturing Company—and turned over to it the old Yellow plants and virtually all of General Motors' truck production. Only Knudsen protested, resisting vociferously and profanely the loss of his truck line, arguing that Chevrolet's delivery trucks were potentially profitable. Sloan permitted Knudsen to keep his light trucks; Yellow would concentrate on heavy-duty vehicles, including buses, taxicabs, and large trucks.*

The Yellow Cab acquisition in 1925 launched General Motors on a new expansion program, one it would follow for the next thirty years, until government attorneys threatened to tear the corporation apart with antitrust suits. The strategy involved entering new businesses with as little risk as possible, Sloan told a Great Neck, Long Island, neighbor one Saturday afternoon about this time: "Our business has grown so large and our available cash surplus so ample that from now on, instead of starting new units, whenever we see a promising field we will enter it by purchasing an existing company. We feel it is better to take a going concern; we get under way more quickly."

Sloan pushed a similar expansion program overseas, where prior to the coming of John David Mooney in 1920 General Motors had hardly distinguished itself. Mooney was a cross between an overage Irish club-fighter and a polished "cookie pusher," as his friend Cordell Hull called career diplomats. Mooney could tick off the vintage years for French wines, region by region, as easily as he listed the batting averages of the starting Detroit nine. Brash, vigorous, and unencumbered with anything other than his pugnacious attitude, Mooney doubled and then redoubled sales of cars and trucks in his first three years as head of the export division. By 1923, he was selling 45,000 vehicles—worth $40 million—annually, more than 7 percent of the corporation's output. Buick, the most popular line, sold in Europe as a prestige automobile.

Mooney's ambitions came a cropper as, one by one, European countries sought to restore their own war-damaged auto industries. To circumvent high protective tariffs against imported motor vehicles, Mooney suggested building assembly plants abroad since tariffs on automobile parts remained low. In 1924, William Knudsen joined Mooney in Europe long enough to set

---

* In 1943, General Motors purchased the remaining 43 percent of Yellow Truck and Coach, ultimately organizing the GMC Truck and Coach Division. Ten years later, it sold Hertz Drivurself, though General Motors was to remain the favored supplier of Hertz fleets.

up, as he had earlier for Ford, assembly lines for Chevrolet near London and, of course, his native Copenhagen.

When the British elected to impose horsepower-based taxes, thereby penalizing the larger Chevrolet, General Motors changed direction. Mooney and Knudsen approached Sir Herbert Austin, majority owner of England's largest auto company, with an offer to buy the corporation entirely in 1925. Knudsen had reservations, for the Austin was a small car—perhaps suitable for England, but not for import to the United States. There "everything is bigger; railways cars are bigger; street cars are bigger; in the United States, when anyone sits down he stretches his legs, and a motor car that doesn't permit people to do that isn't going to get very far in the United States."

At the last minute, Austin's directors raised difficulties, and Mooney turned immediately to Vauxhall Motors, a much smaller firm that made a somewhat larger, more prestigious auto. The price was a bargain $2.5 million, reminiscent of the sums Billy Durant had laid out earlier to pick up struggling automobile manufacturers. At the time, Vauxhall was in no better shape than the Durant acquisitions of old. Four years later, Vauxhall finally turning a profit, General Motors purchased 80 percent of Germany's largest automobile company, Adam Opel A.G., for $26 million. In contrast to Vauxhall, which never would capture more than 10 percent of the British market, Opel was a huge success, garnering half of German auto sales by the beginning of World War II. (It was Opel's success that prodded Nazi Chancellor Adolf Hitler to sponsor development of a *Volksauto* in 1937, a car that two decades later would be both boon and bane to General Motors in the United States.)

By the end of 1925, Mooney presided over six assembly plants in Europe, one in New Zealand, and another in South Africa. Together, these plants imported from the United States parts to build more than 100,000 automobiles with a value of $75 million. Local managers were largely nationals of the country in which they worked, for "General Motors took pains not to seem so foreign as Ford. . . . In England the Vauxhall was considered English, in Germany the Opel was German. Both cars were adapted to local laws and tastes," a later historian noted. Simply stated, General Motors intended "to produce in Europe European cars for European consumers." Only a handful of American production and financial experts were sent overseas, usually for limited periods to install American managerial techniques.

Domestically, General Motors more than matched its overseas success. The recession year of 1924 was quickly forgotten as sales boomed in the spring of 1925, increased in the summer, and, for the first time, continued strong in the fall, when closed cars operated more or less comfortably. The year's profits—$106 million—were more than 135 percent greater than in 1924. Tightened management controls and increased manufacturing efficiency had proved their worth. General Motors, which produced about one-fifth of all automobiles in 1925, garnered one-third of the industry's profits.

With a car "for every purse and purpose," Sloan "smote the rock of the national resources, and abundant streams of revenue gushed forth. He touched the dead corpse of Public Credit, and it sprung upon its feet." Time payments coupled with what later would be termed "planned obsolescence" transformed the industry. "In order to make more people purchase more cars," Sloan explained frankly, "we build cars so they will last the average person four or five years. This provides for a greater turnover of automobiles, labor and raw materials." The cars did not necessarily wear out in five years; they merely *looked* unfashionable, and therefore undesirable.

The economic recovery spread widely throughout the industry. Total automobile sales topped four million; there was one car for every twenty people in the country. Only Ford seemed to miss the general boom. That company sold 100,000 fewer Model-T's in 1925, and its profit slipped for the second year in a row—this while the Model-K increased rival Chevrolet's sales 70 percent. Here was more evidence of Ford's vulnerability, Knudsen pointed out.

On the basis of sheer numbers, Knudsen's optimism was schoolyard bravado. Ford had sold 1.6 million autos that year, Chevrolet just 512,000. But the Ford juggernaut was slowing.

Chevrolet's dealers were heavy with a new-found prosperity

and Knudsen was supremely confident when they gathered at Chicago's Palmer House for their year-end sales meeting. Expected to deliver a complimentary address to the assembled dealers at the annual banquet, Knudsen, suddenly shy, raised two fingers in the air and shouted, "I vant vun for vun!" There was a moment of silence as the general manager abruptly sat down, his "remarks" concluded; then the dealers broke into a roar. Chevrolet had declared war.

Hand-to-hand combat it would be, with revived Chevrolet pitted against the automobile that had become legendary and had transformed its inventor into a mythic figure. But the upstart held a formidable weapon, one that Ford refused to wield: installment buying. The more cars dealers financed to clear their lots—especially cheaper, used vehicles taken in trade—the more they cut into the Model-T's natural market. By his very unwillingness to adopt a time-payment plan, Henry Ford was contributing to his own defeat.

In 1925, more than 1,000 automobile finance companies loaned $2.64 billion on three of every four cars sold. In less than a decade, installment credit had become the foundation of the nation's fastest-growing industry. Promoted by "easy credit," automobile ownership was the premier symbol of success in an era plunged, like Jay Gatsby, into "the service of a vast, vulgar, and meretricious beauty." More costly than tailored clothes—which, after all, any thrifty laborer might buy—but less expensive than a home, the automobile conferred an aura of affluence, and hence status, upon its owner. Even in the anonymity of larger cities, though the driver might be unknown, he or she motored in a mantle of prosperity displayed for all to admire. Automobiles that best conveyed that prosperity, as the stick-in-the-mud Model-T could not, sold best.

No community was immune to "automobile madness." In sheltered, insular Muncie, Indiana, "among the high school set, ownership of a car by one's family has become an important criterion of social fitness; a boy almost never takes a girl to a dance except in a car; there are persistent rumors of the buying of a car by local families to help their children's social standing in high school," Robert and Helen Lynd reported in *Middletown,* their classic study of midwestern America. Residents of Muncie would mortgage homes, set aside a week's salary to make their monthly payment on the new closed Essex or Hupmobile, and abandon the long-treasured virtue of thrift to own a car. "We'd rather do without clothes than give up the car," one working-class mother told the Lynds. "I'll go without food before I'll see us give up the car," insisted another.

In its rush to wheels, the nation abandoned any restraint except concern for the size of the monthly payment. A signature on a sales contract meant freedom, as well as the opportunity to keep up with, or ahead of, the neighbors—for pennies more per day.

Time payments fueled industrial expansion and the seemingly limitless Coolidge prosperity. Thus, buying and selling on credit was virtually every patriot's duty, argued one auto dealer: "To keep America growing we must keep Americans working, and to keep Americans working we must keep them wanting; wanting more than the bare necessities; wanting the luxuries and frills that make life so much more worthwhile, and installment selling makes it easier to keep Americans wanting."

Stung by criticisms of frivolous or irresponsible credit practices, finance companies periodically tightened their requirements, but just as quickly loosened them when auto sales slackened. To broaden their own market base, they began financing installment purchases of other goods, especially refrigerators and home furnishings. Rather than curtail their operations, they expanded, for fear a poor automobile-sales year would leave them in jeopardy.

Providing immediate gratification had become sound business policy. At the end of the decade, President Hoover's Research Committee on Social Trends acknowledged a "new attitude toward hardship as a thing to be avoided by living in the here and now, utilizing installment credit, and other devices, to telescope the future into the present."

Nowhere was criticism quite so shrill as in rural America, which had turned to the Model-T with an acceptance that bordered on the doctrinaire. Farmers were mortgaging land to buy automobiles even as farm foreclosures escalated. Some 450,000 small farmers already had lost their family holdings to banks between 1920 and 1925; bought in the belief that crop prices would continue to rise, the land proved too costly in periods of low farm prices. "During Wilson's time," one Ohioan fretted, "I made enough money to buy my farm but now, during Harding's time, I am not sure I can hold on to it."

If any Ford machine was responsible for farm foreclosures, it was not the Model-T, but the equally successful Fordson tractor. In the great heartland of the Midwest, where the bulk of the nation's staple crops were grown, tractors compelled consolidation of acreage into larger, more economical units; a man with a tractor could do the work of two or three hired hands, men who no longer could find jobs in their communities. "Rather than fitting itself unobtrusively into our agriculture," concluded a presidential committee in 1929, the tractor "sets a new pace and creates a demand that agriculture be quite drastically readjusted . . ."

The inexpensive Fordson tractor increased farm productivity, and that, in turn, forced down grain prices. Farmers without sufficient acreage inevitably lost their quarter- and half-sections. They too bundled families into autos, joining their former hired hands in an unceasing pilgrimage for work. They sang a Book of Job in accented 2/4 time:

> Back in nineteen twenty-seven
> Had a little farm and I called that heaven,
> And the price was up and the rain come down,
> And I hauled my crops all into town.
>> I got the money,
>> Bought clothes and groceries,
>> Fed the kids and raised a family.
>
> But the rain quit and the wind got high,
> And a black old dust storm filled the sky,
> And I swapped my farm for a Ford machine,
> And I poured it full of gasoline.
>> And started—rockin' and rollin'
>> Over the mountains, out towards
>> The old Peach Bowl—California.

Such families became "gasoline gypsies," one unsympathetic observer complained. In California, where fruits and vegetables grew year-round, ten thousand children followed the crops. Auto camps built to accommodate overnight tourists "are now occupied by large numbers of families who stay for indefinite periods. Last year California camps registered 140,000 machines and a million and a quarter people."

It was the unrecognized onset of the largest internal migration in American history, a westward tilt of empire that in the decade of the 1920s would bring 1.3 million people to Los Angeles county alone. The gasoline engine had both unleashed it and made it possible. "Like a swarm of invading locusts, migrants crept in over all the roads," another reporter wrote. "For wings they had rattletrap automobiles, their fenders tied with string, and curtains flapping in the breeze; loaded with babies, bedding, bundles, a tin tub tied on behind, a bicycle or a baby carriage balanced precariously on the top. Often they came with no funds and no prospects, apparently trusting that heaven would provide for them."

Heaven in this glorious year of 1925 provided little for such wanderers, despite the country's runaway industrial prosperity, while the rich waxed fat. General Motors, the fastest-growing of the nation's industries, suffered only one setback, and that, ironically, stemmed as much from its very success as from the accidental explosion on October 24, 1924, at the Baywater, New Jersey, laboratory of the Standard Oil Company. Sloan had opposed Standard of New Jersey's attempt to manufacture the new "doping compound" developed by Charles Kettering to be added to gasoline to eliminate engine knock. Sloan argued futilely that it was best left to a chemical company, such as eager E.I. du Pont de Nemours, which had experience in handling such dangerous compounds. Four workers had died already in accidents involving tetraethyl lead at Kettering's laboratory and at Du Pont research facilities. But Standard, claiming a cheaper manufacturing process than Du Pont's, "would never get it out of its system unless they did go into it," Sloan lamented. Instead, Standard brushed aside "friendly remonstrances and warnings" about safety factors just a month prior to the accident.

Standard's accident was calamitous for the newly organized Ethyl Gasoline Corporation, which it owned jointly with General Motors. Thirty-five men who had inhaled the poisonous fumes were gravely ill, eight requiring treatment in New York City hospitals. Within five days, five of the eight had died, one of the five violently insane, bound in a strait jacket. Newspapers bannered the accident, triggering a national panic. State legislators rushed to introduce bills banning the sale of "loony gas." New Jersey suspended sales of Kettering's doping compound and convened a grand jury to investigate the accident. Across the country, sales plummeted at the 10,000 service stations selling ethyl-doped gasoline for three cents per gallon more than the untreated "regular." No one wanted loony gas in his automobile, not with all the rumors circulating about people going crazy while out for a Sunday drive.

Sloan was slow to move, fearing lost sales were he to suspend ethyl gasoline production and believing the company might ride out the loony-gas storm. What was potentially the most important advance in automotive engineering since the self-starter, and a hugely lucrative one at that, hung in jeopardy. Ten years' work by Kettering and his young assistant, Thomas Midgley, Jr., in search of a compound that made high-powered, highly profitable engines possible appeared to be wasted.

Kettering's interest in the problem of engine knock had grown over the years. He first looked into it in 1913, after Cadillac engineers blamed the premature ignition that caused the knock on Kettering's then-new self-starter and battery system. Having satisfied the engineers that the violent banging in the cylinders did not stem from faulty firing of the spark plugs, but was a fuel problem, he dismissed it. The problem turned up again when Kettering began work on a simple farm lighting system with electricity generated by a small gasoline motor. Cheap kerosene, a relatively low-grade petroleum distillate, also prematurely ignited.

Kettering assigned the problem of engine knock to Midgley in 1916. The auto industry was using engines with increasingly higher compression—that is, motors whose pistons more tightly compacted the gasoline vapor in the cylinders before ignition. The greater the compression, the greater the propulsive force against the piston heads—and the greater the engine knock, "the nightmare of all automotive engineers," Kettering groused.

The problem loomed larger than merely making cars go faster, Kettering had explained to Billy Durant. The best estimates obtainable suggested that the world's supply of crude oil would last only twenty-five years, perhaps to 1940, when motorists would be forced to switch to alcohol fuels. If automobiles had the high-compression engines necessary to burn alcohol. Until then, they needed an antiknock compound, something to retard the premature combustion in the cylinder.

Even after estimates of crude-oil reserves ballooned with further Texas finds, Durant continued to encourage the research. In the process, Kettering discovered that eliminating the knock—this had been accomplished with some highly expensive, scarce compounds—also increased gasoline mileage. If they solved the knock problem, cars also would go faster at less cost.*

In March 1922, Midgley announced his new doping compound, a long-known chemical product, claiming it would increase gasoline mileage by 25 percent. They organized the General Motors Chemical Company, with Kettering as president and Midgley as vice-president and general manager, and the company contracted to buy the basic additive, tetraethyl lead, from E.I. du Pont de Nemours. Du Pont also furnished the dye to give the otherwise colorless gasoline a distinctive red tint.

The first ethyl gasoline went on sale at the Refiners Oil Company station on South Main Street in Dayton, Ohio, on February 1, 1923. That first day, 310 gallons were sold at the premium price of twenty-five cents per gallon, three cents more than the regular price. ("Premium" and "regular" would enter the language as measures of gasoline octane, not price, in short order.) Within a year, Standard Oil of Indiana was marketing its adver-

---

* Among the antiknock chemicals, tellurium showed real promise. It had one drawback: a penetrating garlic-and-onions odor. Once tellurium touched either skin or clothes, the odor was almost impossible to expunge; water only made it worse. Tellurium was abandoned.

tised "ethylized gasoline" throughout the Midwest, and General Motors had approached Standard of New Jersey with a national distribution plan. The two created the Ethyl Gasoline Corporation, a nicely profitable venture until the Baywater accident in October 1924. Because of those profits, the partners delayed taking action.

In the midst of General Motors' best sales year ever, six more men died at Du Pont's Deepwater, New Jersey, tetraethyl plant. The partners took one look at the newspaper headlines and suspended further tetraethyl sales on May 4, 1925. General Motors needed "the good will of the public for the sake of our car products and in view of the position we were placed in by attacks which we did not have the ammunition to meet, I felt that in deference to public opinion and to our position, we should retire . . ."

The ammunition would come from a special committee convened at the behest of Standard Oil by a complaisant surgeon general of the United States. They could have no better validation, and Du Pont representatives, now that Standard had decided it did not want to produce the compound after all, were actively lobbying the committee. They expected a favorable report; for whatever the dangers in manufacturing tetraethyl lead—dangers Du Pont was willing to accept—the chemical was perfectly safe in its diluted public form of one part tetraethyl lead to 1,300 parts gasoline.

As the partners anticipated, the committee report released in January 1926 exonerated ethyl in its diluted form. Five months later, after a concerted advertising campaign to prepare the public, ethylized gasoline went back on the market. It would prove hugely profitable, especially after 1927, when automobile manufacturers rushed to duplicate the high-compression engine Walter Chrysler put into the car bearing his name.*

* Between its formation in 1924 and the expiration of its patents in 1947, the renamed Ethyl Corporation recorded net sales of $1 billion. General Motors' patent royalties totaled $43.3 million; its half-share of the 17.5-percent net profit on sales amounted to $82.6 million. As the manufacturer of the chemical additive itself, Du Pont posted profits of $86 million. Still, Irénée du Pont, as president of Du Pont, complained in a letter on June 29, 1936: "Personally, I feel that the Standard Oil Company is somewhat grasping and have [sic] not demonstrated that they are very good partners in this particular enterprise."

Lucrative ethyl immediately helped General Motors narrow the gap in total income that separated it from front-running Ford to just $16 million. The tide was ebbing fast for the Model-T. Market analysts freely predicted that General Motors "would gain the supremacy of the industry in forthcoming years." Ford professed no public interest in what his rivals did; time spent worrying about them was time not spent on their own production, he told his executives. The master of Dearborn cleaved to the utilitarian Model-T. Meanwhile, General Motors marketed fifty models of trucks and automobiles, open and closed, ranging in price from $525 to $4,485. General Motors sold, as Sloan boasted, "a car for every purse and purpose."

Flush with record sales, General Motors roared into 1926 with plans for a major expansion that would give it "supremacy." Sloan's first move was to acquire the remaining 42-percent interest in the Fisher Body Corporation for $118 million. The purchase transformed the mammoth Fisher enterprise into an operating division of General Motors, no longer a partially independent enterprise paying its minority owners fat profits.

With more than enough Fishers to manage the body-building plants, Sloan enticed Lawrence P. Fisher from the family enterprise to become general manager of Cadillac. It was a significant move—until then the brothers had hung together with a fierce loyalty enforced by their aged mother—and a move that would have lasting impact on the corporation and the national economy. Sloan's dissatisfaction with Cadillac had grown as rival Packard outstripped it. Sloan believed Cadillac deserved at least half of the market for prestige automobiles, and he intended to capture it, not necessarily for the profits alone, but especially for the esteem. Fisher was just the man to imbue Cadillac with whatever qualities Packard had exploited to become the favored automobile of those with established fortunes.

There were few men in the automobile industry with as much managerial experience as the thirty-six-year-old Lawrence P. Fisher. The fourth of the brothers, he had followed the oldest, Fred, to Detroit in 1905 to become a bench hand in the C.R. Wilson Body Company. Three years later, he and his older brothers had organized the first Fisher-owned firm, with Law-

rence assuming the title of factory manager at the age of nineteen.
In the years since, he had taken on much of the production
responsibility, and in the days when Fisher produced Model-T
bodies for Knudsen, he had matched the Dane's production,
body for chassis.

Lawrence had a reputation as the most innovative and daring
of the brothers. Like Sloan, he had long been dissatisfied with
the appearance of the automobile in general—"a high, ungainly
contraption, with a dangerously high center of gravity," as Sloan
disparaged. Part of Sloan's reason for purchasing Fisher Body
outright had been to bring its body designers into closer cooperation with the division mechanical engineers who designed the
chassis—and both of them into contact with the sales force
closest to public taste. From the earliest days of the industry,
engineers had designed fenders and radiators, while body manufacturers had designed cabs to plop down on the chassis. The
two parts had not always melded well—or sold well, which was
more important than the offense to Sloan's aesthetic sensibilities.

Fisher had a suggestion. On a trip to California earlier in 1926,
he had visited a Cadillac dealer in Los Angeles who maintained a
custom body shop catering to the newly rich of the motion-
picture industry. The young man in charge of the custom rebuild-
ing, Harley J. Earl, designed lavish body shells and then fitted
them to the chassis of either American or foreign autos. The son
of a carriage builder, like Fisher, Earl had a fine sense of hand-
craftsmanship; each of his designs was different, conceived
three-dimensionally in modeling clay by the young man before
his craftsmen took hammer to sheet metal. Scornful of the ponderous boxes on wheels produced in Detroit, Earl advocated
longer, lower bodies, with rounded corners and lines flowing
from headlights to rear bumper. The notion was revolutionary,
and his creations had a panache lacking even in the work of such
prestigious custom carriage builders as Fleetwood and LeBaron.

Since young Earl worked so fast, they still had time for him to
design the body for the Cadillac Division's new family car
scheduled for release in early 1927. Sloan agreed to hire Earl as a

consultant on the forthcoming model. Within weeks Earl was installed in an office—which he promptly dressed up with mauve drapes—and was working on plans with startled engineers. Whatever he thought of the drapery, Sloan was delighted with Earl's first sketches. Hood and fenders still belonged to the mechanical engineers—Earl had been unable to wheedle many changes there—but the cabin at least blended with the running gear. Wider doors and reproportioned windows gave the auto the appearance of sitting lower to the ground. The car appeared "racy," but not too much so; the La Salle was, after all, to be a family car.

With the new design in hand, Fisher turned to the frumpy standard Cadillac. "What shall we do with these cars?" he asked Earl, pointing to the blueprints for the 1927 Cadillac about to go into production. Major changes were out of the question.

"Let's paint them up so they look like something," the young designer suggested. "Put a lot of color and some wire wheels on them and doll them up."

Fisher nodded. The 1927 Cadillac was announced as available in five hundred color and upholstery combinations, a thoroughly astounding offer by a company that had never marketed a single model in more than three colors. In Earl, however, they had a man with the vision to match Sloan's conviction that the company's future sales rested not on technology, but on their body designs, the paint schemes, the richness of the interiors, all of which had to be presented in a manner that differentiated them from their mechanically identical competitors.

The following year, Earl joined General Motors as the director of a newly organized, fifty-member-strong "Art and Color Section." Sloan's sponsorship overcame divisional resistance to the concept of styling itself, and his even-tempered arguments beat down complaints of interference by corporate headquarters. The coming of Harley Earl and what he called "dynamic obsolescence"—others would sneer at it as "Sloanism"—simply accelerated a long-standing policy within the industry. Neither Sloan nor Earl invented it; they simply institutionalized it.

Automobile companies had long made a point of installing

improvements in the models to be exhibited at the important New York Automobile Show in the first week of each new year. In the earliest years, the bulk of the improvements were mechanical, for the automobile was still a mechanical contrivance and less a social force. By the end of the second decade of the century, however, the mechanical improvements were fewer each year. "New, improved" models that the public had come to expect from Detroit necessarily were "new and improved" only by the addition of conveniences and the dint of advertising. Certainly some of the conveniences were utilitarian—the electric windshield wiper replacing the hand-driven wiper, for example—but having reached market saturation, the industry was forced to rely on new sales devices to convince automobile owners to trade in the old machine for this year's spanking "new" model. Advertising had to breed dissatisfaction with the automobile that just last year or the year before had marked the very zenith of industrial accomplishment.

Price reductions on the more comfortable, more convenient closed cars stimulated sales early in the 1920s, prompting owners of open roadsters and touring cars back into dealers' showrooms. "A little later," the *Nation* editorialized, "appeared new closed cars with low rakish lines, so that even those who did own closed cars found themselves quite out of fashion." Duco and other lacquer finishes and four-wheel brakes provided new sales appeal, but if in any given year, "a middle-class man can go to the local automobile show without feeling an irresistible urge to exchange his car for the latest model," sales tumbled. The industry's erratic production in the face of apparent saturation troubled the *Nation* editorial writer: "So far as the automobile serves an economic function, its future is assured; but so far as its use represents a pastime, so far as it is a means for advertising one's social position, and so far as it is a craze, its future is uncertain."

The merry-go-round of annual style changes was costly to ride, the brass rings scarce for those with short arms. The *New Republic* noted that year by year:

The number of makers has shrunk considerably, both by failures and mergers; soon we shall have a comparatively few large stabilized producers. . . . Meanwhile, such competition as survives is mainly along the line of needless variations in external fashion—variations not demanded by consumers but thrust upon them by snobbish and expensive advertising and salesmanship. This industry, so highly efficient in production, is wasteful to a degree in merchandising, since it presses so avidly for continually enlarging volume. Only a few cars in the United States cost more than $500 to make—the rest of what we pay is what it costs to sell them.

The annual model change joined installment credit in fueling the saturnalia of Coolidge prosperity. Everywhere but Florida's Gold Coast, where a crazed land boom had lured thousands of eager marks down the eighteen-foot-wide Dixie Highway in frenzied pursuit of the quick buck. The boom had died abruptly, done in by overspeculation in underwater lots and barren sand dunes and by two successive hurricanes that significantly rearranged the local topography and induced hasty reconsideration of the climate's healthful properties. Elsewhere, the carnival sped on—if one ignored the flurry of migrant workers, the scattered labor agitation, and the vastly inflated prices of even poorly performing stocks.

When land values in Miami, Florida, could grow tenfold and Radio Corporation shares quintuple without ever paying a dividend, no statistical evidence of American prosperity seemed beyond belief. General Motors sales increased from $734 million in 1925 to over a billion dollars in 1926, the company becoming the first to reach that Olympian height. Buick sales jumped 20 percent, enough to retain its place as the most prosperous of the corporation's auto lines, despite the death of its capable general manager, Harry Bassett. Chevrolet ran a close second, as Knudsen rammed production to 732,000 vehicles. But the great surprise was the Pontiac, fitted with a stylized Indian-head logotype and shoved into the price gap between Chevrolet and Oldsmobile late in 1925.

Albert Glancy had taken charge of the Oakland division and development of the new Pontiac in the fall of 1924. Trained as a mechanical engineer at Lehigh—Sloan had a decided preference for engineers—Glancy had knocked about American industry until he drifted into E.I. du Pont de Nemours. From there he had been transferred to General Motors with instructions to bury first

Sheridan Motors and later Samson Tractor. Dissatisfied with industrial undertaking, Glancy was about to quit when Sloan asked him to take on slipping Oakland. This time he was to revive a General Motors property.

Glancy was an ironic choice. His graduating thesis from Lehigh in 1903 was a study of the automobile industry based upon tests of the Cadillac, the Knox, and the Stanley Steamer. Glancy was unimpressed; the final paragraph of his thesis concluded: "The automobile is a rich man's toy and has no commercial future."

The Pontiac was essentially a lengthened Chevrolet with a newly developed six-cylinder engine. The similarity between the Pontiac and Chevrolet was hardly accidental. At the New York Automobile Show, C.S. Mott complained, "On one side was the Chevrolet and on the other was the Pontiac, but they had painted the two cars exactly the same and you would have sworn it was the same body."

But the Pontiac had hidden advantages, Glancy inadvertently revealed in praising his engineering team: whopping profits. His men were "commercial engineers, because never was anything costing one dollar incorporated in the car that could not sell for a dollar sixty." The Pontiac, scheduled for a production run of 65,000, would generate a return on investment of 60 percent, approximately $180 per vehicle. This was new income for the corporation, pried away from competitive Hudson, Dodge, Nash, and Durant. Oldsmobile was unaffected; *its* sales rose as well. Pontiac surpassed the company's expectations, with production reaching 77,000 coaches and coupes in its first year. Even before the selling season ended, the finance committee had appropriated another $5 million to expand Pontiac's production facilities.

By the end of 1926, the automobile industry had sold 4.4 million cars and trucks, worth $3 billion. (Motorists laid out another $10 billion to travel 141 billion miles that year; they would motor billions more miles when the first transcontinental highway opened the following year.) Between them, Ford and General Motors had skimmed off 60 percent of all sales, leaving the dwindling number of "independents," as the smaller companies were then called, to scramble for the balance. Ford still outsold General Motors, narrowly, but its gross receipts and profits were slipping. If the old man of Highland Park was still immensely rich, probably the richest man in the country, his automobile company was fast losing its ability to compete with General Motors.

Just how flush it was, General Motors quickly established. Having spent $106 million for expansion in 1926, the company announced that it would construct a twenty-eight-story Fisher Building in Detroit for an estimated $34 million. Such tokens of faith in the future, as well as a stock dividend in August 1926, which the New York *Times* labeled the largest in history, were reassuring. An editorial in the Baltimore *Sun* optimistically concluded: "An enormous number of people are employed in the industry, and as its activity, coupled with that of iron and steel and building operations, constitutes the basis upon which the present gratifying business condition largely rests, what the future holds out for it is of serious concern to the public. As depression in it would be widely felt, its prosperity would seem to foreshadow a healthy and vigorous era . . ."

General Motors' affluence prompted yet another rise in stock prices. The Great Bull Market, as it would be known ever after, was under way. Who could afford to miss out? waitresses, insurance clerks, and cab drivers asked. Had an investor purchased $1,000 in the original General Motors stock of 1908, it would be worth more than $100,000 at 1926 market prices. What greater proof of the success of the capitalist system and Coolidge prosperity could there be? And 1927 would be even better. The industry had built its production capacity to seven million cars a year and expected to produce five million.

Whatever trouble the industry would have meeting its goal would come from Ford, financial panjandrums whispered confidentially. The Model-T was in trouble. Ford had done virtually everything possible to keep his auto competitive. He had permitted his son Edsel to modestly restyle the bodies. He had cut prices, in February and again in June 1926. He had incorporated the self-starter, balloon tires, and demountable rims—the most critical of driving conveniences—as standard equipment at no extra cost. He even had added smart wire wheels to his closed sedans at no extra cost. And still his sales fell. Once Ford had sold six of every ten cars in the United States; now he supplied one in three. General Motors, with its ever-changing array of vehicles, had pulled even; if Chevrolet's sales were no more than half of Ford's, the one was rising while the other fell. Nevertheless, as late as May 1926, despite failing dealerships, despite desertions by even the best dealers to other companies, despite the ever more grim sales figures, Ford insisted, "Most of your trouble at the present time is a question of your mental attitude."

The Model-T's illness was systemic—and incurable. It was poorly sprung, and the ride, at best, was jarring. It needed constant care; the spark plugs, for example, required cleaning every two hundred miles, and even then the ignition was sporadic compared to Chevrolet's reliable Remy device. The Chevrolet had a foot accelerator; the Ford driver kept one hand on the wheel and the other on the accelerator. (Psychologically, this allowed the Chevrolet owner more freedom, since one hand was free to light a cigarette, hold a child, or caress a companion.) But most vexing to customers and dealers alike, Ford hewed to his antiquated, cranky transmission, which required the driver to depress a floor pedal to keep the car in low gear.

Late in 1926, Ford learned that Knudsen had scheduled a one-million-car production for the coming year and that the ebullient R.H. Grant intended to support it with a $10 million advertising campaign. Morale dipped throughout the Ford Motor Co., but still the owner held firm. In January 1927, Grant's wave of advertising broke over the floundering Model-T, whose sales plummeted to one-third the total of a year earlier; both Chevrolet and, even more shocking, Essex outsold Ford that month.

Stubbornly, Ford held out as long as he could, blaming everybody and everything but his beloved Model-T for having failed him. Finally, worn down by the pleadings of his son and the handful of executives not totally intimidated by their boss, Ford gave way. He announced that on May 27, 1927, Model-T production would end with the fabrication of the fifteen-millionth copy of the venerable machine. The Ford plants then would shut down while the owner himself designed a new automobile. (The shut-down was not quite so absolute as the announcement indicated; Ford intended to work off his inventory of raw materials and to continue to turn out replacement parts. In fact, Ford's assembly lines were halted only after they turned out 15,458,781 Model-Ts.)

An era, as these things are marked, had ended. With the exception of the telephone, no single product had done more to change American life. In nineteen years, the Model-T had carried half of the nation into the auto age. It had fostered mobility, especially in rural America, breaking down the provincialism that isolated farm from city. (Ford's personal provincialism remained unaffected.) It had freed millions to travel beyond the confines of birthplace, to see a larger world beyond, or merely to enjoy the countryside that surrounded squalid urban centers. It had helped to transform a country 60-percent rural at the beginning of the century to just 44-percent rural by the Census of 1930. In building the Model-T, Ford had purchased almost $5 billion worth of raw materials and another $5.5 billion in labor. He had paid taxes of more than $500 million—in an era when the federal government's total corporate tax in any one year barely reached $1.2 billion. Most important, Ford had proved that mass production stimulated economic growth.

Ford had done all this with an auto as cranky as its creator, as plain and functional as a broom, and as long-lived as any industrial product in history. "That car had integrity. Perhaps nothing in it was beautiful—but nothing in it was false," historians Allan Nevins and Frank Hill concluded.* Its production had ended in a single, peremptory, stunning order from its creator. It was fitting.

The end came with the country sliding into a recession aggravated by a general tightening of credit, which served to reduce the number of cars sold on time payments to 58 percent of those manufactured. The ten surviving independents in 1927 suffered most—General Motors, after all, had its own captive finance

* It was just that imbued integrity that so captured popular imagination. In 1949, twenty-two years after the last Model-T had been manufactured, some 200,000 were still registered in the United States.

company with ample reserves. The smaller companies were left to divide profits totaling $106 million, with Chrysler taking almost 20 percent of that. Even collectively, the independents could not keep pace with General Motors, which raked in the largest industrial profit in history: $235 million.

Knudsen more than achieved "vun for vun." Unhindered by a large competitor, Chevrolet easily moved into first place in sales in 1927, dealing off 1,001,880 cars and trucks. Pontiac sales picked up to 140,000 cars. Harley Earl's newly introduced La Salle became "the first stylists' car to achieve success in mass production," as Sloan put it; its sales were hardly spectacular, but they did not need to be. Sharing the Cadillac chassis, as Pontiac did the Chevrolet, any La Salle sold was, in effect, a boost to Cadillac volume and profits.

General Motors' first million-vehicle year came largely at the expense of the independents. Chevrolet sales increased 270,000 over the year before, but hardly enough to make up for the unmanufactured Fords. (Industry sales in the low-priced field dropped by 800,000 that year.) The combination of an economic downturn, which would affect workingmen's buying before it touched managers', and the absence of a favored car simply kept hundreds of thousands of potential buyers out of the market. Others decided to wait, to see what Ford wrought.

The squeeze on the independents was fierce. Only a handful of rivals understood that Sloan's policy of "a car for every purse and purpose" gave to General Motors a competitive advantage the rest of the industry lacked. Walter Chrysler, who had grown personally close to Sloan once the two men began working apart, was quietly taking a step toward fulfilling the full-line concept; his engineers were working on a low-cost auto to compete with Ford and Chevrolet that he would call the Plymouth. Billy Durant made a half-hearted effort to induce other independents to join his Star in a new Consolidated Motors, asserting they otherwise had no chance of survival; they ignored him and his lagging Star. Durant would prove to be right, but by then the independents would be so reduced in sales that even a merger would not save most of them.

The Ford shutdown in May, as idiosyncratic as everything else about Henry Ford's operations, aggravated a worsening economic situation. Ford began furloughing more than 100,000 workers and ended raw-material purchases, contributing to the nation's unemployment and depressing iron and steel production to its 1920 level. None of this was unusual. Automobile manufacturers traditionally shut down for two to four months annually while converting models and waiting out the slow sales season; but when they did so, they had in hand designs for the new cars, dies to stamp metal, and firm timetables for reopening.

Ford had nothing: no engine, no chassis, no designs at all. For years Ford engineers had purchased competitors' autos, stripped them down, and analyzed each part (a practice still common in the industry), then compiled a catalog of improvements to incorporate into the new Ford. If Henry Ford himself approved of them. For Ford personally, the shutdown initiated a return to the early days of the industry—to experimentation and constant testing, to the "cut and try" of old. He intended to build a light, strong car, powered by a four-cylinder engine, and he intended it to be as reliable as the Model-T had ever been. The decision to use a four-cylinder engine was crucial; when word leaked to Knudsen at Chevrolet, he ordered a speed-up on the six-cylinder engine with which his engineers had been tinkering.

Characteristically, much of Ford's design work was trial-and-error. After an accident in which a test driver was thrown through the windshield of the new car, mangling his right arm, Ford summarily ordered production models equipped with newly available safety glass. According to the definitive history of Ford's company: "Still another touch was needed. When the model seemed almost ready, Henry Ford stepped to the front with his jaw set. 'Somebody must represent the public,' he said. He slid his lanky form into a sedan, slammed the door, and stepped hard on the throttle. Always he drove at a reckless gait. He hurtled across a rough field, bumping over stones and fallen timber. Alighting on his return, he issued a curt demand: 'Rides too hard. Put on hydraulic shock absorbers.' "

Ford's designers worked throughout the summer, their dealers posting hopeful window signs reading "Wait for the new Ford," the banners becoming fly-specked as Chevrolet production reached 4,000 vehicles per day late in the spring. Ford himself remained indifferent; besides, the company already had orders, cash in hand, for 120,000 cars purchased sight unseen by customers.

The country waited through 1927, seemingly with bated breath, certainly with closed pocketbook, for "the most titanic industrial struggle in its history," as the Scripps–Howard newspaper chain described it. The putative combatants denied that they were to do battle, certainly not to engage in the price war every newspaper in the country was predicting.

Said Curtis C. Cooper, president of the General Motors Acceptance Corporation, which would provide much of the armor for its champion, Chevrolet: "The idea of a battle between two individuals for control of automobile sales never enters the minds of the directors of General Motors. Product, not financial strength, will be the issue."

For his part, Ford assured the country that "We have no desire to take business away from any automobile manufacturer. . . . If any particular automobile company's success meant putting out of business some other automobile manufacturer, there would be no gain in that; it would only mean putting thousands of men out of work, letting valuable power go to waste, and maybe, throwing a great industry out of balance."

Neither man and neither corporation was entirely forthright, to put it as mildly as possible. Both Ford and General Motors intended to do battle, beginning with Ford's announcement of his new auto in December 1927. In the meantime, "there is not on record a single instance of a refusal of a Chevrolet dealer to sell a car to a Ford owner," financial commentator Merryle Rukeyser wryly observed.

On August 10, 1927, the design of Ford's new model was fixed, and the company began converting its factories. Major production was to be at River Rouge, a factory that would grow to gargantuan size during the next years, but thirty-six other assembly plants around the world also had to be reorganized. The work was slow. There were 5,580 parts in the new automobile, each requiring special machine tools to produce. By mid-

October, the assembly lines were in place, and production workers were coming back to work in increasing numbers.

The long-awaited car was announced in a teaser ad campaign that ran beginning on November 29 for five consecutive days in 2,000 newspapers across the country. The cost was a boggling $1.3 million, but the consequent nationwide excitement in a decade periodically galvanized by fads, fancies, and bizarre enthusiasms was unprecedented.

Ford had named it the Model-A.

Curious about the styling, which had been kept a carefully guarded secret, hundreds of thousands stormed dealer showrooms in the first hours on December 2. "Excitement could hardly have been greater had Pah-wah, the sacred white elephant of Burma, elected to sit for seven days on the flagpole of the Woolworth Building," the New York *World* pronounced. The crowds could only be compared to the tumultuous reception given Charles A. Lindbergh, when the aviator returned from his pioneering transatlantic flight. No sports hero—not Gertrude Ederle; not the awesome New York Yankees of 1927, led that year by Babe Ruth's sixty home runs; not Jack Dempsey—ever stirred as much excitement in a single day. Pushing throngs in front of the Ford Motor Company's New York showroom spilled onto Broadway for blocks around; the managers rented Madison Square Garden that afternoon and moved cars and crowds there through the rain. Police struggled to control mobs in front of the showrooms in Cleveland and Detroit. The Kansas City Convention Hall closed its doors in desperation. In Los Angeles, 30,000 waited in 86-degree heat outside Ambassador Auditorium waiting to see Ford's machine.

Many were coming to admire an automobile they already had purchased on faith in Henry Ford alone. The company held 400,000 orders by the time the showrooms opened that morning. What the crowds discovered, Edsel Ford admitted, was hardly a radical innovation. The Model-A was, he told reporters, more conventional than the original Model-T had been in its day. Still, the car embodied its manufacturer's commitment to sturdy workmanship, reliability, and low price. The forty-horsepower engine provided quick acceleration for what was, essentially, a light car on a short chassis. The automobile would deliver twenty to thirty miles per gallon of gasoline, "depending upon speed," the Los Angeles *Times* reported.* The old irritants of transmission, ignition, and throttle were gone, replaced with improvements upon conventional systems. Gone, too, were the rattles of the bolted-together Tin Lizzy. The Model-A's assembly depended heavily on welding. The Model-A was comfortable to ride in, and, though some thought the body "looked a little as if it had been put on as an afterthought" (it had), the car came in a variety of colors. A Ford buyer could specify, *mirabile dictu,* either Niagara blue, Arabian sand, or Copra drab.

The Model-A was at least as up-to-date as the competition, and in a few touches—the safety-glass windshield and the hydraulic shock absorbers—well ahead. Most important, Henry Ford had priced it close to the Model-T it replaced, still intent on underselling his competition. The closed coupe listed at $495, $100 less than Chevrolet, and the sedan at $570, $125 below Chevrolet. The open coupe also sold for $495, $130 less than Chevrolet's competing model. Oddly, the once despised "convertible" models had increased in price as closed cars took more than 80 percent of the market; in a few years, with little improvement in their "one-man" tops, they would become prestige vehicles, tagged with the highest prices. Such were the benefits of mass production.

With the opening of the 1928 New York Automobile Show, General Motors countered with $10-to-$50 price cuts on Chevrolets. John Willys followed suit, cutting the Whippet by as much as $200. Finally, Billy Durant, making one last attempt to salvage an automobile empire, announced that he was bringing out a new Star and would match Ford's prices and models. Willys and Durant, precariously financed, risked everything on this throw of the dice. The price war had begun.

* Appropriately enough, the *Times'* lead story was headlined "Nation Rich and Happy/ Hoover Reports We Prosper/American Living Standard/Highest Ever Known,/Says Commerce Secretary." A short item in the paper reported that "Miss Soong, a Wellesley graduate, married Gen. Chiang in Shanghai."

Automotive Industries whimpered that the Model-A's prices were "too low for the conventional type of industrial organization which is publicly owned [Ford, of course, was owned entirely by the family] and under a moral obligation to pay a more or less regular return to its stockholders." In fact, the posted prices were far too low for Ford himself. Confronted with interminable delays in getting his production line up to speed, the company actually lost as much as $335 on each car sold. But with cash reserves of $200 million, Ford could dismiss these losses until his production increased and he could begin working off the backlog of 700,000 orders in hand by the end of January.

Despite the excitement swirling about the Model-A, General Motors remained confident. Sloan was certain that the old man would hew to his ways and keep the Model-A in production indefinitely. Meanwhile, as Sloan wrote to Lawrence Fisher, "the great problem of the future is to have our cars different from each other and different from year to year." Eventually, the unchanging Model-A would appear to have aged, even if Ford and Chevrolet remained on a par mechanically.

For 1928, Knudsen was introducing a Chevrolet with two design changes: a chassis lengthened to 107 inches to accommodate the six-cylinder engine that would be ready the following year, and a hasty restyling of the body by Harley Earl. The Model-A might have the lower silhouette of more-expensive automobiles, but the 1928 Chevrolet conveyed an aura of size and distinction.

The burden now rested on R.H. Grant, the bespectacled salesman with a passion for the histrionic. Richard Ralph Hallam Grant was part showman, part technician, and all salesman. Short, with small hands that constantly punctuated his conversation, Grant was as voluble as Knudsen was laconic, as slight as Knudsen was huge. Grant had made selling not only a life's career, but a "science" to be mastered since his graduation from Harvard in 1901. At National Cash Register, he had become a demon salesman of pneumatic delivery devices for sales receipts at department stores. Lured to Delco Light, he sold electric generators to farmers and then 20,000 Frigidaires in the first year he was given responsibility for selling them. As a result of his success at Delco, Grant had been transferred to Chevrolet, where he became Knudsen's general sales manager. "You make them; I'll sell them," he told the production manager in his distinctive down-East accent. A lack of confidence was never one of "Dynamic Dick's" faults.

Taking advantage of Ford's difficulty in bringing his assembly lines up to full production, Grant whipped his dealers with quotas, sales campaigns, and cash prizes. By the middle of the year, Chevrolet production had reached 5,300 vehicles a day. Meanwhile, Ford was still shuffling his River Rouge assembly lines, substituting stamped metal for cast parts, and shaving pennies here, nickels there. Even Ford's last capitulation to the new realities of automobile sales—the creation of his own captive finance company, Universal Credit—could not help Ford keep pace; he simply lacked the cars to sell. At its peak late in the spring, the backlog of Model-A orders reached 800,000 vehicles. Not until September would dealers begin getting adequate deliveries, and by then sales supremacy for the year clearly would go to Chevrolet—and Grant.

Amid the hoopla celebrating the clash of titans, Walter Chrysler made a series of moves that by the end of the year would rank him as a member of the newly designated "Big Three." In April, he introduced the new, six-cylinder De Soto as a low-cost complement to the car bearing his own name. That same month, banker-broker Clarence Dillon, ruing an earlier enthusiasm for automobiles, put the fading Dodge Brothers on the market. Dillon apparently first approached General Motors, assuming it was the only company large enough to relieve him of his white elephant, but Sloan declined. (Three years earlier, Dillon had outbid General Motors for the Dodge properties; since then, General Motors' expansion program had eliminated the need for additional factories.) Instead, Sloan recommended that Dillon sound out Chrysler, who desperately needed both production facilities and the 4,600 Dodge dealers.

In five days of marathon bargaining in a suite at New York's Ritz-Carlton, Dillon and Chrysler came to terms. While the Dodge and the Chrysler were directly competitive, Chrysler would adjust the price of the car bearing his name. The Dodge alone would compete with the Buick, while the Chrysler squared off against the Cadillac and La Salle. More importantly, Chrysler had acquired the necessary production facilities for the four-cylinder Plymouth, which would be introduced in July. Actually a refurbished Maxwell, Plymouth was at best a weak, overpriced competitor to Chevrolet and the Model-A, but Chrysler expected to follow the Ford blueprint of lowering prices as his production climbed. Chrysler had become, in the space of just three months, the second automobile company with "a car for every purse."

Sloan was more pleased for his friend than worried about the possible competition, and, as a gesture of friendship, he, Kettering, and Mott each bought 1,000 shares. There was more than enough business in these years of four- and five-million auto sales. In fact, none of General Motors' executives ever had fancied that such prosperity was possible. General Motors was selling one of every three new cars driven from dealers' lots. Gross sales reached almost $1.5 billion, and the corporation had posted a profit of $296 million, or 50 percent on its investment. Every car sold produced an average profit of $150; each of the automobile divisions was profitable; and laggard Oldsmobile was catching up.

Success conferred prestige. As chairman of the powerful finance committee, John Raskob acquired a prominence on Wall Street that gave him a reputation among the press as a "maker of millionaires." A hint from Raskob and the stock market gyrated in manic spasms. Sailing for Europe in March 1928, Raskob casually confided to dockside reporters that he thought General Motors should be selling for fifteen times its current earnings. Over one weekend the stock jumped $13, and before year's end it had reached the suggested figure. The investors' faith knew no bounds; if General Motors was worth fifteen times its earning power, why not twenty times, or twenty-five? Confidence fueled prosperity, and prosperity inspired confidence.

A photograph taken late in 1928 of a group of General Motors executives, on the occasion of a dinner in their honor hosted by the Muncie Chamber of Commerce, demonstrated their sense of well-being. Sloan stood with his hands clasped in front of him, staring straight at the camera, deadpan, defying it to probe beneath the surface. Knudsen bulked tall in the center, his inevitable derby set squarely on his head, no nonsense; his dapper white spats flashed below the cuffs of his black pants. In the front row, a young man grinned broadly under a wide, snap-brim fedora; later, someone would inform Charles E. Wilson, the recently appointed special assistant to the president, that rising young executives at General Motors did not wear light-gray suits. Altogether, the twelve men assembled looked quite like the men in charge of the nation's largest business.

There were two faces conspicuously missing from the photograph taken on the steps of the Chamber of Commerce: Pierre du Pont and John Raskob. Raskob had resigned under pressure, and Pierre du Pont had followed his friend voluntarily. Perhaps Raskob's departure could have been predicted; Sloan never had appreciated Raskob in his role as "self-appointed spokesman of General Motors." As chairman of the finance committee, Raskob was responsible for explaining to increasingly avid newspapermen the company's rapid earnings and stock-market increases, and had acquired a prominence out of proportion to either his value to the corporation or his contribution to those elevated profits.

Had Raskob's tie to General Motors been less public, perhaps Sloan would have disregarded the finance committee chairman's deepening involvement in politics. Through Pierre du Pont's interest in a national committee to end Prohibition, Raskob had been drawn into the anti-dry campaign. Another committee member introduced Raskob to New York's governor, Alfred E. Smith, and the two men—both Catholic, both poor boys who had bootstrapped their way to success, and both wets—became fast friends. When the jaunty Smith, the band blaring "The Sidewalks of New York," captured the Democratic nomination for the presidency in June 1928, he asked his new friend to become chairman of the Democratic National Committee. Such an appointment would go far to proving that Al Smith was the businessman's friend. With Pierre du Pont's encouragement,

Raskob, a lifelong Republican who listed his occupation in *Who's Who* as "capitalist," accepted.

No sooner had Raskob moved the national headquarters of the Democratic Party to rented space in the General Motors Building high above Fifty-seventh Street—the better to view America— than a prickly rash of editorials questioned his appointment. Alarmed editors, who had overlooked similar appointments by Republicans, questioned the implications of having a powerful "capitalist" as chairman of the committee. (Actually, it is an appropriate appointment for either party, since the chairman's job, above all else, is to raise campaign funds.)

Backed largely by the Fisher brothers on the board of directors, Sloan insisted that Raskob resign either as chairman of General Motors' finance committee or as Democratic Party chairman. "The management of General Motors, particularly myself, felt it would be very unsound for an individual who was managing a political campaign to continue as a spokesman of General Motors," Sloan later explained. (Sloan conveniently disregarded the precedent set by C.S. Mott, who served three terms as mayor of Flint, then ran unsuccessfully in 1920 for the governor's seat in Michigan, all without resigning his General Motors offices.)

Raskob refused, claiming a leave of absence would be sufficient. Sloan dismissed the suggestion on the grounds a leave would appear merely convenient.

The intracompany battle was savage, the conflict heightened by the fervid support of Herbert Hoover by Sloan and the Fishers. Despite Pierre du Pont's hint that he would resign as chairman of the board were Raskob forced out, Sloan put the issue to the board of directors. The vote was split, with a majority favoring Raskob's resignation. Sloan later insisted, "It was not a question of partisanship. It was a question of principle." After all, four members of the board—Knudsen, Pratt, Mooney, and chief counsel John Thomas Smith—were Democrats.

Raskob was deeply hurt, and du Pont pained for his friend. Both resigned their posts, du Pont to be succeeded by his brother

Lammot, though they would continue as nominal members of the board of directors. Neither again would play a truly active role in General Motors.*

Despite the departure of Raskob and du Pont, the corporation they had helped to restore continued to flourish. Virtually everything General Motors fondled turned to gold. It was clearly the largest automobile manufacturer in the United States and would sell 1.8 million automobiles before the end of 1928. The export business had grown until General Motors, the sixth-largest corporation doing business in Europe, was the continent's largest automobile manufacturer.

The company's alchemic powers spilled into refrigeration. It would sell the one-millionth porcelain-coated Frigidaire in the next year, and wizard chemist Thomas Midgley, Jr., had begun the search for a nontoxic refrigerant that eventually would transform home refrigeration.

When the du Pont family in 1927 and 1928 invested in United States Rubber, eventually to buy 30 percent of that company and a controlling interest, General Motors promptly signed a contract to purchase one-half of its tire requirements at favorable prices. So favorable were they that the company eventually bought up to two-thirds of its tires from the sister corporation. (It was safer than an earlier $3.4 million effort to crack the British-managed rubber cartel by stockpiling raw rubber at low prices. The cartel merely cut its price temporarily below General Motors' cost.)

New industries that, like the automobile, symbolized this age of prosperity, attracted the corporation. General Motors Radio Corporation would begin next year. Sloan had assigned his special assistant, Charles E. Wilson, to look into Kettering's sugges-

---

* Du Pont thereafter devoted himself to the gardens at Longwood, to the directorates of various banks and industries, to collecting family memorabilia in France, and, most notably, to building schools in Delaware for black children. Because he was no longer a corporate employee, Raskob cashed in, as the bylaws required, the $20 million in General Motors stock he had purchased as part of the Managers Securities plan. Together with a combine of other Smith supporters, Raskob built the Empire State Building, investing his General Motors profits there. That real-estate venture turned out badly; for all its fame, the building was as impractical as the dirigible mooring mast with which Raskob planned to top the 102-story structure. Du Pont and Raskob drifted apart in the late 1930s, du Pont turning to Delaware and Raskob to New York City, neither ever to understand the social and political upheaval that was taking place.

tion that the struggling airplane industry was close to achieving a
"flying flivver." If so, General Motors' mass-production skills
would stand them in good stead. Wilson was recommending
major investments, not only in manufacturers, but in airlines as
well. It would make a strong hedge against saturation in the
automobile market and at least give them parity with Henry
Ford's earlier investment in aircraft production.

Meanwhile, Sloan and Kettering had turned their interest to
diesel engines, long neglected and relegated largely to powering
boats. It was a personal interest; both men owned yachts. Kettering spent more time in the engine room of the *Olive K.* than he
did at the helm, tinkering with the balky diesel. Sloan promised
manufacturing facilities if Kettering solved the diesel's problems. By 1930, General Motors would be launched on a development program that would doom that venerable symbol of
American enterprise, the steam locomotive.

Meanwhile, the automotive divisions expanded. Chevrolet
alone had achieved profits of $75 million in 1927 and $92 million
the next year, while rival Ford, crippled by its shutdown, posted
net losses of $121 million for those two years. Knudsen had a
new six-cylinder engine ready for the 1929 Chevrolet, the first
counterblow against the fast-growing Model-A. Priced just $30
more than Chevy's four-cylinder model of 1928—Grant's advertising fudged a bit, claiming "a six for the price of a four"—the
new car would be in the hands of dealers just sixty days from the
time the last 1928 Chevrolet left the factory.

Buick would have an entirely new model for 1929—the first
automobile totally designed by Harley Earl for the corporation.
Cadillac and La Salle, with a novel synchronized transmission,
which made shifting gears easier, were closing on Packard. Oldsmobile had introduced its higher-priced Viking to share parts
with Buick, while Buick had a low-cost car, the Marquette,
ready for 1929. In all, General Motors would have seven car and
two truck lines to offer to the avid public when the New York
Automobile Show opened in January.

There never had been anything to compare with such industrial success. And 1929 would be even better.

11

The Siege

"The big men in the country have got to get together and do something about it," former President Calvin Coolidge declared from his retirement home in New Hampshire. "It isn't going to end itself."

The "big men"—the bankers and industrialists who had battened on Coolidge prosperity—were paralyzed with fear. They watched as once-vast fortunes, whole industries, the work of a lifetime vanished with the streaming lights on the Trans-Lux: Radio down 50, Motors down 30, Telephone down 25. Down. Everything down.

At first, the Crash on Black Thursday seemed nothing more than a temporary setback, a wringing out of overinflated stocks. If thousands of small investors were wiped out and millions upon millions in paper values erased, the big men could be philosophical. "Wall Street Lays an Egg," *Variety* joked in what was to become a classic headline. The fundamental economy was sound, Secretary of the Treasury Andrew Mellon insisted, be-

264

fore the decline affected the big men themselves. Investor confidence soon would set matters to rights.

The flash of panic between Black Thursday and Blacker Tuesday—October 24–29, 1929—abated momentarily. Some stocks even recovered slightly when such investors as Billy Durant returned to the market scavenging for bargains. Even more reassuring, the Rockefellers too were buying stocks, the senior John D. announced, for the fundamental economy was sound.

There were too few true believers, however, and too many pessimists. The market did not turn about, but instead began a long slide. Wall Street's fear percolated through the country. One by one, then in droves, people began to curtail their purchases and to hoard small savings. The Crash had not directly touched the great majority of Americans, who merely watched the stock market as if it were some sort of spectator sport. But when that sweet bird of prosperity tumbled from the skies, confidence evaporated; suddenly it seemed wiser to hold off, to wait and see what happened, to put off buying the refrigerator, to postpone the vacation, to make the two-year-old Nash do for another twelve months.

A million such individual decisions slowed sales and consequently slackened production. The federal government's index of industrial output sank from 1929's high of 125 to a low of 58 in the summer of 1932.

Automobile production had been the one pre-eminent symbol of American prosperity, and, in turn, the President's Research Committee on Social Trends concluded in 1933, had "created an 'automobile psychology'; the automobile has become a dominant influence in the life of the individual and he, in a very real sense, has become dependent on it." In "Middletown" (Muncie, Indiana), gas stations were "one of the most prominent physical landmarks of the city"; a traffic policeman wrote citations for overparking in the downtown business district; and the city of 47,000 recorded 2,500 traffic accidents a year. Even in the worst of the Depression that set in after the Crash, "the local sentiment, as heard over and over again, is that 'People give up everything in the world but their car.' "

But the pre-eminent symbol of prosperity became the pre-eminent victim of the Depression. In 1929, the last and greatest of the boom years, the industry had sold 5.3 million motor vehicles, a million more than the previous record year of 1925. On the eve of Black Thursday, General Motors stood as the largest of a dwindling number of automobile companies, though Ford's Model-A, finally in full production, had outsold Chevrolet's six-cylinder competitor by 400,000.

Within a year, "mass idleness" at Henry Ford's 1,100-acre factory on River Rouge dragged "like a dead weight on the city—on the world," Anne O'Hare McCormick telegraphed the New York *Times*. Nothing seemed to stimulate sales. Even price cuts that brought Chevrolet and Plymouth within $90 of Ford's $500 Model-A were not enough. Between 25 and 33 percent of automobile dealers, heavy with used-car inventories, sank with barely a trace. Already burdened local banks found themselves with unsaleable used cars weathering in the summer sun.

Amid the crash, Sloan stood resolute, assuring stockholders, as Rockefeller had, that "Business is sound." But business was not sound, nor was the financial underpinning, and no simple benediction would restore it. General Motors' stock had stood at $73 a share on September 3, 1929, the last day of the Great Bull Market. It had fallen to one-half that in the Crash and would continue down until it bottomed at $8 in 1932. Sales of $1.5 billion in 1929 fell by one-third, profits by 40 percent, and employment by 50 percent a year later; the company's best-selling line, Chevrolet, operating just four days a week, had sold one-half million fewer cars.

The entire automobile industry was suffering the hangover from the party President Coolidge had hosted. Through the 1920s, accumulating wealth had gravitated into a black hole of the already affluent, never to emerge. Less than 3 percent of the nation's population held two-thirds of all savings; sixteen million families could not afford the $800 per year the government believed necessary for an adequate diet. There simply were not enough people able to afford used cars, let alone new ones.

Size then became fundamental to survival. (In 1931, only those corporations with assets of $50 million or more showed a profit; by 1937, concentration would be so severe that just six companies, General Motors among them, would garner one-quarter of all industrial profits.) Declining sales riddled the already dwindling band of independent producers. Gone were such long familiar marques as Jordan, Velie, Jewett, Marmon, Peerless, and Stutz, which were done in even before the Crash. The Depression wiped out even more, notably Overland and Studebaker, both of which went into receivership to re-emerge gravely ill in 1935. Six of the fifteen best-selling automobiles of 1923 no longer were in existence a decade later.

Three major firms captured the bulk of what few automobile sales were to be had by 1932: General Motors, with 41 percent of the market; Ford, with 24 percent; and Chrysler, their one emergent rival, with 17 percent. Sixteen others scrambled for the remains.

Despite the automobile slump, or because of it, General Motors used a portion of its rainy-day surplus of $400 million to expand into new fields: radio, aircraft and airlines, and, most lucrative of all, diesel engines. All were "natural acquisitions," logical areas of expansion, Sloan asserted. "Natural" they were, but only for a corporation that was, as financial editor B.C. Forbes put it, "rapidly becoming in reality an investment trust."

The first investment, and what appeared to be the most immediately profitable, was in radio. General Motors Radio was a $10-million joint venture with Radio Corporation of America, General Electric, and Westinghouse; the auto company owned 51 percent of the stock and was to manage the venture into "radio sound and picture receiving."

The most complicated of the expansions was into the nascent aircraft industry. Intrigued by possibilities of a "flying flivver," an airborne version of Ford's Model-T, Charles Kettering and Sloan's special assistant, Charles Wilson, urged the expansion of their long-moribund Dayton aircraft laboratory. Aircraft production could prove a hedge against the ultimate saturation of the automobile market. Between 1929 and 1933, General Motors purchased Allison Engineering Company, a tiny Indianapolis firm that had developed a small engine for a "family-style" plane; helped organize Bendix Aviation; and invested in a succession of holding and operating companies that evolved into

North American Aviation, one of the three largest aircraft holding companies formed by Wall Street interests.*

The third of the three new investments was the least likely to produce immediate profits, but, ironically, proved to be the most profitable over the years. Kettering's experiments aboard the *Olive K.* and in his laboratory had pointed to an innovative type of diesel engine, one that might be fitted to trucks as well as to ships. In June 1930, Kettering arranged the purchase of the small Winton Engine Company of Cleveland, which had built the two diesel motors for his yacht; Winton would become General Motors' diesel manufacturing plant when Kettering had the new engine perfected.

Six months later, one of Winton's customers for gasoline engines, Electro-Motive Company, sold out to General Motors. Electro-Motive built gasoline-powered rail cars but lacked an engine powerful enough to meet railroad needs, as well as the cash to develop it. The railroad market intrigued General Motors; sheer survival animated Electro-Motive. For a total of $7 million, General Motors had bought both Winton and Electro-Motive, and with them a revolution in railroading.

Yet even expansion-minded General Motors could not escape the Depression entirely. Marquette and Viking died after only one year, victims of anemic sales and a corporate decision to concentrate efforts on Buick and Oldsmobile. Oakland, overwhelmed by its offspring Pontiac, succumbed in 1931. Cadillac sales plummeted to just 3,900, and Sloan convened executive-committee meetings to discuss that division's future; the majority favored closing the line in favor of the cheaper La Salle. Chevrolet sales had fallen well below the point of being able to

---

* By 1934, General Motors controlled or owned a plurality of the stock in North American Aviation, Eastern Air Transport (later Eastern Air Lines), Western Air Express (later Western Air Lines), and Transcontinental & Western Air (later TWA), as well as holding large interests in Bendix, Douglas Aircraft, and the Northrup Corporation. According to Alfred Sloan's *My Years with General Motors,* General Motors' major contribution to the industry was managerial, not technological. The corporation began dealing off its airline interests after the passage of the Air Mail Act of 1934, which required divestiture of airlines by manufacturers. Thus, General Motors lost the rich air-mail subsidies it and two other Wall Street combines had obtained in closed meetings with Herbert Hoover's postmaster general, Walter Folger Brown. General Motors held onto its manufacturing facilities—North American Aviation and Bendix Aviation—until 1948.

make up for the losses of the other divisions; in 1932, General Motors actually lost $4.5 million on its automobile production. Only the income from its outside investments and its finance companies enabled the corporation to post a slender $8.3 million profit.

Reviewing the long slide, William Knudsen argued, "The low-priced cars hung on the longest, but finally they started to slide, too, and the only thing the automobile business could do was to follow the trend of dropping income, try to hit for the lowest priced field, and give the best possible car for the money so we could tempt people to go back in and buy some more cars."

Others had the same idea. Plymouth had proven a formidable contender when its 1931 model, with eight body styles, made that automobile the most technologically advanced in the low-cost field. John Willys had scuttled the Whippet in favor of a new, low-priced Willys, and from the wreckage of Durant Motors emerged the short-lived DeVaux. In 1931, Studebaker introduced the Rockne (named for Notre Dame's football coach), had a losing season, and abandoned it the next year.

The crucial element was building mass production fast enough to overcome the high initial costs, and "tempting people" with mechanical improvements as Walter Chrysler had with the Plymouth. For General Motors, it meant a major shift in policy and the necessity of overcoming corporate inertia. As early as July 29, 1929, Sloan complained to the corporation's sales committee, "You have no idea how many things come up for consideration in the technical committee and elsewhere that are discussed and agreed upon as to principle well in advance, but too frequently we fail to put the ideas into effect until competition forces us to do so." The competition would soon be even more fierce.

In the early summer of 1929, Albert Bradley had spotted a decline in the national index of production. According to his working hypothesis, automobile sales were most vulnerable and would presage either a downturn or an upturn in the national economy. The ten-day sales reports from General Motors dealers confirmed Bradley's hunch. On October 4, three weeks before the Crash, Sloan hinted to stockholders that for an indefinite period they would be confronted with lower returns, while the corporation gave "more detailed consideration to value in respect to price."

That consideration to value first involved safety glass. Despite its introduction with the 1928 Ford Model-A, and its adoption by competitors the following year, Sloan resisted the improvement he acknowledged was "bound to come": "Two or three years ago I would have felt that perhaps it was a desirable thing for General Motors to take an advanced position similar to what it did on front wheel brakes, but the way things stand now with our volume increasing at a decelerated rate, I feel that such a position can not do other than to materially offset our profits."

Cadillac had installed safety glass; competitive Packard had not, Sloan continued. Yet Packard actually had increased its sales lead over Cadillac–La Salle by 9,000 vehicles. "In other words, I do not think that from the stockholders' standpoint the move on Cadillac's part has been justified," Sloan wrote Lammot du Pont, the president of E.I. du Pont de Nemours.

Both men recognized that safety glass was a major improvement over conventional plate glass used till then in automobile windows. "However, irrespective of accidents or no accidents, my concern in this problem is a matter of profit and loss." General Motors, Sloan wrote du Pont, could install safety glass, but only by "absorbing a very considerable part of the extra cost out of our profits." Such a move would be detrimental to "the comparatively large return that the automobile industry enjoys and General Motors in particular." The 48-percent return on its motor-vehicle investment was inviolate, whatever the carnage among the motoring public.

By 1932, Sloan still resisted the installation of safety glass on Chevrolets, though Knudsen, the division's general manager and soon to be promoted to executive vice-president for all motor-vehicle production, wanted it all the more. Ford had it; he would have it too. Sloan believed motorists were "entitled to this extra protection to the degree that they are willing to pay for it, but I do not feel that it is equitable to charge the General Motors stockholders with the cost of it if the public shows it is not interested to pay a reasonable extra for it and so far they have not evidenced that willingness. . . . You can say perhaps that I am selfish, but business is selfish. We are not a charitable institution—we are trying to make a profit for our stockholders."

The single-minded Sloan was not alone in that fetid summer of 1932. Coolidge's "big men" remained paralyzed, unwilling to take risks to stimulate sales, or like Herbert Hoover, Coolidge's successor, ideologically opposed to tampering with the national economy. Things would get better if only the public had confidence.

Some sixteen million people were unemployed as Democrats gathered in Chicago in June 1932 to pick a presidential nominee. Another of the big men, purblind John Raskob, still chairman of the party, stepped down from the Broadway Limited and told assembled newsmen, "Prohibition is the greatest economic and social question of the day." Perhaps it was to the wealthy Raskob, but not to those sixteen million who could not feed their families, let alone toss off a glass of needle beer in the neighborhood speakeasy. In industrial cities like Buffalo, Akron, and Pittsburgh, unemployment ran as high as one-third the labor force; the frightened wage-earner took home but 40 percent of his 1929 pay. Since 1929, some $26 billion in wages, salaries, and farm income had been lost; the nation's gross national product had plunged from $104 billion to $58.5 billion in the same period.

The bellwether industry was withering. General Motors produced only 570,000 motor vehicles in 1932, and the industry recorded a deficit of $122 million. Not only were people not buying new automobiles, they were driving less. For the first time in history, gasoline sales were down, Sloan wrote Lammot du Pont, "indicating that the economic situation has reached the point where people must use their cars less."

Sloan intended to wait out the storm. Wearing the stiff, high collars of an earlier age, he still rode to work each day from Snug Harbor or his Park Avenue apartment in a chauffeured Cadillac, the sandwich wrapped in a brown paper bag on the seat beside him an oddly humanizing element. Once at work in his office in the General Motors Building, he could see far below him, if he bothered to look at all, the biggest bread line in New York City. William Randolph Hearst "had a big truck with several people on it, and big cauldrons of hot soup, bread. Fellows with burlap on their shoes were lined up all around Columbus Circle, and went for blocks and blocks around the [Central] park, waiting."

The longer the slump, the worse were conditions in Detroit. At its peak in 1929, the automobile industry had employed 475,000 production workers. By the end of 1931, fewer than half were working four or less days each week; payrolls fell even further, to one-third 1929's $733 million. Among blacks, unemployment was estimated at 80 percent. Numbed men looked for work, then slowly succumbed to despair and stopped looking for jobs that were not to be found. Eventually they swallowed their pride—usually the day their children went without their first meal—and applied for relief. Already spending $2 million a month, Detroit's welfare department could expend only five dollars per family each week.

Meanwhile, tax collections fell, and interest on the city's debt took $43 million of the $51 million the city raised in 1932. The banks had to be paid, for if a city the size of Detroit defaulted, the banking crisis would paralyze the country.

Detroit's bankers, hard hit when their own speculative investments turned to ashes, stood in line for their own form of welfare handouts: "While the mortgage and consumer markets were starved for funds, and the bankers' committee damned 'welfare chiselers' and insisted on further reductions in the municipal budget, the banks cannibalized the money of savers and investors." One of the city's two major bank holding companies also used its own shares as security for loans, a violation of both federal and state banking laws; loaned money to officers—$33 million, more than its total capital; and issued fraudulent financial reports and met daily withdrawals only because the city's welfare fund was on deposit.

When all else failed, the Union Guardian Trust Company turned to President Hoover's belatedly created Reconstruction Finance Corporation for $51 million, counting on the fact that the ex-president of the Hudson Motor Company, Roy Chapin, was not only a trustee of the bank, but Hoover's secretary of commerce. Henry Ford refused to permit his own loans to the bank to be subordinated in favor of the federal government and thus blocked the RFC loan. Confronted with the prospect of the bank's failure, Michigan Governor William Comstock ordered the 436 banks in the state closed on February 14, 1933. Better a moratorium in the face of incipient panic than collapse.

Business in the automobile industry, the city of Detroit, and the entire state was frozen. Five weeks later, General Motors stepped in at the request of the federal government to organize a new bank. General Motors announced that it intended to stay in the banking business only for the emergency, but the big men were finally doing something.*

They were too late to save the dispirited Herbert Hoover. Having stood against the economic tide for three years, he had little left to throw into the 1932 presidential campaign. Within his circumscribed economic view, he had done all he could; the system had failed him, not he it. Yet millions blamed him personally for the continuing Depression. Hoover had little taste for the fall campaign.

The Democratic Party's nominee feasted on it. Franklin Delano Roosevelt traveled 25,000 miles, criss-crossing the country by train. His speeches were never very specific—the Democratic platform was as heavy in economic pieties as Raskob could make it—but Roosevelt did talk about a New Deal for "the forgotten man on the bottom of the economic pyramid." It was a vague promise, Walter Lippmann warned: "Franklin D. Roosevelt is no crusader. He is no tribune of the people. He is no enemy of entrenched privilege. He is a pleasant man who, without any important qualifications for the office, would very much like to be President."

Roosevelt promised just enough to stir hope and anger in such stalwart Republicans as Alfred P. Sloan, Jr. The Democratic nominee called for a public-works program, unemployment insurance (a long-forgotten Progressive Party plank), public power, and, most threatening to Sloan, "regularization and

---

* General Motors sold large blocks of its bank stock to company executives and the public at cost. In April 1945, it disposed of the remaining 51 percent for $20 million. By then, the bank had assets of $1 billion and was the thirteenth largest in the country.

planning for balance among industries and for envisaging production as a national activity." Business, the Democratic nominee bellowed from the back of his campaign train, "must think less of its own profit and more of the national function it performs." Roosevelt took his heresy into San Francisco's Commonwealth Club, a donjon of privilege: "Private economic power is a public trust. . . . Continued enjoyment of that power by any individual or group must depend upon the fulfillment of that trust."

The promise of some governmental action was enough. On November 8, 1932, Roosevelt defeated the exhausted Herbert Hoover and six minority candidates by seven million votes, capturing 472 electoral votes to Hoover's 59.

In the interregnum between election and inauguration on Saturday, March 4, Roosevelt sought a program. The answers were vague; many, including Bernard Baruch, who loomed larger and larger as a presidential advisor, could suggest only the old panacea of balancing the budget. Sloan, along with others, refused to cooperate at all, turning down a Senate Finance Committee invitation to contribute his thoughts on the grounds that he was "entirely out of sympathy" with the senators, and what was really needed was "relief from government expenditure."

Washington was chilled by blustery winds as the president-elect, leaning on his son James' arm, shuffled to the platform erected on the east front steps of the Capitol. As yet Roosevelt had no program, only a farrago of proposals contributed by a hastily organized "Brain Trust," as the newspapers called his advisors. But the Bible upon which Roosevelt swore the oath of office was opened deliberately to Corinthians I:13: "And now abideth faith, hope, charity, these three; but the greatest of these is charity."

Speaking to the frightened people huddling in makeshift "Hoovervilles," the angry farmers he had been warned were near revolt, and the numb men who had for three years stuffed cardboard into their shoes because they could not afford new soles, the thirty-second president of the United States said, "So first of all, let me assert my firm belief that the only thing we have to fear is fear itself—nameless, unreasoning, unjustified terror which paralyzes needed efforts to convert retreat to advance." Then he set to work saving the old order.

Sloan's antipathy to the New Deal was instant, pervasive, and vocal. As early as May 1933, at the opening of the Chicago Exposition boasting a century of progress, Sloan's banquet address scored "taxation, government regulation, and the elimination of freedom." (Sloan's political sensibilities were acute: upon discovering that Mexican artist Diego Rivera was a communist, General Motors canceled its contract to have him paint the murals for its exhibition hall in Chicago.) After the dinner, one of the well-fed industrialists ignored the crowds waiting to ogle Sally Rand's coy flirtation with a handful of fans to wander instead through the General Motors exhibit. Ralph Budd, the president of the Chicago, Burlington & Quincy, was intrigued with the company's display of two small diesel engines that Kettering and the former Winton Engine Company had developed. Budd decided these were just the power plant needed for the crack passenger train he envisioned. With some reservations, General Motors agreed to produce a special version of the engine, intended for use on navy submarines, so that Budd might have his Burlington Zephyr. That much-publicized train was a major factor in convincing both General Motors and the railroads that diesel power was more economical than steam. Had Budd been of more prurient mind, the introduction of the diesel locomotive would have been delayed by ten years.

Though Sloan never would concede the fact, the very presence of Franklin Roosevelt in the White House went far to stir a sense of confidence across the nation. *This* president would not sit by while the country went to hell in a hand basket. With long-hoarded caches, people began to make modest purchases. Individual sales multiplied, one upon another, and soon local merchants began ordering more goods. When those sold as well, the more optimistic butchers and druggists and haberdashers decided they just might go down and look over the new 1934 models after all.

There was much to see, though most of the changes since 1929 were cosmetic—rearrangements of trim or newly reshaped fenders. Mechanical improvements came slower. Whether from inertia, or a conscious policy of not being first with new technology, General Motors lagged behind other manufacturers in incorporating mechanical changes in its automobiles. Stressing "the car's the thing," Chrysler had quickly gained a reputation for its innovative engineering. Ford was first to bring out a new model with a V-8 engine in the low-priced field in 1932. (The Model-T had lasted nineteen years, its successor, the Model-A, just four, done in by what the public took to be major improvements in competitive automobiles each year.) In the meantime, Chevrolet hewed to the six-cylinder engine Knudsen had introduced in 1929, adding refinements but retaining the basic design. While the company resented sorely the nicknames that motor acquired, the "Cast Iron Wonder" or "Stove Bolt Six" would be the basic power plant for all Chevrolets until 1953.

Unless mechanical improvements could be sold to the public in terms of riding comfort or ease of handling, General Motors shunned them. Instead the company concentrated on an improved front suspension and automatic transmission, but, most of all, on the evolutionary styling changes flowing from Harley Earl's design section. None were *too* novel: the built-in, rather than bolted-on, trunk incorporated as part of the body rather than an appendage; wind wings in the windows; gently sloping windshields; twin taillights and headlights protruding from, rather than perched atop, fenders. All were touted in iridescent advertisements timed to coincide with the annual model announcements on November 1. (The industry had agreed to that date, beginning in 1935, to help smooth out peaks and valleys of employment; the usual winter slump would correspond to the layoff period necessitated by model changeovers. Before the end of the decade, the annual model announcement would be transformed into a kind of national holiday for an automobile-avid public.)

The restyling of General Motors' automobiles, after Earl's first go-round, was never to be too radical, too innovative, Sloan ordered. There was always the example of Walter Chrysler's Airflow, introduced in 1934 as the very zenith of streamlining.

The teardrop design did slightly improve the car's top speed. "You have only to look at a dolphin, a gull, or a greyhound to appreciate the rightness of the tapering, flowing contour of the new Airflow Chrysler," the company advertised. Customers attending the festive opening for the automobile turned away cold, however. Chrysler sold just 11,000 of the cars its first year and 4,600 in its last, 1937. The smaller De Soto Airflow did no better. Industrial designer Henry Dreyfuss shrugged off the tapered front and rear as "the classic example of going too far too fast" in outdistancing public taste. The usually discerning editor of *Harper's* magazine, Frederick Lewis Allen, dismissed the Airflow as "so bulbous, so obesely curved as to defy the natural preference of the eye for horizontal lines."

Neither Dreyfuss nor Allen would appreciate just how much General Motors—its automobiles still fitted with vertical radiators, high hoods, and bulky contours—contributed to the public's rejection of the Airflow. Fearing acceptance of the design, and the necessity of undertaking what would be a $100-million retooling effort to remain competitive, General Motors discovered that a quarter of those who saw the car disliked it, while half had no opinion one way or another. "Our job was subtly to suggest that Chrysler had made a wrong guess," the advertising man handling the General Motors corporate account later confessed. The resulting campaign was keyed to the slogan "An eye to the future, an ear to the ground." The first clause "obviously implied that GM also was looking ahead, not back. The second half was the real keynote of the campaign, interpreted to mean that GM did not make rash changes, without consulting the people's desires."

The corporation's conservative strategy was successful. Chevrolet, which built its ten-millionth automobile in 1934, produced its fifteen-millionth just five years and two $25-million retoolings later. But the greatest success was Buick, which had sunk to just 40,000 sales in 1933. A new general manager, Harlow Curtice, revived the division with a "higher speed and lower price" policy.

The promotion of "Red" Curtice to Buick general manager was a significant departure for the corporation. Until then, the managers of the automobile divisions had been engineers or production experts, men skilled in the mechanics of automobiles. Curtice was one of a new breed—the professional manager—making its way upward in Corporate America. He had gone to work as a bookkeeper in the AC spark-plug factory in Flint and in nineteen years had climbed to the presidency of that division. From there he was shifted to anemic Buick.

Curtice was but the first. The more the General Motors form of industrial organization served as a model for other companies, the more the demand for professional managers and highly trained staff. The "growth of corporate enterprise in America has been drying up individual independence and initiative," Russell Leffingwell, a partner in J.P. Morgan, told the Senate Finance Committee in 1935. "We are becoming a nation of hired men, hired by great aggregates of capital." The shift had come rapidly, accelerated by the massive concentration of American industry in the 1920s; yet word had filtered to even such smaller communities as Muncie, Indiana, where "Andrew Carnegie's advice to enterprising young men to begin at the bottom no longer appears to be sound advice. Men of his type are advising young men today to get a toehold in one of the managerial or technical departments halfway up the ladder."

The rise of the professional manager did not, for the while, prevent all enterprising young men from forcing their way to the top, but enthusiastic go-getters such as Cadillac's new general manager would become corporate rarities. Nicholas Dreystadt had come to the United States in 1912 as a thirteen-year-old apprentice mechanic on the touring Mercedes racing team. By the time the Depression laid Cadillac low in 1932, Dreystadt had worked his way up to works manager for the division, a job he might have lost soon but for a bold stroke.

Learning that General Motors' executive committee was meeting on the fourteenth floor of the corporation's Detroit headquarters in June of 1932 to decide whether to continue manufacturing its grievously overpriced Cadillac—consensus favored abandoning it for the cheaper La Salle—Dreystadt crashed the meeting. It was audacious—a thirty-three-year-old ex-mechanic in a tweed jacket scarred by pipe embers bursting in upon the well-appointed, formal Alfred P. Sloan and Donaldson Brown. In a heavy Swabian accent, Dreystadt asked for ten minutes' time and blurted out a scheme to save the automobile.

As Cadillac service manager, Dreystadt had earlier discovered that the car was very popular with the small black bourgeoisie of successful entertainers, doctors, and ghetto businessmen. A surprising number brought Cadillacs in for service—surprising because corporate policy was not to sell Cadillacs to blacks at all; the Cadillac was reserved for the white prestige market. "But the wealthy Negro," business critic Peter F. Drucker recalled, "wanted a Cadillac so badly that he paid a substantial premium to a white man to front for him in buying one. Dreystadt had investigated this unexpected phenomenon and found that a Cadillac was the only success symbol the affluent black could buy; he had no access to good housing, to luxury resorts, or to any other of the outward signs of worldly success."

Overwhelmed by Dreystadt's audacity and bemused by his proposal, the committee gave him eighteen months in which to develop the Negro market. By the end of 1934, Dreystadt had the Cadillac division breaking even, and by 1940 had multiplied sales tenfold. In the process, he redesigned Cadillac's system of production, renewed a stress on quality that would have done the late Henry Leland proud, and transformed a failing automobile into the premier symbol of the upwardly mobile. (Packard reserved for itself the old-money, landed gentry. However, there were more arrivistes in the decades of the 1940s and 1950s than gentry; thus Packard went under, while Cadillac prospered as America's status symbol.)

Dreystadt notwithstanding, it was Buick's renaissance under its new manager that was to be the corporation's model for the future. Harlow Curtice's formula was fitted to individual lines, then to the entire company, and finally adopted by the entire industry.

The year before Curtice took command of the fast-failing Buick, the corporation had melded the line with the equally sluggish Oldsmobile and Pontiac into the "B-O-P" sales division. The quintessential salesman, R.H. Grant, was given responsibility in a desperate effort to salvage the lines. The three marques had sold just 110,000 cars in 1932, slightly more than one-fifth of 1929's high. Once the flagship of the General Motors fleet, Buick was saddled with a reputation as "the doctor's car," fit for old men, "sturdy and reliable, but no fun to drive, and completely lacking in glamour."

In the language of the times, Curtice set out to "jazz up" his cumbersome beauty. The low-end Buick, the Series 40 "Standard," became the "Special." The Series 60, a light car with a large engine capable of doing 100 miles per hour, became the "Century." The Series 80 was dubbed the "Roadmaster" for 1936, and the top of the line Series 90 was tagged the "Limited." "Hot? It's a ball of fire!" shrieked the advertisements for these "great-powered, trigger-quick, light-handling" machines. "The day of the 100-mile-an-hour stock car is here," Buick advertisements proclaimed.

Curtice made one other contribution to automobile mythology: his personal taste. His preference ran to large hoods: dominant, preferably chrome-plated radiators; and as much bright trim as the market would bear. In his Buick, speed, size, and glittering ornament became linked forever in the Automotive Gospel According to General Motors. Curtice would ram the refurbished Buick into a comfortable fourth place in industry sales by 1939, behind only the low-priced trio of Chevrolet, Ford, and Plymouth.

By the end of 1936, General Motors not only was the largest of American corporations, but by virtue of its success had become independent of Wall Street financing. Future growth could be paid for out of profits and depreciation allowances. "All in all," the editor of *Harper's* concluded, "the General Motors inner management—a few men in New York and Detroit—exercised a power in American life probably greater than that of any state government."

In 1936, the corporation captured 43 percent of the 4.5 million motor vehicles sold in the United States. Its automotive lines were healthy again—the grateful citizens of Pontiac, Michigan, home of that car's once threatened production, presented Sloan a life-sized portrait of Chief Pontiac paid for with 90,000 pennies collected by school children. Frigidaire had snared the bulk of the refrigerator market, but found it difficult to compete with companies that made washing machines and other home appliances. Despite the failure of General Motors Radio, the corporation still ranked as the fourth-largest manufacturer of electrical goods. The new LaGrange factory of the Electro-Motive division had produced its first demonstrator models of diesel locomotives for switching and passenger service, while other locomotive manufacturers steadfastly insisted on the steam engine's superiority. The complex of aircraft companies appeared to be profitable for the first time; the army air corps was to expand in the next years, and British buyers, concerned about their country's defensive strength, had pointedly inspected the corporation's aircraft plants. Thus had free enterprise restored itself, Sloan smugly announced. Government merely impeded industrial progress, interfering with the laws of economics.

Each of President Roosevelt's successive legislative acts goaded Sloan the more, but none so much as the National Industrial Recovery Act, creating the National Recovery Administration (NRA). The bill, passed as the capstone to Roosevelt's first, furious hundred days, was a conflation of experiments that tinkered with classic free enterprise. It was what state-house politicians called a "Christmas tree bill," with something for everyone hung on it. At first intended to spread work by reducing the work week, it acquired minimum-wage and child-labor provisions, amended the Sherman Antitrust Act to permit voluntary trade associations to fix prices, gave labor the right to organize and bargain collectively, and created a $3.3 billion public-works program.

Henry Ford obstinately refused to participate in the automobile trade association, thereby scuttling any thought of that industry avoiding "ruinous competition" by the tidy expedient of price fixing. Thus died the bill's one advantage for industry; the other automobile manufacturers signed on only because of presidential pressure.

Under the NRA's Blue Eagle banner, an Automobile Labor Board functioned for just over two years, mediating disputes between labor and management. In its short lifetime, the board did more than enough to alienate Sloan and not enough to avoid the NRA being dubbed the "National Run Around" by auto workers. Nothing provoked Sloan's jeremiads more than the Blue Eagle. "Industry, if it has any appreciation of its obligations to future generations, will fight this proposal to the very last," he averred. Industry did. The NRA died under the headsman's axe on May 27, 1935, when a unanimous United States Supreme Court ruled it unconstitutional.

The president's "experiments in economics" morally offended Sloan. He opposed the Social Security Act of 1935, which established unemployment insurance and old-age pensions, for its "dangers are manifest." By September 1935, declaring "the depression is definitely behind us," Sloan warned that "we certainly are not going to tolerate any further interference with recovery." Emboldened by sales of 3.9 million cars and trucks that year, Sloan wanted no more "deflationary force of adverse political action." A rearmament boom, set off by Mussolini's invasion of Ethiopia, Hitler's reoccupation of the Rhineland, and the Spanish Civil War, had American steel mills running near capacity, and General Motors had all but doubled its employment from the low of 1932 to meet consumer demand.

Sloan's personal outrage was that of the pilgrim confronted with sacrilege. The New Deal, he asserted, sought to repeal natural economic laws. "As a people, we know, to get something for nothing is an economic absurdity," he declared. His own fear that, in fact, the people did not appreciate such economic wisdom led him, in December 1937, to set up a $10 million foundation under his brother Harold's chairmanship. The foundation's goal was to promote "a wider knowledge of basic economic truths generally accepted as such by authorities of recognized standing. . . ."

As head of the nation's largest business—United States Steel had greater assets but smaller annual sales—Sloan was an early and dedicated recruit to the conservative, even reactionary, American Liberty League. Founded in 1934 with the express aim of denying Franklin D. Roosevelt the renomination of his party, the ostensibly nonpartisan league was heavily funded by the du Pont family. Its membership was comparatively small, but represented a goodly share of the nation's financial peerage, men who feared for their fortunes under a "sovietized America." Sloan not only tithed $10,000—he could afford it, for as General Motors' largest single stockholder his dividends amounted to $2.5 million in that second year of recovery—but for the next two years spoke widely on the advantages of free enterprise and the threat posed by the New Deal.

Among the lavishly printed speeches, articles, and position papers the American Liberty League produced was a carefully reasoned legal brief dismissing the Wagner Labor Relations Act, which was passed immediately after the Supreme Court throttled the NRA, as equally unconstitutional. General Motors fastened upon the brief as *legal* authority for refusing to obey the Wagner Act's provisions permitting labor to organize freely and to bargain collectively.

The league stirred first anxiety, then ire, in the White House, but had no impact on voters. Deaf to Liberty League screeds, the Democratic Party renominated President Roosevelt by acclamation in 1936. In his acceptance speech at Franklin Field, Philadelphia, the president chided "the economic royalists who complain that we seek to overthrow the institutions of America. What they really complain of is that we seek to take away their power."

Nettled, the league abandoned nonpartisanship to support the "Kansas Coolidge," Alfred M. Landon, the Republican nominee. In a transparent attempt to sway votes, Sloan mailed a letter to all General Motors employees two weeks before the election, stating: "With the many proposals now coming forth almost daily we appeal to you all to examine carefully into their economic foundations. In other words, be sure that they are sound. Regardless of what the promises are, be sure that you understand who is going to pay for them. The economic load of our country is a matter for us all to consider and to be hardheaded is not the same as to be hard-hearted." Lest the threat be too vague, Sloan cautioned, "Class strife or economic shackles can break the company up or retard its progress."

Sloan's letter, Landon's efforts, and the Republican campaign all were for naught. Roosevelt crushed Landon, taking 61 percent of the vote and every state except Maine and Vermont. Sloan would not easily accept the bitter defeat, and less easily still the repudiation of his economic philosophy; but never again would he be so outspoken, so partisan. The president of the United States was about to teach Sloan a basic rule of American politics: Reward your friends and punish your enemies.

12

The Assault

"Shut it down!"

The young men in the patched work shirts dodged along the assembly line of the Cleveland plant of the Fisher Body Corporation, shouting at the startled workers. "Shut it down, goddamnit! They refused to talk."

One by one, the assemblers stepped away from the workbenches and lighted cigarettes.

"Shut it down!"

The command flashed through the factory. The line of all-metal, turret-top bodies for the nation's best-selling automobile ground forward, missing door hinges, windows, and side panels.

"Shut it down!"

The plant manager had postponed a meeting scheduled for that afternoon to discuss the reduced piece rate paid during this changeover to the 1937 models. From the quarter-panel section, word passed to steel stock. The warehousemen snapped off the power to their cranes and climbed down.

"Shut it down!" the men in the work shirts shouted over the

clanking of the assembly line and the distant thump of the steam press. Men in the metal assembly and trim departments folded their arms as the line ground on.

Within minutes, the command had skittered through the building. On December 28, 1936, the most important strike in American labor history had begun. It had come prematurely, a week before the fledgling United Auto Workers of America had planned it, and it had come in the wrong plant. It was in Flint where union leaders had planned to lay siege to the largest industrial enterprise the world had ever known.

There had been sporadic attempts to organize automobile workers as early as 1913, when the Industrial Workers of the World targeted Henry Ford's Highland Park plant. Ford's five-dollars-per-day wage offer and the flood of 10,000 job applicants had crushed the first attempt at an industry-wide union. The recession of 1920–21 had shattered the one craft-centered union of Carriage, Wagon, and Automobile Workers, which at its peak claimed a membership—mostly in body factories—of 40,000. What the recession did not do, Duco paint accomplished; layoffs in finishing departments, where the union was strongest, wiped out its membership.

In the years since, the American Federation of Labor had ventured hesitantly into Detroit, hampered by its craft-union orientation in an industry that recognized few skills beyond tool and die makers and by its own conservatism. AFL president William Green was derided by rebellious members of his own unions as "Sitting Bill."

For all the organizing efforts, "G.M., like its rivals, was a complete and rather skittish virgin in collective bargaining." Until the coming of the NRA, Sloan wrote later, General Motors had dealt only with a bare handful of craft unions in the construction industry. The corporation was not ready for the burst of union activity the New Deal loosened, and Sloan was "unaccustomed to the whole idea."

Under the sponsorship of the National Industrial Recovery Act, the unions had sought qualified representation in the auto factories. But without a closed shop, confronted with toadying company unions, harassed by management and especially foremen who had virtually unfettered power to bestow favors or fire workers, the hardly militant AFL had floundered. With the Supreme Court's decision in June 1935 ruling the NRA unconstitutional, even that limited form of representation had evaporated.

At the same time, General Motors adopted a policy of what later would be called welfare capitalism. From Billy Durant's days of building needed housing for workers in Flint—"shotgun" houses that stretched for dreary blocks between the factories he heaved up—to the more recent employee savings plan, General Motors sought to portray itself as a benevolent, paternal figure. The fatherly posture stopped short of providing real security. The automobile industry had taken one major step toward eliminating long winter layoffs by moving the introduction of new models from January 1 back to November 1. But whatever spirit of generosity prompted the change, it was more than overshadowed by economic considerations of another sort: the shift in the introduction date made it possible to overlap the usual model-turnaround layoffs with winter layoffs, thereby extending the selling season by about two months.

During the depths of the Depression—and pushed by the demands of the NRA—the corporation had limited workers to forty-eight hours per week, with a long-term average of forty hours. The purpose was to stretch out available work; the employees took proportionate wage cuts. Nevertheless, the principle of the eight-hour day was established. William Knudsen, raised to executive vice-president in charge of operations in 1933, hewed to the limit.

Auto companies also had granted wage increases, an average of nine cents per hour, in hopes that sixty-four cents per hour would keep workers from organizing. Why pay dues to a union when the corporation was so generous without a union to prod it? Average annual earnings of $749 during the 1933–34 model year had increased to $1,399 by 1936. In the assembly plants, where the pay was some 17 percent higher than in the parts plants, there was little discontent over wages by the time the strike of 1937 erupted.

The grievances ran deeper. Increasing auto sales and steadier employment had wiped away some of the fear with which auto workers had lived since October 1929. First the NRA and then the Wagner Labor Relations Act of 1935 gave them heart. The overwhelming reelection of President Roosevelt in 1936 had reinforced their courage. There would be no better time for the born-again United Auto Workers, split from the somnolent American Federation of Labor little more than a year earlier, to begin recruiting in General Motors plants. No more than 700 Cleveland–Fisher employees held union cards; about the same number were members at the sprawling Chevrolet complex in Flint—counting the company spies.

Yet something of the Depression-born fear did not easily vanish; it never would for these men and women. At the worst of the Depression, employment in the industry had fallen from 1929's high of 470,000 to just half that. Paychecks were chopped from $33 to $20 a week, and still "men eye each other with distrust and compete in their efforts to maintain their places. Every bad quality of a human being comes out at this time, and every man is deliberately made an enemy of the others by this trickery of the company."

The distrust was pervasive, fostered by the corporation. Labor spies were everywhere. The world's largest industrial corporation was also the world's largest employer of detective agencies; between the end of 1933 and July 1936, General Motors paid $1 million for the services of no less than fifteen agencies. There were never fewer than fifty company spies in the city of Flint, the heart of the corporation's factories. They had infiltrated the plants and burrowed into the AFL locals. Fearing exposure and instant dismissal, workers had dropped away from the union; the Flint local's membership of 26,000 in 1933 under NRA protection had declined to just 122 by the summer of 1937—and two of its officers were company spies. The spying was not solely focused on union members, the head of the Pinkerton office in Detroit acknowledged. It was extended to "somebody who may have arrived at certain conclusions himself and wanted to force them into the minds of others, and thus get them a little excited, and have them join some radical organization."

General Motors was acutely sensitive about its elaborate espionage network. In the month after a Senate committee sub-
poenaed Pinkerton records relating to "industrial espionage,"
Harry Anderson, General Motors' director of labor relations,
stripped the company's files of material relating to its intricate
spy system. Anderson testified in February 1937 that he had
"about one drawer" of files, kept no copies of correspondence,
and did "most of his business over the telephone."

Senator Robert La Follette was skeptical. "Did you make an
examination of Mr. Sloan's files?"

"No, sir; I did not," Anderson testified. In fact, he had ordered Sloan's secretary to dispose of the reports forwarded by
Anderson.

"Did you make one of Mr. Knudsen's?"

"I did, sir."

"And whose idea was it that you should go through Mr. Knudsen's files?"

Anderson was protective. "It was my idea."

"Did you get permission from him to do it?"

"No; I just done it."

"Sir?" La Follette feigned disbelief.

"I just done it," Anderson stubbornly reiterated. "I told the
secretary I wanted to go through his files."

"What did you tell her you wanted to go through his files for?"

"I gave her no explanation; I mean I gave him. It was a male
secretary. I mean, I gave him no explanation." La Follette's
cross-examination evidently had rattled Anderson.

"Is it possible for officers who are subordinates to Mr. Knudsen to walk in his office and just tell his secretary they would like
to look through his files?"

"It is so far as I am concerned."

"Who ever gave you permission to do that?"

"No one gave me permission. I went ahead and done it."

"What did you have in mind in making this search?"

"This investigation."

"What did you do with the papers you found that you thought
might relate to the general subject matters of this inquiry in the
Knudsen file?"

"I threw them in the wastebasket."

Again the feigned incredulity. "You threw them in the wastebasket?"

"Yes, sir."

"How about Mr. Wilson's files?"

"I did the same with Mr. Wilson's."

"With the same purpose?"

"Yes, sir."

"And to accomplish the same result?"

"Absolutely."

Fearing union organization, General Motors also had taken what it steadfastly termed "defensive measures," including the purchase of more than $24,000 worth of tear gas from 1933 through 1935. The purchases were handled with some secrecy; deliveries often were made to the homes of plant managers rather than to the factories, and some of the purchases were then turned over to local police for their use in the event of a strike.*

Shortly before Christmas in 1936, the antagonists began probing. An emboldened United Auto Workers union, affiliated now with the Congress of Industrial Organizations, announced that it would seek to represent the workers in collective bargaining. "We are hoping there will be no necessity for a strike," CIO president John L. Lewis asserted. "That will be up to General Motors."

In a speech opening a new factory in Indianapolis, Knudsen countered. The company would not discourage organizing "done on legal and constructive lines," he stated, adding, wistfully as it turned out, "I think collective bargaining is here to stay but I do think collective bargaining ought to take place before a shutdown rather than after." Point, counterpoint; the fugue was running.

Four days later, Knudsen sat down with UAW president Homer Martin for the first time. Martin came primed to discuss union recognition, complaints of a speed-up, job insecurity and

* General Motors' arsenal did not approach the lethal capacity of Youngstown Sheet and Tube, which armed itself with eight "Army type machine guns" and 40,000 rounds of ammunition. See Report, Part III, *Violations of Free Speech and Rights of Labor* (Washington, D.C., 1937), p. 72.

especially the firing of workers for suspected union activity, and the union's proposal to shift from piecework to weekly wages. Significantly, actual wage increases were not among the demands.

Knudsen evaded discussion of the issues, asserting that the corporation itself was not responsible for these matters; each was in the province of local plant managers. It was a clumsy ploy, coming at a time when Chevrolet's division manager, Marvin Coyle, required his plant managers to teletype his office when they left for lunch. Union officials took Knudsen's response as a refusal to bargain. Martin left the General Motors Building on West Grand Boulevard realizing that the union would have to strike.

Still, when it came, the strike stunned General Motors. In the preceding six months, corporation executives had watched the nationwide index of production slowly creep back up until it reached 121, just four points shy of the magical level of October 1929. Automobile production had climbed with it; the industry would produce more than 4.4 million cars and trucks in 1936, a half-million more than in 1935. The recovery promised to continue into 1937.

There was no better antidote to labor fever than strong sales and continued production. If that did not eliminate the virus, so the industrialists' prescription ran, then a nickel-an-hour increase would end all complaints. Before the darkness of 1932, the nickel palliative might have been sufficient, but no longer. The automobile worker had lost faith in an industrial cornucopia. Instead, he had learned to fear summary dismissals by high-handed foremen, unexpected plant shutdowns ordered by distant, barely recognized bosses, and killing speed-ups that drained him of anything but the will to survive for another day. Above all, he was terrified of growing old. Only the young could stand the pace in the factories. "Men near forty find great difficulty in securing jobs with the industry or being rehired after layoffs," economist Leon Henderson noted in a 1935 report for the National Recovery Administration.

"At the end of nine hours, after a man has worked that way, he can hardly move," one auto worker testified before a Senate investigating committee. Even after a half-hour lunch, "my shoulders and arms got so stiff that I could not raise them with the level of the machine when I got back to work." A man did not have time to rest in a half-hour, and after work, "You go home and go to bed. You are just tired out, just feel like sitting down or laying down and resting."

Even then, a man could not rest, an auto worker's wife told one of Henderson's investigators in Flint. Her husband came home so tired that he lay in bed at night, shaking, unable to sleep. The Buick and Chevrolet plants sucked the workers of vitality and poured it into a 38-percent return on investment. "They're not men anymore—if you know what I mean," another woman said. "They're not men. My husband, he's only thirty, but to look at him you'd think he was fifty and all played out."

Henderson's report, disparaged by those auto makers who did not ignore it entirely, concluded: "Labor unrest exists to a degree higher than warranted by the depression. The unrest flows from insecurity, low annual earnings, inequitable hiring and re-hiring methods, espionage, speedup and displacement of workers at an extremely early age."

Earlier strikes in the automobile industry also might have served to warn the corporation. In April 1934, workers in Kansas City and St. Louis had staged "quickies," short sit-down strikes lasting a few minutes or a few hours, to protest the speed of the assembly line. Plant managers, especially in the onrushing Chevrolet division, reported increasing "skippies"—workers deliberately refusing to tighten every fourth bolt, or screw in the sixth spark plug.

The company had clamped down. Foremen and supernumerary straw bosses ordered more men to pick up their time. The divisions installed tougher factory managers, men like the arrogant Arnold Lenz in the crucial Chevrolet No. 2 plant in Flint. A German immigrant, Lenz was understandably anti-union. As a young man, he had refused to join one in a solidly organized foundry in the old country; as if by accident, a fellow worker poured molten metal on his legs. Years later, he still carried the scars—and the anger. But he had never joined the union.

The corporation had increased the number of detective agencies watching for incipient union activity, what the La Follette committee labeled "a far-flung industrial Cheka . . . the most colossal supersystem of spies yet devised in any American corporation." Spies spied on spies, for lack of anything better to do. Much of what they turned up was useless: "Employee 556545 (Milton Struble) was heard to say he intended to buy one of the new Fords next Saturday and when another employee asked why he did not buy a Chevrolet, replied that he knew how Chevrolets were built and he would not advise anyone to buy one."

In the face of such determined opposition, Wyndham Mortimer, the UAW's first vice-president, slipped into Flint in June 1936 to begin organizing. He immediately received an anonymous telephone call in his hotel room warning him to get out of town.

Mortimer did not scare so easily. He was fifty-two, a veteran organizer, the oldest of the UAW's leaders. Yet like the younger men—whom Chevrolet plant manager Arnold Lenz complained were "full of piss and vinegar"—Mortimer was dedicated. His father had been a member of the Knights of Labor, and the young Mortimer had marched behind the parades of striking miners. He had gone to work in the pits himself when he was twelve, became a railroadman, then a steelworker before settling down in Cleveland to take a job at the White Motor Company. While there, he had organized a strong union. He was personally close to John L. Lewis, the new head of the Congress of Industrial Organizations—in part because of their shared Welsh heritage, in part because Mortimer had dug coal and still held a United Mine Workers card. Most important, Mortimer was intelligent and a tenacious, soft-spoken negotiator, as General Motors was to learn.*

Mortimer came to Flint with the certain knowledge that General Motors, for all its paternalism, was not to be trusted. He had learned that lesson with the demise of the UAW's Toledo local. When 2,000 workers at the Chevrolet transmission factory in that

---

* A dedicated communist, Mortimer was soon to be purged from the union he helped create. The labor revolution ate its children too.

city walked off in April 1934, they effectively halted production of the automobile across the country. More than 35,000 workers in other Chevrolet plants were laid off until the Toledo strikers won a four-cents-an-hour wage increase and the unwritten agreement of the corporation not to form a rival company union.

Five months after the workers went back and the flow of transmissions was resumed, the plant shut down, ostensibly for the 1935 model changeover. Plant manager Alfred Gulliver had assured the union that "as many men would be hired by the company as before." Instead, three-quarters of the machines in the plant were shipped to factories in other cities without unions, and the Toledo plant dismantled. Gulliver followed his machines to Saginaw, explaining, "But I didn't say *where* the men would be hired."

The Toledo strike also had taught UAW organizers—especially Wyndham Mortimer and Robert Travis, the major strategists—just how vulnerable was the world's largest corporation. If the loss of transmission production in one plant could shut down virtually all Chevrolet output, perhaps there were other "bottleneck" factories, despite Knudsen's vow "never to be in such a position again."

That vow was more easily made than fulfilled. The Depression had forced General Motors to abandon Sloan's "car for every purse and purpose," with the high-priced market evaporating to just 1.5 percent of all automobile sales. To stay alive, Pontiac, Oldsmobile, and Buick had crowded new models into the under-$1,000 market, sharing parts to keep costs down. Between the most expensive Chevrolet and the cheapest Buick was but a $170 spread.

Interdivisional competition and executive bonuses provided the incentive for each of the automobile lines to attempt to maintain a separate identity. Where there were no differences, the nation's largest advertising budget—$20 million—went to maintaining the illusion of difference. At one time, the corporation's automobile lines had been clearly distinguished by price: "Chevrolet for *hoi polloi,* Oakland (later Pontiac) for the poor but proud, Oldsmobile for the comfortable but discreet, Buick for the striving, Cadillac for the rich." But the class distinctions had blurred as the price range compacted. Demarcations came not from equipment, but largely from gradations in body design, trim, and upholstery. Cadillac, La Salle, Buick, Pontiac, and Oldsmobile used the same body shell, which was merely decorated with somewhat different fenders, radiators, and rear decks. Both the Pontiac and Oldsmobile Light Sixes were no more than redecorated Chevrolets. The interdivisional borrowing was so extensive that the same assembly lines turned out Buicks, Oldsmobiles, and Pontiacs.

Such corporate borrowing had left General Motors woefully vulnerable at two points the company itself called "mother plants": Fisher No. 1 in Flint and Cleveland–Fisher. Cleveland produced all of the new, all-metal bodies for Chevrolets assembled around the country. Flint manufactured the bulk of the body stampings for the corporation's other automobiles.* As much as three-quarters of General Motors' $1.4 billion in sales depended on these two factories, and it was there that the union centered its organizing efforts.

The union's weapon was the newly rediscovered sit-down, a tactic raised to strategy since the Wobblies had first used it in the United States early in the century. The sit-down had major advantages over the classic walkout and picket line. First, and most important, it left the factory in the hands of the workers; they could not be ousted and replaced with scabs without violence and possible serious damage to the plant. Clearly enough, the sit-down striker was illegally expropriating property, or trespassing; no court was quite ready to accept the arguments of

---

* The five-piece bodies being welded together in these plants included safety glass for the first time. The decision to install the glass came as a result of a nationwide furor stirred by a particularly graphic magazine article complaining of the 36,000 killed annually in highway accidents. Wrote J.C. Furnas in *Reader's Digest* for August 1935: "Flying glass—safety glass is by no means universal yet—contributes much more than its share to the spectacular side of accidents. It doesn't merely cut—the fragments are driven in as if a cannon loaded with broken bottles had been fired in your face, and a sliver in the eye, traveling with such force, means certain blindness. A leg or arm stuck through the windshield will cut clean to the bone through vein, artery and muscle like a piece of beef under the butcher's knife, and it takes little time to lose a fatal amount of blood under such circumstances." Apparently, General Motors' chief stylist, Harley Earl, ignored Furnas' warning of "the lethal array of gleaming metal knobs and edges and glass inside the car." Thirty years later, these metal knobs and edges would be central to consumer advocates' demands for automotive safety.

union lawyers that the workers had a coequal right to their jobs. (Years later, the illegality of the 1937 strike still rankled. C.S. Mott burned with indignation: "They were illegally occupying it. The owners had the right to demand from the Governor to get those people out. It wasn't done." In 1939, with the *tsunami* of sit-downs past, the Supreme Court would rule them illegal.) Second, the sit-down averted violence, for any assault on picket lines outside the plant by police, national guardsmen, or hired thugs would only provoke retaliation against valuable machinery. Lastly, a comparative handful of men could do the deed.

That was all they had when Cleveland–Fisher jumped the gun. Though the union had planned to sit-down at that plant, the strike was intended to begin in Flint after the January inauguration of Frank Murphy, the former major of Detroit, as governor of Michigan. Better someone sympathetic to the rights of labor in the governor's mansion than the conservative Republican whom Murphy was replacing; the governor would have the power to enforce any court order General Motors was sure to obtain. (The union did not know that, when elected, Murphy owned a considerable block of General Motors stock, which he sold quietly in the middle of the next month.)

Sparked by the cancellation of the meeting to discuss the reduced piece rate by the plant manager, 700 of the 7,100 rank and file at Cleveland–Fisher took matters into their own hands four days early. Chevrolet body production came to a halt. Two days later, some two hundred members of the Flint local on the night shift—tipped that the corporation was about to move the vital body-stamping dies out of the plant—seized the huge Fisher No. 1, while another hundred captured companion Fisher No. 2, a mile away. Workers who wanted no part in the strike peacefully walked off, many leaving their lunches behind for the strikers' larder.

Within a week, the General Motors Corporation had been paralyzed. Sympathetic sit-down strikes broke out in Remy and Delco factories in Anderson, Indiana, and Toledo, Ohio, and in Detroit's Cadillac plant. One by one, the company began closing assembly plants across the country as the supply of automobile bodies and parts dwindled, then vanished.

The strike centered in Flint by tacit agreement; the Cleveland sit-downers abandoned their hostage factory with the corporation's pledge not to attempt to reopen it until the Flint strike was settled. In that city, pickets paraded in the freezing winds along the quarter-mile plant frontage while the union marshaled forces for a long siege. With the tacit cooperation of the company—a cooperation that neither side could quite acknowledge for fear of losing face, but a cooperation that made the eventual settlement possible—the union fed the sit-down strikers from field kitchens set up across the street from Fisher No. 1.

The men inside the building, once the main plant of defunct Durant Motors, organized. Not wanting to give Lenz an excuse to reoccupy the plant by force, they hewed to self-imposed discipline. The building was swept daily, and trash collected for company trucks to haul away. Toilets and showers were cleaned, with the company providing soap, brooms, and toilet paper.

Meanwhile the strikers settled in as best they could. Unfinished auto bodies became sleeping quarters for the men not on guard, hung with signs reading "Hotel Astor" and "Mills Hotel." The most luxurious, its interior smothered in sheepskin used to polish finished bodies, was dubbed "Papa Sloan." Short of the nominal clean-up duties, there was nothing to do but wait.

To combat the dreary routine inside the plant, the men entertained themselves. The Fisher Body Stay-In Band organized to play country music, including the quickly dashed off "The Fisher Strike," a parody of "The Martins and the Coys":

> These four thousand union boys,
> Oh, they sure made lots of noise,
> They decided then and there to shut down tight.
> In the office they got snooty,
> So we started picket duty,
> Now the Fisher Body shop is on a strike.

There were organized sports inside the plant, including football games played in front of lackadaisical company guards in the fields surrounding the plant. Liquor was banned after a few ugly incidents, and on a couple of occasions enterprising prostitutes made house calls. Those uninterested in the hookers could get occasional furloughs to spend a night at home.

Despite the overtly peaceful setting, the men inside both plants prepared for an expected assault by company guards, deputy sheriffs, or some combination of the two. They arranged fire-hose drills and bored machicolations in sheet metal and placed them in window frames. They heaped nuts, bolts, and door hinges at strategic locations. Others turned to producing "Blackjacks out of rubber hoses, braided leather, and lead, and the blackjacks became a sort of symbol of the strikers' readiness to defend themselves. Some of the left-wing observers of the strike were impressed with the communal aspects of life within the plants, but private enterprise reared its head inside the strike community in the No. 1 plant as the strikers began selling blackjacks to the souvenir hunters. The 'No. 3A' blackjack plaited in leather sold for $1.25, and the 'Model 9F skull crusher' for $2.00 or $2.50 if autographed."

For the while it was a fine holiday. The real struggle was elsewhere in smoke-begrimed Flint: this was General Motors' home turf, and the corporation's influence was pervasive. An estimated 80 percent of Flint's 150,000 residents directly depended on the weekly paychecks of the company's 47,000 employees in that city. The city manager had once owned a foundry that manufactured automobile parts for General Motors. The three local judges were Republicans. Since 1911 and the election of a Socialist as mayor, General Motors had strongly influenced, if not absolutely controlled, city government. Union organizers could not get a city permit to pass out handbills. The Flint *Journal* refused the union's ads and left union activities unreported.

General Motors' attorneys worked over the New Year's holiday to prepare a court petition requesting an injunction to order the strikers out of the two Flint plants, end picketing outside, and permit nonstrikers to go back to work. In a city with three Republican judges on the bench, the injunction was a foregone conclusion. But of the three judges, only Circuit Judge Edward Black was available when company attorneys came to court.

Black dutifully issued the injunction on January 2, 1937. Within a day, the union discovered that Black held 3,365 shares of General Motors stock valued at $219,900 and was therefore in violation of a state law barring a judge from hearing any case in which he had an interest. The torrent of embarrassing publicity severely undercut the corporation's defense of outraged morality; the strikers' illegal seizure had been more than matched by the judge's apparent collusion. Black hardly helped matters when he whimpered, "It sounds like communist talk to me. I pay taxes in Genesee County too. But no one criticizes me when I sit in a case which involves the county." General Motors abruptly dropped the injunction tactic for a month.

The Black embarrassment forced General Motors to shift its strategy to convincing the residents of Flint and the idle workers that "What happens to General Motors happens to me." A public-relations consultant reminded the company's executives in a memorandum to Donaldson Brown that the corporation was "peculiarly vulnerable," since it was so big, so successful, and its leaders had so vigorously opposed President Roosevelt just months before: "Our position at all times must be that of a reasonable employer who is unfortunately being victimized by irresponsible professional agitators whose demands exceed all reasonable limits. Any other attitude at this time would place our whole case in jeopardy, regardless of the basic merits of our side, and would be politically about as stupid a blunder as we can commit. We must not forget that there has been an election."

The first move was to set up the "Flint Alliance—for the Security of Our Jobs, Our Homes, and Our Community." Dominated by General Motors, this ostensibly civic-minded body was headed by George Boysen, a Buick paymaster for twenty-four years and a former mayor of Flint. His ex-boss, Harlow Curtice, the bookkeeper who became Buick general manager, was Boysen's contact with corporation executives. The Flint Alliance began signing up hundreds of local residents—men, women, and schoolchildren, General Motors employees or not—all pledged to getting the strikers out and the workers in. The larger the Alliance, the more it would appear that the strikers were a small minority of workers (true) who did not represent the sentiments of the bulk of General Motors' employees (dubious at best). The Alliance's intended role was to demoralize the strikers.

Any strike is a test of will, of the capacity of the workers to go without paychecks and the corporation to forgo production. Short of intervention and forced arbitration—unheard of at the time—the winner is that party able to hold out the longest, or that feels it has the most to gain by holding out. General Motors, for all its size, enormous profits, and dedication to the prerogatives of free enterprise, was vulnerable to the lost production. Idle plants pained Knudsen personally, and the threat of lost profits—other manufacturers were building vehicles at full production—vexed Sloan. The auto workers' union, buttressed by the support of the CIO, was not in desperate straits. A comparatively small number of men had to be fed daily, and strikers' families were banding together to pool their resources. The big worry concerned the nonstrikers idled by the sit-down—whether they would sign up with the Flint Alliance, or support the strike tacitly while their families went hungry.

On January 4, 1937, Sloan released to the New York press a notice to be posted on company bulletin boards responding to union demands. Ostensibly addressed to employees, the notice urged that they "have no fear that any union or any labor dictator will dominate the plants of General Motors Corporation. No General Motors worker need join any organization to get a job or to keep a job. . . . You do not have to pay tribute to anyone for the right to work." It was a straw man. The union had not asked for a closed shop, but Sloan, every bit the rhetorical equal of union organizers, was intent on public opinion, not a strike settlement. Sloan departed for Detroit in his private railway car the next day, spoiling for the fight: "Let them pull the workers out. That's the only way I know to find out how strong the union is."

To bring pressure on the strikers, now estimated to number no more than five hundred, General Motors began closing factories that were still in production. By January 10, approximately 106,000 workers were idle, some 25,000 of them in tense Flint. Minor scuffles between pickets and laid-off workers ruptured the uneasy truce; then what labor men afterward dubbed the "Battle of the Running Bulls" shattered it completely. The corporation's direct complicity was never clear, and probably unimportant. But the pitched battle in the early dark of January 11 did not improve General Motors' standing.

The skirmish began when company guards at the small Fisher No. 2 plant suddenly barred the way to union members bringing the evening meal for the hundred men inside the building. When the supply train moved around to the side of the building and attempted to carry the food up a ladder through a second-floor window, guards snatched the ladder away. The conflict escalated, suddenly serious, the truce unraveling. Despite a temperature of 16°F, a company official turned off steam heat to the building. City police, coordinating their efforts with company guards, sealed approaches to the factory.

The union ordered reinforcements, some from as far away as Detroit, where the president of the Kelsey–Hayes wheel local, Walter Reuther, recruited the biggest men he could find from Jimmy Hoffa's teamsters local. Together they set off to join Reuther's younger brother Roy, already in Flint and a celebrity because of his clever use of the union's sound truck.

Before Reuther's group arrived, a force of men inside Fisher No. 2, armed with factory-made billy clubs, seized the main gate. The company guards fled, as if by prearrangement, to a women's restroom, and barricaded themselves in there while their chief called local police to report his men had been "captured." Arriving police formed a line, firing tear gas at the union sympathizers clustered around the gate. At close range, the gas shells—purchased by General Motors and secretly furnished to the department—exploded amid the workers. The pickets scattered, but the wind blew the gas back upon the police. As the officers retreated in choking confusion, the strikers in Fisher No. 2 turned a fire hose on them, and followed up with a barrage of two-pound door hinges.

The police fled beyond the strikers' range—soaked, gassed, and humiliated. They regrouped and charged again, only to be driven off a second time by a fusillade of bottles, hinges, and stove bolts. Again they retreated, but a handful, safely out of range, drew their pistols and fired wildly at the exhilarated men milling about the gate. Fourteen strikers fell, one wounded seriously.

Governor Frank Murphy and 1,200 members of the National Guard arrived the next day, Murphy moving into the Durant Hotel to assume a personal role in the escalating struggle. The governor was risking a great deal politically in tense Flint. Ambitious enough to consider the presidency within his reach, Murphy was a dedicated civil libertarian unwilling to temper principle to ambition. His election in November, riding on the coattails of President Roosevelt, had fortified his conviction that working-class and Catholic voters—he represented both—were the future of the Democratic Party. More dogged than brilliant, he saw himself as the quintessential democratic man, convinced he could rise by virtue of conscientious public service. His own career, thus far, had proved him right.

At age forty-six, his red hair thinning, Murphy still liked to box to keep fit, a decided advantage for the burden he was about to undertake. Fewer men were better suited. Despite his own working-class background, he gamboled among Michigan's growing number of millionaires, squiring a succession of notable beauties to the delight of gossip columnists. Lawrence P. Fisher was a close personal friend. Murphy felt comfortable among workers and executives alike.

His first priority, Murphy believed, was to prevent further violence; he confined the National Guard to an empty schoolhouse. "The state authorities will not take sides. They are here to protect public peace," Murphy announced. If it had been General Motors' ploy to invoke the National Guard to break the strike, it had failed. Further, Governor Murphy ordered the use of state relief funds for the families of striking workers.

General Motors was "in no spiritual shape to fight an honest holy war." The corporation's public position had been eroded by the Battle of the Running Bulls and the fourteen wounded strikers; by the concurrent revelations of the Senate Civil Liberties Committee detailing General Motors' vast purchases of tear gas and extensive use of labor spies; and by the lingering embarrassment of Judge Black's investment portfolio.

Both sides accepted Murphy's invitation to mediate the dispute in his office in Lansing. After fifteen hours of negotiation, the union promised to evacuate the plants, and General Motors agreed not to resume production. Both parties also agreed to begin formal negotiations on Monday, January 18, four days later.

As scheduled, sit-downers evacuated three General Motors plants in Detroit on Saturday. The strikers were met by a band and Walter Reuther singing hoarsely into a mobile sound system, "The boss is shaking at the knees, / He's shaking in his B.V.D.'s. / Hinky dinky parlez-vous."

Just hours before the strikers were to leave the key Flint plants, the détente ruptured. On Sunday morning, United Press reporter William Lawrence casually informed union leaders that he had seen the text of a telegram from William Knudsen in the offices of the Flint Alliance assuring the organization that "we stand ready always to discuss with your group or any group of our employees any questions without prejudice to anyone." Fearing the Alliance as a potential rival in the plants, and keenly aware that the organization had never before asserted itself as a *labor* union, United Auto Workers officials termed the Knudsen telegram a "double-cross." They canceled the planned evacuation of the critical Fisher Body plants. Murphy's carefully wrought truce had broken down.

At this point the federal government stepped in. President Franklin D. Roosevelt and his secretary of labor, Frances Perkins, combining with the governor to maintain a "steady pressure upon the corporation, and upon me personally, to negotiate with the strikers who had seized our property, until finally we felt obliged to do so," Alfred P. Sloan complained, his outrage still clear more than a quarter of a century later.

Sloan, Donaldson Brown, Knudsen, and corporate counsel John Thomas Smith met with Secretary Perkins only after she agreed to their two conditions: "absolute silence" and no face-to-face negotiations with union representatives. The four traveled to Washington in Sloan's private railway car; reporters discovered them anyway. Just as there was no secrecy, there would be no negotiations. Sloan lost his temper, stalking up and down the secretary's office, denouncing John L. Lewis, the union, and the sit-downs that had deprived General Motors of its plants and its lawful profits. Sloan peremptorily broke off his tirade and the negotiations.

The next day, January 20, President Roosevelt took the oath of office for the second time. In his inaugural speech, he recalled the "economic royalists" of his earlier Franklin Field address and his pledge to drive them from "the temple of ancient faith"—a pointed reference to the four General Motors executives who had left town furtively the night before.

Still Sloan stood inflexible. "We cannot see our way clear to accept the invitation to negotiate further with the union while its representatives continue to hold our plants unlawfully," he announced from New York. Meanwhile, the corporation sought to improve its public-relations posture. It offered to open the parts plants closed earlier, to put men back on the job while stockpiling parts for future production. Since the cars still could not be assembled, the union privately encouraged its men to go back to work.

On the last day of January, the syndicated Gallup Poll reported that 53 percent of those who had an opinion sided with "the employers." (One week later, Gallup would tabulate public opinion favoring by two to one General Motors' refusal to negotiate until the plants were cleared.) The stalemate favored the corporation.

General Motors then went back into court, seeking an injunction ordering the strikers out of the plants. Even with a new judge, the union had no hope of winning even a delay in the issuance of the order.

Clearly on the defensive, a tight handful of union leaders conceived a bold counterstroke: seizure of the massive Chevrolet No. 4 plant in Flint, probably the most important factory in the far-flung GM enterprise. One million Chevrolet engines issued from the factory each year, and while depriving the bodiless Chevrolets of motors was overkill, capture of the plant would signal union vitality and corporate weakness. It also would have a stimulating effect on lagging morale among the strikers.

Aware that the company had infiltrated spies into its ranks—at least two were among the men holding Fisher No. 1—union leaders formulated a multilevel deception. Ostensibly to protest discrimination in rehiring by the Chevrolet factory manager, Arnold Lenz, they would stage a protest rally. That rally, the planners leaked to the suspected spies, was in reality a cover for a quick move to capture Chevrolet No. 9, a nearby plant.

Lenz "discovered" the plot. When a decoy group of strikers started through Chevrolet No. 9, shouting for the mingling day and swing shifts to sit down, company guards, Lenz himself in the van, came down on them. For almost an hour, the two groups fought, blackjacks and clubs against weapons *trouvés*. Lenz ordered his men to fire tear gas in the unventilated factory and finally drove the strikers from the building.

Meanwhile, a hand-picked group of union members working in the No. 4 engine plant emerged from the latrines as the swing shift settled in, then raced up and down the lines, demanding a shutdown. Here and there workers resisted, then gave way. Strikers turned off machines; supervisors and straw bosses turned them back on. Reinforced with men from an adjacent plant, the strikers slowly overwhelmed the dwindling opposition. Moments later they escorted the supervisors to the gates, dismissing them "in the words so familiar to the frequently laid-off auto workers, 'We'll let you know when to come back.' " Forty minutes after they began, the strikers were in effective control; Lenz, duped, was left to rage bootlessly against "the communists."

The following day, Judge Paul Gadola issued the expected injunction. Governor Murphy was confronted with the problem of enforcing it. Murphy preferred to temporize, rejecting the sheriff's suggestion that he declare martial law, turning down a National Guard plan to scatter the growing picket lines with troops. Still seeking a negotiated settlement, Murphy had one crucial supporter, his friend Lawrence Fisher, a director of General Motors, who pleaded, "Frank, for God's sake, if the Fisher brothers never make another nickel, don't have any bloodshed in that plant. We don't want blood on our hands."

Murphy was a tormented man, ground fine between his re-

spect for the law and his sympathies for the working man. A
liberal who valued human rights over property rights, unyielding
in his opposition to capital punishment, Murphy finally told the
wife of Michigan football coach Fielding Yost, "I'm not going
down in history as 'Bloody Murphy'! If I send those soldiers
right in on the men there'd be no telling how many would be
killed."

As long as Murphy refused to invoke the National Guard,
except to patrol the perimeter of the plants and keep company
police outside, General Motors was helpless. Meanwhile, Ford
and Chrysler each had boosted production above 25,000 units
per week while General Motors could turn out no more than
6,100 vehicles in scattered plants around the country.

Apparently it was Knudsen who finally prevailed. The president of the United States had requested that they bargain. "Besides," said Knudsen, "this strike has gone on so long that
women and children are hungry and cold, and when this happens, there is no issue but to get their men back to work."
Knudsen believed that Governor Murphy had let them down in
not enforcing the court order; but, being pragmatic, he preferred
"to settle now and let the public decide later who was right and
who was wrong."

It would take another week of determined bargaining to produce a settlement, the corporation intent upon putting on the best
face possible. Sitting in separate rooms of Detroit's Recorders
Court, Murphy bouncing between them "like a jackrabbit," the
two sides struggled for a compromise. Of the three General
Motors representatives, Knudsen was the most anxious for a
settlement, union attorney Lee Pressman believed. "It was just
hurting him that his machinery was idle." Better to have Knudsen negotiating than Sloan—though Donaldson Brown and John
Thomas Smith were bad enough. Knudsen sincerely liked
people, and he loved his factories. His politics were comparatively simple, old-fashioned perhaps in an age of increasing ma-
nipulation of the consent of the governed, but they permitted him
to avoid the pitfalls of pride and prejudice into which the more
rigid Sloan had stumbled. As the negotiations dragged on, Knudsen complained to Wyndham Mortimer, "This is a hell of a conference." Of all the negotiators, the two of them were the only

former auto workers there. Left alone, they might have settled matters quickly.

But Brown and Smith kept a tight check on Knudsen. Brown was there as Sloan's personal representative, to make certain Knudsen did not give away the store, to defend Sloan's corporate policy. The man whom few in General Motors could understand impressed Pressman as "about as cold a human being as I've ever met in all my life. He gave you an impression of dollars and cents."

Though they wrangled over every sentence of the settlement, there was one major sticking point: exclusive representation of the workers. Lewis demanded it, unconditionally; General Motors refused, just as unconditionally. After five days, General Motors proposed a neat compromise. The corporation would promise verbally not to bargain for three months with any other labor group in the seventeen struck plants unless Governor Murphy approved. In effect, the UAW would have exclusive bargaining rights, and General Motors would not have to put any such embarrassing policy reversal into writing.

Lewis, the more experienced labor negotiator, held out for a six-month bargaining period, in writing. Murphy, still confronted with the unenforced court order, and President Roosevelt, worried that a prolonged strike would undercut industrial recovery, turned the screws. Murphy threatened Lewis with enforcement of the court order if he did not give up his demand for a written agreement. Meanwhile, the president personally urged Sloan, at Knudsen's suggestion, to extend the bargaining period. Sloan gave way. The entire General Motors Corporation had produced just 151 cars during the first ten days of February.

Finally it was over, John Thomas Smith telling a bedridden Lewis, "You beat us, but I'm not going to forget it. I just want to tell you that one of these days we'll come back and give you the kind of whipping that you and your people will never forget."

Early on the morning of February 11, 1937, a tired, drawn Governor Murphy, sustained only by his own excitement, announced the settlement. Ever pragmatic, Knudsen shook hands with the union negotiators, urging, "Let us have peace and make automobiles."

The strike had lasted forty-four days. A handful of union members, never more than 2,000 in all the affected plants, had barred 44,000 others from working by a tactic as illegal as it was effective. Some 110,000 other General Motors employees, in sixty factories across fourteen states, had been laid off. It had cost $25 million in lost wages and the production of 280,000 motor vehicles worth $175 million, but as John L. Lewis put it, the CIO had broken "the united front of capital." Knudsen shrugged it off, declaring that the main thing now was "to get people back to work, to get them some income, and to get the public some cars."

The settlement was relatively simple. The corporation agreed to negotiate with the union on issues raised early in January. There would be no retaliation against those who had participated in the sit-downs or against union organizers. The union was free to sign up as many as it could. In the seventeen pivotal plants, according to the unwritten rider, the union had exclusive representation for six months. Elsewhere, the company was free to negotiate with any labor organization.

The prestige of the United Auto Workers was assured. Workers who had lived in constant anxiety flocked to join. "Even if we got not one damn thing out of it other than that, we at least had a right to open our mouths without fear," one Fisher Body employee said later. By October 1937, the UAW had signed up 400,000 workers—the bulk from General Motors; a smaller group from threatened Chrysler, which settled shortly after; and a scattering from violently anti-union Ford, which would hold out until May 1941.

Sloan would not go quietly. On April 1, 1937, he wrote stockholders; "Briefly stated, the strike against General Motors Corporation was not actuated by any fundamental causes that affected, in an important degree, the welfare of the workers. I am quite convinced that this is an unprejudiced statement of fact." To the extent that unions succeeded in securing the closed shop, he continued, "It means the economic and political slavery of the worker, and an important step toward an economic political dictatorship." Whatever the totalitarian threat, union and management observed the truce. Unhindered by anything more than wildcat sit-downs, which the union sought to curb, automobile sales escalated through the model year.

Yet Sloan remained dissatisfied. Greeting visitors, the restless president of General Motors paced high above Columbus Circle, appropriately enough the starting point for measuring highway mileage from New York City. Sloan was sixty, his hearing had worsened, and he had taken to wearing an oversized hearing aid that he had to remember to turn down before speaking himself, lest he shatter his remaining eardrum. The deafness embarrassed him, like some public revelation; he was aging, and even the lock of hair brushed like a peninsula into his sea of forehead could not hide the baldness.

Sloan still spent long hours in his office. There was little to distract him from the business of running the world's largest industrial enterprise. He and Irene, his wife of thirty-eight years, were childless. The 245-foot yacht *Rene,* moored at the dock in front of his estate at Great Neck, provided no distraction. It was as if the yacht, like the private railway car in which he still made his biweekly trips to Detroit, were expected of the highest-paid executive in America, no more. That year Sloan would make $561,311 in salary and bonus, approximately 352 times the annual wage of a factory worker.

General Motors paid well, which, like his deafness, Sloan disliked revealing. It was a private matter, and the annual public report listing executive salaries to the newly organized Securities and Exchange Commission Sloan considered just another example of New Deal meddling. Eight other General Motors executives, headed by William Knudsen's $459,000, made more than $300,000 that year, most of it in bonuses dependent upon the corporation's profit margin.

The continued growth of those profits prompted Sloan to take one further step toward removing the corporation from outside influence. The pending retirement of Lammot du Pont as president of Du Pont and chairman of General Motors' board of directors provided the opportunity. Without the need for outside financing—Sloan had approved a $50 million expansion program financed entirely out of current earnings—he moved to reorganize the corporation's board of directors. His intent was to reduce the influence of Wall Street and other outside directors, to turn over more decision-making authority to the heads of the operating divisions by the simple expedient of combining the board's finance and executive committees into a single policy committee. At the same time, he would turn over the presidency to Knudsen, moving up to the chairman's seat on the board.

While the Du Pont representatives had some reservations about the combined committee, Sloan prevailed. He also arranged to have the bylaws of the corporation amended to give him the added title of "chief executive officer," fearing "the public impression would be that he had been 'kicked upstairs.' " Sloan demanded not only the reality but the appearance he "was still active and the head man," as Lammot du Pont wrote to another board member.

In May 1937, Sloan succeeded du Pont, acquiring the definitive title of chief executive officer as well. The net effect of the corporate reorganization, which would be changed back in 1946, was to provide the Detroit production people, led by Knudsen, with more authority in corporate decision-making. General Motors was now entirely Sloan's creature.

Then, in the late summer of 1937, just as R.H. Grant was about to unleash bands, pretty girls, and entertainers in his festive new model showing for dealers, the four years of industrial recovery came to an abrupt halt. The bottom fell out precipitously; once again production had overtaken the public's ability to buy all the goods offered. Automobile sales suffered severely. Knudsen reported that December's decline was the worst drop in corporation history. On January 1, 1938, General Motors laid off 30,000 employees and put the remaining 230,000 on a three-day week to spread the work. Confronted with the same problem they had faced in 1929, manufacturers responded the same way. "It is better to curtail production than to work off inventories through reduced prices," Knudsen told a Senate Committee on Unemployment.

Knudsen was offering "a prime example of the social spectacle that President Roosevelt called 'rigid prices and fluctuating payrolls,' " *Fortune* magazine observed. "Just as Detroit's generally low-price, big-volume philosophy has more than once led us out of a depression, so the abrupt surrender of its production to a falling demand hurries us into them; Detroit is probably the birthplace of both good times and bad."

Without price reductions, there was no way to stimulate sales—short of government's artificial "pump priming," precisely the sort of budget unbalancing industrialists most feared. "The main obstacle to the general revival of American enterprise is the fear the foundation of the national economy is in jeopardy," Sloan told the Association of Life Insurance Presidents. To restore confidence, he urged, "the budget must be balanced by reducing expenses of government—not by increasing taxation."

With the economic downturn, the UAW membership drive skidded to a halt. Of the two million unemployed nationally, some 320,000 were auto workers. Another 196,000 auto workers were on short work weeks. The fear had returned.

President Roosevelt waited only until spring brought no seasonal upturn. On April 14, 1938, he devoted a fireside chat to the announcement that he would send to Congress a $3 billion relief and public-works bill. The news alone was enough to stimulate confidence—if not in the economy, at least in the federal government. The president's exasperation with big business and corporate executives who "can't see further than the next dividend" also led him to invoke a new governmental policy emphasizing competition. He revived the dormant antitrust laws.

The Big Three, as they were firmly dubbed by the business press, were logical targets. Between them, General Motors, Ford, and Chrysler virtually monopolized the automobile market, capturing more than 90 percent of all new-car sales. Ten independents had been reduced to half that in just the previous two years; Cord and Auburn ended production in 1937, while venerable Reo, Hupp, and Graham were near collapse. Sloan apparently recognized the risk of growing too big, and placed a brake on General Motors' continued growth. "Our bogie is 45 percent of each price class. We don't want any more than that," he averred.

Furthermore, the Big Three were vulnerable politically: Ford had refused to cooperate with the NRA; Walter Chrysler had supported the Liberty League; and Sloan, despite General Motors' profits of $880 million in the six years of Roosevelt's presidency, still scored the New Deal as a destructive force.

The hammer fell in May 1938, when a federal grand jury in South Bend, Indiana, indicted the three companies, a swarm of subsidiaries, and the very cream of Detroit society on charges of conspiring to monopolize automobile financing. Both Ford and Chrysler signed consent orders agreeing not to force their dealers to use the corporations' captive finance companies. General Motors refused, asserting that its policy, among other things, was intended to protect its customers from the fly-by-night operators among the nation's 370-odd independent finance companies. Sloan, Knudsen, and fifteen other uncomfortable General Motors executives found themselves in the criminal dock, facing a jury of their peers.

The verdict was as odd as the confrontation in the drab courtroom. After six weeks of testimony, a jury of farmers and small businessmen found General Motors and three of its finance subsidiaries guilty of conspiracy to restrain interstate commerce. The jury then decided that the seventeen executives of the convicted companies—men who, like Sloan, testified that their tasks were policy-setting rather than administrative—were not guilty. It was, said *Time* magazine, as if "there had been a conspiracy without conspirators." *

General Motors and its three subsidiaries each received the maximum rap-on-the-wrist under the law: a $5,000 fine. More important from the government's point of view, General Motors Acceptance was forced to compete on an equal footing with independent finance companies, without General Motors' dealers steering clients to the house lender. The decision had one other effect, intended or not: it effectively silenced Alfred P. Sloan as a political spokesman. Firmly convinced that the corporation had been singled out because of Sloan's vehement attacks

---

* The United States Supreme Court denied *certiorari*, letting the convictions stand, on October 13, 1941. That same day, the court also declined to review a tax-court ruling that Pierre S. du Pont and John Raskob could not deduct from their 1929 federal income tax claimed losses on stock sales to each other that year. Raskob was to pay about $1 million and du Pont $600,000 in additional taxes.

on the New Deal—such retaliation was not beyond the cunning of Franklin Delano Roosevelt, to be sure—General Motors executives would maintain a resolute nonpartisanship in public for the next thirty years.

It had not been a good year. Sales for 1938 were way off, slightly more than half those of 1937. The Depression-born paralysis of will returned, only momentarily lightened by Sunday evening broadcasts featuring an insolent wooden dummy named Charlie McCarthy; by swing bands and jitterbugs; and by Walt Disney's *Snow White and the Seven Dwarfs* (an animated allegory for the times, the popular picture advised the nation to "whistle while you work" and "someday a prince will come").

Even as he grappled with the economic crisis at home, President Roosevelt kept a wary watch on international events. The German chancellor had annexed Austria and was demanding the return of the Sudetenland. The French and British prime ministers were to discuss the German demand with Herr Hitler in Munich.

13

The Cadet and the Shadow Dancers

V-J Day seemed anticlimactic somehow, after the German surrender in May 1945 and the fateful Hiroshima and Nagasaki bombings in August. The crowds in the streets seemed less raucous than on V-E Day, their excitement subdued. This was not a time to rejoice publicly; what thanks one had were better delivered in private, perhaps with prayers, more likely with tears.

The war was over, and the corporation could get back to the business of producing and selling cars and trucks once again. A huge market waited expectantly. There were some 25.8 million cars on the road or garaged for the duration—a number had been put up on blocks for want of tires or replacement parts. Nearly half of all motor vehicles were more than seven years old, sure to be replaced just as soon as the industry could reconvert to civilian production. Sloan estimated a six-million-unit auto market for the first two years—twice the 1941 figure and larger than record-setting 1929, a great feast just waiting for guests.

The days of 35-mile-per-hour speed limits and two-gallons-per-week gas rationing were over. Chevrolet already had begun manufacturing light civilian trucks, which were desperately needed, and since May had increased its production of replacement parts. Yet the reconversion, even with all the corporation's planning, would be a massive undertaking.

In the five years of war production, General Motors had turned out $12.3 billion worth of military supplies, only one-third of it comparable in form to its civilian production. The conversion from peacetime to wartime production, beginning with the prewar planning of 1940, had been a gigantic task made the harder by the company's agreement to take on government contracts for only the largest, most difficult projects.

The corporation had maintained contact with the War and Navy departments since 1933, revising estimates of General Motors' "allotment" in case of war and the kinds of contracts on which it would bid. The first of its military orders, for 75-millimeter high-explosive shells, went to Chevrolet in April 1940. Still the company—like the great majority of American industry—had taken few steps to actually prepare for war until June 1940, when France collapsed before the Wehrmacht and Britain evacuated the remnants of its army from the resort beaches of Dunkirk.*

---

* British and United States government officials suspected General Motors executives of pro-Nazi sympathies. British intelligence noted that James D. Mooney, in charge of General Motors Export, attended a dinner in New York on June 21, 1940, hosted by a German trade attaché, celebrating Nazi military victories in Europe. (Mooney, according to the *Saturday Evening Post* of October 30, 1937, once practiced the Nazi salute as a gesture of courtesy before meeting Hitler in 1935, certainly a suspicious act when recalled in the days of panic after the fall of France.) Mooney, a Democrat, was expected to bring pressure on President Roosevelt to suspend aid to Britain "so that the Germans would allow GM to continue business in Europe," according to William Stevenson, *A Man Called Intrepid* (New York: Harcourt Brace Jovanovich, 1976), pp. 114–15. On May 31, 1941, Assistant Secretary of State Adolf A. Berle, Jr., requested that FBI director J. Edgar Hoover conduct "a most discreet investigation" of Sloan, Mooney, and Graeme K. Howard, a General Motors vice-president who had written a book Berle believed defended German aggression in Europe. Whatever Hoover uncovered could not have been too damning. Mooney was General Motors' first Washington representative on military contracts until called to active duty as head of the production engineering section of the Navy's Bureau of Aeronautics; he ended the war on the staff of the chief of naval operations. Howard moved to Ford Motor Company to head its foreign operations after the war. For General Motors' rebuttal and a defense of Mooney, see *The Industrial Reorganization Act,* Hearings before the Subcommittee on Antitrust and Monopoly, Senate Judiciary Committee, Part IV (Washington, D.C., 1974), pp. 2378 ff.

It was in June of 1940, against the wishes of Sloan and Donaldson Brown, that William S. Knudsen took a leave of absence to go to Washington as a member of the National Defense Advisory Commission. Knudsen insisted that it was his duty, even if it were to cost him the title of General Motors chief operating officer; the Nazis had overrun his native Denmark on the night of April 8–9. At age sixty-one, the president of General Motors, still wearing blue work shirts occasionally, enlisted in Roosevelt's undeclared war. Knudsen's very presence in the capital seemed to assure that the necessary job would be done.

"Can you build those 50,000 planes the President is calling for?" newsmen had challenged Knudsen the day he left for Washington.

"I can't," Knudsen answered, "but America can."

On September 3, 1940, Knudsen resigned both as president and as a member of the board of directors of General Motors "to remove any possibility of conflict of interests," Sloan explained. Charles Erwin Wilson, the one-time Delco engineer, having learned among other things to wear dark suits befitting the office of executive vice-president of General Motors, became acting president. Alfred P. Sloan remained in effective control as chief executive officer. At the same time, Harley Earl was elected a vice-president of the corporation in recognition of the importance to General Motors' prosperity of what Sloan himself called "Hollywood" styling.

The nation made good use of the year between the fall of France and the German invasion of the Soviet Union. Industrial production increased by 30 percent and employment by 20 percent. Three million men who had been unemployed in 1939 found themselves working on the first of the war contracts Knudsen approved as head of what became the Office of Production Management.

Before the end of 1940, the executives of the nation's largest business had absorbed the lessons of modern warfare taught by Roosevelt's chief of staff, General George C. Marshall. "The nation that is able to produce the most effectively . . . is the one less vulnerable from attack," Sloan said in a radio interview. There was one difficulty, he added. "We haven't got enough 'economic royalists' among us to do this job for national defense." Sloan was not one to miss an opportunity to twit the man in the White House—especially in an election year. Indefatigable Sloan, loyal to class and principles, had endorsed Hoover and lost, then Landon and lost. Like some clumsy club fighter with more courage than skill, Sloan heaved himself back to his feet each time Roosevelt knocked him down, then gamely tried once more. In 1940 he endorsed Wendell L. Willkie.

By the end of 1940, General Motors had undertaken $410 million in defense work for the United States, Great Britain, and Canada. Eight months later, the total had reached $1.2 billion. The New York-directed staff turned the research skills that had armored the corporation in peacetime to analyzing wartime conditions. They had determined that the great need would be for manpower, that government contracts should be assigned to factories with ample labor pools, even if it meant moving machinery or renting factory space from other companies. It was a crucial policy decision—that and the board's early determination to ask for only a 10-percent pretax profit, just half the corporation's average peacetime yield.

Through forty months of war after Pearl Harbor, the corporation lived in a state of suspended commercialization. Automobile rationing began on January 1, 1942; the last civilian passenger cars rolled off the Flint assembly lines on a cold, snowy January 31. Then the tool and die men had removed the $7 million stamping dies and engine molds for each of the car lines and placed them in storage; sometime in the future they would refit them to the presses and once again turn out "pleasure" cars.

Division managers were free to bid on any war contract they wished and to accept any the government awarded. Saginaw Steering and Frigidaire made machine guns; Olds turned out artillery shells; Delco produced fuses; and Pontiac anti-aircraft guns. With a speed and flexibility not seen since the hyperventilated years of Billy Durant, General Motors adapted to wartime production. If the corporation ever had a supreme moment, a period of unqualified contribution to the commonweal, it was during the war years of 1940 through 1945. General Motors was second only to E.I. du Pont de Nemours in expansion for the war effort, spending $911 million for new factories and tools, $809 million of that from the public treasury. By July 1942, the entire automobile industry had accepted contracts equal to its annual peacetime production. Less than a year later, the industry's output was double its prewar capacity. "American superiority in mass production techniques developed in the automobile industry was indeed the main reason why the Allies won World War II," concluded a later automobile historian and critic.

Despite the low-profit mandate, General Motors fared well during the war years. Its total sales from 1942 through 1945 topped $13.4 billion, more than 90 percent of it in war materiel and the balance in such civilian products as replacement parts, trucks, and buses deemed essential for the war effort. The net, even after excess-profits taxes, topped $673 million, and production capacity had increased by 50 percent.

As the staff had predicted, the great shortage was in workers. In 1940, the last year before wartime production began adding significantly to the payroll, General Motors employed 250,000 people. Three years later, the company had 460,000 employees, a quarter of them World War II's celebrated "Rosie the Riveter." For the first time since 1929, the workers outnumbered the stockholders. To meet the labor shortage, the division managers hired indiscriminately and thereby helped spread prosperity to men and women who had seen few dollars since the 1929 Crash. However, none could match the ingenuity of Cadillac general manager Nicholas Dreystadt.

Dreystadt had accepted a contract to produce delicate aircraft gyroscopes, despite mutterings on the fourteenth floor that the job was a killer and the needed skilled hands unavailable. The dissent turned to outrage when Dreystadt and his personnel manager, Jim Roche, hired 2,000 overage black prostitutes from Paradise Valley—uneducated, untrained, but willing workers. Dreystadt hired the madams too, blithely explaining, "They know how to manage the women."

Dreystadt himself machined a dozen gyroscopes, then produced a training film detailing the step-by-step assembly process. Within weeks the women were surpassing quotas, and the outrage turned to chagrin on West Grand Boulevard. Jokes about

Cadillac's "red-light district" angered Dreystadt. "These women are my fellow workers, and yours," he insisted. "They do a good job and respect their work. Whatever their past, they are entitled to the same respect as any one of our associates."

Dreystadt knew he would have to replace these women at war's end—returning veterans had job preference, and the United Auto Workers, heavily white male with a southern-states orientation, wanted the women out of the plant. "Nigger-lover" and "whoremonger" Dreystadt fought to keep some, pleading, "For the first time in their lives, these poor wretches are paid decently, work in decent conditions, and have some rights. And for the first time they have some dignity and self-respect. It's our duty to save them from being again rejected and despised." The union stood adamant.

When the women were laid off, a number committed suicide rather than return to the streets. Nick Dreystadt grieved, "God forgive me. I have failed these poor souls."

With war production in full bore in mid-1943, Sloan and his staff turned to planning an orderly conversion back to peacetime work. The automobile shortage was already critical, and the nation was scrapping 4,000 cars per day. The immediate demand would be for twelve million to fourteen million new cars, more if the war continued beyond 1945. To meet that demand, Sloan's staff estimated, the company would have to increase its own production capacity at least another 50 percent. Not to do so would risk others creaming off sales, of General Motors losing its position in the marketplace. The cost would be $500 million, and it still would take the corporation eighteen months to reach peak production.

The pent-up buying demand—it would reach $200 billion by the end of 1944—was a volatile gas bag. If government controls did not act as a safety valve, it would explode in inflation when returning veterans and purse-heavy production workers sought scarce goods. For Sloan, that presented a dilemma: "This will increase the temptation to continue the New Dealish tendency toward planned economy which in turn would interfere with a proper interplay of free enterprise and defeat a return to normal economic life."

In a speech before the National Association of Manufacturers, Sloan warned industry "that it must make good by providing plenty of jobs to a people who have seen what it can do in the way of employment, payrolls and other benefits during the war, or permit the enterprise system to be supplanted by some form of socialism. Mr. Sloan asserted that there are three 'musts' in our national postwar program: Maximum employment, national defense policies designed to prevent a third world war, and foreign trade on a 'two-way street' basis, 'with no world WPA at the expense of the American taxpayer.'" His eye on the presidential election less than a year off, Sloan assured his audience of industrialists that he had faith that the nation had put aside "something for nothing" and "rabbit out of the hat" economic panaceas. New governmental economic policies—Sloan had come to accept *some* role for government, but best it be minimal—would reflect the turn away from the New Deal.

Groggy from repeated political pummeling, Sloan gave only a tepid, dutiful endorsement to Thomas Dewey as the Republican Party's standard-bearer in 1944. Speaking before the New York State Chamber of Commerce, Sloan stated that the election would have a direct bearing on the planned $500 million postwar expansion program: "I do not need to tell an audience of this type that if Governor Dewey is elected President next November it would change the entire aspect of the American enterprise system." Wary perhaps of the president's uncommon resiliency, Sloan diluted his endorsement: "If Mr. Roosevelt should be reelected, I still think that that doesn't end the whole thing; I still think we are going to go on."

Some of the passion had burned out in Sloan since the death in 1940 of his close friend Walter Chrysler. He stood aloof, separated by formal reserve from his coworkers; to them he was always "Mr. Sloan," and they "Mr. Knudsen" or "Mr. Wilson." Only one man had managed to transcend Sloan's reserve, his fear of showing favoritism among his subordinates—Charles F. Kettering. Perhaps Sloan envied the laboratory man his friendly image in the press—carefully promoted by the corporation's expanding public-relations department. Perhaps it was

Kettering's ability to relax, to enjoy the pleasures Sloan denied himself.

Increasingly, the two men found themselves talking after board meetings, Sloan relaxing with the single highball he drank to be sociable. Until then, Sloan had kept some distance from the man who headed the corporation's research laboratories; Kettering seemed too involved with science and the wonders of the future, too little interested in the pressing social and economic issues that grated on Sloan. For years Sloan had kept Kettering away from policy committees because "through his personality and the interest that he can always develop, the meetings become one of listening rather than one of doing business." As a gesture to his new friend, however, Sloan reversed himself and urged Kettering's appointment to the policy committee. He wrote Lammot du Pont in 1943 that Kettering had become interested in matters beyond the technical: "Altho [sic] I know he has always been critical of me in my tirades against the New Deal, yet, in a different way, he now finds himself in about the same position."

In Kettering's friendship, Sloan found comfort and, more important, reassurance. Something had ruptured Sloan's aura of infallibility and with it his position of unquestioned authority—something Sloan did not well comprehend. The first hint had been the sit-down strike of 1937, the next a severe personal loss—to his pride, mastery, and pocketbook—when a federal judge ruled that he and seven other members of the board had wasted corporation assets in distributing the executive bonus fund. Judge Vincent L. Leibell had ordered the eight men to refund $4.3 million, plus $2.3 million interest, in a 1942 case brought by three small stockholders. While the judge had ruled specifically that the bonuses paid were not excessive, at least not in view of the competition among automobile companies for good executives, he had faulted various methods used to compute the bonuses.

During the trial, the judge unknowingly had stung Sloan, and two years later the slight still rankled. "We do not want to furnish too much ammunition," he wrote the Du Pont Corporation's Walter S. Carpenter, "for those who think that nothing can be done in General Motors except we consult J.P. Morgan and Company . . . Judge Leibell was heard to say that I, as President of General Motors Corporation, could not adopt any policy without it was approved by Mr. Morgan."

It was as if Sloan no longer were recognized for the power he wielded. Once men in his position had been exalted, their opinions sought by politicians and press alike. Not so in this new and uncomfortable social order. Industrialists had to share their once unquestioned authority—not only with labor leaders, but with the government as well. Franklin Roosevelt had demonstrated just how much economic power the government had, first during the Depression and even more effectively during the national emergency. Sloan might pray publicly for the comforts of the old order in his endorsement of Tom Dewey, but the public never would permit the president—be he Dewey, Roosevelt, or anyone else—to give business the free rein it once had enjoyed.

One could reach accommodation in this new environment, Sloan realized. Knudsen and Wilson had been right about labor; he and Brown wrong, unable to believe that union leaders were to be trusted. Organized labor actually helped impose discipline in the plants, thereby increasing productivity.. Furthermore, Sloan sensed, the wartime experience had proved to the government that it was better to deal with a handful of large firms than myriad small ones, that only large corporations like General Motors were capable of meeting the military production needs of modern warfare.

Sloan considered setting the corporation's sights higher, to something more than the 45 percent of the civilian passenger-car market he had thought the antitrust flash point. Beyond motor vehicles, the opportunities in diesel locomotives were huge; the railroads' wartime use of General Motors' diesel electrics had convinced all but the most stubborn steam hogs. The board also could consider funneling more money into the newly organized truck and bus division for the conversion of streetcar and trolley systems to buses; the corporation's partners in the conversion plan, Standard Oil and Firestone Tire, were eager enough. Not only domestically, but overseas as well, the prospects were bright; foreign sales could reach one million vehicles annually, at least until war-shattered Europe and Japan rebuilt their domestic industries. Never in all the history of Christendom had there been such a rich market awaiting businessmen.

In planning to meet the pent-up demand, General Motors' president, Charles Wilson, pressed for a favored project: a small automobile that could meet the need for low-cost transportation. C.S. Mott had suggested it in a letter to Wilson in 1944, even detailing specifications he thought most suitable. Kettering, too, had pondered such an auto, one he thought of as a "Market Wagon," a machine similar to the prewar German *Volksauto*.

The concept squared with the corporation's own market research as well as a survey conducted by the Society of Automotive Engineers just before the end of the war. According to the SAE, prospective automobile purchasers in New York, Chicago, New Orleans, and San Francisco wanted smaller, less expensive, and more functional automobiles. (The survey apparently reflected a prejudice of urbanites, 70 percent of whom drove to work even during the war years.) Powell Crosley had used his radio and television fortune to introduce a small car in 1939, had sold a few, and then had ended production when the war began; he would be ready to capitalize on any postwar shift to small cars if he could built a network of dealers.

Wilson's proposal met immediate opposition from Sloan and the New York finance people. Small cars meant small prices and lower per-unit profits. Further, an inexpensive automobile would compete with used cars, and no matter how much the demand for used cars in the immediate postwar shortage, the seller's market eventually would evaporate.

Wilson also confronted a general prejudice; a small, lightweight car was anathema to the majority of men in the automobile industry, including his executive vice president, Harlow Curtice. Small cars *seemed* retrogressive; for decades the entire industry had worked to produce bigger, more powerful cars. Increased size and Harley Earl's cosmetic ministrations represented automotive progress. Ford executives, considering the purchase of the Volkswagen company in Germany shortly after the war, sneered at the "Bug's" tear drop design, one dismissing it with "You call that a car?" The general attitude was inadvertently summed up in a publication released by the Automobile Manufacturers Association in 1945:

Manufacturers who have tried to compete with the used car market by offering a "stripped down" low-cost *new car* have fared badly. During the Depression, attempts to sell "standard" models in competition with "masters" and "de luxes" made little headway. Efforts to sell the European small car met with little success. People could get a full-sized car for less money. There has been little chance in this country of introducing a low-cost people's car, as Germany planned to do in the 1930s. We already have it. The used car is it.

Wilson's opposing argument was simple: "The higher the prices of automobiles, the fewer will be sold. . . . If people cannot raise the money or credit for new cars, they will simply get along with their old ones. They showed they could do it during the war."

Wilson persisted, supported only by Marvin E. Coyle, general manager of Chevrolet. Coyle's support was crucial, for under the corporate scheme of decentralization, he was free to develop new products, short of actually setting up an assembly line. On May 15, 1945, Wilson publicly announced the plan to build "a lighter weight and more economical car in the postwar period. Because of the necessity of putting war production first, the car is only in the idea stage, and therefore, it cannot be placed in production until a considerable period of time after the close of the war with Japan."

Coyle assigned the small-car project to his new chief design engineer, Earl MacPherson, a veteran automobile engineer with a visionary jumble of ideas he wanted to put into the automobile. MacPherson's design, fitted to the dimensions of the 1935 Chevrolet, was an "engineer's dream," an automobile that would seat four, with a wheelbase of 108 inches (eight inches shorter than the 1942 Chevrolet going back into production as the division's 1946 model). The prototype small car weighed just 2,200 pounds and rode easily on its novel four-wheel, independent suspension. In its first months, the design project was an orphan tucked away in a rented Detroit loft MacPherson's team nicknamed "Cockroach Canyon,'' an indication of the low priority the small car had in General Motors' plans. Suddenly MacPherson's group was abruptly moved to a converted bank building across the street from General Motors' headquarters, and the corporation's chief of styling, Harley Earl, detailed a team of designers to work with the engineers on the new car.

Corporate interest in the auto—dubbed the Cadet—had perked up when word leaked to them that Ford also had a small car on the drawing board and that Chrysler was quietly investigating the possibility of buying Volkswagen's factories. Wilson and Nicholas Dreystadt, replacing Coyle as Chevrolet's general manager, decided that the car should go into production in mid-1947, once the engineers reduced the costs so that the car could sell for no more than $1,000. Chevrolet's Arnold Lenz was assigned management of the Cadet program and set to work building two factories in Cleveland to produce the automobile.

But the Cadet was in trouble. Not only was MacPherson forced to compromise his design to bring down costs—not something he did willingly—but a materials shortage gripped the country. Chrysler had thrown up its hands at Volkswagen's tangle of public and government owners, and Ford had put aside its small-car project. At the same time, General Motors' $600 million reconversion and expansion program—increased by $100 million since it had been announced three years earlier—was running behind. Wilson estimated that it would take not one year, but as long as three, to increase the corporation's plant capacity from 2.5 million to 3.4 million vehicles annually. Until the company could do that, and meet the demand for higher-priced standard-size vehicles, the Cadet would have to wait.

MacPherson built a succession of prototypes, each cheaper than its predecessor, with Dreystadt's continuing support. But Dreystadt's sudden death from cancer late in 1946 deprived the car of its last support. The financial picture was cloudy; it would take the production of 300,000 cars per year for three years to amortize the tools and dies for the Cadet, and the sales department was skeptical that dealers could sell that many. Why should they? They could move every full-size car they got their hands on, at full price, with much more profit per unit. Dreystadt's successor, James Crawford, dismissed the Cadet "as too much of a jewel of a car."

On May 15, 1947, the corporation aborted the Cadet, announcing simply: "The proposed Chevrolet lighter car project has been indefinitely deferred due to a continuing material shortage, both for new plants and car production, and the desire of the General Motors Corporation to devote all the productive facilities and available materials of the Chevrolet Motor Division to meet the overwhelming demands of the motoring public for the established line of Chevrolet vehicles." The decision to abandon the Cadet was to have profound implications for the next thirty years.

An overwhelming demand for all cars created another problem for the nation—a place to put the thirty million registered motor vehicles. If cars were in short supply, so, too, were the roads to run them on; the country needed a highway-construction program on the scale of its war effort.

But what an opportunity this need afforded for remaking urban America, General Motors believed. The company first had presented its concept at the most popular exhibit of the New York World's Fair in 1939. General Motors' "Futurama" offered a "magic Aladdin-like flight through time and space" twenty-some years into the future. Fair-goers stood in long, winding lines waiting to travel on a moving sidewalk above a huge model created by designer Norman Bel Geddes. Miniature superhighways with 50,000 moving model cars wove past model farms to model cities. For sixteen minutes, the five million eavesdroppers on the future peered at such novelties as elevated freeways, expressway traffic traveling at 100 miles per hour, and "modern and efficient city planning—breath-taking architecture—each city block a complete unit in itself [with] broad, one-way thoroughfares—space, sunshine, light and air." As impressive as was "Futurama"—a million to-scale trees and a half-million structures—the message was even more awe-inspiring: "The job of building the future is one which will demand our best energies, our most fruitful imagination; and that with it will come greater opportunities for all."

Bel Geddes' vision was not revolutionary, but merely an elaboration of ritual chant by city planners and automotive companies alike. Even during the Depression, newly built suburbs had grown 17 percent in population, three times as fast as the urban centers—all of this made possible by the great equalizer, the private automobile. (It was no accident that automobile devotee Robert Moses of the New York World's Fair Commission had given the Big Three the place of honor hard by the fair's cynosure and trademark—the Trylon and Perisphere.) Bel Geddes' self-contained city blocks would come, so the chant continued, because "with fewer people in our central cities, and with the stores spreading out, property values in the center of town have decreased. . . . This has given us a chance to tear down buildings, widen streets, and turned our 'blighted' areas into more pleasant-looking places by letting in the light."

Nor were the superhighways of "Futurama" beyond belief— that was part of the fascination the exhibit held. Pennsylvania already was building its toll-road turnpike along the former roadbed of the defunct South Pennsylvania Railroad. Connecticut was at work on the Merritt Parkway and its extension, the Wilbur Cross Parkway—67 miles of limited-access toll road connecting that state's bedroom communities with Manhattan.

Across the continent, a motley band of Los Angeles businessmen, traffic engineers, and city officials had introduced a large-scale master plan to build what appeared to be "a dream castle by traffic experts" joining the residential suburbs with the downtown business district twenty miles away. The state of California had adopted a statewide program envisioning "express" traffic arteries, the first of which would open—with a chain-reaction rear-end accident involving three cars carrying dignitaries—between central Los Angeles and the city of Pasadena, 8.2 miles to the north. Opened on December 9, 1940, the six-lane Arroyo Seco Parkway was the first leg of what would become the most extensive freeway system in the world, a veritable symbol of Motoropolis, and the model for expressways, parkways, and freeways across the country. The Arroyo Seco Parkway had been envisioned first in 1911, but not until Los Angeles' downtown department stores backed the project was the $1.3 million "speedway" launched. Planned to draw shoppers into the urban core, instead, it lured even more people out of the city. The value of residential lots in the Pasadena area increased 25 percent, more than enough to enlist real-estate interests and builders in future parkways elsewhere.

Cities everywhere looked upon these works, judged them to be good, and rushed to emulate them. The more highways built, the more they encouraged automobile travel. The pioneering Arroyo Seco Freeway of 1940, with a capacity of 45,000 cars per day, was carrying 70,000 twenty years later. Motorists groused it was "the world's longest parking lot."

With or without the new highways, traffic would increase. The solution, then, was to build more high-speed expressways through and around congested urban centers and to pave the 1.6 million miles of unimproved roads. Only some 700,000 of the 3.3 million miles of state and federal highways had asphalt or concrete surfaces capable of handling high-speed traffic. Priority lay upon so-called "interregional highways," some 40,000 miles of roads that carried one-fifth of all traffic. "The roads already exist, but they need to have curves widened, grade separations provided, concrete [center] strips added. By-passing roads will be added where needed," the Automobile Manufacturers Association predicted in 1945. "When our total car registration in the United States reaches 40 million, as it soon will, we'll sadly need all this highway improvement. The question is whether it will come in time."

It would. The Automobile Manufacturers Association intended to see to that.

Highway construction would lag far behind automobile and truck production, even though the conversion to peacetime production was slower than anticipated, hampered by severe shortages of raw materials and component parts. A rash of strikes, particularly among the traditionally low-paying parts manufacturers, aggravated conditions. Assembly lines frequently shut down for lack of such parts as seat springs or rear-view mirrors. In the waning days of 1945, the industry turned out only 70,000 passenger cars. In 1946, production reached 2.1 million, less than half 1941's total.

A gray and black market flourished, with customers willingly or unwillingly paying considerable "vigorish" above the ceiling prices set by the Office of Price Administration. When the OPA clamped down in an effort to keep inflation in check, dealers resorted to a variety of cunning ploys to circumvent the rules. Used cars were deliberately undervalued at trade-in, or, if the customer had no trade-in, he was expected to buy extra equipment, wanted or not. (The extra item was not always practical; one veteran paid the ceiling price for his new car, as well as $300 for the cat asleep on the front seat.) The lucky ones—those who could pay cash for their cars as well as a "fee" to be placed high on the waiting list—became accustomed to strangers approaching them, offering to buy the new De Soto or Hudson or Studebaker for a price well above the legal ceiling. Those who sold went back on the dealer's waiting list while their car passed to others at even higher prices.

A considerable failure, automobile price ceilings died for lack of enforcement in November 1946. As late as May 1948, dealers were scoring $700 above list price for a Chevrolet, $500 for Pontiacs and Dodges. The lasting stereotype of the auto dealer as a shady character was born.

The continuing automobile shortage gave heart to the remaining "independents," especially struggling Studebaker, which had commissioned industrial designer Raymond Loewy to style its first postwar car for 1947. In the last year before the war, the independents had captured 10 percent of auto sales, and in the postwar seller's market flourishing around them, they expected to capture an even larger share—providing they could get scarce raw materials. What better proof of the untapped potential of the market than the announcement that West Coast steel manufacturer, cement maker, dam builder, and World War II Liberty-ship contractor Henry J. Kaiser was entering the automotive business? Kaiser's partner was Joseph W. Frazer, president of the moribund Graham–Paige Motor Company. Their Kaiser–Frazer automobiles thus combined proven automotive experience with an industrial wizard's ability to achieve the seemingly impossible. If the company could survive, it would be the first successful entry into the marketplace since Chrysler twenty years earlier.

For General Motors, by far the most critical question was the immediate survival of its once-dominant rival. The Ford Motor Company by 1941 was in grim straits, its share of new-car sales fallen to less than 19 percent, well behind Chrysler's 24.2 percent. Henry Ford's creaking enterprise wheezed through the war years on military contracts with guaranteed profits, but faced the return of peacetime production in a dreadful state. The company was losing $10 million a month; its executives had no idea where the hemorrhage was, its books "about as good as a small tool shop would have."

Henry Ford lived on, feeble, barely interested in cars any longer. He had progressively ceded management responsibilities to pistol-packing Harry Bennett, a former boxer whose industrial knowledge was limited to strike-breaking. Playing upon Ford's increasing fears—paranoia would not be too strong a word— Bennett had amassed ever more power at the expense of Edsel Ford, the founder's long overshadowed son and the nominal president of the company. Edsel's death in 1943, "of stomach cancer, undulant fever, and a broken heart," had merely strengthened Bennett's hold. Twice afflicted with strokes and near senility, Ford again assumed the presidency, in effect leaving the brutish Bennett in command. Executives worked without clear responsibilities, found their orders countermanded capriciously, or were fired by finding their personal effects literally thrown into the street when they came to work in the morning. Fearing the company's collapse and the loss of needed industrial capacity, William E. Knudsen as coordinator of war production arranged for the discharge from the navy of Edsel's oldest son, Henry Ford II. If young Ford, just twenty-six, could not keep the company going, or so Washington rumors had it, the Ford Motor Company would be nationalized.

Henry Ford II, as vice-president, could do little better than his father, as president, had done. Peace came just in time, removing at least the threat of nationalization, if not total collapse. The company had slipped further and further into chaos, for Bennett had no more interest in sound management than had the elder Ford—and far less automobile experience.

In September 1945, Henry Ford II outmaneuvered Bennett by

enlisting the support of his grandmother. Clara Ford worked to sway her doddering husband; as a last resort, she gave the young man authority to vote her considerable block of stock. That, with the holdings of Edsel's heirs, made a majority. On September 21, 1945, Henry Ford the elder resigned; his grandson was elected president in his stead, with full authority. That same day young Ford fired Bennett.

Ford moved rapidly to take hold of the floundering corporation. His first move was to hire a team of former air-force officers headed by Charles "Tex" Thornton, a group of brilliant young men who had managed air-force procurement and logistics during the war. To these so-called "Whiz Kids" he turned over the organization of Ford's accounting and purchasing.

Ford also intended to copy General Motors' decentralized staff and line management, the very antithesis of Henry Ford's autocratic rule. Other large companies, especially those that were Morgan Bank-influenced, including General Electric and International Harvester, already had adapted it. Young graduates of the prestigious Harvard Business School had suckled on it in class, then gone out to the hinterlands to convert the heathen.

Ford, however, needed someone familiar with it—in short, a General Motors executive. He settled on Ernest R. Breech, the president of Bendix Aviation. (While General Motors owned only one-third of Bendix, Breech was considered one of the family and still shared in the management bonus and retirement plans.) Breech was forty-nine, a former accountant who had worked for General Motors for twenty-one years, rising to head successive divisions as a trouble-shooter. He had succeeded so well that he was considered one of the possible heirs to Sloan and Wilson.

Ironically, Breech had been the watchman over the activities of General Motors' competitors and had charted the decline of the once-potent Ford empire with "contempt and pity." He turned down Ford tactfully—Ford Motor Company bought Bendix products—but the company's young president persisted. Ultimately, Breech gave way, telling his wife, "Well, here is a young man that is only one year older than our oldest son. He needs help. This is a great challenge. . . . I hate to take on this job, but if I do not do it I will always regret that I did not accept the challenge.'' The executive, considered to be General Motors' clean-up man, left to restore the fading competitor in August 1946.*

Breech immediately began a massive reorganization of the Ford Motor Company, modeling it upon General Motors' decentralized lines, implementing the long-tested concept of standard volume and the staff–line division. The copy was so complete that Breech even set up a Small Car Division to match the Chevrolet Cadet. The major difference was that Ford's interest in small cars persisted, even after its program was shelved.

Henry Ford, Sr., had outlived his best years. Alfred P. Sloan, Jr., did not intend to make the same mistake. The burden of meeting all the new competition would fall on younger men, those who better understood the realities of the postwar era. Sloan was tired; much of the excitement had gone out of the business for him. "It's been terribly lonely since Walter P. died," he confessed, and only under the dreadful weight of that loneliness had he unbent enough to become personally close to Charles F. Kettering. Sloan was seventy-one, and for the past twenty-three years had, with or without the title, served as chief executive officer of General Motors. He had taken on a sickly company and had built it into the world's largest industrial organization. Its automobiles, refrigerators, aircraft, diesel and electric motors, buses, trucks, locomotives, ball bearings, and electrical equipment were either first, second, or third in sales in their fields. He had spun a corporate structure of line and staff, the model for every large company in the country, an accomplishment of which he was enormously proud. He had guided the transformation of the corporation from threatened weakling to in-

---

* Alfred P. Sloan played a covert role in helping Breech make the decision to become executive vice-president of the Ford Motor Company. He arranged for Breech to preserve his accrued stock bonuses, thus unlocking the golden handcuffs. It was done discreetly; none of the principals ever discussed Sloan's cooperation publicly. Sloan may well have been acting out of enlightened self-interest, since Ford's demise would have brought even more attention upon General Motors by the United States Department of Justice's Antitrust Division. One wonders if Breech would have moved to Ford at all if one of his major rivals for General Motors' presidency, Nicholas Dreystadt, had died a few months earlier than he did.

dustrial titan, then had supervised the transformation of that enterprise into a vital component of President Roosevelt's arsenal of democracy. It was time to let someone else shoulder the burden.

Shaken by Chrysler's death—they were the same age—Sloan had considered stepping aside in 1940. Knudsen's resignation over Sloan's entreaties to head the war-mobilization effort had forced Sloan to stay on; there was simply no one ready to replace him. As executive vice-president, Wilson was in line for the presidency, but Sloan was unsure Wilson was quite ready to assume the chief-executive-officer title as well. Wilson was shy the necessary fiscal experience, and maybe, just maybe, was *too* familiar with his fellow vice-presidents, *too* friendly to make the hard decisions that a chief executive officer sometimes had to make. Sloan retained that title and the final authority it conveyed.

Promoted to president on January 6, 1941, Charles Erwin Wilson had shouldered the operational responsibilities of the wartime conversion. He worked long hours, sleeping more often in the executive apartments in the General Motors Building than at home. Even for a man of fifty-one, he maintained a brutal schedule, until his collapse with what doctors called a "circulatory episode" early in 1944. Advised to rest for six months, he recuperated for three, then returned to his office on the fourteenth floor. For the rest of his life he suffered from crippling headaches; when he was tired, his speech slurred.

His wartime efforts and his planning for reconversion had proved Wilson's merit. Sloan determined to cede to Wilson in Detroit the chief executive officer's title and responsibilities, while tapping Donaldson Brown as the new chairman of the board. Brown would have little responsibility; Wilson would not report to him at all, but to the entire board of directors, his ultimate bosses in any event.

A delegation of executives headed by Wilson asked Sloan to reconsider Brown's role. Under the new organization, they argued, Sloan could handle the nominal duties of board chairman and would preserve a presence, some continuity with the corporation. Moreover, they had difficulty understanding Brown, and always had; over the years Sloan himself had been Brown's translator. Without Sloan, the decisions they needed—already slow, Wilson pointed out—would come slower still. Sloan acceded; the mandatory retirement at age seventy, instituted the year before, was waived in his case.

The changing of the guard came quietly on June 3, 1946. Sloan surrendered the chief executive officer's title, staying on as chairman of the board with minimal duties. Donaldson Brown retired "from further executive responsibilities" to tend his Maryland cattle.

Wilson was just fifteen years younger than Sloan, but a generation apart in his perception of a larger corporate responsibility, some reciprocal obligation to the community. Sloan believed "the interests of G.M. and of the society in which it lives are really the same," an attitude common enough throughout the company, James Truslow Adams noted. "GM people have a sort of motto which pretty well sums up their philosophy. . . . 'What's good for the country is good for General Motors.' What it means is that General Motors, and many other businesses too, have so fitted themselves into the pattern of our American life, have become such a part of it, that anything that benefits the country *has* to benefit them and, on the other hand, anything that is harmful to the country is bound to injure them." If that which was good benefited the company, Wilson pondered, what could General Motors offer, in return, to promote further benefits?*

Wilson first gave serious thought to this mutuality of interests during the winter of 1941–42, while convalescing from a broken hip suffered while ice skating. (That injury put an end to Wilson's ice skating and horseback riding, but not to his raising prize cattle.) While lying in his hospital bed, he had undertaken to work out a guaranteed annual wage for factory workers—a plan the corporation had first pondered five years earlier, then cast aside as too costly. Looking beyond the full employment pro-

---

* In repeating this motto before the Senate Armed Services Committee (see the Introduction), Wilson was both misunderstood and misquoted. Wilson actually said, ". . . [F]or years I thought what was good for our country was good for General Motors—and vice versa." Popular usage has corrupted this to a pejorative comment on big business: "What's good for General Motors is good for the country."

vided by the war effort, Wilson saw the need to plan for the peacetime conditions that would follow. Memories of the Depression were too strong, both in Wilson's mind and in the popular imagination, to ignore the question of providing income security. Wilson grappled with the concept for three years, borrowing ideas from everyone—including the newly named head of the UAW's General Motors Department, Walter Reuther.

Wilson and Reuther discovered that they had much in common: both were sons of immigrants who put a great deal of stock in education, and both had been youthful admirers of Eugene Debs. Wilson, too, had once joined a union; his framed membership card in the pattern-makers' union sat on his cluttered desk. When he and Reuther argued, Wilson would point to the card and insist, "Goddamit, I know something about unions too."

Despite the different careers they had followed—Wilson would earn $459,000 in 1945, Reuther $7,000—during the war years the two became friends, privately, relaxing behind the closed doors of Wilson's office when Reuther ostensibly came to discuss grievances or contract interpretations. Each man's constituency demanded that its champion hold the enemy in contempt, yet both men understood that corporation and union were partners in an orchestrated minuet. "A union is a political organization and needs adversary relations and victorious battles. And a company is an economic organization and needs productivity and discipline. At GM we get both," Wilson explained.

Despite Reuther's vanity and rhetoric—he was not one ever to pass up an opportunity to flay "the bosses"—Wilson believed his adversary "the ablest man in American industry. He, not I, should be the chief executive of GM, and he'd love it. In fact, if Walter Reuther had been born a few years earlier and gone to work before 1927, when the near-collapse of the Ford Motor Company destroyed opportunities for machinists to move into management [as Knudsen had done earlier], he'd be president of GM today."

If Wilson saw in Reuther a strain of business judgment labor leaders were thought to lack, Reuther considered General Motors' president atypical of management, "a very decent, genuine human being. The test of that is whether you can still act human after going through the GM corporation machine, and he passed the test."

Their relationship was the exception—in General Motors and in the auto industry as a whole. As late as 1945, one observer permitted into the highest councils of the corporation decided: "Far too many people in management prefer even today to escape into the belief that workers are a race apart and almost subhuman, and that all labor leaders are crooks and gangsters." Managers with their roots sunk deeply into the small towns of the Middle West nursed a primal fear of the workers, newcomers all, blacks and poor whites alike. There was a tendency, Peter Drucker continued, "especially among the lower ranks of management, to feel superior to the worker, or at least to see him as an alien."

Neither Wilson nor Reuther, for all his soap-box posturing, wanted union–management relations to return to the bloody class war of the 1920s and 1930s. When eventually Wilson did shape his guaranteed-wage plan, he quietly passed it on to Reuther, knowing it ultimately would surface as a union demand in some future contract negotiation. "*I* am never going to put it into effect. I grudgingly yield to a union demand for it when I have to," Wilson explained. It was part of the illusory shadow dance. "If it's to be of any value to a union"—or to an ambitious union leader such as Reuther, he might have added—"it's got to be a hard-won gain. No union can believe that what management offers can be anything but harmful to the union and its members as well."

Despite their warm personal relations, perhaps because of them, both Wilson and Reuther knew they must eventually do battle. To some extent, both men wanted it—Reuther to further his own ambitions and Wilson to test the union's resolve. The timing was also appropriate. General Motors, like all automobile manufacturers, was severely hampered by material shortages anyway, and whatever losses in sales it endured because of a shutdown could be written off against excess profits accumulated before V-J Day. For his part, Reuther would be able to use a strike as proof of his militancy and leadership when he ran in 1946 for the presidency of the United Auto Workers union.

The battle began on August 16, 1945, two days before the war's end, when President Harry Truman's executive order defrosted the wartime wage freeze—as long as a wage increase would not result in a corresponding price increase. Within hours, the UAW had delivered a seventy-six-page brief asking the Big Three for a 30-percent wage boost, coupling that with a demand that the companies open their books to determine whether they had the ability to pay without raising prices. In effect, Reuther wanted to tie wages to profits, to share the wealth anticipated in the postwar boom.

For six weeks General Motors executives sat quietly, their silence a deliberate attempt to force negotiations up against the deadline of the auto workers' contract expiration on November 21. Wilson rejected the demand on October 2, stealing a bit of Reuther's thunderous rhetoric: "We shall resist the monopolistic power of your union to force this 30 percent increase in basic wages." Were General Motors to grant the increase, Wilson thundered on, "automobiles would shortly cost 30 percent more to produce. Prices to consumers would have to be raised 30 percent." (The latter was intended to recruit public opinion to General Motors' cause.) "If wage raises in automobile plants forced such increases in car prices, the market for automobiles would be restricted. Fewer cars would be sold; fewer people would be able to afford and enjoy them; and fewer workers would be employed in making them."

With contract negotiations scheduled to begin on October 19, Reuther adroitly outfoxed General Motors' chief negotiator, Harry Anderson, by inviting a dozen reporters to sit in on the session. Since the public had a vested interest in the price of automobiles, the press should be there to report, Reuther said disarmingly. Anderson took one look at the grinning reporters and led his delegation from the room, leaving the public impression that the corporation had something to hide. The opponents reached a compromise—there would be no reporters, but both sides were to hire court reporters to take down the proceedings. They could put comments off the record if they chose, but the choleric General Motors delegation frequently forgot in its anger. Reuther took some pleasure in baiting them, at least getting on the record what reporters called "Elizabethan" language more often associated with the shop than the board room.

Each day Victor Reuther and an aide, A.Z. Zwerdling, read favorable portions of the transcript to reporters in the hall. Detroit reporter William Serrin later described their theatrical presentation: "Once Victor stopped as he read a passage, almost like a heroine in a silent movie, and insisted that the next section was too indelicate, that Zwerdling must read it. Zwerdling did—a passage in which Anderson, incensed at Walter Reuther, said, goddammit, he wasn't going to talk with Reuther any longer, goddammit, he wasn't going to do it, because his father had always warned him not to get into a pissing match with a skunk."

For a week, the union presented its case "to the soles of their shoes perched on the edge of the negotiating table, and to the back of *Liberty,* which they said was 'more interesting than the crap you are giving us.'" Reuther could make a case for some wage increase. Auto workers' basic hourly pay had gone up from 93.5 cents per hour in 1939 to $1.13 six years later, but wages had not kept pace with the cost of living. Auto workers had more than made up the difference with an average of 5.5 hours overtime weekly, but with wartime shortages had been unable to spend the money anyway. No one expected prices to go down in the postwar period; they had learned the lesson of the 1920–21 depression after World War I and would prevent that. Reuther essentially was asking, demanding, that the corporation give the shop hands fifty-two hours' pay for a forty-hour week so that his members could share in the expected prosperity. If the demand was too high, General Motors had only to open its books to prove it, he suggested disingenuously.

Meanwhile, the negotiations wandered far from wage demands.

"Unless we get a more realistic distribution of America's wealth," Reuther argued, "we don't get enough to keep this [industrial] machine going."

Harry Coen, assistant director of personnel for the corporation, snapped, "You can't talk about this thing without exposing your socialist desires."

"If fighting for a more equal and equitable distribution of the wealth of this country is socialistic, I stand guilty of being a socialist."

Coen agreed. "I think you are convicted."

"I plead guilty."

The talks adjourned with no counterproposal, Wilson turning the screws tighter with each silent day. Ten days later, General Motors announced its counter: 10 cents an hour—if the union would join the corporation in asking Congress to increase the work week from forty to forty-five hours and join in an appeal to the OPA for a price increase of 10 percent to cover the wage hike. Wilson had called Reuther's bet and then raised him.

Two weeks later, no closer to a settlement, and with Reuther's suggestion for arbitration ignored, 180,000 union members hit the bricks—to be met by another 140,000 men already laid off as a result of the peacetime reconversion. Now came the time of testing—for a militant union leader who grasped business principles, and a less than humble corporation seeking to defend what it considered its sacred rights. General Motors' ability to pay 30-percent higher wages was not the issue for Sloan, Wilson, or the balance of the board; the real struggle was to retain the right to set prices, but above all, to keep its secrets locked in the company's books. "We don't even open our books to our own stockholders," Anderson growled, an inadvertent admission that the professional managers had assumed virtually unfettered control of the nation's largest enterprise.

Reuther's oratory—"You are asking for a fight, and, brother, you are going to get it"—was just that, stemwinders for the troops. More important were his resolve to keep the men on strike and his political judgment of when to settle without damaging his chances of election as president of the UAW. If he held out too long—and the $4 million strike fund would not last indefinitely, with 320,000 families siphoning it off each week—he could antagonize supporters.

In December, President Truman stepped in, terming the strike a "major obstacle holding up our reconversion program." For the first time, General Motors was confronted with an explicit affirmation that its quarrels with the union involved an unrepresented third party, the public; that the union–management quarrel could not be permitted to effect the economy as a whole.

On his own authority, President Truman appointed a three-member fact-finding board, though the corporation held firm, warning that if its ability to pay were to be an issue, it would not cooperate.* As the commission opened its proceedings, chairman Lloyd Garrison, who was also chairman of the War Labor Board, read a telegram from the president asserting that inspection of the company's books was "essential to enable the board to determine the ability of the employer to pay an increase in wages where such ability is in question." The General Motors delegation stalked out.

The corporation's boycott was a public-relations gaffe, and no amount of advertising in the nation's newspapers stating the company position could rectify it. "A look at the books" seemed reasonable; what did the corporation have to hide?

On January 10, 1946, the president's board recommended a wage increase of 17.5 percent—a raise of 19.5 cents per hour—with the stipulation that the corporation was not to increase its prices. General Motors turned down the settlement proposal the next day, Wilson hewing to the principle that the company not "be forced to pay higher than competitive wages because of its financial ability."

Late in January, first Chrysler, then Ford settled their contracts with the autonomous UAW locals in their plants, accepting 18.5-cent wage hikes, half of what Reuther was asking of General Motors. Neither Ford nor Chrysler agreed to hold down automobile prices. (Henry Ford II had complained publicly that, restricted to a 1942 price ceiling of $780, his company was losing $261 on every car manufactured.) The settlements with rival Ford and Chrysler undercut Reuther's position, and he opted to

---

* Ability to pay was, of course, a spurious issue, even as it was foolish. Twelve years later, General Motors president Harlow Curtice told a Senate committee, "We would not negotiate at any time on the basis of ability to pay." Senator Estes Kefauver then asked, "You mean if you were losing money, you would not feel that was important to bring out before a presidential committee?" Curtice was snared and could only evade: "I think if we were losing money, I think it would probably be a matter of taking a good look at our management." (See *Administered Prices,* Hearings before the Subcommittee on Antitrust and Monopoly, Senate Judiciary Committee, 1958, p. 2490.)

accept the 19.5-cent boost recommended earlier by the federal panel. Wilson refused—not for the penny difference, which the corporation could well afford, but because Reuther still insisted that there be no increase in the price of General Motors' cars.

Time was running out for the labor leader. First President Truman backed down on his opposition to price increases in an effort to settle a bitter concurrent steelworkers' strike. The steelworkers' negotiated settlement contained the touchstone 18.5-cent-an-hour boost, and the OPA subsequently allowed a hike in basic steel prices. The final blow came on February 12, when the United Electrical Workers, with some 25,000 members in scattered General Motors plants, accepted the corporation's offer of 18.5 cents, with no strings. (UEW President James Mattles opposed Reuther's bid for the auto workers' presidency on the grounds that Reuther had pledged to purge communists from the CIO.) General Motors offered the same settlement to Reuther.

A month later, after 113 days out, CIO president Philip Murray and Charles Wilson signed a two-year contract providing for an increase of 18.5 cents an hour, with various fringe benefits, including equal pay for women, seniority preference on job transfers, the checkoff, and improved overtime and vacation pay. Petulantly, Reuther boycotted the last negotiations, then put on the best face he could, claiming the fringe benefits boosted the total wage package above the 19.5 cents he had demanded. Practically, Reuther had lost, yet within the union he never stood higher. Two weeks later, on March 27, 1946, he was narrowly elected president of the United Auto Workers at its Atlantic City convention. American labor history would never be the same.

John Thomas Smith had finally won, just as he had promised John L. Lewis he would in 1937. Long after, General Motors executives still savored Reuther's defeat—the only one he would experience. They had beaten him on a matter of principle, they believed, which made the victory so much sweeter. Yet the total cost of the strike, some industry sources estimated, may have been $1 billion in lost sales, unearned wages, and dealers' profits.

A year after the settlement, Wilson shrugged off charges of poor union relations: "We have the union relations *I* designed, and they are right for our industry and our union. They suit both of us. The test of labor relations isn't rhetoric. The test is results. We lose fewer days to strikes than any other major company in this country or in any other unionized country. We have great continuity of union leadership. And both the union and we get the things the country, the company, and the union need: high discipline, high productivity, high wages, and high employment security.''

The 113-day ordeal permanently reordered labor relations in the industry. Unlike the sit-downs of 1937 and the bloody struggle to organize within the Ford Motor Company, it was entirely peaceful. The violence had been rhetorical.

Contract negotiations in 1948 were models of fraternal felicity. In full cry, selling everything the corporation could make, Wilson wanted no work stoppage. For its part, the union, too, preferred to stay on the job. The passage, in 1947, of the Taft-Hartley Act—a bitter union loss, or so it appeared at the time—suggested caution, lest the unions bring down even stronger legislation. Further, Walter Reuther was in Grace Hospital, recovering from an assassination attempt in which his right arm was shattered by a shotgun blast.

Wilson's 1948 proposal was two-pronged. Wages would be tied to the Bureau of Labor Statistics cost-of-living index; further wage increases would come from increases in worker productivity. In effect, workers were assured that they would remain the highest paid in the country, and that they would at least keep pace with inflation. Further, they would share in the corporation's expanded prosperity, for as productivity increased, so would their salaries. The proposal did not provide a guaranteed annual wage; Wilson was still working on that element of a comprehensive labor policy. But the innovative contract, widely praised even within business, assured General Motors of what it most wanted: continued production. "The treaty of Detroit," said *Fortune,* "may have cost General Motors a billion for peace, but it was a bargain." Wrote a later auto historian: "The result was a contract of historic importance in American labor relations since it established a pattern that was widely followed in the next decade" in other industries. Wilson's proposal—for which the union later would claim credit when it suited its needs—demonstrated that General Motors did not have to be the eternal nay-sayer.

Wilson's leadership as president *and* chief executive officer had marked more than just the passage of generations, though it was that too. (Another automobile pioneer, Charles F. Kettering, retired as vice-president in 1947, and William Knudsen, returned to General Motors as a member of the board, would die the following year.) Wilson had shifted the locus of power in the corporation from New York's financially oriented General Motors Building to the production-minded executives in Detroit. By 1948, for the first time since World War I, more than half of the board of directors were production people.

That year Wilson anointed his successor, selecting Buick general manager Harlow Curtice for the training role Wilson himself had once filled: executive vice-president in charge of the staff. Curtice had turned it down the year before, telling a friend, "I'd rather be able to walk out in the factory and see things going on." He was a line man, the small-town boy from Eaton Rapids, Michigan, who had started as an accountant at age twenty with the spark-plug division in Flint. He had worked his way to the presidency of AC, then had been shifted to Buick in 1933. There he found his calling, as a sales-minded executive with an uncanny ability to gauge public taste.

At Curtice's order, Buick had introduced a styling innovation that would persist for twenty years—the "mouseholes" in the hood. They had begun as a joke, when Ned Nickles, Buick's chief designer, had punched holes in the side of his own car and fitted them with small lights that flashed in sequence with the cylinder firing. Curtice happened to see the Nickles family car, liked the sockets empty at the moment, and summarily ordered three holes for the Super and four for the Roadmaster. Buick publicists named the holes "ventiports," but, with or without a name, they remained resolutely unfunctional—except they sold cars.

With such hunches, Curtice had succeeded as had no other division head, ramming Buick from a slumping eighth spot to press Plymouth for third place in sales behind Chevrolet and

Ford. The corporation had had finance men and production men as presidents; soon it would have a super-salesman.

Wilson then turned to a newly vexing problem that had surfaced only with his promotion: the shortage of qualified executives to move up the ladder. For years the corporation's management had thought itself well-staffed, with platoons of younger men eager for advancement. That might have been true at lower echelons, might still be, but they had discovered rudely just how few were the seasoned executives ready for the highest offices. Most of the men running the divisions were at the end of their careers; like Sloan, Knudsen, and Kettering, they were men who had known Billy Durant, Ransom Olds, and Henry Ford from the early days. With the new mandatory retirement age, which would be lowered to sixty-five in 1950, they would be gone.

The untimely death of Nicholas Dreystadt in 1946 literally left only Curtice ready to assume the chief executive officer's title when Wilson himself retired. The corporation had to get younger men into managerships and had to season them with a rotation of assignments that imparted some comprehension of the entire corporation. Because the shortage was so acute in 1948 Wilson ignored tradition and protests to bring in an outsider with no automobile experience to serve as his "special assistant." The title deceived no one; Roger Kyes was meant as an alternative in case Curtice could not cut it.

In part because its management was spread thinly, the board of directors made a critical decision to sell off its minority investments in other companies, to become purely an operating rather than a holding company. These sales simplified operations and also had the effect of removing criticism of General Motors as the editorial-page cartoonist's grasping octopus with tentacles in a host of corporations only vaguely related to automobiles. In the uncertainty of postwar America, with the specter of a revived federal antitrust effort, some discretion by the board seemed appropriate.

General Motors sold its aircraft interests—Bendix Aviation and North American. While both were profitable, there was no immediate prospect of the "flying flivver" that would permit mass production of airplanes.

The corporation's 3.5-percent interest in Greyhound went next. The bus lines had come to General Motors as part of the purchase two decades earlier of Johnny Hertz's Yellow Cab. During the Depression, Yellow had invested in financially strapped bus lines, conditioning the investments on exclusive purchase of Yellow's motor coaches. As the bus lines replaced interurban trolleys, General Motors' bus sales increased, leading Yellow to consider converting unprofitable streetcar systems to buses.

A Yellow subsidiary purchased the electric-streetcar lines in Springfield, Ohio, and in Kalamazoo and Saginaw, Michigan, then converted them to buses and promptly sold out, leaving behind three new customers for motor coaches. That experiment considered a success, in 1936, General Motors, with Firestone Tire and Standard Oil of California, organized a similar company, National City Lines. NCL worked on a larger scale. It purchased streetcar systems, converted them to buses, and then sold out—with the stipulation that the new owners would not buy "any new equipment using any fuel or means of propulsion other than gas." By 1949, when General Motors disposed of National City Lines, that company had been involved in replacing rail systems in forty-five cities, including New York, Los Angeles (the largest system converted), Philadelphia, Baltimore, St. Louis, and Salt Lake City. At least one critic charged that "the National City Lines campaign had a devastating impact on the quality of urban transportation and urban living in America," but General Motors had built a grand market for its GMC coaches.

The last of the major investments to be dealt off was wholly owned Hertz Drivurself and companion Sterrett Operating Service, a truck-rental company. Organized originally by Johnny Hertz, the car-rental company had limped through the Depression, gained ground through the war, and now stood on the brink of prosperity. Already the largest such business in the country, it stood to grow substantially as long-distance air travel increased in the postwar years of jet transport. General Motors' announced reason for disposing of Hertz was more self-serving than accurate: "It was felt that General Motors' original objective of demonstrating the need and profitability of the car and truck rental business had been accomplished. Since Hertz was a service business, in which General Motors had no special competency, rather than a manufacturing business, General Motors decided to dispose of its interest in accordance with its policy of getting out of businesses in which it could no longer make a real contribution."

In fact, the decision to sell was impelled as much by other considerations. Hertz, a marginally profitable operation, would need large sums of investment capital to keep pace with the expected expansion of the airline industry and the nation's airports. While finding capital would be no problem, the corporation believed the money would be better spent on ventures with a higher return on investment. Secondly, ownership of Hertz vertically integrated General Motors; the manufacturer, in effect, rented its cars to the public. General Motors already was integrated vertically, but as a manufacturer; further integration, dealing with the public, provided high visibility and high risk of the federal government filing an antitrust action. The corporation was coping with enough of these risks already, and there were hints of others in diesel locomotives and bus manufacturing. Plainly enough, they could do without the headaches of the automobile-rental business.

In 1953, General Motors sold Hertz Drivurself for $6.5 million to a group of Chicago investors, though the fraternal bond that led to Hertz using General Motors cars would endure for the next twenty years. (Similarly, Ford had a fleet-sales arrangement with Avis, the second largest of the car-rental companies, and Chrysler with third-ranked National.)

Wilson consciously girded General Motors for a great boom in automobile sales during the 1950s. Given population projections, highway construction, and widespread prosperity, the future appeared rich with opportunity, especially with the new Kettering engine. The corporation's retired vice-president had left one last innovation, not as advanced as others he had contributed, but one that would be as influential in its own way as the self-starter was nearly forty years earlier. Kettering had presented a technical paper in mid-1947 proposing a V-8 engine with overhead valves and a potentially high compression ratio that would practically double the industry standard of 6.5:1. All that was needed was a higher octane gasoline for these super-horsepower brutes.

"It is difficult to determine what was so revolutionary about the engine," one automotive historian wrote later. "The V-8 designs had been around for over thirty years; the standard Ford had a V-8 engine. Overhead valves, or valve-in-the-head, had also been around; the Buick straight-eight engine had them at the time of Kettering's paper. Everyone knew the effects of high octane gas in permitting high compression (more efficient) engines. But somehow the combination of these elements excited the industry."

The reason was simple: the Kettering engine provided surplus power beyond what was needed to move the 3,000-pound family car. That additional power could be employed to make cars bigger and more comfortable, with more lavish and heavier appointments. It could be diverted for a host of accessories; some, such as air-conditioning and power seats, merely conveniences; others, such as power-assisted brakes and steering, necessities as the cars themselves grew in size. The industry's excitement was visceral—and contagious. Manufacturers could build machines embodying the very essence of the new American prosperity, mobile palaces of creature comforts that proclaimed the affluence of the nation. They would be creating nothing less than patriotic symbols, even as they were contributing to ever-increasing prosperity.

With the introduction of the 1949 Cadillac, sporting more horsepower than any other production engine before it, the great race was on. What Detroit engineers cast aside was Kettering's concern for efficiency—and with it, gasoline economy. The 1949 Cadillac got twenty miles per gallon at highway speeds, a mileage figure the division could not match in the next thirty years of automotive development.

For Charles Wilson and General Motors, the future could not have been brighter. Industry production in 1949 reached 6.2 million cars and trucks, an all-time record, yet more than half of the vehicles on the road were still prewar models, begging for replacement. General Motors had garnered 43 percent of all new-car sales, grossing $5.7 billion, a billion dollars more than 1948's record. Chevrolet had brought out its first new automobile since 1941, the tooling costs of $50 million, twice those of prewar models. Even though it was powered by the same "Hot Water Six" introduced twenty years earlier, sales spurted by 300,000—proof again of Harley Earl's ability to sell automobiles. The "Hot Water Six" had four more years of life before Chevrolet, too, joined the horsepower contest.

The major concern at the moment was prices. The Chevrolet was priced at more than $1,000; the mid-range Pontiacs, Buicks, and Oldsmobiles at $1,500. Radios and heaters were optional. When reporters asked if there would ever be a cheap car—below $1,000—again, Wilson shook his head no: "People don't want the kind of car you would have to make in order to price it under $1,000. You would have to take too much out to get the price down, and there are many things you couldn't cut. Fenders, just to take one item, cost just about the same to make whether they are large or small."

The lifting of the twenty-four-month ceiling on installment payments eased the price problem. The public rushed to buy the new Buick, Oldsmobile, and Cadillac hardtops introduced that year, increasingly opted for costly automatic transmissions, radios, and heaters, but above all selected those models with an abundance of chrome, which proclaimed that for their owners the years of austerity were over.

General Motors was entering the Decade of the Automobile in American history—with only one cloud to rain on its parade. In June 1949, the United States Department of Justice filed suit to force E.I. du Pont de Nemours to divest itself of its controlling interest in General Motors.

14

The Bazaar

For all his reservations, Charles Wilson could not refuse his president. Dwight David Eisenhower, elected in the landslide of 1952, had asked "Engine Charlie" to become secretary of defense. It was a risk—a move from the familiar routines of General Motors to the strange labyrinths of the Department of Defense at an age when most men would be considering retirement. Moreover, it meant selling his 39,000 shares of General Motors stock, a sacrifice ordered by the president himself. The conflict-of-interest law was clear, Ike had insisted, and General Motors was the nation's largest defense contractor. However Wilson sought to remove himself from the awarding of contracts, there always would be the suggestion that underlings favored the boss's old employer in order to please him.

The offer was tantalizing for other, private reasons, not the sort discussed on the fourteenth floor of the corporation's executive offices in Detroit. Wilson had been with General Motors for thirty-three years; the ambitious engineer had become president of the corporation, his hair now gray and thinning, his once

349

roseate cheeks sagging to jowls. He had spent more than twelve years guiding General Motors through a war, then peacetime conversion; had refined production methods in the process; and presided over the greatest sales market the corporation had ever known. In the last few years, the job—as big as it was—had felt confining. Even the once-troubled relationship with the United Auto Workers had settled into something near contentment. The UAW had so liked the 1948 contract that it had proposed a renewal in 1950 for an unprecedented five years.

Both Walter Reuther and Wilson were intent upon keeping the labor force at work when their negotiators sat down in the spring of 1950 to hammer out a new agreement. Both sides were happy with the wage formula of 1948, which provided an escalator clause linking wages to the government's cost-of-living index, and the concept of an annual productivity award. The union had three major demands: an increase in the productivity payout to five cents per hour, a pension, and health insurance. General Motors played Br'er Rabbit, pleading not to be thrown into the briar patch.

Wilson had anticipated the pension demand and, in fact, had conceived a plan to fund it by investing in the stock market "the way a prudent financial manager would invest," he told writer Peter Drucker.

"But that would make the employees, within twenty-five years, the owners of American business," Drucker pointed out.

"Exactly what they should be," Wilson shot back. "And what they must be. For the income distribution in this country surely means that no one else can own American industry unless it be the government."

The productivity payout they compromised at four cents an hour. The health plan was to cover workers and their families, a major contribution to the sense of security Wilson wanted to provide employees.

For its part, the union agreed not to stand in the way of either automation or technological innovations that might displace workers—a key concession to the corporation then embarked on a comprehensive capital-investment program.

Critics of the settlement ignored the long-term impact of the pension plan—which would be the largest of its kind in the country and thus the most influential—to savage the cost-of-living provision. "There are two inflationary forces in the U.S.—Washington and General Motors," a rival auto-industry executive snorted.

Prepared to lead a General Motors independent of the industry, Wilson countered: "I contend we should not say 'the wage-price spiral.' We should say 'the price-wage spiral.' For it is not primarily wages that push up prices. It is primarily prices that *pull* up wages."

Two years later, with labor mollified and the end of the Korean War imminent, the corporation turned again to the undistracted business of building and selling automobiles. It had barely satisfied the pent-up demand from World War II, the industry producing more than 19.4 million vehicles before the outbreak of the Korean War in 1950. Once the burgeoning market might have stirred his competitive juices, but for Wilson it lacked the challenge the president of the United States was offering—to bring big-business management techniques to government.

"Engine Charlie" Wilson left Detroit to become one of three men associated with General Motors in the Eisenhower cabinet—an unprecedented and unmatched achievement by one corporation. The incoming secretary of the interior was Douglas McKay, a one-time Chevrolet dealer from Salem, Oregon, who had gained a substantial regional reputation as a conservationist. The postmaster general's office went to Flint's Arthur Summerfield, owner of one of the largest Chevrolet agencies in the world, a considerable fund-raiser for the Republican Party and its national chairman during the 1952 presidential campaign.*

Wilson's move to the Pentagon opened the door for Harlow Curtice, crown prince of the corporation, to move into the presi-

---

* Earlier, as state party chairman, Summerfield had earned a formidable reputation as a political fund-raiser. Between 1946 and 1948, he levied party contributions upon Michigan auto dealers of one dollar for each car sold, upon pain of not receiving factory shipments of cars they had ordered. Summerfield raised some $250,000 for the GOP, but eighteen dealers who made the mistake of sending in their tithes on company checks were convicted of violating the Corrupt Practices Act. In subsequent years, dealers were careful to use personal checks. See Drew Pearson's "Washington Merry-Go-Round" column for October 21, 1952.

dent's office. Curtice was fifty-nine and for three years had stood
at Wilson's right hand as executive vice-president. Of all the
corporation's presidents—Durant, du Pont, Sloan, Knudsen,
and Wilson before him—Curtice was to be the most influential in
shaping Automobile America and the least recognized for that
influence.

Raised in Eaton Rapids, Michigan, Curtice was the small-town
boy who made good. A graduate of tiny Ferris Institute in nearby
Big Rapids, he had moved to Flint, then still comfortably small,
yet large enough with Billy Durant's expanding enterprises to
offer opportunities to an eager young man. Answering an ad for a
bookkeeper, Curtice had gone to work in 1914 for Champion
Ignition; within a year he was controller of that General Motors
subsidiary, at twenty-one the youngest executive in the corpora-
tion. Thirty-eight years later—still known to his friends as
"Red," though his hair was a sandy gray—Curtice still lived in
Flint, still played poker with cronies from AC Spark Plug and
Buick on Saturday afternoons in a private room at the Hotel
Durant, and hewed still to the values learned as a boy in Eaton
Rapids.

The former bookkeeper had gained a reputation in the corporation as a man who could "pitch, catch and cover first base at
the same time." From the confines of the controller's office, he
had moved to the presidency of AC, where he displayed a flair
for sales not usually associated with bookkeepers or accountants. It was that which earned his promotion to the presidency
of stumbling Buick in 1933.

At Buick Curtice had prodded stylist Harley Earl for new and
bigger models, then hustled them with single-minded zeal. Curtice liked big cars—he reveled in them, the bigger the better—
and assumed all America shared his attitude. The big men in
town drove the biggest cars. So it had been in Eaton Rapids, Big
Rapids, and Flint in the first decades of the twentieth century,
and so it was in Harlow Curtice's memory and value system.
Small cars simply did not command the status nor convey the
affluence, the greatness, of America today; for just that reason,
Curtice had led the opposition to the subsequently aborted
Chevrolet Cadet.

So it was that General Motors' automobiles were to grow progressively larger during Curtice's tenure, acquiring bulk, longer wheelbases, and, most important, highly profitable accessories. Curtice made no claim to engineering or styling skills, but he had cultivated a keen faculty for selecting just the innovation that would most likely sell cars. In 1953 it was to be air-conditioning, which Curtice had decided General Motors would offer as an option on its biggest cars, the first automobile manufacturer in the industry to do so.

As president of the corporation and its chief executive officer, Curtice tended to ignore the New York office and its financial staff. However ironic, the former bookkeeper left financial matters to Albert Bradley, the ex-university professor who had resolutely hid his doctorate in the era of grease-stained executives such as Knudsen and Dreystadt. Instead, Curtice concentrated on building and selling automobiles; it was more fun.

Job and man were well met. Curtice relished the work beyond all measure, setting a pace telling on lesser men, yet invigorating to the president. Despite extensive publicity describing Curtice as a devoted family man and father, he frequently spent entire weeks in the General Motors Building on West Grand Boulevard, leaving only to eat occasional meals with close friend Anthony DeLorenzo, the corporate vice-president in charge of public relations. From eight o'clock on Monday morning, when the two flew from their homes in Flint the sixty-seven miles to Detroit in a two-engine Lockheed Ventura (one of twenty airplanes in the corporate fleet), until late Friday night, Curtice worked, ate, and slept in the General Motors Building.

In operational matters, Curtice was Billy Durant reborn— given to quick decisions, disposing of problems with lavish hand and absolute authority. Like Durant, he toured factories and instantly dispensed millions of dollars for expansion without so much as a by-your-leave to the finance committee. The committee system of which Alfred Sloan and Pierre du Pont were so proud gradually slipped into disuse; Curtice was frank to assert, "The best committee is the committee of one."

The new president wrought an almost immediate shift in corporate policy. Wilson had kept a rein on automobile sales, warily staying around a 45-percent market share, directing sales energies into such nonautomotive areas as refrigerators, ball bearings, and diesel engines. Harlow Curtice would have none of it. "You never stand still in this business. You either go up or down," he told associates, senators, and newsmen repeatedly—and heatedly. Refrigerators were all very well and good, but Harlow Curtice was not put on earth to sell iceboxes. He was an auto man, a true believer, and autos he intended to sell.

The change from Democratic to Republican administrations altered the political climate enough, Curtice calculated, to allow General Motors to strike out for a larger market share. Holding 46 percent of domestic motor-vehicle sales in 1953, General Motors, he boldly announced, would aim for 48 percent in 1954. When President Eisenhower announced in his annual economic message to Congress in January 1954 that size alone would not be the criterion for bringing antitrust actions, Curtice had his license to plunder.

The election of a Republican administration, the first in twenty years, was as some electric stimulus applied to the neurons of American industry. Hundreds of business executives, fairly twitching with anxiety, swooped down upon the nation's capital to open offices from which to press for special favors. In this Cold War era of United States–Russian confrontation, national defense dipped into the Treasury first.

General Motors stood at the head of the line, for the nation's largest industrial enterprise was a favored air force and army contractor. As early as 1953, there were complaints that General Motors had been singled out as the sole supplier of trucks and of light and medium tanks for the army; three other firms—Ford, Chrysler, and American Locomotive—were eliminated as suppliers on the grounds that single-source procurement would be more efficient. (The policy of a single-source contractor, approved by Secretary of Defense Wilson, actually contravened General Motors' own system of having at least two contractors for parts purchased outside the corporation; should one suffer a breakdown in production, the other could take up the slack.)

As a favored supplier, General Motors repeatedly received

contracts that unsuccessful rivals challenged as overly costly to the taxpayer, or unwarranted on the basis of competitive bids. In 1952, Fisher Body snared a contract for turret lathes although its bid was more than twice as high as a rival's, and as late as 1968, the army awarded General Motors a contract to manufacture M-16 rifles though two other firms had underbid the automotive firm by sizable margins. A Senate subcommittee concluded the rifle procurement "so questionable as to present the appearance that the Army did not expect them to be questioned or to be subjected to on-the-spot inquiry . . ."

Through 1953 and the Korean War, the corporation ranked as the nation's largest defense contractor, with $5.7 billion in military orders. By 1955, it had slipped in both the number of contracts awarded and the amounts; the Pentagon was caught up with intercontinental ballistic missiles and nuclear arms, for which the corporation lacked scientific background. Future contracts would be harder to come by, dependent upon the company's ability to expand into the unfamiliar fields of electronics, rocketry, and computers.

All were far afield, however, and even the procurement contracts that would follow research and development were for limited numbers of items, production simply not fitted to the corporation's greatest strength. Caught between the guaranteed profits of cost-plus defense contracting and the great consumer market of the 1950s, General Motors vacillated, then settled on token efforts more symbolic than effectual.

In 1956, the corporation finally opened a long-planned, much-delayed technical center twelve miles north of Detroit with a dedication speech by its doyen of research, Charles F. Kettering:

To me a technical center is a place where people can think and develop ideas. One thing worries me about this technical center. I am afraid that the people here may lean too heavily on the facilities and forget that ideas are developed in the mind . . .

It may be fifty or sixty years sometimes before an idea develops. But if we will recognize that there is a definite time before an idea can become a product, provided the customers are available for it, the future is the greatest natural asset we have.

Kettering clearly feared that the $150 million center would be devoted to technology rather than research, to the quick buck rather than the long-term investment. His fear was justified. The corporation had let Kettering give his why-grass-is-green speech one last time and was now going to get on with its real concern. General Motors was not about to sit around fifty or sixty years waiting for a scientific discovery to become commercially useful.

Despite his background in physics and his earlier direction of the Atomic Energy Commission's reactor-development program, the newly hired vice-president in charge of research, Lawrence R. Hafstad, Ph.D., warned that he did not want "to go overboard" in favor of basic scientific investigation. Nor could he. Research is an expensive, often fruitless business, and Hafstad's budget in 1956—no more than $20 million, or less than two-tenths of one percent of sales—would not alter reality. One critic noted that "G.M. has not yet proved that it has a research laboratory of front rank. Until very recently, Detroit had never done much true research as scientists understand it. Most of its so-called research achievements have fallen, rather, under the head of advanced engineering."

Into the 330-acre complex of twenty-five buildings designed by internationally recognized architect Eero Saarinen, the corporation put 4,000 employees. Thirteen hundred were assigned to nominal research functions, 700 to engineering and manufacturing developments, and 1,200 to styling. Of the three, styling was to be the most influential in the next decade and a half, even after the shock of Sputnik in October 1957.

But if research and defense were not to be profitable, General Motors still meant to benefit from a second government spending program. Hard after the would-be defense contractors had come Coxey's Army reborn, this time not unemployed laborers beseeching their government to put them to work building local roads, but well-fed representatives of industrial associations descending upon Washington to pry open the public purse to build a vast national highway system. They formed a potent, irresistible lobby: sand, gravel, and concrete companies, highway contractors, unions, oil and tire manufacturers, the American Automobile Association, the National Limestone Institute, the Automobile Manufacturers Association, state highway administrators, motor-bus operators, the American Trucking Association, and even the American Parking Association—for the more cars on the road, the more cars would be parked for a fee at the end of the journey.

These diverse groups had banded together in 1943 as the American Road Builders Association, with General Motors its largest contributor, to form a lobbying enterprise second only to that of the munitions industry. This band of corporate mendicants came intent upon expanding a wartime measure that authorized the expenditure of $1.5 billion in federal funds to create a 40,000-mile interstate highway system.

By 1953, the appropriation had long since vanished. While paved highways for the first time equaled unimproved tracks in length—there were about 1.5 million miles of each in the nation—the interstate network remained incomplete. Moreover, the highways of the 1940s were not adequate to the speeds of the 1950s or the expected volume of traffic of the 1960s and beyond. The road builders envisioned no mere widening of existing roads, but the creation of an entirely new superhighway system. It would be nothing less than the largest peacetime construction project in history.

To ease the bill's way, the so-called "Road Gang" inaugurated a comprehensive public-relations program. General Motors contributed in 1953 by sponsoring a national essay contest on the need for adequate roads. The winner of the $25,000 prize was, *mirabile dictu,* Robert Moses, coordinator of New York City's public-works program, passionate advocate of the urban expressway, and chairman of the 1939 New York World's Fair. Moses intended to implement the vision of Norman Bel Geddes on Manhattan Island.

Anticipating passage of the act, General Motors also purchased the Euclid Road Machinery Company to serve as the nucleus of its entry into the heavy earth-moving equipment business. Major governmental road expenditures would mean major sales and profits.

In August 1954, sensitive to political pressure, President Eisenhower appointed a hand-picked committee to "study" the nation's highway requirements. The committee's conclusion was foregone; its chairman was Lucius D. Clay, a career soldier retired to big business and a member since 1951 of the board of directors of General Motors. Later critics would complain that the Clay commission was misguided, since its members began with the premise that "the penalties of an obsolete road system are large, and that the price in inefficiency is paid not only in dollars, but in lives lost through lack of safety, and also in national insecurity."

The committee considered no alternatives to a massive highway system; it had not intended to. In the two years before the committee's recommendations were adopted as the National System of Interstate and Defense Highways—in the Cold War era, "defense" was a righteous mantle in which special interests sought to cloak themselves—no one weighed the merits of mass transit or rehabilitated railroads. The emphasis and concern were solely upon the automobile and truck. In effect, a major redirection of national policy had been predetermined by companies that would most benefit from that redirected policy.

The nation needed super-fast highways for continued industrial progress, witness after witness told the Clay commission. There were fifty-seven million automobiles registered in 1954, and manufacturers forecast another twenty-four million crowding the roads within ten years. James T. Nance, president of the Automobile Manufacturers Association, claimed that America's antiquated byways were costing motorists $2.5 billion annually. The states, eager for federal aid, already perceived a need for $25 billion to build urban freeways to speed commuters to and from the suburbs. The freeways were desperately needed; city auto traffic moved but eight to twelve miles per hour, and much less in rush hour. Transit ridership had peaked in 1947, then sunk to 1920's level as auto manufacturers rushed to fill the war-created passion for private cars. (Before passage of the act in 1956, transit patronage would fall another 17 percent, rail traffic 78 percent, and intercity bus travel almost 30 percent.) Americans wanted automobiles, ran the litany, and roads to drive them on.

In 1956, the Road Gang presented draft legislation that provided for a 41,000-mile interstate system, with the federal government paying 90 percent of the cost. The key provision of the bill as it was enacted provided for a highway trust fund—an accumulation of federal taxes on gasoline, tires, new buses, trucks, and trailers—and a use tax on large trucks plying the "toll-free" highways. The bill passed both houses with only twenty-four nay votes and was signed into law by President Eisenhower. The $25 billion highway system was to be built pay-as-you-go, with the trust fund expiring in 1972. Ostensibly, the highway system was to be designed to meet traffic loads anticipated for 1975.*

The proposed highway system never quite fulfilled public expectations in urban areas, no matter how many miles of freeway were built. (The general manager of Los Angeles' traffic department complained that they were building only six miles of six-lane freeway annually when thirty miles were needed just to keep pace with traffic increases; at that, Los Angeles was the world's most thoroughly macadamized city.) Still, the massive enterprise, twenty-nine times the size of the Panama Canal, St. Lawrence Seaway, and Grand Coulee Dam projects lumped together, was considered "one of the greatest engineering wonders of the 20th Century." It transformed the trucking industry into a mighty rival of the railroads; it made cross-country and vacation travel more pleasurable (until one reached the clogged urban portions and learned to take belatedly constructed bypasses); and it entrenched the automobile as the dominant form of transportation in the United States.

Meanwhile, General Motors was unilaterally determining what kinds of cars would ply these superhighways. As early as 1944, while planning for postwar production, automobile manufacturers had invested considerable effort in market research seeking to determine consumer needs. Motorists said they wanted economical, easy-to-repair automobiles; and 85 percent of their car trips were short, made for essential rather than recreational purposes.

The logical move was to build smaller, more practical auto-

---

* By 1959, the trust fund was draining faster than motorists could fill it; Congress responded by raising the tax on a gallon of gasoline by one cent. Furthermore, costs had jumped from $25 billion to $41 billion. Undeterred, the road builders built on. Congress meekly increased taxes again, even as the program's cost rose to $47.8 billion. By 1960, the average commuter was paying $63 annually in gas and excise taxes for the privilege of riding on already congested urban "speedways."

mobiles. With the end of the war, Paul Crosley again produced his tiny runabout. Nash began importing a small European "city car," the Metropolitan. Kaiser–Frazer introduced its Henry J, with a 100-inch wheelbase. Chrysler straddled the fence in the immediate postwar period, then designed a "shortie" Plymouth to be introduced in 1953. All were to suffer gravely. The market research had been faulty, centered on what consumers said they *needed*, not what they—often secretly—*desired*. It had failed to devalue motorists' immediate wartime concerns for parts and tire shortages, gas rationing, and increased prices—concerns that would disappear with postwar production.

Further, the research failed to gauge accurately the attitude of consumers toward the small car itself. The long-time General Motors strategy of selling the automobile as a symbol of success had rooted deeply in the public mind. Through the depressed thirties and the wartime forties, a probable majority of Americans had yearned for these merit badges of affluence. Now, in the fifties, when millions of middle-class workers finally could afford automobiles, they were not to be denied the status that seemingly surrounded such a major purchase. Even when budget forced them to purchase the comparatively mundane Chevrolet, Ford and Plymouth, they sought accessories to enhance the vehicle. And if by straining they could trade up, trade up they did. It was a market tailor-made for the merchandising skills of Harlow Curtice, who had restored Buick in the 1930s with just such a sales strategy. Two decades later he had an entire corporation with which to play.

Both General Motors, with Harley Earl ever in favor of longer and lower cars, and a management certain that bigger meant better; and Ford, with its nucleus of well-indoctrinated former General Motors managers at the helm, chose to build bigger cars. Set on a contrary course, Chrysler's market share would fall to barely 13 percent of all cars sold, while General Motors and Ford together accounted for eighty-one of every one hundred cars sold in 1954. Chrysler, which had once garnered 25 percent of American automobile sales, would never regain its customary market share.

By the end of 1952, as Curtice assumed the presidency, the

surviving independent auto makers were in grim condition; together, six snared but 14 percent of the market, a share that shrank as fast as their numbers. After four years of losses, Crosley ended production of cars that year. In April 1953, struggling newcomer Kaiser merged with venerable Willys–Overland. A year later, Hudson and Nash melded into American Motors. Five months after the Nash-Hudson merger, flagging Packard and lagging Studebaker joined forces.

Their weakened condition undercut whatever efforts the surviving independents made toward solvency; the press speculated constantly about possible bankruptcies. Despite the long career some of them had enjoyed—Packard was, after all, eight years older than General Motors—they acquired the status of "off-brands," according to automobile historian Lawrence White. Customers were concerned that their Nash or Willys would be orphaned, left parts-less by the manufacturer's demise. Trade-in values fell sharply, further undermining the autos' worth.

One by one, the independents guttered to insolvency, leaving the passenger-car field to the Big Three, American Motors, and Studebaker. Potential new entrants were scared off by the formidable barriers they confronted: a lack of dealers, a paucity of experienced talent to staff what necessarily would be a large corporation from its onset, but, most of all, a lack of capital. In 1945, when Henry Kaiser told an auto-industry group that he was prepared to risk $25 million of his own money in the new Kaiser–Frazer, a voice from the back of the room growled, "Give the man one white chip." Within a decade, $25 million would hardly make the ante; one estimate suggested that it would cost as much as $1 billion to create a viable new automobile company, and that firm would have to snatch at least 8 percent of the market to survive.

Paradoxically, the number of manufacturers shrank even as the market grew, from an average annual output of 4 million vehicles in the 1940s to 6.3 million vehicles in the late 1950s. America was determined to spend itself to prosperity in this decade of boomlets and slumps.

In the ten years between 1950 and 1960, the gross national product rose 37 percent. Corporate profits climbed by only one-third, as strongly organized labor unions pressed for wage hikes and fringe benefits. Personal income jumped 42 percent, faster than the gross national product but at about the same rate as industrial productivity. By the end of the decade, employment had risen 10 percent and workers had more disposable income to spend.

Spend it they did—on television sets, home appliances, and vacations, but most of all, on automobiles. In 1950, there were 49.3 million motor vehicles registered in the country; ten years later, 73.8 million jammed the roads, despite scrappage rates running as high as 4.5 million vehicles annually.

Led by General Motors, the nation's automobiles reflected this economic growth in physical terms. Even the low-priced cars bulked seventeen-and-a-half feet in length and more than six feet in width. If there was one automobile that seemed to most embody the nation's optimistic mood, it was Cadillac—two-and-a-half tons of rolling affluence blatantly advertised as the automobile for the executive on the way up. In postwar America, millions turned to the siren call of Cadillac's appeal to the nouveaux riches:

Let's say it was thirty-one years ago, on a beautiful morning in June. A boy stood by a rack of papers on a busy street and heard the friendly horn of a Cadillac. "Keep the change," the driver smiled, as he took his paper and rolled out into the traffic. "There," thought the boy, as he clutched his coin, "is the car for me!"

And since this is America, where dreams make sense in the heart of a boy, he is now an industrialist. He has fought—without interruption—for the place in the world he wants his family to occupy. Few would deny him some taste of the fruits of labor. No compromise this time!

As simple as the ads were, they sold automobiles: "'Here is a man,' the Cadillac says—almost as plainly as the words are written here—'who has earned the right to sit at this wheel.'" It was a naked appeal to ego, Harlow Curtice's hard sell.

To the uninitiated—and there seemingly were few in this age of hokum surrounding the annual introduction of new cars—passenger cars appeared to be homogeneous creatures, a Del Rey (Chevrolet) no different in appearance from a De Soto—if indeed the Chevrolet could be identified as a Del Rey at all.

Concluded one Senate report: ". . . Apparently in the minds of those who establish car designs and formulate advertising policy, appeal to specific groups of buyers must be subordinated to a generalized appeal to a synthetic, homogeneous buyer whose prime, if not sole, interests are in show, bigness, power, speed and snob appeal."

At the same time, the automobile companies sought to infuse their passenger cars with an individuality the cars, in fact, did not and could not have. Taking advantage of computers newly introduced to production, computers that could tabulate and keep track of a virtually infinite number of possibilities while directing production lines, General Motors introduced ever more body styles in its five automotive lines and ever more combinations of trim and engine. By 1957, the company was offering seventy-five body styles—in two-doors, four-doors, station wagons, soft-top and hardtop convertibles—and no less than 450 trim combinations that might be affixed to the three basic bodies the corporation manufactured. (By 1969, the corporation offered 175 body styles and 918 trim combinations, automobile critic Kenneth Schneider marveled.)

The public bought, and paid for, such custom comforts. The average wholesale auto cost of $1,270 in 1950 rose to $1,822 by 1960, twice as fast as all wholesale costs during the decade. A generation earlier, motorists had spent 10.6 percent of their disposable income on transportation; by 1941, as mass production and a depression forced prices down, that figure had fallen to 9.5 percent. Amid the prosperity of the 1950s, transportation costs had risen once more to 11.5 percent.

General Motors' success was neither uniform nor untroubled. In this era of chrome-plated affluence, Chevrolet had fallen behind its corporate brethren and had lost ground to a revitalized, onrushing Ford. The 1952 Chevrolet appeared banal compared to the newly redesigned Fords of that year—one critic decided Chevrolet "looked as though it had been designed by Herbert Hoover's haberdasher"—and the organization was dispirited.

Late in 1951, after seeing the new Fords, then-President Charles Wilson had directed Curtice to restore the aging Chevrolet's image. Division manager Thomas Keating finally decided that his engineers were "too six-cylinder minded. They thought the six-cylinder engine would be tomorrow's best." In the immediate postwar years, when a salesman such as Keating could deal off everything that rolled, the competitive disadvantage of the "Hot Water Six" was not apparent. Now, in the fifties, younger buyers deserted the drab Chevrolet for the sprightly eight-cylinder Ford, boding ill for the corporation: today's young Chevrolet buyer was ostensibly tomorrow's middle-aged Oldsmobile and Buick customer.

Pushed by Curtice, Keating lured forty-three-year-old engineer Edward Cole from Cadillac and told him to build an eight-cylinder Chevrolet from the ground up. Curtice gave Cole a little more than two years in which to design the car—a task that normally takes three or more years. While Cole worked on an engine and chassis, Curtice himself prodded the styling section for what he fondly called the "hound dog" look—a car that was sleek and appeared to be lunging forward even when parked at the curb.

Even as Cole worked, Ford closed in. The two companies put increasing pressure upon their dealers, delivering unordered cars, threatening cancellation of franchises if dealers were deemed laggards, and drastically cutting margins near the end of the year to deal off the last of the 1954 models even as the factories ran full tilt until the model changeover.

Among themselves, dealers complained of the pressure. When one dealer grumbled that reduced prices and the need to sell new cars piling up in inventory had made profits impossible, a friend remarked that the wives of the dealers still were wearing mink and sable coats. "Sure," the dealer snapped, "but those coats are last year's models."

Both Ford and Chevrolet ended the 1954 model year with a blizzard of phony registrations in an effort to claim to be the best-selling automobile in the country. When the last flurry of dealer registrations of 1954 automobiles to friends and salesmen settled, Chevrolet had retained the top-selling spot by a scant, illusory 14,000 vehicles. Each company had sold 1.4 million of the 6.6 million cars and trucks manufactured that year. The other four General Motors automobile lines combined sold 1.9 million cars, giving the corporation half of the new-car market for the first time. General Motors had held off Ford, and the new Chevrolet was ready. In Detroit and in Flint, confidence ran unchecked. Fifty percent? "You know what the boss says—it means we're losing almost five out of every ten deals," they joked.

The competition was to be even more fierce the next year. The new 1955 Chevrolet had blossomed to an ostentatious nineteen feet long, no more a car that inspired customers to think of their grandmothers, but a zero-to-sixty phenomenon overpowered by Cole's V-8 engine, which delivered more than 180 horsepower. The arching tail fins set off rumors of the car "flying off the road at high speed," appeal enough for the youth market, but somewhat unsettling for the older majority.

The new Chevrolet, at a tooling cost of $100 million, did not exactly overwhelm either Ford or the twenty million people General Motors claimed had turned out to see its heralded debut. (Chevrolet spent some $3.5 million promoting the unveiling, passing out two million balloons to the kids, a million bottles of perfume to the ladies, and uncounted thousands of potholders, yardsticks, key rings, and beanies to everybody else who picked his way through the bubble machines and spotlights.) Curtice's "hound dog" look and the V-8 engine had kept sales leadership for Chevrolet, but not by as much as General Motors had expected its new model to generate against the year-old Ford and a Plymouth struggling up from the depths.

For twelve furious months, the industry hosted a carnival that would generate sales of $65 billion, almost one-fifth of the nation's gross national product. Amid the spectacle, it was somehow fitting that General Motors would produce its fifty-millionth automobile, and appropriate, too, that Curtice ordered that car to be a Chevrolet especially prepared for the well-publicized occasion.

The event was quintessential Curtice. He ordered the fifty-millionth car sprayed with a special "golden glint" paint and more than six hundred of its parts, from screws to body trim, plated in 24-karat gold. Even the seat covers were one-of-a-kind golden vinyl, and the upholstery was woven of gold metallic thread. If any one automobile could embody the era, it was the glimmering Chevrolet hardtop that moved down the Flint assembly line in forty-five minutes while a beaming Harlow Curtice waited to present it to a properly awed and well-fed press. Here was conspicuous consumption incarnate, proudly displayed and highly publicized. The golden Chevrolet toured briefly, then was retired to storage. But what better way to celebrate the golden corporation that in 1955—with the help of a "big stretchout" lengthening auto-finance terms from twenty-four to thirty-six months—would become the first company in the world to earn more than $1 billion in a single year?

Years later, the automobile industry would recall the great sales war of 1955 with varying degrees of fondness. Confronted with suddenly doubled sales quotas, dealers turned to a range of sales devices half-forgotten in the salad days since World War II: the "pack," the "mooch," the "low-ball," and half a hundred other schemes based on the simple premise that "car buyers were larcenous at heart and therefore if they were offered something to steal, they would come in and steal it." Complaints about automobile dealers' advertising ranked first among cases handled by Better Business Bureaus across the country.

Coupled with defects in both the design and manufacture of automobiles themselves, the continuing dealer practices would foster a vast mercantile system in which 150 million customers actively distrust the 26,000 merchants from whom they buy. With the manufacturers' tacit blessing, the nation's largest industry came to be uneasily grounded upon an elaborate confidence game that customers inevitably must lose. The only saving grace is that rarely does the customer realize that he has been fleeced; thus he is spared the humiliation.

The following year was to produce one of the enduring myths of the motor industry: safety doesn't sell. Chevrolet spent an additional $40 million to provide more horsepower in its V-8 and for an instant face lift on its 1956 model; $1 million went into new dies that flattened the top of the front fenders, giving the automobile a broader, more powerful appearance. Meanwhile, Ford all but ignored its exterior sheet metal, leaving the impression of an unchanged auto resting in dealers' showrooms. The two companies also stressed different promotional themes. While Chevrolet trumpeted, "The hot one's even hotter," For inaugurated a calculated advertising campaign stressing safety.

Seat belts and padded dashboards lacked the sales appeal of record Pikes Peak climbs, however, and Ford sales slipped in the first months of the model year. "Ford sold safety," the wags joked, "and Chevrolet sold cars." In fact, Ford managed to increase its market share—while General Motors held steady at 50.8 percent—but it did so only after abandoning the safety campaign midyear. Ford's advertising director, Edward Rothman, sadly concluded that "Safety does not appear to create an emotional urge to buy." Ford had reached its high-water mark; the ebbing was to follow.

Confronted each year with the need to surpass the last, General Motors whirled in frenzied hedonism. Its advertising budget, already the nation's largest, topped $100 million, 80 percent of that spent touting the physical and psychic comforts of driving a General Motors automobile. Another 5 percent went to institutional advertising, and the balance on products as varied as ball bearings and clothes driers.

Automotive advertising began in September, keyed to the introduction of the carefully hidden new models later that month. The secrecy shrouding new cars reached antic proportions, with automobiles shipped under canvas tarpaulins or in moving vans to scenic sites for advertising photographs, while newspaper photographers lurked around Michigan back roads on the weekends hoping for chance shots of the new cars when GM executives took them for test drives. Yet the more the public's appetite was teased, the more people seemingly turned out on opening day.

Even with the uncritical assistance of a complaisant press, General Motors did not rest. The corporation's most lavish promotion device was pure Curtice: an annual touring road show, "Motorama," offered a movable feast of new models; handmade, experimental "dream cars" not yet in production; bands; and flossy hyperbole. "It's pure schmaltz," a rival public-relations man harumphed, adding enviously, "but it sells cars." By the time the 1955 show closed and was stored in its 1,183 crates for the last time, 2.1 million people had turned out in five cities to see the new cars, to ogle the college girls hired as hostesses, and to ponder the shape of the automotive future. More than two million of the curious, one of every eighty-two Americans; no figure could better explain the pivotal role of the automobile at midcentury.

A similarly expensive "Powerama" inaugurated later that year was less successful. Devoted to earth-moving equipment from the new Euclid division and diesel motors for a variety of industrial uses, "Powerama" featured all the schmaltz of "Motorama," including a massive off-road dump truck converted into a swimming pool, replete with bathing beauties. Harlow Curtice hugely enjoyed himself at the Chicago opening, hinting broadly that General Motors intended to expand the 15 percent of its business that was nonautomotive, especially in the billion-dollar market for construction equipment.

By the end of the decade, Chevrolet was securely installed as the number-one manufacturer of cars and trucks, while Cole had replaced Keating as Chevrolet president and had become a certain contender for the presidency of the corporation. Cole had raised what Chevrolet considered its "normal, rightful share" of the American automobile market from 23 to 26 percent, and the corporation had boosted its market penetration from 50 to 52 percent.

Unlike Wilson, no self-imposed restraint bounded Curtice's ambition to drive General Motors to dominate each field it entered. With every new success, Curtice gathered to Detroit powers that a younger, more active Sloan once had carefully retained in New York. But Sloan was eighty, an honored figurehead but a figurehead no less, with Kettering and C.S. Mott virtually the last of the pioneers. Pierre du Pont had died two years earlier, on April 5, 1954, leaving the states of Delaware and Pennsylvania to squabble between themselves for the right to levy an inheritance tax on his estate. Mott seemingly would go on forever; at age sixty-two he had fathered a son.

The death of Sloan's wife, Irene, at the couple's winter home in Palm Beach in February 1956 was another tolling of the hour. Six weeks later, on April 2, 1956, after thirty-eight years with the corporation, the last nineteen as its chairman, Sloan retired in favor of Albert Bradley. Perhaps Bradley could reclaim some of the authority that had passed from Sloan and New York to Curtice and Detroit. Bradley would have his work cut out for him; how to argue organizational theory in the face of 1955's stunning 28-percent return on investment?

Bradley's succession opened the way for a series of orderly promotions on the financial side. New York always did things in orderly fashion. Two of the three men who moved up a rung would, in their turn, serve as chairman of the board: first Frederic G. Donner, later Richard Gerstenberg; the third, George Russell, would become vice-chairman. All had accounting or fiscal backgrounds—Gerstenberg described himself as "Old Dick the bookkeeper"—with no experience in Detroit. Curtice saw none of these gray men as a threat to Detroit's continued control of the company when he himself retired in two years.

The problem was to find a successor for Curtice. Outsiders praised General Motors' "management in depth," likening it to the Notre Dame football roster, yet the corporation lacked any formal management-training program. "The biggest myth in Detroit is GM's management in depth," an executive at a competitive firm noted. "They don't have lots of management. All they have is lots of people. They keep trying various combinations until they get one that clicks."

The situation suited Curtice. Without a formal promotion scheme, the would-be candidates were always on trial, always on their toes. Curtice's successor would come from one of the automotive divisions, that much was clear; thus his shuffling of personnel in July 1956 was considered the anointment of the heirs apparent. John F. Gordon moved from Cadillac to become executive vice-president for automobile production. Cole took over the management of Chevrolet. James Roche, the late Nick Dreystadt's one-time personnel manager, became Cadillac general manager. And in a surprise move, Curtice tapped Semon E. Knudsen as the man to restore slipping Pontiac.

The son of Signius Poul Wilhelm, forty-four-year-old "Bunkie" Knudsen had a reputation as a hard-driving, ambitious engineer. He had gone to work for the corporation in 1939 at Pontiac, working on army tanks, then had supervised the postwar installation of new automated machine tools. It was a major responsibility, and the appointment marked Knudsen as a "comer" in General Motors. Knudsen was so successful that in coming years General Motors was able to boost production by 50 percent while adding just 5 percent more workers.

At the same time, Knudsen and his colleagues in Process Development were implementing a new industrial objective, what had come to be known as quality-control engineering. The concept abandoned the notion of perfectability in machine-made parts, intending instead to set standards of allowable imperfection. Theoretically, the system permitted the economical organization of factories to produce products with a minimum of defects or parts that exceeded tolerance limits. In practical effect, cost-conscious manufacturers worked to insure that no part was made any better than it had to be. Once the statistical controls for sampling nonuniformity were perfected—a matter of some fifteen years—automobile manufacturers could offer warranties. By then they knew to the fifth decimal place the likelihood of any part breaking down before the minimal life span expected of it. How Henry Ford—dead on the night of a power failure at the River Rouge plant in 1947—would have scorned them. And how quick his grandson was to emulate them.

In 1953, Knudsen went off to Allison, charged with putting that airplane-engine manufactory into civilian production. Two years later, with that task done, he was dispatched to Cleveland Diesel, once again to whip a faltering operation into shape. As General Motors' Mr. Fixit, Knudsen confronted his biggest task in 1956, when Curtice tapped him to revive the Pontiac division. If he performed well, he believed, the corporation presidency ultimately would be his.

The problem with Pontiac, Knudsen decided, was its image—that of a stolid, middle-aged citizen who blended into a crowd with ease. It was an automobile for plumbers or bank clerks, and there simply were not enough of either bank clerks or plumbers to keep the return on investment high. Knudsen determined to change the car's image, to bring some excitement to the line. His first move was to hire a young automobile engineer with ideas enough for three Pontiac divisions and ambitions that matched Knudsen's own.

In hiring the lanky, chain-smoking John Zachary DeLorean, Knudsen was tacitly conceding that General Motors lacked engineers and designers with verve enough to turn Pontiac around. Under thirty, DeLorean had spent eight years in the industry—four of them at Chrysler, where the corporation "was too big for me to be noticed," and then four more at smaller Packard, where he not only was noticed, but tapped to head research and development. Knudsen offered DeLorean a similar post at Pontiac; the two were to spark a rush of sales and a firestorm of controversy.

By 1958, the corporation's fiftieth anniversay, it was the undisputed king of the hill. Would-be rivals had fallen far behind, or dropped out of the contest entirely, or sought safer niches in specialized production. Ford was to make a last run at General Motors, introducing the ill-fated Edsel in an effort to carve a larger share of the middle-priced market, would fail badly, and would leave Pontiac, Oldsmobile, and Buick virtually unchallenged thereafter.

In its fifty years, General Motors had posted sales of $129 billion and had collected net profits, after taxes, of $11.3 billion. It had sold more than fifty-six million motor vehicles in that period, nearly sixteen million refrigerators, and 20,000 diesel locomotives. If an investor had purchased 100 shares in 1908 for the posted price of $10,000—though no one did since Billy Durant had discounted stock with abandon—and had saved both the stock and the dividends, that investor would be worth $10.6 million by 1958, better than a thousandfold increase.

Not only was General Motors the nation's and the world's largest manufacturer of automobiles, buses, and railroad locomotives, it ranked among the four largest firms turning out diesel engines, trucks and truck tractors, bicycles, aircraft engines, and propellers. Its refrigerators, air-conditioning units, water heaters, electric ranges, and ball bearings were similarly ranked. Paradoxically, it was probably the major supplier of automobile components to its rivals in the industry, selling everything from spark plugs and wiring harnesses to air-conditioners and automatic transmissions to Ford, Chrysler, and American Motors.

Within the auto industry, the corporation was the price and styling leader. General Motors determined its prices unilaterally, unconcerned about the competition, Harlow Curtice all but conceded in testimony before a Senate subcommittee in 1956. The corporation grandly set its prices "as low as they can be and still produce the indicated return on the net worth at the standard volume."

Vexed Senate subcommittee members repeatedly sought to probe how the company could avoid price competition, but made little headway. A new line of Buicks, Curtice acknowledged, "probably was priced more in relation to its brothers than it was in relation to outside competition." And the prices for its "brothers" were governed not by traditional marketplace considerations, but by Donaldson Brown's hallowed return-on-investment formula.

But if its return on investment averaged 25 percent for 1950 through 1955, well above the corporation's target and the highest return in American industry, why couldn't General Motors reduce the prices on its cars, the senators puzzled.

"They are as low as they can be and still produce the indicated return on the net worth at the standard volume," Curtice insisted doggedly. "We can never be sure whether we are going to exceed the standard volume or whether the market place will be such that we will sell less than the standard volume."

But in the competitive commercial world, wasn't it usual to give consumers the benefit of any decline in costs?

"So that we would have to raise the prices with the declining volume?" Curtice countered. "No, I don't think that is the case."

General Motors set prices within the industry to suit its own arbitrary profit goal, heedless of the competition. There was little to worry about, as Ford's embarrassment in 1956 proved.

Ford had introduced a new car in September 1956 to compete

against a Chevrolet model that was three years old. Fearing that General Motors would competitively shave the price of its three-year-old model—after all, the tooling had long since been paid for—Ford raised its prices only 2.9 percent, "no more than our actual costs for materials and labor have gone up." Two weeks later, Chevrolet announced its prices for the merely face-lifted models, increasing them from $50 to $166. A week later, Ford responded by raising its prices $50 and within three months had adjusted all of its prices to bring them within $10 of Chevrolet.

Testifying before the Senate Subcommittee on Antitrust and Monopoly, Ford vice-president Theodore O. Yntema explained: "I mean this is the kind of thing that happens in a competitive situation. It is like a boxing game where you try to guess what your opponent is going to do. . . . We made a very bad guess."

Schooled in an economic theory that stressed price as a major competitive tool, Senator Estes Kefauver asked, "If you had kept your prices lower, might not Chevrolet and other cars have come down to meet yours?"

"Conceivably it would have happened. I do not know if it would have happened."

"If you had kept yours lower, would you not have gotten more sales, more business?"

"Probably some more," the Ford executive conceded.

Instead, Ford had matched General Motors, taken higher profits on fewer units, and avoided any risk of a price war that it inevitably would have lost.

United Auto Workers president Walter Reuther contemptuously dismissed Ford's "double shift": "This is the first time in the history of a free enterprise economy where a company raised the price of their products in order to be competitive. They raised their prices to be competitive. Why? Because prices in the automobile industry are set by General Motors."

Industrial dominance had imbued General Motors with magisterial arrogance and smug assurance. During the hearings, the bemused Senator Kefauver asked Harlow Curtice, "Do you regard the growth of your company from about one-third in 1929 to over one-half and the decline of the independents from one-fourth to less than 5 percent as a healthy trend in the economy and in the automobile industry?''

''I regard that as a healthy situation as far as General Motors is concerned; yes,'' Curtice replied.

''Not so far as General Motors is concerned, Mr. Curtice. I am talking about the country and the industry generally.''

''I think it is a healthy situation for the country and the industry in general.''

By virtue of its very size, General Motors was also the de facto leader in creating styling trends. No matter how *outré* the innovation, General Motors could shape consumer preferences.

The first reaction to the 1949 Cadillac's tail fins at its New York introduction was decidedly negative. About half of the would-be customers registered distaste for the P-38 appendage on the firmly grounded automobile. Charles Wilson subsequently ordered Harley Earl to quickly design a rear end without fins. ''But somewhere along the line,'' *Fortune* magazine discovered, ''opinion began to change. The more fins that appeared on the road, the more people got used to them, and finally they began to like them. 'We would have been murdered [had we been first with fins],' a competitor says, in open admiration.''

As George Romney, president of American Motors, put it: ''A company doing 45 to 50 percent of the business can make an aspect of car appearance a necessary earmark of product acceptance by the public. . . . If one of the smaller companies had put a wraparound windshield on its car, it probably would have been a flop, but the fact that it was put on cars by a company doing as much business as the company that put it on [General Motors] helped to make the thing a success, because in the field of fashion . . . familiarity brings acceptance.''

Both the hardtop convertible, whose roof did not convert, and the wraparound or panoramic windshield, as General Motors stylists referred to it, were demonstrably hazardous to motorists. The hardtop roof offered no real protection to the passenger should an automobile roll over, and at least one-third of the glass of the panoramic windshield optically distorted the driver's vision. (According to former automobile writer John Jerome, the curved windshield lasted only so long as the cost of glass was cheaper than the cost of steel. As glass prices increased, the wraparound windshield disappeared.)

Year after year, Earl and his styling director, William Mitchell, had used Cadillac as the testing ground for what Mitchell called "cross-ups," novel design innovations. And year after year they succeeded, even when the innovations were as useless as 1954's "Dagmars"—tumescent bumper guards, named after a handsomely endowed television actress, which offered no protection to the bumper and were themselves costly to replace. The "Dagmar-ed" Cadillac's sales jumped 25 percent.

"I've never seen a study that said styling is the one thing that makes people buy—but we know it's true," Chevrolet's sales manager, William E. Fish, said. Daily, monthly, annual sales figures proved, as Harlow Curtice insisted, "The annual model change has been the most important single factor responsible for the growth and vitality of our industry."

No styling innovation seemed more emblematic of this golden age of the automobile industry ("not of the automobile," Jerome cautions) than the great jutting, thrusting, and chromed fins that sprouted on the rear fenders of automobiles. Nursed by Mitchell, who succeeded Earl as General Motors' chief stylist in 1954, the fins grew both in nonfunctional size and lethal potential, reaching their peak in 1959, then shrunk under critical scorn and the need for novelty until they disappeared in the mid-1960s. That tail fins were deadly weapons mattered not at all. "A car *should* be exciting," Mitchell exhorted, and tail fins appeared to provide excitement.

So long as Mitchell hewed to the gospel according to Earl, General Motors' automobiles increased in length and weight. Between 1955 and 1970, the average two-door or four-door standard-size "family car"—Detroit's staple—ballooned a foot and a half in length and gained one-half ton in weight. It was no longer a transportation vehicle, but a rack upon which to hang literally hundreds of accessories, providing "living room comfort," as the advertisements put it. Beyond the power steering necessary to turn eighteen-and-a-half-foot-long salons and power brakes to stop the forward progress of their two tons of sheet metal and upholstered seats—both of which had a detrimental effect on the driver's ability to "feel" the road—the most popular accessories were radios, heaters, automatic transmissions, and air-conditioners. Not one of them improved the automobile's performance; indeed, they detracted.

In 1955, the average automobile on the road obtained about twenty miles per gallon of gasoline—up from fifteen miles per gallon in 1930, yet still below the Model-T's twenty to thirty miles per gallon. (Twenty years later, the average of all American cars would be just twelve miles per gallon.) The reason, General Motors maintained, was customer preference for power-draining accessories, quick acceleration, and leaden bodies that provided bumpless rides.

But the preferences were none too subtly guided by auto manufacturers themselves, first by stressing sheer horsepower and speed in advertisements and then by "loading" automobiles with accessories. (A customer who wanted a manual transmission, ostensibly standard equipment, had to order it from the factory in the heyday of the automatic transmission, one reason why 95 of every 100 automobiles were sold with automatic shifts.)

Such "options" were highly profitable, both for the corporation and for dealers, who might make more on the white-wall tires, radio, heater, electrically powered seats, and deluxe chromium trim package than on the automobile itself. At least from 1948 on, the corporation admitted, though the practice was older if less widespread, "General Motors countered its rising costs with imaginative efforts to increase efficiency and to develop and sell 'more car per car'—more optional equipment and a higher proportion of top-of-the-line models."

The stress upon performance, as measured in acceleration, and the comfort provided by weighty accessories fueled a horsepower race that would continue for twenty years. General Motors had achieved eminence by offering customers more than bare-boned frugality, later maintaining its position by transforming luxuries into essentials. First Ford, under Ernest Breech, and then Chrysler, frightened by its inability to market the small Plymouth, followed the General Motors pattern. Only American

Motors stood aloof, seeking to thaw what its president, George Romney, termed "this frozen 'big car mentality.'"

Continued success bred corporate hardening of the arteries, Romney told the Kefauver subcommittee: "You become muscle-bound. You get so darned much invested in the way you are doing things today that it takes a heck of a lot more to change. . . ."

The slow adoption of unibody construction by the Big Three proved his point, Romney continued. Traditionally, the automobile was built on a heavy frame, with the body merely bolted in place, a vestige of the automobile's carriage-and-wagon roots. But modern airplane construction had introduced the box section, in which formed structural members supported and shaped the body at the same time. The box section was lighter, stronger, and welded into a single unit, less prone to rattles, and more likely to last longer. There was less weight, and thus improved performance, and the roomier automobile could be better sprung, providing a more comfortable ride, Romney argued.

The smaller cars General Motors was building overseas—the Holden, Vauxhall, and Opel—all employed unibody construction, yet none of the Big Three had adopted it in the United States principally "because it would cost so much money to scrap their body facilities and tool them for this type construction." Because the box section could not be seen, and because smaller manufacturers such as American Motors could not invest enough money in advertising to make it the *sine qua non* of the modern automobile, the Big Three had been able to ignore it.

"The availability of large sums of money for advertising can perpetuate an archaic and old-fashioned product concept if it is drummed home sufficiently," Romney noted. The wraparound windshield had "no basic advantage over the straight windshield, and yet through advertising and promotion you can make an item of that type become absolutely the hallmark of a modern car, if you have got a large enough percentage of the total market to do it." General Motors had.

The sources of General Motors' dominance were many-splendored. Even such a disparate division as Frigidaire fitted neatly into the enterprise; it purchased electric motors from other divisions, and it could combine its sheet metal purchases with the auto divisions to bargain reduced prices for both. As the nation's largest manufacturer of refrigerators, with approximately 20 percent of the market in the 1950s, Frigidaire sheet requirements were not inconsequential.

But of all the nonautomobile divisions, the most profitable, the most smoothly running, was the General Motors Acceptance Corporation. As corporate auto sales grew, so did the number of finance contracts written by GMAC: for dealers needing credit to increase their inventory, for buyers of new or used cars, and for other General Motors products ranging from locomotives to home appliances.

By 1954, GMAC was extending 33 percent of all dollars loaned on automobiles, despite stiff competition from banks, finance companies, and the growing number of employee credit unions. Neither the government's prewar criminal case nor a civil action begun in 1940 to divorce the corporation from its financing arm had curbed GMAC growth. The civil suit ended in November 1952 with a consent decree in which the corporation agreed to let its dealers use whatever finance companies they wished. The consent decree, rather than curbing GMAC's voracious appetite, smaller competitors charged, had only "made them impregnable to competition" by the end of the decade; GMAC was responsible by then for eleven of every one hundred dollars of retail installment credit extended nationally.

For all of its power, however, General Motors was vulnerable in the last half of the 1950s as the market began to shift along the urban-suburban fault line. The ever-expanding suburbs were filled with tracts of identical homes and obligatory attached garage. Roadside billboards touting Greenbrier Estates or Glenside or some other faintly English-sounding name suggestive of rustic peace staked the radial arteries of American cities. The GI Bill and "easy terms" afforded millions of families their own home on their own land—even if the "estate" was but a fraction of an acre, with a single, nonindigenous maple seedling providing the only rusticity. On land once given over to truck farms, orange groves, and pastures, a new lifeway emerged, a lifeway in which the automobile was the linchpin.

Suburban America made use of the automobile as urban America did not. "The automobile has shifted from the role of being a family necessity to a personal necessity," George Romney explained in 1957. "People need cars today for their personal mobility, and that is resulting in this new stage of multiple-car ownership. Actually, we have got a situation where people are beginning to own car wardrobes, cars of different types to serve different purposes . . ."

It was a new market, far more fragmented, in which individual requirements outweighed Detroit's dictates, in which station wagons outsold four-door sedans, and the obligatory garage grew to accommodate not one but two cars. In California, where tract subdivisions outnumbered in-town construction permits, even the two-car garage would not be enough. In the 1960s, as the children of the postwar baby boom reached driving age, a third or fourth car would be parked in the driveway or under the thirty-foot maple.

The automobile industry might have read the shift in consumer attitudes in the deflated sales of 1956 and 1957, when General Motors' return on investment, once as high as 28 percent, skidded to 17 percent. They might have read it in the slump of Buick, from 530,000 cars and third place in sales in 1956 to sixth place and 395,000 sales the next year. Buick, after all, pushed its top-of-the-line models, and the suburban family, however affluent, really needed only one car capable of seating mom, pop, and their statistical mean of 2.3 children. Instead, the manufacturers missed the shift, assuming the customer was still there to be force-fed whatever deal was offered. The two-year slump was merely the expected aftermath of the great sales year of 1955, they argued. The auto industry always had been cyclical, they assured themselves.

Wall Street wags had a rueful joke to explain what happened: "GM sneezed and the country caught a cold." Because the automobile industry was so intrinsically tied to national prosperity, its decline in 1957 inevitably led to a recession in 1958. Auto sales dropped even further, from 5.7 million to 4.2 million in 1958. Dealer showrooms, once crowded, were empty; customers ignored the "You Auto Buy Now" signs in the windows. Measured against its own standard of achievement, General Motors fared poorly, recording a 12.6-percent return on investment.

At the mandatory retirement age of sixty-five in 1958, Harlow Curtice was leaving at the right moment; the coming era was not one for either tail fins or golden chariots. With Curtice's retirement looming, a five-member committee from the board of directors sat down to pick his successor. The committee, which included Curtice himself and Alfred P. Sloan, decided that the management of the corporation should be split once again, a return to pre–Charles Wilson days. Increasing responsibilities— to labor, the government, and the public at large—simply placed too great a burden on one man. The function of chief executive officer was returned to New York to be vested in the man who would succeed Albert Bradley as chairman of the board. The chief operating officer, the president, would stay in Detroit as head of production.

Before the jobs were filled, the committee was forced to consider the future role of both the two men and the board of directors. Within a few years, there would be a major upheaval in the company's ownership: Sloan, Kettering, Mott, John Pratt, and Donaldson Brown—all members of the board—held huge blocks of stock. All were well over seventy, and none had heirs interested in serving on the board of directors.

Sooner or later, all the members of the board would be relatively small stockholders, no longer the dominant owners that Sloan, Mott, Kettering, and the du Ponts had been. The board members would be representing the stockholders collectively, and, like the president and chairman of the board, would be, in fact, professional managers. By implication, the board would be forced to pay more attention to the stockholders, many of whom held larger blocks of stock than did the directors and officers themselves. By necessity, then, the board would take on more managerial authority; it would mean a return to the committee system that Sloan and du Pont had created thirty-five years earlier and to shared responsibility. (Much later, the strong-willed John DeLorean would contend, "Harlow Curtice was really the last guy who was president of GM who really ran it.")

The choice of the new chairman of the board was clear-cut: Frederic G. Donner, fifty-five, a thin-lipped accountant with a sharply analytical bent. Recruited in 1926 from the University of Michigan campus by Albert Bradley, Donner had spent his entire career at Bradley's right hand in New York. Unlike his predecessors, Donner's detailed knowledge of the corporation had been garnered not from the shops in Detroit, Flint, or Lansing, but from the executive suites on Columbus Circle.

In other ways Donner was reassuringly like Wilson and Curtice. Born in Three Oaks, Michigan, population 1,500, the son of the accountant for a plant that made whale-bone corsets and buggy whips, Donner shared the small-town values that dominated the corporation. And like Wilson and Curtice, he had few interests beyond General Motors, virtually nothing other than an occasional round of golf. Said a colleague, "What he really thinks about all the time, day and night, is this corporation." Largely in financial terms. Meeting a young executive for the first time, he often would ask afterward, "How much are we paying that man?"

Donner was virtually unknown beyond the company, a precise cipher who resented his invisibility. "I am not taciturn. I am not shy. I am not afraid of people, and I don't even own a slide rule," he insisted in the first interview he granted after his election as chairman. He was a colorless man who had served anonymously, who seemed to resent Curtice's dash and charm, and who would now be the chief spokesman on corporate policy, financial, and public affairs.

In contrast, newly named president John F. Gordon was a comforting figure to the auto makers in Detroit; he was a bald, hearty engineer who had spent most of his career at General Motors with Cadillac. For the eight years preceding his presidency, he had served as group executive in charge of body and assembly plants, and it was he who had been largely responsible for bringing out new models of all five General Motors cars in 1959—the first time in company history that had been accomplished.

Donner and Gordon were to lead the corporation into the 1960s. And remake it in the process.

The 1925 Chevrolet Model K (for Knudsen), the automobile with which General Motors challenged Henry Ford's supremacy.

Charles W. Nash, in the mid-1920s, after leaving General Motors.

The 1927 La Salle, the first of that short-lived, fondly remembered "low-cost family car" built by Cadillac.

less grace and balance. Windows and windshield framed in nickeled ing; nickel trimmed rear deck with rumble seat for two. When the in position the rear curtain may be folded upward out of the way

The Two-passenger CONVERTIBLE COUPE

Alfred P. Sloan, Jr.,
about 1927.

The last Model-T, built in
1927, still powered by the
four-cylinder, twenty-
horsepower motor. The body
had been modernized, but the
mechanical system lacked
competitors' refinements, and
the Model-T would be re-
placed by the Model-A the
following year.

You can't help but appreciate the distinc-
tiveness and individuality of the Tudor
Sedan especially when it is equipped with
natural wood wheels. Add to this the
comfort of Balloon tires and you have a
car of which you may be genuinely proud.
Like all Ford cars, the Tudor Sedan is
roomy inside but compact and readily
parked in small space.

Ford's 1928 Model-A roadster, successor to the famed Model-T, probably the most eagerly awaited car in automobile history. The Model-T was in production nineteen years, the Model-A just four.

The New FORD ROADSTER

A long, low, chummy car. Steel body, of course. Wide doors. Deep cushions. Rich upholstery. Nickeled hardware. Rumble seat optional. Artistic colors.

The men of General Motors in Muncie, Indiana, in May 1928, after a meeting at the Delco plant. From left to right, *front row:* George Whitney, Junius S. Morgan, Jr., Alfred P. Sloan, Jr., Charles E. Wilson, William S. Knudsen, Walter S. Carpenter, and Samuel McLaughlin; *second row:* C.F. Kettering, Donaldson Brown, Henry M. Crane, John L. Pratt, Charles S. Mott, and Earle F. Johnson.

The ill-fated 1936 Chrysler Airflow, the design precursor of the Volkswagen Beetle.

William S. Knudsen, about 1940; the president of General Motors on the eve of his resigning to head industrial mobilization in World War II.

Charles E. Wilson, about 1940, newly named president of General Motors.

C.F. Kettering, about 1950.

The 1949 Buick Roadmaster was the first hardtop convertible, and the first of a long line of Buicks fitted with the nonfunctional "mouseholes" in the fender.

Pierre S. du Pont, left, and John Jacob Raskob, in 1950.

Harlow Curtice, Alfred P. Sloan, Jr., and Charles E. Wilson in 1956.

The 1959 Cadillac El Dorado, nineteen and one-half feet long, its tailfins the height of that decade's taste in automobile design.

The 1960 Chevrolet Corvair, the automobile that made Ralph Nader famous.

James M. Roche, president of General Motors, appearing before the U.S. Senate Government Operations Subcommittee on March 22, 1966, to apologize for the harassment of Ralph Nader. His attorney, Theodore Sorensen, former special assistant to President John F. Kennedy, is at left.

The 1976 Chevrolet Chevette, General Motors' response to both the gasoline shortage and the import invasion, fitted out in its sporty Rally garb.

Part III

THE OZYMANDIAS SYNDROME

"A car is like part of your wardrobe, man. You can't go nowhere without one."

—Unidentified black youth to Attorney General Ramsey Clark
(Los Angeles, 1965)

'My name is Ozymandias, King of Kings:
Look on my works, ye Mighty, and despair!'

—Percy Bysshe Shelley, "Ozymandias"

15

Base Metal

The Supreme Court decision of June 3, 1957, came as no surprise. Eight years earlier, the antitrust attorney hired by E.I. du Pont de Nemours & Company had suggested that the corporation sell its 23-percent interest in General Motors and end the government's antitrust case right there. But Pierre S. du Pont had ignored Hugh B. Cox's advice, instead directing the veteran lawyer to defend the suit; even as they slogged through the legal mire, the Du Pont Corporation would rake in almost 25 percent of all General Motors' dividends, many millions more than Cox's legal fees.

For eight years, Cox and a battery of thirty-three assistants—they reserved eighty-six rooms in Chicago's Palmer House during the seven dreary months of the trial—had battled squadrons of government attorneys up to the maroon-draped chambers of the United States Supreme Court. Pierre du Pont had died and General Motors had tripled in value before a majority of the court had ruled, four votes to two (three justices took no part in the deliberations), that the decades-old acquisition of General

Motors by the Wilmington crowd violated the Clayton Antitrust Act.

The telling evidence was the Raskob report of December 19, 1917, urging the Du Pont finance committee to invest $25 million in Billy Durant's automotive combine. The investment, Raskob had written on that wintry day four decades earlier, "will undoubtedly secure for us the entire Fabrikoid, Pyralin [celluloid], paint and varnish business of those companies, which is a substantial factor." Du Pont had come close, despite sometimes frosty dealings between the two companies, with Sloan attempting to maintain an arm's-length relationship and then acceding because Du Pont was "a member of our family." By the time the trial started in Chicago in 1949, General Motors was purchasing from 50 to 70 percent of its finishes, fabrics, and anti-freeze from Du Pont and paying more than $26 million for those products.

At the time that Du Pont's investment buoyed the hard-pressed Durant, neither Du Pont nor General Motors dominated their respective markets. Both had ample competition: Du Pont faced rival paint manufacturers, General Motors the giant Ford Motor Company and a host of smaller rivals. But, the Supreme Court held, the passage of time had changed all that, and what was a benign investment in 1917 had become a violation of the law by 1957. The myriad automobile manufacturers of 1917 had dwindled to just five, and General Motors, spurred on by the heedless Harlow Curtice, held half of the automobile market. In the eight years since the filing of the suit, three more venerable marques had packed it in: Willys, Hudson, and Nash. The threat that Du Pont might monopolize the automobile fabric and finish market through its special relationship with General Motors—a threat that had not existed in 1917—was very real in 1957.

It would take four more years of litigation—during which Du Pont snared another $550 million in profits on its General Motors holdings—and yet another appeal to the United States Supreme Court before the trial court would order Du Pont to sell or disburse to its stockholders the controlling interest it held in General Motors. Even before then, Alfred P. Sloan would resign from the board of directors of Du Pont, complying with the judge's order that no individual sit on the boards of both corporations. Five Du Pont directors similarly quit the councils of General Motors at the end of 1959.

Harlow Curtice, by ignoring the self-imposed restraints of Sloan and Wilson, had helped tip the balance, and ended an era in American industrial history. No longer could some successor to Johnny Raskob crow, "There is no group, including the Rockefellers, the Morgans, the Mellons, or anyone else that begins to control and be responsible for as much industrially as is the du Pont Company."

The sundering of the two corporations left General Motors entirely in the hands of professional managers, men whose stock holdings were comparatively small. Executives and board members—Sloan, Pratt, and Mott the aging exceptions on the board, Kettering dead in 1958 at the age of eighty-two—no longer could muster a controlling interest in the company's stock in order to enforce their decisions. Ironically, the shift in leadership, which might have induced corporate "democracy," with the individual shareholders' votes more crucial, had virtually the opposite effect. Stockholders with relatively few shares and no more interest in management than the company's annual yield allowed the managers free rein. Even without the great block of shares voted by Du Pont representatives, the new elite routinely would pile up massive majorities on the few ' roposals upon which the stockholders at large were permitted ιo vote. As long as the dividends continued—and they were a punctual two dollars per share per year—the small stockholders continued to endorse management decisions without demur.

But new legal problems loomed. At first the suggestion—break up General Motors—seemed quaint, a throwback to the Supreme Court's Standard Oil decision of 1911, which shattered the oil trust. Any notion of dismembering General Motors appeared quixotic now when businessmen and economists considered the corporate state that gigantic enterprises had fashioned. Moreover, President Eisenhower was their man, and no foe of big business; in his economic message to Congress in January 1954, the president had declared that sheer size would not be sufficient cause for an antitrust case during his tenure, for "it is clear that size alone does not preclude effective competition."

Still, the rumors tumbled from government office buildings, underscored by the Du Pont ruling, so inconceivable before.

Break up General Motors. The head of the Department of Justice's antitrust division, Stanley Barnes, launched an investigation of the automobile industry in 1954.

Break up General Motors. Republican Attorney General Herbert Brownell warned the members of the august Economic Club of New York of the "developing pattern of concentration in the automobile industry." General Motors quickly retained well-connected Washington attorneys to make certain Brownell did not wander off the political reservation. In short order, White House aides were cooing reassurances that the Eisenhower administration did not intend to use the antitrust laws to experiment with "novel economic doctrine," and that enforcement would be confined to "hard-core" violations.

Break up General Motors. Senator Joseph O'Mahoney, a Wyoming Democrat with a populist heritage and a constitutional opposition to monopoly in any guise, opened Senate hearings in November, 1955 to study the relationship of sheer size and economic competition.

Alfred P. Sloan's appearance before the committee was, in effect, a last performance in defense of free enterprise. Like a scarred old lion still guarding the pride, the chairman of the board intimidated the senators and brushed aside annoying questions by the committee's counsel.

"Mr. Sloan"—even the formal address was unusually deferential—"is there any limit to the number of activities which your corporation can enter, before you would say that the growth would not be economically justified?"

Sloan turned the dials of his oversized hearing aid. "Accessories?"

"No, not accessories. Is there any limit to the number of activities—"

"Number of what?" Sloan struggled to hear, unsure whether to point his hearing aid at the committee counsel or at the loudspeaker booming his questions. Perhaps the forum was new to him, but the question and the underlying issue were not. ". . . [T]here is no policy. And each case is decided on the basis of its own merits. If your question is centered around the question of efficiency relative to size, if that is in the back of your mind, let me say that efficiency and size have nothing to do with one another. Where size comes in, it simply requires a certain type of administration technique, that is where the difference is.''

Sloan was in control again, the minister lecturing his flock against heresies. He turned to the committee chairman at the table in front of him. "General Motors is generally recognized—even the Senator recognized it as an efficient organization. Is that right, Senator?''

"Yes. Of course I do,'' Senator O'Mahoney agreed hastily.

Acquisitions, Sloan continued, were judged on their capacity to strengthen the corporation, and secondly on whether General Motors had "technique or knowledge or know-how that makes that particular thing better for the consumer.''

Could General Motors be reduced in size and still be as efficient?

"I don't think the size of General Motors, Mr. Burns, has anything to do with its efficiency. I think the efficiency depends upon the administrative technique and the people who comprise General Motors.''

Committee counsel Joseph W. Burns probed here and there, seeking some weakness in the immaculately tailored rebuttals of the old man at the witness table. "The question has been raised whether or not in the field of diesel locomotives, for example, it is necessary to have your corporation making locomotives when it has a competitive advantage over all other locomotive manufacturers who are not able to ship as many products.''

"All right, Mr. Burns,'' Sloan flared. "Let me tell you something: When we created the diesel electric locomotive, there was not a single part of that locomotive but what the functioning and the engineering had been known to the mechanical arts for fifty years. The diesel engine was fifty to seventy-five years old. It took an organization with courage, with capital, and the know-how, to put the known parts together and make the diesel electric locomotive.''

His patience exhausted, Sloan rushed on. "I maintain it was a great accomplishment. I think we contributed a great deal in more employment, in improving the economic position of the railroads."

The old man pounded home the point. In twenty years the diesel electric had driven steam from the rails. The steam locomotive manufacturers could have been the pioneers, but declined to produce diesels until General Motors had proved to the railroads that the new locomotives were more economical than . their beloved steam engines.

Through the morning it went. Republican senators anxious to appear as friends of big business relaxed. Despite his age—he was eighty, slowed by the years, and distracted by his wife's lingering illness—he was still Alfred Pritchard Sloan, Jr., the single most influential man in the history of American industrial enterprise. As he walked from the hearing room at the end of the December 2 session, the thirty-member General Motors delegation stood and applauded. "It was like they knew he was one tough sonovabitch, but, by God, he was our sonovabitch."

Break up General Motors. When the O'Mahoney subcommitttee report suggested the corporation divest itself of General Motors Acceptance Corporation, the company dismissed it as a reflection of "the same emotional, rather than factual, approach to the 'case study' of General Motors that pervaded the hearings themselves."

Break up General Motors. Stanley Barnes, the assistant attorney general in charge of the Department of Justice's antitrust division, whose lawyers had been pecking through corporate documents, warned, "If economic concentration in the automobile industry continues as in the recent past, someday soon action will have to be taken."

When the action came, it did not attack General Motors' automobile business at all. On July 6, 1956, the Department of Justice filed suit in Detroit charging General Motors with monopolizing the manufacture and sale of both transit and intercity buses. The suit alleged that General Motors had captured 85 percent of the nation's bus sales by successively driving twenty rival manufacturers out of business through unfair competition.

The bus case was narrowly drawn, as much a warning to the expanding corporation as it was an effort to stimulate competition in a declining industry. The government did not seek divestiture at all; selling the bus and coach division merely would transfer the virtual monopoly to another owner, nor could the single factory readily be sold to multiple buyers. Even then, the Eisenhower administration moved slowly in this election year, anxious to appear a friend of the straphanger, yet not to seem an enemy of free enterprise. "GM has come to represent the biggest and best in American mass production and business efficiency," *Business Week* noted. At a moment when the nation considered itself locked in an ideological crusade against communism, an antitrust suit seeking to stimulate free enterprise might, paradoxically, appear un-American.

Break up General Motors. On October 16, 1959, the government brought a civil action to force the corporation to sell the Euclid division purchased six years earlier. If General Motors wanted to enter the off-road earth-moving industry, the government claimed, the company had the resources to do so without first buying out an erstwhile competitor.

Prior to the acquisition, Euclid had produced more than half of all off-highway dump trucks and had begun design work on both rubber-tired and crawler tractors. It lacked capital, some $30 million, but rather than seeking to borrow it from banks, allowed itself to be wooed into oblivion by General Motors.

Euclid was intended to be the nucleus of a new corporate division, just as the purchases of Yellow Cab, Winton, Electro-Motive, and Allison Engine had provided the core of the bus and coach, diesel engine, locomotive, and aircraft engine divisions. As early as Billy Durant's creation of United Motors in 1917, General Motors had entered new businesses by acquisition, not by innovation.

Unlike the earlier acquisitions, however, the Euclid purchase seemingly violated amendments to the Clayton Antitrust Act, though the Republican Department of Justice had given its tacit approval in 1953. Three years later, Senator O'Mahoney's Democratic-dominated judiciary subcommittee scored both the acquisition as "potentially dangerous to competition" and Justice for failing to challenge it. In 1959, Euclid a formidable competitor to long-standing leaders Caterpillar and Allis-Chalmers, the Department of Justice had reversed itself and filed suit to dissolve the merger.

Break up General Motors. After a lengthy presentation by federal prosecutors and the election of John F. Kennedy as president, a grand jury in New York returned an indictment in April 1961 charging Electro-Motive with monopolizing the diesel-electric locomotive business. General Motors, the complaint alleged, had snared 80 percent of all locomotive sales by enforcing reciprocity with the railroads: the auto manufacturer would ship its autos and parts via those lines that bought EMD locomotives.

The O'Mahoney hearings in 1956 had never moved beyond the "study" stage, done in by a smoothly orchestrated lobbying campaign. It was just that smoothness, the smug assurance of the company's advocates, that piqued the curiosity of another senator.

Estes Kefauver was too easily dismissed and too often under-rated, as a young senator from Massachusetts discovered in 1956 when he sought the Democratic Party's nomination for vice-president. Kefauver had turned back John F. Kennedy's convention bid, winning the nomination and delivering a lesson in politics the younger man never forgot.

Kefauver seemed too much the homespun yokel to be taken seriously. He was not a member of the inner circle of mostly senior Democrats from the South, the men who really ran the world's most exclusive club. But that same Kefauver had chaired a select commitee early in the 1950s that documented the existence of a well-organized network of criminals known loosely, if inaccurately, as the Mafia. And he had done so in the Senate's first televised hearings, a daily crime show on television that made him a national celebrity.

Kefauver in 1957 was to pick up where O'Mahoney had left off—an odd interest for a man to whom the simplest of mathematics remained puzzling. And as the new chairman of the Anti-trust and Monopoly Subcommittee, Kefauver could thoroughly stir the waters once again. He enjoyed favorable press attention; no reporter ever lacked a good quote after an interview with the lanky Kefauver. For all his cultivated folksiness, Kefauver was an adroit legislator and floor leader. He recognized that legislation to curb the growing concentration of economic power would meet serious opposition; it had since Roosevelt's Temporary National Economic Committee hearings in 1939. O'Mahoney had been unsuccessful for another reason as well: antitrust was no longer a touchstone of American political policy. If there were to be a successful bill, it would take time.

Kefauver set out to "build the record," in Washington terms, to accumulate a massive pile of documentation showing the depredations of big business; to promote, proselytize, and eventually convert or neutralize opponents.

Break up General Motors. Kefauver never mentioned it in the hearings that began in January 1958 and stretched through May. Instead, he focused the hearings—as he had earlier while investigating the dairy and baking industries—upon administered prices, a new concept fashioned primarily by economist Gardiner C. Means to describe "a price set by someone, usually a producer or seller, and kept constant for a period of time and for a series of transactions. The opposite of an administered price is a market price, a price that fluctuates on the basis of supply and demand as these forces are felt in the market."

An administered price did not require a monopoly, but only a company, such as General Motors, so dominant that it set the pace for the industry. It required no collusion among the members of the industry to follow the prices set by the largest, for the largest made certain it achieved handsome returns. Selling too far below the "administered" price, competing on price alone, would leave even large rivals, such as Ford, the third largest corporation in the country, or even less efficient Chrysler, the tenth largest, with unacceptably low profits. Selling too far above, so as to increase profits, would leave competitors at a serious disadvantage at the retail level. Administered pricing was neat, it was efficient, and it curtailed the contemporary businessman's nemesis—price competition.

The hearings themselves were far more a summary than an exposé of the automobile industry. Kefauver was dealing this time with respected business leaders, not swarthy men with foreign-sounding names who mumbled repeated invocations of the Fifth Amendment. Further, he was building the record, laying the groundwork for future legislation.

Harlow Curtice, as president and chief executive officer, represented General Motors, accompanied not by the imposing Alfred P. Sloan, who had evoked such solicitude from the sub-committee just two years earlier, but by executive vice-president Frederic G. Donner, the chairman of the financial policy commit-tee. Donner's cold manner and seeming disdain nettled even the normally friendly Wisconsin Republican Alexander Wiley.

"I think you have got to consider the cities, the highways in relation to your cars," Wiley scolded the General Motors delega-tion. "You are going to make tremendous expenditures neces-sary if these cars keep growing bigger and bigger, and I think more and more people want medium-sized cars. . . . I have talked to municipal people who are very much concerned about this tremendous car business, what it means in the life of the community, what it means in parking not only on the thoroughfares, but parking places, what it means for the con-venience of the other fellow."

The most telling witness—as he had been earlier for O'Mahoney—was George Romney, the former president of the Automobile Manufacturers Association and then president of struggling American Motors. "Romney was too straight to be in the auto business," a veteran of Detroit automobile companies said twenty years later. "He was a very moral man, enlightened, not like the myopic men who built cars the way Detroit wanted instead of the way the consumer wanted." Romney's disaffec-tion had grown through the years—during the Korean conflict, when General Motors received preferential steel shipments while others had to cut back, and then later, as its cars swelled in ostentation, making economy a last-considered factor.

Romney's testimony was to be a momentary capstone on the effort to dismember General Motors. "There has not been enough competition in the automobile business in the United States," he told the Senate subcommittee, "to compel the Big Three to keep their products as modern in this country as the products the two biggest ones [General Motors and Ford] are building in Europe and in Australia and places like that."

The previous fall, American Motors had reintroduced its 1950 Nash with a new name and a new body. Staking the company's last $100 million on a single entry in what he called the "compact" size, Romney was gambling that the 1957 Rambler could exploit a market the Big Three had overlooked in their quest for bigger-means-better.

Responding to the perceived market for smaller cars, Romney's American Motors confronted "this frozen 'big car mentality,' because we had to break that down in order to succeed in the automobile business." For the moment, American Motors and the eight-year-old, smaller Nash were successful. The company had jumped from twelfth in sales among all automobile marques to seventh, ahead of such large cars as Mercury, Cadillac, Dodge, and De Soto.

Romney's strategy was to position the compact between the large American car and the small European import—which was coming into the country in ever increasing numbers—while trying to retain the best of each:

The things that the American car have [*sic*] excelled in down through the years have been comfort and room and performance. We haven't had to worry about availability of raw material, cost of gasoline.*

We have had long distances. In the early days we had very bad roads and families wanted to travel, so putting room in them and comfort in them was a big factor.

Now the small European car has excelled because of the environment in which it was born, in providing high economy and providing as much room as possible in a small space, albeit a tight space, and ease of maneuverability in handling, because they had short distances and crowded urban areas right from the start, and they had better roads from the start than we did.

General Motors had recognized before its major rivals that people wanted more luxury, comfort, and style in their cars in the years following World War II. Now the large manufacturers had "so darned much invested in the way [they] are doing things today that it takes a heck of a lot more to change and do things differently than it does somebody else who hasn't quite reached that point. One of the Big Three problems is that they are

---

* A joke of the day, retold by *Time* magazine, September 8, 1958: "Cadillac owner drives into filling station, tells attendant, 'Fill her up,' lets motor idle. Desperate attendant finally yells, 'Turn off the motor. You're gaining on me.'"

muscle-bound, and they have got heavy fixed investments in building cars the way they have been building them in this country.''

The muscle-bound corporation was slow to innovate, Romney continued: ''The smaller companies historically have been the principal innovators. In the early days this was apparent. As a matter of fact the philosophies of the large, more successful companies has [*sic*] been to be not the first to try the new and not the last to drop the old.'' General Motors' financial resources did not produce a significantly better car, cheaper, but rather ''went to perpetuate an archaic and old-fashioned product concept'' through advertising drummed home convincingly. As the largest advertiser in the country, its annual budget more than $150 million, General Motors drummed loudest and longest.

Sheer corporate size, Romney asserted, was a handicap: ''Stockholder interest isn't what it ought to be, and it gets to be less as the stockholder's influence declines, as it gets so darn big that his viewpoint doesn't count for much anyway.'' Professional managers—Donner sitting impassively in the hearing room, Curtice fuming as the square-jawed Romney scored the industry that had nurtured him—then retained de facto control. But men such as these had lost touch with the world beyond Bloomfield Hills, the Detroit Athletic Club, and Columbus Circle. ''It is my observation when companies acquire as much power as the Big Three, it is difficult for the management to realize the economic, social, and political impact flowing from the exercise of that power.''

Romney proposed splitting both Ford and General Motors into two, perhaps three, independent companies. Standard Oil's stockholders, he maintained, had benefited when the Supreme Court ordered that trust splintered into thirty-four parts. ''General Motors and Ford stockholders, executives, employees and customers could reasonably be expected to benefit as did those of Standard Oil,'' Romney continued. There would be no detrimental impact on ultimate profits, for sheer production volume was not the determining element in creating profits. The optimum volume for a single auto-manufacturing plant was about 180,000 cars per year. After that, economies leveled off.

Mitosis was the only possible solution to the dominance exerted by a single company, Romney testified. To start a new company capable of producing 250,000 automobiles annually would require approximately $900 million in investment capital, and the company could reasonably expect a $33.4 million loss in its first year because of high initial overhead and selling expenses. It was not an appealing prospect for a potential new entry—especially since Henry J. Kaiser's effort had failed in the midst of the greatest automobile-sales bonanza in history.

The Kefauver hearings would come to naught in these waning days of the Eisenhower administration, even though the president had become disenchanted with "big business" and would warn of a military-industrial complex in his valedictory address as president. Yet even as lobbyists put out that fire, another erupted in a new and unexpected quarter—California.

The "Golden State" was the richest of automobile markets, the first state to adopt a lifeway predicated on the internal-combustion engine, the first to build freeways as basic traffic arteries, the first to quarter and section itself by those multilane thoroughfares, the first to ask not "How far is it?" but "How long does it take to get there?" Now Californians were the first to question the subculture they had so willingly created in the preceding fifty years.

Smog—the brown, tear-provoking atmospheric haze about which comedians joked—was the product of the photosynthesis of automobile emissions, Arlie Haagen-Smit of the California Institute of Technology reported. The jokes brought no laughs in California; by 1956, three of every four people in Los Angeles reported that they were affected by smog. Though the automobile companies studiously ignored the charge, in fact, they were aware as early as the 1920s that automobile emissions were injurious to automobile paint, and rubber tires and hoses. Even earlier, automobile fumes were recognized as a local irritant:

That the fumes of the exhaust of an automobile are not tonics is well known. The remarks which pedestrians make as they get a whiff of them show that they are hard on the throat and irritating to the temperament. When vapors are mingled with smoke from oil, a visible rise in temperature is experienced by all who happen to be behind the offending car . . .

Dr. D. Bryson Delevan of this city discussed in a paper read by him before the American Laryngological Association the effect of motoring on the upper air passages. He referred to the unpleasant odors of the vapors and their harsh and irritating effect on the mucous membranes of nose and throat.

The influence of the automobile was even more pervasive, often more subtle, a growing number of critics charged. The automobile was the one single factor that most contributed to the deterioration of the urban environment, Felix T. Thoeren, Los Angeles president of the Institute of Real Estate Management, noted. His proposed solution was to group structures in self-contained clusters separated by wide automobile causeways—Norman Bel Geddes' scheme from the New York World's Fair of two decades earlier, a plan that would provide even more space for traffic and engender more automobile sales.

The automobile had become something more than "a tool of mobility. To many it is a way of ego satisfaction; to some a way of sublimation for inferiority complexes," urban planner Victor Gruen despaired. How could one plan a city to cope with an individual's inferiority complex?

Outspoken Methodist Bishop G. Bromley Oxnam condemned the automobile as a symbol of "stumbling capitalism," as dangerous to national survival as "creeping socialism." Detroit's cars represented a "luxury-mad and gadget-crazed" people, the head of the Methodist church in the United States complained. "Who are the madmen who built cars so long they cannot be parked and are hard to turn at corners, vehicles with hideous tail fins, full of gadgets and covered with chrome, so low that an average human being has to crawl in the doors and so powerful that no man dare use the horsepower available?"

Oxnam was outraged, writer John Keats sardonically mused in the first book critical of the automobile industry and its products, *The Insolent Chariots,* published in 1958. A New York *Times* reviewer concluded that Keats' book scorned autos as "overblown, overpriced monstrosities built by oafs for thieves to sell

to mental defectives." For all his humor, Keats was also perceptive. The Midwest, he wrote, "land of simple plowmen," had
purveyed "the Midwest's culture to the nation; Detroit has
shaped us in its image. Today, most Americans join in the shout,
'The biggest means the best!' and the echo responds from Detroit, 'More of the same'!"

California seemed to have more than its share of the latter.
There, high school students gained enviable reputations for their
ability to "soup up" Detroit's stock cars, especially the Fords
and Chevrolets of the early 1950s. More than a few of the mechanical and styling improvements eventually found their way to
Detroit to be adopted by the industry.

But as teenagers' car ownership rose, high school grades fell.
"Cars consume time that might otherwise be spent on study or
school activities," Leon Meeks, the dean of boys at Santa
Monica High School, noted. "A boy may have to work to make
payments or maintain his car. He spends additional time joyrid-
ing and still more time working on his car." Henry Blunt, dean of
boys at Culver City High School, raged, "Automobiles are a
curse."

All such complaints, scattered and diffuse, Detroit could readily dismiss as the protests of cranks, virtually un-American, even
when they emanated from that richest of automotive markets,
Los Angeles. Californians were strange, "kooky" (to use their
own term), and quick to embrace fads. How else could one explain the number of Californians asking Chevrolet dealers to
install optional seat belts? Or the number buying foreign cars?

Clearly, Californians were the exception; everywhere else,
America was buying automobiles—the recession year of 1958
excepted—in unprecedented numbers, six million a year, as
many as half of them built by General Motors. That, plus the
most careful projections of future sales, proved them right, corporate executives assured each other in committee meetings
throughout 1958. By 1975, the number of vehicles on the road
would virtually double to 120 million as the postwar baby boom
came of age. In those seventeen years, Americans would spend
$1 trillion for motor transport—not only for passenger cars, but
for trucks (already hauling half as much as the competitive rail-

roads), for tires, gasoline, repairs, replacement parts, insurance and finance charges.

In theory, it might have been more difficult for General Motors to brush aside the complaints from restive dealers, for, after all, they not only were part of the industry, but the foundation upon which the corporation's sales rested. In fact, General Motors treated its 16,217 dealers in similar cavalier fashion, forcing slow-moving models on them, setting severe sales quotas, demanding that they purchase "genuine" General Motors parts at inflated prices, but most of all threatening summary cancellation of franchises at the slightest provocation.

The threat was real. In the four years between 1951 and 1955, a total of 4,600 General Motors dealers accepted what the corporation euphemistically called "voluntary terminations." Some might have been justified, for dealers, long accustomed to a seller's market, had grown complacent. But many of the cancellations came because dealers could not meet arbitrary quotas, or the competition from General Motors–owned "company stores" set up to stimulate sales in areas the corporation deemed underserved. Others succumbed before the overt favoritism shown high-volume dealers, who received hot-selling models and bootlegged the cars across country. (The company winked at the extensive practice of favored dealers selling new autos at fifty dollars above list so that the cars might be transported cross-country to be sold again as "used" cars in other states. One estimate placed the number of bootlegged cars sold in California, the nation's largest auto market, at one in every five sales. When a Lake Orion, Michigan, dealer complained publicly of "factory bootlegging," Harlow Curtice branded him "a Red" and denied a renewal of his twenty-one-year-old franchise.)

For all the corporation's public deference—"General Motors is the servant of the dealers," Curtice had assured the O'Mahoney subcommittee—dealer and corporation were not equal partners. The local businessman was forced to keep his books as General Motors directed, to take all of a division's models, and to participate in any company-mandated sales campaign, the costs of which he more than likely would have to absorb. Ostensibly an independent businessman, the dealer lived with year-to-year renewals. Until 1954, he could not even pass on the dealership to his offspring when he retired. Even a successful dealer could not rest easy; his money was invested in a lease and service facilities that could be rendered useless if he alienated a corporation representative.

Dealer and corporation were pitted against each other. Confronted with pressure from zone representatives or high new-car quotas, dealers yielded generous trade-in allowances, hoping to balance inevitable losses on used-car sales, 70 percent of the business, against the profits on new-car sales. (Ironically, many franchised dealers made more money during the years of World War II, when they could sell used cars at inflated prices, even though there were no new cars manufactured.)

By the mid-1950s, the extensive dealer network set up so carefully by R.H. Grant two decades before was a shambles. Dealer complaints prodded Senator O'Mahoney to his "study of the antitrust laws," in the middle of which Harlow Curtice was forced to announce publicly that General Motors would extend the annual dealer contract to a five-year term. The public-relations gesture fell short, largely because the company insisted on retaining the power to cancel a dealer agreement unilaterally.

Eight months after the O'Mahoney hearings closed, President Eisenhower, remembering all the campaign contributions Art Summerfield had wrung from auto dealers, repaid the debt. He signed into law the "Auto Dealers Day-in-Court Act," partially protecting the nation's 25,000 local auto dealers from capricious summary cancellations. It was the first of an ongoing series of bills that would curb the untrammeled power of automobile manufacturers. Still, General Motors continued to pare its dealer roster in the declining central cities while building up mammoth suburban dealerships. By 1961, five years after the O'Mahoney committee hearings, the corporation had trimmed its rolls of another 2,400 dealers, 15 percent of its franchises.

Beyond the high-handed treatment they received from the manufacturers, dealers nurtured another grievance, especially on the two coasts. Because they had no directly competitive car, they were beginning to lose sales to foreign imports. At first foreign competition was just a nuisance in an era when dealers could sell all the new cars the factories turned out. Then it became an irritant, those cars with funny names—Renault, Toyopet, Simca, Sunbeam—cars with odd shapes like that prewar relic, the Volkswagen, which even capitalized in its advertising on its homely appearance; cars with the hard rides and cramped interiors the British favored in their MGs, Triumphs, Austin-Healys, and Minors.

Detroit sniffed and then dismissed the invaders as "shitboxes" hardly worth bothering about. Only George Romney at American Motors had recognized that these smaller, spartan vehicles offered a salable alternative to the Big Three's hyperthyroid designs. Romney's perception was all the more remarkable in that such imports collectively were taking less than 1 percent of the 6.6 million sales in 1954, the year he assumed the presidency of the new American Motors and redirected its product line.

By 1956, a year of slumping sales, the Big Three had lost some 15 percent in sales while the imports were virtually doubling their market penetration. The trend puzzled Detroit, for the industry that had so long prided itself on its consumer sampling simply did not know who was buying the "shitboxes." It defied all their experience, knowledge of the market, and certainty that they knew what the American consumer wanted. How explain that two out of three people who bought Volkswagens—the car even lacked a gas gauge—had incomes about 40-percent higher than the average new-car buyer, that two out of three owned more than one car? Worse still, few of those who bought the car they fondly dubbed the "Bug" ever considered a Chevrolet, Plymouth, or Ford, opting instead for an automobile with less power than the cars of the Depression and a wheelbase almost two feet shorter than the current Chevrolet.

The longer Detroit's automobiles grew, the more import sales rose. The Chevrolet had stretched more than one-and-a-half feet from 1953 to 1958; by 1957, automobile imports had exceeded exports and had swallowed more than 8 percent of the market—

despite a national recession. The Big Three no longer could dismiss their foreign competitors.*

Division General Manager Edward Cole believed he had a solution to the problem for Chevrolet—a long-dreamed-of rear-engine automobile. As early as 1946 he had worked on a prototype at Cadillac, a plan that was shelved when it was determined the car would need four rear wheels. It was all right for the Cadillac to be as big as a truck; it was not all right for it to *look* like a truck.

Still Cole harbored the dream. When he assumed the general manager's post at Chevrolet in the summer of 1956, he detailed a team of engineers to begin design work on a small car with an engine in the rear that might challenge the American Motors Rambler if that car proved successful. At the same time, a smaller Chevrolet would compete with imports for those customers seeking economy and a bit more leg room.

The debate within the executive committee on West Grand Boulevard was sharp, with Cole pitted against his former boss at Cadillac, John Gordon, executive vice-president and soon to be president of the corporation. A Cadillac man, and to that extent a disciple of the big-is-best credo, Gordon's opposition was instinctive, "gut-level," one former General Motors executive insisted. Furthermore, Gordon doubted that the market for small cars was big enough to support Cole's entry, a compact Ford that was in the works, the expected Rambler, and the economic Studebaker Lark due in 1958. General Motors' compact car might easily bankrupt American Motors or Studebaker, or both, and provoke the antitrust action leading to the break-up of General Motors they all feared.

Once before the corporation had considered entering the small-car market, with the since long-forgotten Cadet, only to

* Foreign manufacturers, many of them owned at least in part by their governments, had not so much entered the American market because they saw ready sales but to equalize the balance of payments. Desperately short of American dollars, France, Britain, Germany, and Japan happily discovered the gold field and rushed to exploit it. The importance of foreign exchange was underscored by the fact that European buyers were forced to wait from six months to three years for delivery, while Americans drove about in imported Fiats, Porsches, and Jaguars.

see that market vanish. Sales of the company's big cars were off
for 1957 but that was attributable to the general decline in business, a decline that probably would continue through the next
year. After that, the public would return to dealers' showrooms
looking for the same things the public always looked for: roominess, comfort, power, and the "feel" of a big car, even if it were
the smallest Chevrolet made. Even at that time, General Motors
had more engineers working on door frames and latches, seeking
a "big car" sound when the door closed, than they had designing
safety equipment.

Equally important, Gordon argued, they had learned long ago
that the used car was America's bargain vehicle, its second car in
the family, the answer to the need for cheap transportation. A
good used American car would appeal to the American buyer
long after the imports had disappeared.

Harlow Curtice waffled between increased sales and the antitrust threat, then chose to straddle the fence. He approved the
decision to go ahead with the new compact-car project, but ordered Cole to go slowly, figuring on an October 1959 introduction. The timing would give him another year before he had to
commit to the expensive tool and die making, a year in which
they could see what the market might do. In the meantime, they
would import the English Vauxhall and the new German Opel.
At the same time, Curtice began a calculated investment program in the corporation's revitalized overseas subsidiaries;
company studies suggested European sales would grow proportionately faster than domestic sales. (The combined worth of
Opel and Vauxhall would double to $1 billion between 1957 and
1962.)

Curtice placed one further restriction on Cole. At least one
model of the new auto had to be pegged below $2,000, in line
with Volkswagen's $1,950 list price. If, for economy's sake, con-
trary to all they believed, Americans would settle upon a small
new car rather than a big used car, the compact Chevrolet must
offer economy as well.

Publicly, General Motors denied rumors that it was bringing
out an auto to challenge the imports. As early as October 1957,
Cole gracefully evaded a reporter's question by saying that

Chevrolet could produce a compact car only when that segment of the market reached a size of half a million vehicles per year. (The figure was revealing for its implication that General Motors realized it had to leave room for both American Motors and Studebaker.)

Curtice was even less frank in his testimony before Senator Kefauver's antitrust subcommittee on January 30, 1958. Asked if General Motors intended to build a small car "to compete with imported smaller cars," Curtice replied, "For over the years that has been the subject that we have constantly studied. Thus far it has not been practical from the standpoint of the economics to offer the small car . . . because you take the value out so much more rapidly than you can take the cost out." (Viewed another way, Curtice was conceding that the cost of constructing a car, regardless of size, was relatively the same. Sheer length and width, accessories, ornate trim—these constituted "value" in Curtice's terms. Yet these high-profit, low-cost elements were the first to go when engineers designed a small car. Thus the "value" fled before the selling price was reduced significantly.)

By spring 1958, both General Motors and Ford had committed themselves to the compact. Ford was to call its new car the Falcon; Chevrolet had named its entry the Corvair.

Final approval of the Corvair was Curtice's last contribution to the corporation that had nurtured him all his adult life. In August 1958, at the mandatory retirement age of sixty-five, Curtice withdrew to the golf courses of Palm Springs, California, a king exiled, his counsels coolly ignored. At the same time, Albert Bradley, the former economics teacher, resigned as chairman of the board, opening the way for a major reorganization of the company.

The board of directors tapped Frederic Donner, one of its own, to assume both the chairmanship of the board and the role of chief executive officer, the title that indicated where real corporate power lay. Donner was to have a profound and lasting effect on the corporation, regathering to New York the authority lost during Curtice's rampaging tenure.

Donner had spent his entire career in finance; he knew comparatively little about operations. The men in the automotive divisions complained—with only a touch of hyperbole—that Donner had never set foot inside a factory. Whereas Curtice had been an outgoing, back-slapping super-salesman, Donner was a cold-blooded financial expert, keenly aware that he did not command the esteem of the automotive divisions. Precise to a fault—he carried in his breast pocket a small card listing pertinent statistics about the corporation—Donner intended to whip the automotive men into line.

Intolerant of dissent, Donner's insistence upon executive loyalty above all else was to eventually gut the automotive divisions of their independence and what little creativity remained in the corporate world dominated by professional managers.

Donner's first move was to select former Cadillac general manager John F. Gordon as president. Gordon was the "unobvious choice," as a then-aspiring Pontiac engineer, John DeLorean, later complained. By passing over other, stronger executives to tap Gordon, Donner was binding the new president to him, securing his loyalty with a promotion Gordon otherwise might never have expected. At the same time, Donner was disciplining the automobile men. All those ambitious general managers would have to pay fealty to him.

Over the next half-dozen years, Donner progressively trimmed the authority of the automotive divisions to design their own cars, insisting instead that preliminary design work be done at the corporate level and that the divisions share as many parts as possible. The divisions resisted, fighting futile, petty, rear-guard actions as long as they could, even denying Gordon a key to their separate styling studios. There was little support for them on the board of directors, even less when Charles E. Wilson died in 1961 and Curtice the following year. One by one, the division general managers succumbed to their ambitions, exchanging independence for consideration as Gordon's successor. Under the leadership of Bunkie Knudsen, Pontiac was the last holdout, caving in only after Knudsen moved to Chevrolet and was succeeded by the more pliable Elliott "Pete" Estes in 1961.

Donner assumed the chief executive officer's chair in the midst of the second "Eisenhower" recession. Motor-vehicle sales had peaked in exuberant 1955 at 9.2 million, then had slumped sharply. By August 1958, when Donner took command of the corporation, industry sales were running at a rate of five million per year, national unemployment had soared, and some 400,000 men and women were out of work in hard-pressed Michigan. Donner prickled at criticisms that the recession could be laid to the auto industry's open-handed credit extensions, preferring to blame what he called, vaguely, "business excitement."

General Motors *needed* excitement at that point. The corporation was in poor competitive shape. Its net income had tumbled steadily since 1955. Its automobiles were dated, their befinned styling gone stale; Curtice had stayed too long with his "jukebox" designs, and consumer resistance had set in. Curtice had taken the first steps to set matters to rights—installing Bunkie Knudsen in the "old ladies' division" at Pontiac and planning new models for all five divisions—but the corporation was top-heavy with executives short on ideas and long on years. The market had slipped from their grasp.

In 1957, for the first time since the introduction of the Model-A, Ford had edged Chevrolet for first place in industry sales. Buick had dropped from 10 percent of all new-car registrations in 1955 to 6 percent in 1957 and would slip to 4 percent the next year. Oldsmobile and Pontiac had no more than held their own in the market. The truck division was losing money, and even Frigidaire was casting about for a company to buy its lagging small-appliance lines. Meanwhile, foreign-car importers and enterprising American Motors were soaking up 12 percent of all passenger-car sales with smaller autos.

Immediate help was on the way. All five automotive divisions would have new, de-finned models for 1959—the first time in corporate history the company had refurbished its entire line-up at one time. (At Donner's retirement dinner in 1967, a bitter John Gordon reportedly took full credit and lashed out at the assembled executives, many of whom still were secretly critical of the Donner administration: "When Fred and I took over this corporation in 1958, it was in trouble. Executive morale was low. People were horribly depressed. We were coming apart inside. It was like that because Harlow Curtice let it get that way. He almost wrecked this company." According to Gordon, whose remarks Donner reiterated, "Fred and I recognized these problems and by busting our rears with hard work we were able to turn this company around.")

The new models failed to generate the excitement General Motors had counted on, the company's market share slipped to just 42 percent of 1959's new-car sales, and Ford again topped Chevrolet. Paradoxically, because of higher selling prices and Donner-mandated cost cutting, the corporation recorded its second-highest profit in history, $873 million. Reluctantly, never fully committed to the rear-engine concept, the corporation turned to its first "import fighter," developed at a cost of $150 million, to stimulate the excitement the new-model announcement once generated each October.

Edward Cole's automobile was conceived as a "sporty" car with low, rakish lines; even the name selected, Corvair, was intended to conjure images of the high-powered, limited-run Corvette, a Chevrolet sports car introduced in 1953. Though the compact would seat six people nominally, if uncomfortably, it would weigh 1,300 pounds less than the standard-size Chevrolet and would be priced just two hundred dollars less than the least expensive "full size" (implying that a car fifteen feet long was less than full, less than adequate). Here was an all-new car, ostensibly an engineering marvel. Even the engine was novel: an air-cooled "pancake" of cast aluminium with its six cylinders horizontally opposed, weighing only half what the conventional Chevrolet engine weighed, yet capable of delivering eighty horsepower. It was an echo, however faint, of the copper-cooled engine Charles F. Kettering had conceived three decades earlier.

The marvels were tempered, however, by compromises between Cole's original designs and the corporation's Procrustean standard of return on investment. The tire diameter was too small for the weight of the vehicle, saving a dollar per car on cost while enhancing the "sporty," low appearance. The original aluminum engine was scrapped in favor of a half aluminum and half cast-iron hybrid. The well-appointed interiors of other General Motors cars were not intended for this "economy" car—in part to keep costs down, in part to avoid luring too many customers from the "full size" market. The Donner-mandated cost cutting extended to the smallest parts, including a fifteen-dollar stabilizing bar stripped from the auto on the grounds that it was too expensive. Its deletion would prove even more costly. A Chevrolet test driver tried the first handcrafted prototype of the Corvair on a test track and accidentally rolled it over. Other roll-overs followed, including those involving Ford test drivers who had swapped their new compact, the Falcon, for two of the competitive Corvairs. As early as May 31, 1960, senior Ford executives had discussed the Corvair, agreeing "the poor handling and stability characteristics of the Chevrolet Corvair . . . would have little or no adverse affect [*sic*] on sales . . . [S]uch factors have less direct affect on vehicle sales than more easily discernible product characteristics . . ."

Fred J. Hooven, a former engineer at Ford, explained in 1971 that his company's decision to remain silent rested on fear. "*Everybody* knew the truth would get lost. And Ford's credibility would be challenged, and that would institute an era of dirty advertising and dirty P.R., and Ford said, in effect, 'We're in no shape to tell the truth about this.'" Ford would remain silent, "keeping secrets—this is an endemic disease. It's positively pathological."

Secrecy was, if anything, even more an ingrained policy at General Motors, where Cole had been told that on high-speed turns, sometimes only in stiff crosswinds, the rear end of the Corvair tended to lift or "jack" and the tires to tuck under. "In the high performance Corvair, the car conveyed a false sense of control to the driver," then Pontiac chief engineer John DeLorean explained later, "when in fact he may have been very close to losing control of the vehicle." If the car did not overturn, the tubeless tires, their edge forced away from the rim, could suffer a sudden "airout," a loss of pressure that could send the car careening out of control. Further, because 60 percent of the car's weight was in the rear, like all other rear-engine vehicles, it tended to oversteer—that is, to turn farther than intended. When the driver sought to correct the oversteering, he aggravated the jacking motion.

The combination of jacking and oversteering would prove "disastrous. I don't think any one car before or since produced as gruesome a record on the highway as the Corvair. It was designed and promoted to appeal to the spirit and flair of young people. It was sold in part as a sports car. Young Corvair owners, therefore, were trying to bend their car around curves at high speeds and were killing themselves in alarming numbers," DeLorean raged.

The fundamental instability of the Corvair triggered "a massive internal fight," according to DeLorean, who observed from the relative safety of the Pontiac division. Cole, the automobile's sponsor, and the Corvair design team stood on one side, struggling to fit the new car to fixed profitability formulas. Ranged against them were Charles Chayne, corporate vice-president of engineering, and a clutch of engineers who had worked on chassis and suspension systems for the corporation. Despite their entreaties, Cole stood firm; though the necessary mounting studs were already in place, the 1960 Corvair would not have the fifteen-dollar stabilizing bar or the larger, more expensive tires that could reduce risks.

Yet, apparently, none of the dissenters, including Chayne, who as a staff engineer and vice-president had direct access, took the matter to the fourteenth floor. Nearly six years after the introduction of the Corvair, John Gordon stated in a deposition that he could not recall the Corvair's design—touted as "revolutionary"—having come before the engineering policy committee. Further, he asserted that he did not know "what kind of rear-end suspension was on the Corvair design that was approved for production by his committees," Corvair critic Ralph Nader noted.

If Gordon had not known in 1957, by 1961 he would have been the most isolated president in corporate history to have remained ignorant. According to DeLorean, that year Bunkie Knudsen refused to succeed Cole as Chevrolet general manager unless he was permitted to make changes in the Corvair's rear suspension. He carried the fight to the fourteenth floor, where he was turned down on the grounds that the fifteen dollars in new parts was too costly. "Bunkie was livid," recalled DeLorean. "As I understand it, he went to the Executive Committee and told the top officers of the corporation that, if they didn't reappraise his request and give him permission to make the Corvair safe, he was going to resign from General Motors."

Knudsen's threat apparently carried the day. He installed the roll bar on the 1964 Corvair and, six years after the first roll-over at the proving grounds, approved designs of an entirely new suspension system for the 1965 model. The corrections came belatedly, however, and not before some 1.1 million Corvairs had been sold. Nor before the auto's twitchy handling had come to the attention of a young Harvard Law School graduate with a deeply felt interest in automotive safety—Ralph Nader.

At thirty-two, the slender, tense Nader was a crusader with no following in 1965, an attorney with a Harvard law degree turned to freelance writing to sustain himself. Unlike most of his Harvard classmates, Nader was interested in using the law to remedy larger social problems than the tax turmoils of large corporations, an attitude that had made him few friends among the smoothly ambitious men of the class of '58. A loner since boyhood, the young man born of Lebanese parentage in Winsted, Connecticut, seemed barely to notice. Instead, as editor of the school's *Law Record,* he attempted to use that publication as an instrument of social change, to reflect his own interest in the rights of the American Indian, in the Swedish *ombudsman* system for the redress of grievances, and in automotive safety—indeed, a broad range of subjects he called "public-interest law."

His degree in hand, Nader had opened a law office in Hartford, a city where insurance litigation far outweighs the public-interest suits Nader would have preferred to handle. Between cases—Nader was then and remains a man of eighteen-hour days and frantic travel schedules—he continued gathering information about automobile defects. In effect, he was expanding on the work done earlier for his senior paper, a study of manufacturers' liabilities for the designed-in defects of automobiles.

In 1964, Nader packed in his law practice, moving to Washington, D.C., to become a self-appointed lobbyist for the public. Nader's was an austere life, supported, barely, by the odd lecture and freelanced articles published in *The New Republic,* the *Nation,* and the *Christian Science Monitor.* He found work for a time as a consultant to Under-Secretary of Labor Daniel P. Moynihan, who himself had written about automotive safety for *The Reporter* in the 1950s, an assignment that momentarily fixed Nader's attention on motor vehicles.

Nader, as he was quick to concede, had come late to automobile safety. As early as 1905, newspapers and magazines had assailed the growing traffic death toll. In high dudgeon, the Chicago *Record-Herald* had shrilled, "No longer need the juggernaut of Pagan India hang its head in shame. Its horrors are mild in comparison with the slaughter of the innocents by the modern juggernaut of the auto in this Christian land of America." Despite such outraged editorials, more than one million people had died in automobile accidents since the first recorded traffic death in 1899, when one H.H. Bliss had stepped off a New York City streetcar into the path of a passing motor vehicle.

In 1936, the automobile industry organized the Automotive Safety Foundation, as effective a public-relations tool as it was ineffective as a curative. Funded by auto manufacturers, tire companies, the oil industry, and insurance firms, the foundation deflected criticism from the vehicle itself, laying blame for the rising annual death toll—49,000 by 1965—on highway conditions and drivers themselves. Beyond lobbying for more and better roads—a position which fitted neatly into the effort to create the vast interstate freeway system—the Automotive Safety Foundation promoted mandatory state motor-vehicle inspections. While such programs, along with antidrunk driving campaigns, could reduce the traffic death toll, they studiously ignored what the determined Ralph Nader was calling the "designed-in defects" of the automobile.

The Automotive Safety Foundation, again with an eye on the public-relations aspects, then induced President Eisenhower to create the President's Committee for Traffic Safety. Chaired by General Motors President Harlow Curtice and supported entirely by the privately funded safety foundation, the president's committee gave the appearance of an industry taking forward strides for the public good.

Still the slaughter of innocents and not-so-innocents alike provoked criticism of the automobile, prompting Congressman Kenneth Roberts to pressure the House of Representatives Interstate and Foreign Commerce Committee to create a subcommittee on traffic safety in 1956. The Alabama Democrat lacked the political influence to bring about major reform legislation—a failing more of the House of Representatives than of the congressman himself—but he was to midwife some remedial bills before being voted out of office in 1964.

That same year Congress adopted legislation requiring that all cars purchased by the General Services Administration for federal government use meet sixteen particular safety standards—including the installation of seat belts, outside rear-view mirrors, back-up lights, and headrests. Using the bait of annual government purchases of 36,000 passenger cars, Congress hoped to lure the industry into modest safety measures. The legislation came despite the auto industry's voluntary agreement in January 1964 to make seat belts standard equipment—a bone thrown in hopes of delaying the hounds of Congress baying after a reform bill. The placating concession failed, in part because the growing anti-automobile lobby was too sophisticated to be gulled any longer.

Both Chrysler and Ford had offered seat belts as an optional accessory since 1955; in less than eighteen months of their introduction, Ford had sold 400,000 seat-belt-equipped vehicles. According to then company vice-president Robert S. McNamara, no other optional accessory had "ever caught on so fast." Despite McNamara's assertion, General Motors steadfastly maintained that "there is not sufficient factual information on the protective value of seat belts in automobiles to form any definite conclusions." Moreover, "there is little interest on the part of the motoring public in actual use of seat belts."

Fearing anything, however slight, that might intrude on the romance of the automobile, General Motors resisted installation of seat belts for nine years while conceding that "further enhancement of the inherent safety of automobiles . . . clearly demands that automobile manufacturers continue and intensify their efforts to make safe driving as easy as possible and to afford

maximum possible protection to those involved in accidents."
Yet there was room for improvement, a General Motors engineer
tacitly inferred. "If we made a car that was completely safe to
ride in, I wonder if it would sell," he told a *Fortune* magazine
interviewer. Commented the magazine: "Translated, this means
that it might appeal only to 'squares,' and as G.M.'s styling
director [William Mitchell] observes, 'There ain't any squares
any more.'"

By 1964, Ralph Nader was convinced that General Motors,
accounting for almost half of the domestic automotive market,
was the great roadblock to safety legislation and safe motor vehicles. It was the 1960 Corvair that most infuriated Nader, a man
whose anger rarely surfaced but was sublimated into even more
frantic scheduling and longer work hours. Not only was the Corvair inherently unstable, Nader believed, but its air-cooling system leaked deadly carbon monoxide fumes into the passenger
compartment, and in front-end collisions, there was a significant
chance that the steering shaft would be jammed rearward, impal-
ing the driver.

Nader began collecting information about the Corvair and its
accidents and making that information available at no charge to
attorneys around the country handling suits against General
Motors for victims of accidents in the sporty car. Meanwhile, he
was serving as an unpaid consultant to a new Senate Subcommittee on Executive Reorganization.

The subcommittee's chairman, freshman Senator Abraham
Ribicoff, had long held an interest in auto safety. As governor of
Connecticut, he had campaigned unsuccessfully in the previous
decade to reduce that state's highway death toll. It was at the
suggestion of subcommittee counsel Jerome Sonosky that
Ribicoff decided to make his debut as chairman in hearings designed to investigate the federal government's role in automotive
safety. It was a legitimate use of the Congress's investigative
powers, however strained; the General Services Administration
standards had been watered down by industry lobbyists to permit seven current—and, Nader charged, unsafe—automobiles to
qualify for sales to the government. Moreover, Sonosky argued,
there was a good deal of information available concerning high-

way safety, and he happened to know a young attorney, someone from the senator's home state, who was something of an
expert on the subject. There was the additional political bonus:
the publicity would enhance Ribicoff's reelection chances.

In February 1965, the senator announced that his obscure subcommittee would hold hearings on "the fantastic carnage"
wrought by the automobile on the highways and invited the chief
executives of the five American manufacturers to testify. On
July 13, 1965, the pivotal hearings began, virtually unreported in
the press, as various government bureaucrats testified. A week
later, with such "celebrities" as General Motors' chairman of
the board Frederic Donner and newly installed president James
Roche scheduled to testify, the hearing room in the lavish New
Senate Office Building was crowded with newsmen and spec-
tators.

Donner and Roche were ill-prepared. They had come with the
smug assumption that Ribicoff could be handled as summarily as
the corporation earlier had dealt with Representative Roberts,
and before that with the "studies" of Senators O'Mahoney and
Kefauver. General Motors had been for so long at the pinnacle of
American business, had contributed so much to the economy,
that Donner and Roche believed it unassailable in its business
wisdom. Privately, they knew all politicians were vulnerable,
especially when 13,000 General Motors dealers from around the
country could be mustered to lobby their elected representatives.

A week before the hearings, the corporation had announced a
$1 million grant to the Massachusetts Institute of Technology to
study the interrelationship of the highway, the automobile, and
the driver in automotive safety. That transparent gesture—too
little, too late—merely angered the subcommittee's Democratic
majority.

Still hoping to smother the committee before it was properly
launched, the company announced it would incorporate as standard equipment on all its automobiles an outside left-hand rear-
view mirror, dual-speed windshield washer-wipers, a padded instrument panel, back-up lights, padded sun visors, and rear seat
belts. Nine years after Ford first offered such safety features,

General Motors had come around—in no small measure due to the GSA requirements, as well as growing public concern about automotive safety. The costs, of course, would be passed on, with appropriate profits added, to the consumer.

Donner led off. The safety question was "complicated," it was "variable," it was full of unknowns. The consumer played a large role, for, according to a Gallup Poll released on July 4, only 36 percent of automobile owners "always" used the front seat belts then standard equipment on cars. (Donner did not tell the whole story. That same Gallup Poll reported 56 percent of all respondents believed there should be "a law requiring automobiles now being built to be equipped with seat belts." More than 40 percent of the car owners already had seat belts on their cars.)

"As manufacturers," Donner continued, "we need the support of the public—public acceptance of the new safety devices that become available. These items must also be thoroughly tested, under the controlled conditions of the proving ground and laboratory . . . we do not propose to sell our customers untried equipment items."

Go slow, the chairman of the board was cautioning. He droned through his prepared statement while the television cameramen zoomed in for close-ups—the obligatory, dull "talking heads" television abhorred.

"The decision to offer an item as optional equipment recognizes what I believe is the basic freedom of the customer to pay the cost of tailoring a car to his own specifications or rejecting whatever he may not want," Donner continued. "From a commercial standpoint, in a competitive marketplace, this must be the approach until a very high proportion of customers selects the item or unless there are other compelling reasons for standard installation. When this point is reached, the items can be included as standard equipment and required selling price adjustments made to cover the additional costs involved."

Forty years earlier Sloan had delayed installing safety glass until the customer demanded it. Now Donner was warning against infringing on the freedom of the individual and the operation of a free market.

James Roche had been president of General Motors for just

one month when he sat down to testify in front of the bank of microphones. He was another of Donner's "unobvious choices," tapped to replace the retired John F. Gordon over men with more experience and more success building and selling automobiles. Perhaps that explained why the grandfatherly Roche, virtually alone among General Motors executives, found the brittle Donner a warm friend and why he tended to follow Donner's lead.

In one respect Roche was atypical of General Motors' officers, this son of an Elgin, Illinois, undertaker father and school-teacher mother. A devout Catholic, Roche had a troubled social conscience. As personnel manager at Cadillac, he had attempted to break down segregation in the plants; confronted by union opposition, he nevertheless ended the black–white drinking fountains and separate lunch areas. It was a start, and he would attempt to do more—much more—later, once Detroit was scorched by a race riot.

An accountant by virtue of a correspondence-school course—he never went to college—Roche had spent virtually his entire General Motors career at Cadillac. Though not a product man—Harlow Curtice and Harley Earl had given him the cars he was to sell—Roche had presided over the befinned sales bonanza of the late 1950s. Still, he was an unlikely president of General Motors, neither aloof like Sloan, ebullient like Curtice, nor brusque like Donner. Nothing about him suggested the towering figure one would imagine was president of the world's largest corporation.

Roche sat before the microphones, his hands shaking and his voice faltering in a stutter that surfaced when he was nervous. Donner having stated corporate policy—"We will continue to study . . . all aspects of the safety situation"—it fell to this un-obvious choice to tick off General Motors' accomplishments in the field of safety ("door locks have undergone constant improvement over the years"); to detail the company's testing facilities (including the Milford, Michigan, proving grounds where the Corvair had rolled over); to gratuitously praise the interstate highway system, without mentioning General Motors' pivotal role in bringing that network into being; and to note the

40,000 cars loaned over the years to high schools for driver-training classes, without mentioning that dealers willingly shared the cost since it helped sell cars.*

"We believe that automotive design for safety is most important and General Motors has always considered this a number one priority in its forward product design," Roche assured the subcommittee. The long statement ended with his warning that "safer automobiles cannot be viewed as a panacea for this highway safety problem."

The statement was artfully crafted to lend substance to the diffuse, intermittent programs initiated within the corporation. At another time, in another forum, it might have been effective. But committee counsel Jerome Sonosky had briefed Senator Ribicoff well, and sitting in the wings, the unpaid consultant was scribbling questions for senators to ask the two executives.

"You talked about safety door latches and hinges. You say you already meet GSA's requirements. Could you explain then, why the doors on General Motors cars seem to tear off to a far greater extent than other cars'?" Ribicoff asked. "I read this from a 1964 study made by John W. Garrett at Cornell. For 1963, percentage of cars with doors torn off [in accidents]: Chrysler, 0.8; Ford, 0.6; and General Motors, astronomically, 5.1. Have you seen this report? . . ."

Neither Donner, Roche, nor vice-president of engineering Harry F. Barr knew of the report released by the prestigious Cornell Aeronautical Laboratory.

Senator Robert F. Kennedy interposed. "Isn't it well known in your company that Cornell makes these studies?"

"Yes, sir," Barr answered.

"As everybody considers this an important matter, I would think that you would have a close working relationship with Cornell."

---

* Driver-training classes provided a subtle way of influencing young customers-to-be. "I've lost a lot of deals this way," one Ford dealer complained to Hal Higdon in "The Big Auto Sweepstakes," New York *Times Magazine,* May 1, 1966, p. 99. "A kid will learn to drive with a Chevy just because that's what they use in school" and buy a familiar Chevrolet later. By 1965, General Motors was supplying free of charge 5,235 driver-training vehicles, and Ford approximately 5,400.

"We do have," Barr insisted.

"And with their studies?"

"We do have."

Kennedy snorted. "How can you appear before this committee and not even know about it?"

The company's well-calculated appearance before the committee began to unravel. The television lights and cameras suddenly flipped on again; talking heads were fine when there was controversy.

"What surprises and somewhat shocks me," the senator from New York continued, "is the fact that the institution makes this study, it has been continuously making this study, makes this material and information available to you. Yet here are the three top executives of the company and not anybody, not one of them knows anything about it. It does seem to me that that is not giving it the highest priority, or the kind of priorities that it deserves."

Robert Kennedy, first-term senator from New York, was no longer John F. Kennedy's little brother "Bobby." In the eighteen months since the president's assassination, he had gradually come to accept the responsibilities that fell to him as his brother's political heir. It would evoke in him a sense of social justice he had carefully masked in earlier years as his brother's campaign manager and as attorney general of the United States. Far more than had his older brother, Robert Kennedy nursed an aroused social conscience.

Kennedy was unlike any senator since Robert La Follette in his open disdain for General Motors' executives. A skilled advocate—nine years before, as counsel for the Senate Rackets Subcommittee, he had hounded Teamsters president James Hoffa—Kennedy, a millionaire himself, was unawed by the covey of well-groomed executives sitting uneasily at the witness table. Kennedy had known such men from youth, men who were associates of his father Joseph P. Kennedy, whose opinions of most industrialists were scarcely flattering.

The three General Motors executives shifted uncomfortably. No one within memory, perhaps ever, had bullyragged the chairman of the board of the world's largest corporation. In the hermetically sealed world of the elite who managed the automobile industry—living in exclusive residential communities ranked by corporate status, joining the "right" clubs at the "right" time—men such as Donner and Roche moved as lords of the realm.

Suddenly the late president's younger brother was cuffing them with impudence. "When did you make the arrangements with MIT?" Kennedy asked. Merely asking the question suggested that General Motors' grant was made in bad faith, a tithing to the new god of safety in hopes of producing yet another unread study.

"How much money have you spent to find out how many children, for instance, fell out of the back of an automobile because of a faulty latch or lock?"

Donner dabbed at his forehead. "I think it is hard to define how much money you spend on a specific thing. . . ."

The evasive answers of unprepared, chastened executives angered the senator. What was General Motors spending on automotive safety research outside the company?

About $1.25 million, Roche finally estimated.

"What was the profit of General Motors last year?"

"I don't think that has anything to do—"

"I would like to have that answer if I may," Kennedy broke in, a prosecutor once again. "I think I am entitled to know that figure. I think it has been published. You spent $1.25 million, as I understand it, on this aspect of safety. I would like to know what the profit is."

Donner sought to fend him off. "The one aspect we are talking about is safety."

"What was the profit of General Motors last year?" Kennedy demanded.

"I will have to ask one of my associates," Donner replied while the television cameras zoomed in on the blue-suited men huddled together. Inconceivably, the chairman of the board of General Motors, the man who carried a "pony" in his breast pocket with up-to-date statistics about the company, seemingly could not remember the corporate profit of the year before. The flustered Donner gave the impression that he did not know very much at all about the corporation he headed and could not talk authoritatively about General Motors and auto safety.

Roche interjected, "One thousand seven hundred million dollars."

At that moment, the future of General Motors changed.

"You made $1.7 billion last year?" Kennedy asked, using a hoary prosecutor's trick to hammer home a telling point.

"That is correct," Donner replied.

"And you spent $1 million on this?" Kennedy's disdain lay heavy in the hearing room. Moments later he snapped, "If you gave just 1 percent of your profits, that is $17 million." Kennedy would try once more to learn just how much the corporation spent annually on safety research and testing, only to fail. Donner, Roche, and Barr, the three men who should have known, could not answer.

It was a "dismal" performance that enhanced chances of federal auto-safety legislation, the *Wall Street Journal* editorialized. General Motors and later Chrysler "underestimated the opposition and failed to prepare adequately," the commentary continued, quoting an unnamed senator: "I really wouldn't have believed they could be so bad." According to the Washington *Post,* Kennedy had "dealt with Donner ($653,000 in salary and bonuses last year) and Roche ($482,000) much as if he were examining a couple of youthful applicants for a driver's license who hadn't done their roadwork."

Even viewed charitably, the corporation's appearance before the Ribicoff subcommittee was a public embarrassment. General Motors no longer could pretend it held the best interests of the motoring public foremost, that what was good for America was good for General Motors. But General Motors unmasked as a profit-hoarding corporation did not mean Ribicoff could persuade enough senators to vote for remedial legislation; it merely meant General Motors no longer could pretend to some lofty stature immune to criticism.

If the July hearings were "dismal," there was worse to come—a humiliating, humbling ordeal unprecedented in either the history of American business or politics, and one that guaranteed passage of a strong automobile-safety bill.

Working out of his rooming house, living on a spare budget, unpaid consultant Ralph Nader had rushed in 1965 to complete the manuscript of a book about automotive safety for a small New York publisher. Some weeks before the formal publication date of Nader's book, General Motors' chief counsel, Aloysius F. Power, learned about the book and its special attention to the Corvair. Power ordered a confidential investigation of the young man. Such investigations are routine in civil cases, and Power's legal department was awash in Corvair suits—more than a hundred already filed, thirty in California alone, and more threatened. Nader was making available to attorneys his own research material, some of which could prove both embarrassing and costly to the corporation; conceivably, Nader also might turn up as an expert witness in these cases. If they were to prepare for his testimony, General Motors trial attorneys needed to know about the man.

Unhappy with the results of the first investigation, Power ordered a more intensive effort. On January 11, 1966, Eileen Murphy, the law librarian for the corporation, contacted a friend in Washington and asked him to undertake a more thorough investigation.

Richard Danner was, in the parlance of espionage, a "cut out," an intermediary who shielded the identity of the spymaster from the field agent. Danner retained Vincent Gillen, a former agent for the Federal Bureau of Investigation, who told his employees, "Our job is to check his life and current activities, to determine 'what makes him tick' such as his real interest in safety, his supporters if any, his politics, his marital status, his friends, his women, boys, et cetera." While some of Gillen's investigators interviewed Nader's friends and former associates—on the pretext that they were conducting a background check for an unnamed firm that wanted to hire Nader—other investigators shadowed the young lawyer.

Meanwhile, Nader was making his first appearance as a witness before a congressional committee. Sniffing constantly—a nervous habit that led many to think the young man either suffered from a perpetual cold or was pneumonic—Nader appeared before the Ribicoff subcommittee on February 10, 1966. With the publication of his book, and the good reviews it had received, Sonosky and Ribicoff decided that Nader could now surface as an automobile-safety expert rather than remain in the background as an unpaid consultant. They needed his testimony, they needed something to get a reform bill through the Senate. If General Motors had bungled its public presentation, it had followed through brilliantly in its private lobbying effort.

Nader hardly had begun his testimony before Senator Carl Curtis, a Nebraska Republican considered friendly to the auto industry, querulously interrupted, complaining that the young attorney was using big words the senator did not understand. Sniffing through Curtis' repeated interruptions, Nader argued for:

a genuine democracy . . . to provide for the participation of the public in decisions relating to technology whose use is so fraught with tragedy to millions of people. . . . A democratic policy should not permit an industry to unilaterally decide how many years it wishes to hold back the installation of superior braking systems; safer tires; fuel tanks that do not rupture and incinerate passengers in otherwise survivable accidents; collapsible steering columns; safer instrument panels, steering assemblies, seat structures and frame strengths; or to engage in a stylistic orgy of vehicle-induced glare, chrome eyebrow bumpers and pedestrian impalers—to take only a few examples of many.

Senator Curtis hectored the increasingly impatient Nader, exploring his career in Washington—in effect, asking him the questions General Motors ostensibly wanted answered when it had retained Danner earlier. Nader finally lost patience when the senator asked, "When did you do the work on this book?"

"That book, Senator," Nader retorted, "had its gestation almost a decade ago when I saw a little girl decapitated when a glove compartment door opened in a car that collided at 15 miles per hour."

The following day, two of Gillen's agents tailed Nader into the Senate Office Building, lost him, and, describing Nader to a guard, asked which way he had gone. The guard, coincidentally a Ribicoff patronage appointee, told the committee staff. Sonosky telephoned the news to Ribicoff, "Senator, I think we've got a bill."

On Sunday, February 13, 1966, the Washington *Post* ran a short article about the incident, adding that Nader had suspected he was under surveillance but had lacked clear evidence. The *New Republic* picked up the story, locating a flustered Gillen, who admitted he had made inquiries about Nader but refused to name Danner. The New York *Times* took the story a step further on March 6, adding that Nader also claimed to have received anonymous threatening telephone calls and that women he did not know had attempted to place him in compromising situations.

The story had grown into a nationwide issue. On March 8, Senator Ribicoff took the floor of the Senate to condemn the surveillance and harassment, asking for a federal investigation of what he described as an attempt to intimidate a congressional witness. Under pressure from clamoring newsmen, first Ford, then Chrysler and American Motors, flatly denied any involvement. General Motors, the New York *Times* reported on March 10, "declined comment."

Roche faced his first crisis as president of the corporation alone. Donner was touring New Zealand and Australia, and was not to return until the crisis had blown over. Twenty-four hours after Roche first learned the legal department had put detectives on Nader's trail, he personally drafted a public statement. It was released only after a day of wrangling within the executive suites on the fourteenth floor, with ranking executives divided about the content and tone of Roche's statement. Some wanted to maintain silence. Others, notably members of Aloysius Power's legal department who believed their careers at stake, insisted on claiming that the investigation was both legal and proper.

Roche was still unaware of the full scope of Gillen's prying when he released the statement late on March 9, asserting, "The investigation was limited only to Mr. Nader's qualifications, background, expertise and association with such attorneys [as those handling Corvair suits against the company]. It did not include any of the alleged harassment or intimidation recently reported in the press."

At least some members of the legal department were aware that Gillen's men had looked into Nader's sexual preferences and rumors that he was anti-Semitic. David Lewis, at the time a

General Motors public-relations man, later told writer William Serrin about a lunch he had had with one of the legal staff shortly after Nader's book was released. According to Serrin, "the staff member informed Lewis that the legal staff was investigating Nader and, Lewis recalls, that it would 'make a case for him being a homosexual and an anti-Semite. . . . I was assured that the corporation was indeed going to smear Nader and that, after it had done so, Nader would stand discredited. Anything he might say or do afterward . . . would carry no weight with the great American public.'"

If anyone was to lose credibility, it would not be Nader. Nationwide news coverage inevitably cast General Motors as a bully, an impression reaffirmed two weeks later when Ribicoff reopened his hearings to probe the alleged harassment.

Nader was to be the first witness, but, ironically, he was unable to find a taxi in congested Washington and arrived late. Instead, white-haired James Roche, attended by his newly retained attorney, former Kennedy White House special assistant Theodore Sorensen, opened the hearings.

There was little Sorensen could do for his client, even though Sorensen was a friend of Senator Kennedy and even though it had been Sorensen as the late president's speechwriter who, more than anyone else, had created the illusion of a new Camelot in Washington. "Deny the girls," Sorensen reminded Roche *sotto voce.*

Roche had come to apologize, having shouted down the outraged company executives who insisted that General Motors did not apologize, that such an act was unseemly for the world's largest corporation. Goddammit! Roche raged. What the hell do you want me to do? This is the only thing that can be done.

Grandfatherly-looking, obviously sincere, Roche made the best of what was for him, personally, a painful obligatory appearance. (Five years later he would recall to the minute the anniversary of his humbling before the Ribicoff subcommittee.)

"Let me make clear at the outset that I deplore the kind of harassment to which Mr. Nader has apparently been subjected," Roche read from his prepared statement. "As president of General Motors, I hold myself fully responsible for any action authorized or initiated by any officer of the corporation which may have had any bearing on the incidents related to our investigation of Mr. Nader.''

Roche was sweating, perhaps from the hot television lights, perhaps from the strain. "To the extent that General Motors bears responsibility,'' Roche paused a moment, then plunged on, "I want to apologize here and now to the members of this sub-committee and Mr. Nader. I sincerely hope that these apologies will be accepted.''

It was done. The rest of the statement came more easily. "There has been no attempt by, and it has at no time been the intention of General Motors Corporation, or any of its officers or employees to annoy, harass, embarrass, threaten, injure or in-timidate Mr. Nader . . . I personally have no interest what-soever in knowing Mr. Nader's political beliefs, his religious beliefs and attitudes, his credit rating or his personal habits re-garding sex, alcohol, or any other subject. Nor for the record was any derogatory information of any kind along any of these lines turned up in this investigation.'' Roche had apologized *and* cleared Nader of any suspicion.

There remained only for Senator Kennedy to force Roche to admit that the statement released the night of March 9 had not been accurate. "If the statement were written today,'' Roche agreed, "it would be in different language.''

Had Roche checked the statement with the legal department before issuing it, Kennedy pressed. "Did you ask them whether they knew it was inaccurate at the time? Did you raise questions about the fact that they permitted you to put out a statement that was itself inaccurate?''

"Yes. We have discussed that. We have discussed that,'' Roche repeated.

"I can't see how you can know the facts, I don't see how you can order the investigation . . . as to what was taking place, including what the chairman described, and then put out a state-ment like this, which is not accurate, which you agree is not accurate, and which was reviewed by the very people who knew the facts and who ordered the investigation. That, Mr. Roche, disturbs me as much as the fact that you conducted the investiga-tion in the way that it was conducted in the beginning.''

The damage was done. Despite Roche's apology, General Motors had been marked as arrogant and mendacious. Said one senator, "Everybody is so outraged that a great corporation was out to clobber a guy because he wrote critically about them. At that point, everybody said the hell with them."

The result, ultimately, was the passage of the National Traffic and Motor Vehicle Safety Act, which empowered a new government agency to set standards for automotive safety and to order recalls of vehicles with safety-related defects. While the National Highway Safety Bureau would wax and wane in its enforcement vigor, for the first 'time the nation's largest industry had come under formal and abiding federal scrutiny. In its first year of operation, manufacturers voluntarily recalled 4.7 million vehicles for repair; by the end of 1967, one of every three new cars sold was subject to recall for safety-related reasons.

The Corvair travail would not end with a simple apology, no matter how contrite the president. Before the year was out, Nader filed suit against the corporation and private detective Vincent Gillen, asking $6 million for compensatory damages and an additional $20 million in punitive damages. Gillen charged that the corporation was trying to fix the blame on him for exceeding his instructions, adding, "I was not going to take the rap for doing what I had clear instructions to do and which I had done . . ." Four years later, Nader accepted a settlement out of court for $425,000—which his attorney claimed was the largest such settlement for an invasion-of-privacy action—though the corporation steadfastly denied any wrongdoing. After his legal fees were paid, Nader pumped the remaining $284,000 into consumer advocacy programs, including a revived attack on the Corvair.

That car was doomed. In 1965, Chevrolet sold 209,000 Corvairs, equipped with a new, more effective suspension, but with an exhaust system that leaked fumes into the passenger compartment. The next year, that car's sales totaled 86,000 and by 1968 had plunged to a meager 12,887. The company had sold 1.5 million Corvairs prior to the Senate hearings and just 125,000 in the four years after. On May 12, 1969, after ten years of Corvair production, General Motors announced that it was ending the manufacture of Edward Cole's dream car. The corporation offered no other explanation than "It is our regular practice to review our products." In an oblique reference to the unstable Corvair of earlier years, General Motors emphasized that it had not lost a single Corvair suit. The claim was true enough; there were an estimated five hundred cases stemming from deaths and injuries in Corvair-related accidents, an undisclosed number of which had been settled out of court when it appeared General Motors might well lose at trial.

The Nader furor aside—after all, it had not touched him—Frederic Donner neared the end of his tenure as chairman of the board with some satisfaction. In the eight years since his ascension, General Motors had doubled its annual automobile sales to $21 billion. Its stock had reached an all-time high on the market and was considered the bellwether in good times and bad. The corporation had levered itself from a 45–50 percent share of the market to 50–55 percent, all the while returning profits equal to those Donner's more celebrated predecessors had achieved. Under his direction, the corporation had been fundamentally reorganized, ending the engineer's hallowed "cut-and-try" design methods in favor of computer-generated design parameters, saving tens of millions of dollars annually. Moreover, this had been done while totally revamping company products—not once, but repeatedly—bringing out new cars to meet new markets at less cost.

In the twenty years since the first true postwar automobiles, the industry had virtually doubled the number of models available, to 370, as Ford and Chrysler sought to emulate the Sloan dictate of a car for every purse and purpose. Beyond the nameplates—the million-seller-a-year Impala, and Chevelle, Caprice, Bel Air, Biscayne, Chevy II, Monza, and Corvette in the Chevrolet array alone—and the body configurations of two- and four-door sedans, convertibles, vans, pickup trucks, and hardtops, General Motors offered limitless combinations of engines, drive trains, and accessories. A New York *Times Magazine* article noted in 1966:

Last year a Yale University physicist calculated that since Chevy offered 46 models, 32 engines, 20 transmissions, 21 colors (plus nine two-tone combinations) and more than 400 accessories and options, the number of different cars that a Chevrolet customer conceivably could order was greater than the number of atoms in the universe. This seemingly would put General Motors one notch higher than God in the chain of command. This year, even though the standard Chevrolet never accounts for less than two-thirds of Chevy's sales, Chevy is offering still more models (a total of 50) and options, indicating that while they may not be increasing their lead over Ford, they are pulling away from God.

By any reasonable standard, both Donner and the corporation he headed were successful, offering consumers more choice, more of what Detroit called "value"; yet the company had never come under such attack—from "self-appointed" safety experts, from the government, even from consumers themselves.

For eight years Donner had held himself aloof from the press, especially television, once warning Roche at a news conference, "Don't tell them anything." Here, at the end of his career, when he might have expected honors, he faced contempt or, even more galling, indifference. He groped for an explanation in one of the rare interviews he granted. Safety wasn't the real issue, Donner believed, Nader notwithstanding: "I'm arguing that we have a fundamental problem that involves things not normally considered as safety factors. I think the [automobile] owner is groping for something more than safety. I call it reliability."

If Donner perceived the corporation's responsibility for the loss of public esteem, it went unmentioned. Embattled and defensive, he insisted, "I am not ashamed of General Motors."

16

The Heretics

North and west the summer sky was striped with the oily black smoke of tarred roofs burning. Squinting in the sun's glare, the men on the roof of the General Motors Building, sixteen stories above West Grand Boulevard, strained to see the flames feeding the black columns. Even at night the homes and storefronts no more than a mile away seemed to glow rather than burn.

For hours James M. Roche, chairman of the board, and the corporation's senior executives had nervously watched the tendrils of smoke through the torpid haze. They could hear the police and fire sirens, faintly reassuring reminders that law and order still existed somewhere, for all the anarchy and the palpable anger welling from Detroit's black ghetto.

"I never thought I would see anything like that in the City of Detroit," Roche said later of the July 1967 riots along Twelfth Street. "I went to sleep and heard gun shots. I never thought I would hear that in the City of Detroit."

Five days after the shaken Roche finally fell asleep in the

executive suite on the fourteenth floor, gunfire still ringing in his ears, police and national guardsmen quelled the nation's worst urban riot. Forty were dead, damage estimates improbably ranged into the hundreds of millions of dollars, and police were attempting to sort out thousands of arrestees.

James Roche had never paid much attention to the city of Detroit. Few General Motors executives did—beyond obligatory tickets to Detroit Symphony concerts and an occasional Tigers or Lions ballgame. Each day they drove to and from their mock Tudor or ranch-style homes on wooded tracts in Bloomfield Hills, heedless, unseeing, oblivious to the dank inner city, that decaying rabble of neighborhoods their parents had fled a generation earlier. One out of five young men in the black community was unemployed; the tuberculosis and neonatal death rates ran twice the national average; and as many as one of every two youngsters dropped out of school. Yet as corporate executives they were unconcerned.

The 3,500 other men and women of General Motors who worked on West Grand Boulevard did not think about the rotten neighborhoods lapping at the granite of the General Motors Building. Few people of the middle and upper classes anywhere gave thought to the inner city. The blacks they encountered were faceless menials, certainly not coworkers. "General Motors is a white man's corporation and it's going to stay a white man's corporation," executives believed.

So it had always been. As early as 1936, there was only one black—Roscoe Van Zandt—among the strikers who sat down in Flint's Chevrolet plant. Chevrolet then had few black employees, and those were confined to janitorial work, "while the ban on colored workers in the corporation's body plants was absolute."

General Motors had never had an *official* policy; its silence on the subject became de facto policy, and individual plant managers were free to hire as they saw fit. Bowing to pressure from locals of the United Auto Workers—made up largely of white southerners—personnel men had hired few blacks over the years and had confined those few to the most menial, undesirable jobs. Four out of five blacks drawing General Motors paychecks prior to World War II worked among the blast furnaces of the foundry departments. As late as 1958, only one of 5,346 white-collar employees in eleven General Motors assembly plants scattered across the country was black. In the southern states, where General Motors was opening ever more factories, there were few jobs available to blacks even as production workers. "When we moved into the South," a plant manager in Atlanta explained, "we agreed to abide by local custom and not hire Negroes for production work. This is no time for social reforming in that area and we're not about to try it."

Even as Roche stood peering into the burning city below him during the riots of July 1967, the corporation had made little progress. Despite considerable national attention focused on equal opportunity in the years following *Brown* v. *Board of Education* in 1954, and the Southern sit-ins of the early 1960s, only 12 percent of the company's work force in 1967 was black. Further, they still held the least desirable jobs throughout the industry. A black worker in the aged Dodge plant at Hamtramck—he might have been speaking about any of the auto makers—snarled, "Black workers, they work on the dirtiest, nastiest, filthiest, noisiest jobs. You go find the dirtiest, nastiest, filthiest, noisiest, mother-fuckingest jobs and that's where you'll find the black man."

Worse still, just two of General Motors' 12,000 dealers were black as Roche took the chairmanship. Lack of capital and training was not an adequate explanation or excuse. In 1929, General Motors had set up Motors Holding Corporation, which, according to Alfred P. Sloan, was "to assist capable individuals who lacked capital to become the owners of profitable General Motors dealerships." Motors Holding "found qualified operators, backed them with adequate capital, and enabled them to produce profits sufficient to retire Motors Holding's interest and become independent."

General Motors was barely integrated when the riots struck. The week of chaos erupting from a police raid on a blind pig at the corner of Clairmount and Twelfth avenues had stunned Roche. There was nothing in the background of the Elgin, Illinois, native to enable him to understand such fury. Yet within

days of the organization of a prestigious New Detroit Committee, of which the prominent James M. Roche was a member of
the board, General Motors had copied a recruiting program initiated by Ford Motor Company and had begun hiring blacks from
the inner city. In the three months following the riots—the gutted
hulks of some thousand dwellings and stores a daily reminder of
the urgency—General Motors hired 5,000 blacks. Many, unused
to the discipline, some unable to read, would not stay; yet non-
white employment at General Motors reached 13.4 percent in
1970. By the end of 1971 and Roche's retirement, minority employment had surpassed 15 percent, and the company had more
than 5,000 blacks in higher-paying white-collar positions, some 3
percent of all management and staff jobs.*

Though General Motors could be slow to face a problem, once
that was accomplished, the company was capable of effective
efforts to correct the deficiency. Too few black dealers? By June
1972, the corporation's marketing staff and the University of
Detroit had worked out a joint twenty-one-month course to train
candidates for dealerships. Within three years, the two black
dealerships had grown to thirty-two.

Roche's effort to redress the imbalance of minority-group employment was made easier by the general economic prosperity of
the times and General Motors' expansive plans to take advantage of that prosperity. In what later became known as the "go-
go" years of the 1960s, as large manufacturing companies trans-
mogrified into conglomerates, the Democratic administrations of
both John F. Kennedy and Lyndon B. Johnson had deliberately
stimulated an expansionary—and inflationary—fiscal policy.
Businessmen who for decades had reviled government "med-

---

* In 1974, incoming board chairman Thomas Murphy reaffirmed the new-found commitment to equal opportunity in a message to corporate personnel directors that concluded:
". . . the position of GM in these matters is unmistakably clear: there is no room for
prejudice in General Motors—and we mean just that. If we have any person at management level in any GM facility who cannot function within this policy, or is not giving it full
attention, then he will simply no longer be able to work for General Motors." By the end
of 1978, the corporation reported, minorities held 17,526—or almost 12 percent—of all
white-collar positions. Nine percent of the company's 56,500 managers and officials, the
highest ranked of white-collar employees, were minority-group members. Lacking
seniority or experience, most were in comparatively lower-paying positions; only time
will prove if General Motors can promote minorities as easily as it has hired them.

dling,'' bitter men who still condemned Franklin D. Roosevelt's New Deal as rampant socialism, swarmed to Washington to batten on defense contracts; farm, oil, and ship-building subsidies; and space-research grants. Corporate sales and profits, superheated by military and space expenditures, soared to annual records after the recession of 1960. Five years later, after-tax profits for industry in general reached a 13-percent return on investment, the highest in history. General Motors soared from 16.5 percent to 25.8 percent in the same span.

So long as conglomerate mergers did not involve competitive firms, the Department of Justice and the Federal Trade Commission looked benignly upon the acquisitions. Thus International Telephone & Telegraph, once a communications company, became ITT, owner of insurance firms, a mutual fund, an airport parking company, the nation's second-largest auto-rental firm, a phonograph-record manufacturer and music publisher, and a housing developer. Conventional wisdom held that acquisition by a conglomerate brought in new capital and brighter management and stimulated intellectual and research cross-fertilization.

In such a time, the earliest of the conglomerates, General Motors—encompassing autos, home appliances, insurance, locomotives, electronics, ball bearings, electric motors, air-conditioning, banking, and financing, among other enterprises—prospered. Not all of those divisions were doing equally well, but the automobiles spilling from its factories in a multiplicity of models and configurations had touched off a sales binge in 1962 that set records three years in a row. By 1965, Americans had invested $185 billion to tool about in sixty-six million automobiles, enough to permit every man, woman, and child in the country to ride in the front seat of a car at the same time. And ride they did: 90 percent of all vacation travel was by automobile, seventy billion miles in 1961 alone. Twenty-eight states ranked travel expenditures as one of their three major sources of business income. (Expanding on a travel-promotion campaign put forward in 1960 by the American Petroleum Institute, Chevrolet exhorted the public throughout the decade to "see the U.S.A. in your Chevrolet.")

The boom in sales seemed endless. From 1963 to 1968, automobile dealers sold twenty-two million new and used cars each year. Happily anticipating the financial returns to investors, Chase Manhattan Bank predicted the public was ready to buy "a different car for each occasion—work, errands, sport, long trips and city living. . . . The widespread desire for more than one car," the bank's economic forecast burbled, "could put two cars in every family's garage by 1980."

Though the forecast was too optimistic, by 1970 multiple-car ownership was no longer a privilege of the upper classes: 22.5 million families had at least two cars, and as many as 3.5 million had three or more. Traffic clogged even the expanding interstate highway system, and one powerful California legislator—who already had secured stiff air-pollution control laws—was proposing that the state outlaw possession of more than one internal-combustion automobile per family. The auto industry, Chevrolet general manager Edward Cole had predicted in 1959, was entering "the era of specific driving needs," when people bought cars to suit personal requirements. Detroit intended to fulfill the demand, relying on compact cars and their progeny.

General Motors' first compact, the Corvair, had not done as well as anticipated, though in one sense the corporation was grateful. The compact car yielded a net profit of only two hundred dollars, half that of the cheapest full-size Chevrolet. But with Ford's strong-selling Falcon, Plymouth's Valiant, and the Rambler, the Corvair had helped curb the import invasion. Within three years of their introduction, the domestic compacts had halved import sales to just 5 percent of new-car registrations in the United States. Only the defiantly ungraceful Volkswagen prospered in the new market, doubling its sales to 240,000 vehicles between 1959 and 1963. Weakened by inadequate dealer organizations, the other imports silently folded their tents.

The automobile industry congratulated itself. While the compacts had winkled some sales out of their larger, more profitable cars, approximately four of every ten compacts sold were second cars in a family, transportation that freed housewives from suburbia, or put the coming-of-age postwar babies into "passion wagons."

But if Dad had a radio, power steering, luxurious interiors, and such in the family car—which spent most of the day in a parking lot anyway—spouse and offspring meant to have these accoutrements of good living too. Within a year of the introduction of their compacts, the Big Three realized that for all the claims of the compact's economy—10-percent lower insurance rates and gasoline savings estimated at sixty dollars per year—small-car customers were opting for expensive accessories. Compacts fitted with extra-cost "performance" engines could be made more profitable still. Larger engines permitted additional accessories as standard equipment, larger bodies to accommodate the package, and higher list prices. Like Alice, the compact car was to grow magically throughout the rest of the 1960s in size, price, and profitability.

General Motors' profits hinged on size. The Cadillac Coupe de Ville, for example, cost only $300 to $400 more than a mid-size Chevrolet Caprice to assemble, depending on the options ordered, but carried a sticker price between $2,700 and $3,800 more.

Even with federal and state taxes swallowing 58 percent of the gross profit, General Motors benefited most when consumers opted for larger cars. For a full-size car, with a sticker price of $4,500, the dealer paid $3,375. Its assembly costing between $1,900 and $2,000, the corporation grossed as much as $1,475 on each Oldsmobile 88 or Impala and netted, after taxes, $855. By comparison, an intermediate-size car such as the Chevrolet Chevelle yielded $200 less profit, and the compact Chevrolet Nova, Pontiac Ventura, or Oldsmobile Omega $400 less.

On particularly popular cars, such as the 1969 Pontiac Grand Prix, General Motors favored loading the autos with profitable options. The intermediate-size "muscle car" sold briskly for $4,000 retail, yielding dealers a tidy $1,000 and the corporation $1,500 gross profit.

The more accessories or optional equipment provided, the greater the profits. Fifteen dollars spent on chrome strips, a larger tire size, and more attractive upholstery produced a "new" model with a $300 larger price tag. Twenty-five dollars for heavy-duty shock absorbers, bucket seats, a tachometer, and a chrome gear-shift lever became a $400 performance package for those favoring a sporty car.

"We were living off the gullibility of the consumer combined with the fantastic growth of the American economy in the

1960s," John DeLorean, former general manager of both Pontiac and Chevrolet, confessed.

Selling "more car per car" by 1970, General Motors and its dealers were putting automatic transmissions in nine of ten cars produced, V-8 engines in more than eight of ten, air conditioning in three of four, and power steering in nine of ten. General Motors led the industry in all four categories of these, the most expensive of options.

The first of the loaded compacts was Chevrolet's Monza, a tricked-up Corvair with bucket seats shown as a designer's dream car at the New York Automobile Show in 1960. The display model had attracted hundreds of curious shoppers interested in buying the mock-up; Edward Cole, Chevrolet's general manager at the time, took the hint, introducing the dressed-up vehicle with an extra-cost, optional performance package that included the stabilizing bar banned from the mundane Corvair.

The Monza's success unleashed a pack of so-called personal cars aimed largely at the young and the single, notably Pontiac's "muscle cars." To promote them, Bunkie Knudsen and his chief engineer, Elliot "Pete" Estes, secretly launched a stock-car racing team that shattered the "old lady" image of the division, this despite the industry's 1955 agreement not to engage in factory-sponsored racing programs. Once violated, the agreement collapsed. By the mid-1960s, Ford and Chevrolet reportedly were spending more than $20 million annually on their covertly sponsored stock-car racers.

Catering to the young with muscle cars and a de-chromed styling that stressed power rather than size, Pontiac became General Motors' most successful division through the 1960s. Its engineers given their head, Pontiac originated three-quarters of the innovations on General Motors' automobiles from 1962 to 1969, DeLorean boasted.*

As the compacts grew in size and weight, eventually to become "intermediate" cars, they opened a gap at the low end of the market once again. Into that opening a relative handful of

---

* Among the innovations: a radio antenna molded into the windshield, which "left something to be desired in performance," DeLorean acknowledged; and concealed windshield wipers, a DeLorean styling innovation, which had the disconcerting habit of freezing tightly in their hidden position during winter months.

chastened foreign producers crept back. Detroit paid scant heed; American industry had demonstrated it could turn back the interlopers any time it wished to. There were more pressing concerns, including a threat to the internal-combustion engine itself.

As reluctant as it was to install safety devices in motor vehicles, the automobile industry was even more resistant to pollution control. Seat belts, padded dashboards, and deep-dish steering wheels might cost money, but those costs would be passed on to the consumer in any event. Beyond tarnishing the aura of the automobile as a stressless, floating palace, safety devices had no lasting sales impact.

Not so pollution control. The subject was complicated, with more variables than engineers could manage: the amount of automotive pollutants pumped into the atmosphere—86 million tons in 1966 alone—depended on gasoline formulae, the efficiency of the internal-combustion engine, local climatic conditions, and the very concentration of cars in a given area. Worse still, from the automotive industry's viewpoint, pollution-control devices would necessarily reduce performance, and that, General Motors feared, would hurt sales.

From the early 1950s, the industry had desultorily investigated the problem of noxious emissions. In 1953, the auto makers reached an informal agreement to share among themselves any devices to control pollution one or another might discover. The following year, under the sponsorship of the Automobile Manufacturers Association, they ratified the share-and-share-alike pact with a formal agreement.

Despite increasing pressure, especially from smog-laden California, the companies dallied. When a Los Angeles County supervisor, Kenneth Hahn, visited Detroit to urge that the auto makers take some remedial action, he was turned aside by a senior executive of one company.

"Well, Mr. Hahn, will that device sell more cars?"

"No," Hahn conceded.

"Will it look prettier, will it give us more horsepower? If not, we are not interested," the unusually frank executive told the unsuccessful envoy.

That attitude armored the automobile industry, though both

American Motors and Studebaker were more inclined to bend with the wind. Social responsibility simply did not figure high on the list of priorities in Detroit's concept of a freely enterprising economy. The men of General Motors resisted any criticism, no matter how couched in praise, and any suggestion that it look beyond the balance sheet to the social impact of its operations and products. When in 1946 the decidedly pro-business writer Peter Drucker published his widely heralded *Concept of the Corporation*, based on an intensive study of General Motors' management system, the company's executives rejected it as "unfairly critical" and "fundamentally 'anti-business.'" Drucker found himself unwelcome in the corporation:

. . . I had clearly accepted the fact that the existing policies were optimal for all major parties to GM itself—workers, managers, stockholders, and dealers. I had criticized these policies because I had adjudged them as not fully acceptable to the "outsiders," e.g., society and community. I had, in other words, asked GM to assume authority in matters in which it had no authority, and to step beyond being a "business" with a clear and defined area of authority and responsibility. Instead I had asked GM to make political judgments, to make moral judgments, to make value judgments—all areas in which a business had absolutely no business to be and in which it would be clearly beyond the limits of its authority as well as of its competence.

Such single-minded focus on the well-being of the corporation ignored the obligation of all societal institutions to support consensual social good. General Motors underestimated the importance of air pollution as a political issue in the Los Angeles basin, and from there to other parts of California. Smog choked Republican as well as Democratic lungs and shrouded political oratory. Even the most conservative of politicians found it unwise to resist the growing consensus. The dominant newspaper of the region, the Los Angeles *Times,* which for seventy years had unabashedly promoted boosterism—"it's the climate we're selling, not the land"—served to put spine to the weak. Los Angeles was the smog capital of the world and resented the title. California, with automobile registrations growing faster than the population, was a state bathed in air pollution and meant to do something about it.

Detroit responded with desultory research. Seven companies had budgeted $1 million for smog studies by 1955, the Automobile Manufacturers Association proudly announced. By 1959, General Motors had discovered that a fifty-cent part used even before World War II on military vehicles was effective in reducing automobile pollution by about 25 percent. (The device, a positive crankcase ventilation valve, or PCV, had been patented in 1909.)

Still the automobile industry had no intention of rushing to fit the PCV valve to American automobiles. When Representative Kenneth Roberts, the industry's periodic thorn-in-the-flesh, suggested the device be installed on all cars built, a spokesman for the Automobile Manufacturers Association testified it would be impractical. The smog problem should be attacked on a community basis, he added vaguely.

Yet when the California Legislature did grant local communities such power, the manufacturers were still in no hurry to comply. "We decided we had to make the manufacturers control emissions," S. Smith Griswold, the director of Los Angeles County's Air Pollution Control District, told a reporter. "The companies said it couldn't be done. So we got independent companies to design emission control devices and ordered the auto makers to put them on their cars. Then we discovered the auto makers *had* the devices, and finally, when they were forced too, they put them on." Rather than have the profits go to two nonautomotive firms, the industry in 1964 rushed to install its "impractical" devices—at a cost of ten dollars per car on the 1966 models.

Even though California would require control devices, the automobile industry had no intention of installing similar valves on all cars built. When Congressman Roberts repeated his request to put PCV valves on all cars sold in the country, the Automobile Manufacturers Association polled its members in June 1961 for reasons why the suggestion was not feasible. "It must be recognized," General Motors engineer G.R. Fitzgerald noted in a memo, "that they [the Association] are specifically looking for problems that will justify a negative decision."

In 1965, prodded by a complaint from Ralph Nader, the Department of Justice began an investigation of collusion in suppressing antismog research and devices. A federal grand jury in Los Angeles heard testimony for eighteen months, the antitrust division attorney in charge of the case finally recommending that a criminal action be brought against the companies. Instead, just ten days before the inauguration of President-elect Richard Nixon in 1969, the lame-duck Johnson administration filed a civil antitrust case, disregarding the attorney's recommendation. The suit charged that the four automobile manufacturers had conspired to delay installation of the PCV valve on cars outside of California before 1963 and of an auto exhaust device until 1967. General Motors issued a statement defending the auto makers' 1954 compact as "a program of cooperative research and development," entered into "in good faith, in the public interest and with the knowledge of governmental authorities . . . General Motors will continue as it has in the past to devote its resources and its experience to finding a solution for the nation's air pollution problems."

That was precisely what the corporation would do, dragging its feet for the next seven years as it had for the previous sixteen, pleading that it could not meet ever more stringent emission standards, then suddenly, miraculously, finding a way after all.

Ten months after the suit was filed, Republican Attorney General John Mitchell agreed to settle it with a consent agreement—a legal document in which, as more cynical attorneys argue, "the defendant claims it never did it and promises never to do it again." The consent decree had the effect of suppressing fifty-seven volumes of grand-jury evidence, as well as a pointed memorandum summarizing that evidence, which might have been used against the automobile manufacturers in parallel suits filed by a dozen cities, counties, and states charging irreparable damage by automobile emissions. Attorney General Mitchell claimed in a statement released with the announcement of the settlement that his decision "represents strong federal action to encourage widespread research and marketing of more effective auto anti-pollution devices."

Under authority of the federal Clean Air Act of 1965, the Secretary of Health, Education, and Welfare set modest standards for emissions from 1968 models, then delayed their enforcement until 1970 after the automobile manufacturers pleaded they could not meet the criteria. (The Clean Air Act was adopted over the protests of the manufacturers, who argued that the subject required "further research" and that national standards were not necessary because Los Angeles' photochemical smog was not a major problem in other cities.) So it would go for the next half-decade, with government agencies promulgating ever more stringent emission controls and the industry invariably pleading that it could not meet them and asking for more time.

Disturbed by the dilatory tactics, in 1968 California State Senator Nicholas Petris carried a bill through the upper house that would have banned the sale of automobiles powered by unclean internal-combustion engines. The bill was intended as a warning; one legislative aide compared it to the man whacking a mule he was about to train with a two-by-four bat, explaining, "First you have to gain his attention."

To that extent, Petris was successful. The following year a General Motors spokesman turned up in Los Angeles to claim victory in the struggle to reduce air pollution. Fred Bowditch, the corporation's director of emission control, asserted that automobile-produced air pollution had peaked, "and will never be as high again." Los Angeles motorists were pumping 1,459 tons of pollutants into the air each day, compared to a high of 1,860 tons three years earlier. Had the industry not adopted PCV valves and exhaust traps, Bowditch noted, the daily total would have reached 2,377 tons. He was, in effect, claiming credit for the automobile industry, which had resisted the very imposition of such devices.

Moreover, under questioning by Los Angeles *Times* reporter Dan Fisher, Bowditch grudgingly conceded that the reduction had come in only two of the three major pollutants: unburned hydrocarbons and carbon monoxide. The third major contaminant, oxides of nitrogen—which medical authorities considered a major health hazard, and which, when exposed to sunlight, produced the brown pall characteristic of Los Angeles' smog—were actually on the increase. In fact, Louis J. Fuller, the new head of the county's Air Pollution Control District, told Fisher that the 1969 models produced three times the oxides of nitrogen generated by 1965 models.

Little more than a year later, General Motors' president, Edward Cole, complained that the federal antismog standards which would be upgraded in 1975 asked too much of the auto industry in too short a time. Contrary to Bowditch's earlier victory claim, Cole predicted: "The 1975 emission control systems will remove the automobile as a significant factor in the nation's air pollution problem. . . ."

By the end of 1972, the industry had shifted its stance yet again. Taking the lead, Cole suggested General Motors could meet the 1975 mandates with a new device, if it could have an extra year in which to test its catalytic converter. But, said one critic, Cole sought only to "dangle a plum" while gaining a year in which to lobby Congress for a broad review of the Clean Air Act itself. "Automobile executives," charged Leon Billings, a senior Senate staff member and the man most responsible for drafting the stricter standards, "are among the most arrogant of America's oligopoly. They have decided that if they can meet the standards with the internal combustion engine, it will be done. If they can't, they'll change the standards."

Flailing in all directions, seeking any argument that might pressure relaxation of the mandate, General Motors' new board chairman, Richard C. Gerstenberg, pointed out in February 1972 that the catalytic converter developed by the company to reduce emissions would cost the American public $2 billion per year. "We must ask ourselves, is this the best use of our resources, or could this $2 billion—or at least a good part of it—be better applied to the solution of our society's other serious problems."

A year and a half later, Ernest S. Starkman, a former University of California at Berkeley mechanical engineer hired in February 1971 as vice-president in charge of General Motors' environmental staff, contradicted the chairman. Because the new converter improved fuel economy and reduced maintenance costs, consumers would recover the $150 premium in the first year, Starkman said. Pollution control was, then, in the words of businessmen themselves, "cost-effective."*

On April 12, 1973, William D. Ruckelshaus, administrator for the Environmental Protection Agency, delayed for one year imposing the stringent standards called for in the Clean Air Act. Loosening the noose, Ruckelshaus disregarded the fact that two Japanese firms and Germany's Mercedes-Benz, with differing solutions, already could meet the most stringent standards proposed. The Honda used a stratified charge engine, an internal-combustion engine developed by an American inventor that Detroit had tested and cast aside because it was too small to power the large cars the industry favored in the 1950s and 1960s. The Mazda employed a rotary engine with a thermal reactor that burned off the noxious gases. The Mercedes sported a diesel engine that, for all the smell and smoke of the exhaust, was less polluting than any of Detroit's internal-combustion engines. Significantly, all three alternatives to the conventional automobile engine had been developed outside Detroit, once the unchallenged automotive capital of the world.

While engineers grappled with the air pollution their internal-combustion engines generated, corporate lawyers massed to defend their employer against attack from yet another quarter—the threat of an antitrust action, specifically a move to sever Chevrolet from General Motors.

From the last days of the Eisenhower administration, a small team of attorneys within the Department of Justice had studied the automobile industry, weighing possible antitrust suits. In 1961, they focused upon General Motors, by that time firmly the industry leader, and after the Ford double-shift in prices, the acknowledged price-setter as well. By 1965, Eugene Metzger, a young staff attorney, had drafted a 104-page complaint arguing,

---

* Starkman's hiring was virtually unprecedented for General Motors, which prided itself on promotion from within. It also could be read as a confession that the company lacked a candidate of sufficient authority in its own ranks. As assistant vice-president of the university, Starkman also served on the state of California's Air Resources Board. Accepting General Motors' offer, Starkman told reporters, "I wanted to be sure I'd be doing something worthwhile and not just being a front piece . . . I became convinced the corporation wasn't willing to continue wearing the black hat" (Los Angeles *Times,* February 2, 1971, p. 3). Within a year, General Motors also had hired as vice-president for personnel a Harvard School of Business professor, Stephen Fuller.

as did the successful Du Pont divestiture case, that the mergers Billy Durant had brought about a half-century earlier were no longer legal. Because of those mergers, Metzger's draft alleged, General Motors "monopolizes the manufacture, sale and distribution of automobiles." Metzger was going for the jugular, challenging forty of the acquisitions and seeking a court order that would require the corporation "to divest itself of said acquired companies and to reconstitute itself into a sufficiently large number of companies to accomplish a restoration of competitive conditions."

In the closing months of the Johnson administration, eight years after the Department of Justice had begun its investigation, and despite virtual unanimity among the staff lawyers and economists that the suit should be brought, the case was effectively shelved. Because of indecision, fear of the untested theory of a "shared monopoly," and the extensive investment of staff resources the case inevitably would require, and perhaps for presumed political reasons, the head of the department's antitrust division never recommended that the action be filed. As a former Department of Justice lawyer testified, "The fact that most Antitrust staff members who worked on the GM matter during my tenure did so with only one eye on the law may largely account for the Division's failure to act. Assistant attorneys general as well as attorneys general, regardless of their background, promptly learn about politics and the risks involved in sticking out their necks."

While President Johnson's Department of Justice was reluctant to pursue the big case, it was quick to settle two significant suits filed during Eisenhower and Kennedy years. In 1965, the department and General Motors agreed to a consent order mandating that General Motors aid would-be competitive bus manufacturers. Seeking divestiture, the federal suit had been brought nine years earlier, after General Motors had captured 85 percent of all new buses sold, leaving four rivals to scramble for the meager crumbs. Instead of forcing the case to trial, government attorneys drafted a court order by which GM agreed to sell to competitive bus manufacturers General Motors parts, engines, and transmissions; to permit bus companies to use General

Motors Acceptance Corporation financing even if they purchased non-General Motors buses; and to allow other bus manufacturers free use of General Motors' bus patents.

Though the reasons for the settlement never were revealed, the government apparently had opted for the consent agreement because General Motors had but one bus-manufacturing facility. Its forced sale, in effect, would merely transfer the monopoly from General Motors to another company, without stimulating competition. The suit was, in any event, successful. By the time the consent order expired in 1975, General Motors' competitors—then including American Motors and Grumman Aircraft—had snared more than 50 percent of the enlarged bus business.

Nonetheless, to those who insisted on breaking up General Motors, the bus case appeared a "sellout" and a parallel locomotive case an abandonment of principle. In 1961, a federal grand jury in New York City had returned a criminal indictment charging that General Motors monopolized production and sale of diesel locomotives through reciprocity: the corporation allegedly promised to ship its automobiles and parts over those railroads which bought General Motors locomotives. Compounding the criminal case, the Kennedy Department of Justice also brought a civil action seeking General Motors' divestiture of the locomotive business.

The government abandoned the criminal case in 1964, saying only that its evidence was "stale" and too scanty to prove the reciprocity allegation. Three years later, the civil suit was closed out for the same reason. By then General Motors held more than 90 percent of the business and was turning out five locomotives per day. It had one competitor, a company making switch engines.

The federal government did press one merger challenge to divestitute during the Johnson years, a case attacking General Motors' acquisition in 1953 of the Euclid Road Machinery Company. In August 1967, the corporation announced that it would sell two Euclid plants manufacturing off-highway dump trucks while retaining a third factory where it produced crawler tractors, front-end loaders, and scrapers. (The three had been developed after the 1953 acquisition of Euclid and, in effect, represented an entry into a new field by innovation rather than acquisition.)

Department of Justice attorneys did score a major victory against the corporation and three Chevrolet dealers' organizations in southern California in an antitrust case that sprang not from manufacturing, but from sales practices. The corporation and dealers' groups had brought pressure on twelve dealers to stop them from selling automobiles at substantial markdowns through discount houses. After federal judges kicked both the government's criminal and civil cases out of court, the government appealed, with the United States Supreme Court ruling unanimously that the corporation and the dealers' groups had engaged in "a classic conspiracy in restraint of trade." Within days, the discount houses were selling Chevrolets again, as well as other automobiles, for as little as $250 above wholesale prices.

Over the years the federal government had brought no less than eighteen antitrust actions against the world's largest industrial enterprise. The government claimed victory in thirteen— either by convictions, pleas, civil judgments, or consent decrees—yet the nation's largest manufacturer when the first action was filed during the Depression remained the nation's largest manufacturer thirty years later.

Paradoxically, by 1974, General Motors was defending its mammoth size as crucial to its very survival. Pointing out that the four largest firms in Japan sold 81 percent of all cars in that country, the four largest French companies 80 percent in France, the British "Big Four" 79 percent, and the Italians 78 percent, General Motors argued that "the nature of the automobile business seems to call for large size which will result in fairly high levels of 'concentration.'" The four largest in the United States sold 85 percent of all passenger cars and had never sold less than three-quarters since 1922. Size, even of monopolistic proportions, was necessary for survival.

The likelihood that the courts could or would address the situation dwindled year by year. The Nixon administration openly favored the conglomeration movement; the abbreviated Ford administration remained passive. "It doesn't seem to matter

which party is running Washington," retired government economist E. Wayles Browne sighed in an interview in 1974. "Nothing really happens to any of the big companies like General
Motors, Exxon, or Telephone." Even the most passionate of
big-business critics could not be sanguine. There is a *Realpolitik*
of big business. "General Motors will not be decomposed because that company is accepted as an integral component of the
country's structure, having parity with at least the Commonwealth of Pennsylvania," political scientist Andrew Hacker decided in 1971.

From the beginning to the end of the 1970s, the focus on antitrust would shift from the courts to half-hearted attempts at legislative reform. In 1977, Attorney General Griffin Bell said
shared-monopoly cases in which three or four companies effectively dominated an industry had become "too large for the
courts and would be most appropriately considered by the legislative branch." But just such a bill had died three years before in
the Senate Judiciary Committee after extensive hearings on an
industrial reorganization act. There simply was no consensus.
"It's hard to arouse people," Mark Green, director of the Corporate Accountability Research Group in Washington, D.C.,
concluded. "People don't die in antitrust."

Moreover, what attorney or judge could unscramble the eggs
Frederic Donner had whipped together more than a decade before? Ostensibly, Donner's plan to fashion a single unit out of the
far-flung assembly plants run by the automotive divisions was
intended to create a more efficient, responsive organization.
Never mind that this centralization was Sloanist heresy; the creation of the General Motors Assembly Division was also a cunning antitrust strategy.

If threatened Chevrolet no longer controlled its own manufacturing plants, and those factories turned out as many as four
different marques, it would be harder for antitrust attorneys to
break up General Motors. Thus, in 1965, ignoring the objections
from the automotive divisions, Donner transferred six paired
Fisher Body and Chevrolet factories, eight Buick–Oldsmobile–
Pontiac facilities, and a new "4-in-1" plant in Oakland, California, into a single assembly division. (The remaining Chevrolet
factories fell to GMAD in 1968 and 1971.)

The new boy on the block set out to prove that it was as hard-nosed as any of the auto divisions and even more cost-conscious. As GMAD asserted control, new managers reorganized assembly lines, trimming "excess" workers, enforcing a discipline not seen in the auto industry since World War II, when employees had accepted the pace in the interests of the war effort. Workers rebelled; strikes followed in eight of the first ten plants the new division took over, the young taskmasters of GMAD boasted.

In a parallel move, the corporation instituted an ongoing effort to standardize the 15,000 component parts of an automobile among the five car lines. The more parts the automobiles shared, the easier the changeover on the production line from slower- to quicker-selling models and the easier to produce on the same line virtually identical Chevrolets, Buicks, Pontiacs, and Oldsmobiles. The family differences that had distinguished a Buick from an Oldsmobile disappeared one by one. No more were division general managers permitted such idiosyncratic trademarks as the "mouseholes" of the postwar Buick. Mouseholes cost money.

Before the end of the 1960s, the Chevrolet Monza, Pontiac Sunbird, and Buick Skyhawk; the Buick Special and Pontiac Tempest; and the Chevrolet Camaro and Pontiac Firebird were strikingly similar. The more the cars blended into a General Motors crowd, the less important was their divisional name. In keeping with the centralization effort and the resulting loss of individuality among the automotive divisions, General Motors instituted a $275 million corporate-identity program in mid-1968. Signs announcing "GM—Mark of Excellence" were to go up over the rooftops of 12,000 dealers, overshadowing the Chevrolet, Pontiac, or Cadillac nameplates.

None of Donner's centralization effort sat well with the auto men, many of whom spent their entire careers in one division, sometimes in one department. As a later General Motors president recalled, "When I moved from Oldsmobile to Pontiac, I thought it just terrible."

It fell to Edward Cole to convince them, *his* people, that the centralization of engineering and marketing was best for the corporation. After all, Ed Cole himself had come to understand the wisdom of it, but then Edward Nicholas Cole knew when an argument was lost on the fourteenth floor and how to take orders. Those two capacities outweighed all the shortcomings that might have barred him from the presidency of the company in another era.

The former student at General Motors Institute—the wholly owned technical school that produced cadres of narrowly focused engineers for the company—had learned the intricacies of corporate politics well enough to overcome his past errors. It was the single-minded Cole who was responsible for the Corvair, who had defended it beyond the endurance of everyone but Ralph Nader, and who, as the legal settlements piled up, defended it still. Not his engineers but the financial men had vetoed the necessary stabilizing bar as too costly.

Cole's ability to compromise with Donner, Roche, and the financial figures dominating the board of directors even overcame what would have been a further black mark irredeemable but a few years before: he was divorced and had remarried—his second wife an outspoken woman. As the New York *Times* discreetly put it, "Some thought this sealed his career in an industry whose leaders have come from small Midwestern towns and have stayed married to their high school sweethearts."

Cole once had a reputation as a man who liked to "kick hell out of the status quo," to innovate. But at fifty-eight, after thirty-seven years scrambling over dead and wounded rivals, by 1967 Cole had come to accept the dominance of the financial men within the corporation. Ordered to discontinue the corporation's covert racing endeavors after criticism of the renewed attention upon speed and horsepower, Cole dutifully clamped down. When Jim Roche complained of a revived emphasis on youth and speed in General Motors' $250 million worth of advertisements, Cole warned advertising executives that "we simply are not being realistic to put such heavy emphasis on appealing to the under-thirty-one group in our advertising. The potential simply isn't there—either in numbers or in purchasing power." Confronted with government "meddling" in auto safety, Cole had pressured the divisions to conform, a logical position, but one that in its very logic angered the auto men. But most irritating to his former colleagues in the divisions, Cole endorsed the increasing centralization Donner had outlined and Roche was implementing daily. Abandoning the "cut-and-try" engineering the divisions favored, the construction of multiple prototypes and testing of them, Cole as vice-president in charge of the car and truck divisions, and then as head of the operations staff, opted for computer-generated designs. The computer eliminated the engineers' intuition, turning them into servants of a printout, building what the numbers told them to build.

With Donner's retirement on November 1, 1967, Roche moved up to the chairmanship of the board, and Cole, "the engineer who understood the financial side," stepped into Roche's old office. In tapping Cole, Donner and Roche passed over Bunkie Knudsen, the only other serious candidate, who had a string of successes at both Pontiac and Chevrolet, in favor of a team player. Three months later, Knudsen, the most successful of the automobile men in the previous decade, resigned. Independent, a man who bore the auto-making tradition of his father, Knudsen realized that he would never follow in Big Bill's footsteps as president of General Motors. One week after he resigned, Knudsen was named president of the Ford Motor Company, a bittersweet appointment perhaps, for his father might have idly dreamed of that office a half-century earlier when the Danish machinist first made his mark on Henry Ford's production lines.

Ostensibly, Roche and Cole complemented each other—one the grandfatherly administrator, the other the dedicated engineer. But if Cole had believed he was to direct the production aspects of the business, he was gradually disillusioned; even there, financial analysts held sway, forcing more and more uniformity upon the automotive divisions, erasing long-nurtured product differences.

Soon rumors of antagonism between Cole and Roche circulated in the General Motors Building. Not once, the gossipmongers said, had Roche ever set foot in Cole's office; instead, Roche summoned the president. The Cole–Roche antagonism seeped into the open by 1969, the two men disagreeing in public statements. Cole was complaining of financial staff "meddling in product decisions about which they knew nothing." Retaliating,

Richard Terrell, head of the financial staff, wandered about Bloomfield Hills cocktail parties, sneering, "No one is president of General Motors. Ed Cole is just the chief engineer."

Nearing the end of his forty-four-year career with the corporation, Cole had lost the zest that had marked his rise through the engineering ranks. "If I was your age," he told forty-eight-year-old John DeLorean, "I'd get the hell out of here so fast that you wouldn't believe it. The opportunities in this business are gone. Especially for a guy like you who can get things done. There are a lot of people around here who should stay up here [on the fourteenth floor] because this is the best they can do. The system protects them. But the opportunities for you are too great."

Lost opportunities, centralization, whatever the reason, General Motors seemingly had lost momentum by the end of the decade. In the United States, its market share had dropped to 45 percent, where it stood in 1940; the revitalized imports, with a 15-percent share, had replaced the flagging independents of old. Overseas, despite a growth rate of 250 percent in car sales during the previous decade, General Motors subsidiaries had grown by only 85 percent. With increased prosperity in Europe and Japan, the foreign market would grow twice as fast as the domestic, yet General Motors had no clear design to nab a larger share.

In the United States, where motor vehicles multiplied twice as fast as the population, the corporation had left the lower end of the market to imports, preferring to concentrate on the big-ticket, big-profit intermediate and large cars. Ceded a 10-percent market share—industry observers believed General Motors was prepared to tolerate that much infringement on its turf—the Lilliputians had gone on to take another 5 percent. Gulliver seemed helpless; General Motors had no domestically produced alternative.

The malaise spread to the non-automotive divisions. Frigidaire was losing money. Defense sales continued to decline, despite the corporation's investment in research and development facilities; the nation's largest corporation, the foundation of an established, low-technology industry, ranked just seventeenth among contractors for the increasingly sophisticated Department of Defense.

Roche and Cole had bulled the massive enterprise into a re-structured alignment. Roche had imparted some sense of social responsibility to corporate officers—though its implementation too often was in inverse relationship to corporate profits. There were still embarrassments that caused Roche "to go limp," as one General Motors executive put it.

Confronted with rising costs due to warranty claims, Chevrolet's general sales manager, Robert Lund, notified his 6,000 dealers that "Unless a safety defect is discovered, no warranty work is to be performed unless requested by the customer and needed." The letter reflected a "shocking insensitivity" to the public, one rueful General Motors executive groaned. Ed Cole could only growl, "We've got to find a way to communicate to the public in their [sic] terms, not our terms. This is one of the things we've been a little stupid about, in my view."

Try as Roche and Cole might to stir the corporation, General Motors remained the nay-sayer—opposing reform as unnecessary and protesting ever more stringent safety, pollution, and crashworthiness regulations as "impossible to meet," then grudgingly coming up with devices to meet the standards a year before the deadlines set by unyielding legislators.

General Motors' opposition seemed reflexive. Angered by testimony that the average five-mile-per-hour crash resulted in a $200 damage claim, Congress mandated in 1969 that auto makers fit bumpers capable of withstanding a five-mile-per-hour bump on their 1973 models. General Motors' lobbyists bitterly opposed the legislation as costly, unnecessary, unwanted by the public—on every conceivable ground but the real reason, the fear that crashworthy bumpers of uniform height would restrict styling options. Rebuffed, the automobile companies promptly introduced such bumpers with no visible effect upon sales a year before the deadline. The corporation's credibility slipped another notch.

Even when General Motors did move voluntarily to install the energy-absorbing steering column, a significant safety device, the accomplishment had all the thumbprints of a face-saving move after the losing struggle against federal safety legislation. There were still too many other innovations the corporation overlooked, or refused to adopt: disc brakes, standard on European automobiles for a decade; Chrysler's electronic ignition; radial tires; but most important, most basic of all, the development of economical, fuel-efficient automobiles. The average imported car easily doubled the gas mileage of General Motors' fleet, was generally cheaper to repair and insure, and appeared better constructed—matters of some concern to the average motorist who spent from sixteen to twenty-one cents per mile on his ever-depreciating automobile in 1970.

Yet to judge from the progression of new models, General Motors stood firm against change—because it would involve costly retooling and because it might upset even further the long-settled marketing strategies that assumed customers bought on the basis of ego-appeasing design. From the vantage point of the fourteenth floor of the General Motors Building, there was little reason for overhaul. The company was selling more twelve-miles-to-the-gallon autos and trucks than ever before, 5.2 million in 1969 alone. But at the same time it was groping, living off accumulated fat while fumbling for new products and new customers. It no longer led the market, dictating consumer choices by its offerings. For all of its marketing surveys, the corporation had lost touch with its customers and, noting the rising level of small-car sales, sensed vaguely that something was out of joint.

Despite staggering advertising budgets, General Motors—all of Detroit—no longer could generate the excitement that once surrounded the automobile. "The novelty and status of car ownership are long gone," the sober *Wall Street Journal* concluded. "People today look at their cars as appliances to get them economically from place to place and to be replaced when they wear out."

To General Motors, this was the ultimate betrayal.

17

Taking on the Big Guy

They came early, crowding through the doors of Detroit's Cobo Hall and sporting red-and-white badges that urged the stockholders to "Tame GM." For most of these young people General Motors' annual stockholders' meeting on May 22, 1970, was the first they had ever attended. While they owned a share or two, they did not consider themselves capitalists, or even investors, but more like poker players anteing before the cards were dealt.

Members of a hastily organized Campaign to Make General Motors Responsible—that cumbersome name quickly shortened to "Campaign GM"—these young people had few illusions. Visionary they might have been, intent on transforming the corporation into a force for what they deemed social good, but as practiced veterans of earlier political and civil-rights campaigns, they were realistic enough to understand that huge institutions did not budge without huge pushes. Newtonian laws applied to social movements too.

The playfully provocative "Tame GM" badges and the deadly

455

serious Campaign GM had grown out of a Project on Corporate Responsibility, organized late in 1969 by two Washington attorneys, lately Harvard roommates, Geoffrey Cowan and Philip W. Moore III. Though endorsed by Ralph Nader, the project to open General Motors to public scrutiny was not one of Nader's rapidly expanding investigative groups.

On February 7, 1970, with Nader's blessing, the project launched Campaign GM. Owners of twelve shares of General Motors common stock, Cowan, Moore, and two colleagues intended to solicit stockholders' proxy votes for two propositions: creation of a shareholders' committee for corporate responsibility, and the addition of three public members to the board of directors. It was a modest start; originally they had proposed nine ballot measures to be voted on by shareholders, only to be rejected by the corporation. With the intervention of the federal Securities and Exchange Commission, they succeeded in placing those two on the ballot.

Campaign GM began soliciting votes for its proposals, largely by contacting institutional investors, especially foundations and universities that might be thought of as more civic-minded than the average investor. Roche reacted by mailing a letter to the company's 1.3 million stockholders claiming the proxy proposals were meant merely "to harass the corporation and its management and promote the particular economic and social views" of the sponsors. If adopted, the proposals "would restrict management's ability to meet its responsibilities to the stockholders and the public."

The proxy votes were returned and counted, the outcome settled as expected in management's favor by the time Roche gaveled the stockholders' meeting to order. Cobo Hall was crowded, the 2,895 stockholders and 130 reporters spilling over to a second room where loudspeakers had been set up. Campaign GM could claim that much of a victory; both reporters and stockholders had quadrupled in attendance since the *pro forma* 1969 convocation. The meeting rambled for six-and-a-half hours, sometimes tense, Roche as chairman on his feet the entire time, courteous and unflinching, but quick to cut off the microphone when Campaign GM spokesmen pressed questions.

A decade earlier, the four organizers of Campaign GM—holders of twelve shares of General Motors common stock, or .0000042 percent of the company's 286 million shares—might have been sitting impassively among the dark-suited executives in the first row. But a decade of social activism, a civil-rights movement, an anti-Vietnam war campaign, and the rise of a potent environmental lobby had transformed these young people from potential corporate plodders into minority stockholders determined to remold the massive corporation in their own socially aware image.

The meeting ran late into the dinner hour when Roche finally turned to Campaign GM's proposal to add three public members—a black, a woman, and an environmental scientist—to the corporation's board.

A young black woman then studying law at the University of California at Los Angeles asked Roche, "Why are there no blacks on the board?"

"Because none of them have been elected," Roche answered coolly.

Unimpressed, Barbara Williams snorted, "I expected better of you. Why are there no blacks on the board?"

The young black woman had nettled Roche. *He* asked such probing questions; he did not answer them like some schoolboy remiss in his homework.

"No black has been nominated, and no black has been elected."

Even from the paternal Roche, the answer infuriated Williams. "Why are there no blacks on the board?" she repeated.

"I have answered the question."

Williams, her voice trembling, dismissed him. "You have failed not only the shareholders but the country. Why are there no women on the board?"

Roche struggled to control his temper-triggered stutter. Blacks or women, as representatives of special-interest groups on the board, he replied, would not serve the interests of management and the stockholders. "Our directors are selected on the basis of their ability to make a contribution to the success of General Motors," he continued.

It was an evasive, even foolish explanation in the eyes of the Campaign GM activists, a typical example of the unaccountable authority they believed General Motors wielded.

Williams would have none of it. "You have not adequately answered those questions," she concluded, then sat down amid cheers from her supporters.

Whatever Barbara Williams' moral victory, as expected, the stockholders overwhelmingly turned down the two Campaign GM proposals, the reformers polling less than 3 percent of the outstanding shares. Still, the young people had scored a tactical victory: several large institutions—not including Harvard, to the chagrin of Campaign GM's founders—voted for the reform measures. Others, led by the Massachusetts Institute of Technology, Alfred P. Sloan, Jr.'s favorite educational charity, abstained. MIT's neutrality came as a shock to the corporation; James R. Killian, Jr., honorary chairman of MIT's governing board, had served for eleven years on General Motors' board of directors, a measure of both the close link between the two organizations and the school's extensive stock holdings. Other institutions, though voting with the directors, warned that unless changes were made, they might cast their votes for the insurgents the following year. The Rockefeller Foundation, scoring General Motors for its "defensive and negative attitude," added: "As stockholders and citizens we urge that management respond affirmatively to the goals of the proposals and search for acceptable ways to realize them."

Roche would do just that. Out of pride, he could not accede to the public pressures brought down by the reformers and "radicals" of Campaign GM. But privately, the gunfire of that hot July in 1967 still faintly remembered, he acknowledged the need for change.

Roche's first move was to recruit the Reverend Leon H. Sullivan, minister of Philadelphia's largest black church, to the board of directors. The founder of a minority job-training program that had spread to ninety cities, and a one-time strategic planner of Southern boycotts promoted by the Reverends Martin Luther King and Ralph Abernathy, Sullivan was a hardheaded proponent of black capitalism who dismissed black militants with a reminder: "Black power without brain power and green power is no power."

Sullivan was a departure in more than race. "I told Mr. Roche he should have no illusions about what I am," said Sullivan. "He knows I am a man who expresses his opinions, and that I will not be tied to the traditions of the board. I'm more interested in human returns than capital returns. My main concern is helping to improve the position of black people in America. I want to be a voice from the outside on the inside."

This first step was easy, for Roche himself was determined to implement an equal-opportunity program. Other steps were more difficult, but necessary, as the 1971 stockholders' meeting and the threatened return of Campaign GM loomed. In August 1970, Roche effectively co-opted one Campaign GM plank by creating a Public Policy Committee composed of nonemployee directors. The committee was charged with overseeing "every phase of corporate activities that relate to public policy and [to] make appropriate recommendations to management or the full board." By the time the advocates of corporate reform returned to Cobo Hall, Roche also had arranged for the deposit of $5 million of company funds in black-owned banks, had recruited an outside science advisory committee to guide a new corporate vice-president for environmental affairs, and had allocated an additional $26 million for research on pollution control.

Campaign GM was not the only stockholder group critical of corporate policy. In February 1971, the presiding bishop of the Episcopal church in the United States, John E. Hines, wrote to Roche urging that the corporation end its manufacturing in undeniably racist South Africa. The church, which held some 12,500 shares of General Motors stock, warned that South Africa's apartheid policies "would inevitably result in the destruction of foreign investments."

In the face of Roche's conciliatory moves during the preceding year—Nader remained dubious, wary that they were merely "cosmetic"—Campaign GM fared less well in 1971 than it had in 1970. Despite Reverend Sullivan's passionate backing—the first time a director publicly deviated from corporate policy—the Episcopal church's recommendation that General Motors withdraw from South Africa went down to overwhelming defeat. Borrowing Sullivan's argument of being "a voice from the outside on the inside," Roche argued that by example General Motors could improve conditions for black and colored (mixed racial parentage) peoples.*

In dealing with Campaign GM, Roche showed himself able to co-opt the best ideas of others, at least those that would not "be unsound business practice for us." Within months of Campaign GM recommending that the corporation publish "hard statistics" in its annual report revealing its progress in pollution control, safety, and minority employment, General Motors was preparing just such a report. Confronted again at the 1971 annual meeting with the proposal that the corporation add women to its board of directors—National Organization for Women President Patricia Burnett pointed out that the majority of stockholders were women—the board would do just that. (By 1976, there were two women directors—one a trust banker and the other the former United States Ambassador to the Court of St. James, Anne L. Armstrong, not exactly the average housewife-consumer NOW originally had in mind, but women nonetheless.)

The seven-hour annual meeting, the longest in the company's history, was to be Roche's last as chairman. For seven hours he had benignly, even paternally presided. He made only one slip— one that suggested neither he nor the corporation he headed had been purged of a lifetime's thoughtless prejudice. In the midst of questions from Campaign GM supporters, while defending the stockholder elections, Roche blurted, "We are a public corporation, owned by free, white—" He faltered, suddenly embar-

*After 1972, the corporation apparently devoted considerable effort—and at least $4.5 million in integrating its facilities in South Africa—to providing equal employment opportunity for its more than 2,000 non-white employees, and much-needed housing loans. It also has secured specific exemption from various government acts intended to reinforce apartheid, permitting General Motors South Africa to promote non-whites to supervisory and skilled jobs, to negotiate with black unions, and to integrate its plants, cafeterias, and restrooms. General Motors also has taken the initiative in enlisting other corporations to follow what it has dubbed the "Sullivan principles," six measures contrary to South African government policy but in keeping with the spirit, if not the strategy, of the original Episcopal church motion. General Motors has an abiding interest for remaining in South Africa: GMSA is a $200-million-a-year enterprise. Though GMSA barely managed to break even in the last half-decade of the 1970s, General Motors believes future corporate growth will necessarily come from overseas markets.

rassed, then recovered to add over the groans and sardonic cheers of Campaign GM members, "Umm . . . and . . . and black and yellow people all over the world."

Roche was less successful in coping with the newly aroused United Auto Workers, but by 1970, both the company and the union realized a strike was inevitable. Not since the dismal winter of 1945–46 had the United Auto Workers singled out General Motors, preferring instead to deal with the much weaker Ford and Chrysler. A settlement with the second- or third-largest of the auto makers had the same effect as an agreement wrung from General Motors; a tacit agreement among the three companies held that a settlement for one was a settlement for all. If nothing else, more or less uniform labor contracts removed a possible variable in setting prices and helped confirm General Motors as the industry's price leader.

After twenty-five years—good years economically, but years of growing discontent among assembly-line workers who had grown old in grimy factories—it was General Motors' turn. "The average person, the average worker," said the vice-chairman of the UAW bargaining committee, James Hensley, "likes to take on the big guy, the giant. And GM is a giant." By comparison, Chrysler, the seventh-largest manufacturer in the country, was "a pygmy," Hensley explained. "I think people kind of felt it was their duty to take on GM rather than Ford, Chrysler, or AMC."

In addition, rank-and-file union members nursed a long-standing animus toward the largest of the auto companies, an antagonism that had grown since the assembly division assumed control of manufacturing. Incessantly pressured to boost their productivity, workers had become rebellious. Minor grievances once settled by foremen erupted into costly local strikes. In the decade prior to 1970, work stoppages increased fourfold and days lost rose to five times what they had been in the 1950s.

"A strike against General Motors isn't just a strike, it's a crusade," Douglas Fraser, then head of the union's Chrysler department and later president of the UAW, insisted.

The union had three demands: a wage increase of $2.50 per hour; a return to the unlimited cost-of-living clause Walter

Reuther had bargained away in 1967 in order to get skilled workers a larger pay raise than production-line employees; and full retirement after thirty years of service, regardless of age. The first two were pragmatic, while the third became the emotional war cry. Initially, Reuther had opposed the retirement concept; he had taken it as his own only when he realized the depth of rank-and-file sentiment in favor of it. "Thirty-and-out" buttons sprouted throughout Detroit.

As militant as the UAW was, General Motors' management was equally determined to hold the line. A recession, reborn competition from foreign manufacturers, and reduced productivity all had cut profits, even as labor costs increased. In February 1970, James Roche threw down the gauntlet in an uncharacteristically harsh speech, asserting that General Motors had "been able to recover only a fraction of recent costs through greater efficiency, only another fraction through price increases." Because of rising costs—$45 million in health insurance premiums alone in just the last year—General Motors in 1964 earned "about $25 million *more* on a sales volume that was some $7 billion *less* than in 1969."

Two months later, Reuther effectively took up the challenge, telling delegates to the annual UAW convention in Atlantic City, "In the last ten years, including 1969, where Mr. Roche said they were suffering a serious profit squeeze, the General Motors Corporation earned $14.8 billion. Or to put it another way, every three and a half years, General Motors had an income—a profit—equal to its total investment." If there was a squeeze, "it was on the workers who haven't enough money to do the things they need to do for their kids. That is where the squeeze is," Reuther retorted.

Roche dug in his heels, stiffened by Frederic Donner, now retired, but still the major influence on the board of directors. Behind them stood the Nixon administration, which had made control of inflation its first priority even as it fueled that inflation with increased appropriations for the widening war in Southeast Asia.

Inflation struck hardest at the workingman, including the relatively better paid auto worker earning an average of $5.76 per hour, including fringe benefits. Reminded of the late Charles Wilson's contention that "it is not primarily wages that push up prices, it is primarily prices that pull up wages," a General Motors executive told reporter William Serrin that sometimes "we would like to go out and piss on his grave."

The corporation could afford to stand firm—for the moment anyway. Anticipating eventual concessions, General Motors had announced a price increase averaging $208 on its automobiles. Meanwhile, despite the recession abroad, the company luxuriated in record totals of working capital and stockholders' equity. The company also held some $3 billion in nonautomotive investments, time deposits, and government bonds, cushion enough for even a protracted walkout. A strike certainly would slow recovery from the national recession and hurt corporate sales and profits, but a strike was preferable to capitulation.

Donner especially felt the erosion by unions and government of General Motors' once unhindered power. Throughout the 1960s, the corporation had bent to increasing government demands for auto safety, smog control, and curbed factory pollution; for improved working conditions in the plants; for less flamboyant advertising claims and broader warranties; and even for dismemberment of the corporation itself. While General Motors would go to court on the most onerous of these, the company gradually came to realize that it was easier to work with the government than against it.

"Business and government can ill-afford to be adversaries," Roche concluded in a conciliatory address to the Illinois Manufacturers Association in 1968. "So mutual are our interests, so formidable are our challenges, that times demand our strengthened alliance." Without acknowledging that General Motors was clearing its annual price increases with the White House—Lyndon Johnson was "jawboning" the nation's pivotal manufacturer to reduce inflationary pressures—Roche concluded, "Today, business and government are each becoming more involved in the affairs of each other."

If government and corporation had drawn closer together, corporation and labor had not. A bewildering sea change had come over the work force, younger now, more heavily populated with less-educated blacks who settled on the unattractive assembly-line jobs only because there was nothing else available. Rejecting values their trusting parents had held to disillusionment, confronting their own insecure futures amidst rising inflation and escalating taxes, younger workers were demanding more control over their lives.

Employees, noted one personnel manager for an automobile manufacturer, were less concerned about losing their jobs, or staying with the same employer; less willing to tolerate the unpleasant working conditions of the assembly line; even less ready to accept the monotony of producing an automobile every minute for seven hours and forty-five minutes each day; and quick to challenge anyone in authority who sought to enforce work rules. "The traditional American work ethic—the concept that hard work is a virtue and a duty—will undergo additional erosion," he lamented.

In 1969, Roche asserted, General Motors had lost 13.3 million man-hours in work stoppages. (He failed to note that the union had filed 250,000 formal contract grievances that year, one for every two workers in domestic factories. Unsatisfied grievances led to wildcat strikes.) Absenteeism, once negligible, had grown to 5 percent of the work force each day, and in some plants soared to a crippling 15 percent on Mondays and Fridays.

The anecdote had become part of the folklore of the automobile industry by the time Douglas Fraser retold it to reporter William Serrin. Someone asked a welder why he had taken a day off, willing to live on four days' pay a week rather than five. "The welder stopped, raised his welding gun, tipped back his visor, and said, 'Because I can't get by in three.'"

By the spring of 1970, union–management negotiations were swept along by an inevitability of their own. Having staked out unyielding positions, neither side could back down. The union position hardened even more when on May 9, before the two sides had met formally, Walter Reuther and his wife were killed in the crash of a light plane. Long-winded, vain about it, Reuther had understood how to make the canny compromise look like a grand victory; his replacement as union president, Leonard Woodcock, for all his intelligence, lacked Reuther's capacity for leadership and oratory.

Woodcock had waited long for this opportunity. Forced to drop out of Detroit City College during the Depression, he had worked at Detroit Gear and Machine seven twelve-hour days a week for $29.40. He became a union organizer for the American Federation of Labor at Detroit Gear; when the UAW incorporated all automobile-related plants in 1936, the Detroit Gear local became the largest in the struggling union. A former socialist, like Reuther, Woodcock had worked his way up to head of the union's General Motors department. Offered an ambassadorship to either Taiwan or Pakistan, or a subcabinet post in the Kennedy administration, Woodcock the loyal subaltern had turned down the offer when Reuther vetoed the move. (Ultimately, Woodcock would get his ambassadorship, a far more important position, when President Carter appointed him as the United States' envoy to the Peoples Republic of China.) With Reuther's death, Woodcock suddenly found himself in the post he had all but given up hope of holding, and believed he had to win major concessions from General Motors to retain his office. "If that Woodcock don't get 30-and-out, he is a short-term president," one Flint union member threatened.

Neither management nor union was prepared to compromise. At 12:01 on the morning of September 15, 1970, nearly 350,000 General Motors workers officially went on strike. Within a month, another 150,000 would be laid off by the corporation or its suppliers, though General Motors and the union cooperated to keep open fifteen plants manufacturing parts General Motors sold to its three domestic rivals.

By comparison with the earlier confrontations in 1936 and 1946, this was a placid, decidedly nonmilitant strike. The picketing was largely symbolic; only one local was overtly militant, and that was at the General Motors Proving Ground, where the major issue was social parity between the union's blue-collar skilled labor and white-collar, nonunion professionals.

Neither was there the hardship of earlier walkouts. The union began with a $120 million strike fund from which it paid as much as forty dollars weekly to a married worker with children. Supplementing this, the strikers obtained government food stamps, with some strikers also receiving welfare payments. Additionally, the union undertook to maintain the life and health insurance plans negotiated earlier, borrowing $23 million at 5-percent interest from General Motors to pay the premiums. Earl R. Bramblett, General Motors' vice-president for personnel, explained that the loan—to be repaid after the strike was settled—was extended to avoid bad publicity and the public image of the remorseless factory owner of old.

The two sides were far apart when they sat down on November 9 for the first serious bargaining session in seven weeks. The company had proposed a thirty-eight-cents-per-hour average wage increase; the union wanted an average of 61.5 cents. While willing to improve the cost-of-living adjustment (COLA), the corporation would not accede to the union's demand to "uncap" the COLA. General Motors also insisted on a minimum age of fifty-eight before a worker could take advantage of thirty-and-out, a stipulation the union already had rejected.

Both sides were running out of time, however. The union's strike fund would be depleted by December 1, raising the prospect of a levy on the salaries of 900,000 UAW members still employed. Meanwhile, General Motors was losing money, as much as $90 million in sales every day. The corporation had intended to hold out, regardless of how long it took, committed to gaining clauses in the contract which would increase productivity and reduce absenteeism. Privately, Donner, Roche, board of directors Vice-Chairman Richard Gerstenberg, and President Edward Cole already had agreed they could afford the wage demands, even if Roche had called them "inflationary."

General Motors could not hold out indefinitely. One-third of the lost sales never would be made up, as customers opted instead for Fords, Chryslers, or, even worse, the imports. Ford's new compact, the Pinto, had broken all sales records that company claimed, while the strikebound Chevrolet Vega compact languished. Roche also was feeling pressure from Richard Nixon's White House. While presidential advisors wanted to hold inflation in check, they were equally worried about the ongoing recession. A strikebound General Motors could not fulfill its expected role in leading the nation out of the slump.

Both sides, then, needed a settlement—and, needing a settlement, found the means on the fifty-ninth day. General Motors agreed to an average wage increase of fifty-one cents per hour, less than Woodcock had demanded originally, but enough to put the settlement in line with agreements reached in other industries by both teamsters and printers. The corporation agreed to uncap the COLA, but secured a postponement for a year. Both sides compromised, too, on thirty-and-out. At age fifty-eight, a worker could retire on a $500-per-month pension, with the retirement age to be lowered to fifty-six in 1972. Those who retired before reaching fifty-eight would receive reduced pensions. When a worker reached sixty-two and began receiving social security, the $500-per-month company pension would be reduced.

To help raise productivity, the union agreed to participate in a joint management–labor indoctrination program for new employees and accepted a twenty-cent wage differential for employees with less than three months' service. An automatic twenty-cents-per-hour wage boost at ninety days was thought a greater stimulus to keep new hires on the job.

The agreement ratified by the 379,000 General Motors employees who were union members, the majority of strikers went back to work on November 23. (A handful of local disputes had yet to be ironed out.) The walkout had lasted sixty-seven days and had cost General Motors at least $1 billion in profits. It also had cost the corporation the production of 1.5 million cars, Roche complained later, production that would not be made up. It had cost some twelve states an estimated $30 million in welfare benefits paid out to the families of striking workers. The federal government, the corporation estimated, had lost $1 billion in taxes. Hundreds of millions of retail dollars were never spent, $375 million in Michigan alone. It was by far the most costly strike in history.

In other ways, too, the settlement came dearly. An angry Nixon administration immediately termed it inflationary. General Motors would raise its prices—$24 within two weeks of the union's ratification of the contract—to cover the $1.40-per-hour wage boosts over the three-year term of the compact. The settlement also provided a model for contracts in other industries over the next six months; the post office, the copper and aluminum industry, aircraft and communication workers, and

steelworkers successively received 50-cents-per-hour wage
boosts and/or cost-of-living clauses.

Whatever their disagreements had been, company and union
were bonded more firmly than ever. The United Auto Workers
argued that the General Motors contract was "counter-
inflationary" since the anticipated wage increases would come
only after the government released its quarterly cost-of-living
reports. Similarly, Roche protested—resting his argument on the
twenty-year-old Wilson concept of a price–wage spiral—that
only six cents of the fifty-one-cent hourly boost in the first year
was "not tied in some way to past inflation or to productivity."
And if the historic productivity trend held true, even that six
cents would be covered.

Corporate executives and labor leaders agreed, necessarily,
since both were professional managers with an interest in keeping the assembly lines at work and increasing profits. (Woodcock, for example, had not worked in what Walter Reuther
called "the gold-plated sweatshops" since 1946, and that was
only for a short period in which to qualify as a delegate to the
union's annual convention.) Corporate executive and union official needed each other, used one another to prove managerial
competence. As one union member put it, "The union and the
company, they are more or less business partners."

The strike did more than savage General Motors' profits for
the year; it crippled the introduction of Chevrolet's Vega, the
promised "American car with size, economy, and performance
to serve the American people." With an additional flourish of
patriotic trumpets, General Motors had announced in 1968 that
its new small car, code-named the XP 887, would be launched
"to improve this country's balance of payments."

Once again General Motors had pirouetted with clumsy grace.
The failing Corvair lingering long on its death bed, General
Motors had happily turned its back on the low-profit, small-car
market. Only Ford and American Motors—Studebaker having
closed its doors once and for all in 1966—had covered the retreat
with compact cars.

General Motors' management was confused. The persistent
interest in a small car defied all the executives had been schooled

to believe: Americans wanted luxury, comfort, roominess—in short, the status that could come only from owning a large car. Yet foreign automobiles, including the impossibly ugly Volkswagen, steadily gained ground. Their styling similarly ran counter to Detroit's precepts. Italians were "exhibitionists" and the Mercedes was "laughable," General Motors' styling vice-president William Mitchell concluded. Indeed, was Mercedes' styling department "still alive?" he asked facetiously. As life itself seemed to Thomas Hobbes, so, too, the automobile industry considered the imports poor, nasty, brutish, and short, *Fortune* magazine concluded.

To attract those buyers interested in economy—a relative few, management assured itself—General Motors stepped up sales through its Buick dealers of its "captive import," the German-built Opel. Roche explained the decision in mid-1968 as a patriotic gesture of "fighting the foreign car problem by building the cars overseas and importing them to the United States."

Disdaining that feeble gesture, the Johnson administration issued a pointed warning in September 1968. The auto industry, said Assistant Secretary of the Treasury John R. Petty, was "an example of an area where new thinking is called for." Detroit's compact automobiles were "so far from what is needed that they have recently had to invent a new name—the subcompact—to describe the size of cars which are now entering our markets in volume from abroad," Petty asserted.

The criticism stung, implying that Detroit, once the very pride of American industry, no longer knew how to compete in the very market it had created. Two weeks later, Roche suddenly announced the XP 887, denying that government pressure had any influence on the decision to build a new small car. General Motors simply did not wish to appear to be "asleep at the switch," Roche explained.

The XP 887, widely publicized under that name during the next two years of its development, would be more than a foot shorter than any car in the General Motors array. It would be powered by "a new and entirely different engine, made possible only through the important advances in technology accomplished in our GM laboratories," Roche promised. "The new engine will allow a combination of economy, performance and durability not now available in this type of car." Equally important, the design would remain unchanged for at least four years, thus reducing the largest hidden cost of driving—depreciation.

Patriotism aside, the major factor in the decision to reenter the small-car market lay in Chevrolet's weakened position. During the early years of the 1960s, that division had done handsomely, happily filling the gap left by the retreating imports. Under Bunkie Knudsen, the division had sold as many as three of every ten passenger cars delivered in the United States. But the Corvair waned, and the second of General Motors' compacts, the Chevy II, was less an economy car than a somewhat scaled-down Buick. In time, Chevrolet bore the brunt of the resurgent imports, slipping steadily to just 22 percent of the passenger-car market by 1968. Whatever else was wrong with the division— model proliferation, overstaffing of white-collar positions, massive parts inventories—its sales and profits would never improve without a competitive small car.

Chevrolet also had management problems. An empire within an empire, it had grown unwieldy. "Chevrolet is such a big monster that you twist its tail and nothing happens at the other end for months and months. It is so gigantic that there isn't any way to really run it. You just sort of try and keep track of it," Knudsen's successor as general manager, Elliot "Pete" Estes, complained.

Sheer size had increased Chevrolet's inertia. Rival Ford seemingly had captured leadership in marketing innovations—first with the compact car, next with the sporty Mustang, then with a luxurious top-of-the-line model, and later in the recreational truck–van market. If nothing else, Chevrolet needed the XP 887 to lift its morale.

The division would have its new car and, soon enough, a new general manager, John DeLorean, to shepherd it into production. Peremptorily summoned from a Palm Springs golf course in February 1969, DeLorean was the third Pontiac alumnus following Knudsen and Estes to succeed to threefold larger Chevrolet. All three were auto men, engineers who had equated improved sales with greater horsepower, but DeLorean stood out.

DeLorean was young, at forty-four the youngest of all General Motors general managers, and he had been with the company just seventeen years. Further, he was the highly visible corporate rebel—a tall, strikingly handsome man who affected stylishly tailored clothes in a world of uniform wool suits. Vain about his looks—he dyed his graying hair black and lifted weights thrice weekly in a gymnasium—DeLorean had been twice wed and twice divorced. When he again began dating, as was his wont, the young models and actresses to whom he was attracted, a sympathetic Dollie Cole, second wife of the corporation's president, Edward Cole, warned him: "They are all shook up on the Fourteenth Floor. God! Don't get married again. You'd better cool it. All you've got to do is lay low and wait them out. Those guys will be gone in five years. Don't kick away your career now."

By his own admission General Motors' "token hippie," John DeLorean had not always been the maverick. As a young engineer, he had clipped his hair short and played the corporate game, never forgetting the story of the executive sent home in the late 1950s for wearing a brown suit. It was with his first successes as chief engineer at Pontiac in the early 1960s that he blossomed in long hair and colorful plumage, dieted off twenty pounds, and emerged, to the delight of otherwise bored reporters, as the auto industry's resident "character." DeLorean himself enjoyed press attention; he was always good for a quote or a story idea on a slow day, and his reputation grew correspondingly.

To Roche, Cole, and Knudsen, DeLorean appeared the ideal choice for Chevrolet; he was "with it," tuned to the younger market, the people they hoped to attract to the XP 887. Over no little opposition from other executives on the fourteenth floor, John Zachary DeLorean was named general manager of Chevrolet.

DeLorean's first problem with the XP 887 was its origin. "Chevy engineers were almost totally disinterested in the car," he later acknowledged. Their competitive concept had been passed over in favor of the XP 887, the first "corporate" car, designed not in an automotive division, but at the corporate level, and then farmed out to Chevrolet for production. The auto had been conceived by former Chevrolet general manager Ed Cole sometime around 1965, largely as a prospective entry, something to keep his own engineering juices flowing. Promoted from Chevrolet to the corporate staff as a vice-president and then in 1967 to the president's office succeeding John Gordon, Cole took the small-car designs with him.

When Donner and Roche determined to enter the subcompact market, Cole pushed hard for his design over rivals from both Chevrolet and Pontiac. The XP 887 was selected in part because Cole was president of the corporation, in part because he was a determined salesman in staff meetings, but largely because development of the car itself furthered the Donner–Roche program of centralization. Cole was the responsible engineer and styling vice-president William Mitchell the designer of the final product.

By all odds the XP 887 promised to be the most innovative automobile General Motors had produced in a generation. It would have a new aluminum engine. It would be built in a newly redesigned, highly automated, heavily publicized plant in Lordstown, Ohio, whose production the corporation touted as the acme of workmanship in America. Not since the Model-A had an automobile received the advance publicity afforded the XP 887. When in April 1970, a skywriting plane puffed, "Chevrolet Names It Vega 2300," virtually everyone in Detroit and millions elsewhere knew "it" was the widely heralded import fighter.*

The decision to promote the car long before its actual production, contrary to policy of old, was significant in itself. The corporate marketing staff finally had realized that the majority of those who bought imports simply were not interested in larger American cars. The Vega would compete only with the smaller imports, and since General Motors as yet had no entry in that market, any postponed purchase of an import could only benefit General Motors. The trick was to convince the public, by playing on patriotic themes, to wait and then buy American.

* Among other names tried and rejected in favor of the vaguely foreign-sounding Vega marque was "Gemini," an acronymic of "G-Mini"; and "Jiminy," from the Walt Disney cartoon character Jiminy Cricket.

The $18-million advance build-up also increased public expectations, which the car ultimately could not meet. Roche's first announcement of the size, a foot shorter than the Corvair, a foot longer than the Volkswagen; of the weight, 1900 pounds; and the price, under $2,000, was based solely on computer studies, not on a prototype. The promises evaporated with the delivery of the first prototype to the Milford Proving Grounds. After eight miles of driving on the test track, the front end of the Vega literally fell off. It would be only the first of many problems with the car: the cooling system proved inadequate and the engine block warped; the front disc brakes wore rapidly, or, worse, gave out suddenly; the combination of a faulty carburetor and ruptured muffler could lead to the automobile catching fire; the accelerator could jam open; and, most disconcerting of all, the rear wheels were liable to drop off due to an error in production that left the axle a fraction of an inch too short.

Roche's promised car was forgotten. As finally built, the aluminum engine with a cast-iron head weighed more than the conventional engine Ford intended for use in a rival compact, the Pinto. A foot longer and $300 more expensive, the Vega really did not compete with the lighter Volkswagen, Datsun, and Toyota.

DeLorean attempted to put up a brave front. At a press preview, he predicted that about half of Vega's anticipated 400,000 sales in the first year would be "conquests," largely over foreign-car dealers. Import sales, he predicted, would fall from the current 13 percent of the market to as little as 8 percent by the end of the model year. The Volkswagen would wither.

The key question, DeLorean told newsmen, was producing a car of high quality and overcoming "a basic skepticism about American manufacturers' ability to compete effectively and responsibly in this market. It's the American system that's being tested." Those who bought foreign cars carried with them into dealers' showrooms "an image of craftsmen in the Black Forest, building cars by hand," DeLorean conceded. His answer was the Lordstown plant itself, with its rows of automatic welders— indeed, an assembly line that had automated 88 percent of production, compared to the 20 to 40 percent in most automotive factories. In addition, "The high level of enthusiasm among employees at the Lordstown plant," he later enthused, "is producing craftsmanship to challenge any auto maker in the world."

Despite the handicaps—the sixty-seven-day strike throughout the corporation coinciding with the Vega's introduction in 1970 was the biggest—sales of the new car reached 323,000. It was not the 400,000 that had been thought a reasonable target; the Volkswagen continued unfazed, and the balance of payments dipped closer to a deficit.

Whatever remained of Vega's promise vanished on October 1, 1971, when the General Motors Assembly Division took over direction of the Lordstown plant. Seven hundred workers, including the bulk of those assigned to quality control, were summarily dismissed as supernumeraries. Four months later, harassed and angry, the remaining workers walked off the job in a three-week strike, shattering the image of craftsmanship the corporation had cultivated for Lordstown. Craftsmen did not strike—but then craftsmen were not asked to turn out 102 automobiles an hour, one every thirty-six seconds.

The press descended on Lordstown, seeing it, in the words of a *Wall Street Journal* editor, as Paradise Lost, a revolt of militant, youthful auto workers against the numbing, repetitive tasks assigned by subservience to automation. For six months the "Lordstown Syndrome" was a staple of newspaper editorials and television reports. Striking back at a corporation they considered ruthless, the workers were quick to point out to reporters defects in the cars; even the massive robot welders misfired, betraying the image so carefully wrought since mid-1968. Foremen approved faulty parts for installation—under pressure from plant managers, the workers claimed. In all, it appeared that the Vega was not assembled so much as it was flung together.

At Lordstown the dream died. The Vega was no more or no less a Chevrolet, a General Motors car after all, shoddy, tawdry, and eternally suspect. Interment followed with three mandatory safety-recall campaigns between April and July of 1972. The first concerned the fire threat, the second the possibility of the accelerator jamming, and the third and largest the undersized axle. By the time these campaigns were completed, 95 percent of the

Vegas built to that time had been recalled, with *Time* magazine editorializing:

If the world's largest and presumably most advanced manufacturing company cannot mass-produce a product without making a mistake that inconveniences half a million customers, who can? In a recent Harris Poll, only 30 percent of the people interviewed believed that the quality of American products had improved in the past year, down from 37 percent last year. Probably the time has come for the auto men and other manufacturers to slow their production lines and spend more time and money on checking out quality instead of concentrating on quantity.

The workers themselves resented descriptions of the strike as a sociological upheaval or generational clash. "*Playboy* called us long-haired hippies, spaced-out, or whatever words they used. They're a bunch of idiots; it makes no difference how long a guy's hair is. Most of the long-haired dudes in there, they're not dummies any of them. Nor are the short-hairs. It makes no difference," Dennis McGee, a union committeeman, insisted.

The issue was the same one that had triggered the Flint sit-down thirty-six years earlier: working conditions. "General Motors' attitude's no damn good! They break their agreements. You settle a grievance, then they turn right on you and break the agreement," Al Alli, a second committeeman, charged.

"From day to day," an assembler chimed in, "you don't know what your job's going to be. They always either add to your job or take a man off. I mean management's word is no good. They guarantee you—they write to the union—that this is the settlement on the job, this is the way it's going to run—102 cars an hour, and . . . two weeks later management comes down and says, 'Hey listen, let's add something else to that guy.' They don't even tell the union."

Lordstown, coming after Campaign GM and the repeated attacks by Ralph Nader, pierced James Roche's reserve. Despite the corporation's best efforts—honest efforts, he insisted—the critics remained dissatisfied, unwilling to acknowledge that General Motors was moving, was changing, was serious about its social responsibilities. The corporation had brought out a small car. It was spending millions to clean up factory pollution and was on the verge of a breakthrough in controlling smog. Despite opposition from oil companies and his own division engineers, Roche had come down in favor of the catalytic converter, which required unleaded gasoline so as not to ruin the rare metal elements in that pollution-control device. Unleaded gas would cost the oil companies millions in new capital investment and deprive Roche's engineers of the quick acceleration and sense of power that had marked General Motors cars for a generation.

Yet, despite these changes, people such as Nader and Consumers Union continued to carp. "This unjustified harassment—and much of it is unjustified—is a covert danger we can no longer ignore," Roche avowed.

When Nader urged workers to blow the whistle on their employers, to publicly reveal product defects, he nurtured a philosophy "antagonistic to our American ideas of private property and individual responsibility." Critics were seeking to erode "another support of free enterprise—the loyalty of a management team, with its unifying values of cooperative work. Some of the enemies of business"—Roche could not bring himself to mention Nader's name publicly—"now encourage an employee to be disloyal to the enterprise. They want to create suspicion and disharmony and pry into the proprietary interests of the business. However this is labeled—industrial espionage, whistle blowing, or professional responsibility—it is another tactic for spreading disunity and creating conflict."

Roche's protest might have been more convincing had not a final "buy" inspector in the St. Louis Chevrolet plant proved the need for whistleblowers, and already cost the corporation an estimated $100 million. Edward Gregory took his job as a final inspector seriously. He was feisty, persistent, and if his suggestions cost the company too much money, that was tough. He had an old-fashioned notion that the public was entitled to safe automobiles.

For two years Gregory had recommended better sealing of rear quarter panels on Chevrolets coming off the assembly line in St. Louis; for two years management had ignored his formally submitted suggestions. Frustrated, angry that the defect permitted carbon monoxide to leak into the passenger compartment, he had relayed information about the flaw to Ralph Nader. Although Nader went public with Gregory's data, the corporation still refused to correct the defective sealing or to recall the potentially lethal Chevrolets already on the road.

Edward Gregory received grim affirmation on July 11, 1968, when Utah highway patrolmen discovered the bodies of three people and two dogs in a Chevrolet Impala parked on the shoulder of U.S. Route 40. They had been asphyxiated by carbon monoxide fumes leaking from a damaged exhaust system into the passenger compartment.

Seven months later, after twenty-nine other cases of carbon monoxide poisoning and a fourth death had turned up, General Motors recalled 2.5 million Chevrolets built between 1965 and 1969 to repair the defective quarter-panel sealing about which Edward Gregory had complained two years earlier. In announcing the recall, General Motors protested that only thirty cases had surfaced, and "the whole affair is like calling in the haystack to find the needle."

The former director of the National Highway Safety Bureau, Dr. William Haddon, disagreed: "If there are thirty cases when carbon monoxide is suspected, the actual number probably is considerably higher." Exact figures are unobtainable. Police often do not investigate the reasons for accidents, superficially noting the cause instead as "reckless driving" or, perhaps, "heart attack" if the victim has died. Moreover, the early symptoms of carbon monoxide poisoning—drowsiness and disorientation—are identical to those exhibited by a drunk driver. Police understandably assume intoxication instead of asphyxiation as the cause of nonfatal accidents, especially if the driver admits to having taken a drink before driving.

To correct the sealing defect, Chevrolet used the remedy suggested by Edward Gregory two years earlier, awarding him the maximum bonus, $10,000, for his suggestion. (Gregory used part of the unexpected prize to buy a small motorboat with which he cruised the Mississippi River near his home, taking photographs of the industrial pollution that had ruined his favorite recreation, fishing.) At the same time that the corporation recalled the leaking Chevrolets, it also called in a staggering 2.9 million cars and trucks produced by all divisions in 1968 and 1969 to correct a defective part that might jam the carburetor in an open position. The one-day total of more than 5.4 million vehicles stood as a record until December 1971, when Chevrolet recalled nearly 6.7 million cars and trucks built between 1965 and 1970 to repair a defective motor mount.

Ed Cole had resisted the motor-mount recall for two years, arguing with more passion than logic that even when the motor mount broke, jamming the throttle open, anyone who "can't manage a car at twenty-five miles per hour shouldn't be driving." Even when a broken motor mount caused the death of an elderly woman in Florida in 1969, General Motors refused to recall the automobiles. When John DeLorean, the new division general manager, asked to "quietly recall all the cars with these problem mounts," he was refused by the fourteenth floor, he claimed. Only the torrents of bad publicity, threatening to unleash government action, forced Cole to relent and the company to institute the recall campaign.

Defensive, uncertain of this new order of things, Cole declined to accept responsibility for the corporation's laxity. "We're under the gun more from the critics because of what we are. The biggest is the most vulnerable. It's easier to get headlines by attacking GM." Roche agreed, adding that automobile safety and pollution problems "have been used in an attempt to get at the system." General Motors "would be a natural target for anybody who wanted to find a basis for criticizing American business in the free enterprise system of our society."

Since 1968, his last four years as chairman of the board, James Roche had spent much of his time and energy explaining the corporation to the public, so much so that General Motors had expanded its dual leadership to a troika to spread the responsibility. Yet on the eve of his retirement, with the board of directors squabbling about the seeming lack of impact he had had, Roche was still optimistic, though guardedly so. "America's romance with the automobile is not over," he insisted. "Instead it has blossomed into a marriage."

With James Roche scheduled to retire at the end of 1971, the still influential, though retired, Frederick Donner began looking for a replacement. The most likely candidate, President Edward Cole, would not do. Cole was not a financial man, and for all his willing service at the direction of Roche, he simply had not demonstrated the firmness it would take to cut costs further, lay off workers, and standardize the company's products for maximum cost-effectiveness.

Instead, in the spring of 1970, Donner reached down to tap Richard Gerstenberg, the company's executive vice-president for finance, as vice-chairman of the board and chairman of the powerful finance committee. For those who followed such sweepstakes, it was clear that Gerstenberg, the son of a Mohawk, New York, factory inspector, was going to be the next chairman of the world's largest corporation. The *Wall Street Journal* noted, "He is taking over as the top money man at a time when profit is sliding; as the chief man for overseas at a time when GM's market share is slipping in a growing market; and as the chief overseer of external relations at a time when the threats of more government regulations are growing."

Gerstenberg was the paradigm of General Motors executives; he was cautious, colorless, virtually unknown beyond the confines of the industry, and a diplomat who brokered adroit compromises between factions on the fourteenth floor. He had spent his entire career in financial affairs since the Depression year of 1932, when he joined the company as a timekeeper in the Frigidaire division for $125 a month. "When I got that job in 1932," he later recalled, "it was a big event for a little town; one of their guys got a job with General Motors."

The University of Michigan graduate's accomplishments since then had been equally modest, yet he rose steadily upward after a report he had written impressed Donner in 1949. Within the company he became known as an expert on pricing, budgets, and cost control—the very heart of the corporation's new emphasis on profits. If Gerstenberg had one moment of public celebrity, it was in 1968, while testifying before Senator Ribicoff's Government Operations Subcommittee on the prices charged for motor-vehicle safety equipment. Confronted with a detailed question from Senator Kennedy, Gerstenberg demurred, "You are talking to old Gerstenberg the bookkeeper, Mr. Chairman. I am not an engineer." At that, the self-deprecation would evoke no comment until three years later, when "old Gerstenberg the bookkeeper" became chairman of the board of the world's largest automobile manufacturer.

At the same time Gerstenberg became vice-chairman of the board, Donner placed yet another financial wizard in direct line of succession. Skipping over a half-dozen men from the automobile side, the Donner-manipulated board of directors named the corporation's treasurer, Thomas A. Murphy, as vice-president in charge of the auto and truck divisions.

No appointment could have been more disheartening to the handful of unreconstructed automotive men who dreamed of a return to old glories. Affable Tom Murphy, he of the "Irish" wit, also had spent his entire career in finance since joining the company in 1938 fresh out of the University of Illinois. Four years earlier, Murphy had been far down the organizational charts, serving as General Motors' comptroller. Now he was on a fast track, with twenty months to gain something of an insight into the manufacturing side before Roche retired and the chosen successors moved up.

The appointments of Gerstenberg and Murphy underscored the shift from a production and merchandising company to a financial and marketing firm. General Motors, explained Jean Frere of Bank Lambert in 1970, was best understood as a major financial institution with some automobile and other manufacturing subsidiaries. That year, American automobile manufacturers would extend $35 billion in credit to finance two-thirds of all automobiles sold.

General Motors' fortunes rose and fell with national prosperity. With or without engineers and salesmen in its highest offices the corporation would do well in good times; the keen-eyed financial men were needed when the economy was less healthy, as it was in the middle of 1971. Imported cars had scored heavily in the last model year, as much as 40 percent of all sales in southern California—long considered a telltale of national trends—and more than 16 percent across the country. The impact was considerable, Henry Ford II told reporters: "If our figures are right, for every 1 percent of import penetration, there are 20,000 fewer jobs available in the United States." According to Ford, as many as 320,000 people were unemployed because of the imports. In Michigan, unemployment ran 8 percent, two points higher than the figure the Nixon administration had considered acceptable as a deflationary measure. Thirty thousand members of the UAW had been laid off, and by mid-1971 thousands more were expecting pink slips. Bumper stickers sprouted on domestic autos proclaiming, "Built in Detroit by Americans"; in California, defiant Volkswagen owners retaliated in Gothic blackletter, "Built in Der Black Forest by Elves."

Meanwhile, inflation ran on, fueled by military expenditures. Anomalous inflation during a period of high unemployment defied classical economic theory. Frustrated, pressured by the business community to take steps to curb inflation, President Nixon abandoned his pledge "not to take this nation down the road to wage and price controls" to do just that. Acting under the authority of the Economic Stabilization Act of 1970, which authorized the president to "issue such orders and regulations to stabilize prices, rents, wages and salaries," Nixon announced on August 15, 1971, that he was imposing a ninety-day freeze on all four. At the same time, he proposed ending the 7-percent excise tax on automobiles, a tax that had been in effect, despite industry opposition, for thirty-nine years. He coupled to that a 10-percent surcharge on all imports, including automobiles.

General Motors was elated with the president's "New Economic Policy." The Vega, $311 more costly than its major foreign competitor, was in one neat stroke suddenly within $23 of the Volkswagen Beetle.

Furthermore, the president refused to sell the nation's gold reserves at the long-fixed price of thirty-five dollars an ounce, thus forcing other countries to reevaluate the exchange rate. The mark, the yen, and the pound sterling suddenly bought more dollars, thereby effectively reducing the cost of United States exports while simultaneously raising the prices of imported goods. The dollar simply bought less foreign-manufactured products. The administration dropped the 10-percent surcharge on imports in November, but two later rounds of currency re-

evaluations effectively replaced that "protective tariff."
Foreign-car prices jumped as much as 40 percent before the year
was out.

There was hardly any secret about the president's intention.
"Autos Back from the Brink," the New York *Times* headlined.
One Wall Street analyst described the combination of proposals
as "the auto industry relief act." Roche and Cole welcomed the
president's program, predicting "passenger car sales in excess of
10 million units, including imports, with 10.5 million clearly possible if consumer confidence is restored in the months ahead."

Well they might have been delighted. One of the major architects of the plan, perhaps *the* singular figure in drafting it, was
Richard Gerstenberg, vice-chairman of the board of directors of
General Motors. Gerstenberg had shuttled between New York
and Washington for a full year as a member of the President's
Commission on International Trade and Investment Policy,
working on a then-secret study that would, among other things,
recommend just the sort of import surcharge the president eventually put forward.

Unable to compete head-to-head with the imports, especially
those from Germany and Japan, General Motors had turned to
the government for assistance. The freeze, Phase I of the new
Nixon economics, became a government program of wage- and
price-screening boards, with annual 5.5-percent pay increases
and 2.5-percent price boosts allowed. Domestic sales re-
bounded; the backlog of 1.5 million unsold new cars evaporated.
In October, the Big Three sold nearly one million motor vehicles,
then tapered off to a less giddy 10.5 million production year. By
July 1972, General Motors was on a record-setting profit pace,
despite lower total employment, higher per-unit costs, and the
end of the model year's reduced output. Granted the 7-percent
rebate with the end of the excise tax, "car buyers apparently
have used that saving to buy more expensive cars—and it's the
costlier models that fetch car makers the most profit," the *Wall
Street Journal* concluded.

For the first time in history, domestic automobile production
surpassed nine million, with importers adding another 1.5 million
sales to the total. General Motors garnered just over half of all

American cars sold in 1972; its net income was the highest of any company in history, though in deflated dollars, and the 18.5-percent return on investment its best since 1966. Jubilant, General Motors declared victory. "The inroads of foreign manufacturers" had been "checked."

The celebration was premature. Import sales had fallen only one percentage point and would rebound the next year. About all the president's New Economic Plan had accomplished was the refurbishing of General Motors' return on investment. It was one last flush of untroubled affluence.

The world General Motors had made—a chrome-festooned world of large cars and luxurious salons; of unfettered, air-conditioned mobility—came crashing down on October 19, 1973.

18

Juggernaut

The lines snaked for blocks—Buicks, Fords, Toyotas, and Jaguars queued to suck the life-giving underground tanks. Temper-raddled drivers waited hours for a dollop of fuel doled into voracious gasoline tanks, the vestiges of their blighted lifestyle mocking them: "Cheap gas"; "Speed Limit 75"; "See America First"; "Drive Now, Pay Later."

The oil embargo announced by Saudi Arabia on October 19, 1973—an act of *Realpolitik* by a presumed ally—and the unilateral pricing policy of the Organization of Petroleum Exporting Countries capped a year-long trend. Here and there spot shortages had erupted in a rash of boarded-up service stations and penny-by-penny increases in the cost of gasoline. Senator Henry Jackson, outspoken foe of the major oil companies, predicted that gasoline would be rationed by spring, then later charged that the shortage was rigged by those "Seven Sisters" to boost already unconscionable profits. There *was* an oil shortage, contrived or not, and the embargo which followed only made that reality more stark.

The anger receded, leaving 126 million American motorists

484

resigned to ever-increasing prices posted on gasoline pumps. By spring 1974, a gallon of gasoline that had cost thirty-eight cents the year before sold for fifty-two cents. But at least there was gasoline, and grateful motorists paid the higher premium. A nation conditioned to private mobility—to great machines transporting solitary passengers (and getting less mileage from a gallon of gas than their grandparents' twelve miles per gallon in 1916)—a nation that had long abandoned coherent mass-transit planning for incoherent traffic jams, while permitting its rail systems, bus service, and interurban lines to dwindle and deteriorate, had no alternative. America discovered that miles-per-gallon was far more important than miles-per-hour.

What could not be cured, ran the homily, must be endured. The oil shortage, legitimatized as an energy crisis, would last "as long as most of us will live. We will have to adopt a whole new way of life," Frank Ikard, the president of the American Petroleum Institute, warned. "The love affair of the American with the large automobile has to come to an end."

The automobile industry reeled as customers for the new 1974 models contemplated increased sticker prices and decided to make the old bus do for another year. The longer the lines at gas pumps, the fewer people kicking tires in showrooms. By March 13, 1974, the day the oil embargo ended, the worst recession since the Depression had ensnared the United States.

If any company appeared threatened by the oil embargo, it was the largest, the most heavily reliant on big-car sales, the corporation that had waxed rich on cheap energy. General Motors depended so heavily on large cars that its corporate average fuel economy was the worst in the industry, just 12.2 miles per gallon, substantially below the 14 miles per gallon average of all cars. "That was the reality we had to face," then-vice-chairman Thomas Murphy said later. If the company was to survive, it would have to adapt, or, like some ponderous beast trapped in a tar sump, slowly sink under its own weight. "We had to take the risk and revamp our entire product line," Murphy argued.

The corporation had come out of 1972 with the second-best year in the history of the industry, selling 11.2 million cars and trucks. In that year too the automobile industry had produced its 300-millionth motor vehicle, enough to have given one motor vehicle to every man, woman, and child who had ever lived in the United States. Despite December's sudden plunge in sales, 1973 had been all the industry had hoped for and more—a record 12.6 million domestically manufactured cars and trucks and 2 million imports. But expectations for a fourth boom year in 1974 disappeared as gasoline supplies dried up. Worse still, both General Motors and Chrysler had been caught with restyled large cars, just at the moment when customers were small-car-conscious.

Richard Gerstenberg put the best face on it he could. Domestic sales for 1974, he predicted in the corporation's annually optimistic forecast—General Motors had cultivated the art of silver-lining—"would be composed of 10 million to 10.5 million passenger cars and about 3 million trucks. This would be a good year for the auto industry by most past standards—although clearly not a record year."

The magnitude of Gerstenberg's error—he had forecast an 8-percent slackening when the final tally would show sales down 21 percent—was a measure of Detroit's lack of understanding of what had happened. Wall Street was less Panglossian; prices for auto stocks fell almost 50 percent from the 1973 high, a paper loss of $17 billion. General Motors languished at an eleven-year low; floundering Chrysler was off a demoralizing 62 percent. Economists stared wide-eyed at an abrupt decline of $10 billion worth of auto production, a figure they multiplied by factors of two or three to estimate the economic impact that rippled from Detroit.*

* According to the 1972 edition of *Auto Facts and Figures,* published by the Motor Vehicle Manufacturers Association, "A slow down in the automotive market may mean a layoff for rubber workers in Akron, a reduction in the work force of steel mills in Pittsburgh and reduced markets for the fabric mills of the Carolinas. Perhaps hardest hit will be the hundreds of small towns whose main industries center on supplying vehicle makers with components or parts." A supplier employing 1,000 workers "supports 1000 households, involving 3100 persons, with more than $10.3 million in personal income annually. These families will in turn support 30 retail establishments through expenditure of $4.7 million and create 650 jobs." If the layoff lasted long enough, it could produce business failures, reduced tax collections, increased unemployment and welfare payments, and a resultant greater public debt to be repaid with interest.

One of every seven workers in the country owed his or her livelihood to the internal-combustion engine, either in its construction, care, or operation, or because his or her firm was dependent upon the automobile to bring in customers. Some 500,000 jobs in allied industries—glass, steel, heavy machinery, plastics, oil, and rubber—hinged on automobile sales. Economists attributed one of every ten dollars spent in America to the automobile and its roadways.

The wellspring of economic well-being dried up, dammed by rising gasoline prices and falling sales. The normal sixty-day inventory of large cars swelled to twice that, a horde of unappreciated, ornamental artifacts of a suddenly ancient age. Unsold automobiles sat stagnating in the car makers' employee parking lots; the commuting workers who would have filled those parking spaces, 135,000 of them, were on indefinite layoff, or "furloughed" for varying periods.

While large cars wintered wherever they could be stored, their sales off by 35 percent, 1974's compacts and subcompacts rose steadily to a 40-percent market share. The Big Three had been caught by a vast shift in consumer demand, and General Motors, the largest producer of "full-size" autos, shouldered the greatest losses.

Only a handful of automobile men understood what was happening. "The Arab embargo," said John DeLorean, now resigned from General Motors in favor of a Cadillac dealership in Florida, "just took a curve and accelerated it. The small car trend has been growing in momentum for ten years." A piqued Richard Gerstenberg snapped back, "All of us are blessed with almost perfect hindsight, and DeLorean's is no exception." The criticism stung most sharply when the corporation found itself awash with automobiles too large and too heavy to deliver more than 10.5 miles per gallon while consumers lined up at their neighborhood gas stations.

Lights in the executive offices on West Grand Boulevard burned long past the accepted 7 P.M. quitting time. Vice-presidents placed repeated calls to lowly field representatives for daily sales reports. The figures came in, ever down. Vice-president and field representative alike grew more anxious. Evening after evening, corporate and division officers pondered the sales figures, agreed on a plan of action, then tore it up the next morning and started over. The longer they waited, the worse matters became. "In November of 1973, the President made his speech that we had to turn the thermostats down," Pete Estes later recalled, "and by December we couldn't sell a big car to save our ass from first base. No way. The curtain came down."

There was something akin to panic on the fourteenth floor. "Our sales of large cars just stopped. We couldn't even get people into our showrooms, and we were in deep trouble. It was an emergency as far as General Motors was concerned, and we decided that we had to move fast, just like in a war. We had the reputation for being the slowest in the industry on small cars and frankly our competition had beaten us in that part of the market several times previously. So we said this was not going to happen again," Estes explained.

The first decision was the crucial one: General Motors, after a half-century of promoting ever larger cars, would reverse itself. The public wanted economy *now*. If the corporation sought to ride out the storm, hove to with shuttered factories, the government, sooner or later, would compel them to make more fuel-efficient cars. Were the oil shortage ever to force a choice between refining heating oil or gasoline from available crude, politicians and public alike would opt for heating oil. General Motors dared not align itself with heavy-footed teenagers joy-riding in oversized automobiles while shuddering children and widows huddled by lifeless heaters.

"Down-sizing," the engineers called it, and a new word entered the language. Shrinking, pruning, hacking, substituting, but, above everything else, paring weight from the company's automobiles. There was plenty to trim; during the preceding twenty years the top-of-the-line Chevrolet had swollen almost three feet, gained 1,120 pounds, and doubled in horsepower.

Later there would be the cost estimates: a mile per gallon gained for each four hundred pounds eliminated; $2 billion in research, design and new capital investment to produce cars delivering each of those additional miles over the next decade; an immediate outlay of $3 billion, $600 million of which the corporation would have to borrow—its first outside financing in twenty-two years. At the moment, Estes' mandate was clear enough: "Anyone who can't meet his target had better walk west until his hat floats."

The company started with its largest cars—the "B-" and "C-" bodies. These, the strongest sellers, consumed the most gasoline, individually and collectively, of all American automobiles. The luxury cars, with wheelbases of 130 inches, were to be no longer than 121 inches by their introduction in 1977. The "B," or standard, wheelbase was to come down to 116 inches that same year, the length of the 1974 intermediate-size car. In 1978, the intermediates would shrink to the size of compacts.

At the same time, the executive committee scratched immediate plans for the Wankel rotary engine—a final defeat for Ed Cole. General Motors had intended to introduce it in the 1975 Vega, with production to begin in August. But with the new fuel consciousness-raising, the Wankel would not do. The company would continue research on the engine, perhaps to use it in the future if the engineers could improve the engine's fuel economy.

Company engineers welcomed the new corporate direction. "The engineers are just delighted," an assistant to General Motors engineering vice-president enthused. "It's great! At last we're working on something people want."

Meanwhile, Chevrolet's engineers put forward designs for a model they had dubbed the SFC, the Small Family-Car. It was a nebulous concept that took form only under the pressure of the oil shortage. However much it was shortened, Chevrolet engineers had decided early on that the SFC would have a transversely mounted front engine and front-wheel drive; that arrangement would allow them a shorter hood and more cabin space. It also would eliminate the transmission and drive-shaft hump that took up so much interior leg room.

Chevrolet's concept became a corporate design. First Pontiac, and later Oldsmobile and Buick—the latter two under orders from the executive committee—enrolled in the SFC, now envisioned as a prospective compact, or X-body, that could carry five adults comfortably. It would take until February 1976 for final approval by the executive committee, but General Motors had its most innovative, market-responsive, and perhaps socially responsible automobile in history.*

All Detroit was frantically caught up in "the midst of the greatest industry conversion in history, at least in peacetime," said the president of the Ford Motor Company, Lee Iacocca. The men of Detroit, as to wisdom revealed, became small-car disciples. "Regardless of the energy thing, we were due to dehydrate our cars. They were *too* overstuffed. *Too* inefficient. *Too* much sheetmetal for the people," General Motors' styling vice-president William Mitchell acknowledged. (But Mitchell himself, driving a custom-modified Cadillac, was a reluctant convert. "Small cars are like Vodka. Sure, people will try them out, but they won't stay with them.")

General Motors was to shift two, three, and then four assembly plants from full-size and intermediate vehicles to compacts, Richard Gerstenberg announced, enough to boost the company's capacity to two million small cars a year. But that was next year. For the moment, only one of every four automobiles coming off company assembly lines was a compact. But even 1975's two million, 40 percent of General Motors' automobile production, would not be enough to keep pace with the market, Gerstenberg conceded. Sales of small cars would swallow up half of all sales by 1977 or 1978. "The company can't change overnight," he grumbled. The public was overreacting to the gasoline shortage, "tending to lose sight of long-term perspective, and we are feeling an undue degree of pessimism about the current [gasoline supply] situation."

In mid-December 1973, Gerstenberg, Cole, and the executive committee decided on a series of measured countermoves. The company would produce as many compacts as possible, but would load them with the high-markup accessories that would produce the desired 20-percent return on investment. The "upgrading" was blindly based on the corporation's unwavering be-

---

* Introduced in April 1979 as the Chevrolet Citation, Pontiac Phoenix, Oldsmobile Omega, and Buick Skylark, the SFC replaced a fifteen-year-old group of compacts. The new cars were nearly two feet shorter and some eight hundred pounds lighter than the cars they replaced, yet offered more passenger and luggage space. Because the Environmental Protection Agency classifies automobiles by interior volume, the SFC ironically "grew" from compact to mid-size in classification.

lief it could induce or pressure consumers to buy those automobiles General Motors wanted to sell. One of every three Vegas would come equipped with air conditioning by the end of the year, compared to just one in seven in 1971; such "add-ons" and a new luxury version of the Vega had "started to get the Vega price where it should be." Where it should be, Thomas Murphy, the corporation's senior financial officer, explained to a group of investment analysts, was a return of 15 to 20 percent on stockholders' equity—the first time a corporation official publicly conceded the corporate goal.

Despite inflationary rates that made consumers flinch, General Motors was to load its "economy" cars with power assists, larger engines, and the pile carpeting, imitation leather, and wood paneling that constituted an extra-cost luxury interior. Gerstenberg rationalized: "A few years ago, the public valued small cars as only basic transportation; now customers are looking for the same luxury and convenience in a small car that are usually associated only with full-size cars." The corporation's new cars were "attuned to this shift in the public's preference, and we intend to take full advantage of the new sales opportunity it presents."

The men of the fourteenth floor were to be betrayed by an inability to grasp the extent of the market shift. Unlike the housewife who absorbed small weekly inflationary increments, the automobile buyer who went shopping for a new car once every three years was shocked by the 20-percent, $1,000 increases on 1974 models. At such a moment, an option-laden car was too expensive for strained budgets.

Down-sizing and upgrading were to be complemented with two crash efforts to produce small cars: a luxury Cadillac fitted to a reinforced frame from a compact Nova; and American production of a subcompact—the German-designed, Brazilian-built Chevette. Both were to come out as soon as possible in the 1975 model year.

The executive committee had debated inconclusively the introduction of a small Cadillac for two years. The majority opposed the concept, whether it was an entirely new car from the tires up or merely an enlarged Opel. "We were conditioned to selling cars by the foot and by the pound, and in a bigger car it's easier to perceive the additional value," Cadillac's sales manager L.B. Pryor later explained.

There were good arguments in favor of a smaller Cadillac: the dealers needed a car to appeal to younger, upwardly mobile buyers who disdained the nineteen-and-a-half-foot, 5,000-pound Cadillac as "a bit showy." Equally compelling, Mercedes-Benz, priced $7,000 higher than the standard Cadillac, had carved out sales of 40,000 cars per year with an automobile three-and-a-half feet shorter and 1,000 pounds lighter. "The imports were eating our lunch," Pryor complained.

The puffed-up Nova would be smaller—"international" size the marketers called it—but heavily appointed and equipped with enough accessories to justify a $12,000 sticker price. With a truncated hood and rear deck and a higher roofline to provide head room, the new Seville would compete directly with the imported Mercedes. That company's styling department was not dead after all, but alive and well in William Mitchell's shop; the small Cadillac's profile smacked of the larger Rolls-Royce, while its front grill and overall size were drawn from the Mercedes.

The corporate decisions of late 1973 were a last, bitter triumph for Ed Cole. Year after year he had given way to the cold, analytic arguments of the financial men, buried under computer printouts that mocked his "gut" instincts. With each retreat he had lost esteem in the eyes of Richard Gerstenberg and, worse, his own self-confidence. In 1970, he had waffled in support of DeLorean's "K-car" plan to build both compact and intermediate-size cars on a single frame. One day he argued that the plan would permit quick production shifts from smaller to larger cars in response to market conditions; the next he acknowledged that it was a costly gamble, and if they were to risk any money, Cole wanted it to continue development of the rotary engine. When Cole backed DeLorean's K-car concept, it seemed to move forward; when William Mitchell opposed the automobile's "European" look, the concept lost ground. The K-car plan finally died a lingering death in late 1970—never quite vetoed, but never approved either.

On the eve of his retirement, that part of Cole that had wanted a new small car—a new automobile in reality—had been vindicated. General Motors was about to begin down-sizing— belatedly. Had the executive committee approved DeLorean's proposal in 1970, General Motors would have been set to introduce that timely small car in October 1973—just when the committee finally was concluding that the corporation needed such an auto.

By January 1974, General Motors' production of cars and trucks had slumped 27 percent from the previous year. The trough deepened; for the first quarter, the company's output fell 35 percent from the record rates of 1973, and the optimistic predictions of yet another boom year tasted like ashes.

Detroit became dead weight, dragging down the national economy. As the automobile industry slowed its production, layoffs increased. Still sales spiraled downward. For every 250,000 cars, $1 billion in lost sales, Detroit furloughed another 23,000 workers, and automobile suppliers an additional 34,000.

Throughout the winter, General Motors executives attempted to maintain the façade of normality. The company steadily denied it had any intention of shrinking all of its automobiles, fearing that potential customers would wait for the smaller cars. Asked about the rumors of down-sizing, Richard Terrell, vice-president of the automobile divisions, shrugged: "I don't see any difference in the size of people walking around."

Even with the lifting of the Arab oil embargo in March, sales failed to recover. "We don't know what the hell is going on," *Business Week* quoted "a frantic middle manager at GM's Oldsmobile" division. But if General Motors did not understand, there were others who did. The buying habits, the judgments of taste, the very importance placed upon the automobile as a status symbol, suddenly were following the pattern long established in California. An "increasing percentage of Americans . . . don't want what Detroit offers and specifically what General Motors offers," financial analyst Ronald Glantz concluded. While many might have turned to imported autos, as Californians had done for almost two decades, progressive dollar devaluations and overseas inflation had jacked the foreign car out

of the "economy" class. Inflation-chivvied customers wanted
economy, but the first economy came on a lower sticker price.

Sociologist David Riesman explained it as a "downward
spread of aristocratic values." The trend-setting upper-middle
class had lost its taste for ostentation, no longer needful of rein-
forcing its tenuous status with the flash and glitter of a be-
chromed behemoth. "Showiness has been so long satirized that it
has become an embarrassment," Riesman continued.

Those who went shopping for a domestic compact found
themselves confronting automobiles with more equipment and
higher prices than they had expected. (General Motors was to
raise sticker prices four times during 1974.) Stripped-down
cars—traditionally held out until the end of the model year, when
dealers hustled for every last sale—were in short supply and still
too expensive.

General Motors' cumulative price increases—the other
domestic manufacturers, with narrower profit margins, gratefully followed—not only had an immediate inflationary effect,
but a long-term, more invidious one as well. Confronted with
higher sticker prices, would-be buyers began searching for longer
terms to repay the larger loans necessary to buy a new car.
Increasingly, finance companies granted four-year payment periods, sometimes more. By September 1975, one out of four
loans was a "mini-mortgage," stretched out past forty months.
Those who elected longer payment periods, with lower monthly
installments, actually increased the effective cost of the average
$4,000 car by $1,000. They rarely considered the total price
seriously—making the monthly installment payment was the
budgeting problem.

Higher interest rates were only one of the "hidden" charges of
automobility. From dealer's showroom to the scrapyard, 100,000
road-weary miles later, the full-size family car would cost the
owner $15,893 to maintain and operate, the federal government
estimated. The greatest single cost was depreciation—$4,258—
followed by maintenance costs of $3,521, and gasoline sufficient
for those 100,000 miles totaling $2,026. Over the same life span, a
compact would cost the increasingly dissatisfied owner $12,875,
and a subcompact $11,153. Those costs would rise steadily, ap-

proximately one cent per mile per year, until by 1979 the full-size car would require twenty cents per mile to own and operate.

Double-digit inflation coupled with deepening recession produced "one of the most turbulent years in automotive history," Gerstenberg admitted. Yet with the resolute optimism expected of the chairman of General Motors, he publicly forecast industry sales for the 1975 model year totaling thirteen million cars and trucks, which, if realized, would make it the third best in history.

The "hyperinflation" of 1974 would subside over the coming year if they could but fix a "moratorium on unnecessary cost," the retiring chairman argued in one of his last official statements. Chief among these, Gerstenberg asserted, restating a leitmotif that was to thread its way through subsequent General Motors statements, was the "cost of a number of governmental requirements that have been placed upon cars and trucks; costs that are in many cases well beyond whatever value these regulations provide. . . . The need to examine the relationship of environmental improvement and economic growth is urgent . . . The mandated equipment added to our cars and trucks over the four model years (1972 through 1975) to meet regulations for emission control, occupant protection, and bumpers, has added about $270 to the cost of every vehicle we produce for the United States. If other car manufacturers have had similar experience, this would amount to a total cost of some $3.5 billion in a 13-million-vehicle year. We cannot but question whether our society can afford such a cost in this time of inflation when so much of it is unproductive."

Gerstenberg's roseate projection collapsed even as the corporation introduced its 1975 models with their $500 price increases. Sales in the month of the unveiling, October 1974, would have ranked as only the eighth-best month in record-setting 1973. Things grew steadily worse, despite a 28-percent increase in gasoline mileage on the new models. (The catalytic converter, a smog-control device that permitted finer tuning of engines, was responsible for most of that increase.)

The recession wore on. In Detroit, unemployment surpassed 9 percent of the labor force; in the ghetto, more than one in five idled away the days, waiting for the upturn that did not come.

"It's simply a crisis," Detroit Mayor Coleman Young declared. If so, it was a crisis that had spread far; in Pontiac, another General Motors plant city, unemployment was almost as bad. Nationally, 6 million men and women were out of jobs, 1.7 million more than the year before.

Optimistic industry sales forecasts of as many as 10.5 million cars and trucks for the 1975 model year gave way to a figure of 9 million, then a dismal projection of 7.5 million. The tidy marketing world turned upside-down by December 1974. The automobile industry had lost control of its markets, its merchandising strategies lay in disarray and its advertising echoed hollowly. Newly promoted General Motors chairman Thomas A. Murphy was frankly puzzled. "I keep scratching my head and asking myself, 'Why?' When I look at all the pluses, I can make a case for a record automobile year."

Whatever the pluses Murphy spied—a sudden, unprompted boom in the sale of small, usually imported pickup trucks and made-in-America vans as second "cars"—there were too few of them to provide a lift. Murphy was left only with plaintive optimism: "We just know this thing is going to turn around."

He could not say when the turnabout would come, but then Tom Murphy had not yet taken upon himself the papal authority or prophet's mantle of his predecessors. The silver-haired "Murph" had served General Motors for thirty-seven years, ever since his graduation from the University of Illinois, all but the last four spent in the corporation's New York financial offices. Hired by the company's general accounting office in Detroit fresh out of college, he was detailed to New York two weeks later on a "temporary assignment." The assignment had lasted until 1970, when then-chairman James Roche, at Frederic Donner's prompting, tapped the former accountant and statistician to be vice-president in charge of the car and truck group.

The vice-presidency was a major shift, an unnerving one, and Murphy was dubious. "For once in my life," the dutiful graduate of St. Leo's in Chicago told Roche, "I have to question that. I'm a bookkeeper. I've been in the financial end all my life. I can count the plants I've been in. I don't know the first darn thing about running a plant."

Roche prevailed, for Murphy understood the corporate pecking order and yearned as much as any man for the chairmanship of the world's largest corporation. Detroit was "a very humbling experience" for Murphy, part of his seasoning as a future chairman. "Growing up in financial we think we know everything . . . I suddenly realized I didn't know the first thing about an automobile, let alone the mechanics of meeting a production schedule."

Twenty-one months after his promotion, having acquired a belated introduction to motor-vehicle manufacturing, Murphy became the heir apparent with his expected promotion to vice-chairman to replace Richard Gerstenberg. On December 1, 1974, he was once again picking up the small plaque he kept on his desk reading "Bless this mess," this time to move into the largest of the blue-carpeted offices on the fourteenth floor.

Despite his sense of humor—and reading tastes that ranged from "Peanuts" to biographies of Ralph Nader—Murphy was cut from the same conservative cloth as his predecessors. Unlike Donner, Roche, and Gerstenberg before him, he was taking charge with the company mired in the worst national recession since the 1930s. The problems were immediate, pressing in on him, leaving no time for reflection or to plan ahead. Sticker prices on the company's automobiles had climbed so high since 1972 that Murphy worried if the cars had been priced beyond the reach of the average worker; a similar situation already had developed in the housing industry, and the automobile was the second-largest purchase most people ever made. Corporate profits had plummeted 75 percent since the oil embargo of a year earlier, further eroding the wondrous returns on investment of the mid-1960s. Morale was low, with the friction between the increasingly powerful corporate staff and the weakened automotive divisions worse than ever. While many of the men throughout the corporation yearned for the fat days of old, before government regulation, Murphy would have none of it. "One of the worst things we could do is wish ourselves back to another era. These are the times in which we're living and operating. We'll give a damn good accounting of ourselves," he promised, "but I'm not going to worry about where our margin was in the 1960s."

To complement Murphy, the board named Elliott Estes as

president in place of the retired Ed Cole. "Pete" Estes was an automobile man, like Cole, and it was precisely because of his engineering experience at Oldsmobile and Pontiac, as well as his management experience at Pontiac and Chevrolet, that he was selected. His putative rival, Richard Terrell, had worked for General Motors since he was nineteen—he was the last of the senior managers who had not attended college—but he had spent his entire career in Electro-Motive and Frigidaire before moving to corporate headquarters as group executive in charge of nonautomotive and defense divisions. When he, too, was moved for seasoning to head the car and truck group, Terrell noted wryly, "They picked a guy who had never worked in the auto industry."

Both Estes and Terrell were "team players" as General Motors defined it—loyal, self-effacing, and deferential. If blunt-speaking Pete Estes found it difficult to remain silent, remain silent he did until he became boss, taking what solace he could with the perquisites of office. Left unmet once at San Francisco International Airport, Estes, then Pontiac's chief engineer, exploded at John DeLorean, "Why the hell wasn't someone out to meet me at the airport this morning? You knew I was coming, but nobody was there. Goddamnit, I served my time picking up my bosses at the airport. Now you guys are going to do this for me." As president, Pete Estes would not have to worry about anyone failing to pick him up. The president of General Motors traveled with an entourage that usually included a personal chauffeur, an ex-policeman who carried a gun and had been trained in evasive driving.

The presidency had come as no surprise to Estes. "I started thinking of it a year before it happened," he told Desmond Wilcox, an interviewer for the British Broadcasting Corporation. Until then, Estes "never had the idea I wanted to push to the top. It never entered my mind I'd be president of General Motors."

Dark-haired and stocky, Estes was the model General Motors executive. He too was from a small town, Mendon, Michigan, where his father was the town banker. At eighteen he entered General Motors Institute, and there met his first wife, a nurse.

He married again two years after his first wife died in 1965. Connie Estes was "doing a great job for me too," Estes told Wilcox during a stiff, uncomfortable walkabout of his million-dollar home in Bloomfield Hills. Mr. and Mrs. Estes spent Friday nights together, while "the rest of the nights belong to General Motors. That's not too bad for General Motors," he laughed. If there was anything at all unconventional about the man, it was his May-to-November early-morning dips in the family swimming pool—nude.

More palatable than Terrell might have been as president, Estes still could not wholly satisfy the younger executives in the far-flung automotive divisions. Though he was an automobile man, Estes had no reputation as an innovator, as Cole had had. He would sponsor no Corvairs, no Vegas, no $100 million efforts to develop a rotary engine, no costly project to create a passive-restraint safety system such as the inflatable air bag. If he had any favorite project, it was the battery-powered automobile Chevrolet engineers sometimes trotted out to impress innocent reporters and congressmen. But Estes was a big-car man and the champion of all the senior executives in the automobile divisions who recalled the glorious days of old and who, as if by second nature, resented the accountants dispatched by Tom Murphy. The resentment ran deeper now as Murphy began pushing for small cars.

None of the factionalism escaped the carefully cloistered executive suites, however. Instead, as one business publication editorialized, the new, generally younger management team—Murphy and Estes both were fifty-nine—brings "a badly needed fresh and imaginative outlook to the badly wounded giant."

Almost immediately Murphy and Estes were at odds. Increasing numbers of oil tankers from the Middle East had refilled storage tanks. Motorists again found gasoline, at higher prices, in goodly supply. That stirred a faint pulse of renewed confidence and brought the more affluent back into automobile showrooms. Large cars began to move once again, while option-laden compacts languished on dealers' lots. Estes and the automobile men who followed him took heart, sniffing the long-expected upturn, failing to realize that lower-income, economy-minded buyers had dropped out of the market entirely. For them the recession was not over, regardless of the supply of gasoline.

Small cars, Pete Estes insisted, were not the way to go. "It's not really big vs. small," he argued. "It's the difference between 10 miles per gallon and 20 miles per gallon. If we had a big car that was getting 19 miles per gallon right now, the party would be over." Estes wanted to move cautiously, to preserve General Motors' lock on the large-car market and the large profits they generated. Even if small cars were to take six of every ten cars sold, "We'd like to be about 45 percent small cars and 55 percent large." But the computers vomited their printouts, and General Motors scheduled its 1975 production to include just 32 percent big cars.

Estes did not stand alone; faith in the large car ran strong at General Motors. "The car purchase and buying up to bigger cars in the market are the fundamental concepts of American life," table-pounding Mack W. Worden, the corporation's marketing vice-president, trumpeted. An inadvertent echo of hucksters "Carload" Collins and Dick Grant, Worden urged everyone "to help sell America out of its troubles. The way to keep the economy from sliding further downhill," he told the American Marketing Association, "is for the salesmen and the saleswomen of this country to get out and sell something, and for everyone to begin to reverse the gloom-and-doom psychology that seems to control the attitudes and adversely influences the action of too many people." One could almost hear Herbert Hoover cheering from the Elysian Fields.

Pep talks would not reverse economic realities in 1975 any more than they had in 1930, however. Auto makers would remember 1974 as the year "the patterns of the marketplace went awry," and 1975 would be worse. "There's a saying around this town," a Ford executive explained, "that when the rest of the country sneezes, Detroit gets pneumonia. Well, I got news for you. This time the pneumonia is contagious."

The contagion leaped from the pest house. One-third of all American automobile workers—250,000 people—were on layoffs, and another three-quarters of a million who worked in supplier industries and dealerships were idle. With autos leading the lemmings into the sea, the stock market plunged to its worst year since the all-but-forgotten Depression; stocks lost 30 percent of their paper value, with General Motors dropping thirty-five dollars a share in just three months.

The automobile moguls were desperate by February 1975. For six weeks they offered customer rebates of up to $600 on the biggest, slowest-moving family cars, rebates that eventually would total $30 million. It was in February, too, that General Motors removed, belatedly, the options which had been loaded onto its cars, cutting list prices up to $300. "We are responding to an economy-minded public," Thomas Murphy explained. The rebates came too late, however, to salvage the worst sales year since 1962. General Motors' production bottomed out at 5.2 million cars and trucks. Its domestic competitors fared worse, leaving General Motors with 53 percent of all domestic automobile sales. Ford and Chrysler both lost market share to the imports, which garnered 18 percent of American sales despite their higher prices.

There was a brief moment of optimisim in the spring of 1975 with the introduction of the "baby" Cadillac, but that optimism faded quickly. Priced above $12,000, the Seville was never intended as a mass-market car; Cadillac would produce no more than 60,000 a year—enough to blunt Mercedes perhaps, but hardly sufficient to cope with the Japanese too.

The Chevette, however, was theoretically "the right size at the right time." Its introduction in September, replete with patriotic trappings, symbolized Detroit's decision "to go small, to respond to the established need for cheaper and more efficient transportation, a need enforced by both the pain of inflation and the strain of the energy crisis," the Los Angeles *Times* editorialized.

Starting with the original Opel designs, and incorporating refinements suggested in Germany, Brazil, and Japan, Chevrolet engineers had produced the Chevette in just eighteen months. Though originally intended to be fitted with the balky rotary engine, as introduced, the $2,900 Chevette was a conventional automobile in miniature. Just over thirteen feet long, the small auto was "GM's first line of attack against the imports," Murphy announced. The company had tooled up to produce 225,000 in the car's first year and expected that two of every three sold would be "conquest" sales over the imports.

General Motors launched the Chevette with the hoopla of old and a campaign calculated to evoke buy-American sentiments in the Bicentennial year. Yet General Motors was tentative, riding on an inadvertently awkward advertising theme announcing, "It's about time!" The production scheduled was far smaller than the initial Vega run of 400,000 five years earlier; there was serious concern that at six hundred pounds lighter, with 40-percent fewer parts and that much greater reliability, Chevette would simply cannibalize Vega's sales. The corporation, Pete Estes fretted, had to learn "how to sell small cars in the same way we sell the so-called regular-sized cars. That's a big problem. We've got to catch up with this *fast*. We think over the long term the small car is going to gain maybe 3 percent of the market each year."

The Chevette did not do well. Seven months after its introduction, the corporation cut its output and reduced its sales estimate to 200,000. Taking a leaf from the elder Henry Ford, for the first time in its post-Sloan history, General Motors lowered the price of a car in midseason. Rumor suggested that the company was losing $300 on each Chevette sold. But even with seventeen options made standard and a price that was $124 cheaper than the competitive Toyota, the Chevette failed to woo import owners back into a made-in-America automobile.

The Chevette did, however, help to stanch the flow of buyers to the imports, an early market survey suggested. Based on a national sample, a market-research firm in Los Angeles concluded that "Chevette owners appear to be long-time American car buyers who have decided that the time has come to buy a fuel-efficient car." Nearly one of every three Chevette owners polled would have bought an import had General Motors not brought out the Chevette.

Only with the introduction of the 1976 models in October did optimism return. Goaded by promises of a cut in income taxes and the ready availability of fifty-seven-cent gasoline, the great beast of consumerism awakened, and, to the special delight of

General Motors, lumbered into dealers' showrooms for one last fling at luxury, comfort, and sheer size. Long accustomed to ten-miles-per-gallon cars, bemused buyers looked at thirteen-miles-per-gallon claims and judged them good.

By the end of the year, confidence had returned to the four-teenth floor. Murphy and Estes privately joked of "60-60-60"— 60 percent of domestic sales and the stock back up to sixty dollars per share by their sixtieth birthday. The chairman's fancy became the vice-presidents' passion; excited executives talked openly of the new goal, until the press learned of it. The embarrassed corporation denied that the slogan was a formal policy.

With the Seville and Chevette on the market already and the slimmed-down big cars to be introduced in fall 1975, General Motors had stolen the march on Ford as the innovative company in Detroit. Beyond that, the company had installed a number of research and design programs in "project centers," an idea borrowed by Richard Terrell from the National Aeronautics and Space Administration. A group of Chevrolet engineers were working on electric cars; Delco was investigating possible batteries; Oldsmobile had a fuel-efficient light diesel under development, an engine that could power as many as 25 percent of General Motors' automobiles and light trucks in ten years, when a 27.5-miles-per-gallon fleet-average mandate fell due; Chevrolet had resurrected its antique six-cylinder Cast Iron Wonder; and Buick had a lighter-weight V-6 ready for the corporation's 1978 models.

Despite the accomplishments—which improved fuel economy nearly 40 percent between the 1974 and the 1976 models—Estes was apprehensive about meeting the 27.5-miles-per-gallon corporate fleet average. Even with the down-sizing program and the diesel engine, doubling the fleet's mileage figure would be difficult. It certainly would limit the number of profitable Cadillacs and large station wagons the corporation could sell; every thousand pounds of weight on the tires represented a loss of 2.5 miles per gallon, a loss that had to be made up by sales of lighter, more fuel-efficient, less profitable automobiles.

The corporation was well embarked "on a massive program to

improve the fuel economy of our cars,'' Estes told the Senate
Finance Committee when it considered minimum mileage bills
that eventually were embodied in the Energy Policy and Conser-
vation Act of 1975, ''. . . because it is the only way we can sell
enough cars to earn a profit.'' Despite his argument—''There is
no other energy consuming sector of our economy that is approaching this 'negative energy growth' ''—Congress paid no
heed. Automobiles accounted for 40 percent of all oil consumption. Estes' threat of ''substantial adverse effects on auto sales
and employment . . . because consumers will not be able to buy
the kinds of cars they want'' went ignored as self-serving argument. (Similarly, when Murphy later argued that large cars were
a necessity for the one in six families with three or more children, legislators turned a deaf ear; after all, in Europe, where the
Roman Catholic church's proscription of birth control made
large families more the norm, there was no production automobile the size of General Motors' family cars.)

Estes and Murphy wanted large cars in the line for their profit
margins. As professional managers, if nothing else, they intended
to restore General Motors' profits to the heights. ''We want all
the business we can get,'' Murphy proclaimed. ''Cars are sold
one at a time, and we plan to try for every sale.'' There were no
more worries of antitrust action on the fourteenth floor; as the
largest company in the automotive industry, General Motors had
reinforced its pivotal role in the national economy. The government *needed* a General Motors, a company so big that it could
single-handedly wrest the nation from the coils of recession.

With General Motors apparently so far ahead not only in sales,
but in bringing out newer, smaller cars, other auto makers worried openly. ''GM has never been so aggressive. If they don't
watch it, they may find themselves selling the whole market,''
fretted Gerald C. Meyers, the executive vice-president of withered American Motors. A second competitor warned, ''If they
wanted to wipe everybody out by 1980, the only one that could
stop them is the government.''

The recovery of the automobile industry during 1976 came
sporadically, pocked by irrationality if not lunacy. The best-
selling ''car'' during the first quarter of the year was not Chev-

rolet's full-size Impala, the traditional leader, but the Ford pick-up. Its Chevy competitor ran a close second. The pickup truck, as large and as expensive, though hardly as comfortable, as the full-size car, had become "a high fashion thing—the latest life-style vehicle." There was a resurgence of the "muscle cars" of the 1960s, compacts and subcompacts splashed in brassy colors and decalcomania stripes, ready to "paint down twin 50-foot patches of surplus rubber," according to *Car and Driver*. These hairy-chested cars, capable of speeds twice the fifty-five-mile-per-hour national speed limit, were not expected to sell in great numbers, but were to refurbish the pallid image of corporate look-alike motorcars. Old values died hard.

Except in southern California—where compact and subcom-pact autos were taking three of every four cars sold—small au-tomobiles were not doing well at all. "Give 'em large, they wanted small; give 'em small, they wanted large," a harried General Motors market analyst sighed. Once again General Motors shifted its production plans, this time to cope with a "big-car backlash." Small-car sales would continue to grow, but at a slower rate than during the preceding two years.

The return of prosperity spread unevenly. Detroit's unem-ployment rate of 17 percent was the nation's highest. Industry-wide unemployment, which had peaked at 300,000 a year earlier, was down to 60,000 by 1977, but more than 100,000 other posi-tions had been eliminated in factory-wide, company-wide econ-omy moves. No longer would that 100,000 take home the ten-dollar-per-hour wages and fringe benefits that had made the auto worker the highest paid factory hand in the world.

By the end of 1977, General Motors had creamed 56 percent of all domestic sales, the largest market share the company had ever posted. Intermediate-size cars—apparently compromises between size and economy—provided most of the gain for the corporation. Alfred P. Sloan's dictum of "a car for every purse and purpose" still paid dividends. General Motors sold 6.2 mil-lion motor vehicles during the year, recording net sales of $47 billion and a record income of $2.9 billion, a 20-percent return on investment. After a three-year absence, the corporation returned to its accustomed place as the largest of all American corporations on the annual *Fortune* 500 listing, displacing the oil-rich Exxon Corporation.

The wash of prosperity buoyed executive salaries. After two niggardly years, Chairman Murphy received a record $950,000 in salary and bonuses, an increase of 65 percent over dismal 1975; as president, Estes took home $225,000 in salary and $600,000 in bonuses. Six other General Motors executives earned more than $760,000 in the largest payout in corporate history.

Despite this affluence, General Motors still groped for a larger share of the still-growing small-car market. Four-hundred-dollar price cuts on the Chevette in seven western states had neither curbed import sales nor helped fulfill the once-grand expectations the corporation had had for the automobile two-and-a-half years earlier. Toyota, Datsun, Volkswagen, and Honda all outsold the vainglorious import fighter; imported cars held a firm 18 percent of the market, and their distributors were covetously eyeing the almost virgin territory lying between the Rocky Mountains and the Appalachians. If the Chevette—the corporate car—had accomplished anything, it was only to siphon sales from the Vega, Edward Cole's last automobile, mercifully putting the *coup de grâce* to the last General Motors vehicle that might be attributed to a single, strong-willed engineer.*

There were two other fly specks on the windowpane: pending bills to place a heavy tax surcharge on gas-guzzlers (or to ban them altogether) and what mocking newspaper reporters called "the Chevymobile affair."

The gas-guzzler tax would be little more than a nuisance; by 1980–81, the down-sizing program would have reduced the "full-size" car to the equivalent of the compact, or back to the length of the family car of 1955. Despite public protests that such a federal restriction on the market was an invasion of free enterprise, corporate executives agreed privately that they could live

---

* A second Cole project, development of the rotary engine, also was formally terminated in 1977. After seven years of trial and a claimed expenditure of $150 million, General Motors tersely reported that "its rotary engines do not demonstrate the potential for low emissions levels and fuel economy equal [to] those of current reciprocating piston engines." General Motors had simply backed the wrong horse; Ford, meanwhile, was planning to introduce in its own mini-car a stratified-charge engine licensed by Honda.

with it. As one Detroit sales analyst put it, "Putting a stiffer price on gasoline or big cars just isn't going to do it. A $50 or $500 tax isn't going to make any difference to a big car buyer who's plunking down between $6,000 and $10,000. If people are putting in $600 sunroofs and $500 air conditioning in record numbers, obviously price is not a major consideration."

Even a proposed ban on automobiles that delivered less than sixteen miles per gallon by 1980 would be no more than a nuisance. The nine-passenger limousine would have to be fitted with a diesel engine, and three of the "sporty" muscle cars would be in jeopardy. "But if certain cars are banned today," Pete Estes argued in a speech at the Lawrence Institute of Technology, "what will be next?" If you must drive a car that gets more than x-miles per gallon, isn't it reasonable to expect that the next step might be to say, you can't live in a house with more than two bedrooms?"

The "Chevymobile" controversy could not be brushed aside so easily. Not after the attorney general of Illinois sued "Mr. Giant Manufacturer" on behalf of "the poor consumer" on the grounds of deception. A dissatisfied Oldsmobile owner from Chicago had complained to the consumer fraud division of the attorney general's office that his brand-new car had a nondescript Chevrolet motor, not the once widely touted Oldsmobile Rocket engine he had come to know and love. The attorney general estimated that 43,000 of his fellow citizens each had paid an additional $175 for the Oldsmobile engine that wasn't.

The day after the suit was filed, "Mr. Giant Manufacturer," in the person of Pete Estes, released a bland admission calculated to burnish its image: "In recent days, questions have been raised about the use of Chevrolet-produced 350 cubic inch V-8 engines in some Oldsmobile Delta 88s. This decision was made knowing that the Oldsmobile Delta 88 customer—no matter which engine he received—would be the owner of an automobile that would give him the quality, performance and service he expects and associates with any General Motors product."

The two engines were comparable, if not identical. (The fan belts and oil filters differed, and some Oldsmobile dealers did not stock replacements on the grounds that those were Chevrolet parts.) The practice of substituting engines, the statement continued, had gone on for years. Buick, for example, made the engines for General Motors' intermediate-size cars, and a second Buick V-6 powered no less than thirteen different models of Pontiacs, Buicks, and Oldsmobiles. Nor was the interchangeability limited to engines. "Major mechanical components such as transmissions are also shared across a number of GM product lines," the statement continued.*

Papered with legal summonses—ultimately there were to be some seventy suits, including fifty filed by state attorney generals—General Motors offered the owners of Buicks, Pontiacs, and Oldsmobiles with Chevrolet engines either new cars or special long-term warranties. (Only 5,725 people accepted the new-car offer, probably because it was subject to a discount of eight cents for each mile the owner had driven his Chevymobile. Rocket 88 engines were not available anyway, the Center for Auto Safety charged.)

The nationwide hubbub caught the corporation by surprise. "I guess it didn't occur to us that people were interested in where the engines were built," Thomas Murphy said, an odd admission in view of the extensive promotion efforts the corporation had expended on its engines since 1904 and David Dunbar Buick's

---

* In September 1979, the Federal Trade Commission began an ongoing investigation of the reportedly "inordinately high repair rate" of overtaxed automatic transmissions installed in General Motors cars. Clarence Ditlow, director of the Center for Auto Safety, charged that the automatic transmission designed originally for the 2,100-pound Chevette had been installed in as many as 3.5 million autos of various sizes up to the 3,765-pound Caprice. General Motors was picking up the estimated $400 repair bill "on a case by case basis," said J.G. Vorhees, the vice-president for consumer relations, but a corporation spokesman insisted, "There has been no widespread failure" of the transmissions. General Motors' handling of the repairs was akin to the practice of "secret warranties" widespread throughout the industry. In some thirty instances where significant numbers of parts failed after the warranty had expired, manufacturers quietly informed dealers that repair work would be indemnified by the corporation. But owners were not informed, nor the cars in jeopardy recalled; federal law requires recalls only for safety-related defects. According to Ditlow, "After new-car warranties expire, many people take their cars to independent repair shops, where prices usually are lower than at dealerships. Others are not given the warranty work even when they take their cars to dealers because they don't know to ask for it. Many consumers who might benefit are excluded." *Automotive News,* an influential trade publication, scored the practice, editorializing, "If it technically is not illegal, it is indeed immoral." The secret warranties are described in an Associated Press dispatch of October 10, 1978, and a *Newsday* article on December 26, 1978.

original L-head motor. The great Chevymobile flap would not be settled until 1979, when the company agreed to pay the 132,000 affected owners a $200 indemnity and provide an extended warranty on the entire power train of engine, transmission, and drive axle. The total cost would reach $40 million, Illinois Attorney General William Scott estimated.

However much General Motors might have wished to dismiss the Chevymobile matter, the nationwide publicity sorely embarrassed the company. The corporation appeared to be sly—or worse, deceitful—when actually it had only become ensnared by its own upgrading publicity. The corporation could, in good conscience, substitute a "Chevrolet" engine for an "Oldsmobile"; the ongoing standardization of parts fostered by corporate headquarters had effectively homogenized General Motors automobiles.

Despite its virtually identical lines, General Motors sold yet another record number of motor vehicles during 1978, almost 6 percent more than the year before. Ford struggled to keep pace, while hapless Chrysler and tiny American Motors edged closer to insolvency. The 5.4 million new autos General Motors peddled represented 57 percent of all domestic cars sold; only the imports, collectively holding 20 percent of the market, managed to avoid the juggernaut that was General Motors.

Thomas Murphy was more than a little irritated by the imports' continuing strength, and their armoring mystique. "I think it is time we Americans took national pride in something else besides our prowess at mass production and our ability to get things done. We in this country are far too ready and willing to defer to foreign traditions and to attribute to imports an aura of superiority, whether it be in wine making or the quality of our automobiles." The chairman seemingly did not understand the link between Detroit's use of secret warranties, product integrity, and the imports' "aura of superiority."

The importers did. C.R. Brown, the director of Mazda's American sales network, explained, "We've lost our competition in the U.S. automobile industry. There is no more competitive environment in terms of product differentiation. The excitement is no longer there except in the minds of a few. The flair, excitement, integrity of the industry is dissipated. It's 'So goes GM, so goes the industry.' "

The juggernaut rolled on, with predictions of yet another boom year, the fourth in a row, for 1979. With the introduction of the new X-bodies, the front-wheel-drive compacts, new cars pegged perfectly to hit the fastest-growing part of the market, even double-digit inflation would not slow General Motors' march to 60 percent.

Those prospects vanished abruptly in February 1979. A coalition of Muslim conservatives, liberal political figures, and militant students ended the regime of the shah of Iran, nationalized the oil fields, and cut off sales to the shah's long-time protector, the United States.

American motorists, who had almost forgotten the lines at gasoline stations five-and-a-half years earlier, discovered them once again. While the fear of oil shortages was greater than the reality—oil-exporting nations merely raised their prices and resourceless importing countries paid more dearly—President Carter's proposal of a stand-by rationing plan was enough to send the automobile market into turmoil. Gasoline prices jumped to more than a dollar a gallon, literally doubling in less than a year. Inflation-pinched, anxious about possible future fuel shortages, buyers sought out automobiles with the best reputation for gasoline economy. (The rush to the fuel-stingy diesel-powered automobiles, once scorned for their "poor" performance—that is, slow acceleration—was so great that would-be buyers were paying premiums as high as $2,500 above the $4,800 list price for Volkswagen's diesel Rabbits. At 1980 fuel prices, it would take the entire lifetime of the automobile to recoup that $2,500 through savings on fuel.)

Still down-sizing, its corporate fuel average dragged down by far too many fuel-inefficient automobiles, General Motors was caught mid-stride. Only its miles-per-gallon leaders—the newly introduced X-bodies, the Chevette, and the diesel-powered Oldsmobiles—prospered. Company sales were down almost 11 percent from 1978's record. Ford and Chrysler suffered even more, Ford's profits reportedly coming entirely from its overseas operations, Chrysler hemorrhaging red ink with each worsening quarterly report.

Yet despite the fuel shortage; despite a threat to diesel engines from the Environmental Protection Agency, which suspected that motor's "soot" emissions to be carcinogenic; despite the sale after sixty years of Billy Durant's Frigidaire division because it had become a steady money-loser; and despite Federal Trade Commission legal actions that threatened the 400-percent markups on crash parts, General Motors remained optimistic.

This was not the same corporation that had begun the decade as king of the hill, dispenser of sufferance to faltering competitors, intolerant of government and consumer alike, weathervane of the national mood, litmus paper and catalyst alike of the national economy. The era of barely accountable authority had ended, the emperor of capitalism cast down. In its place stood a strange hybrid, at once arrogant in its economic power and bewildered by its responsibility to the public.

19

The Corporate State

Once it was a toy of the wealthy, then a source of mobility for the more affluent, and finally a lifeway for Everyman. Now, in the ninth decade of the century, the automobile had become a trillion-dollar prison, locking the richest nation in the world into an economic structure from which it could not, and probably did not want to, escape.

The automobile was blessing and curse both, a harbinger of concrete enough to cement over the entire state of West Virginia; a berserker which killed 55,000 people a year, injured three million more, and permanently maimed 150,000. No nation ever had spent so much on a single transportation system. Perhaps no nation ever again would spend as much.

The automobile ruled the nation's economy, and the motor vehicle's voracious appetite for fuel governed foreign policy. Allies might be cast aside and enemies taken to the bosom in the eternal search for the life-giving distillates of microscopic sea life that died a hundred million years ago.

512

The cars and trucks flowed, sixty or more an hour from the assembly lines, 480 per shift, streams from half a hundred factories pouring together into a flood tide of fourteen, fifteen, and soon sixteen million new vehicles every year.

And astride it all stood the colossus of roads: General Motors.

The corporation was no longer, as it once was, an insular monolith, arrogantly unresponsive. The nation's largest industry had transformed itself into a quasi-public utility, grudgingly accepting government regulation for the privilege of continuing to build and to profit.

General Motors had not adopted government's mandates gracefully, for government regulation is costly. One out of nine General Motors employees, Thomas Murphy has maintained, worked at tasks dictated by the federal government—auto safety, pollution control, the working environment, waste management, taxes, and a host of other legally mandated responsibilities. General Motors spent $2.25 billion in 1974 and 1975 alone to fulfill local, state, and federal regulations. By the end of 1977, that figure had doubled, provoking yet another screed from Murphy against "lost opportunities, misplaced priorities and misused resources." Regulations had to be measured against benefits derived, he insisted.

Even when consumer demand for more fuel-efficient automobiles underscored federal mandates, the corporation balked. The $1.5 billion spent in 1978 for improved fuel economy, Executive Vice-President Roger B. Smith acknowledged, was a competitive expense, "even though our efforts to achieve the very stringent 27.5-miles-per-gallon fleet average mandated for 1985 are requiring substantial spending that will go well beyond cost-beneficial levels to meet consumer demands."

The opposition to government "intrusion" in the marketplace came couched in the fiery slogans of the nineteenth century's economic buccaneers. "Concerned about the slide toward economic regimentation in the United States," Murphy proclaimed with splendid indignation, "Government, rather than the buying public, is increasingly determining the kinds of products and services offered for sale, and government regulations are influencing their costs and consequently their prices. What is of greatest concern is that each intrusion of government, because it takes decision-making power away from the individual consumer, diminishes his economic freedom."

Murphy's complaints might have been more warmly received if, in fact, holding the industry's feet to regulatory fires had not produced results. Some, less doctrinaire than Murphy, agreed. "There's been a lot of moaning and groaning about the burdens of government regulation on the industry, and a lot of people say Washington is killing the business and taking the fun out of it. I don't think so. On the contrary, I think the revolutionary changes in automotive design that the regulations have initiated are creating a great new market for our products," the president of Ford Motor Company, Philip Caldwell, rebutted.*

Whether responding to proposed orders requiring more effective smog control, safety appliances, antitheft devices, or increased gasoline mileage, General Motors has balked. "When government insists on certain regulations, Japan hires engineers, and GM hires lawyers," scoffed Mark Green, one of the corporation's more perceptive and enduring critics. Then, confronted with a deadline, sometimes after going to court to forestall its imposition, General Motors has just as invariably made it a practice to comply voluntarily one year before the deadline falls due. Thus it can continue to complain while simultaneously appearing to be a model of civic overconformity.

With far more grace, the corporation has accepted a social responsibility it once considered beyond its expertise or management's moral purview. It has launched a program in predominantly black schools to locate and train future factory workers.

---

* In 1979, executives of the financially exhausted Chrysler Corporation attempted to blame the costs of meeting safety, mileage, and pollution standards for the company's woeful position. Seeking a billion-dollar loan from the federal government, Chairman John J. Riccardo argued that those expenditures hit the nation's tenth-largest industrial corporation "a lot harder than they have the bigger manufacturers." One dubious financial analyst quoted in the *Wall Street Journal* wryly commented that the argument allowed Riccardo to shift blame for the company's problems away from himself and his fellows. Scapegoating government regulation—and especially the head of the National Highway Transportation Safety Agency, strong-willed Joan Claybrook—is "ridiculous," the analyst said. "Several other observers, including some Chrysler insiders as well as people at other auto makers who generally favor a federal bailout, share the view that Chrysler's government-regulation argument involves tactics more than truth," the newspaper reported on August 3, 1979.

Enlightened self-interest it may be, to the extent that some of these youngsters eventually will draw down General Motors paychecks, yet it also is serving the 1,700 young men and women who otherwise might have no marketable skills, Further, in the wake of the 1960s civil-rights campaign, the company has voluntarily made continuing and determined efforts to buy goods from minority-owned suppliers. That program surpassed $199 million annually in 1979, a total that has grown steadily, if not spectacularly, since the procurement staff launched it a decade earlier.

The corporation also has hired blacks and women in increasing numbers. Of 126,000 women working for the corporation in the United States in 1979, 1,500 held what the corporation called "first-line supervisory jobs." Minorities fare somewhat better, occupying 9 percent of all "officials and managers" slots, slightly less than half of the rate of all minority employment at General Motors. Similarly, the corporation has hired, at least for white-collar positions, handicapped workers, though their numbers are comparatively few.

Apparently the effort will continue. The company's wholly owned General Motors Institute, an accredited college of engineering and management that provides a goodly portion of the trainees for those two job classifications at General Motors, has a student enrollment that is one-third female and almost one-fifth minority.

Beyond the confines of General Motors itself, the corporation has increased its deposits in minority-owned banks, placed $4.9 billion in insurance with minority-owned firms, and invested through minority-owned brokerage houses. It has loaned more than $13.7 million to black and Chicano businessmen and provided managerial guidance to them to repay the money. The number of black and brown dealers has increased to 142, while another 134 car and truck dealerships are owned by women, usually widows of the original owners.

In September 1978, the company announced that it would provide an initial $1.3 million to begin the revitalization of a six-block neighborhood just north of the General Motors Building on West Grand Boulevard. "New Center" was to be a refurbished community, its streets closed to through traffic and its homes rewrought in the image of suburban condominiums with common lawns and small parks. It was an ambitious plan, profitable, part of a slow ingathering of former suburbanites taking place in a number of cities. (This return to the central city, largely of "empty nesters"—unmarried professional people and couples who have decided not to have children soon or at all—will have long-term effects on multiple-car ownership.)

General Motors had not reckoned, however, on the community reaction to what Murphy conceded would be "inconvenience and displacement of some persons living in the area." Resistance was widespread and vocal, especially from working-class renters who inevitably would be forced out of the refurbished homes by higher rents. "Frankly, I'm a bit frustrated," Murphy admitted, when the people most affected did not seem to appreciate the socially responsible motives that lay behind General Motors' planning.

Ultimately, the corporation struck a compromise, but as one commentator put it, General Motors had stubbed its toe: "Although GM dealt with the technical and planning side of the project with breathtaking speed and efficiency, the project moved forward more slowly than originally envisaged. Dealing with people problems is messy, inefficient, and time consuming. But as GM found, not dealing with them at the outset may be more so."

Such well-meaning if clumsy efforts pile upon the day-to-day management of a company and an industry churning in turmoil. Market shares are shifting, some dramatically, both in the United States and abroad. The overseas market—really two or three markets grouped by level of economic development—will grow faster than sales in the nearly saturated United States, Canada, and Japan. By 1990, North American auto sales will average 15.6 million annually, one respected economic study suggests, while European sales will swell to 14 million cars per year. Sales in the less developed nations of Asia, Africa, and Latin America will total 14.9 million cars annually.

To meet this demand, auto makers will resort increasingly to so-called "world cars"—small, more fuel-efficient vehicles with relatively unchanging designs that are built in comparatively small plants in the countries in which they are marketed. General Motors already has its first such car, the Chevette, produced now in six countries. Ford has the Fiesta, Volkswagen its Rabbit, and Chrysler the Mitsubishi-built Omni and Horizon.* There will be more—and, ultimately, an international trading war that will pit government against government, trading group against trading group, and protectionists against free traders.

Contending for overseas sales, American auto makers have had to overcome greater burdens literally and figuratively, in the international trading derby. Even after President Nixon imposed a 10-percent surcharge on imported cars in 1973 so as to give the beleaguered Big Three a respite, the American tariff was substantially less than the protective tariffs fixed by some other foreign governments. Japan hewed to a 35-percent duty on cars with wheelbases longer than 105.5 inches, which is to say on all American-made cars. Germany laid down a 20-to-22-percent tariff, and the United Kingdom 25 percent.

Even with later tariff reductions and the lifting of the Nixon surcharge, the United States still confronted local users' taxes abroad based on gross weight or engine size. The average American car measured one-third longer and weighed 50 percent more than the analogous European model. (France levied a $30 annual tax on the 1975 Mercedes compared to a $203 charge on the competitive Oldsmobile; the American car weighed 1,300 pounds more and had an engine three times the size of its German rival.)

For American companies, the solution in the 1970s remained the same as it has been a half-century earlier: overseas investment, with expansion of factories to build smaller versions of American cars. In theory, growing prosperity was to lead Euro-

* General Motors also has designed a small truck, the Basic Transportation Vehicle (BTV), to be manufactured in underdeveloped countries. General Motors provides assistance in setting up the manufacturing plant, which is "about the size of a large barn," and sells the complex engine and drive train to the local manufacturer. In 1973, there were locally owned BTV plants in Malaysia, Ecuador, Portugal, and the Philippines. While these plants, of course, do buy parts from General Motors, the corporation deserves recognition for its acceptance of what it termed "the moral obligation of industrialized societies to help the less industrialized countries get started on the way to a higher standard of living."

peans to emulate the earlier American experience of "trading up" and displaying one's position in life with the car one drove.

It was a serious miscalculation. Local conditions and parochialism governed automobile development and sales. Cold German winters led Volkswagen to favor air-cooled motors, since an air-cooling system would not freeze. Rough roads throughout Europe called for independent, four-wheel suspension, and icy roads in winter led engineers to place more weight on the drive wheels for traction. Poor drainage of roads favored disc brakes, which did not fade when wet. Narrow, winding roads in England, Italy, and France required quick steering response. In all of these areas, as well as in automobile tire development, European engineers had a demonstrable edge over their smug or disbelieving American counterparts.

While the American automobile was standardized, European engineers combined a "technical know-how with social know-why" to create cars with "such diverse factors as front engines with front drive, rear engines with rear drive, engines with two, three and four cylinders (in some cases air-cooled and others liquid-cooled), traditional rear axles and all independent suspension, springs made from torsion bars, coils, and rubber. In fact, the only features common to all cars are four-speed manual transmissions and restriction to four passengers."

Hampering its international subsidiaries with operating policies that reeked of paternalism until the early 1970s, General Motors had not fared as well overseas as it might have. Though employing as many nationals as possible—in 1972 Adam Opel had a payroll of 61,000, of whom only twenty were United States citizens—General Motors did not permit its overseas divisions to operate independently. As the most successful company in the most heavily motorized nation in the world, the corporation presumed it best understood automobile production and marketing.

"Unlike Ford, GM have always controlled Vauxhall's product policy very tightly from Detroit," British automotive writer Graham Bannock observed, "even to the extent of forcing Vauxhall to follow the American styling trends of the 'fat fifties.' They were spectacularly out of place in Britain at the time and were probably responsible for Vauxhall's unhappy 'tin-can' image." Finally allowed to produce a smaller car in the late 1960s, Vauxhall's new Viva was, in appearance and technical design, "clearly derived from GM products in the United States."

Even into the 1970s, Adam Opel had not yet worked free of William Mitchell's styling dictates; its strong-selling Manta distinctly resembled the decade-old Corvair. Not until Detroit realized that the corporation had lost substantial ground to foreign competition did the board of directors scuttle the paternalistic policies of old.

The changes were abrupt, ultimately capped by the naming of the heads of the overseas companies as corporate vice-presidents—on a par with the general managers of the domestic divisions. By 1973, Alexander Cunningham, Opel's general manager, could assert, "There is a strong feeling today that Opel is first a German company, second a multinational, and third a subsidiary of a U.S. company."

The new sensitivity to international realities reached to exquisite delicacy in the courtship of Isuzu Motors executives. Newly acquired by General Motors, Isuzu, a truck manufacturer, intended to remain a Japanese company, serving Detroit from afar. In allusion to a Buddhist legend, Isuzu managers fancied their company as the balls of the bull. "Although only a small part of something very big, we want to be a very important part," Toshio Okamoto, an executive vice-president, announced.

The Japanese managers of the financially distressed truck manufacturer hardly rushed to embrace the *gengi* who now owned more than one-third (a controlling interest) of Isuzu's stock. It took no little tact and patience to win Isuzu over. One engineering consultant waited eighteen months before he was welcomed to weekly staff meetings. "The Japanese don't warm up to strangers very quickly," the American consultant explained with some understatement.

Rather than force themselves upon the Japanese, General Motors waited for almost three years before convincing Isuzu in 1974 to build a passenger car based upon the Opel. (In the meantime, the Japanese firm was constructing small pickup trucks to be marketed in the United States as the Chevrolet Luv.) This unaccustomed deference was necessary, for the Isuzu purchase, maneuvered around the opposition of protectionist-minded government ministries, was the only way General Motors could penetrate the lucrative Japanese market. (As early as 1936, Ford Motor's applications to build cars and trucks in Japan were turned down with the bald assertion, "We want to protect Japanese industry.")

As late as 1977, of the 4.1 million new cars sold in Japan, only 15,000 were made in America. Rather than explain its own protectionist policies, the Japanese government chided American manufacturers for poor quality of workmanship; because of high prices, up to four times the American sticker price, the Japanese buyer considered an imported car as a "luxury and even as a kind of status symbol" and sought "perfection in detail when purchasing an imported car." Such perfection was missing from the mass-produced American car.

Despite the handicaps, self-imposed or otherwise, American automobile manufacturers have continued to advocate free trade. "Restricting the ability of the automobile industry to compete for world markets could endanger what has historically been a favorable contribution to the United States balance of payments and trade surplus," the Automobile Manufacturers Association maintained as late as June 1968. General Motors alone claimed to have taken as profits from its overseas operations $11.7 billion from 1946 to 1967, $782 million in that last year alone.

But 1967 was to be the last year in which the United States would enjoy a favorable balance of automotive payments—that is, would sell more cars and parts overseas than importers sold in this country. The following year was the first of an unbroken run of debit balances, reaching $3.3 billion in 1973, the year the oil embargo threw the world into recession. That year General Motors claimed for itself a $396 million positive balance of payments, a meaningless figure since the calculation did not, could not, include the millions of dollars the corporation lost because it refused to compete at home with smaller imported cars, especially those streaming from Japan.

By 1974, UAW President Leonard Woodcock claimed that

185,000 production jobs had been lost to imports—ignoring the 143,000 Americans employed by foreign-car dealers, importers, and suppliers, who did not carry UAW cards. The United States sinking fast into a recession, Woodcock abandoned labor's traditional free-trade stand to ask Congress for temporary restrictions on foreign-car imports. Denying that the UAW served as "GM's spear carriers," he warned that foreign manufacturers could "seize" as much as 30 percent of the American market before Detroit brought out its own smaller cars. Unemployment in Flint already stood at 25 percent; the industry confronted a debacle "more disastrous than anything since the Great Depression."

Woodcock made no impression on the Senate Finance Committee, but he did stir the anxieties of at least one manufacturer. Toyota elected to maintain its exports to the United States at the same level in 1974 as it had in 1973, "thereby steering a middle course between its U.S. dealers, demanding more cars to sell, and the United Auto Workers, whom Toyota fears will intensify its calls for import restrictions on small cars."

While Toyota displayed forbearance, European manufacturers could not. Confronted with the same recession that had cast down American auto companies, Fiat, Renault, Volvo, Volkswagen, Triumph, and nineteen other foreign companies began dumping their overproduction on the American market. The "dumpers" included Opel, selling its Corvair look-alike, the Manta, in dealers' showrooms for $3,744, nearly $1,200 less than the *wholesale* price in Germany.

Contrary to UAW claims, "dumping" was not responsible for the continuing lag in American automobile sales, both in total and as a percentage of all cars sold. The two most successful importers, number-one ranked Toyota and second-place Datsun, as well as prestigious Rolls-Royce and Porsche, were not among the dumpers.

The dumping probe was summarily settled without imposing the mandatory punitive tariffs called for by a half-century-old law. The offenders contritely promised to go and sin no more and then raised prices in the United States, ironically ending significant price competition with domestic manufacturers. Eventually, currency revaluations pushed foreign-car prices well above those of the newly introduced smaller American cars.*

Smiling through gritted teeth, foreign auto makers applauded the first of those smaller cars, General Motors' Chevette. "The American auto industry has learned its lesson and finally is becoming market-oriented instead of trying to push the market with their earlier products," Umberto Agnelli, president of Italy's Fiat, approved. With the Chevette, "General Motors has legitimized the small car in the eyes of many American buyers," Datsun Vice President Mayfield Marshall said. Scorning protectionist sentiment, the general manager of Renault, Georges Basiliou, told a group of automotive writers in Detroit that imports were "salutary for the American consumer and the automotive industry here. . . . Without pressure of the import competition, I wonder how quickly Detroit would have moved on minicars, if it would have moved at all."

Despite mutual assurances within the world automobile industry that each favored free trade, protectionist impulses throbbed in the breast of every hard-pressed manufacturer. "There is a ceiling past which imports cannot be tolerated by any country that wishes to retain a healthy domestic industry," Sir William Batty, chairman of Ford Motor Company of Britain, warned. "When imports reach 40 percent"—British imports were then at 33 percent—"we have gone past that ceiling." Sir William be-

---

* According to "a Ford administration official" quoted in the *Wall Street Journal* of May 6, 1976, the investigation was throttled because it "might have done irreparable damage to certain manufacturers whose sales have dropped off greatly," specifically Volkswagen. Like Ford and its Model-T, Volkswagen had stayed with the basically unchanged Beetle and its dated technology for too long, and though Americans had purchased more than four million in the twenty years following its 1952 introduction, sales no longer were enough to keep the company's production lines at full volume. The deference to Volkswagen illustrated the complex intertwinings of multinational corporations and governments; two weeks earlier, after years of discreet pressure from the United States government, Volkswagen finally had announced—over the protests of German labor unions—that it would build an assembly plant in Pennsylvania. Enforcing the penalty for dumping would deprive the company of the $200 million needed to raise up that factory. Just how critical the American automobile market is to overseas manufacturers, and how closely it is monitored by Europeans as a matter of national pride, is illustrated by an article in *Le Figaro* of April 27, 1979, "Guerre mondiale de l'automobile" ("The Automobile World War"), with the subhead, "Carter lance les 'petites Americaines' dans la bataille" ("Carter throws the 'little Americans' into the battle").

seeched Her Majesty's government for "short term restraints" upon imports "to protect the principle of free trade."

With each slump in the market, similar instincts of self-preservation flamed anew in other countries. At the end of 1979, with the American automobile industry again subsiding into recession and automobile unemployment approaching 150,000, UAW President Douglas Fraser threatened to ask Congress for a "local content" law, which would require foreign manufacturers to open factories in the United States. Cut imports, the late president of the AFL-CIO, George Meany, insisted, or manufacturing capacity will be crippled and Americans reduced to "shining one another's shoes."

While General Motors remained silently stoic, other auto manufacturers have echoed the unions' concern. Japanese auto makers are "exporting unemployment," the president of American Motors, Paul Tippett, said heatedly. Philip Caldwell, Ford's president and chief executive officer, also called for local-content laws, noting, "In 19 or 20 countries, we've had to operate in this manner for years. It's not a novelty, except in this market."

It was a world turned upside-down. The American automobile industry, once the unrivaled master, found itself hard-pressed to compete even on its own turf. Not since the earliest days of the automobile had so many manufacturers contended for the public custom. Some twenty companies, many of them bearing the colors and investment of their nation of origin, with at least two more entries from Japan in the offing, vied with the four survivors of America's great industrial bloodletting. Two of the four automobile manufacturers—the American truck industry had a number of smaller, successful competitors—were sick unto their deaths. American Motors held on by building its Jeep, a utility vehicle forty years old, and by the sale of a 5-percent interest to ambitious French manufacturer Renault. Struck dumb by repeated blows to the pocketbook, Chrysler arrogantly turned to the federal government to demand a loan in mid-1979 because managerial ineptitude had led the company close to bankruptcy. Yet even the $1.5 billion in loan guarantees finally approved by Congress at the end of 1979 cannot assure that Walter Chrysler's once formidable creation will not go belly up.

Hornbook maxims of free enterprise gave way to expediency in the case of Chrysler. Were that company to go bankrupt, the financial reverberations would thunder throughout Wall Street, bringing down smaller, Chrysler-dependent suppliers as well. The closing of the tenth-largest industrial enterprise in the country would mean the loss of thousands of jobs, enough perhaps to send the economy into recession. (At first General Motors objected on principle to federal aid to Chrysler because "it removes and compromises that discipline [of failure] from the marketplace." Two months later, board chairman Tom Murphy grudgingly acceded to a government loan guarantee "if that were the only way.")

Chrysler's dilemma reflected the problems of the entire industry as it attempted to meet the competition of foreign imports while coping with ever more stringent government mandates for safety, air-pollution control, and mileage. Detroit would spend an estimated $70 billion by 1985—General Motors $37 billion of that—to redesign its automobiles to meet government standards, a challenge "more economic than technical," according to General Motors President Pete Estes.

To reach the required 27.5-miles-per-gallon average for all General Motors cars sold, the company would lighten its vehicles by another five hundred pounds. It also would build fewer large cars; by the due date of 1985, autos with wheelbases longer than the compact's 111 inches would make up only 5 percent of General Motors' production.

Still, General Motors and its domestic competitors lagged behind the realities of the marketplace. As late as January 1979, Estes stubbornly maintained, "The fuel economy standards are not necessary and they are not good for America." Within a month, the shah of Iran had fallen; within two, spot shortages had reminded Americans once more of the precariousness of oil supplies. By March, Toyota and Datsun, the two leading auto importers, were well on their way to selling more than one million motor vehicles in the United States. Before a year had passed, Estes would concede that consumers already were demanding automobiles that delivered mileage equivalent to the 1985 federal mandate of 27.5 miles per gallon. General Motors had but one automobile, the three-year-old Chevette, that could meet that standard.

The American automobile industry, General Motors included, was in grave jeopardy. Looking at figures for the automotive balance of payments, the doyen of financial journalists, retired *Wall Street Journal* editor Vermont Royster, concluded, "Obviously the American auto industry is no longer king of the road":

> Historically our economic growth was built on imaginative innovation not only in products but in production methods. By the end of World War II our major industries—autos, for example, or steel—were preeminent; the world begged for their products.
>
> Complacency was the result. The steel industry lagged in new production methods as many of its plants became antiquated. The auto industry remained unruffled by the innovative imports from Volkswagen or Toyota until they became a flood. It simply sat by and let a good part of the market, at home and in the world, be taken away from it.

It had become an industry momentarily unable to compete, tacitly aligned with former antagonists—government and labor—against the common enemy. In Tokyo, United States Ambassador Mike Mansfield urged reluctant Japanese manufacturers to emulate Volvo, Honda, and Volkswagen in opening factories in the United States, warning that the alternative was protectionist legislation.

While such a move might be a solution to the problem of "exporting unemployment," as American Motors' president termed it, it can only enhance competitive pressures domestically. Publicly, General Motors welcomes the competition; privately, executives are anxious. At least one widely circulated market study, citing what it calls "consumer overreaction" to the gasoline shortage of 1979, predicted that import penetration of the American market could grow from 1979's 21.5 percent to 27 percent in 1980 and 30 percent in 1981. The survey noted that the shift from larger automobiles would continue: four of every ten Cadillac owners and one of every two Buick drivers said they intended to buy smaller cars in the future. Such predictions make General Motors executives nervous. For all of the company's "down-sizing," it still lacked a reputation for mileage per gallon comparable to the imports. Equally important, it did not have the reputation for quality and economy of operation the imports enjoy.

As great as it was, General Motors was at risk. Even a relatively small loss of market share would send the national economy into a downturn, bringing the federal government into a more active role. Just what steps the government might take to shore up American manufacturers would be decided in the first years of the 1980s. "We are not going to let what happened to the steel industry [obsolete factories, high prices, inability to compete with imports] happen to the automobile industry," a senior official in the Carter administration vowed.

Some protectionist measure—probably a local-content law, perhaps substantial tariff increases as well—appeared likely. "If we export all the dollars saved in buying [fuel for] fuel-efficient cars to other countries to buy the cars, then we haven't gained anything from the point of balance of payments," Transportation Secretary Neil Goldschmidt noted.

In not letting automobiles go the way of steel, the government would necessarily play a greater role in Detroit's decision-making, probably through tax incentives and increasingly stringent mileage and pollution mandates. Federal agencies already had begun funding research in an effort to stimulate the advances or breakthroughs that the industry itself has ignored in its infatuation with the internal-combustion engine. Until now, "research" in the automobile industry has been short-term and product-oriented, "necessarily aimed at immediate product improvement, which can translate more easily into increased revenues," as one government bureaucrat put it.

Short of unforeseen scientific or technological discoveries, the familiar internal-combustion engine will dominate America's roads to the year 2000, still spewing pollutants into the air and still contributing to a slaughter of innocents—as many as 64,000 persons annually, one government study projects. Diesel engines may power one-quarter of all cars—certainly the biggest of the surviving gas-guzzlers. General Motors will have in limited production short-range delivery vans and, perhaps, "city cars" with electric motors. In 1985, it also will have ready for production, under the terms of a National Aeronautics and Space Administration grant, a gas turbine engine that will deliver 42.5 miles per gallon, be able to use alternative fuels, and surpass federal emissions standards.

These vehicles will continue to burn conventionally derived petroleum distillates, only gradually switching to alternative fuels as the rising price of gasoline makes these now-expensive alternatives competitive in price. A future service station conceivably will carry stocks of gasoline; fuels derived from shale, tar sand, or coal; alcohol brewed from organic waste, either "straight" or diluted with gasoline into gasohol; and hydrogen, either in gaseous or metallic form. Electric cars will be "fueled" at home, plugged into the wall overnight for a recharge; their ultimate source of energy will depend upon what fuel the local public utility uses to generate electricity—coal, oil, wind, wave, solar, or nuclear energy.

Planet Earth is not running out of energy; that is an Einsteinian impossibility. It is running out of cheap energy, and nothing will shape the future so much as the availability of energy forms made relatively cheap by mass production.

The greatest single factor in the demand for energy is now, and will be for the near future, the automobile. Urban mass-transit systems and high-speed interurban lines such as Japan's "Bullet Train" will not lure significant numbers of motorists from their automobiles. Further, such fixed-route lines are costly to build and, once laid down, are inflexible. Instead, traffic will increase on the nation's roads between two and three million motor vehicles each year, tripling congestion, smog, and fuel consumption. The only viable alternative to the private automobile, which sits idle twenty-two of the twenty-four hours in each day, is the bus, especially in the less densely crowded suburbs.

On the twenty-fifth anniversary of the passage of the National System for Defense and Highways, the 42,500-mile network of interstate roads was obsolescent. Still incomplete, the system that was to cost $37.5 billion to build had reached a total of $112.9 billion by the end of 1979. It would be more costly to complete the unfinished 6 percent than to build the first 94 percent, and the interstates were deteriorating faster than state and federal governments could raise money to restore and upgrade them. Building new roads to drain off some of the congestion was no longer a practical solution, despite the highway lobby's enthusiasm for the attempt.

America was dependent on motor vehicles, not only for transportation, but to maintain the nation's prosperity. It would remain so as long as Americans tolerated the inconvenience and the cost in exchange for the personal freedom and whatever psychic pleasure the automobile offered. The judgment process already had begun, manifested in speed limits, pollution-control laws, safety requirements, and mileage standards. General Motors dared not ignore the social consensus as it earlier ignored market demands.

Whatever the shape of the future General Motors automobile—three of four would be compacts or smaller in size—it would cost more to own and operate. Higher sticker prices—forcing most customers to stretch out their payments, thereby raising interest costs—will send the average monthly payment on those smaller cars to $200 by 1981. Yet that figure, twice that of a decade earlier, is only one of the manifold costs of America's personal mobility. According to the Hertz Corporation's annual survey, Los Angeles had become by 1979 the most expensive city in which to own a compact car; drivers there spent forty-four cents per mile, or $44,000 over a ten-year, 100,000-mile life span. A used car, the Hertz report indicated, was cheaper to operate because savings from the depreciation costs in the first years more than repaid higher maintenance costs later.

In the surge of inflation following the Arab oil embargo of October 1973, the cost of living climbed 56 percent by 1979, driving wages ever higher. By absorbing through greater productivity some of the costs—including increases for its own employees which had the hourly worker earning $15 in wages and fringe benefits at the end of the 1970s—General Motors could claim the price of its average automobile had climbed but 38 percent in that same period.

Yet even that "modest" 38 percent—and $200-per-month car payments—was enough to speed a socioeconomic trend that will have a vast impact on the corporation and its myriad competitors. In increasingly strapped households, married women are going back to work, their earnings no longer put away for the family vacation or a new sofa, but spent to supplement their husbands' inadequate incomes. Almost one-half of all married women now have jobs, including four of every ten with preschool children.

Women who work have fewer children, one reason for the decline in the national birth rate. Smaller families do not need large cars. In a period when economy is paramount, those smaller families are innocently sabotaging General Motors' grand scheme for the 1980s of wringing every dollar possible from big-car sales while taking lower markups on small cars to increase market penetration.

Content with their past success, General Motors' marketing experts erred badly in the early 1960s. They failed to take into account the nascent trend toward households headed by women, especially young women freed from early marriage by the Pill. In 1962, the editor of *Cosmopolitan,* Helen Gurley Brown, titillated America with her how-to manual, *Sex and the Single Girl.* The male guffaws echoed, but Mrs. Brown's book sold one million copies to young women already living single—and liking it. They, their sisters, and their future mates were the vanguard of a lifestyle that placed less emphasis on possessions and more upon experiences. (The acquisitions that conveyed status were to come later, when they settled down.) Those women did not need, or want, and perhaps were intimidated by big cars.

When Mrs. Brown's readers did marry, large numbers of them chose career and residential alternatives to the traditional home in the suburbs and motherhood. Again, they were playing away from General Motors' great strength, the large family car. In buying automobiles to fit their needs—especially along the two seaboards—these budget-conscious women were opting for ease and economy. They tried unfamiliar automobiles with foreign names, switching from one to another. Every new-car purchase was an adventure into uncharted lands.

That lack of brand loyalty has since spread to the small American cars that followed, further complicating General Motors'

marketing problems. Consumer demands for economical transportation flout the merchandising laws of Sloanism—trading up
and planned obsolescence—the very foundation of the corporation.

As the decade of the 1980s opened, General Motors still grappled with that shift in consumer expectations, and with its own
reluctance to accept this new reality. Imported automobiles
snared more than one out of every four new-car sales nationally,
in large part because General Motors and its domestic rivals
simply lacked enough small vehicles to sell. Bemused by the last
effloresence of the large car in 1975, General Motors forecast
only a slow growth of small car sales and happily restored large
automobiles to the place of honor in its factories. That error in
judgment would only be clear after the second energy crisis in
1979.

Even were its small-car capacity increased, General Motors
and its domestic competitors had yet to confront the equally
critical problem of automotive quality and reliability. Though the
corporation would defend its automobiles as the equal of any
made, General Motors lacked a reputation for finely designed,
well-built machines comparable to the German and Japanese
imports. In the fat years of the 1950s and 1960s, consumers
hardly considered the automobile's durability; new-car buyers
intended to trade in their automobile two or three years after
they bought it. Not so in the 1980s; no longer psychic pacifiers,
automobiles had simply become too expensive for such rapid
resale. Thus the corporation found itself attempting to explain
how long a Buick or a Pontiac would last, not how fast it would
go.

Overtaken by events, burdened by its own preconceived strategies, General Motors struggled to catch up at home, and to keep
pace abroad. It was compelled to build small cars, automobiles
for which it had no great reputation and hardly any more enthusiasm, and then sell them to a public unconvinced that the
world's largest automobile manufacturer produced competitive
vehicles. Yet if this quasi-public utility did not build such economical cars, it would ultimately collapse under its own weight.

Once General Motors was the grand arbiter of automotive

taste, molding public opinion to suit its own prejudices. No longer. It had become instead a ponderous, slow-thinking beast of burden, weighed down by an unforgiving responsibility for the state of the national economy. In decades past what was good for General Motors was indeed good for the nation's well-being; in the ninth decade of the century, what was good for General Motors might be disastrous for the nation.

No corporate executive in the days of twenty-cent gasoline could have imagined the costly energy dependence that General Motors' large cars would foster. No executive, no soothsayer anywhere, could have foretold the dire effects of America's wholehearted reliance on the automobile as personal transportation. In the opulent years, it had all seemed so appropriate for the richest nation in history.

But the wealth was not unlimited. General Motors' policies, predicated upon continuous expansion—the philosophical mainspring of the corporation—were inadequate for the new order of things. Bewildered, General Motors lumbered into the future.

Acknowledgments
Notes and Bibliography
Index

ACKNOWLEDGMENTS

The author attempting a history of this scope quickly comes to appreciate the contributions others make in what is, ostensibly, the lonely business of writing. Mere listing does not properly acknowledge the value of their guidance, criticism, hospitality, or encouragement over the five years it took to write this book. Beyond those cited in the notes which follow, I would like to express my gratitude to:

Jack Anderson, of Washington, D.C., who allowed me to rummage in his files; James J. Bradley, director of the Automotive History Collection, Detroit Public Library; E. Wayles Browne, of Fullerton, California; George Clifford, of Washington, D.C.; Clarence Ditlow, Public Interest Research Group, Washington, D.C.; Lowell Dodge, Center for Auto Safety, Washington, D.C.; M.J. Duberstein, Washington, D.C.; James J. Flink, University of California, Irvine; Mark Green, Corporate Accountability Research Group, Washington, D.C.; Mark Grody, Mark Grody Associates, Venice, California; Lawrence Gustin, automotive editor of the Flint, Michigan, *Journal;* John P. Holmstrom, Detroit, Michigan, whose hospitality is remembered still; Judy Howald, General Motors Institute Alumni Collection of Industrial History, Flint, Michigan; Robert Irvin of the Detroit *News;* Carol Lehman, General Motors Corporation; David D. Martin, Washington, D.C.; Joyce Olin, government documents librarian at the University of Southern California, Los Angeles, whose knack for finding obscure technical reports is unsurpassed; Candy Pearce, Harrah's, Reno, Nevada; Warner Pflug, of the Archives of Labor History and Urban Affairs, Wayne State University, Detroit; Richard P. Scharchburg, General Motors Institute; Amy Sherman, formerly of the Los Angeles *Times;* John C. Waugh and Lynn Waugh of Washington, D.C., loyal friends; Renee Weisenberg, Pacific Palisades, California branch librarian; and James Zordich, associate curator of the Automobile History Section, Los Angeles County Museum of Natural History, who guided me through the myriad early automotive journals.

A number of people in sensitive positions chose discreet anonymity for good and sufficient reason; their wishes are respected, their contributions silently acknowledged.

I should make special mention of the staff of the University of California at Los Angeles Research Library, directed by an old friend from another life,

534

Norman Dudley. It is painful to note the burdens imposed on these worthy librarians by the last two governors of California who seemingly believe that the "era of limits" extends to the preservation and dissemination of human knowledge. I am grateful too that James Mink, curator of that library's Department of Special Collections, will permanently archive the research material which went into the making of this book.

Finally, three others must be acknowledged: Michael Hamilburg, who kept the faith; Ernest Scott, who encouraged when I became discouraged, and prodded when I needed that; and Diane Kovacs, who came back smiling.

NOTES AND BIBLIOGRAPHY

Bibliographical Note
In the interest of the reader's patience, and to keep these endnotes within manageable proportions, I have elected to cite specifically only that material actually quoted from other sources. Only when the facts are in dispute, as, for example, concerning the invention of the self-starter, do the notes become remotely comprehensive.

Anything else would bulk this already long book to two-volume dimensions. I estimate I worked through 15,000 separate items, and used material from as much as two-thirds of these in writing this book.

I have attempted to credit as many sources as possible and certainly those that contain unique or proprietary information. However, the reader is cautioned not to dismiss an entry cited only once or twice. James J. Flink's superlative *America Adopts the Automobile 1895–1910* comes quickly to mind as the sort of touchstone one comes to rely on far more than these notes suggest. A number of sources provided excellent information without quotations extracted and thus without specific citations. The most important of these are credited in general headnotes to the chapters.

E.C.

INTRODUCTION
(pages 1–10)

Information for this introduction was drawn from *Statistical Abstract of the United States*, "Motor Vehicle Facts and Figures," published annually by the Motor Vehicle Manufacturers Association, and the corporation's annual reports. Other sources include:

Page

1 ff.   The quotations are drawn from the published hearings of the Committee on Armed Services, United States Senate, 83rd Congress, 1st Session, (Washington, D.C.: Government Printing Office, 1953).

7   Probably the birthplace: *Fortune,* March, 1939, p. 145.

7   Car and truck sales: "Motor Vehicle Facts and Figures, '77'' (Detroit: Motor Vehicle Manufacturers Association, 1978).

7   The giant GM: Robert L. Simison in the *Wall Street Journal,* February 14, 1979, p. 1.

10   There is probably no company: *A Study of the Antitrust Laws,* Staff Report of the Subcommittee on Antitrust and Monopoly, Senate Judiciary Committee (Washington, D.C.: Government Printing Office, 1956), p. 3.

10   The public decisions of General Motors: "On the Economic Image of Corporate Enterprise," in Ralph Nader and Mark Green, eds., *Corporate Power in America* (New York: Grossman Publishers, 1973), p. 6.

CHAPTER 1: A MATTER OF TIMING
(pages 13–30)

In addition to the sources specifically cited, the following works were valuable in their accounts of the early history of the automobile industry: *Automobiles of America* (Detroit: Automobile Manufacturers Association, 1968); *The American Car Since 1775* (New York: E.P. Dutton, 1971), especially for the production figures, pp. 138 ff.; George S. May, *R.E. Olds, Auto Industry Pioneer* (Grand Rapids, Mich.: Wm. B. Eerdmans, 1977); William Greenleaf, *Monopoly on Wheels* (Detroit: Wayne State University Press, 1961); *Horseless Age,* 1904–05; Waldemar B. Kaempflert, *A Popular History of American Invention,* Vol. I (New York: Scribner, 1924); Arthur Pound, *Detroit: Dynamic City* (New York: D. Appleton-Century, 1940); John B. Rae, *The American Automobile: A Brief History* (Chicago: University of Chicago Press, 1965), and his *American Automobile Manufacturers, The First Forty Years* (Philadelphia: Chilton, 1959); and *Scientific American,* 1900–1905, especially the annual automobile numbers each January.

Page

21 Assume that the man: Durant's autobiographical notes left incomplete at his death, quoted in Lawrence R. Gustin, *Billy Durant: Creator of General Motors* (Grand Rapids, Mich.: Wm. B. Eerdmans, 1973), p. 41.

23 "Automobile" was first printed in Emile Littre's monumental *Dictionnaire de la Langue Français, Supplement* (1876). By 1899 common usage in the United States had shortened it to "auto."

23 I was blissfully ignorant: Hiram Maxim, *Horseless Carriage Days* (New York: Harper, 1937), pp. 3–4. Maxim's father invented the machine gun; the son, the hand-gun silencer.

24 Those who have taken the pains: Quoted in Philip Hillyer Smith, *Wheels within Wheels* (New York: Funk & Wagnalls, 1968), p. 32.

24 The first horseless carriage: Quoted in Frank B. and Arthur M. Woodford, *All Our Yesterdays* (Detroit: Wayne State University Press, 1969) who do not identify the paper; that comes from Allan Nevins's definitive *Ford: The Times, the Man, the Company* (New York: Scribner, 1954), p. 150.

25 Between the first of January: *McClure's Magazine*, July 1899.

26 No accidents: Larry Freeman, *The Merry Old Mobiles* (Watkins Glen, N.Y.: Century House, 1949), p. 49.

27 The automobile will in time: quoted in James J. Flink, *America Adopts the Automobile, 1895–1910* (Cambridge, Mass: M.I.T. Press, 1970), pp. 34–35.

28 Period of experiment: *Scientific American*, January 30, 1904, p. 74.

28 Humor the skittish horse: *Scientific American*, January 14, 1905, quoted in Flink, *America Adopts the Automobile*, p. 36.

28 Unsuited to American needs: "Letter to the Editor," *Horseless Age*, May 6, 1903, p. 554.

29 Extreme simplicity: *Motor Age*, August 9, 1906, p. 8.

CHAPTER 2: THE FOUNDER
(pages 30–53)

For the early history of the Buick companies, I relied on "Buick Catalogue," 1905, courtesy of James Zordich, associate curator, Automobile History Section, Los Angeles County Museum of Natural History; Richard Crabb, *Birth of a Giant* (Philadelphia: Chilton, 1969), pp. 119–148; Carl Crow, *The City of Flint Grows Up* (New York: Harper, 1945); J. R. Doolittle *et al.*, *The Romance of the Automobile Industry* (New York: Klebold Press, 1916);

Horseless Age, 1904–1907; *Scientific American,* January 28, 1905; François Therow, *Buick, "The Golden Era," 1903–1915,* Vol. I (Brea, Calif., 1971); and Cullon Thomas, "The Bug that Roared," *Automobile Quarterly,* VII (1969), No. 1, pp. 106–109.

Page

31   More than enough: Hugh Dolnar (Horace Arnold), "The Buick Motor Company's Side-Entrance Tonneau," *Cycle and Automotive Trade Journal,* October 1, 1904, pp. 112 ff.

36   This motor car business: Eugene W. Lewis, *Motor Memories* (Detroit: Alved Publishers, 1947), pp. 67–68.

37   The general finish: *Horseless Age,* January 25, 1905, p. 113.

37   People at the show: *Ibid,* p. 125.

37   The winter's rest: *Horseless Age,* May 3, 1905, p. 503. See also the issue of November 30, 1904, p. 545.

39   Would you entertain: Clarence H. Young and William A. Quinn, *Foundation for Living* (New York: McGraw-Hill, 1963), p. 1. For an explanation of how Michigan, specifically Detroit, became the center of automobile manufacturing, see George S. May, *A Most Unique Vehicle* (Grand Rapids, Mich.: Wm. B. Eerdmans Publishing Co., 1975).

42   Buick will discontinue: Richard Crabb, *Birth of a Giant* (Philadelphia: Chilton, 1969), p. 143. A photostat is in Lawrence R. Gustin, *Billy Durant: Creator of General Motors* (Grand Rapids, Mich.: Wm. B. Eerdmans, 1973), p. 76.

43   I listed all the assets: Arthur Pound, *The Turning Wheel* (Garden City, New York: Doubleday, Doran, 1934), p. 81.

43   High, wide and handsome: Carton is quoted in Arthur Pound, "General Motors' Old Home Town," *Michigan History,* March, 1956, n.p.

43   Few of the subscribers: Gustin, p. 78.

45   I see a new girl: Bessie McGinnis Van Vorst and Marie Van Vorst, *The Woman Who Toils* (New York: Doubleday, Page, 1903), pp. 35–36. Sister Marie also posed as a working girl to report on conditions in a shoe factory.

45   Driven by a reckless: *The Breeders Gazette,* August 24, 1904, p. 290, quoted in Reynold M. Wik, *Henry Ford and Grass-roots America* (Ann Arbor: University of Michigan Press, 1972), p. 15.

46   We farmers are not opposed: James J. Flink, *America Adopts the Automobile, 1895–1910* (Cambridge, Mass.: M.I.T. Press, 1970), p. 70.

46   Nothing has spread: Wilfred Owen, "Automotive Transportation in the United States," *Annals of the American Academy of Political and Social Science,* 320 (1958), p. 1.

46   American aristocracy: Quoted in Keith Sward, *The Legacy of Henry Ford* (New York: Rinehart, 1948), p. 23 fn.

47   Growing demand: *Horseless Age,* January 16, 1907, p. 26.

50   For men with red blood: Bernard A. Weisberger, *The Dream Maker: William C. Durant, Founder of General Motors* (Boston: Little, Brown, 1979), p. 109.

51   One hell of a gambler: Gustin, pp. 85–86. See also Young and Quinn, *Foundation for Living,* p. 30, for another Mott comment on "the visionary Durant" during the panic. Obviously the near-failure of Weston-Mott, saved only by Buick's continued orders and partial payments when other customers stopped buying axles, had a profound impact on Mott.

51   That small car: George Humphrey Maines, "Men . . . a City . . . and Buick . . . 1903–1953" (Flint, Mich.: privately printed; Advertisers Press, Inc., 1953), p. 8.

52   There wasn't an executive: Beverly Rae Kimes, "Wouldn't You Really Rather Be a Buick?" *Automobile Quarterly,* VII (1969), No. 1, p. 84.

CHAPTER 3: MORGAN'S MINIONS
(pages 54–69)

In addition to the sources specifically cited, I have relied upon, among others, the following: Richard Crabb, *Birth of a Giant* (Philadelphia: Chilton, 1969); Ralph Epstein, *The Automobile Industry: Its Economic and Commercial Development* (New York and Chicago: A. W. Shaw, 1928); Federal Trade Commission, *Report on Motor Vehicle Industry,* 76th Congress, 1st Session, House Document 468 (Washington, D.C.: Government Printing Office, 1939); B.C. Forbes and O.D. Foster, *Automotive Giants of America* (New York: B.C. Forbes, 1926); W.A.P. John, "*That* Man Durant," *Motor,* January, 1923, pp. 70 ff; E.D. Kennedy, *The Automobile Industry* (New York: Reynal & Hitchcock, 1941); Arthur Pound, *The Turning Wheel* (Garden City, New York: Doubleday, 1934); Lawrence Seltzer, *A Financial History of the American Automobile Industry* (Boston: Houghton Mifflin, 1928); as well as runs of various newspapers, including the New York *Times,* the *Wall Street Journal,* and *Commercial and Financial Chronicle.*

The history of the various Olds motor companies is drawn from *The Automobile,* December 29, 1908, p. 904; *Cycle and Automobile Trade Journal,* December 1, 1908, p. 55; Merrill Denison, *The Power to Go* (New York: Doubleday, 1956), pp. 110–115, 156–164; Forbes and Foster, *Auto-*

motive Giants; C.B. Glasscock, *The Gasoline Age* (Indianapolis: Bobbs-Merrill, 1937), pp. 40–41; Pound, *The Turning Wheel,* pp. 50–65; and Frank B. and Arthur M. Woodford, *All Our Yesterdays* (Detroit: Wayne State University Press, 1969), *passim.*

Page

56   Silly season: Benjamin Briscoe, "The Inside Story of General Motors," *Detroit Saturday Night,* January 15, 1921, p. 2.

57   Many of us thought: *Ibid.*

57   I told him frankly: Gustin, *Billy Durant: Creator of General Motors,* p. 97.

58   First see Henry Ford: *Ibid.*

58   Gumshoed separately: Briscoe, "Inside Story," January 22, 1921, p. 4.

59   Durant is for states' rights: Gustin, p. 99.

60   It is very rare: Harry W. Perry, "The Dependability of the Automobile," *Harper's Weekly,* February 1, 1908, p. 24; the description of the automobile of 1908 follows Flink, *America Adopts the Automobile, 1895–1910,* p. 250.

61   Ford was in favor: Gustin, p. 100.

62   Mr. Satterlee was quite put out: Gustin, p. 100–01.

64   A long, hot session: Michigan Historical Collections, University of Michigan, Ann Arbor, quoted in Gustin, p. 102.

65   The best move ever made: Frederick L. Smith, "Motoring Down a Quarter Century," *Detroit Saturday Night,* September 29, 1928, p. 7; October 27, 1928, II, p. 2; reprinted with revisions under the same title as a pamphlet (Detroit: Detroit Saturday Night Publishing Co., 1928). Glenn A. Niemeyer, *The Automotive Career of Ransom E. Olds* (East Lansing, Mich.: Michigan State University Press, 1963), pp. 34–35, argues that plans for other Olds vehicles were saved from the fire, that the decision to concentrate on the curved dash model was made because its parts were sub-contracted, then assembled by Olds; there would be little or no "slippage" from lost orders, delays, or failure to get back into production.

66   We came to a provisional understanding: Smith in *Detroit Saturday Night,* October 27, 1928, p. 37. Smith added, "It helped to restore one's self-respect, later, to find that Durant stood the case-hardened experienced New Yorkers upside down with the same ease that marked his *bouleversement* of us country boys."

67   A title of that kind: Gustin, p. 104.

67   No place in the world: Briscoe, "Inside Story," January 22, 1921, p. 4.

68   The first big combination: New York *Times,* July 31, 1908, p. 13.

68   Why they should feel: Gustin, p. 106, citing a letter from Briscoe to Durant, August 4, 1908, in the Durant papers.

68   It would be possible: *Ibid.*

69   He selected one: Weisberger, *The Dream Maker: William C. Durant, Founder of General Motors*, p. 132, credits Hatheway with originating the name. But see Smith, "Motoring Down a Quarter Century," p. 7.

CHAPTER 4: L'AUDACE, TOUJOURS L'AUDACE
(pages 70–97)

The titles cited at the head of the notes to Chapter 3 and Robert Paul Thomas, *An Analysis of the Pattern of Growth of the Automobile Industry 1895–1929,* Dissertations in American Economic History (New York: Arno Press, 1977) provided useful background information for this chapter.

Background information on the birth of General Motors was drawn from *The Automobile* magazine, 1908–1910; Crabb, *Birth of a Giant,* pp. 234–41; Crow, *The City of Flint Grows Up,* pp. 70–83; *Cycle and Automobile Trade Journal,* October 1908, through January 1, 1910; Ralph Epstein, *The Automobile Industry: Its Economic and Commercial Development* (New York and Chicago: A. W. Shaw, 1928); *Horseless Age,* February 1907, through December 1907; Anne Jardim, *The First Henry Ford* (Cambridge, Mass.: M.I.T. Press, 1970), pp. 64–67; *Motor World,* October 29, 1908, and May 13, 1909; and M.M. Musselman, *Get a Horse!* (Philadelphia: Lippincott, 1950), pp. 196–98.

Leland's career and Cadillac's history are based largely on *The Automobile,* February 11, 1909, p. 297; Crabb, *Birth of a Giant,* pp. 99–107; *Cycle and Automobile Trade Journal,* January 1, 1909, p. 68; Ottilie Leland and Minnie Millbrook, *Master of Precision* (Detroit: Wayne State University Press, 1966), *passim,* but especially pp. 52–57 and 88–96; and Pound, *The Turning Wheel,* pp. 102–110.

Page
71   Mr. W.C. Durant present: Gustin, *Billy Durant: Creator of General Motors,* p. 111.

73   Neither have I: *Ibid.,* p. 112.

74   A hell of a price to pay: Beverly Rae Kimes, "Wouldn't You Really Rather Be a Buick?" *Automobile Quarterly,* VII (1969), No. 1, p. 87.

74 An especially striking array: *The Automobile,* February 11, 1909, p. 268.

75 I cultivated Murphy: Gustin, p. 118.

76 A high reputation in the trade: Federal Trade Commission, *Report on Motor Vehicle Industry,* 76th Congress, 1st Session, House Document 468 (Washington, D.C.: Government Printing Office, 1939), p. 449.

79 Can you produce: Gustin, p. 123.

80 Dignity, proportion and richness: *Cycle and Automobile Trade Journal,* January 1, 1909, p. 68.

81 We have written assurance: *Cycle and Automobile Trade Journal,* August 1, 1909, p. 69.

81 Debutante of the season: *The Automobile,* December 31, 1909, p. 1–8.

82 Durant bought a lot: Lawrence Seltzer, *A Financial History of the American Automobile Industry* (Boston: Houghton Mifflin, 1928). p. 157.

82 Nobody at the time: Maines, "Men . . . a City . . . and Buick 1903–1953," p. 15.

83 I've got no use: Booton Herndon, *Ford: An Unconventional Biography of the Men and Their Times* (New York: Weybright and Talley, 1969), p. 70.

84 All matters of importance: Frank L. Klingensmith in Sward, *The Legacy of Henry Ford,* p. 46.

84 Durant's version(s) of the Ford negotiations are in "Memorandum of Conference with Honorable W.C. Durant. . . . Had by Joseph W. Davies, on Monday, November 22, 1926," prepared for Additional Income Tax Case—1919 (*IRS* v. *Ford Stockholders*), Accession 96, Box 7 (Dodge Estate-Legal), Ford Archives, Dearborn, Michigan; and in Gustin, pp. 128–30. A more romantic and none too accurate version is in Theodore F. MacManus and Norman Beasley, *Men, Money and Motors* (New York: Harper, 1929), pp. 70–72.

85 The nature of the General Motors Company: *Wall Street Journal,* October 30, 1909, p. 8. As a suggestion of General Motors' and the automobile industry's lack of importance, the article appeared on the last page of the last column of the paper. In fact, it was the only article about the industry run during the entire month.

85 The strides taken: *Ibid.*

85 Hitherto unequalled size: *The Automobile,* November 25, 1909, p. 933.

86 Utmost strain: *Wall Street Journal,* October 30, 1909, p. 8.

86   When Mr. Durant visited: Pound, *The Turning Wheel*, p. 95.

87   The $5 million of General Motors stock: Briscoe, "The Inside Story," January 29, 1921, p. 4.

88   Second formative period: *The Automobile*, December 23, 1909, p. 1109.

88   To what extent this nucleus: *Ibid.*, February 3, 1910, p. 279.

89   To sweeten the deal: Briscoe, "The Inside Story," January 29, 1921, p. 4. See also the issues of *Detroit Saturday Night* for January 15, 22, and February 5, 1921. Other information on the stock watering is extracted from Seltzer, pp. 158–59; *Poor's Industrials,* 1910, p. 1559, 1912, p. 2040; and the Federal Trade Commission Report, pp. 453–54. Conventional wisdom has a spendthrift Durant rashly buying the worthless Heany properties for approximately $8.3 million. MacManus, who claimed to be a Durant confidant, and Beasley in *Men, Money and Motors,* p. 109, naively wrote of the Heany deal: "William Crapo Durant missed on that one . . . Strangely enough, everyone told him the facts; apparently he flaunted them." Similarly, Arthur Pound's laudatory history, *The Turning Wheel,* p. 196, terms it the "Heany fiasco." Industry figures such as Glasscock, in *The Gasoline Age,* p. 156, are equally critical of the purchase, though claiming to be friendly with Durant. Even the Federal Trade Commission report misses the stock watering; see pp. 453–54. A number of writers assume that the Heany purchase price was so costly that General Motors had to begin borrowing money, and thus Durant lost control. In fact, Durant was not so foolish. Of the $8.3 million paid out, only $112,759 was in cash, a relatively small sum considering that General Motors owed some $12 million at the time. The balance of the $8.3 million was in both preferred and common stock, which, given the company's poor financial position, was unsaleable anyway. However, Seltzer noted, the Heany deal cost General Motors' stockholders a considerable sum: "It is not a little striking to record that on October 1, 1927, the securities issued for the Heany companies (as multiplied by stock dividends) had a market value in excess of $320,000,000; that, by this date, more than $50,000,000 in cash dividends had been paid on them; and that they now command annual dividends in excess of $10,000,000." See his *Financial History,* pp. 159–60. Hofheimer and Hatheway were pivotal figures in most of Durant's early maneuverings, though little seems to be known about them. According to the *Universal Jewish Encyclopedia,* Hoffheimer was born in Buttenhausen, Bavaria, came to the United States in 1866 and "played a role in the development of General Motors Corporation and Durant Motors and was a great philanthropist." Hatheway was a senior partner in Ward, Hayden and Satterlee, but seems to have left that firm around 1910, judging from the entries in Hubble-Martindale legal directories.

90   The great new life: *Detroit News* quoted in Gustin, p. 94.

91   He would explain: Leland and Millbrook, *Master of Precision* pp. 105–06.

92   The train stopped: Pound, p. 126.

92   Mr. Durant wore: Gustin, pp. 139–40.

92   McClement's biography is based on the approved sketch in *The National Cyclopaedia of American Biography.*

93   To effect a reorganization: Margery Durant, *My Father* (New York: Knickerbocker Press [G.P. Putnam's], 1929), p. 129.

94   Up to the time of your testimony: Leland and Millbrook, pp. 106–08, has the only account of the meeting, drawn from Wilfred Leland's semi-autobiographical notes.

95   If you will only reorient your thinking: *Ibid.,* p. 107.

97   The $15 million loan: Gustin, pp. 143–44.

CHAPTER 5: THE INTERREGNUM
(pages 98–123)

Page

98   Storrow's biography is drawn from Henry Greenleaf Pearson, *Son of New England: James Jackson Storrow* (Boston: Thomas Dodd Co., 1932), *passim.*

99   The terms of the loan are from Seltzer, *A Financial History of the American Automobile Industry,* pp. 164–65. See also *The Automobile,* October 6, 1910, p. 597, and December 1, 1910, p. 936.

100   Private subscriptions: C.W. Barron's Boston News Bureau, quoted in Seltzer, p. 166.

100   Details of the Guggenheim loan appear in the *Wall Street Journal,* November 12, 1910, p. 1.

101   Nash savings: Kennedy, *The Automobile Industry,* p. 78. Nash's career is outlined in Pound, *The Turning Wheel;* Forbes and Foster, *Automotive Giants of America;* and Gustin, *Billy Durant: Creator of General Motors.*

101   I craved responsibility: Nash's obituary in the New York *Times,* June 7, 1948.

102   I doubt if a man ever lived: Pearson, *Son of New England,* p. 144.

102   A title and a position: Gustin, p. 143.

103   The bankers were too skeptical: Seltzer, p. 171.

104   Frank salaciousness: Paul Angle, *Crossroads: 1913* (Chicago: Rand McNally) p. 89. For the general history of the period 1900–1915, see Barbara Tuchman, *The Proud Tower* (New York: Macmillan, 1966); Ernest R. May, *The Progressive Era*, The *Life* History of the United States, IX (New York: Time-Life Books, 1969); Richard Hofstadter, *The Age of Reform* (New York: Alfred A. Knopf, 1956); and Jacob Riis, *How the Other Half Lives*, reprint edition (New York: Hill and Wang, 1959).

107   Which corpse gets: May, *The Progressive Era.*

107   The summary of Ford's five-dollar-per-day plan follows Robert Conot, *American Odyssey*, reprint edition (New York: Bantam Books, 1975), pp. 211–231. The assembly-line data is from Frank Donovan, *Wheels for a Nation* (New York: Crowell, 1965) and Thomas, *An Analysis of the Patterns of Growth of the Automobile Industry, 1895–1929*, pp. 134 ff. Frederick Winslow Taylor was moved to write his seminal *Principles of Scientific Management* in 1911 to make labor easier; instead the assembly line became a symbol of capitalist oppression. See Daniel S. Boorstin, *The Americans: The Democratic Experience*, reprint edition (New York: Vintage Books, 1974), pp. 363–66.

111   Too much of a plunger: McLaughlin's memoirs are quoted in Weisberger, *The Dream Maker*, p. 146.

111   Durant is a genius: Pearson, *Son of New England*, p. 139.

112   Stock prices: *Wall Street Journal*, August 4–12, 1911.

112   Most of the time: Pearson, *Son of New England*, p. 131.

113   For Chrysler's career, see Allan Nevins and Frank Hill, *Ford: Expansion and Challenge* (New York: Scribner, 1957), p. 472; Walter Chrysler and Boyden Sparkes, *Life of an American Workman* (New York: Dodd, Mead, 1950), *passim;* Forbes and Foster, *Automotive Giants of America*, pp. 30–43.

113   A rich railroadman's vocabulary: Nevins and Hill, p. 472.

114   Selling is 90 percent: Forbes and Foster, p. 212.

114   A Flint man of sterling character: Chrysler and Sparkes, p. 130.

114   I saved the Buick Motor Company: Chrysler and Sparkes, p. 135.

114   I was a machinist: Crabb, *Birth of a Giant*, p. 298.

116   I'm sorry I ever built an automobile: Leland and Millbrook, *Master of Precision*, pp. 129–30. Other versions quote Leland saying, "I won't

have Cadillacs hurting any more people that way," suggesting it was a Cadillac that had been the instrument of Carter's death.

116   Always pull up on the crank: May, *The Progressive Era*, p. 133.

118   There are two distinct versions of the invention of the self-starter. T.A. Boyd's uncritical biography of Kettering, *Professional Amateur* (New York: Dutton, 1957), pp. 61–77, arrogates credit to Kettering. Isaac F. Marcosson's *Colonel Deeds, Industrial Builder,* (New York: Dodd, Mead and Company, 1947), pp. 118–27, similarly boosts Kettering, Delco, and Deeds. On the other hand, Leland and Millbrook in *Master of Precision*, the biography of Henry M. Leland, favor Cadillac, pp. 132–33. Late in their lives, an irritated Wilfred Leland, feeling that Cadillac's role was ignored by historians and biographers, wrote to Kettering, outlining the history. Kettering agreed with Leland's summary in a letter dated May 24, 1946 (see *Master of Precision*, p. 133). In contrast, General Motors' official position seemingly plumped for Kettering. The uncritical history by Pound, *The Turning Wheel*, p. 272, ignores Sweet's group, but when it was published in 1934, the Lelands had long since left the firm and General Motors' public-relations office was self-consciously promoting Kettering as its resident research genius.

119   Cadillac advertisements: various editions of the New York *Times*, December 1912 and January 1913. Cadillac retained "the deep, soft upholstery" line verbatim at least through 1914 in advertisements that spoke of the car's "liquid smoothness, luxurious environment, buoyant springs, [and] appointments in good taste."

121   "The Penalty of Leadership": *Saturday Evening Post*, January 2, 1915. The ad was written by Theodore MacManus, head of an advertising agency that specialized in automobile accounts and an anecdotal historian of the industry itself.

122   Everybody has predicted: New York *Times*, December 13, 1914, Part III, p. 5. For "public," read "banking fraternity."

122   In fostering this growing industry: New York *Times*, December 6, 1914, Part VIII, p. 9. See also that paper for November 8, 1914, Part VIII, p. 6.

123   The most expert occulists: Editor John B. Foster is quoted in Paul Angle, *Crossroads: 1913*, p. 93.

CHAPTER 6: SECOND EMPIRE
(pages 124–162)

In addition to the sources cited, I have relied upon Thomas, *An Analysis of the Pattern of Growth of the Automobile Industry 1895–1929;* William

H.A. Carr, *The du Ponts of Delaware* (New York: Dodd, Mead, 1964); *Study of the Anti-Trust Laws,* United States Senate, Committee on the Judiciary (Washington, D.C.: Government Printing Office, 1954); Jeremy Brecher, *Strike!* (San Francisco: Straight Arrow Books, 1972); and Seltzer, *A Financial History of the American Automobile Industry.*

Page
125   We're going to need a car: Gustin, *Billy Durant: Creator of General Motors,* p. 146.

125   I had found a name: Durant's autobiographical notes, *ibid.,* p. 151. The first year's sales figures are given in what appears to be the received history of Chevrolet: Karl E. Ludvigsen, "The Winner and Still Champion," *Automobile Quarterly,* VII (1969), No. 3, p. 249. Had the Chevrolet actually sold that many cars, it would have outsold both the Packard and Franklin, similarly high-priced, prestige automobiles, and today would probably still be a top-of-the-line car.

126   Grown-up people: Gustin, p. 152.

127   I sold you my car: Gustin, p. 157, citing Walter W. Ruch, "A Great Chevrolet Named Louis," *Friends* magazine, July 1971. Chevrolet returned to racing, designing the cars that won both the 1920 and 1921 Indianapolis 500. He was never to achieve the fame of rival racer Barney Oldfield or the business success of Durant. He died in 1941, the automobile bearing his name the largest-selling vehicle in the world.

127   Man on the make: Samuel Eliot Morison, Henry Steele Commager, and William E. Leuchtenburg, *The Growth of the American Republic,* 6th ed. (New York: Oxford University Press, 1969), p. 340.

127   No more important factor: Mrs. A. Sherman Hitchcock, "The Social Side of Motoring," *Suburban Life,* July 1911, p. 9.

128   Modern civilization: Quoted in Kenneth R. Schneider, *Autokind vs. Mankind* (New York: W.W. Norton, 1971), p. 42.

128   Pretty well saturated: Reginald McIntosh Cleveland quote; *Ibid.*

132   Worthless shares: In fact, the bankers sold their shares of bonus stock throughout the five-year interregnum. According to Arthur Pound in *The Turning Wheel,* p. 129, "If the latter [the bankers] had retained until 1929 the $2,000,000 worth of common stock they received in 1910, its value would then have been more than ninety times the face value of the loan," that is, $1.35 billion.

133   Remote generations: Alfred D. Chandler, Jr. and Stephen Salsbury, *Pierre S. du Pont and the Making of the Modern Corporation* (New York: Harper & Row, 1971), p. 11.

133   Rarely amount to much: *Ibid.*, p. 15.

134   Easily worth: Pierre S. du Pont to William A. Brady, February 28, 1914, in a letter entered as a defendant's trial exhibit in *U.S.* v. *E.I. du Pont de Nemours et al.*, 353 U.S. 586. Du Pont predicted: "This stock will be selling about 120 within a year or eighteen months at the outside and it may be that it will be selling there within six weeks. The Company is most excellently managed, has tremendous resources, and a very small capitilization indeed, and I do not hesitate in strongly advising you to buy this stock even at present market prices." Du Pont apparently had some idea of Durant's plans since he accurately predicted a price rise, but had no quarrel with the bankers' management.

135   Turning point: *Automotive News*, quoted in Nevins and Hill, *Ford: Expansion and Challenge*, p. 8.

136   In number and utility: *Ibid.*, p. 9.

136   The 270 companies: Darwin S. Hatch in *Motor Age*, *Ibid.*

137   Durant's letter to Bishop is quoted in Richard P. Scharchburg, "W.C. Durant, 'The Boss,' " (Flint, Mich.: General Motors Institute, 1973), p. 36, and Gustin, pp. 162–63.

138   Lugging it: Durant, *My Father*, p. 181.

139   I'm in control: Weisberger, *The Dream Maker, William C. Durant, Founder of General Motors*, p. 188, citing a letter from H.C. McClement to Dr. E.R. Campbell, Durant's former son-in-law, written the night of the meeting.

140   Absolute deadlock: Chandler and Salsbury, p. 436. *See also* Pierre S. du Pont's direct testimony in the trial exhibits, *U.S.* v. *E.I, du Pont de Nemours*, 353 U.S. 586, and du Pont's letter to J. Amory Haskill, September 17, 1915, reprinted as Government Trial Exhibit 116.

142   General Motors' extra dividend: *Wall Street Journal*, September 18, 1915, p. 1.

143   Paying basis: *Horseless Age*, December 1, 1915, p. 511.

143   Wizard of automobiles: New York *Times*, December 22, 1915, p. 16.

144   Storrow's dismay was reported in the New York *Times*, December 24, 1915, p. 12.

144   Furnish Wall Street: Forbes and Foster, *Automotive Giants of America*, p. 54.

145   Flavor of weakness: Durant, *My Father*, pp. 196–97, quoting the analysis of the Harvey Willis Company of New York City.

145   Those who accepted: New York *Times,* April 7, 1916, p. 17. Chandler
        and Salsbury (pp. 440–42) take a benign view of du Pont's "neutrality,"
        ignoring the well-positioned Coley du Pont and H.M. Barksdale. Theirs
        is not the only partisan biography of the central figures in the drama.
        Durant's *My Father* and Pearson's *Son of New England: James Jackson
        Storrow* are similarly hagiographical.

146   Well, Charley, you're through: Weisberger, p. 198, relying on an unpub-
        lished interview of Durant's secretary, W. W. Murphy, by Richard P.
        Scharchburg.

146   I am not at all surprised: Durant to Pierre S. du Pont, an undated letter
        in the du Pont papers, quoted by Weisberger, *Ibid.*

146   I'd like to hire you: Chrysler and Sparkes, *Life of an American Work-
        man,* pp. 143–45.

147   As necessary as blood itself: Quoted by Romulo Betancourt, *Ven-
        ezuela: Oil and Politics* (Boston: Houghton Mifflin, 1979), p. 19. The
        chief of the German General Staff, Count Erich Ludendorff, blamed the
        loss of the war on the lack of fuel for his motor vehicles. Postwar
        negotiations were to turn largely on control of oil supplies, French
        Foreign Minister Aristide Briand complaining, "In our days petroleum
        makes foreign policy."

149   Everlastingly digging: Unpublished Associated Press obituary for A.P.
        Sloan, Jr., dated October 25, 1927. The quotation was dropped from a
        rewrite of the obit dated April 1, 1942.

149   Unsung American hero: Boorstin, *The Americans: The Democratic Ex-
        perience,* p. 373. Among other things, Boorstin details, Hyatt invented a
        method of making emory wheels; celluloid ("Since he was not a
        chemist, he did not realize that he might easily have blown himself up
        by heating gun-cotton [nitrocellulose] under pressure"); a system of
        water filtration; a sugar-cane mill; an improved sewing machine; a new
        way of making school slates; a technique for solidifying wood for bowl-
        ing balls and golf clubs; and the roller bearing, a device familiar to every
        boy and girl who has taken apart the coaster brakes on a bicycle. To
        Hyatt, then, Americans are indebted for the billiard ball, the golf club,
        the bowling ball, and the base for photographic film.

150   More than half: A.P. Sloan, Jr., in collaboration with Boyden Sparkes,
        Adventures of a White-Collar Man (New York: Doubleday, 1941), p. 93.

150   I have always thought: *Ibid.,* p. 99.

152   His duty to protect: Chandler and Salsbury, p. 449.

153   The growth of the motor business: *U.S.* v. *E.I. du Pont de Nemours,*
        Government Trial Exhibit 124.

154 The Finance Committee will be ours: *Ibid.*

154 Amount of appropriations: *Ibid.* Deposition of Pierre S. du Pont, May–June 1951.

155 This war should stop: The Lelands' version of their leaving is in Leland and Millbrook, *Master of Precision,* p. 174. Weisberger, p. 222, says Durant had cooled to the Lelands and had decided to replace the pair anyway.

156 You might think: Sloan, *Adventures,* pp. 109–10.

156 Baruch telephoned the railway administrator: Ernest R. May and the editors of *Life, War, Boom and Bust, Life* History of the United States, Vol. X (New York: Time-Life Books, 1964), p. 13.

157 John and I agree: A letter from Pierre S. du Pont to H.M. Barksdale, dated June 29, 1918, entered as Government Trial Exhibit 133 in *U.S.* v. *E.I. du Pont de Nemours.* This letter suggests that du Pont was not quite the benign observer his biographers have made him out to be, a critical factor in view of what was to happen.

159 Nothing we need more: *Ibid.,* Defendants' Trial Exhibit 27.

160 As an answer: New York *Times,* April 4, 1919, p. 17.

160 The industry was possessed: Irving Bernstein, "The Automobile Industry: Post-War Developments, 1918–1921" (United States Department of Labor, Bureau of Labor Statistics, History Study Number 52, September 1942), p. 19.

160 Kaye's predictions are taken from *Automobile Topics,* February 1, 1919, p. 1384.

161 Donaldson Brown, *Some Reminiscences of an Industrialist* (Privately printed, Port Deposit, Md., 1957), p. 41.

161 All my feeling: Chrysler and Sparkes, *Life of an American Workman,* p. 161.

162 Not a few highways: New York *Times,* January 8, 1920, p. 12.

162 The vast majority: Los Angeles *Times,* April 25, 1920, courtesy of Bruce Henstell.

CHAPTER 7: THE ONLY SPORTS IN THE COUNTRY
(pages 163–182)

Page
163 The enormous expenditures: Durant to Raskob, October 31, 1919, cited by Richard P. Scharchburg, "W.C. Durant: 'The Boss,' " p. 51.

165   I believe in changing the policies: Chrysler and Sparkes, *Life of an American Workman*, p. 148.

167   The shorts in this issue, etc.: New York *Times*, March 31, 1920.

167   But in so doing: W.A.P. John, *"That* Man Durant," *Motor,* January 1923, p. 254. Durant's killer instinct failed him, according to John. "Men . . . from all levels of the social strata who had speculated and were faced with ruin and disgrace . . . communicated with Durant, either by piteous letters or through their friends. He took time to see them and LOANED THEM ENOUGH OF HIS OWN STOCK WITHOUT COST TO SAVE THEM" (emphasis John's).

169   The company was headed: *They Told Barron*, edited by Arthur Pound and Samuel Taylor Moore (New York, London: Harper, 1930), p. 104.

169   I need not tell you: Edward R. Stettinius, Sr., to Pierre S. du Pont, July 20, 1920; Government Trial Exhibit 145, *U.S.* v. *E.I. du Pont de Nemours and Co.,* et al., 353 U.S. 586.

169   Entire charge . . . to buy: Government Trial Exhibit 1312, *U.S.* v. *du Pont, Ibid.* With Raskob's refusal to subscribe, his relationship with Durant began to cool.

170   Decentralization with a vengeance: A.P. Sloan, Jr., *My Years with General Motors* reprint edition (New York: Anchor, 1972), p. 35.

170   Frankly, the difficulty: Alfred D. Chandler, Jr., and Stephen Salsbury, *Pierre S, du Pont and the Making of the Modern Corporation,* p. 479.

171   I was endeavoring: Pound and Moore, eds., *They Told Barron,* p. 105.

171   Constructive and upbuilding side: *Ibid,* p. 109.

172   Almost a betrayal of trust: Gustin, *Billy Durant: Creator of General Motors,* p. 209. Gustin also interviewed Durant's widow, Catherine, who "remembers that her husband felt he was the victim of 'a well-conceived plan to take over his holdings.' "

172   A new change of clothes: A.P. Sloan, Jr., Direct Testimony, April 28, 1952, in *U.S.* v. *du Pont,* 353 U.S. 586.

173   Salesman-promotor: A.P. Sloan, Jr., Direct Testimony, *U.S.* v. *du Pont, op. cit.*

173   I did not feel: A.P. Sloan, Jr., *My Years with General Motors,* p. 36. Sloan does not explain why he suddenly scuttled his plans, or what brought him back to the United States so summarily—presumably, one example of the rather heavy-handed editing of Sloan's original manuscript, reportedly by General Motors' legal department.

174   Acting well in the market: Gustin, p. 212; see also Chandler and Salsbury, pp. 483–84.

175   Market influences in Wall Street: New York *Times,* October 12, 1920, p. 15.

176   The only way open: Lawrence P. Fisher, trial testimony, *U.S.* v. *Du Pont,* record on appeal, p. 2782 fn.

176   The partners in ownership: Chandler and Salsbury, p. 484. They rely largely on a letter from Pierre S. du Pont to Irénée du Pont, president of E.I. du Pont de Nemours, written on November 26, 1920, which recounts Durant's last weeks with the corporation. Since Irénée du Pont was a participant in some of the events the letter details, the letter smacks of self-justification for the record. The letter was Defendants' Trial Exhibit 50 in *U.S.* v. *du Pont;* it is reprinted in Alfred D. Chandler, Jr., ed., *Giant Enterprise:* Ford, General Motors and the Automobile Industry (New York: Harcourt, Brace and World, 1964), pp. 81 ff., and in Sloan, *My Years with General Motors,* pp. 37 ff.

176   With the impression: Defendants' Trial Exhibit 50. Du Pont maintained this was the first he knew of Durant's straits—unlikely in view of the earlier loan of 1.3 million shares. One did not loan some $20 million without knowing why the money was needed or where it would go.

177   The bankers have demanded: Defendants' Trial Exhibit 50, *U.S.* v. *du Pont,* 353 U.S. 586.

177   As casual and amiable as ever: Durant, *My Father,* p. 268.

177   Mr. Durant was very busy: *Ibid.*

178   He would be practically ruined: Chandler and Salsbury, p. 486.

179   Proving very embarrassing: *Ibid,* quoting a letter from Whitney to Pierre du Pont, January 17, 1921.

179   Are you in trouble, etc.: Reconstructed from Chandler and Salsbury, p. 487; Defendants' Trial Exhibit 50; Harold Nicholson, *Dwight Morrow* (New York: Harcourt, Brace, 1935), pp. 156–7.

180   We told him that his position differed: Chandler and Salsbury, p. 486.

180   Panic that might result: *Ibid.*

181   There are only two firms: *Ibid.*

182   Durant thanks us: Nicholson, *Dwight Morrow,* p. 157. According to Catherine Durant, "There was never any doubt in his mind that he was the victim of a plot . . . that the collapse of GM stock was artificially created." See Gustin, pp. 217, 222. While Durant had in later years

nothing but contempt for the timorous Raskob—comparing him to sheep chips on one occasion—Durant remained grateful to Pierre du Pont. See John Lee Pratt's direct testimony in *U.S. v. du Pont. op. cit.* Curiously, the 1920 annual report of the corporation, written by Pierre du Pont and dated March 26, 1921, makes no mention of the dramatic change in the presidency or the Durant bail-out. The 1922 report then exonerated Raskob of responsibility for the huge losses:

[T]he troubles of past years were not related to an ill-financed expansion program or to delay in receiving the proceeds of financing. It is quite certain that the funds provided before the close of the year 1920 were sufficient to carry out the whole program and also to finance new business offered during the year 1921 and the first half of the year 1922. It is equally certain that disregard for control of inventories and purchase commitments cost the Corporation a very large sum of money, of which the greater part might have been saved by proper safeguards in Divisions now differently managed. Further, it is important to the stockholders to know that the financial misfortunes of the Corporation in the past were only slightly related to the manufacture and sale of its products, but that these misfortunes were directly related to loose and uncontrolled methods which are now corrected.

The two annual reports are reprinted in *A Study of the Antitrust Laws,* Hearing before the Subcommittee on Antitrust and Monopoly of the Committee on the Judiciary, United States Senate, 84th Congress, First Session (Washington, D.C.: Government Printing Office, 1955), pp. 4212 ff. The committee's report, published the next year, concludes, p. 29, "It would appear that Durant was squeezed out of the corporation."

CHAPTER 8: THE WILMINGTON CROWD
(pages 185–208)

Page

186   The prestige and respect: A.P. Sloan, Jr., *My Years with General Motors,* p. 46.

186   Set his mind at rest: Quoted by Chandler, Jr., and Salsbury, *Pierre S. du Pont and the Making of the Modern Corporation,* p. 491, citing du Pont's personal papers.

187   All is ready: *Ibid.*

187   We do not expect: Irving Bernstein, "The Automobile Industry, Post-War Developments, 1918–1921" (United States Department of Labor, Bureau of Labor Statistics, History Study Number 52, September 1942), p. 55.

188 Cut out the hard times talk: Quoted in Smith, *Wheels within Wheels,* p. 75.

188 Banks will extend credit: *Forbes,* December 25, 1920, p. 1.

188 America's first need: Quoted in Howard R. Smith, *Economic History of the United States* (New York, Ronald Press, 1955), p. 516.

189 The purchase of a big block: *Commercial and Financial Chronicle,* November 27, 1920, p. 2072.

189 Details of Durant's dinner with colleagues recalled by John L. Pratt, Direct Testimony, *U.S.* v. *E.I. du Pont de Nemours,* 353, U.S. 586. Just how much Durant salvaged is unclear. In an interview with Clarence Barron on October 1, 1923, he acknowledged he had "fixed Mrs. Durant and my children long ago, thank God, when I had the money; and Mrs. Durant pays all the bills." Mrs. Durant held at least 56,250 shares in 1949, worth more than $3 million, Los Angeles attorney Mitchell Ezer told the author on February 6, 1975. (Ezer represented Mrs. Durant's granddaughter in a private suit over control of those shares.) Once Durant paid off his creditors, he had "nothing left." See *They Told Barron,* edited by Pound and Moore, pp. 107–08. Before the end of 1920, Durant agreed to exchange his 40-percent interest in the du Pont–created holding company for some $13.6 million in cash and General Motors securities. This, too, went to pay his debts; Durant himself estimated he lost $90 million in the vain effort to stem the plunge that year. The complicated settlement is detailed in various government trial exhibits in *U.S.* v. *E.I. du Pont,* and summarized in Chandler and Salsbury, pp. 505–506.

190 To make a real good car: Pratt testimony in *U.S.* v. *E.I. du Pont,* Defendants' Exhibit 196.

192 General Motors has never been operated: A.P. Sloan, Jr., Direct Testimony, *U.S.* v. *E.I. du Pont de Nemours.*

192 Mr. du Pont didn't know: *Ibid.*

193 A great driving force: John L. Pratt, Direct Testimony, *U.S.* v. *E.I. du Pont de Nemours.*

193 They tightened up the bolts: *Ibid.*

196 To compete with the market: C.S. Mott in Young and Quinn, *Foundation for Living,* p. 180.

198 Necessary to lead: Sloan, *My Years with General Motors,* p. 72.

198 We proposed in general: *Ibid.,* p. 74.

201   Upstart du Ponts, and poor white trash: Peter Drucker, *Adventures of a Bystander* (New York: Harper and Row, 1979), p. 265.

201   Junior assistant treasurer: Sloan, *My Years with General Motors,* p. 133.

201   He is the brains: Drucker, p. 263.

202   Standard volume: Reviewing *My Years with General Motors,* Daniel Bell noted: "Although Mr. Sloan spends some five pages on this concept, he omits the actual figures which would make it meaningful." Using statistics developed by the Kefauver committee (see Chapter 14) Bell continued: "Now the company estimates that in its best year, because of seasonal fluctuation and the like, its plants would operate at only 80 percent of capacity. It figures, further, than in an *average* year, it would operate only at 80 percent of the capacity of its best year (80 percent of 80); in other words, it estimates that on a long-run basis, standard volume is 64 percent of capacity." (See the *New York Review of Books,* March 19, 1964, p. 12.) Brown outlined the concept of standard volume in "Pricing Policy in Relation to Financial Control," *Management and Administration,* February 1924, pp. 197 ff; and the forecasting model in "Forecasting and Planning," *Survey,* April 1, 1929, pp. 34–35. Bradley's explanation is far more detailed in "Setting up a Forecasting Program," *Annual Convention Series, American Management Association,* No. 41 (March 1926), pp. 3–18, and reprinted in Alfred D. Chandler, Jr., *Giant Enterprise: Ford, General Motors and the Automobile Industry,* pp. 127–141. See also *Administered Prices: Automobiles, Report together with Individual Views of the Subcommittee on Antitrust and Monopoly, Committee on the Judiciary, United States Senate,* November 1, 1958, pp. 104–115.

203   When business, and hence national income: Sloan, *My Years with General Motors,* p. 156.

204   When cars were novelties: Edgar C. Wheeler, "To-morrow's Motor Car," *The World's Work,* May 1, 1927, p. 81.

205   Man made the automobile: Madelaine G. Ritza in *The Michigan Manufacturer and Financial Record,* quoted in *Literary Digest,* March 18, 1922. Nevins and Hill, *Ford: Expansion and Challenge,* p. 399, outline the demands the women's market made on automotive design.

205   While men buy the cars: Nevins and Hill, p. 400.

206   Increased labor efficiency: Nevins and Hill, p. 519.

206   What the hell is this?: Retold by Nelson Algren in "Chicago Industrial Folklore," manuscript of the Federal Writers Project, Works Progress Administration, State of Illinois, reprinted in Benjamin A. Botkin, *A Treasury of American Folklore* (New York: Crown, 1944), p. 542.

206 Say, I'm goin' to Detroit: Bob Campbell, "Starvation Farm Blues," Vocalion 02798, ca. 1934, quoted in Paul Oliver, *The Meaning of the Blues* (New York: Collier Books, 1963), p. 54.

207 A most disquieting period: Pierre du Pont, quoted by Chandler and Salsbury, p. 503.

207 I am convinced: Government Trial Exhibit 159, *U.S.* v. *E.I. du Pont de Nemours*, 353 U.S. 586. This letter is another bit of evidence pointing to the fact that du Pont was not the industrial simpleton later writers made him out to be.

CHAPTER 9: WAITING FOR THE CIRCUS
(pages 209–230)

I have relied upon a number of sources for this and the next chapter beyond those cited. They include: *American Magazine*, 1923–1925; *Literary Digest*, 1920–1925; *The Nation*, 1920–1925; *Saturday Evening Post*, 1923–1925; Federal Trade Commission, *Report on the Motor Vehicle Industry* (Washington, D.C.: Government Printing Office, 1939); various articles in *The Annals of the American Academy of Political and Social Science*, CXVI, November, 1924; Kennedy, *The Automobile Industry;* Pound, *The Turning Wheel;* and John B. Rae, *American Automobile Manufacturers* (Philadelphia: Chilton, 1959).

Page
210 Wizard of mass production: Matthew Josephson, "Production Man," *The New Yorker*, March 9, 1941, p. 23.

211 Knudsen's physical presence: December 1938, p. 178. According to his Associated Press obituary, number 3372, issued July 1, 1947, Knudsen later established a $250,000 fund to improve health conditions for mothers and babies, explaining, "Saving lives of babies and mothers appeals to me as a cause with which I can do honor to my wife."

212 I learned to shout: Allan Nevins and Frank Hill, *Ford: Expansion and Challenge*, p. 587.

212 I can't avoid it: *Ibid*, p. 168.

213 Pretty hard for shipments: The conversation is recorded in Sloan and Sparkes, *Adventures of a White-Collar Man*, p. 138; and with slight variance in Norman Beasley, *Knudsen: A Biography* (New York: McGraw-Hill, 1947), pp. 112–13. The salary figures come from Nevins and Hill, p. 393, and Defendants' Trial Exhibits 29 and 30, *U.S.* v. *E.I. du Pont de Nemours*, 353 U.S. 586.

214 People's car: *Literary Digest*, September 22, 1923, p. 43.

214 Pay a little less: *American Magazine*, January 1923, p. 86.

214   Almost the perfect low-priced car: *Time,* October 5, 1969, p. 92 fn.

214   I am beginning to feel: Alfred D. Chandler, Jr., and Stephen Salsbury, *Pierre S. du Pont and the Making of the Modern Corporation* p. 520.

217   Completely discouraged: Thomas A. Boyd, *Professional Amateur* (New York: E.P. Dutton, 1957), p. 123.

217   My only regret: Sloan, *My Years with General Motors,* pp. 99–100.

218   Accounting always kills research: see also *Corporate Strategies of the Automotive Manufacturers,* prepared for the United States Department of Transportation, process (Boston: Harbridge House, Inc., 1978), Vol. I, p. 125, where Sloan is quoted as insisting, "GM is a production company, not a research-oriented company."

219   We shall soon with the help of God: Hoover's acceptance speech is quoted in Arthur M. Schlesinger, Jr., *The Crisis of the Old Order* (Boston: Houghton Mifflin, 1957), p. 89.

219   A close chewer: New York *Call,* August 4, 1923. That paper credited Coolidge with "the mentality of a small town Rotarian." Walter Lippmann could not fathom Coolidge's enormous popularity, complaining, "Mr. Coolidge's genius for inactivity is developed to a very high point. It is far from being an indolent activity. It is grim, determined, alert inactivity which keeps Mr. Coolidge occupied constantly."

220   The case of cheaper cars: Henry G. Hodges, "Financing the Automobile," *Annals of the American Academy of Political and Social Science,* CXVI, November 1924, p. 49.

221   The magazine advertising figures are from James Flink, *The Car Culture* (Cambridge, Mass.: M.I.T. Press, 1975), p. 145.

221   The Government of the United States: *Literary Digest,* June 30, 1923, p. 43.

222   A pretty little cottage: *Ibid.,* June 16, 1923, p. 39. Note the early interest in selling a second car to a family.

222   Built particularly: *Ibid.,* September 8, 1923, p. 43.

222   Artistic appearance: *American Magazine,* February 1923, p. 105.

222   See the children safely: *Ibid.,* April 1923, p. 125.

222   Ownership of a Buick: *Literary Digest,* June 16, 1923, p. 37.

223   The way the motor truck has succeeded: Mark Sullivan, "The Reckless Driver Must Go," *The World's Work,* January 1923, p. 299.

224   Imperative that something be done: *Motor Age,* December 13, 1923, cited by Flink, p. 145.

225   The faster the speed: Sullivan, p. 293.

225   Preventable causes of death: *The Nation,* March 8, 1922, p. 279. See also *Literary Digest,* September 8, 1923, p. 84.

225   The child, the aged person: *Nation,* March 8, 1922, p. 279.

225   Occasional "safety" movements: Mark Sullivan, "The Reckless Driver Must Go," pp. 291–2.

226   To keep our organization lined up: Defendants' Trial Exhibit 30, *U.S.* v. *E.I. du Pont,* 353 U.S. 586.

226   Make its executives partners: *Literary Digest,* January 5, 1924, p. 64. Details of Raskob's complicated plan, which retained voting control of the shares in du Pont hands, are in Chandler and Salsbury, pp. 538–543; and Sloan, *My Years,* pp. 481–487. The original documents, including allotments approved by Pierre du Pont, are in *U.S.* v. *du Pont,* 353 U.S. 586, Defendants' Trial Exhibits 30 *et seq.*

227   By cutting production schedules: Sloan, *My Years,* p. 149.

227   When nicer cars: Beverly Rae Kimes, "Wouldn't You Really Rather Be a Buick?" *Automobile Quarterly,* VII (1969), No. 1, p. 95.

228   For twenty years: Sloan, *My Years,* p, 310.

230   A very great inclination: A.P. Sloan, Jr., to W.P. Allen of E.I. du Pont de Nemours, February 4, 1924, Government Trial Exhibit 388, *U.S.* v. *E.I. du Pont,* 353 U.S. 586. On November 8, 1926, Sloan wrote Lammot du Pont: "I sometimes come to the conclusion that a big organization like General Motors cannot lead due to the fact that there is so much inertia within itself." See Government Trial Exhibit 475.

CHAPTER 10: VUN FOR VUN
(pages 231–263)

In addition to the sources cited in the headnote for the previous chapter, the following provided background information here: Charles Wertenbaker, "The World and Jim Mooney," *Saturday Evening Post,* October 30, 1937, pp. 22 ff.; Frederick Lewis Allen, *Only Yesterday* (New York: Harper, 1931); George E. Mowry, ed., *The Twenties* (Englewood Cliffs, N.J.: Prentice-Hall, 1963); General Motors Corporation Annual Reports for 1925 through 1929; Seltzer, *A Financial History of the American Automobile Industry;* and Thomas, *An Analysis of the Pattern of Growth of the Automobile Industry 1895–1929,* Dissertations in American Economic History.

Page
233   Our business has grown: Richard D. Wyckoff, *Wall Street Ventures and Adventures Through Forty Years* (New York: Greenberg, 1930), p. 286.

Wyckoff was founder and editor of *The Magazine of Wall Street*. Various congressional committees later spent considerable effort (after 1954) attempting to get General Motors executives to concede this was corporate policy.

234   Everything is bigger: Beasley, *Knudsen, A Biography*, p. 131.

234   General Motors took pains: Allan Nevins and Frank Hill, *Ford: Expansion and Challenge*, p. 361. The foreign summary is extracted from Forbes and Foster, *Automotive Giants of America*, pp. 196–97.

235   To produce in Europe: "American Capital Motorizing Europe," *Literary Digest*, May 4, 1929, p. 82.

235   Sloan "smote the rock": Paraphrase of Daniel Webster's comparison of Alexander Hamilton to Moses.

235   In order to make more people: *Consumer Reports*, June 1936, p. 10, quoted by Ralph Nader, *Unsafe at Any Speed*, new edition (New York: Grossman Publishers, 1972), p. lxxii.

236   Among the high school set: Robert S. and Helen Merrell Lynd, *Middletown* (New York: Harcourt, Brace, 1929), p. 137.

237   To keep American growing: Walter Engard, "The Blessings of Time Sales," *Motor*, April 1928, p. 112, quoted in Flink, *The Car Culture*, p. 149.

237   New attitude toward hardship: *Recent Social Trends in the United States*, Report of the President's Research Committee on Social Trends (New York and London: McGraw-Hill, 1933), I, p. 302.

238   During Wilson's time: Mark Sullivan, "The Corn Belt from a Car Window," *The World's Work*, December 1922, p. 216. On Ford and the Model-T, Sullivan added: "In a period when everything else he buys was going up in price, this one machine which the farmer already felt was well worth the money relative to other things was sharply lowered. . . . The farmer sees him [Ford] as a man who is able to make and sell automobiles very much lower than anybody else. He also sees Ford as a man who, according to all trustworthy accounts, pays higher wages to his workers than any other automobile manufacturer. . . . Also the farmer has heard that Henry Ford is trying to get Muscle Shoals in order to make fertilizer cheaper than anybody else, and that the politicians, or 'the interests' are trying to head Ford off."

238   Rather than fitting itself: *Recent Economic Changes in the United States*, Report of the Committee on Recent Economic Changes of the President's Conference on Unemployment (New York: McGraw-Hill, 1929), p. 560.

238 Back in nineteen twenty-seven: Woody Guthrie, "Talking Dust [Bowl] Blues," recorded on *Dust Bowl Ballads,* Folkways FH 5212, copyright 1964; conflated with the text in Alan Lomax, *The Folk Songs of North America* (New York, 1960), p. 434. The specter of being tractored-out loomed large in Guthrie's songs of this period. See "Dust Can't Kill Me," on *Dust Bowl Ballads,* for example.

239 Large numbers of families: Ross Sanderson, "Gasoline Gypsies," *Survey,* December 1, 1924, pp. 265–66. Sanderson concluded these early dust-bowl refugees migrated as a lark. "The players laugh at life, and keep on begging." Two weeks later, *Survey* ran a series of letters from irate social and welfare agencies confronted with "tin-Lizzie-tourists" who had run out of money. Paternalistic solutions ranged from forced labor to "taking the children away from a tramp family."

239 Like a swarm: Mildred Adams, quoted in Carey McWilliams, *Southern California: An Island on the Land,* reprint edition (Santa Barbara, Calif.: Peregrine Smith, 1973), p. 135. The unprecedented automobile migration produced at least three enduring American classics: John Steinbeck's *The Grapes of Wrath;* the celebrated Farm Security Administration photographs, especially those of Arnold Rothstein and Dorothea Lange; and the folklike songs of Woodrow Wilson Guthrie, including "So Long, It's Been Good to Know You" and what has become the unofficial national anthem, "This Land Is Your Land."

239 Standard would never get it: Sloan to Irénée du Pont, August 8, 1926, Government Trial Exhibit 704, *U.S.* v. *E.I. du Pont de Nemours,* 353 U.S. 586.

239 Friendly remonstrances: N.P. Westcott, "Origins and Early History of Tetraethyl Lead Business," E.I. du Pont de Nemours report dated June 9, 1936, Government Trial Exhibit 773, *Ibid.*

241 The nightmare of all automotive engineers: Charles F. Kettering, *The New Necessity* (Baltimore: Williams and Wilkins, 1932), p. 75.

242 The good will of the public: Sloan to Irénée du Pont, *op. cit. A Study in Antitrust Laws, Hearing Before the Subcommittee on Antitrust and Monopoly of the Committee on the Judiciary, United States Senate,* December 9, 1955, VIII, pp. 2572 ff., reprints many of the pertinent trial exhibits regarding the Ethyl [Gasoline] Corporation.

243 A car for every purse and purpose: "General Motors," *Fortune,* December, 1938, p. 148.

243 Would give it supremacy: Frank J. Williams, "President Sloan and 'General Motors,' " *American Review of Reviews,* September 1926, p. 258.

244   A high, ungainly contraption: A.P. Sloan, *My Years with General Motors,* p. 310.

245   Dynamic obsolescence: John Jerome, *The Death of the Automobile* (New York: Norton, 1972), p. 55.

246   Appeared new closed cars: "The Pace of the Auto Industry," *The Nation,* March 2, 1927, p. 225.

246   The number of makers: George Soule, "The Capitalism of Automobiles," *The New Republic,* August 22, 1928, p. 11. Even those less given to rush to judgment were critical of the auto as "one more method of ostentation." J.C. Long, "The Motor Car as the Missing Link Between Country and Town," *Country Life,* February 1923, p. 112, cautioned, "One must wait until a new generation has grown up under this nation-wide condition of motor travel before conclusions can be definitely reached concerning its social effect." The Lynds felt no need to wait a generation. Fifteen years later, they noted that by the mid-1930s (about the time Sloan formally codified the annual model change with elaborate production manuals and timetables) the people of Muncie reeled under "the pounding impact upon the family's standard of living of the commercially manipulated pressure to buy new models. . . . With the exception of women's clothing, at no point is this forcing pressure more apparent than in the deliberately instigated vogue of the annual new model of each make of automobile. . . . This institutionalized pattern of 'deliberate obsolescence' is being extended continually to more and more of the things Middletown consumes." Robert S. Lynd and Helen Merrell Lynd, *Middletown in Transition,* reprint edition (New York: Harvest Books, 1965), pp. 267–68, note 35.

248   A rich man's toy: Quoted by Eugene W. Lewis, *Motor Memories* (Detroit: Alved Publishers, 1947), p. 145.

248   On one side was the Chevrolet: Young and Quinn, *Foundation for Living,* p. 86.

248   Commercial engineers: Lewis, *op. cit.,* p. 147.

249   An enormous number of people: An editorial in the Baltimore *Sun,* quoted in *Literary Digest,* August 28, 1926, p. 54. Less than two years later, Lawrence Seltzer noted General Motors' bellwether status: "In many quarters its position is held to be analogous to that of the United States Steel Corporation: the current volume of its operations is regarded as reflecting the state of the entire automobile industry and as indicative of the trend of general business." See *Financial History of the American Automobile Industry,* p. 136.

250 Most of your trouble: Nevins and Hill, *Ford: Expansion and Challenge*, p. 417. This section is largely based on their definitive history of the Ford Motor Company.

251 That car had integrity: *Ibid.*, p. 433.

252 The first stylists' car: Sloan, *My Years with General Motors*, p. 313.

253 Still another touch: Nevins and Hill, p. 450.

254 The most titanic industrial struggle: Quoted in *Literary Digest*, August 20, 1927, p. 11.

254 The idea of a battle: Merryle Stanley Rukeyser, "General Motors and Ford: A Race for Leadership," *American Review of Reviews*, October 1927, p. 371.

254 We have no desire: *Ibid.* Ford, of course, was most prescient.

254 There is not on record: *Ibid.*, p. 373.

256 Put on as an afterthought: Nevins and Hill, p. 452. Other details on the introduction of the Model-A are from the Los Angeles *Times*, November 29–December 3, 1927; and the *Wall Street Journal*, December 3, 1927.

257 Too low for the conventional type: *Automotive Industries* as quoted by Kennedy, *The Automobile Industry*, p. 201.

257 The great problem: Sloan to Fisher, September 9, 1927, in *U.S.* v. *du Pont*, 353 U.S. 586.

258 You make them; I'll sell them: *Fortune*, February 1939, p. 78.

259 Maker of millionaires: Earl Sparling, *The Mystery Men of Wall Street* (New York: Greenberg, 1930), p. 203. See the New York *Times*, March 31, 1928, p. 21.

260 Self-appointed spokesman: A.P. Sloan, Direct Testimony, in *U.S.* v. *du Pont*, p. 1191.

261 The management of General Motors: *Ibid.*

261 Not a question of partisanship: *Ibid.* Sloan did not indicate that management—that is, the board—was not unanimous, nor how the four Democrats voted. The du Pont version is put forward in Chandler and Salsbury, *Pierre S. du Pont and the Making of the Modern Corporation*, pp. 583–587.

263 Flying flivver: Sloan, *My Years with General Motors*, p. 424.

CHAPTER 11: THE SIEGE¿
(pages 264–284)

The literature on the New Deal and the Depression defies summary. I have relied upon Arthur Schlesinger, Jr., *The Coming of the New Deal* (Boston: Houghton Mifflin, 1958); Irving Bernstein, *The Lean Years* (Boston: Houghton Mifflin, 1960); and Clarence Cramer, *American Enterprise: Free and Not So Free* (Boston: Little, Brown, 1972) for an overview. Frederick Lewis Allen's *Since Yesterday,* reprint edition (New York: Perennial Library, 1972) and Robert S. Lynd and Helen Merrell Lynd, *Middletown in Transition,* provide a social setting for the legislation. Sidney Fine, *The Automobile under the Blue Eagle* (Ann Arbor: University of Michigan Press, 1963) is an exhaustive treatment of that subject. E.D. Kennedy's *Dividends to Pay* (New York: Reynal & Hitchcock, 1939) was also useful.

Page

264 The big men in the country: Frederick Lewis Allen, *Since Yesterday,* p. 56.

265 One of the most prominent: Robert S. and Helen Merrell Lynd, *Middletown in Transition,* p. 265.

266 Like a dead weight: Nevins and Hill, *Ford: Decline and Rebirth* (New York: Scribner, 1963, p. 7.

266 Business is sound: Sloan is quoted in John Kenneth Galbraith, *The Great Crash 1929,* reprint edition (Boston: Houghton Mifflin, 1954), p. 126.

267 Natural acquisitions: Sloan as quoted in *Business Week,* October 1, 1930, p. 20.

269 The low-priced cars hung on: Beasley, *Knudsen: A Biography,* p. 151.

269 The resistance against progress: Sloan, *My Years with General Motors,* p. 197. Eleven days later, Sloan complained to the corporation's sales committee, "You have no idea how many things come up for consideration in the technical committee and elsewhere that are discussed and agreed upon as to principle well in advance, but too frequently we fail to put the ideas into effect until competition forces us to do so." See Federal Trade Commission, *Report on the Motor Vehicle Industry* (Washington, D.C.: Government Printing Office, 1939), p. 34.

270 For the present: Sloan, p. 198.

270 Two or three years ago: A.P. Sloan to Lammot du Pont, August 7, 1929, Defendants' Trial Exhibit 347, *U.S.* v. *E.I. du Pont de Nemours,* 353 U.S. 586; reprinted in *Planning, Regulation and Competition: Automobile Industry—1968,* Hearings before Subcommittees of the Select

Committee on Small Business, United States Senate (Washington, D.C.: Government Printing Office, 1968), pp. 964–68. The correspondence is summarized in Morton Mintz and Jerry S. Cohen, *America, Inc.,* reprint edition (New York: Dell, 1972), pp. 318–321.

270 Irrespective of accidents: Sloan to du Pont, August 13, 1929, Defendants' Trial Exhibit 350, *Ibid.*

270 Entitled to this extra protection: Sloan to du Pont, April 15, 1932, Defendants' Trial Exhibit 353, *Ibid.*

271 The economic situation: Sloan to du Pont, February 27, 1932, Defendants' Trial Exhibit 767, *Ibid.*

272 A big truck with several people: E.Y. "Yip" Harburg quoted in Studs Terkel, *Hard Times,* reprint edition (New York: Avon, 1970), p. 35. Inspired in part by the bread lines, in 1930 Harburg wrote the lyrics of what became the Depression's theme song, "Brother, Can You Spare a Dime?" Harburg hoped his song was speaking for the men in that line, men asking, "Why the hell should I be standing in line now? What happened to all this wealth I created?" he told Terkel.

272 While the mortgage and consumer markets: Robert Conot, *American Odyssey* reprint edition, (New York: Bantam, 1974), p. 387, which retells the Guardian Bank story.

273 Franklin D. Roosevelt is no crusader: Allen, *Since Yesterday,* p. 63.

273 Regularization and planning: Arthur Schlesinger, Jr., *The Crisis of the Old Order* (Boston: Houghton Mifflin, 1957), p. 433.

274 Private economic power: New York *Times,* September 23, 1932.

274 Entirely out of sympathy: Kennedy, *The Automobile Industry,* p. 247.

277 You have only to look: Donald J. Bush, *The Streamlined Decade* (New York: George Braziller, 1975), p. 121, which also includes the Dreyfuss quote.

277 So bulbous, so obesely curved: Allen, p. 182. Chrysler did score one artistic triumph in the Streamline, or Moderne, style with his 1928–1930 Chrysler Building at the intersection of Forty-third Street and Lexington Avenue in New York City. That William Van Alen-designed, seventy-seven-story stalagmite is the finest surviving example of what has come to be known as Skyscraper style.

277 Our job was subtly to suggest, and, an eye to the future: Jim Ellis, *Billboards to Buicks* (London, New York and Toronto: Abelard-Schuman, 1968), p. 102. Ellis does not take full credit, adding that the campaign would have failed if Chrysler had been able to make his car more

visible. But in the Depression year of 1934, with no backlog of production, Chrysler could not put enough Airflows on the road to dent public consciousness. By 1952 and the introduction of the Volkswagen Beetle to the United States, the airflow or teardrop design was no longer radical at all. The Beetle, named the *Kraft durch Freude* (Strength through Joy), and nicknamed the "Baby Hitler," had been designed in 1937 by Ferdinand Porsche. See the New York *Times,* July 3, 1938.

277   Higher speed and lower price: Ellis, p. 148.

278   Growth of corporate enterprise: Russell Leffingwell as quoted by Arthur Schlesinger, Jr., *The Coming of the New Deal,* p. 491.

278   Andrew Carnegie's advice: *Middletown in Transition,* pp. 71–72.

279   But the wealthy Negro: Drucker, *Adventures of a Bystander,* p. 268. Drucker retells the story of Dreystadt's success.

280   Sturdy and reliable: Ellis, p. 147. Buick's image had not been helped when Fisher Body engineers made some slight changes—about an inch—in a curve Harley Earl had plotted and came forth with the "pregnant Buick" of 1929. It was Earl's first completely designed car, and it was a conspicuous failure, the onset of the Depression not helping any. See Sloan, *My Years,* p. 317.

280   Hot? It's a ball of fire!: Ellis, p. 150. With the appearance of a much-circulated article on automobile accidents by J.C. Furnas in *Reader's Digest,* "we were asked to soft-pedal reference to high speed," Ellis added. The embargo would be lifted quickly enough.

280   The General Motors inner management: Allen, p. 227. Allen wrote this prior to 1939. Thirty years later, John Kenneth Galbraith would come to the identical conclusion.

282   Industry, if it has any appreciation: This and the following quotes attributed to Sloan were drawn from the Los Angeles *Times,* September 26, October 17, and December 5, 1935.

282   A wider knowledge: Associated Press dispatch to the Los Angeles *Times,* December 13, 1937. Sloan left no doubt as to the particular aims of his foundation: "Having been connected with industry during my entire life, it seems eminently proper that I should turn back, in part, the proceeds of that activity with the hope of promoting a broader as well as a better understanding of the economic principles and national policies which have characterized American enterprise down through the years."

283   With the many proposals: United Press dispatch to the Los Angeles *Times,* October 21, 1936. For a history of the American Liberty League,

see George Wolfskill, *The Revolt of the Conservatives* (Boston: Houghton Mifflin, 1962), and Wolfskill and John A. Hudson, *All but the People* (New York: Macmillan, 1969). There are further details in Richard O'Connor, *The First Hurrah: A Biography of Alfred E. Smith* (New York: Putnam, 1970), pp. 246–285.

CHAPTER 12: THE ASSAULT
(pages 285–313)

Background information for this chapter, in addition to the sources cited, was drawn from William H. McPherson, *Labor Relations in the Automobile Industry* (Washington, 1940); *Industrial Munitions, Report of the Committee on Education and Labor, United States Senate,* 76th Congress, 1st Session (Washington, D.C.: Government Printing Office, 1939); Walter Linder, "The Great Flint Sit-Down Strike against GM, 1936–37," *Progressive Labor,* February-March, 1967; "The Story of the General Motors Strike" (Detroit: General Motors Corporation, 1937); B.J. Widlick, *Detroit: City of Race and Class Violence* (Chicago: Quadrangle, 1972); and Louis Adamic, "Sit-Down," *Nation,* December 5, 1936.

Page

286   G.M., like its rivals: "General Motors IV: A Unit in Society," *Fortune,* March 1939, p. 146.

286   General Motors had no dealings: Sloan, *My Years with General Motors,* p. 475.

288   Men eye each other: Unidentified auto worker quoted in the Los Angeles *Times,* September 20, 1970.

288   Somebody who may have arrived: Arthur L. Pugmire in *Violations of Free Speech and Rights of Labor,* Hearings before a Subcommittee of the Committee on Education and Labor, United States Senate, (Washington, D.C.: Government Printing Office, 1937), Part II, p. 553. The committee was universally known as the La Follette committee, after its chairman, Senator Robert La Follette.

289   The Anderson testimony is taken from *Violations,* Part VI, pp. 1924–25. Anderson, the good soldier, was retained by the corporation. General Motors' newly hired public-relations men urged reporters not to use the Anderson testimony in their stories. See Drew Pearson and Robert S. Allen, "The Washington Merry-Go-Round" column for February 28, 1937, and *Violations,* p. 1995.

290   We are hoping: John L. Lewis as quoted by Irving Bernstein, *The Turbulent Years* (Boston: Houghton Mifflin, 1970), p. 524.

290   Done on legal and constructive lines: Quoted by Henry Kraus, *The Many and the Few* (Los Angeles: Plantin Press, 1947), p. 75.

291   At the end of nine hours: Testimony of James Mangold in *Violations,* Part VI, p. 2123.

292   They're not men: Quoted by Sidney Lens, *The Labor Wars* (Garden City, New York: Doubleday and Co., 1973), p. 293. See also Kraus, *The Many and the Few,* pp. 12–13.

292   Labor unrest exists: Quoted by Kraus, p. 12.

293   Far-flung industrial Cheka: *Violations of Free Speech, Report,* Part II, p. 123.

293   Employee 556545: *Violations,* Part VI, pp. 2089–90.

293   Full of piss and vinegar: Bernstein, *The Turbulent Years,* p. 501. See also Kraus, p. 59.

294   As many men would be hired: H.S. Grant, "General Motors Strikes Back," *Nation,* December 25, 1935, p. 743.

294   Never to be in such a position again: Sidney Fine, *Sit Down* (Ann Arbor: University of Michigan Press, 1969), p. 49. Fine's skeptical history is the definitive work on the subject.

294   Chevrolet for *hoi polloi:* "General Motors," Part I, *Fortune,* December 1938, p. 148.

296   They were illegally occupying it: C.S. Mott as quoted by Studs Terkel, *Hard Times,* reprint edition (New York: Pantheon, 1970), p. 162.

297   "The Fisher Strike" is printed in Bernstein, *The Turbulent Years,* p. 527. The figure of 4,000 strikers is at least twice as many union members as there were in the local at the time. The most famous labor song to come out of the Fisher sit-down was set, shortly after the settlement, to the tune of "When Johnny Comes Marching Home Again" by Maurice Sugar, one of the union's attorneys:
> When they tie a can to a union man,
> Sit down, sit down.
> When they give him the sack, they'll take him back,
> Sit down, sit down.
> When the speed up comes, just twiddle your thumbs,
> When the boss won't talk, don't take a walk,
> Sit down, sit down,
> Sit down, sit down.
> Sit down on the job. *or*
> Right down on your ass.

298   Blackjacks out of rubber hoses: Fine, p. 165.

299   It sounds like communist talk: Kraus, p. 114.

299   What happens to General Motors: Fine, p. 107.

299   Our position at all times: Fine, pp. 178–79.

300   Have no fear: Associated Press dispatch to the Los Angeles *Times*, January 5, 1937.

300   Let them pull the workers out: *Ibid.*, January 6, 1937.

302   The state authorities will not: *Ibid.*, January 12, 1937.

302   Fight an honest holy war: *Fortune*, March 1939, p. 146. Walter Lippmann observed from Olympian heights: "Mr. Sloan's task is to operate General Motors, and to do that his main objective should be to lift its labor relations from the level of ultimata and coercion to that of negotiation, bargaining and impartial adjudication. The way to do that is to put his emphasis not on abstract principles and legal rights but on ways and means for inaugurating a new tradition of consultation with his men." See Los Angeles *Times*, January 13, 1937.

303   The boss is shaking at the knees: Fine, p. 251.

303   We stand ready always: United Press dispatch to the Los Angeles *Times*, January 18, 1937.

303   Steady pressure upon the corporation: Sloan, *My Years*, p. 461.

304   We cannot see our way: Associated Press to the Los Angeles *Times*, January 26, 1937.

305   In the words so familiar: Fine, p. 270.

305   Frank, for God's sake: Bernstein, p. 540. Some later writers report that William Knudsen, too, wanted no overt use of force, no risk of bloodshed.

306   I'm not going down in history: Bernstein, p. 541.

306   This strike has gone on so long: Beasley, *Knudsen: A Biography*, p. 172.

306   Pressman observations: Fine, p. 232. Brown's view of the negotiations, unfortunately defensive, is in *Some Reminiscences of an Industrialist*, pp. 89–98. Brown says: "In these sessions, I served as spokesman for GM. . . . I represented Sloan, who was the executive head of the corporation."

307   You beat us: Fine, p. 303.

307   Let us have peace: Associated Press to the Los Angeles *Times*, February 12, 1937.

308   United front of capital: Associated Press to the Los Angeles *Times*, February 14, 1937. On March 2, 1937, another great bastion of company unionism, United States Steel, settled with John L. Lewis's Steel Workers Organizing Committee. The great union organizing drive, even before the United States Supreme Court affirmed the constitutionality of the Wagner Labor Relations Act, was on.

308   To get people back: Associated Press to the Los Angeles *Times*, February 12, 1937.

308   Even if we got not one damn thing: Fine, p. 306.

308   Briefly stated, the strike: Los Angeles *Times*, April 2, 1937.

310   The public impression: Lammot du Pont to Walter Carpenter, April 23, 1937, Government Trial Exhibit 196 in *U.S.* v. *Du Pont*, 353 U.S. 586.

310   A prime example: *Fortune* magazine, March 1939, p. 144.

310   It is better to curtail: Kennedy, *The Automobile Industry*, p. 300. Kennedy adds: "This statement is worth thinking about a moment. It was made by one of the more enlightened industrialists, representing one of our more enlightened corporations. It was not a political statement; Sloan did the New Deal-baiting for General Motors, and Knudsen was talking as an expert witness on his own special subject—production and plant management. And 999 industrialists out of 1,000 would echo his statement."

311   Further than the next dividend: Clarence H. Cramer, *American Enterprise: Free and Not So Free* (New York: Little, Brown, 1972), p. 455.

311   Our bogie is 45 percent: *Fortune*, December 1938, p. 158.

312   Conspiracy without conspirators: *Time*, November 27, 1939, p. 69. See also the New York *Times*, May 28, November 8, 1938, and November 17, 1939, for a fuller account of the key events in the case.

CHAPTER 13: THE CADET AND THE SHADOW DANCERS
(pages 314–348)

Though not specifically cited, I have used the following sources as background for this chapter: Norman Beasley, *Knudsen: A Biography;* "General Motors Overseas," *Fortune*, November 1945, pp. 125 ff.; Frank Ernest Hill, *The Automobile* (New York: Dodd, Mead 1967); Harold Katz, *The Decline of Competition in the Automobile Industry, 1920–1940*, Dissertations in American Economic History (New York: Arno, 1977); Nevins and Hill, *Ford: Expansion and Challenge;* John Rae, *The Road and Car in American Life* (Cambridge, Mass.:

M.I.T. Press, 1971); "Report on Detroit," transcript of a talk given February 28, 1942, by Charles E. Wilson over the Columbia Broadcasting Network, courtesy of Archives of Labor History, Wayne State University, Detroit; A.P. Sloan, Jr., *My Years with General Motors;* Howard R. Smith, *Economic History of the United States;* Samuel C. Stearn, "The Financial History of the American Automobile Industry Since 1928," unpublished master of arts thesis, Wayne State University, April 28, 1948; and runs of *Business Week, Time, U.S. News and World Report,* 1940–1950.

Page

316   Can you build: Matthew Josephson, "Profiles: Production Man—I," *New Yorker,* March 8, 1941, p. 22.

316   Conflict of interests: Associated Press to the Los Angeles *Times,* September 4, 1940.

316   "Hollywood" styling: Los Angeles *Times,* August 6, 1941.

316   The nation that is able: Associated Press dispatch to the Los Angeles *Times,* October 19, 1940.

318   American superiority: James J. Flink, *The Car Culture* (Cambridge, Mass.: M.I.T. Press, 1975), p. 190. The fullest account of the industry's contribution to war production, one-fifth of all military hardware, is in *Freedom's Arsenal: The Story of the Automotive Council for War Production* (Detroit: Automobile Manufacturers Association, 1950). See also Carl Crow, *The City of Flint Grows Up* (New York: Harper and Row, 1945). According to Harlow Curtice, testifying before the Senate Subcommittee on Antitrust and Monopoly in 1957, General Motors produced 198,000 diesel engines primarily for tanks and landing craft; 206,000 airplane engines; 13,000 complete bomber and fighter planes; 38,000 tanks, tank destroyers, and armored vehicles; 850,000 trucks, including amphibious "Ducks"; 190,000 cannon; 1.9 million machine guns and submachine guns; 3.1 million carbines; 11 million fuses; 119 million mortar and artillery shells; 39 million cartridge cases; among other purely military products.

In 1974, Bradford Snell, a Yale Law School graduate who had spent a good deal of research time in government archives charged "General Motors and Ford became an integral part of the Nazi war efforts" in a report prepared for the Senate Subcommittee on Antitrust and Monopoly. Snell's argument in the committee print, *American Ground Transport,* (Washington, D.C.: Government Printing Office, 1974) continues, "Had the Nazis won, General Motors and Ford would have reappeared impeccably Nazi; as Hitler lost, these companies were able to reemerge impeccably American." While there is a grave question as to the "nationality" and, hence, the loyalty of any multinational corporation to its nation of "origin" or headquarters, in General Motors' case during World War II, Snell's comments are tendentious. Hitler froze all foreign profits in 1933; General Motors sought to "export" its profits in the form of barter goods—including Christmas-tree ornaments—and Opel sales elsewhere in Europe, but never freed more than $3 million per year. Instead, it plowed back into its Adam Opel works at Russelheim, Germany, some $30 million to create the most integrated European auto plant, hoping for a change in German currency regulations. If Sloan is to be faulted, it is for believing, as did most Americans, that "the petty squabbles" would not involve distant America. After Germany invaded Poland, American managers at the Opel works returned to the United States. With the declaration of war on December 8, 1941, the four American directors nominally on the Opel board resigned; a Reich's commissioner assumed custody of the company in March 1942. General Motors did not reassert its control until November 1, 1948. Similarly, Spanish Loyalists seized both the Ford and General Motors plants in Barcelona, then were succeeded by the Falangists for the duration; in 1943, Perón took over General Motors' Argentinian factory.

Far more serious is Snell's charge that "GM and Exxon joined with German chemical interests in the erection of the Ethyl tetraethyl plants" vital to fueling the Blitzkrieg. As early as December 15, 1934, the resolutely anglophilic Irénée du Pont had cautioned Ethyl Corporation against "disclosing secret information of military importance." Germany and Italy secured the information—as had the British Air Ministry in 1928 and the French government in 1931—only after the United States government had given its assent. The technical data necessary to manufacture tetraethyl lead, which in the event of war the Germans would have pirated from patent documents, actually was sold by Standard Oil of New Jersey, not Ethyl or General Motors. (See Government Trial Exhibit, in *U.S.* v. *E.I. du Pont de Nemours et al.,* 353 U.S. 586, p. 4754.)

Hitler might have looked askance at the German directors of Adam Opel who owned, after 1931, more than 200,000 shares in General Motors (see Government Trial Exhibit 511, *Ibid.*). No matter who won the war, they stood to benefit, if they survived. The Russelheim works, then making airplane engines, was bombed by the Allies, and later stripped of machinery by the Soviets in lieu of reparations. General Motors did not resume operations in Germany until 1948. In 1967, the corporation finally secured $35 million in war-damage payments from the federal Foreign Claims Settlement Commission; the taxpayers thus reimbursed General Motors for its "lost" profits in Germany which had been plowed back into the factory from 1933 to 1940. General Motors has denied all of Snell's charges. See *The Industrial Reorganization Act,* Hearings before the Subcommittee on Antitrust and Monopoly, Senate Judiciary Committee (Washington D.C.: Government Printing Office,

1974), Part IV pp. 2378 ff.; and in a printed public rebuttal, "The Truth About 'American Ground Transport'—A Reply by General Motors" (Detroit: General Motors Corporation, 1974), pp. 5–11.

318 They know how to manage the women: The story of Dreystadt's uncommon humanity is recounted in Drucker, *Adventures of a Bystander*, pp. 270–71.

319 This will increase the temptation: Los Angeles *Times,* August 14, 1943.

320 It must make good: New York *Times,* December 11, 1943. The "world WPA" Sloan feared was, of course, later created as the Marshall Plan.

320 I do not need to tell: Associated Press to the Los Angeles *Times,* October 6, 1944.

321 Through his personality: Government Trial Exhibit 205, *U.S.* v. *du Pont.* Out of this late-blooming friendship sprang the Sloan-Kettering Foundation, perhaps the nation's foremost cancer research and treatment center.

321 Altho I know: *Ibid.*

321 Too much ammunition: Sloan to Carpenter, February 11, 1944, Government Trial Exhibit 208, *U.S.* v. *du Pont.* Details of the suit are in the New York *Times,* April 12 and November 5, 1942. Sloan's fellow defendants in the private suit brought by three stockholders included Morgan partners Junius S. Morgan and George Whitney, Seward Prosser, Donaldson Brown, Albert Bradley, James Mooney, and John Thomas Smith, as members of the bonus committee at various times between 1931 and 1939.

324 You call that a car: Mira Wilkin and Frank E. Hill, *American Business Abroad* (Detroit: Wayne State University, 1964), p. 368.

324 Manufacturers who have tried: Franklin Reck, "A Car Traveling People" (Detroit: Automobile Manufacturers Association, 1945), pp. 44–45. Durant, for one, had made a last effort to save his crumbling Durant Motors by bringing in the small French Mathis.

324 The higher the prices: New York *Times,* September 21, 1946. Wilson added, "The automobile business depends on two things—a confidence and ability to pay. It is a pretty good barometer of the state of the national economy from the point of view of the immediate future."

324 A lighter weight and more economical car: Karl Ludvigsen, "The Truth about Chevy's Cashiered Cadet," *Special Interest Autos,* January–February, 1974, p. 16. Information on the tentative foray into small-car production was drawn from that article; Young and Quinn, *Foundation for Living,* p. 237; and M.M. Musselman, *Get a Horse!,* p. 281.

324   Engineer's dream: Ludvigsen, p. 17.

326   Too much of a jewel: Ludvigsen, p. 19.

326   The proposed Chevrolet: Quoted by Ludvigsen, *ibid.* Shortly after, MacPherson joined the Ford Motor Company, eventually rising to engineering vice-president. Elements of the Cadet, including the MacPherson strut suspension, appeared in various Ford automobiles, but General Motors failed to use any of the advanced engineering concepts embodied in the Cadet. The Cadet appeared in 1948 as the Australian Holden.

326   Modern and efficient: "Futurama" narration script quoted by Donald J. Bush, *The Streamlined Decade* (New York: George Braziller, 1975), p. 162. The Ford building had a similar "Road of Tomorrow" conceived by Henry Dreyfuss; Chrysler's hall was designed by Raymond Loewy. Together the Big Three had employed the three most influential of American industrial designers. Bel Geddes detailed his theatrical designs for "Futurama" in *Magic Motorways* (New York: Random House, 1940).

327   With fewer people: Franklin M. Reck, "A Car Traveling People," p. 41. This see-no-evil pamphlet was published by the Automobile Manufacturers Association. Reck did not explain why the central city needed refurbishing if fewer people lived there, how it would be accomplished in view of the centrifugal force whirling people, stores, and factories out to the periphery, and who would pay for it in any event. Neither did he weigh the automobile's responsibility for the blight left behind.

327   Dream castle: Los Angeles *Times,* December 22, 1939. See also that newspaper for March 23 and October 9, 1938; September 11, 1939; December 30, 1940; and December 30, 1960, for other information about the beginnings of southern California's freeway system. Los Angeles' reliance on the automobile was so wholehearted, the city traffic engineer in 1939 all but disdained mass transit: "Undertakings in transit operations by American cities have usually been with unhappy financial results, but there remain those persistent proponents who harass officials with pressure for municipal operation despite the uniformly unfortunate experience in large cities which have tried it" (Los Angeles *Times,* December 22, 1939).

328   The roads already exist: Reck, p. 45.

330   About as good as a small tool shop: Nevins and Hill, *Ford: Decline and Rebirth,* p. 315, which details the account of the hiring of Ernest Breech and the reformation that followed.

330　Of stomach cancer: Nevins and Hill, p. 300. Clara Ford reportedly came to tears over "this man Bennett who has so much control over my husband and is ruining my son's health." See Nevins and Hill, *Ford: Expansion and Challenge*, pp. 591–593, for the most judicious of the unflattering descriptions of Bennett's pug-ugly tactics.

331　Contempt and pity: *Ibid.*, p. 315.

331　Here is a young man: *Ibid.*

332　It's been terribly lonely: Drucker, *Adventures of a Bystander*, p. 284.

334　From further executive responsibilities: General Motors press release quoted in *Time*, June 17, 1946, p. 86.

334　The interests of G.M.: "General Motors IV," *Fortune*, March 1939, p. 150.

334　GM people have: James Truslow Adams, *Big Business in a Democracy* (New York, 1946), p. 176.

335　Goddamit, I know something: Drucker, p. 275.

335　A union is a political organization: *Ibid.*

335　The ablest man: *Ibid.*

335　A very decent, genuine human being: Frank Cormier and William J. Eaton, *Reuther* (Englewood Cliffs, N.J.: Prentice-Hall, 1970), p. 294.

336　Far too many people: Peter F. Drucker, *Concept of the Corporation*, new edition (New York: John Day, 1972), p. 177.

336　Especially among the lower ranks: *Ibid.*

336　*I* am never going: Drucker, *Adventures*, p. 275.

337　We shall resist: Quoted by William Serrin, *The Company and the Union* (New York: Alfred A. Knopf, 1973), p. 158. Details of the strike also were drawn from *The New Republic*, January 7, 1946, pp. 4–5; Survey Graphic, January 1946, pp. 10 ff.; and the New York *Times*, October 1946 through March 1947.

338　Once Victor stopped: Serrin, p. 159.

338　To the soles of their shoes: Walter P. Reuther, "This is Your Fight!" *Nation*, January 12, 1946, p. 36.

338　More realistic distribution: Serrin, p. 160.

339　We don't even open: Anderson as quoted by Keith Hutchison, "General Motors: Sovereign State," *Nation*, December 8, 1945, p. 620.

Hutchison added, "What Mr. Anderson should have said is that the books are not open to the majority of stockholders. Thirty percent of the stock is owned by the managers and their associates, including 23 percent held by the Du Pont Corporation, which has a large number of representatives on the board of directors. We can be sure that this group of stockholders is given all the facts about the company and thus occupies a specially privileged position."

339   You are asking for a fight: Associated Press to the Los Angeles *Times*, December 15, 1945.

340   Essential to enable: United Press to the Los Angeles *Times*, December 21, 1945.

340   Be forced to pay higher: United Press to the Los Angeles *Times*, January 12, 1946.

341   We have the union relations *I* designed: Drucker, *Adventures*, p. 275.

342   The treaty of Detroit: Quoted by Serrin, p. 170.

342   A contract of historic importance: John B. Rae, *The American Automobile* (Chicago: University of Chicago Press, 1965), p. 174.

345   Any new equipment using fuel: Bradford Snell, *American Ground Transport*, Committee Print, presented to the Subcommittee on Antitrust and Monopoly, Senate Judiciary Committee (Washington, D.C.: Government Printing Office, 1974), p. 31, citing *U.S.* v. *National City Lines*, 1951 Trade Cases, paragraph 64,237 (Northern District, Illinois). Basing his accusation largely on a successful federal antitrust case, Snell implies that General Motors subverted prospering rapid-transit rail systems for its own selfish, public-be-damned purposes. The most obvious flaw in Snell's argument lies in the fact that had they been successful—street transit systems were failing everywhere—the owners never would have sold out. Like the railroads, which needed little inducement to abandon short-haul passenger service in favor of interurban bus routes, the city streetcar systems were inefficient, done in by the auto during the 1920s, even before General Motors began building buses. The conversion to more flexible bus lines helped transit systems reduce losses. (See letter to the editor by Spencer Crump, Los Angeles *Times*, November 17, 1979.) In the antitrust case, *U.S.* v. *National City Lines* (CD California, 1947), the trial judge held the acquisitions lawful, but the subsequent requirement contracts virtually stipulating that the new owners purchase GM buses over all others were a violation of antitrust laws. For GM's rebuttal to Snell, see "The Truth About 'American Ground Transport'—A Reply by General Motors," April 1974, submitted to the Senate Subcommittee on Antitrust and Monopoly. See also *Study of the Antitrust Laws*, Hearings before the

Subcommittee on Antitrust and Monopoly, Senate Judiciary Committee (Washington, D.C.: Government Printing Office, 1956), pp. 2595 ff.

345 The National City Lines campaign: Snell, *American Ground Transport,* p. 31.

345 General Motors' original objective: *Administered Prices,* Hearings before the Subcommittee on Antitrust and Monopoly, Senate Judiciary Committee (Washington, D.C.: Government Printing Office, 1957), p, 3852.

347 It is difficult to determine: Lawrence J. White, *The Automobile Industry Since 1945* (Cambridge, Mass.: Harvard University Press, 1971), p. 218.

348 People don't want: *U.S. News and World Report,* December 30, 1949, p. 35.

CHAPTER 14: THE BAZAAR
(pages 349–381)

Page

350 A prudent financial manager: Drucker, *Adventures of a Bystander,* p. 277. Drucker adds (p. 278) that pension funds "already have made America's employees into America's capitalists. And that, I suspect, rather than employee pensions, was what Charlie Wilson—patternmaker's business agent, Eugene Debs socialist, president of GM, and arch-capitalist—had in mind all along."

351 Two inflationary forces: *Business Week,* February 13, 1954, p. 68.

351 The wage-price spiral: Charles E. Wilson, " 'Progress-Sharing' Can Mean Industrial Peace," *Reader's Digest,* September 1952, p. 27. In an address to the National Press Club in Washington, Wilson had at his critics: "The problem is to work out an American solution for the relations of labor and industry and not attempt to adopt the philosophy of class conflict from Europe, either from the Communists and Socialists on the one hand or the cartel-thinking, non-competitive reactionaries on the other. . . . It sometimes seems to me that some people who talk free enterprise intend it for others and are reluctant to face competition themselves. Some even seem to use free enterprise talk as a cloak for a little extra selfishness." See C. E. Wilson, "Five Years of Industrial Peace," *Vital Speeches,* July 15, 1950.

352 Pitch, catch and cover first base: *Time,* December 1, 1952, p. 68. See also *Business Week,* March 21, 1953, pp. 92 ff.

353 The best committee: *Time,* November 1, 1954, p. 90.

354 You never stand still: *Time,* December 1, 1952, p. 68.

355   So questionable: *Planning, Regulation and Competition: Automobile Industry—1968,* Hearings before Subcommittees of the Select Committee on Small Business, U.S. Senate (Washington, D.C.: Government Printing Office, 1968), p. 584. The turret-lathe contract is outlined in Drew Pearson's "Washington Merry-Go-Round" column for April 23, 1953. See also *Time,* August 5, 1957, p. 68; and the *Wall Street Journal,* January 5, 1959, for General Motors' profiteering on air-force contracts and refunding $9.9 million to the government. The corporation explained the excess profit as "a misunderstanding."

355   To me a technical center: Los Angeles *Times,* May 14, 1961.

356   To go overboard: A.H. Raskin, "Key Men of Business—Scientists," New York *Times Magazine,* May 13, 1956.

356   GM has not yet proved: *Ibid.*

358   The penalties of an obsolete road system: The final report of the Clay commission is quoted in Helen Leavitt, *Superhighway—Superhoax* (Garden City, N.Y.: Doubleday, 1970), p. 30.

359   One of the greatest engineering wonders: Charles E. Davis, Jr., "Highway Project Ranks as Engineering Wonder," Los Angeles *Times,* September 27, 1965. Additional information on the freeway system was drawn from Rae, *The American Automobile,* pp. 186–87; Francis Bello, "The City and the Car" in *The Exploding Metropolis,* edited by the editors of *Fortune* (New York: Doubleday, 1958); and John Burby, *The Great American Motion Sickness* (Boston: Little, Brown, 1971), pp. 297–317.

361   The $1 billion cost of entry is estimated by White in *The Automobile Industry Since 1945,* p. 57. It could be doubled to account for inflation during the decade of the 1970s.

362   Let's say it was thirty-one years ago: A gloss of Cadillac advertisements by William H. Whyte, Jr., "The Cadillac Phenomenon," *Fortune,* February 1955, p. 109.

362   Apparently in the minds: *Administered Prices,* Report of the Subcommittee on Antitrust and Monopoly, Senate Judiciary Committee (Washington, D.C.: Government Printing Office, 1958), p. 100. Seven years earlier, perhaps the first critic of the large postwar automobile, Senator J.W. Fulbright, complained new cars were "big as hearses," according to the Los Angeles *Times,* October 13, 1951. See also White, pp. 203, 217; and Kenneth Schneider, *Autokind vs. Mankind* (New York, 1971), p. 178.

363   Herbert Hoover's haberdasher: Karl E. Ludvigsen, "The Winner and Still Champion: Chevrolet," *Automobile Quarterly,* VII (1969), No. 3, p. 266. See also *Business Week,* October 30, 1954, pp. 45–48.

363 Too six-cylinder minded: Dero A. Saunders, "How Chevy Does It," *Fortune,* December 1956, p. 111.

364 Hound dog look: *Time,* November 1, 1954, p. 88.

364 Those coats are last year's: *Newsweek,* March 21, 1955, p, 84.

364 Phony registrations: Saunders, "How Chevy Does It," p. 106.

365 You know what the boss says: Robert Sheehan, "How Harlow Curtice Earns His $750,000," *Fortune,* February 1956, p. 135.

366 Car buyers were larcenous: Leon Mandel, *Driven: The American Four-Wheeled Love Affair* (New York: Stein and Day, 1977), p. 126. A former editor of *Car and Driver* magazine, Mandel himself had worked as the manager of an automobile dealership. See also Jerome, *The Death of the Automobile,* pp. 151–161. For complaints to the Better Business Bureau, see the Los Angeles *Times,* September 17, 1955.

367 Safety does not appear to create: Saunders, "How Chevy Does It," p. 238. General Motors was evidently less interested in safety than were its customers. In Los Angeles, one of every ten buyers was asking the area's largest Chevrolet dealer for GM's unadvertised seat belts. See Francis Bello, "How Strong is G.M. Research?" *Fortune,* June 1956, p. 194.

367 It's pure schmaltz: *Business Week,* September 10, 1955, p. 75. See also *Newsweek,* May 16, 1955, p. 81.

368 Normal, rightful share: Saunders, p. 244.

369 The biggest myth in Detroit: *Business Week,* January 12, 1957, p. 167.

370 Regarding statistical controls for quality, see Boorstin, *The Americans: The Democratic Experience,* pp. 195–200. Boorstin asks rhetorically: "What must we think of a civilization that aims to make its products just barely as good as they need to be, and not one bit better? . . . Was this the road to industrial progress, to the more democratic society, where the 'quality' [i.e., excellence] of objects was limited by the need to supply them to everybody?"

371 Too big for me to be noticed: Rush Loving, Jr., " 'The Automobile Industry Has Lost Its Masculinity,' " *Fortune,* September 1973, p. 188.

372 As low as they can be: *A Study of the Antitrust Laws,* Hearings before the Subcommittee on Antitrust and Monopoly, Senate Judiciary Committee (Washington, D.C.: Government Printing Office, 1956), p. 3699.

372 Probably was priced, etc.: *Ibid.,* pp. 3609 ff.

373 No more than our actual costs: *Business Week,* September 29, 1956, p. 95. Ford's original press release is in *Planning, Regulation and Competi-*

tion, pp. 208–09. A decade later, Ford and Chrysler were no longer attempting to maintain the fiction of independent pricing policies. In 1966, 1967, and 1968, either Ford or Chrysler announced first, then revised their prices downward to meet General Motors'. Again in 1976, Ford retreated in the face of "some pressure from its dealers and said the decision by General Motors Corp., the traditional pricing leader, not to follow suit, helped force the rollback." See the Los Angeles *Times,* January 6, 1976.

373   The Yntema dialogue is taken from *Administered Prices—Automobiles, Hearings* before the Subcommittee on Antitrust and Monopoly, Senate Judiciary Committee, Part VI (Washington, D.C.: Government Printing Office, 1958), p. 2694.

373   This is the first time: *Ibid.,* p. 2214. On September 25, 1979, newly named chairman of Chrysler's board of directors Lee Iacocca told newsmen in Detroit that his struggling company could not abandon the production of large cars, as some government officials had suggested, because smaller, energy-conscious automobiles were not profitable enough. "You cannot be a small car producer only in the United States and survive against General Motors because General Motors sets the price," Iacocca said. See the Los Angeles *Times,* September 26, 1979.

374   Healthy trend in the economy, etc.: *Administered Prices—Automobiles, Hearings,* pp. 2502–03.

374   But somewhere along the line: Whyte, "The Cadillac Phenomenon," p. 181.

374   A company doing 45 to 50 percent: *Administered Prices—Automobiles, Hearings,* p. 2983. See also *A Study of the Antitrust Laws,* p. 16, for a similar comment by Romney two years earlier.

375   I've never seen a study: *Business Week,* October 30, 1954, p. 45.

375   The annual model change: *U.S. News and World Report,* January 28, 1955, p. 139. As late as 1970, General Motors defended the annual restyling. In April of that year, James M. Roche, the chairman of the board of directors, asserted, "Planned obsolescence in my opinion is another word for progress." See Robert Heilbroner, et al., *In the Name of Profit* (Garden City, New York: Doubleday, 1972), p. 33.

375   Not of the automobile: Jerome, *The Death of the Automobile,* p. 31. In a conversation with the author on July 19, 1979, Jerome said that his deliberately hyperbolic, witty book "was extremely well received, reviewed everywhere but in Detroit." The imagery of those fins lives on, twenty years later. See B. Bruce-Briggs, "Chrysler and the Small-Car Morality Fable," *Wall Street Journal,* September 20, 1979.

375   A car *should* be exciting: Quoted by Ralph Nader in *Unsafe at Any Speed*, new edition (New York: Grossman, 1972), p. 223. Nader cited four cases of people impaled on the sharp fins of the Cadillac; three of the accidents were fatal.

376   General Motors countered: "The Automobile Industry: A Case Study in Competition, A Statement by General Motors Corporation," presented to the Subcommittees of the Select Committee on Small Business, United States Senate, October 18, 1968, p. 37. The full statement is reprinted in *Planning, Regulation and Competition*, pp. 617 ff.

376   Frozen big car mentality: *Administered Prices*, pp. 2857–58.

377   You become muscle-bound: *Ibid*.

377   It would cost: *Ibid,*, p. 2879.

377   The availability of large sums: *Ibid*.

378   Impregnable to competition: Paul Jones, president of the American Security Co., of Marion, Indiana, quoted in the Los Angeles *Times*, February 26, 1959. Other information about GMAC's growth and influence is contained in *A Study of the Antitrust Laws*, pp. 67–76; *Administered Prices—Automobiles*, Hearings, pp. 151–168; Simon N. Whitney, *Antitrust Policies*, Vol. I (New York, 1958), pp. 441–451; *U.S.* v. *General Motors Corp.*, No. 7146 (7th Cir. 1940). The consent agreement was to come under sharp attack for not severing the finance arm from the corporate body. Lee Loevinger, then chief of the United States Department of Justice's Antitrust Division, commented, "Although it is on the books as a victory, [it] may properly be regarded as one of the great failures of antitrust." See *Business Week*, June 17, 1961, and the congressional hearings reported there.

379   The automobile has shifted: *Administered Prices*, p. 2859.

380   Harlow Curtice was really the last guy: DeLorean to Bob Irvin, New York *Times*, October 28, 1973.

381   What he really thinks about: *Time*, September 8, 1958, p. 85. See also Robert Sheehan, "G.M.'s Remodeled Management," *Fortune*, November 1958, pp. 122 ff.

381   I am not taciturn: Donner to George Bookman, *Time*, September 22, 1956, p. 79.

CHAPTER 15: BASE METAL
(pages 385–429)

Page

386   Will undoubtedly secure: Cited in *U.S.* v. *E.I. du Pont de Nemours*, 353 U.S. 586, 602. The memo was Government Trial Exhibit 124 and is

reprinted in *A Study of the Antitrust Laws,* Hearings before the Subcommittee on Antitrust and Monopoly, Senate Judiciary Committee (Washington, D.C.: Government Printing Office, 1956), pp. 2475–2481.

386   A member of our family: Government Trial Exhibit 367, Sloan to Lammot du Pont, November 11, 1926, in *U.S.* v. *du Pont.*

387   There is no group: Quoted in the government's brief on appeal in *U.S.* v. *du Pont.* The disbursement of 71.8 million shares of General Motors stock would not be completed until 1965, and not until the corporation had retained the services of Washington attorney and lobbyist Clark Clifford, former counselor to President Harry S. Truman, who lobbied through Congress and the White House the "Du Pont Relief Bill," which saved an estimated $1 billion in taxes for the recipients of the stock. From the beginning of the suit in 1947 until the start of the stock distribution in 1962, General Motors paid dividends of $7.35 billion, of which $1.69 billion went to the du Ponts and to Du Pont shareholders. For details on the persuasive lobbying effort, see *Du Pont-Christiana,* Hearings before the Committee on Finance, United States Senate, March 17 and 24, 1965 (Washington, D.C.: Government Printing Office, 1965); Jack Anderson, "The Washington Merry-Go-Round" column for April 10, 1965; and Senator Albert Gore's remarks on "Du Pont Tax Favoritism" in the *Congressional Record,* May 24, 1965. On the importance of the *Du Pont* decision itself, see Mark J. Green, et al., *The Closed Enterprise System,* reprint edition (New York: Bantam, 1972), pp. 300–301; F. Boggis, "The du Pont-General Motors Divestiture," *Cartel* XII (October 1962), pp. 147 ff.; and Guy B. Maseritz, "The Relevant Market," *The Antitrust Bulletin* VI (1961), pp. 502 ff.

387   It is clear: Cramer, *American Enterprise: Free and Not so Free*, p. 460.

388   Developing pattern, and novel economic doctrine: *Business Week,* May 8, 1954, p. 30.

388   The Sloan–O'Mahoney dialogue is taken from *A Study of the Antitrust Laws,* pp. 3542–43.

390   One tough sonovabitch: Interview with a retired General Motors executive, December 15, 1974.

390   Emotional, rather than factual: Los Angeles *Times,* May 1, 1956. But not until 1968 and a second, more serious challenge would the corporation put forward a factual defense. See "The Automobile Industry: A Case Study in Competition," in *Planning, Regulation and Competition: Automobile Industry—1968,* Hearings before Subcommittees of the Select Committee on Small Business, United States Senate (Washington, D.C.: Government Printing Office, 1968), pp. 617 ff.

390   If economic concentration: Los Angeles *Times,* March 9, 1956.

391   GM has come to represent: *Business Week,* July 14, 1956. Beyond the antitrust case, there was also a series of Federal Trade Commission cease-and-desist orders dealing with vague or inflated advertising claims. See FTC Decision No. 9181, June 23, 1959, and the cases collected in *Planning, Regulation and Competition—1968,* pp. 453–469.

393   A price set by someone *Administered Prices—Automobiles,* Report together with Individual Views, Subcommittee on Antitrust and Monopoly, Senate Judiciary Committee (Washington, D.C.: Government Printing Office, 1958), p. 219.

394   Consider the cities: *Administered Prices—Automobiles,* Hearings before the Subcommittee on Antitrust and Monopoly, Senate Judiciary Committee, Part VI (Washington, D.C.: Government Printing Office, 1958), p. 2543.

394   Romney was too straight: Interview with former Chrysler executive, Los Angeles, November 1, 1979.

394   Romney's testimony is quoted from *Administered Prices—Automobiles,* Hearings, Part VI, pp. 2849–2897. Romney's estimates of optimum production are critically reviewed in Lawrence J. White, *The Automobile Industry since 1945* (Cambridge, Mass.: Harvard University Press, 1971), pp. 38–53.

397   The fumes of the exhaust: New York *Times,* January 2, 1916, Section VIII, p. 1. Even earlier, Pedro Salom, the inventor-designer of the 1894 Electrobat, noted in the *Journal of the Franklin Institute* in 1896: "All the gasoline motors we have seen belch forth from their exhaust pipe a continuous stream of partially unconsumed hydrocarbons in the form of a thick smoke with a highly noxious odor. Imagine thousands of such vehicles on the streets, each offering up its column of smell!" Salom's Electrobat, of course, produced no such noisome plume. Quoted by Rae in *The American Automobile,* p. 13.

398   Thoeren's criticism: Los Angeles *Times,* February 28, 1957.

398   A tool of mobility: Undated news clip from the Los Angeles *Times,* ca. 1958. Gruen cited the case of an Alhambra, California, woman who repeatedly slammed her 1949 Buick into her ex-husband's brand-new 1957 Chevrolet so that her ex-spouse's new girlfriend could not enjoy the car. The original stories ran in the Los Angeles *Times,* August 5 and 6, and November 27, 1957.

398   Oxnam's comments are quoted from the Los Angeles *Times,* February 21, 1958.

398   Overblown, overpriced: New York *Times* book review, September 23, 1958.

399 The comments by Meeks and Blunt are taken from the Los Angeles *Times*, November 22, 1959. Two years later, Allstate Insurance found an absolute correlation between grades and driving in a national survey. Among "A" students, two-thirds had drivers' licenses, while car ownership reached 82 percent among "F" students. The longer a student owned a car, the survey noted, the poorer his or her grades. However, the automobile itself was not to blame; it was not the use or ownership of a car that was the determining factor, but the parents' laxity in permitting the car to supplant studies. See the Los Angeles *Times*, December 3, 1961.

399 The growth projections are from Wilfred Owen, "Automotive Transport in the United States," *Annals of the American Academy of Political and Social Sciences*, Vol. 320 (1958), pp. 1 ff.; and the Los Angeles *Times*, January 4, 1957 and July 26, 1959.

400 Factory bootlegging: Drew Pearson, "Washington Merry-Go-Round" column for December 18, 1955.

400 General Motors is the servant: *A Study of the Antitrust Laws*, p. 3541.

401 Information on the dealers' plight was drawn from *A Study of the Antitrust Laws*, Hearings, Part VII, pp. 3555 ff.; White, *The Automobile Industry Since 1945*, pp. 157–164; Drucker, *Concept of the Corporation*, pp. 98–103; and *Business Week*, March 3, 1956.

405 Curtice: *Administered Prices—Automobiles*, Hearings, Vol. VI, p. 2483. Other information on the rise of import sales and Detroit's response was taken from White, *The Automobile Industry since 1945*, pp. 182–85; Ralph Nader, *Unsafe at Any Speed*, pp. 18–19; Jerome, *The Death of the Automobile*, pp. 94–95; Wilkin and Hill, *American Business Abroad*, pp. 372–391; *Business Week*, January 11, 1958; *U.S. News and World Report*, April 28, 1958, May 2, 1958. General Motors' policy was to delay announcement of new models for as long as possible on the grounds that the announcement might convince people to keep their old car a year longer; in a replacement market, a purchase deferred was a purchase lost. To keep the Corvair project a secret, tool and die makers were told the parts were for a new Holden to be built in Australia; early prototypes were camouflaged with Porsche and Vauxhall bodies in test drives. In May 1959, board chairman Donner finally confirmed the rumors at the corporation's annual meeting with the announcement that "a smaller and lighter" car called the Corvair would be introduced in October 1959.

406 Unobvious choice: J. Patrick Wright, *On a Clear Day You Can See General Motors* (Grosse Pointe, Michigan: Wright Enterprises, 1979), p. 41.

407   Business excitement: *Time,* September 22, 1958, p. 79.

407   When Fred and I took over: Paraphrased by John DeLorean in, J. Patrick Wright, *On a Clear Day You Can See General Motors,* pp. 206–07. DeLorean considered Curtice "GM's last dynamic leader" (p. 207) and the "last guy who was president of GM who really ran it." See the New York *Times,* October 28, 1973, Part III, p. 1.

409   The poor handling: Internal Ford memorandum written June 17, 1960, by Fred J. Hooven, reprinted as Appendix F in Ralph Nader, *Unsafe at Any Speed,* pp. 396–7.

409   *Everybody* knew: Thomas Whiteside, *The Investigation of Ralph Nader,* reprint edition (New York: Pocket Books, 1972), pp. 192–93. According to an article celebrating the introduction of the Corvair in *Time,* October 5, 1959, p. 91, "Chevy says the car is easy to steer without power steering, gets better traction and braking. Such claims have stirred up an angry argument. Ford contends that a rear-engine car tends to oversteer and veer out on curves because the greater part of its weight is in the rear." This seemingly was as close as Ford was to come to blowing the whistle. Paradoxically, General Motors spokesmen had testified before a congressional committee eleven years earlier that an air-cooled, rear-engine, four-door car with the swing axle the Corvair employed "would not be safe, practical or reasonable;" see Robert Cumberford, "R.I.P. Corvair," in *Car and Driver Yearbook, 1970,* pp. 94–96.

409   DeLorean's comments are noted in Wright, *On a Clear Day,* pp. 54–55. DeLorean adds, "The son of Cal Werner, general manager of the Cadillac Division, was killed in a Corvair. Werner was absolutely convinced that the design defect in the car was responsible. He said so many times. The son of Cy Osborne, an executive vice-president in the '60s, was critically injured in a Corvair and suffered irreparable brain damage. Bunkie Knudsen's niece was brutally injured in a Corvair."

410   What kind of: Gordon as paraphrased by Nader, *Unsafe,* p. 39.

410   Bunkie was livid: Wright, *On a Clear Day,* p. 56. DeLorean himself remained silent until the publication in 1979 of Wright's book, though he was resisting imposition of an adapted Corvair on his own Pontiac division. Instead, he modified a jointly developed Buick–Oldsmobile compact, launched as the Tempest, which was, according to the independent *Road Test* magazine, "probably the worst riding, worst all-around handling car available to the American public. . ." DeLorean did not acknowledge this, but he did concede that "the car rattled so loudly that it sounded like it was carrying half-a-trunkful of rocks." See Wright, p. 91.

412   *Chicago Record-Herald:* Quoted in *Horseless Age,* June 21, 1905.

412   Designed-in defects: The subtitle of Nader's *Unsafe at Any Speed* is
      "The designed-in dangers of the American automobile." On the vehicle
      inspection program, see, for example, the Los Angeles *Times,* July 12,
      1962, "90% of Autos Tested Have Safety Defects"; and similar scare
      stories on December 12, 1962; March 3, 1963; April 3, 1963; April 8,
      1963; and May 27, 1965. The guiding hand of the auto industry in the
      campaign appeared only in the earliest stories; for example, the Los
      Angeles *Times,* April 18, 1954; "More than half of 197,500 motor vehi-
      cles inspected in Washington, D.C., during a one-year period were
      found to be mechanically unsafe, according to Ted Wessen, head of
      Wessen Buick Co., Western Avenue dealership." The boilerplate press
      release was written in Detroit and favored local dealers' names inserted
      for home-town release.

413   Ever caught on so fast: Nader, *Unsafe,* p. 116. See also a Ford press
      release of November 18, 1956, cited by Nader, p. xiv.

413   Not sufficient factual information: *Ibid.,* p. 114. But, automobile histo-
      rian Lawrence J. White noted in *The Automobile Industry since 1945,* p.
      241, "They did not, however, seem to be interested enough to collect
      that information themselves."

413   Further enhancement: Engineering vice-president of General Motors
      Charles A. Chayne's article, "Automotive Design Contributions to
      Highway Safety," *Annals of the American Academy of Political and
      Social Sciences,* Vol. 320, (1958), pp. 78 and 82. According to James M.
      Roche, in the Los Angeles *Times,* October 24, 1965, "Each automotive
      division—competing with other GM divisions as well as with other
      companies—seeks constantly to improve the safety of its products . . . ."

414   If we made a car: *Fortune,* June 1956, p. 194. More than five years later,
      in his keynote address to the National Safety Congress, then General
      Motors President John F. Gordon asserted, "To begin with, it is com-
      pletely unrealistic even to talk about a foolproof and crashproof car.
      This is true because an automobile must still be something that people
      will *want* to buy and use" [emphasis added]. Quoted by Nader, *Unsafe,*
      p. 4.

416   Gallup Poll: Telephone interview of Madri, executive assistant to
      George Gallup, Jr., president of the Gallup Poll, Princeton, New Jer-
      sey, November 30, 1979.

416   Donner's testimony is quoted from *Federal Role in Traffic Safety,* Hear-
      ings before the Subcommittee on Executive Reorganization, Part II
      (Washington, D.C.: Government Printing Office, 1965), pp. 657 ff.

418   The Kennedy–Donner–Roche exchange is taken from *Federal Role in
      Traffic Safety,* Part II, pp. 777–786. Two days after the testimony, in a

letter to the subcommittee, the corporation estimated that it had spent $193 million on safety, durability, and reliability in 1964. That figure seemed inordinately high, the definition of "safety research" stretched out of shape to inflate the total. " 'I saw the "tilt" sign light up,' says one federal official," quoted by Elizabeth Brenner Drew, "The Politics of Auto Safety," *The Atlantic,* October 1966, p. 97.

421   Dismal performance: *Wall Street Journal,* July 20, 1965, p. 12.

421   Dealt with Donner: Washington *Post,* as quoted by Jeffrey O'Connell and Arthur Myers, *Safety Last* (New York: Random House, 1966), p. 92.

422   Our job is to check: *Federal Role in Traffic Safety,* Hearings, Part IV, p. 1552.

423   The Curtis-Nader exchange is quoted from *Federal Role in Traffic Safety,* Hearings, Part III, p. 1275.

424   The investigation was limited: Hearings, Part IV, p. 1389.

425   The staff member: Serrin, *The Company and the Union,* 250–51 fn.

425   Deny the girls: Whiteside, *The Investigation of Ralph Nader,* p. 43.

425   Goddammit: Roche as paraphrased by Serrin, p. 252.

425   The Roche statement and Roche-Kennedy exchange is quoted from Hearings, Part IV, pp. 1381–1401.

427   Everybody is so outraged: Drew, "The Politics of Auto Safety," p. 97.

427   The National Highway Safety Bureau became the National Highway Traffic Safety Administration. For a history of the agency's progress, see the second edition of Ralph Nader, *Unsafe at Any Speed,* pp. xvii-ff. Details of recall campaigns are reported annually in "Motor Vehicle Safety Defect Recall Campaigns," published by the United States Department of Transportation, National Highway Traffic Safety Administration.

427   I was not going to take: Whiteside, *The Investigation of Ralph Nader,* p. 123. In papers filed in the New York Supreme Court, Gillen said under oath that he was instructed to "get something, somewhere on this guy [Nader] . . . get him out of their hair . . . shut him up."

427   It is our regular practice: Los Angeles *Times,* May 13, 1969. Nader was not yet done with Corvair or General Motors. He charged successively that the corporation had hidden test failures in which the car rolled over at speeds as low as twenty-six miles per hour and that General Motors' defense of the car was "a massive lie." Moreover, Nader asserted that the estimated 600,000 Corvairs still on the road in 1970 could leak

carbon monoxide, a deadly poison, into the passenger compartment. General Motors' president at the time, Edward Cole, denied it, charging Nader was waging "a continuing personal vendetta." See the Los Angeles *Times,* November 27, 1970.

In 1970 and 1971, two former General Motors employees came forward to support Nader's claims of a cover-up of Corvair inadequacies, one of whom was "told to hide, not to discuss . . . a series of proving-ground reports on attempts to keep the Corvair from rolling over. . . . I had information which was harmful and could be used against GM in court." See the Los Angeles *Times,* Sept. 30, 1970, and Whiteside, pp. 179–183.

428   Yale University physicist: Hal Higdon, "The Big Auto Sweepstakes," New York *Times Magazine,* May 1, 1966, p. 97.

429   Don't tell them anything: Robert Irwin, "At the Pinnacle of G.M.," New York *Times,* September 8, 1974. According to Irvin, Donner was so inaccessible that two reporters drove two hundred miles for a two-minute conversation with him.

429   I'm arguing: *Business Week,* June 11, 1966, p. 162. The first postwar complaints about the reliability of General Motors products surfaced in 1956, when the president of Greyhound Bus, Arthur S. Genet, charged that the first 570 buses of a $53 million, 1,000-vehicle order suffered lubrication defects in the transmissions and clutches. "Some of them literally caught fire and burned to the ground," Genet charged. See *Business Week,* July 28, 1956.

CHAPTER 16: THE HERETICS
(pages 430–454)

Page

430   I never thought: New York *Times,* November 10, 1967. The riots of July 23–30, 1967, are most graphically described in Robert Conot, *American Odyssey* (New York: Bantam Books, 1975), pp. 679–706.

431   A white man's corporation: William Serrin, "For Roche of G.M. Happiness is a 10% Surcharge," New York *Times Magazine,* September 12, 1971, p. 114.

431   The ban on colored workers: Henry Kraus, *The Many and the Few,* p. 257 fn.

432   When we moved into the South: *Wall Street Journal,* October 24, 1957, quoted in Herbert R. Northrup, "The Negro in the Automobile Industry," The Racial Policies of American Industry, No. 1, University of Pennsylvania Press, 1968, p. 29. General Motors' policy sprang simply from a lack of will. At the same time, Levi Strauss & Company, then a

comparatively small firm making men's work pants, was successfully integrating its Southern plants, at far greater financial risk proportionately than General Motors faced. See Ed Cray, *Levi's* (Boston: Houghton Mifflin Co., 1978), pp. 127–129.

432   They work on the dirtiest: Black worker as quoted by Serrin, *The Company and the Union,* p. 15. Serrin notes that Robert W. Dunn's *Labor and Automobiles* (New York: International Publishers, 1929) earlier asserted: "The writer noticed in one Chevrolet plant that Negroes were engaged on the dirtiest, roughest and most disagreeable work . . . It is more difficult for a Negro to get promoted. Opportunities for more skilled jobs are . . . fewer for him than for the white worker."

432   To assist capable individuals: Sloan: *My Years with General Motors,* p. 336. Ralph Nader first made this point in testimony before subcommittees of the Select Committee on Small Business in 1968.

433   Background material for the description of the "go-go" years was drawn from Richard J. Barber, "The New Partnership—Big Government and Big Business," *The New Republic,* August 13, 1966.

435   Chase Manhattan Bank: Los Angeles *Times,* September 30, 1963. Other figures are drawn from "The Automobile Industry: A Case Study in Competition, A Statement by General Motors," (Detroit: General Motors Corp., 1968), p. 25.

435   Era of specific driving needs: *Time,* October 5, 1959, p. 94.

436   We were living off: Wright, *On a Clear Day You Can See General Motors,* p. 50. Information on automotive profits was drawn from Wright, pp. 25, 92, 130, 133, 177, 180; Serrin, *The Company and the Union,* p. 30; *Business Week,* March 16, 1974; The New York *Times,* March 24, 1974; and *Planning, Regulation, and Competition: Automobile Industry—1968,* Hearings before Subcommittees of the Select Committee on Small Business, United States Senate (Washington, D.C.: Government Printing Office, 1968), pp. 271, 274, 350, 499–500, 736.

438   Hahn's conversation with an auto executive is quoted from Nader, *Unsafe at Any Speed,* pp. 154–55.

439   Unfairly critical, *etc.:* Drucker, *Concept of the Corporation,* pp. 291–296.

439   It's the climate: McWilliams, *Southern California: An Island on the Land,* p. 124, quoting Col. Tom Fitch, circa 1885. The word "smog," a fusion of "smoke" and "fog" (there is little of the latter in Los Angeles), is at least as old as 1940. *Business Week* of December 14, 1940, used it in a headline for a story describing St. Louis's efforts to clean up factory emissions.

440   The comments by the Automobile Manufacturers Association spokes-
       man appeared in the Los Angeles *Times,* February 24, 1960.

440   We decided: Ronald A. Buel, *Dead End: The Automobile in Mass
       Transportation* (Englewood Cliffs, N.J.: Prentice-Hall, 1972), pp. 65–66,
       crediting John Wicklein, "Whitewashing Detroit's Dirty Engine,"
       Washington Monthly, June 1970, p. 10. See also the Los Angeles *Times,*
       August 8, December 7, 1961.

440   It must be recognized: *Congressional Record,* May 18, 1971, p. H4068.
       These "Remarks by Representative Phillip Burton" reprint a confiden-
       tial memorandum written by the late Samuel Flatow, a Department of
       Justice attorney who urged a criminal indictment of the manufacturers'
       association, the four American automobile companies, and a clutch
       of unnamed officers of the companies for monopolistic restraint of
       trade.

441   General Motors' statement is taken from the Los Angeles *Times,* Janu-
       ary 11, 1969.

441   Represents strong federal action: Los Angeles *Times,* September 12,
       1969.

442   Further research: Los Angeles *Times,* April 8, 1965. See also that pa-
       per, March 11 and May 11, 1964.

442   Bowditch is quoted by Dan Fisher in the Los Angeles *Times,* August 6,
       1969. Fisher, currently the *Times*'s Moscow bureau chief, was one of
       the few automotive writers for a daily newspaper who covered his beat
       with the skepticism of a knowledgeable cityside reporter, unconcerned
       with any possible impact on advertising revenues.

443   The 1975 emission control: Associated Press dispatch to the Los
       Angeles *Times,* October 28, 1970. See also *Air Pollution—1970,* Joint
       Hearings before the Subcommittee on Air and Water Pollution of the
       Committee on Public Works and the Committee on Commerce, United
       States Senate (Washington, D.C.: Government Printing Office, 1970),
       Part III, pp. 1056–1081; and Part V, pp. 1576–1584.

443   Billings' comments are quoted from the Los Angeles *Times,* November
       12, 1972, in another Dan Fisher story that embarrassed the automobile
       industry.

443   We must ask ourselves: United Press International dispatch to the Los
       Angeles *Times,* February 11, 1972.

444   Metzger's complaint is quoted by Louis M. Kohlmeier, *Wall Street
       Journal,* October 31, 1967.

445   The fact that most: Former Department of Justice lawyer Thomas R.
       Asher, testifying on *The Industrial Reorganization Act,* Hearings before

the Subcommittee on Antitrust and Monopoly, United States Senate (Washington, D.C.: Government Printing Office 1974), Part III, p. 2005. With some sarcasm, Asher pointed out that the Department of Justice *did* file suits in the softball, bedspring, overhead garage door, hearse, and Christmas-tree decoration industries.

447 Classic conspiracy: Los Angeles *Times,* April 29, 1966. On September 26, 1964, federal Judge John Feikens dismissed a civil complaint against General Motors and Ford Motor charging that the two companies had conspired to fix prices on fleet sales automobile-rental agencies. Nine months earlier, a jury had returned not-guilty verdicts against the two firms in a parallel criminal action. These were the last government antitrust-related cases pending.

447 The nature: General Motors' statement on "Competition," 1968, p. 57.

447 It doesn't seem to matter: Interview, February 26, 1974.

448 Not be decomposed: Andrew Hacker, "Citizen Counteraction?" in Ralph Nader and Mark J. Green, eds., *Corporate Power in America* (New York: Grossman 1973), p. 175.

448 Too large for the courts: Los Angeles *Herald-Examiner,* April 17, 1977.

448 Hard to arouse people: Interview, February 26, 1974. Green's *The Closed Enterprise System,* reprint edition (New York: Bantam Books, 1972), written with Beverly C. Moore, Jr., and Bruce Wasserstein, was helpful in summarizing the General Motors antitrust cases.

449 GM—Mark of Excellence: *Wall Street Journal,* June 12, 1968.

450 Some thought: New York *Times,* October 31, 1967.

450 We simply are not: Los Angeles *Times,* December 28, 1969. See also *Planning, Regulation and Competition,* pp. 455–57.

451 Meddling in product decisions: Wright, pp. 21–22.

452 No one is president: *Ibid.*

452 If I was your age: *Ibid.,* p. 30.

453 To go limp: Unidentified General Motors executive quoted in the Los Angeles *Times,* March 15, 1970.

453 Unless a safety defect: Lund's letter "To All Chevrolet Dealers," December 5, 1969, reprinted in *Automotive Repair Industry,* Hearings before the Subcommittee on Antitrust and Monopoly, Senate Judiciary Committee (Washington, D.C.: Government Printing Office, 1969), p. 1336.

453 Comments by an executive and Cole are taken from the Los Angeles *Times,* March 15, 1970.

454   The novelty and status: Lawrence O'Donnel and Walter Mossberg, "End of the Affair," *Wall Street Journal,* March 30, 1971. As late as 1968, General Motors maintained that the American public held the automobile "closest to the ideal method of transportation for all except long-distance business trips." See *Planning, Regulation and Competition,* p. 687 fn. Apparently, General Motors' error was to assume that "automobile" meant something akin to a General Motors product. Information on the status of the corporation, circa 1970, was drawn from the Washington *Post,* May 24, 1969; the New York *Times,* September 20, 1970; and the Los Angeles *Times,* March 15, 1970.

CHAPTER 17: TAKING ON THE BIG GUY
(pages 455–483)

Page
456   Roche's letter was quoted in the Los Angeles *Times,* April 10, 1970. Background on Campaign GM was drawn from, among other sources, Charles McCarry, *Citizen Nader* (New York: Saturday Review Press, 1972), pp. 222 ff.; Los Angeles *Times,* February 8, 1970. The campaign of "boring from within" was based on principles first put forward by social reformer Saul Alinsky.

457   The Williams–Roche confrontation is based upon reports from the Los Angeles *Times,* May 23, 1970; E.J. Kahn, Jr., "We Look Forward to Seeing You Next Year," *New Yorker,* June 20, 1970, p. 50; *Fortune,* June 1970; and a conversation with Martin Coren, Campaign GM's former press assistant, in June 1979.

458   As stockholders and citizens: *Fortune,* June 1970, p. 31, and undated clip from *Ward's Auto World,* "Campaign GM Pledges Continuing Action," by Marty Coren, furnished by the author.

459   Black power: *Newsweek,* December 10, 1973, p. 105.

459   I told Mr. Roche: *Business Week,* April 10, 1971, p. 100. See also *Wall Street Journal,* May 17, 1974.

459   Every phase: "General Motors Annual Report 1978," p. 31.

459   Would inevitably result: Los Angeles *Times,* February 7, 1971. Information on General Motors' activities in South Africa is drawn from the corporation's public-interest reports, 1972–78; articles in the Los Angeles *Times,* March 2, 1977, August 30, 1978, and July 26, 1979; and Richard A. Jackson, editor, *The Multinational Corporation and Social Policy: Special Reference to General Motors in South Africa* (New York: Praeger Publishers, 1974).

459   Cosmetic: *Wall Street Journal,* March 24, 1971.

460   Unsound business practice: *Ibid.*

460   We are a public: New York *Times,* May 22, 1971. See also McCarry, *Citizen Nader,* p. 226, and the New York *Times Magazine,* September 12, 1971, p. 116.

461   The average person: Serrin, *The Company and the Union,* p. 19. Serrin's book was singularly helpful in explaining worker, union, and management attitudes.

461   A strike against: *Ibid.,* p. 19.

462   About $25 million *more: Ibid.,* p. 11.

462   In the last ten years: *Ibid.,* p. 12.

463   Piss on his grave: *Ibid.,* p. 20.

463   Business and government: Edward Ayres, *What's Good for GM . . .* (Nashville: Aurora Publishers Incorporated, 1970), p. 66. Roche's comment was, of course, nothing so much as a restatement of Charles E. Wilson's by-then infamous comment, "What's good for America is good for General Motors, and vice versa."

464   Traditional American work ethic: B.J. Widick, *Detroit: City of Race and Class Violence* (Chicago: Quadrangle, 1972), p. 218. During the 1970 strike, General Motors prepared a position paper citing "tardiness, loitering, failure to follow instructions, and abuse of employee facilities," wildcat work stoppages, and "careless workmanship," all then unchecked. See Emma Rothschild, *Paradise Lost* (New York: Random House, 1972), p. 125. The best description of the older values and their erosion is in Eli Chinoy, *Automobile Workers and the American Dream* (Garden City, New York: Doubleday, 1955), which makes clear the loss of the Protestant work ethic predates current complaints.

464   The welder anecdote appears in Serrin, p. 14.

465   If that Woodcock: Serrin, p. 7.

466   Inflationary: Los Angeles *Times,* November 13, 1970.

468   Counter-inflationary: Los Angeles *Times,* November 14, 1970.

468   Not tied in some way: Los Angeles *Times,* December 5, 1970. Roche did not discuss the inflationary effect of the thirty-and-out clause. By 1972, a company brochure on employee benefits asserted: "GM pension checks totaling $231.6 million were mailed to approximately 95,000 retired hourly employees and eligible survivors. In addition about $72.5 million were paid by GM in 1972 for their hospital, surgical, medical and prescription drug coverage." Early retirement climbed to 5,000 workers annually by 1974, more than 25 percent of those eligible, with each

drawing $625 per month from the company or from both the company and social security. "About 80 percent of all employees who retire because of age are retiring prior to age 65," George B. Morris, Jr., vice-president of industrial relations, said in a press release dated September 28, 1974.

468   The union and the company: Serrin, p. 306.

468   American car with size: Rothschild, *Paradise Lost,* p. 56.

469   Mitchell's comments appear in Rothschild, p. 230.

469   *Fortune,* March 1969, p. 110. "These executives have a visceral aversion to small, austere cars that cannot be wholly accounted for by their reading of the economics of their business. By all evidence, these men truly love the products of their factories. They have grown used to accepting each year that their cars are the best and most beautiful ever, as well as the biggest, until those three terms have become almost as synonymous in their own thinking as in the prose of their ad writers," *Fortune* writer William S. Rukeyser continued. In one of the more provocative articles published in the so-called automotive press, an iconoclastic Brock Yates earlier noted: "Precious few auto executives understand the motives for purchasing an imported car, except for empirical values like low price and operating costs, but the social implications of such undersized vehicles escape them. Most are still convinced that a majority of Americans aspire toward the ownership of a Cadillac (or replica thereof) and view the marketing and sales problems in the context of producing forgeries of this great upper-middle-class sacred cow. The idea that some of America does not yearn for bogus-Caddies is baffling to a surprisingly large number of Detroit decision-makers. . . ." See "The Grosse Pointe Myopians," *Car and Driver,* April 1968, p. 41.

469   Fighting the foreign car: Dow Jones dispatch to the Los Angeles *Times,* July 11, 1968. Less than a year later Roche concluded that increasing the flow of captive imports "is not going to help solve the balance-of-payments problem" See *Fortune,* March 1969, p. 168.

469   An example of an area: *Fortune,* March 1969, p. 167.

469   A new and entirely: Associated Press dispatch to the Los Angeles *Times,* October 4, 1968.

470   Such a big monster: Wright, *On a Clear Day You Can See General Motors,* p. 100. Wright devotes thirty-six pages to the carefully hidden Chevrolet problems as seen from the perspective of the man who replaced Estes. See also *Business Week,* September 18, 1971, pp. 50 ff.; Los Angeles *Times,* February 8, 1970.

471   They are all shook up: Wright, p. 9.

471   Token hippie: Wright, p. 14. For other stories on DeLorean, all of which make a point of his "mod" dress and lifestyle, see *Business Week*, September 18, 1971, pp. 50 ff.; *Fortune*, September 1973, pp. 187 ff.; *Wall Street Journal*, January 12, 1979; and *Esquire*, June 19, 1979, pp. 75 ff.

471   Chevy engineers: Wright, p. 163.

473   Information on the Vega's design and manufacturing defects was drawn from two letters addressed to Richard C. Gerstenberg and signed by Lowell Dodge, director, Center for Auto Safety, Washington, D.C., dated September 1, 1972, and May 15, 1973; and from Michael Putney, "Burnt at Any Speed," *National Observer*, November 8, 1975, pp. 1, 16. Putney noted that in mid-1973, "GM was quietly moving to quash complaints from Vega owners whose engines had been ruined by over-heating after the 12-month/12,000-mile warranty period. But GM apparently did so without ever acknowledging publicly that the Vega overheated. GM also implemented, but didn't announce, a policy of paying for engine repairs beyond the warranty period under certain conditions." In a letter of the Federal Trade Commission on January 10, 1974, Dodge scorned the "under-the-table extension," pointing out "that neither the public nor the affected owners are told by the manufacturer of such warranty extensions. . . . Usually, only those who complain frequently or strenuously to an authorized dealer in a timely manner succeed in learning of the warranty extension" and get free repairs or replacement. Concerning the spread of what has come to be known as the "secret warranty," see the Los Angeles *Times*, October 10, 1978, and December 26, 1978.

473   Basic skepticism: Los Angeles *Times*, August 7, 1970.

473   Image of craftsmen: Rothschild, p. 57.

474   The high level of enthusiasm: *Ibid.*, p. 100.

474   The complaints of whistle-blowing Lordstown workers are summarized in a letter from Dodge to John A. Volpe, United States secretary of transportation, March 3, 1972.

475   If the world's largest: *Time*, July 17, 1972, p. 67. A survey of 250 American automotive engineers by *Wards Automotive Reports* showed that almost half of those polled believed the best cars were built in Japan. Germany ranked second. Only 27.2 percent said they believed United States-built automobiles superior in quality to those constructed elsewhere. See the Los Angeles *Times*, February 28, 1980.

475   The comments of McGee, Alli, and the assembler, Joe Alfona, are taken from Bennett Kremen, "Lordstown—Searching for a Better Way of Work," New York *Times*, September 9, 1973, Section III, p. 1. In a

subsequent letter to the editor, George B. Morris, Jr., the corporation's vice-president for industrial relations, was defensive, complaining that Kremen had entered the plant without authorization, but agreed, "We had a strike—a typical labor disagreement over manpower, disciplinary action and negotiations of new local agreements" (see the New York *Times,* October 7, 1973, Section F, p. 5). Morris's judgments are more fully aired in Rothschild, pp. 120–22. John DeLorean, general manager of the Chevrolet division at the time, agreed that "what was taking place was a classical confrontation of union and management over the oldest issue in the history of auto-labor relations—a work speed-up" (see Wright, p. 169).

475   Roch's comments are excerpted from a speech before the Executive Club of Chicago, reported by Jerry M. Flint, New York *Times,* March 26, 1971.

477   Calling in the haystack: Ralph Nader, Peter J. Petkas, and Kate Blackwell, eds., *Whistle Blowing,* reprint edition (New York: Bantam Books, 1972), p. 82. See also the *Wall Street Journal,* December 31, 1973, p. 1. Though ostracized and harassed, Gregory was not fired. Moved to another job, he eventually won back his position as final inspector and continued to make suggestions about improvements on Chevrolets.

478   Can't manage a car: Wright, p. 58.

478   Quietly recall: Wright, p. 57. There were other instances of slow recalls. The record delay seems to have occurred with some 140,000 1960–65 three-quarter-ton pickups whose wheels were subject to catastrophic failure. General Motors first recommended that owners replace the wheels at their own cost, then agreed to recall 50,000; and finally, in November 1975, approximately sixteen years after the first of the trucks had rolled off the assembly lines, agreed to replace the rear wheels at company expense. See the Los Angeles *Times,* May 28, 1969, and June 1, 1969; *Wall Street Journal,* June 14, 1974, and January 21, April 30, and November 7, 1975.

478   We're under the gun more: Cole as quoted by *Business Week,* July 11, 1960, p. 72.

478   An attempt to get at the system: Roche as quoted in the *Wall Street Journal,* December 6, 1971.

478   America's romance: *Wall Street Journal,* March 30, 1971.

479   The top money man: Laurence G. O'Donnell in the *Wall Street Journal,* April 7, 1970.

479   When I got that job: New York *Times,* December 29, 1974.

480   Old Gerstenberg: *Prices of Motor Vehicle Safety Equipment,* Hearings before the Subcommittee on Executive Reorganization of the Committee on Government Operations, United States Senate (Washington, D.C.: Government Printing Office, 1968), p. 198.

480   If our figures: Los Angeles *Times,* August 29, 1971.

481   Not to take this nation: Los Angeles *Times,* June 18, 1970.

482   Auto industry relief act: Jerome, *The Death of the Automobile,* p. 240.

482   Passenger car sales: Los Angeles *Times,* August 29, 1971.

482   Car buyers apparently: *Wall Street Journal,* May 12, 1972. Other information on the effects of Phases I and II was drawn from the New York *Times,* August 6, 1972; the Los Angeles *Times,* July 30, 1972; and *Fortune,* January 1972, pp. 99 ff.

483   Inroads: Rothschild, p. 59.

CHAPTER 18: JUGGERNAUT
(pages 484–511)

In addition to the sources cited, I have relied on runs of the Los Angeles *Times,* the *Wall Street Journal, Business Week,* and *Time* for background information used in this and the following chapter. Detailed information also may be found in *The Industrial Reorganization Act,* Hearings before the Subcommittee on Antitrust and Monopoly, Senate Judiciary Committee (Washington, D.C.: Government Printing Office, 1974); Stanley E. Boyle, "A Reorganization of the U.S. Automobile Industry," Committee Print, Subcommittee on Antitrust and Monopoly, Senate Judiciary Committee, February 28, 1974 (Washington, D.C.: Government Printing Office, 1974); *Controls or Competition,* Hearings before the Subcommittee on Antitrust and Monopoly, Senate Judiciary Committee (Washington, D.C.: Government Printing Office, 1972); *Multinational Corporations and United States Foreign Policy,* Hearings before the Subcommittee on Multinational Corporations, Senate Foreign Relations Committee, Part I (Washington, D.C.: Government Printing Office, 1973); *Federal Role in Traffic Safety,* Hearings before the Subcommittee on Executive Reorganization, Government Operations Committee, United States Senate, Part I (Washington, D.C.: Government Printing Office, 1966); *Role of Giant Corporations,* Hearings before the Subcommittee on Monopoly, Select Committee on Small Business, United States Senate, Part I (Washington, D.C.: Government Printing Office, 1969); and *Automotive Repair Industry,* Hearings before the Subcommittee on Antitrust and Monopoly, Senate Judiciary Committee, Part III (Washington, D.C.: Government Printing Office, 1969).

No event in recent economic history has received so much press attention as the Arab oil embargo and its impact on Detroit. Among other articles providing significant information were: Agis Salpukas, "Auto Industry Facing Lasting Changes," New York *Times,* December 14, 1973; that same writer's "Auto Men Thinking Small," New York *Times,* January 6, 1974, and "And for Detroit: Throw Money into Small Cars," *Ibid.;* "The Painful Change to Thinking Small," *Time,* December 31, 1973 (cover story); Charles G. Burck, "Detroit Turns Against the Gas Guzzlers," *Fortune,* January 1974; Robert J. Samuelson, "How Detroit Begat Its Own Nightmare," Los Angeles *Times,* January 6, 1974; "The Small Car Blues at General Motors," *Business Week,* March 16, 1974; Marylin Bender, "The Energy Trauma at General Motors," New York *Times,* March 24, 1974; "Detroit Thinks Small," *Newsweek,* April 1, 1974; Jerry M. Flint, "The Energy Crisis Spurs Demand for Small Cars," New York *Times,* April 9, 1974; and Stephen Shepard and J. Patrick Wright, "The Auto Industry," *The Atlantic,* December 1974, pp. 18 ff.

Page

485   We will have to adopt: Los Angeles *Times,* December 5, 1973.

485   That was the reality: *Business Week,* March 26, 1979, p. 65.

486   Would be composed: Los Angeles *Times,* December 7, 1973.

487   DeLorean and Gerstenberg are quoted in the New York *Times,* March 24, 1974. DeLorean was not the only true prophet. One month before the oil embargo, General Motors Vice-Chairman Thomas Murphy warned, "We in the automobile industry had better be able to swing with the market." See the New York *Times,* September 2, 1973, and the *Wall Street Journal,* July 11, 1973.

488   Turn the thermostats down: David Quintner, "The Man Who Made Detroit's First Minicar," *Car and Driver,* January 1976, p. 39.

488   Our sales of large cars: *Fortune,* July 1976, p. 102.

489   Anyone who can't meet: *Ibid.,* p. 104.

489   Engineers are just delighted: Craig Marks in *Fortune,* January 1974, p. 99.

490   Mitchell is quoted by Brock Yates in "Detroit's Shattered Love Affair," *Car and Driver,* October 1974, p. 50.

490   The company can't change: Los Angeles *Times,* December 8, 1973. Gerstenberg's spirits and predictions of the large-car market share fell apace. By April 1974, he was projecting that compacts and subcompacts would account for two of every three cars sold in the foreseeable future.

491   Started to get: *Wall Street Journal,* June 25, 1974.

491   A few years ago: New York *Times,* April 9, 1974.

491 We were conditioned: New York *Times* News Service dispatch to the Los Angeles *Herald-Examiner*, June 8, 1978.

493 I don't see any difference: New York *Times*, March 24, 1974.

493 We don't know what the hell: *Business Week*, March 16, 1974.

493 An increasing percentage: *Ibid.*

494 Downward spread: *Ibid.*

494 The statistics relating to hidden charges are taken from the United States Department of Transportation, "Cost of Operating an Automobile" (Washington, D.C., 1974 *et seq.*). See also the Los Angeles *Times*, October 27, 1974.

495 Most turbulent years: General Motors press release, September 1, 1974. Earlier Gerstenberg had complained of government regulation in less specific terms. Safety regulations were counterproductive because "most Americans who ride in cars don't use safety belts, unfortunately. . . . Society can understandably require good brakes or good steering mechanisms because these affect the safety of people outside the car—pedestrians and others. But when people are required to buy equipment whose only purpose is to protect the buyer, then government has invaded consumer sovereignty." See Richard C. Gerstenberg, "The Automobile Industry," *The Saturday Evening Post*, Fall 1972, pp. 17 ff.

496 I keep scratching: *Business Week*, December 14, 1974.

496 For once in my life: Murphy as quoted by Bob Irvin in the New York *Times*, September 8, 1974.

497 Humbling experience: New York *Times*, December 12, 1971.

497 One of the worst: *Wall Street Journal*, September 30, 1974.

498 They picked a guy: New York *Times*, March 24, 1974.

498 Why the hell: J. Patrick Wright, *On a Clear Day You Can See General Motors*, p. 35.

498 I started thinking: *Americans: The Company President*, one of a BBC series filmed in 1977 and rebroadcast in Los Angeles on KTLA on January 24, 1979.

499 Great job: *Ibid.*

499 Badly needed: Malcolm S. Forbes in *Forbes*, December 1, 1974, p. 10.

500 Big vs. small: *Wall Street Journal*, September 30, 1974.

500 The car purchase: *Business Week*, October 5, 1974.

500 Help sell America: Worden in a speech to the American Marketing Association, November 12, 1974, quoted in a General Motors press release of that date.

500 There's a saying: Robert Sam Anson, "Will the Last Person Leaving Detroit Please Turn out the Lights," *New Times,* February 7, 1975, p. 21.

501 We are responding: General Motors press release, February 21, 1975.

501 The right size: Los Angeles *Times* editorial, September 18, 1975.

501 GM's first line of attack: Los Angeles *Herald-Examiner,* October 17, 1975.

502 How to sell: *Forbes,* February 1, 1975, p. 14.

502 Chevette owners: David Power, president of Power-Robertson & Co., in the Los Angeles *Times,* January 19, 1976. The survey, forwarded through the courtesy of Mr. Power, indicated that more than three of every four Chevette buyers had owned a Chevrolet previously and that almost nine out of ten cars traded in on the Chevette were domestic cars. In an interview with the author on July 7, 1976, Power speculated that buyers perceived the Chevette merely as a Chevrolet, more of the same. "Not many people saw a major difference from the Vega. What we felt they should have done was position it apart from the Chevrolet line." According to C.R. Brown of Mazda Motors, interviewed by the author on July 14, 1976, General Motors had failed to give the Chevette "an image, a personality. It's just another small car."

503 Massive program: General Motors press release, July 10, 1975.

504 All the business: *Wall Street Journal,* January 1, 1976.

504 GM has never been: *Ibid.*

504 Wipe everybody out: *Ibid.* Unidentified in the article, the "competitor" was probably an executive from crumbling Chrysler Corporation.

505 A high fashion thing: Norman D. Lean, vice-president of Toyota Motor Sales U.S.A., in the Los Angeles *Herald Examiner,* May 23, 1976. Sales figures are from the Los Angeles *Times,* May 24, 1976.

505 Paint down: *Car and Driver* as quoted by the *Wall Street Journal,* December 9, 1976. Explaining that his Buick division only sought to please its youthful customers, the division general manager, David C. Collier, said, "We're trying to satisfy that market, not rebel against being forced into designing boxy cars. If Washington doesn't like that, we'll just hire more lawyers." The social value of an automobile capable of painting down fifty-foot strips of surplus rubber apparently never

entered the equation. Chevrolet also stepped up its quasi-secret racing program. "Officially we're out but actually we're still in," one General Motors source told *Wall Street Journal* reporter Terry P. Brown.

505   Give 'em large: Interview of market analyst by the author, June 9, 1977.

505   Big-car backlash: *Wall Street Journal* subhead, January 7, 1976.

507   Putting a stiffer price: Associated Press dispatch to the Los Angeles *Herald-Examiner,* April 24, 1977.

507   But if certain cars: General Motors press release, October 13, 1977. Estes' argument overlooked the difference between the automobile as a luxury and the automobile as a necessity for a family with children. In an earlier attack, Thomas Murphy was more blunt, more the axe man, labeling the proposed excise tax as "one of the most simplistic, irresponsible, and shortsighted ideas ever conceived" (see General Motors press release, April 1, 1977).

507   Mr. Giant Manufacturer: Quoted in an Associated Press dispatch to the Los Angeles *Times,* March 8, 1977.

507   In recent days: General Motors press release, March 9, 1977.

508   I guess: Los Angeles *Times,* June 12, 1977. The Chevymobile incident was reconstructed from the Los Angeles *Times,* March 8, April 26 and 28, May 23, and June 12, 1977, and February 27, 1979; the San Francisco *Chronicle,* June 2, 1977; Los Angeles *Herald-Examiner,* July 19, 1978; and corporate press releases of March 9, April 25, and December 19, 1977, and March 6, 1979.

509   It is time we Americans: General Motors press release, February 15, 1978.

509   We've lost our competition: Interview with the author, July 14, 1976.

CHAPTER 19: THE CORPORATE STATE
(pages 512–531)

Though not cited specifically, information for this chapter was drawn from Buel, *Dead End: The Automobile in Mass Transportation;* "Technology Assessment of Changes in the Future Use and Characteristics of the Automobile Transportation System," Office of Technology Assessment, Congress of the United States (Washington, D.C., 1979), Vols. I and II; San Francisco *Chronicle,* December 18, 1979; Los Angeles *Times,* August 24, 1975, March 13, 1977, August 20, 1979, and January 22, 1980; *Wall Street Journal,* April 1, 1976; *Christian Science Monitor,* July 2, 1976; and the Los Angeles *Herald-Examiner,* April 16, 1978.

513   Lost opportunities: General Motors press release, November 17, 1976.

513   Even though our efforts: General Motors press release, May 15, 1979.

513   Concerned about the slide: General Motors press releases of April 23, June 5, and June 23, 1975. See also Murphy's criticism of the then-pending Balanced Growth and Economic Planning Act of 1975 syndicated by the New York Times News Service and printed in the Los Angeles *Herald-Examiner,* among other newspapers, on December 21, 1975.

514   Moaning and groaning: Los Angeles *Times,* June 18, 1979.

514   When government insists: Interview with the author, February 26, 1974.

515   First-line supervisory jobs: General Motors press release, March 6, 1979. Women constitute somewhat less than 19 percent of the entire domestic labor force, according to the "1979 General Motors Public Interest Report" (Detroit: General Motors Corp., 1979), p. 44, and just under 6 percent of the "officials and managers" jobs.

516   Inconvenience and displacement: General Motors press release, September 18, 1978.

516   A bit frustrated: *Wall Street Journal,* June 12, 1979.

516   Technical and planning side: Amanda Bennett in *ibid.*

518   Technical know-how: Lawrence Pomeroy, "Contrasts in Europe," *Atlantic,* July 1965, p. 107.

518   Unlike Ford: *The Juggernauts* (Indianapolis: Bobbs-Merrill, 1971), pp. 259–260.

519   Strong feeling: *Fortune,* August 1973, p. 68.

519   Only a small part: *Wall Street Journal,* May 7, 1974.

519   Japanese don't warm up: *Wall Street Journal,* May 8, 1974.

520   We want to protect: Wilkin and Hill, *American Business Abroad,* p. 255. "On July 11, 1936, the official attitude was firmly embodied in a motor car manufacture law the operation of which limited the making of cars in Japan to the Nissan [later sold as Datsuns in the United States] and the Toyoda [Toyota] firms," Wilkin and Hill add.

520   A kind of status symbol: Los Angeles *Times,* February 25, 1978.

520   Restricting the ability: "International Trade and Investment," a statement of Policy by the Automobile Manufacturers Association, June 10, 1968.

520   General Motors' overseas profit figures are taken from *Planning, Regulation and Competition: Automobile Industry—1968*, Hearings before Subcommittees of the Select Committee on Small Business, United States Senate (Washington, D.C.: Government Printing Office, 1968), p. 748. The $11.7 billion represented two-thirds of total profits overseas; corporate policy was to reinvest one-third of profits in factory expansion.

521   GM's spear carriers: Los Angeles *Times*, March 23, 1974.

521   Steering a middle course: *Wall Street Journal*, February 15, 1974, based on a statement of Seisi Kata, executive vice-president of Toyota Motor Sales Company.

522   Legitimized the small car: Los Angeles *Herald-Examiner*, September 24, 1975.

522   Salutary: Los Angeles *Herald-Examiner*, October 19, 1975.

522   There is a ceiling: Reuters dispatch to the Los Angeles *Times*, October 23, 1975.

523   Shining one another's shoes: Los Angeles *Times*, February 22, 1978.

523   Exporting unemployment: Associated Press dispatch to the Los Angeles *Times*, January 16, 1980.

523   In 19 or 20 countries: Los Angeles *Times*, January 16, 1980.

524   Removes and compromises: Associated Press dispatch to the Los Angeles *Times*, October 10, 1979. General Motors took advantage of Chrysler's predicament—or generously aided a cash-short competitor, depending on one's point of view—by buying $230 million in discounted receivables from Chrysler's financial arm. According to Los Angeles *Times* writer Bill Sing, "Industry analysts have said that GM, which has about a 60 percent share of the nation's auto market compared to Chrysler's 12 percent, would not like to see Chrysler leave the passenger auto market for fear that it might bring action from federal antitrust prosecutors." See the Los Angeles *Times*, August 15, 1979.

524   More economical than technical: General Motors press release, February 24, 1978.

524   Fuel economy standards: Interview with Patrick Boyle, Los Angeles *Times*, January 21, 1979. A former consumer-affairs reporter for the Rochester *Times-Union*, Boyle is one of the least of automotive buffs among newsmen covering the industry, far more concerned with policies than with models.

525   King of the road: *Wall Street Journal*, January 31, 1979.

525   Historically: *Ibid.*

525   Consumer overreaction: J.D. Power and Associates in the Los Angeles *Times,* January 17, 1980.

526   We are not going: Senior official as quoted by Larry Kramer in the Washington *Post,* reprinted in the Los Angeles *Times,* December 31, 1979.

526   If we export: Associated Press dispatch to the Los Angeles *Times,* January 16, 1980.

526   Necessarily aimed at: Larry Kramer's Washington *Post* article, reprinted in the Los Angeles *Times,* December 31, 1979. For an analysis of automobile-industry research, see *Economic Concentration,* Hearings before the Subcommittee on Antitrust and Monopoly, Senate Judiciary Committee (Washington, D.C.: Government Printing Office, 1965), pp. 1123 ff; and *Role of Giant Corporations,* Hearings before the Subcommittee on Monopoly, Senate Select Committee on Small Business (Washington, D.C.: Government Printing Office, 1971), Part I, pp. 210 ff.

528   Hertz survey: Associated Press dispatch to the Los Angeles *Times,* January 26, 1980. In six years, the cost of ownership of a mid-size or compact car had risen 120 percent.

INDEX

605

CREDITS FOR THE PHOTOGRAPHS

Courtesy of General Motors Institute Alumni Foundation Collection of Industrial History: Henry Leland's first Cadillac, 1903; Henry M. Leland portrait; 1903 Oldsmobile; 1904 Buick at Flint Wagon Works; Louis Chevrolet and Bob Burman in Buick "Bug" racers; William C. Durant about 1909; Louis Chevrolet in 1914 Buick; C. F. Kettering tinkering with 1912 Cadillac; William C. Durant about 1915; Richard H. Grant with Chevrolet 490; Alfred P. Sloan, Jr. about 1927; the men of General Motors in Anderson, Indiana; William S. Knudsen portrait; Charles E. Wilson portrait; C.F. Kettering about 1950; and Harlow Curtice, Alfred P. Sloan, Jr., and Charles E. Wilson in 1956.

Courtesy of Motor Vehicle Manufacturers Association of the U.S., Inc.: Henry Ford about 1900; Walter P. Chrysler about 1920; and Charles W. Nash in the mid-1920s.

Courtesy of General Motors Corporation: 1925 Chevrolet Model K; 1949 Buick Roadmaster; 1959 Cadillac El Dorado; 1960 Chevrolet Corvair; and 1976 Chevrolet Chevette.

Courtesy of Detroit Public Library (Automobile History Collection): David Dunbar Buick portrait.

Wide World Photos: James M. Roche and Theodore Sorensen at Senate hearings.

Courtesy of Eleutherian Mills Historical Library: Pierre S. du Pont about 1915; Pierre S. du Pont and John Jacob Raskob in 1950.

Courtesy of Harrah's Automobile Collection, Reno, Nevada: Model-T of 1909; 1910 Buick White Streak (on display in the Collection); 1910 Oldsmobile Limited (on display in the Collection); and contemporary advertisements for 1914 Royal Mail Roadster, 1927 La Salle, 1927 Ford Model-T, 1928 Ford Model-A roadster, and 1936 Chrysler Airflow.

616